ORGANIZATIONAL BEHAVIOR

The new edition of this essential resource in organizational behavior provides a balanced framework to understand the impact of increasing dynamism and complexity, the importance of collaboration, and the implications for organizational strategy.

Covering both psychological and sociological perspectives on organizational behavior, this clearly written and presented textbook offers a comprehensive review of classic organizational behavior theories and approaches, illustrated with updated case studies. The sixth edition includes new material on ethical considerations; international contexts, with renewed attention to Africa and Asia; environmental pressures and responses; groups and intergroup processes; and the vital importance of building change readiness in any organization.

Upper-level business and technology students, as well as professionals in executive education courses, will find the book a useful guide to all facets of organizational behavior.

A companion website, featuring an instructor manual, test bank, and PowerPoint slides, provides additional support for students and instructors.

Joseph E. Champoux is a Regents' Professor of Management Emeritus at the University of New Mexico, USA. He has published extensively, in such journals as the *Academy of Management Journal*, *Journal of Management Education*, *Personnel Psychology*, and the *Journal of Organizational Behavior*.

ORGANIZATIONAL BEHAVIOR: INTEGRATING INDIVIDUALS, GROUPS, AND ORGANIZATIONS

Joseph E. Champoux

Sixth Edition

Routledge
Taylor & Francis Group

NEW YORK AND LONDON

Sixth edition published 2020
by Routledge
52 Vanderbilt Avenue, New York, NY 10017

and by Routledge
2 Park Square, Milton Park, Abingdon, Oxon, OX14 4RN

Routledge is an imprint of the Taylor & Francis Group, an informa business

© 2020 Taylor & Francis

First edition published by West Group 1996
Fifth edition published by Routledge 2016

Library of Congress Cataloging-in-Publication Data
Names: Champoux, Joseph E. (Joseph Edward), author.
Title: Organizational behavior : integrating individuals, groups, and
    organizations / Joseph E. Champoux.
Description: Sixth edition. | New York, NY : Routledge, 2020. | Includes
    bibliographical references and index.
Identifiers: LCCN 2019052644 | ISBN 9780367187460 (hardback) | ISBN
    9780367430047 (paperback) | ISBN 9781003000587 (ebook)
Subjects: LCSH: Organizational behavior. | Organizational behavior.
Classification: LCC HD58.7 .C453 2020 | DDC 302.3/5--dc23
LC record available at https://lccn.loc.gov/2019052644

ISBN: 978-0-367-18746-0 (hbk)
ISBN: 978-0-367-43004-7 (pbk)
ISBN: 978-1-003-00058-7 (ebk)

Typeset in Times New Roman
by Servis Filmsetting Ltd, Stockport, Cheshire

Visit the companion website: http://cw.routledge.com/textbooks/champoux

To Linda, Jean-Marc, Jean-André, Suzanne Nicole,
Blaise, Elektra, Milo, Rémy, and Soaring Seagull Bistro and Kennel

CONTENTS

PART 1: INTRODUCTION: THE CONTEXT OF MODERN ORGANIZATIONAL BEHAVIOR AND MANAGEMENT

PART 2: INDIVIDUAL PROCESSES IN ORGANIZATIONS

PART 3: GROUP AND INTERPERSONAL PROCESSES IN ORGANIZATIONS

PART 4: ORGANIZATIONAL PROCESSES

PART 5: ORGANIZATIONAL DESIGN AND ORGANIZATIONAL CHANGE

DETAILED TABLE
OF CONTENTS

PART 1: INTRODUCTION: THE CONTEXT OF MODERN ORGANIZATIONAL BEHAVIOR AND MANAGEMENT

PART 2: INDIVIDUAL PROCESSES IN ORGANIZATIONS

PART 3: GROUP AND INTERPERSONAL PROCESSES IN ORGANIZATIONS

FIGURES AND TABLES

Figures

Tables

PREFACE

Organizational Behavior: Integrating Individuals, Groups, and Organizations, sixth edition, concisely presents essential theories about organizational behavior and concepts for managing in the twenty-first century. This book is a product of more than 40 years of teaching organizational behavior at the undergraduate, graduate, and executive levels. The goal of this book is to show the power of organizational behavior theories and concepts and to help people understand their behavior and the behavior of others in an organization.

This book helps the reader to quickly comprehend essential organizational behavior theories and concepts. Although it is firmly grounded in behavioral science theory and research, it is not a compendium of research findings. I have carefully selected topics and built them into frameworks that are useful for explaining, analyzing, and diagnosing organizational processes.

Organizational Behavior includes topics that apply to issues or problems that people face in organizations. Each chapter develops its content and shows the reader its application through references to the opening episode and other examples.

I designed this book for upper-division undergraduate courses and introductory graduate courses in organizational behavior. It is also appropriate for internal training programs in corporations and government. The descriptions of behavioral science theory and research will help both nonmanagers and managers. For nonmanagers, the book offers insights into personal behavior and the behavior of others, which should help a person perform effectively in an organization. For readers who are managers or will become managers, *Organizational Behavior* offers insight into managerial situations. The discussion of motivation, for example, explains both what motivates a person to behave in certain ways and how managers can affect the behavior of people by using guidelines from motivation theory.

The book combines macro and micro perspectives, because I believe the combined perspectives are essential to understanding organizations and their management. Treating behavioral processes with little reference to organizational design assumes that people behave independently of the organized forms within which they behave. This book describes the relationships between aspects of organizational design and the specific behavioral process under discussion. All chapters are fully updated with current research results and references.

DISTINCTIVE FEATURES

Organizational Behavior has many distinctive features. The organization of the book is based on five parts. The first part has four chapters, which describe the context of modern organizational behavior and management. The next three parts follow the widely accepted individual, group, and organizational perspectives. The last part looks at organizational design and organizational change.

I have built an **integrated perspective** of organizations by linking related theories and concepts, both within chapters and in the chapter sequencing. Discussions also show how the theories and concepts apply to individuals, groups, and organizational processes. The result is a set of useful insights about organizational behavior and management that will serve people well in their careers.

Several **student resources** distinguish this text. Each is designed to enhance learning while reading and studying chapter content. These interactive student resources use multimedia to help students apply the theories and concepts in each chapter. The resources include "Take Five: OB Alive" film scenes and the Companion Site, which has extensive online content. Readers access each online resource using the access code and related instructions bound with this book.

"Take Five: OB Alive" describes a film with scenes that highlight selected concepts discussed in the chapter. Each chapter's scenes give readers a powerful visual anchor that makes organizational behavior concepts truly accessible. Students are encouraged to make notes about what they see, guided by the questions provided. Your instructor has the detailed analysis of the film scene that ties it closely to chapter content. You can view the scenes as often as you wish, making the film scenes a useful study and review resource.

The **Companion Site** has extensive online material that enhances student learning and comprehension of this book's content. This online content includes detailed chapter outlines, PowerPoint slides, online quizzes, a glossary of terms, and much more.

An **"International Aspects"** section in each chapter describes the cross-cultural aspects of the chapter's content and examines the special international issues it raises. For example, this section in Chapter 16, "Stress in Organizations," describes the stressors that expatriates and repatriates experience during their international transitions.

Beginning with Chapter 4, an **"Ethical Issues"** section in each chapter addresses the ethical issues raised by the chapter's topics. Analyses in these sections build upon the ethical theory background presented in Chapter 3, "Ethics and Behavior in Organizations." They also deal with cross-cultural ethical issues as appropriate. This section in Chapter 6, "Organizational Socialization," closely examines the ethical issues surrounding an organization's socialization efforts, especially deliberate efforts to shape a person's behavior.

The **"References and Notes"** section at the end of each chapter has all citations and some explanatory notes. Readers can view this section as a rich resource for library research about a topic, especially for a course paper or term project. The citations often have more detailed discussion of topics than the text.

ORGANIZATION OF THE BOOK

Part 1 has four chapters that describe the context of modern organizations.

■ Chapter 1, "Introduction and Historical Background," outlines the book's goals and how it presents material. It describes organizations, the roles they play in our lives, and how theories and concepts offer different perspectives on organizations. The opening chapter develops functional analysis because it is used throughout the book as an analytical tool. An "Historical Foundations" section looks at the major predecessors of modern thinking.

■ Chapter 2, "The Context of Modern Organizations (Diversity, Quality, Technology, International)," discusses several issues that form the context of modern management: workforce diversity, quality management, technology, and international issues. The first two topics receive detailed treatment, providing a full understanding of the issues. Other chapters weave in these issues as appropriate. I treat emerging and predicted future technologies in a separate section that examines the behavioral and management issues of modern technology. The international section offers a useful framework for thinking about cross-cultural aspects of organizational behavior.

■ Chapter 3, "Ethics and Behavior in Organizations," provides detailed treatment of ethics and behavior in organizations. Several ethicists reviewed this chapter for accuracy. This chapter comes early in the book to emphasize the importance of ethics and behavior in organizations and to point the reader squarely at the issue of building an ethical culture in an organization. Each chapter after Chapter 3 has a separate section that discusses the ethical implications of the chapter's topics. Those sections apply many ideas developed in Chapter 3.

■ Chapter 4, "Organizational Culture," describes organizational culture. Part 1 includes this discussion because of its intimate connection with the issues described in Chapter 2, the emphasis on ethical values in Chapter 3, and the strong context it presents for behavior in organizations. The chapter describes the major elements of organizational culture, and how managers create, maintain, and change organizational cultures.

Part 2 focuses on individual processes in organizations.

■ Chapter 5, "Perception, Attitudes, and Personality," gives a basic background used in later chapters. It includes a discussion of attribution processes, attitude formation and change, and personality development. The discussion of personality development includes the potentially controversial views of the biological bases of personality. It also includes a discussion of the role of emotions in human personality and behavior.

■ Chapter 6, "Organizational Socialization," describes organizational socialization processes and is closely linked to the earlier organizational culture chapter. This chapter's purpose is to inform the reader of what to expect when first considering an organization from an employee's perspective and the dynamics of the socialization process over time. The chapter also describes some limited aspects of careers because different aspects of socialization are experienced as one's career unfolds.

▪ Chapter 7, "Motivation: Need Theories," Chapter 8, "Motivation: Cognitive and Behavioral Theories and Techniques," and Chapter 9, "Job Design and Intrinsic Rewards," develop material dealing with motivation, rewards, and job design. The chapters describe need theories, cognitive and behavioral theories, and job design theory. These chapters let a reader do an analysis and diagnosis of motivational problems.

Part 3 presents material dealing with various aspects of group and interpersonal processes in organizations.

▪ Chapter 10, "Groups and Intergroup Processes," describes groups and intergroup processes in organizations. The chapter focuses on the role of informal groups in organizations, their functions and dysfunctions, why cohesive groups form, and the stages of group development.
▪ Chapter 11, "Conflict in Organizations," describes conflict in organizations and conflict management. Conflict management includes both reducing and increasing conflict. This chapter includes some discussion of the role of groups in conflict.
▪ Chapter 12, "Leadership and Management," describes various approaches to leadership research and outlines the conclusions drawn from that research. The chapter discusses current thinking about trait, behavioral, and contingency approaches to leadership, followed by descriptions of some alternative leadership views. One view is the leadership mystique; another is transformational leadership; a third is charismatic leadership; a fourth is Leader-Member Exchange (LMX) theory; a fifth view focuses on self-leadership, SuperLeadership, and servant-leadership. The chapter contrasts leadership and management and shows the difference between the two concepts.

Part 4 has four chapters focusing on several organization processes: communication, decision making, power, political behavior, and stress.

▪ Chapter 13, "Communication Processes," discusses communication processes in organizations. The chapter first presents a model of the basic communication process. It describes verbal and nonverbal communication, active listening, ways of improving communication effectiveness, and communication networks. A distinctive feature of this chapter is a discussion of technology's effects on communication and how technology will change people's interactions.
▪ Chapter 14, "Decision-Making and Problem-Solving Processes," begins with a discussion of decision-making processes in organizations. The chapter then moves to a discussion of different decision-making models. It

contrasts individual and group decision making, the advantages and disadvantages of each, and the Vroom-Yetton decision process model.

■ Chapter 15, "Power and Political Behavior," discusses both power and organizational politics. This chapter fully develops the concept of power and its many facets and bases. The chapter then moves to ways of building power and power attributions. It includes a discussion of political strategies, political tactics, and how to do a political diagnosis. It also examines the dark side of organizational politics—deception, lying, and intimidation.

■ Chapter 16, "Stress in Organizations," covers types of stressors, incremental and cumulative effects of stress, and ways of managing stress. Descriptions of the various nonwork sources of stress and how these stressors interact with work stressors are the chapter's unusual features. Other sections describe stress-diagnosis and stress management strategies.

Part 5 has two chapters that examine organizational design and organizational change.

■ Chapter 17, "Organizational Design," describes the contingency factors of organizational design (environment, technology, strategy, and size). It follows with a discussion of the configuration view of organizational design that includes two configuration typologies: (1) mechanistic and organic organizations; and (2) the four-part typology of defender, prospector, analyzer, and reactor. The chapter then discusses several alternative organizational forms (functional, division, hybrid, and matrix). The chapter also includes descriptions of some evolving forms of organizational design: self-managing teams, a process view of organizational design, and the virtual organization.

■ Chapter 18, "Organizational Change and Development," discusses why organizations must change, how managers cause planned change, and resistance to change. It includes a discussion of several organizational development interventions.

SUPPLEMENTS

All supplementary material is available on the Companion Site at http://cw. routledge.com/textbooks/champoux.

INSTRUCTORS' MANUAL

I have prepared an Instructor's Manual to accompany the text. This manual has the following special features:

■ Chapter outlines: Three- and four-level detailed chapter outlines.
■ Teaching tips: Descriptions of how to use the chapter material for teaching

college students, for corporate training, and for government training. This section often has current research observations not included in the text.

▪ **Personal and management implications:** Discussion of the chapter's implications for individuals and managers.

▪ **Take Five: OB Alive:** Analysis of the film scene chosen for each chapter with suggestions on how to integrate the scene into classroom activities.

▪ **Answers to review and discussion questions:** Detailed answers to all discussion questions, including ways to probe and direct class discussion.

▪ **Additional chapter material:** These materials are theories and concepts that I could not include in the textbook because of space limitations.

▪ **Instructional television applications:** Observations on ways to make the chapter material effective when teaching by television.

RESPONDUS 4.0 TEST BANK

The Respondus 4.0 test bank has almost 2,300 questions. It includes multiple-choice, true false, and completion questions for each chapter. Respondus is an easy-to-use test-generating computer program. It lets instructors quickly create printed tests, online tests, and import them into online courses. Instructors can enter their own questions, using the software provided, and customize the appearance of their tests. The "Exam Wizard" lets test generators use an existing bank of questions to create a test in minutes, using a step-by-step program.

POWERPOINT SLIDES

A complete set of PowerPoint slides supports each chapter and acts as a guide to chapter content. The slides include many chapter figures, additional figures, and text slides. The slides are available on the Instructor page of the website.

INSTRUCTOR'S ANCILLARIES

Key instructor ancillaries (Instructor Manual, Respondus Test Bank, the Companion Site, and PowerPoint slides) give instructors the vital tool for customizing lectures and presentations. These are available in the Instructor section of the Companion Site.

THE COMPANION SITE

The Companion Site (http://cw.routledge.com/textbooks/champoux) is a student's guide to studying and developing a better understanding of what you are learning from this textbook. It is a content-rich, Web-based teaching and learning aid that reinforces and clarifies complex concepts. You have access to summary materials to complement the text chapters, outlines, a glossary of terms, and more.

AVOIDING SEXIST LANGUAGE

I am sensitive to the need to avoid sexist language, particularly in a textbook. I chose to use a single gender throughout a chapter but alternate female and male gender from one chapter to another. My daughter Nicole chose the male gender for Chapter 1 based on a coin flip. All even-numbered chapters use the female gender; all odd-numbered chapters use the male gender.

ACKNOWLEDGMENTS

My Students. Thousands of my students read earlier versions of this book. They included undergraduate, Masters of Business Administration (MBA), and Executive MBA students. Many have given me feedback, which has led to this improved text.

Reviewers. I thank the following reviewers for their valuable suggestions.

Joseph Adamo, Cazenovia College
Paschal Anosike, University of Wolverhampton
Scott J. Behson, Fairleigh Dickinson University
William H. Bommer, Georgia State University
Don Bowen, Dalton State College
Greg Braxton-Brown, Indiana University East
Lisa Burke, Louisiana State University
Andrea Burleson, Roosevelt University
Matthew Cocks, Cincinnati Bell
Thomas C. Cross, Drake University
Cynthia E. Devers, Texas A&M University
Benjamin L. Dilla, Webster University
Harry Domicone, California Lutheran University
Jaye Francis, University of New Mexico
Edward W. Frederickson, University of Texas at El Paso
Sally R. Fuller, University of South Florida
Janice S. Gates, Western Illinois University
Robert D. Goddard, III, Appalachian State University
Amy Hietapelto, Michigan Technological University
Jacqueline N. Hood, University of New Mexico
Fred Hughes, Faulkner University
Kathryn A. Jackson, Loyola University, Chicago
Deborah L. Kidder, University of Connecticut
Susan Kuznik, Baldwin-Wallace College
Jeong-Yeon (Jay) Lee, Indiana University
Stephen J. Linenberger, Bellevue University

Doyle J. Lucas, Anderson University
Nora Madjar, University of Connecticut
Karen Markel, Oakland University
Jon Monat, California State University, Long Beach
Samuel M. Natale, Adelphi University
Christopher Neck, Arizona State University
Pamela Pommerenke, Michigan State University
Terry B. Porter, University of Massachusetts, Amherst
Joan Benek Rivera, Bloomsburg University
Jeffrey A. Robinson, University of Phoenix
Robert Sands, Rensselaer Polytechnic Institute
Roy Shin, Indiana University
Jonathan Smith, John Carroll University
Gregory K. Stephens, Texas Christian University
Scott L. Stevens, Detroit College of Business
Thomas Sy, California State University, Long Beach
Joe G. Thomas, Middle Tennessee State University
Holly A. Traver, Rensselaer Polytechnic Institute
Linn Van Dyne, Michigan State University
Stephen Vitucci, Tarleton University
Ignatius Yacoub, Loma Linda University

My special thanks to the anonymous reviewers of this edition and the following people at Routledge Publishing. This team brought this book to fruition:

- ▨ To Mary Del Plato, Editorial Assistant, for cordially keeping me well-focused on our production schedule.
- ▨ To Miriam Pilcher-Clayton, Production Editor, for leading me through the production process.
- ▨ To Gail Welsh, Copy Editor, for excellent copy editing observations on the text.

FEEDBACK AND CONTINUOUS IMPROVEMENT

I ask all users of this book to give me feedback about any aspect of its content and design. I want to continuously improve the book and need your help to do that. Please send your comments and observations to me at 10201 Modesto Ave. NE, Albuquerque, New Mexico 87122–3906, USA. You also can contact me at 505.401.1260 or send e-mail to champoux@unm.edu.

Part 1

INTRODUCTION: THE CONTEXT OF MODERN ORGANIZATIONAL BEHAVIOR AND MANAGEMENT

Part 1 introduces you to organizations and discusses some major issues that form the context of modern organizational behavior and management. It also discusses ethics, organizational behavior, and organizational culture.

Chapter 1, "Introduction and Historical Background," introduces you to the world of organizations. This chapter defines an organization and introduces you to theories and concepts. The chapter also describes the historical background of modern thinking about organizations and management.

Chapter 2, "The Context of Modern Organizations (Diversity, Quality, Technology, International)," focuses on four major issues that can affect modern organizations and their management. Those issues are workforce diversity, managing for quality, technology, and the global environment of organizations. Projected changes in the demographic makeup of the domestic civilian workforce will make the workforce of the future more diverse, presenting managers with both opportunities and problems. Managing for quality helps organizations become more competitive and meet the needs of increasingly demanding consumers. The third issue, technology, will have sweeping effects on organizations and their managers well into the future. The global environment of organizations adds still another dimension of diversity, opportunity, and problems. Today's managers can no longer assume their markets and competitors are only within their home country's boundary.

Much behavior and many decisions in organizations involve ethical issues. Chapter 3, "Ethics and Behavior in Organizations," examines ethics and ethical behavior in detail. The chapter first considers the social responsibility of modern organizations and then compares ethical and unethical behavior in organizations. It next describes the sources of ethics for both societies and individuals and reviews several theories of ethics. Finally, the chapter addresses how managers can promote ethical behavior and considers the implications the increasingly global environment of organizations has on ethical behavior.

Chapter 4, "Organizational Culture," describes many aspects of organizational culture and its effects on organization members. The chapter offers several ways of viewing organizational cultures. It describes the functions and dysfunctions of cultures, explains how to diagnose an organization's culture, and discusses the relationship between an organization's culture and its performance. The chapter discusses some international aspects of organizational culture and several ethical issues.

Chapter 1

INTRODUCTION AND HISTORICAL BACKGROUND

After reading this chapter, you should be able to:

- Describe the concept of an organization.
- Distinguish between organizational behavior and organizational theory.
- Explain the role of theory and concepts in analyzing behavioral issues and problems.
- Analyze the consequences of behavior in organizations.
- Discuss the historical foundations of modern organizational behavior and management.

Modern organizations face simultaneous pressures for change and stability. Many organization members view these opposing pressures as paradoxical and difficult to understand.[1] Successful organizations constantly evolve and thrive on change. Managers and nonmanagers in this system must repeatedly innovate to stay competitive.[2] Many employees find these systems exhilarating. Others view them as a source of stress.

Organizations extensively use technology for many organizational processes and interactions. A company's intranet helps manage internal interactions wherever they occur in the world. Organizations use the Internet to manage external interactions with suppliers, customers, and partners. Such technologies help managers sustain the global focus needed for success. Many employees telecommute, working from their homes or other locations using computer technology.[3]

Technology also changes many aspects of organizational form and function. Electronic groups saw extensive development since the 1980s. Group members interact over a network using group-support technology. Group members can be anywhere: in the same room or across the globe.[4]

An emerging organization form called the virtual organization has become increasingly common. These networks of organizations and individuals coordinate their activities electronically. They can span the globe and feature diverse cultures, yet they stay focused on specific goals.[5]

Strategic changes have become the norm.[6] This is the area that will see the greatest pressure for stability and change. Pressure for stability comes from managers who believe they have a successful strategy. Pressure for change comes from managers who believe a new strategy is essential. Electronic business (e-commerce) is a source of continuing pressure. The strategic decisions focus on whether to have traditional outlets for products and services (bricks and mortar) or electronic outlets over the Internet (or both).

Welcome to the modern organizational world! You possibly have experienced much of what this introduction described. If you have not, there is a high probability that you will in the future. This book discusses all the topics mentioned and gives you well-grounded information to let you function successfully in this modern environment.

This chapter starts with the definitions of some basic concepts that underlie all other chapters. It then summarizes some historical foundation writings that are enduring classical observations on organizations and management.

These observations, made many years ago, apply to many issues about modern organizations.[7]

WHAT IS AN ORGANIZATION?

An **organization** is a system of two or more persons, engaged in cooperative action, trying to reach a purpose.[8] Organizations are bounded systems of structured social interaction featuring authority relations, communication systems, and the use of incentives. They usually have a hierarchical form, whether steep or shallow. Organizations have formal legal status and are recognized by state and federal governments. Examples of organizations include businesses, hospitals, colleges, retail stores, and prisons.[9]

We are all part of organizations. You are part of an organization at your college or university. In your daily activities, you move from one organization to another. You might shop at a store, deal with a government agency, or go to work. Understanding organizations and their management can give you significant insights into systems that have major effects on you.

Consider for a moment the various classes in which you are now enrolled. Each class has a different professor, often different students, and a different structure. The relationship between professor and students differs from one class to the next. Each class exposes you to a different organization, a different structure, and a different culture.

Reflect on your reactions to your classes. You enjoy some classes more than others. You are pleased or annoyed by some aspects of the way professors manage their classes. The task of this book is to develop an understanding of such phenomena in organizations.

ORGANIZATIONAL BEHAVIOR AND ORGANIZATIONAL THEORY

Organizational behavior and organizational theory are two disciplines within the social and behavioral sciences that specialize in studying organizations.[10] The term organizational behavior is a little misleading because it actually refers to the behavior of people in organizations—organizations themselves do not behave. **Organizational behavior** focuses on the behavior, attitudes, and performance of people in organizations. **Organizational theory** focuses on the design and structure of organizations.

As Figure 1.1 shows, several social and behavioral science disciplines contribute to both organizational behavior and organizational theory. The discipline of organizational behavior draws on theory and concepts from various branches of psychology, anthropology, political science, and the sociology of work. From the psychological disciplines comes information about human psychological processes that can affect behavior in an organization. For example, psychology has contributed vast knowledge about human motivation. It tells how a system of rewards affects a person's behavior and performance in an organization.

Anthropology, political science, and the sociology of work offer other perspectives, theories, and concepts about organizational behavior. Anthropology emphasizes the importance of culture in human systems. It also offers some analytical tools for studying behavior in organizations, one of which this chapter introduces later. Political science forms part of the base for studying political behavior in organizations. The sociology of work emphasizes social status and social relationships in the work setting.

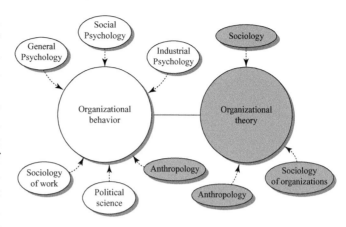

Figure 1.1: Organizational Behavior and Organizational Theory

The discipline of organizational theory strives to understand the existing design of an organization, ways to decide its redesign, and alternate forms of organizational design. Sociology offers theories and concepts about social systems and relationships in them. The sociology of organizations, the core of organizational theory, is a specialized part of sociology that focuses on organizations as social systems. Anthropology's theories and concepts about entire societies also contribute to organizational theory.

Figure 1.1 links organizational behavior to organizational theory by a solid line to show that neither area of study can ignore the other. Because behavior happens within a specific organizational design, you need to understand the perspectives of organizational theory. Similarly, human beings design organizations and are embedded in a behavioral system that can strongly affect their behavior.

Both areas of organizational study are important, although this book mainly discusses topics from organizational behavior, such as organizational culture, socialization processes, motivation, and group dynamics. Chapter 17, "Organizational Design," draws its content from organizational theory. That chapter also links its observations to organizational behavior.

THEORIES AND CONCEPTS

Each chapter describes theories and the concepts derived from those theories. Each theory uses **concepts** to explain parts of the phenomena to which the theory applies.[11] Think of the concepts as tools, a notion that emphasizes their use in understanding behavior in organizations. As the book unfolds, you will develop a large collection of theories and concepts. You will learn to use those tools analytically to look at and solve organizational problems.

Theory

The word theory has many meanings and connotations, not all of which are positive. People often describe theory as abstract, boring, and not associated with the real world. This book has a positive view of theory. As the late Kurt Lewin, a noted social psychologist, said many years ago, "Nothing is as practical as a good theory,"[12] a view with which this book agrees. A simple working definition is: "a **theory** is a plausible explanation of a phenomenon."[13] Theory also describes relationships among its concepts. Of course, some theories are stronger and better-developed than others. This book describes each theory in detail so that you can judge how useful it is in understanding behavior in organizations.

Theories and Concepts as Lenses

Scientists have long recognized that theories from different scientific disciplines give different views of problems, issues, and questions. Different theoretical perspectives help scientists derive multiple answers to a single question.[14] Similarly, using theories and concepts lets you bring different views to the same organizational issue, problem, or question.[15]

Scientists use theories and concepts in much the same way that photographers use zoom lenses or **lenses** of different focal lengths. A normal lens has an angle of view about the same as human vision. A wide-angle lens gives a broad view of a scene. A telephoto lens lets a photographer isolate the part of a scene on which he wants to concentrate. Photographers often start with an overview of a scene. They then move in and out with a zoom lens or lenses of different focal lengths depending on what they want to emphasize. You can do the same with theories and concepts.

Figure 1.2 shows the relationship between theories and concepts and how they can act as camera lenses. Let us assume that you are interested in understanding why someone is not doing a job as well as he could. As later chapters explain, motivation is an important element in job performance (the broad view of the scene). Two theories of motivation are expectancy theory and equity theory. You might choose either theory to help you understand the performance problem.

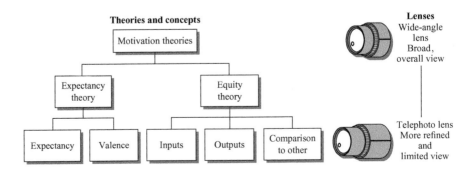

▨ **Figure 1.2:** Theories and Concepts as Lenses

Expectancy theory can help narrow the view of the scene with its concepts of expectancy and valence. Expectancy is a person's belief that performance leads to an expected outcome. Valence is the preference people have among outcomes.[16] These concepts act as telephoto lenses. Applying each concept to the performance problem focuses your attention on limited parts of the problem. Expectancy focuses on a person's performance-outcome belief, and valence focuses on a person's preference among outcomes.

Just as a skilled photographer switches lenses or uses a zoom lens to view a scene from several perspectives, you will learn to use concepts to view behavioral phenomena in organizations from many perspectives. A skilled manager knows the concepts and moves quickly from one to another to analyze and solve problems in an organization.

FUNCTIONAL ANALYSIS

Theories and concepts explain behavioral phenomena from the perspective of the theory's author and the intended results. Unintended consequences often occur with, or instead of, the intended consequences. You will find it useful to examine theoretical concepts according to both what is supposed to happen and what might occur unintentionally.

You can examine the consequences of behavior with **functional analysis**, an analytical tool borrowed from anthropology.[17] When anthropologists study a society, they divide their behavioral observations into two groups. First, they decide whether the consequences of behavior are manifest or latent. Then they determine whether the consequences are functional or dysfunctional for the society.

Manifest consequences are the intended results of an individual's actions. **Latent consequences** are unintended results, often of the same behavior. Latent consequences can occur, but the person does not intend for them to happen. For example, an organization might specify quantity targets for production (manifest consequence), and workers meet the target by accepting poor-quality output (latent consequence).

Functional consequences are results of behavior that are good for the organization and help its adjustment and adaptation. Such results contribute to the organization's progress toward its goals. **Dysfunctional consequences** are results of behavior that have a negative effect on the organization. These results restrict the organization's adjustment and adaptation, impeding it from reaching its goals.

Considering manifest and latent consequences with functional and dysfunctional consequences produces four classes of behavioral consequences. Although four are possible, we are interested mainly in two: manifest functional consequences and latent dysfunctional consequences.

Manifest functional consequences are intended results of behavior that are also good for the organization. People in an organization behave in specific ways expecting something good to happen. They make decisions as managers or employees and want those decisions to have good results.

Organizational change and new technology are common sources of **latent dysfunctional consequences**—results of behavior that have unintended negative effects on an organization. Managers often change their organization design and processes to adapt to a fast-changing, competitive environment. The manifest functional consequence is to improve their competitive position. The latent dysfunctional consequence is an equal response from competitors, making the environment more complex and competitive.[18] Introducing new technologies to an organization also can result in latent dysfunctional consequences.[19]

While reading this book, deliberately test what it says using the perspective of latent dysfunctional consequences. Such an analysis can be a powerful tool because it adds much information to a theory or concept.

HISTORICAL FOUNDATIONS

Modern organizational behavior and management has a rich intellectual history. This section describes some key people and ideas that are the historical base for what we know today.

Division of Labor: Adam Smith (1776)

The division of labor is the way an organization divides its tasks, duties, and responsibilities among its members. The importance of the division of labor in managing an organization led at least one scholar to say, "The division of labor is without doubt the cornerstone among the four elements [of classical organizational theory]."[20]

The importance of the division of labor in manufacturing in early industrial England impressed Adam Smith, the famous Scottish philosopher.[21] He discussed the division of labor in the first chapter of his book, *The Wealth of Nations*. Smith offered the following as an example of the division of labor:

> To take an example, therefore, from a very trifling manufacture; but one in which the division of labour has been very often taken notice of, the trade of the pin-maker; a workman ... could scarce, perhaps, with his utmost industry, make one pin in a day, and certainly could not make twenty. But in the way in which this business is now carried on, not only the whole work is a peculiar trade, but it is divided into a number of branches, of which the greater part are likewise peculiar trades. One man draws out the wire, another straightens it, a third cuts it, a fourth points it, a fifth grinds it at the top for receiving the head; to make the head requires two or three distinct operations; to put it on, is a peculiar business; to whiten the pins is another; it is even a trade by itself to put them into the paper; and the important business of making a pin is, in this manner, divided into about eighteen distinct operations, which, in some manufactories, are all performed by distinct hands, though in others the same man will sometimes perform two or three of them. I have seen a small manufactory of this kind where ten men only were employed, and where some of them consequently

performed two or three distinct operations. But though they were very poor, and therefore but indifferently accommodated with the necessary machinery, they could, when they exerted themselves, make among them about twelve pounds of pins in a day. There are in a pound upwards of four thousand pins of a middling size. Those ten persons, therefore, could make among them upwards of forty-eight thousand pins in a day.[22]

In this passage, Smith described what we today would term the manifest functions of the division of labor. Smith believed higher productivity would follow from the division of labor because it helps workers increase their skill and dexterity in doing their tasks. Because the division of labor limits the number of tasks a person does and the number of places where a person does a task, workers save time by not moving from one task location to another. By repeatedly doing the same task, workers may discover better ways of doing it. These innovations can then be introduced into the work process, improving it. Lastly, from doing the task repeatedly, the workers' skills improved until eventually they have mastered the task.

Smith also felt the division of labor could have some latent dysfunctional consequences. Doing the same task repeatedly could lead to mental degradation. The workers would no longer perceive the task as stimulating, and their mental processes would slow. Smith felt that lack of involvement in work led to decreased political and social involvement. Workers also would become physically inactive because their work did not require them to move about.[23]

Smith described a high degree of task specialization in the 18 operations of making a pin. Division of labor, however, does not always lead to high specialization and routine work. Division of labor spans a continuum from low to high task specialization. Smith's description of making a straight pin is on the far right of the task specialization continuum. The job of a heart surgeon is on the far left.

Scientific Management: Frederick W. Taylor (1911)

"The principal object of management should be to secure the maximum prosperity for the employer, coupled with the maximum prosperity for each employee."[24] Those words appear in the opening paragraph of Frederick W. Taylor's book *The Principles of Scientific Management*. Taylor felt he had developed a new approach to management that produced positive results for both employer and employee.[25]

The usual approach to management in Taylor's day was based on antagonistic relationships between management and labor. Management wanted as much output from labor as possible at the lowest possible cost. Workers tried to protect their interests by not working too hard. They believed they would put themselves or their coworkers out of work if they worked at a faster pace. Neither side felt cooperation could lead to maximum prosperity for both.

Although Taylor made his observation in the early 1900s, it appeared again in the 1998 General Motors strike. The effects of this strike prompted GM to appoint a new vice president for labor relations with a history of a cooperative orientation to labor.[26]

Management wanted to maximize profits, and workers wanted the highest possible wages. Disputes between management and labor centered on what each viewed as mutually exclusive goals. Taylor felt his system of scientific management could maximize both goals. Both sides had to undergo a "mental revolution." Each side had to rid itself of antagonistic views of the other. Taylor felt they should view profits as the result of cooperation between management and workers. In short, management needed the workers and workers needed management to get what they each wanted.

Taylor based his **scientific management** on the following four principles:[27]

■ Carefully study jobs to develop standard work practices. Standardize the tools used by workers.
■ Select each worker scientifically.
■ Management and workers cooperate to ensure that work is done according to standard procedures.[28]
■ Management plans and makes task assignments; workers carry out assigned tasks.

These four principles describe a division of work between management and workers. Managers planned and designed the work. They made task assignments, set performance goals, and made time schedules. Managers also selected and trained the workers to do the tasks according to standard procedures and gave the workers quick feedback about how they were doing. They rewarded increased individual productivity with economic incentives.

Taylor's system, procedures, and behavior irritated many people in business and government, and even some of his supporters. Some observers perceive him as leaving the greatest legacy in modern management history. Frederick Taylor was the twentieth century's first management consultant.[29]

Toward a Theory of Administration: Henri Fayol (1919)

Henri Fayol, managing director of Commentry-Fourchambault Company in France, prepared a theory of administration based on his management experiences.[30] His theory described the major management functions and several principles that act as administrative guides.

Fayol took a broad view of administration. He felt his theory of administration applied to all types of organizations, public and private.[31]

Fayol's five **functions of management** are planning, organizing, commanding, coordinating, and controlling. These management functions have endured the test of time. A review of research that focused on managerial activities showed that an impressive number of activities fell into Fayol's five functions. Managers not only performed those classical functions then, but they should continue to do them today. The time spent on these areas and the skills required to do them were associated with higher performance of the manager's unit or organization.[32]

Fayol believed that managers "all must observe the same general principles."[33] These principles were central to his theory of administration. They are a set of tools a manager needs to perform the functions of management. He did not believe managers should apply his principles rigidly and absolutely in all circumstances; instead, they must tailor the application of the principles to the specific circumstances they face, using a clear **sense of proportion**.

Fayol's first principle was the **division of labor**. His remark, "Specialization belongs to the natural order," shows the importance of this principle to his thinking.[34] The division of labor applied not only to tasks done by individuals, but also to the total organization. Fayol warned, however, that the "division of work has its limits which experience and a sense of proportion teach us may not be exceeded."[35]

The principle of **authority and responsibility** implies a relationship between the two ideas. "Authority is the right to give orders and the power to exact obedience ... and wheresoever authority is exercised responsibility arises."[36]

The principle of **centralization** is an essential element of administration and organization. This principle describes the location of decision authority, at the top of an organization when centralized and at lower levels when decentralized. A sense of proportion rules this principle also. As Fayol noted, "The question of centralization or decentralization, is a simple question of proportion, it is a matter of finding the optimum degree for the particular concern."[37]

Delegation of authority is the management tool used to get the desired degree of centralization or decentralization. Delegating authority moves decision authority to lower organizational levels. Although Fayol did not use the phrase "delegation of authority," he clearly implied its use.[38]

The principle of **unity of command** means "an employee should receive orders from one superior only."[39] Fayol strongly felt that managers should never violate this principle. Modern matrix and project organizations violate it, and conflict occurs. Such conflict does not become dysfunctional when it is properly managed. People often live with violations of the unity of command principle successfully. See Chapter 17 for a discussion of matrix organizations where such violations commonly occur.

A principle related to unity of command is **unity of direction**: "One head and one plan for a group of activities having the same objective."[40] This principle helped determine the division of labor of the organization. Set up a department or work unit and have a single goal for that unit.

Several relationships exist among the principles. Delegation of authority gets the desired degree of centralization or decentralization. Delegation also leads to a division of labor in the organization. Unity of command and unity of direction are guides for an organization's design. Think of these concepts as Fayol's tools for designing and managing organizations.

Bureaucracy: Max Weber (1922)

Max Weber was a prominent German political scientist, economist, and sociologist. He made a major contribution to several fields of study with his analysis of bureaucracy as a form of organization and management. He believed bureaucracy was an efficient, necessary, and successful form of administration—a view endorsed by some contemporary scholars.[41]

Bureaucracy is an administrative structure with well-defined offices or functions and hierarchical relationships among the functions. The offices or functions have clearly defined duties, rights, and responsibilities. Each office or function is designed without regard for who will hold the office. Relationships within a bureaucracy are impersonal. Decisions are made according to existing rules, procedures, and policies. Bureaucracies reach goals with precision, reliability, and efficiency.[42]

Bureaucracies use **legal** or **rational authority**, which is part of a position and exists before a person takes the position or function in a bureaucracy. The bureaucracy defines the authority when it develops its division of labor. The person who takes a position assumes that position's authority. Although authority is initially in the function, the person holding the function can change that authority. Weber felt rational authority brought stability to a bureaucracy because the authority stayed in the function after the person left.

Weber believed the following features account for the efficiency of bureaucracies:

- Clearly defined and specialized functions.
- Use of legal authority.
- Hierarchical form.
- Written rules and procedures.
- Technically trained bureaucrats.
- Appointment to positions based on technical expertise.
- Promotions based on technical competence.
- Clearly defined career path.

Weber felt bureaucracies were rational and predictable systems. The rationality followed from the objectivity and impersonality of decisions. Decisions were based on fact and made according to existing written rules and procedures so they would be consistent. The unusual features of any specific case were not to be considered. Predictability followed from the fixed formal relationships among clearly defined hierarchically organized functions.

Mary Parker Follett's Observations on Organizations and Management (1925)

Mary Parker Follett was a social worker among the poor in the Roxbury section of Boston. Although her work career did not involve management, she made several basic and enduring observations about organizations and management during the mid-1920s to the early 1930s.[43] The following paragraphs describe three of her observations on organizations and management: power, conflict, and leadership.

Follett conceived of **power** as capacity. Although her point was not completely clear, she apparently meant the capacity to get things done. Power cannot be delegated, but authority can. She clearly distinguished between power and authority, treating each separately in her analysis.[44]

Follett distinguished power-over from power-with. **Power-over** is dominance, coercion, and control based on force. **Power-with** is "a jointly developed power, a co-active, not a coercive power."[45] She offered power-with as an alternative to power-over, because she believed human organizations were cooperative systems. Follett had a positive view of power and saw it as basic to organizations and management.

Follett's analysis of conflict appeared in the unusually titled paper, "Constructive Conflict."[46] Follett felt conflict was neither good nor bad. **Conflict** is difference, not warfare. The differences can be in opinions or interests. She felt conflict could not be avoided. Instead of running from conflict, managers should put conflict to use in their organizations.

Follett felt there were three ways to manage conflict: dominance, compromise, and integration of desires. **Dominance** means one side of a conflict wins over the other. **Compromise** means each side gives up something to settle the issue. In each instance, the basic conflict issue is not settled. Although one party wins, or both parties agree on settling the dispute, the reason for the conflict remains. Conflict could later occur about the same matter or issue.

Integration of desires was Follett's creative suggestion for managing conflict. This approach finds a solution that fully meets the goals of each party in a dispute. Both parties get what they want. Neither party gives up anything. Integration of desires unshackles you from existing alternatives and lets you creatively discover alternatives that are not mutually exclusive. Integration discovers something; compromise uses only what exists. With integration, conflict is put to work to help discover new, creative solutions to problems and issues in organizations.

Follett felt the prevailing view of leadership was based on qualities such as aggressiveness and domination. The leader tried to impose his will upon others. Leadership meant giving orders and getting compliance to those orders.[47]

Follett's alternative view of **leadership** has many positive qualities. A leader has a vision of the future and can articulate the common purpose toward which the organization is striving. The leader focuses the energies of people toward that purpose. A leader not only knows the technical aspects of the job, but also understands the total situation and the relationships among its many parts. Problems are not just solved. Events are structured and decisions made to head off problems before they happen.

Decisions are made with an understanding of their long-term effects. Leaders do not make decisions that focus only on the present. They know that any situation constantly evolves and that a decision made now affects future states of the situation.

Leaders train and develop their subordinates to become leaders. By developing leaders below them, Follett believed, managers increased the total power in the situation they manage.

Good leaders do not want passive followers. Follett regarded blind obedience to orders and directives as undesirable. Instead, followers should try to influence their leaders by suggesting alternative courses of action. They also should question directives that are wrong or impossible to carry out.

Follett's view of the personal qualities of a leader is a vivid picture of the characteristics of a good leader: "Tenacity, steadfastness of purpose, tactfulness, steadiness in stormy periods."[48]

The Functions of the Executive: Chester I. Barnard (1938)

Chester Barnard was an engineer who became the president of the New Jersey Bell Telephone Company and later the first executive head of the United Services Organization. His book, *The Functions of the Executive*, is rich in basic contributions to current thinking about organizations and management.[49] The term **executive** refers to managers and supervisors at all organizational levels.

Barnard defined an **organization** as "a system of consciously coordinated activities or forces of two or more persons."[50] Barnard's definition implies that any system of two or more people with consciously coordinated activities is an organization. Organizations are based on cooperation and have a conscious, deliberate purpose.[51]

Barnard believed organizations formed because individuals had a purpose or purposes, but also had limitations. The limitations could be knowledge, financial resources, or physical resources. The person with the purpose needed the cooperation of one or more other people to achieve that purpose. **Purpose plus limitations** leads to a system of cooperative action.

How does an organization get people to join its system of cooperative action? Organizations offer inducements in exchange for contributions. **Inducements** include salary and fringe benefits. **Contributions** are activities and work behavior needed by the organization. Barnard felt a person joined an organization when the inducements exceeded the contributions.[52] Today this relationship between inducements and contributions is called the **inducements– contributions balance**.[53] Maintaining the balance so that people join and stay with the organization is an important executive function.[54]

Barnard distinguished between two types of motivation in organizations: motivation to participate and motivation to perform. **Motivation to participate** is the motivation of an individual to join and stay with the organization and perform at a minimally acceptable level.[55] The minimally acceptable level varies from one organization to another and from one part of the same organization to another. When you first join an organization, you learn the minimum performance standards. If you fall below this performance level, you might experience sanctions, particularly during probationary employment. The inducements-contributions balance is closely related to the motivation to participate. Maintaining the inducements-contributions balance lets managers affect the motivation to participate.

Barnard felt managers must first attend to the motivation to participate. After they have solved the problem of membership, they can attend to the second type of motivation, the **motivation to perform**.[56] This type of motivation focuses on performance levels higher than the minimum expectation. Managers use both monetary and nonmonetary incentives to get higher performance levels.

Notice the relationships among Barnard's observations. First, the simple definition emphasizes consciously coordinated activities of two or more people. Second, purpose plus limitations causes people to engage in cooperative behavior with others. People need to be attracted to this system of coordinated activity and induced to participate. The need to attract them to the system and keep them there leads to a concern about motivation to participate and the inducements–contributions balance. With those five concepts, you can analyze the birth and growth of any organization.

Barnard used the concept of the **zone of indifference** to describe how people could respond to orders and directives from others.[57] Figure 1.3 shows the zone of indifference. People execute orders falling within their zone of indifference without any thought or question. They question, and possibly do not act on, orders that fall outside the zone. These orders might be demeaning, such as being told to sweep the office floor, or they might be orders that could be interpreted as illegal or immoral. In both cases, the order falls outside the zone of indifference, making it unacceptable to the person.

The zone of indifference is closely related to the inducements–contributions balance. Managers affect the width of the zone of indifference by changing inducements offered for contributions requested.

The Hawthorne Studies (1939)

The **Hawthorne Studies** were a large research program at the Hawthorne Plant of the Western Electric Company from the late 1920s to the mid-1930s. The plant produced various parts for telephone switching systems. This research was a landmark work in social sciences in the United States.[58]

The Hawthorne Studies were preceded and stimulated by the illumination experiments done in the Hawthorne Plant in the early 1920s. These studies tried to determine whether various lighting levels affected human productivity. The

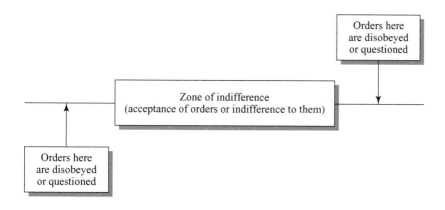

■ **Figure 1.3:** Barnard's Zone of Indifference

experimental design used a control group that had no variation in lighting. An experimental group experienced changes in light levels.

The results of the experiments baffled the investigators. They increased the lighting and productivity went up. Then they decreased the lighting and productivity went up. The lighting was severely reduced, and productivity went up. The lighting for the control group was not changed, but the group's productivity also increased! Eventually, the researchers concluded that simply being part of the experiment, which focused new and greater attention on the workers, increased productivity.[59] Previously, interaction between supervisors and coworkers was limited. It had focused mainly on the work, not on the workers themselves.

Following the illumination experiments, several researchers from Harvard University began studying groups of workers in the plant. Their goal was to understand the factors that contributed to differences in human productivity. The researchers concluded that a more empathic or people-oriented form of management leads to more productivity than a directive, authoritarian, and money-oriented form of management. People wanted more than monetary incentives for working.

Secondary analyses of the experimental data do not show the effects on worker behavior just described. Serious weaknesses in research design also do not allow any strong conclusions from the Hawthorne Studies.[60]

Some researchers doing secondary analyses of data published in the original reports have come to varying conclusions. One researcher found support for a driving form of management and use of monetary incentives. He felt the researchers moved from presenting descriptive results to promoting a new form of management. By doing so, the original Hawthorne researchers went well beyond the results of their research.[61]

Disputes about research design and research results do not reduce the importance of the Hawthorne Studies in developing our understanding of organizations. Although the research did not produce strong conclusions, the studies motivated further understanding of human behavior in organizations.

Theory X and Theory Y: Douglas McGregor (1960)

Douglas McGregor, an MIT psychologist, proposed two sets of assumptions about human motivation that a manager can hold. McGregor called the assumptions Theory X and Theory Y.[62] A manager's behavior toward his workers and his management style will differ based on the assumptions guiding his behavior.

The following are **Theory X** assumptions:

■ The average person dislikes working and will avoid it if possible.
■ Because people dislike working, they must be directed, tightly controlled, and pressured to work toward organizational goals.
■ The average person wants security, avoids responsibility, and has little ambition.

McGregor believed that many managers held Theory X assumptions about workers. Such managers give their workers little latitude, supervise them closely, and punish poor performance. They use few rewards and typically give only negative feedback.

The following are **Theory Y** assumptions:

■ The average person likes work; it is as natural as play.
■ A person who is committed to a set of goals will work toward them without external control.
■ Goal commitment follows from the satisfaction of a person's desire to achieve.
■ The average person can learn to accept responsibility. Lack of ambition is not a basic human characteristic.
■ Creativity, ingenuity, and imagination are human characteristics that are widely dispersed in the population.
■ Modern organizations only partially use the worker potentialities.

Managers who hold Theory Y assumptions have a positive view of people, believe they have much hidden potential, and believe that people will work toward organizational goals. These managers will give workers more job responsibility and rely on self-motivation rather than coercion.

These two sets of different assumptions reigned in the academic literature for many years. They are widely understood by practicing managers. Although called theories, they are not theories as described earlier. They are assumptions or beliefs about human motivation that can strongly affect management behavior.

McGregor's observations on managers' assumptions about human motivation go back many years. You might be tempted to dismiss them as an old set of ideas. Contemporary discussions of the directions of organizations in the twenty-first century are filled with concern that managers largely hold Theory X assumptions. Although these same managers say they favor employee participation, involvement, and empowerment, they often act in the directing, controlling way of Theory X assumptions.[63] (See the citations for an extended discussion of these issues.)

Management Guru: Peter F. Drucker (1995)

Austrian-born Peter F. Drucker ranks among the most widely read, widely quoted, and influential management scholars in the world.[64] Drucker was a professor of management at California's Claremont College starting in 1971. He wrote more than 30 books that cover topics in management, economics, society, and politics. His observations in his 1954 book *The Practice of Management* remain fresh today.[65] The following summarizes some observations from this book and some predictions from his other writings.

Drucker's views of the importance of effective governance of an organization, and his views of integrity as a critical element of a manager's character, set important background for his other observations. Effective organizational governance requires a strongly independent and diverse board of directors.[66] His 1954 observation that board oversight and governance had become largely fictional has a shockingly modern tone to it. Boards should have outside directors, most of whom have never served as the organization's full-time officers. Board roles include reviewing senior management's plans, questioning their assumptions, and taking action in times of crisis. The board is the final court (Drucker called it a "supreme court") when ethical or legal issues arise.

Drucker viewed integrity as a central part of a manager's character.[67] It is especially important at senior organizational levels because it sets the moral example for the entire organization. Drucker wrote about integrity with considerable passion—never can a manager lack it nor can an organization accept its absence. The latter, of course, falls to the board of directors who have the responsibility of removing a manager who lacks integrity.

These background observations appeared in Drucker's 1954 book. Reflect on contemporary events. Do modern managers have the integrity that Drucker believed was important?

Drucker's views on strategy and strategic planning differ from much prevailing practice. An organization's **strategy** describes the organization's long-term goals and the way it plans to reach those goals. Strategy also specifies how managers should allocate resources to reach their organization's long-term goals. He asked managers to move from the question of "What is most likely to happen?" to the question of "What has already happened that will create the future?"[68] Drucker urges managers to understand existing demographics, spending patterns, societal structure, economic forces, and technological changes to see what is shaping the future. His approach to planning focuses not on probabilistic future scenarios, but on existing conditions that will unrelentingly shape that future.

Among his most lasting observations was his proposed philosophy of **management by objectives and self-control**.[69] General Electric was the first company to adopt management by objectives (MBO) and put it into practice with Drucker's help as a consultant.[70]

Senior management defines the long-range goals of the organization. Lower-level managers actively participate in goal setting for units above them. These managers derive their goals from the more senior ones. Drucker emphasized the importance of each manager setting his goals, not imposing them from above. Each manager's goals become the source of self-control of the manager's performance. Drucker viewed self-control as a significant motivator and better than external control.

A key part of self-control management was the quick availability of performance information for each manager. This information went directly to each manager, not to the manager's superior. Managers at all levels guided their unit's performance toward the goal and corrected any deviations that appeared in their performance information.

MBO has endured the test of time. It is a lasting testimony to Drucker's contributions to modern management thinking. Although MBO has had negative moments, when properly carried out, it has positive effects on organizational performance.[71]

Peter Drucker's predictions proposed many challenges that organizations and managers will face well into the future.[72] They include the following:

■ Steady drops in the birthrates of developed nations will produce a population of fewer young people entering the workforce. Older workers will work well past normal retirement ages, making them valuable employee resources.

■ Global competitiveness is a necessary strategic goal for all organizations. Standards for assessing an organization's performance can come from industry leaders anywhere in the world.

■ An unquestionable forming of a world economy in which world markets will become more important than domestic markets.

■ Successfully competing in intertwined global economies requires forming alliances, partnerships, and joint ventures across national boundaries.

■ A compelling need for decentralized organizations in an increasingly uncertain environment with a related increase in using teams in organizations.

■ An increase in the number of knowledge workers (for example, computer technologists and medical workers) and continual decline in the number of blue-collar and agricultural workers in all developed countries. The knowledge workers thrive on autonomy and need continuous learning.

■ Continual change will become the norm. The management challenge is to view change as an opportunity, not a threat.

■ The twenty-first century will see the evolution of knowledge societies in developed countries. These societies will have three sectors: business, government, and nonprofit. Nonprofit volunteer activities will characterize English-speaking countries, but appear less often elsewhere.

Drucker viewed these challenges as the "new certainties" facing modern organizations and their management. Managers who profoundly change their mindset about the present state of their organization's environment will have a strategic advantage over competitors.

SUMMARY

An organization is a system of two or more persons, engaged in cooperative action, trying to reach some purpose. Organizational behavior and organizational theory are both disciplines within the social and behavioral sciences that specialize in studying organizations. Theories and concepts let you view organizational issues or problems from different perspectives. They act much like camera lenses by letting you observe a behavioral scene from different angles.

Functional analysis divides the results of a person's behavior into manifest and latent consequences. Manifest consequences are the intended results of the person's action. Latent consequences are the unintended results of the same action. Functional analysis further divides behavior into functional and dysfunctional consequences. Functional consequences are behavioral results that are good for the organization. Dysfunctional consequences are behavioral results that are bad for the organization.

SUMMARY
1

The historical foundations of modern organizational behavior and management underlie all remaining chapters of this book. Each historical figure discussed in this chapter offered basic insights into organizations and management.

REVIEW AND DISCUSSION QUESTIONS

REVIEW AND DISCUSSION QUESTIONS 1

1 What is theory? Discuss its role in analyzing and diagnosing organizational issues and problems.

2 What are the differences between manifest functional consequences and latent dysfunctional consequences? How are these concepts useful in analyzing and diagnosing organizations?

3 Henri Fayol developed the beginning of a theory of administration. Review the major concepts from his theory. What are the relationships among the concepts?

4 Discuss the differences among dominance, compromise, and integration as approaches to reducing conflict. Mary Parker Follett described these approaches to conflict reduction. Does integration of desires impress you as a feasible approach to conflict reduction?

5 Review the characteristics of leadership described by Follett. Have you ever worked for a person with those qualities? Discuss why those qualities contribute to effective leadership.

6 Review Chester I. Barnard's concepts. Discuss the relationships among them. Have you seen these concepts in your experiences with organizations?

7 What important contributions did the Hawthorne Studies make to our understanding of organizations?

TAKE FIVE: OB ALIVE: *ANTZ* (1998)

Z (voiced by Woody Allen), a member of a massive ant colony, leads a largely insignificant life. He pursues Princess Bala (voiced by Sharon Stone) while trying to finds his life role. Z's life goes to unexpected new places because of General Mandible (voiced by Gene Hackman) and a major termite war.

These scenes begin after the opening credits in DVD Chapter 1, "Insignificantz," Start: 0:00:49. Z says, "All my life I've lived and worked in the big city." The scenes end as Colonel Cutter (voiced by Christopher Walken) and General Mandible leave for a meeting with the queen (Stop: 0:07:59).

While viewing these scenes, note and assess the type of work, worker relationships, and supervisory behavior. Which concepts discussed in this chapter's "Historical Foundations" section appear in the scenes? Draw specific examples from the scenes to support your observations.

REFERENCES AND NOTES

1. Leana, C. R., and B. Barry. 2000. Stability and Change as Simultaneous Experiences in Organizational Life. *Academy of Management Review* 25: 753–59.
   Lewis, M. W. 2000. Exploring Paradox: Toward a More Comprehensive Guide. *Academy of Management Review* 25: 760–76.
2. Drucker, P. F. 1999. *Management Challenges for the 21st Century*. New York: HarperBusiness.
3. Davenport, T. H., and K. Pearlson. 1998. Two Cheers for the Virtual Office. *Sloan Management Review* 39 (Summer): 51–65.
   Nilles, J. M. 1994. *Making Telecommuting Happen: A Guide for Telemanagers and Telecommuters*. New York: Van Nostrand Reinhold.
4. Nunamaker, J. F., Jr., R. O. Briggs, and D. D. Mittleman. 1996. Lessons from a Decade of Group Support Systems Research. *In Information Systems: Decision Support and Knowledge-Based Systems*, Vol. 3, ed. J. F. Nunamaker, Jr. and R. H. Sprague, Jr. Washington, DC: IEEE Computer Society Press, pp. 418–27.
5. Davidow, W. H., and M. S. Malone. 1992. *The Virtual Corporation*. New York: HarperCollins.
6. Brown S. L., and K. M. Eisenhardt. 1999. *Competing on the Edge: Strategy As Structured Chaos*. Cambridge, MA: Harvard Business School Press.
   Drucker, *Management Challenges*.
7. Kilduff, M., and D. Dougherty. 2000. Change and Development in a Pluralistic World: The View from the Classics. *Academy of Management Review* 25: 777–82.
8. Barnard, C. I. 1938. *The Functions of the Executive*. Cambridge, MA: Harvard University Press, p. 73.
   Leavitt, H. J. 2003. Why Hierarchies Thrive. *Harvard Business Review* (March): 96–102.
9. Blau, P. M., and W. R. Scott. 1962. *Formal Organizations*. San Francisco: Chandler Publishing Co.
   Etzioni, A. 1964. *Modern Organizations*. Englewood Cliffs, NJ: Prentice Hall.
   Pfeffer, J. 1998. Understanding Organizations: Concepts and Controversies. In *The Handbook of Social Psychology*, Vol. 2, ed. D. T. Gilbert, S. T. Fiske, and G. Lindzey. Boston: McGraw-Hill Companies, Inc.
   Scott, W. R. 1964. Theory of Organizations. In *Handbook of Modern Sociology*, ed. R. E. L. Faris. Chicago: Rand McNally, pp. 485–529.
10. Heath, C., and S. B. Sitkin. 2001. Big-B versus Big-O: What is Organizational about Organizational Behavior. *Journal of Organizational Behavior* 22: 43–58.
11. Dubin, R. 1978. *Theory Building*. New York: The Free Press.
12. Lewin, K. 1945. The Research Center for Group Dynamics at Massachusetts Institute of Technology. *Sociometry* 8: 126–36. (Quotation from p. 129.)
13. Ibid. Emphasis added.
14. Kuhn, T. S. 1962. *The Structure of Scientific Revolutions*. Chicago: University of Chicago Press.

15. Van de Ven, A. H., and M. S. Poole. 1995. Explaining Development and Change in Organizations. *Academy of Management Review* 20: 510–40.

16. Vroom, V. H. 1964. *Work and Motivation*. New York: John Wiley & Sons.

17. Merton, R. K. 1968. Manifest and Latent Functions. In *Social Theory and Social Structure*, ed. R. K. Merton. New York: The Free Press, Chap. 3.

18. McKinley, W., and A. G. Scherer. 2000. Some Unanticipated Consequences of Organizational Restructuring. *Academy of Management Review* 4: 735–52.

19. Tenner, E. 1996. *Why Things Bite Back: Technology and the Revenge of Unintended Consequences*. New York: Knopf.

20. Scott, W. G. 1961. Organization Theory: An Overview and an Appraisal. *The Journal of the Academy of Management* 4: 9. Emphasis removed.
    Buchan, J. 2006. *The Authentic Adam Smith: His Life and Ideas*. New York: W. W. Norton & Company. This source has a detailed and readable account of Smith's work.

21. Developed from A. Smith. 1893. *An Inquiry Into the Nature and Causes of the Wealth of Nations*. London: George Routledge and Sons, Chap. 1. (Originally published in 1776.)

22. Ibid., pp. 3–4.

23. Ibid., pp. 734–35.

24. Taylor, F. W. 1967. *The Principles of Scientific Management*. New York: W. W. Norton & Company, Inc., p. 9. (Originally published in 1911.)

25. Ibid.

26. Simison, R. L. 1998. GM Turns to Cowger to Repair Labor Ties in U.S., Installs Hendry as Opel Chairman. *Wall Street Journal* (October 27): B7.

27. Taylor, *Principles of Scientific Management*, pp. 36–37, 85.

28. Taylor, F. W. 1916. The Principles of Scientific Management. *Bulletin of the Taylor Society* (December): 13–23.

29. Kanigel, R. 1997. *The One Best Way: Frederick Winslow Taylor and the Enigma of Efficiency*. New York: Viking.

30. Fayol, H. 1949. *General and Industrial Management*. Translated by C. Storrs. London: Sir Isaac Pitman and Sons.

31. Fayol, H. 1973. The Administrative Theory in the State. In *Papers in the Science of Administration*, ed. L. Gulick and L. Urwick. New York: Institute of Public Administration, p. 101.

32. Carroll, S. J., and D. J. Gelen. 1987. Are the Classical Management Functions Useful in Describing Managerial Work? *Academy of Management Review* 12: 38–51.

33. Fayol, The Administrative Theory in the State, p. 101.

34. Fayol, *General and Industrial Management*, p. 20.

35. Ibid.

36. Ibid., pp. 21–22.

37. Ibid., p. 33.

38. For example: A superior can "extend or confine … his subordinate's initiative. Everything which goes to increase the importance of the subordinate's role is decentralization, everything which goes to reduce it is centralization." Fayol, *General and Industrial Management*, p. 34.

39. Ibid., p. 24.

40. Ibid., p. 25.

41. Adler, P. S. 1999. Building Better Bureaucracies. *Academy of Management Executive* 13 (4): 36–47.

Adler, P. S., and B. Borys. 1996. Two Types of Bureaucracy: Enabling vs. Coercive. *Administrative Science Quarterly* 47: 61–89.

Schellenberg, K., and G. A. Miller. 1998. Turbulence and Bureaucracy. *Journal of Applied Behavioral Science* 34: 202–21.

Weber, M. 1946. *From Max Weber: Essays in Sociology*. Translated by H. H. Gerth and C. W. Mills. New York: Oxford University Press, pp. 214–16.

Weber, M. 1964. *The Theory of Social and Economic Organization*. Translated by A. M. Henderson and T. Parsons. New York: Free Press. (Originally published by Oxford University Press, 1947.)

42. Merton, R. K. 1968. *Social Theory and Social Structure*. New York: Free Press, p. 252.

43. Developed from E. M. Fox and L. Urwick, eds. 1973. *Dynamic Administration: The Collected Papers of Mary Parker Follett*. New York: Pitman Publishing.

44. Developed from ibid., Chap. 4.

45. Ibid., p. 72.

46. Developed from ibid., Chap. 1.

47. Developed from ibid., Chaps. 12, 13.

48. Ibid., pp. 224–25.

49. Barnard, C. I. 1938. *The Functions of the Executive*. Cambridge, MA: Harvard University Press.

50. Ibid., p. 73. Emphasis removed.

51. Ibid., p. 4.

52. Ibid., pp. 58, 82.

53. Name of the concept taken from J. G. March and H. A. Simon. 1958. Motivational Constraints: The Decision to Participate. In *Organizations*. New York: John Wiley & Sons, Chap. 4.

54. Barnard, *Functions of the Executive*, pp. 227, 231.

55. Name of the concept taken from March and Simon, *Organizations*, Chap. 4.

56. Name of the concept taken from ibid., pp. 52–81.

57. Barnard, *Functions of the Executive*, pp. 168–69.

58. Mayo, E. 1933. *The Human Problems of an Industrial Civilization*. New York: Macmillan.

Roethlisberger, F. J., and W. J. Dickson. 1939. *Management and the Worker*. Cambridge, MA: Harvard University Press.

The term *Hawthorne effect* refers to an experimental effect on people's behavior because they are part of an experiment. French likely was the first to use the term in his discussions of field experiments. See S. R. G. Jones. 1992. Was There a Hawthorne Effect? *American Journal of Sociology* 98: 451–69. The French discussion appears on p. 452.

59. Ibid.

Hassard, J. S. 2012. Rethinking the Hawthorne Studies: The Western Electric Research in Its Social, Political and Historical Context. *Human Relations* 65: 1431–61.

Rice, B. 1982. The Hawthorne Defect: Persistence of a Flawed Theory. *Psychology Today* (February): 70–74.

60. Cary, A. 1967. The Hawthorne Studies: A Radical Criticism. *American Sociological Review* 12: 27–38.

Franke, R. H., and J. D. Kaul. 1978. The Hawthorne Experiments: First Statistical Interpretation. *American Sociological Review* 43: 623–43.

Moldaschl, M., and W. G. Weber. 1998. The "Three Waves" of Industrial Group Work: Historical Reflections on Current Research on Group Work. *Human Relations* 51: 347–88.

61. Jones, S. R. G. 1990. Worker Independence and Output: The Hawthorne Studies Reevaluated. *American Sociological Review* 55: 176–90.

Yorks, L., and D. A. Whitsett. 1985. Hawthorne, Topeka, and the Issue of Science Versus Advocacy in Organizational Behavior. *Academy of Management Review* 10: 21–30.

62. McGregor, D. 1960. *The Human Side of Enterprise*. New York: McGraw-Hill, Inc.

63. Excellent discussions and debates appear in J. H. Foegen, 1999. Why Not Empowerment? *Business and Economic Review* 45 (3): 31–33.

Ghoshal, S., and P. Moran. 1996. Bad for Practice: A Critique of the Transaction Cost Theory. *Academy of Management Journal* 21: 13–47.

See E. W. Morrison, and F. J. Milliken. 2000. Organizational Silence: A Barrier to Change and Development in a Pluralistic World. *Academy of Management Review* 25: 706–25. (For an excellent summary, see pp. 708–10, 712–14.)

Pfeffer, J. 1997. *New Directions for Organization Theory*. New York: Oxford University Press.

Williamson, O. E. 1996. Economic Organization: The Case for Candor. *Academy of Management Review* 21: 48–57.

64. Edersheim, E. H. 2007. *The Definitive Drucker*. New York: McGraw-Hill. I recommend this highly readable source as an excellent summary of Peter Drucker's work.

Wittmeyer, C. 2003. The Practice of Management: Timeless Views and Principles. *Academy of Management Executive* 17: 13–15.

Wren, D. A., and R. G. Greenwood. 1998. Guru. In *Management Innovators: The People and Ideas That Have Shaped Modern Business*. New York: Oxford University Press, Chap. 12.

Zahra, S. A. 2003. The Practice of Management: Reflections on Peter F. Drucker's Landmark Book. *Academy of Management Executive* 17: 16–23.

65. Drucker, P. F. 1954. *The Practice of Management*. New York: Harper & Row.

66. Ibid., pp. 178–81.

Wittmeyer, The Practice of Management.

Zahra, The Practice of Management.

67. Drucker, *The Practice of Management*, pp. 157–58, 378.

Wittmeyer, The Practice of Management.

Zahra, The Practice of Management.

68. Drucker, P. F. 1995. Planning for Uncertainty. In *Managing in a Time of Great Change*. New York: Truman Talley Books/Plume, Chap. 2.

69. Drucker, *The Practice of Management*, Chap. 12.

70. Wren and Greenwood, *Management Innovators*.

71. Ibid.

72. Drucker, *Managing in a Time of Great Change, passim*.

Drucker, *Management Challenges for the 21st Century*.

2000. Meeting of the Minds: Peter Drucker and Peter Senge Discuss the Future and Why Companies Must Learn How to Walk Away from a Good Thing. *Across the Board* (November–December) 37: 16–21.

Chapter 2

THE CONTEXT OF MODERN ORGANIZATIONS (DIVERSITY, QUALITY, TECHNOLOGY, INTERNATIONAL)

After reading this chapter, you should be able to:

- Explain workforce diversity.
- Describe several diversity dimensions.
- Discuss workforce diversity effects on organizations and management.
- Describe the direction in which many organizations are headed in managing for quality.
- Discuss quality management and its history.
- Explain the likely effects of quality management on an organization.
- Outline how technological changes will affect modern organizations and their management.
- List the effects of specific technologies on modern organizations.
- Discuss some issues and implications of managing organizations in an increasingly global environment.
- Identify some dimensions of country cultures that distinguish one culture from another.

Four issues dominate the context of modern organizations. Those issues center on the increasing diversity of the workforce in the United States, an emphasis on managing for quality, the effects of technology on organizations, and the increasing global orientation required of managers.

Workforce diversity brings people into organizations with vastly different worldviews or ways of thinking about their environment. Managers face the challenge of harnessing those differences to reach organizational goals successfully. Workforce diversity also can increase an organization's conflict potential, presenting managers with the added challenge of managing conflict in a functional way.

Managing for quality asks managers to focus on customer desires, continuously improve quality, and rethink how different parts of their organization contribute to quality services and products. Fully successful quality management usually requires major changes in an organization's culture.

Modern computing and communication technology bring new opportunities and challenges to managers of modern organizations. Communication technologies let people stay connected, no matter where they are in the world. Computing technologies have reshaped manufacturing processes worldwide. Managers now have more organizational design options to build flexible, responsive organizations than ever before.

The global environment of organizations demands a global mindset of modern managers. Understanding cultural differences, and shaping strategies around those differences, is a unique challenge facing modern managers.

Customers demand a focus on their needs and desires. Managers respond to customer needs in many ways, including custom building goods and services to a single customer's requirements. Modern technology, including the Internet, allows fast, flexible responses to customer needs.[1]

WORKFORCE DIVERSITY

Workforce diversity refers to variations in workforce composition based on personal and background factors of employees or potential employees.[2] The **dimensions of workforce diversity** include age, gender, ethnicity, physical and mental ability, sexual orientation, religion, and cultural beliefs. Other dimensions are family status, such as a single parent, a dual-career relationship, or a person with responsibilities for aging parents.[3] A quick look at Figure 2.1 shows you the complexity and scope of the issues surrounding this topic.

The Bureau of Labor Statistics' (BLS) projections of the U.S. civilian labor force growth between 2012 and 2022 show many changes.[4] Those projections show civilian labor force growth of 0.5 percent during the period of 2012 to 2022, a smaller percentage than the previous 10-year period. The number of women and men in the labor force should grow by 0.5 percent. Labor force projections by age show an increase of 2.3 percent for those 55 and over, a 0.4 percent decrease for those in the 16 to 24 bracket, and a decrease of 0.3 percent for 25- to 54-year-olds. Most of the projected increase in the labor force by 2022 will come from minority workers.

BLS projections out to 2050 show further changes. Workers age 55 or over should make up 22.9 percent of the workforce, and non-white workers should make up 48.6 percent of the workforce. The projections for women in the 2050 workforce stay at 48 percent.[5]

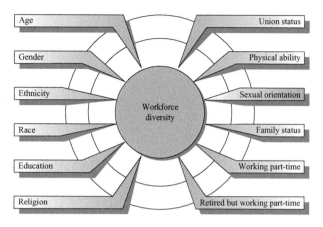

Figure 2.1:   Dimensions of Workforce Diversity

Regional variations also will be significant. The projections discussed so far were for the entire civilian labor force. Local population characteristics will affect the workforce from which a specific organization draws.[6]

People from different social backgrounds, cultures, and language groups bring different worldviews to an organization.[7] They view work issues and problems through different perceptual lenses. If properly managed, these different views present opportunities to organizations, but they also increase conflict potential.[8] The challenge for managers is to focus those diverse views on the mission of the organization while managing conflict to keep it at a functional level.

People with different needs and expectations also present challenges to an organization's human resource policies. Working parents often require adaptations in work schedules or on-site day care. Single parents might need time off to take a sick child to a physician. Native Americans often need special work schedules during their culture's celebration periods. A disabled person could require special access to a building and a specially designed work area. Part-time workers might need to arrange job sharing so that the organization can get the value of their talents.[9]

This chapter proposes three views of managing workforce diversity: managing diversity, valuing diversity, and managing for diversity.[10] **Managing diversity** helps people of all backgrounds have equal access to employment, promotion, and personnel policies. Organizations that manage diversity react to the presence of workforce diversity and do not try to increase diversity. This chapter does not focus on managing diversity. Instead, it offers valuing diversity and managing for diversity as the more likely focus of modern managers.

Organizations and their managers who **value diversity** aggressively embrace it and actively try to build a diverse workforce.[11] Such organizations view a diverse workforce as a competitive advantage. **Managing for diversity** unleashes the potential of a diverse workforce and channels it toward the organization's goals.[12] The challenge for managers and leaders is to provide a vision so everyone understands where the organization is headed. Managers also want to preserve a diversity of viewpoints and help employees get the satisfaction they want from their work experiences.

Managers try to create an environment that harnesses the potential of all sources of difference within an organization's workforce. Managers can actively tap diverse perspectives and rethink approaches to problems, tasks, and markets.[13] For example, after hiring its first Hispanic female attorney, a small Northeastern law firm discovered a new market because of her unique views. She wanted to pursue English-only employment policies in cases involving immigrants. The previously all-white legal staff had never thought of that market.[14]

Valuing diversity and managing for diversity is not affirmative action in disguise. Instead, it is managing to get the greatest contributions from increasingly diverse people. It recognizes that a variety of views enrich organizational life. Managing for diversity does not ask people to give up their individuality and take on the values of the majority. It honors differences among people, but also asks everyone to accept the core values of the organization. Ideally, those core values should be related to the organization's mission, such as "an unending pursuit of excellence in customer service." Such a mission statement states the organization's goal, but not how to reach it. People reach the goal in many different ways because of their diversity.

Why should managers and their organizations care about meeting the expectations and requirements of a diverse workforce? Could they not select people who fit into the organization's existing culture, policies, and procedures? The answer has two parts: (1) managers will have no choice about managing for diversity, and (2) successfully managing for diversity is good business strategy.

The first answer follows from the labor force statistics discussed earlier. Organizations that do not have a diverse workforce now are likely to face one in the future, especially as they pursue scarce skilled labor. Other organizations have followed affirmative action and Equal Employment Opportunity (EEO) guidelines and directives. Those organizations now have diverse workforces.[15]

The second answer implies a more aggressive management position toward workforce diversity. Good business strategy requires unleashing a diverse workforce's potential. The reasons are twofold: (1) the increasing diversity of society in the United States, and (2) the need to think and to compete globally to stay competitive.[16]

As society becomes increasingly diverse, customers also become more diverse. Having a diverse workforce helps managers attract customers from diverse backgrounds. For example, Pizza Hut found that the presence of Muslim workers attracted more Muslim customers.[17]

The global environment of modern organizations adds another layer of complexity to workforce diversity. Many U.S. organizations sell in foreign markets, operate in countries outside the United States, or enter joint ventures with organizations from other countries. Because U.S. organizations operating abroad often employ native-born people at all levels, managers can interact with employees from other countries. To meet customer expectations in foreign markets, they need to understand local customs and business practices. To be successful, U.S. managers must understand cultural differences around the world and not assume customer requirements in foreign markets are the same as at home.

Managing for diversity forces many organizations to make major changes, such as modifying personnel policies concerning work schedules, personal leave, language training, and other basic skills. Managers must manage for fairness when meeting the diverse needs of their workforce.[18] For example, a day-care policy originally created to meet the needs of working women must apply to all employees despite gender and marital status. Managers also must learn new skills, such as accepting differences, appreciating language differences, and even learning new languages. The latter can include sign language to communicate with hearing-impaired employees.

Other changes touch the heart of an organization's culture by asking for shifts in its values, rituals, and assumptions.[19] Values suitable to a homogeneous white male culture need to yield to the heterogeneous values of many diverse groups.[20] Social activities that are rituals in male cultures need to change to give female employees ready access, or rotate the activities to meet the desires of both groups. For example, if social gatherings usually include only male-oriented sports, other activities should be added. Instead of assuming all employees enjoy a game of flag football, the gathering's organizers could poll people for their preferences.

QUALITY MANAGEMENT

The management of product and service quality continues as a major thrust of organizations in the United States and worldwide.[21] Although quality management's roots exist in the early 1920s, U.S. organizations did not embrace it until the early 1980s.[22] Quality management has many names, including total quality control, total quality management, total quality leadership, leadership through quality, market-driven quality,[23] and continuous process improvement. Terms and ideas emphasized since the late 1990s include robust design, Six Sigma quality, and ISO 9000.[24] The term *quality management* includes all quality management and continuous-improvement programs. Such efforts apply to all organizations, ranging from Xerox to Pal's Sudden Service, a hot dog stand in Tennessee and parts of Virginia.[25]

Quality management (QM) is a philosophy and system of management built upon concepts dating to at least the 1920s.[26] QM includes tools and techniques that help organizations manage for quality in services, products, and processes. Although its roots are in manufacturing, it is a management system that can bring major improvements to any organization.

The earliest U.S. antecedents to QM are the works of Walter A. Shewhart, Armand V. Feigenbaum, Joseph M. Juran, and Philip B. Crosby. Shewhart was the first to recognize that variability in manufacturing processes could be attributed to abnormalities or causes common to the process. He developed statistical tools that let managers know when a manufacturing process was out of control and introducing poor quality.[27] In the 1950s, Feigenbaum pressed for total quality control, a method of quality management that required the involvement of people both inside and outside a quality control department.[28] Juran did the economic analyses that showed the long-term payoffs of managing for quality.[29] His phrase *gold in the mine* has become a motto of quality management enthusiasts and consultants. Crosby advocated "zero defects," a strong departure from the prevailing view of quality levels that accepted some defects.[30]

Perhaps the best-known person associated with quality management is W. Edwards Deming, a statistician who started his career with the U.S. Department of Agriculture and the Bureau of the Census.[31] Deming emphasized using statistics to understand and manage process variability. His early teachings had little effect on U.S. managers, but strongly influenced the Japanese, who consider Deming the most important U.S. contributor to their methods of quality management.

The major Japanese contributors to quality management are Kaoru Ishikawa and Genichi Taguchi.[32] Each brought different perspectives and tools to QM and left a distinct Japanese mark on it. Ishikawa emphasized statistical quality control, as did Deming. He also emphasized human factors in QM by introducing the quality control circle (QCC) concept. Ishikawa viewed QCCs as a powerful way of harnessing human potential for quality improvement.[33]

Taguchi developed a QM approach based on advanced mathematical and statistical techniques. His unique philosophy viewed any lack of quality as a loss to society. Taguchi developed a "loss function" to measure the costs of quality losses that decision makers could use to guide their QM efforts. He also applied experimental design to quality assessment, a set of techniques popularly known as the "Taguchi method."[34]

QM is now a worldwide phenomenon and not limited to the United States or Japan. Various quality awards have also accompanied the spread of QM. The following lists the most prominent awards with their start date and country or region of origin:[35]

- ▨ Deming Application Prize, 1953, Japan
- ▨ Malcolm Baldrige National Quality Award, 1987, United States
- ▨ European Quality Award, 1992, Europe.

In addition, the International Organization for Standardization (ISO) developed and published a set of international quality standards. ISO 9000 was its first quality standard that appeared in 1987. This move by the ISO recognizes the global reach of business and a need for international guides for QM.

Effective QM requires a total system's view of the organization that reaches well beyond its boundaries. It uses an understanding of the interdependence of outside people, outside organizations, and groups within the organization to manage for quality. The list of these stakeholders—groups with an interest in the organization's activities—is long and includes employees, suppliers, clients, customers, the community surrounding the organization, coalitions to which the organization belongs, professional or trade associations, and competitors.

QM asks people to view organizations in a new way. It asks people to move away from a typical chain-of-command view and move toward a process view. This view emphasizes processes, customers, interdependence with suppliers, and the critical role of feedback in moving toward continuous quality improvement. Only by directly asking customers and suppliers can an organization discover shifts in expectations and quality requirements.[36]

Many tools and techniques support QM's philosophy of continuous improvement. These **tools and techniques of QM** were developed to let people watch their work processes to ensure a quality product or service. Table 2.1 summarizes some major tools and techniques of QM. Organizations that move toward QM must train employees in the use of the tools to get true quality management.

QM tools and techniques help organizations carefully analyze their processes. Teams of people drawn from all parts of the organization affected by the process typically do such analyses. Analysis teams, usually called process action teams, have diversity in membership to bring many different views to the analysis and improvement of a work process. For example, an analysis team examining an organization's hiring process might include members drawn from the human

■ **Table 2.1: Summary of Total Quality Management Tools and Techniques**

Benchmarking	A method of comparing an organization's processes to those of an accepted leader. It shows how the quality of the organization's process compares to one that has already reached high quality.
Cause and Effect Diagram	A drawing that shows the relationship between a problem and its likely causes. The diagram shows relationships among the factors that can affect the variability of a process.
Checksheet	A structured method of collecting quantitative data about a process's results. Lets the user count items such as the number or types of defects in a product.
Control Chart	A line graph showing the performance of a process over time. The user compares the line showing actual performance to previously computed upper limits and lower limits of process performance. It quickly shows whether the variability in a process is inside or outside the control limits.
Flowchart	A diagram that shows the steps, and the relationships among steps, in a process. It uses different symbols to show action steps, decision steps, and waiting periods.
Pareto Chart	A bar chart displaying the bars in descending order by height. Each bar is a problem measured in the same units. Pareto charts isolate major problems from minor ones.
Quality Function Deployment	A concept and a tool for translating customer needs into engineering requirements. It emphasizes the need for cross-functional teams to truly meet customer expectations.*

* Hauser, J. R., and D. Clausing. 1988. House of Quality. *Harvard Business Review* 66 (May–June): 63–73.

Source: Evans, J. R., and W. M. Lindsay. 2005. *The Management and Control of Quality*, 6th ed. Mason, Ohio: South-Western.

resources department, hiring departments, newly hired employees, and labor union representatives.

Organizations that fuse QM thinking into their culture enjoy many benefits that do not directly result from other approaches to management. Employee commitment to continuous quality improvement increases. The cost of providing a service or manufacturing a product declines. Service processes function more dependably; products are more reliable.

QM is a way of managing that differs from what most managers and organizations have done in the past. It emphasizes a long-term commitment to continuous quality improvement and stresses that quality is everyone's job, not only the job of a quality control or quality assurance department. QM is intensely customer focused and demands that all organization members share that focus.[37] QM emphasizes high involvement in the work process. It also emphasizes communication in all directions—top-down, bottom-up, and laterally. This feature follows directly from the need for cooperation and high involvement. It also is a way QM generates large amounts of information in the system.

QM's emphasis on continuous improvement of all processes in an organization lets people do more with the same resources. Involving everyone in continuous improvement can add challenge to employees' jobs. The long-run result is a committed corps of people with an impassioned focus on mission, customers, and continuous quality improvement.

Moving toward managing for quality typically presents massive change to an organization and its managers. A passionate customer focus, combined with a process view that emphasizes continuous improvement, requires people to reframe the way they think about their organization. Such transformations of thinking are difficult and account for many failures in the journey to quality. Research evidence shows that successful transformation requires top management commitment to QM and widespread supervisory and employee involvement in the change process.[38]

By the mid-1990s, researchers identified the way improved quality can increase profits. Continuous improvement increases process efficiency and reduces costs. Quality can attract new customers and increase the retention of old ones, an especially useful result for organizations with a market-oriented strategy.[39] According to some estimates, it costs five times as much to get new customers as to keep the present ones.[40] High quality also can make a product or service so attractive that an organization can charge higher prices than competitors. Researchers and analysts found that QM efforts often produced poor results because managers did not target improvements to areas with the greatest long-term positive effect on profits.[41]

The financial results of managing for quality often are impressive. One study compared the financial performance of quality award-winning companies to comparable companies that had not won an award. The quality winners had a 38 percent to 46 percent increase in stock value four years after winning. They also had a two to three times increase in assets, employment, sales, and income. Perhaps inspired by such results, Honeywell is using its Six Sigma quality process to increase productivity and reduce costs.[42] Other research also suggests positive organizational results of QM efforts. One study found a positive relationship between QM practices and expert-rated performance in a sample of hospitals.[43]

Not all organizations that adopted QM had successful results.[44] Several prominent failures have occurred, causing some private sector organizations in the United States to reconsider a QM orientation. The Wallace Co., a winner of the Malcolm Baldrige National Quality Award, filed for chapter 11 bankruptcy protection.[45] Moving to QM did not prevent Douglas Aircraft in Long Beach, California, from experiencing massive layoffs. At Florida Power & Light, a leading U.S. example of QM, major layoffs of the QM staff followed the appointment of a new chief executive officer.

These negative results for organizations with well-developed QM efforts, and inconsistencies in research linking QM and organizational performance, have led some observers to question the effectiveness of QM.[46] Critics felt the costs of such programs often exceeded the benefits of quality. Other researchers have observed that top management commitment as noted above, and massive organizational change, are needed to have successful QM efforts.[47]

TECHNOLOGY, ORGANIZATIONS, AND MANAGEMENT

Massive changes in computing power and computer features, combined with various types of **technology**, revolutionize much of what organizations do now and into the future. Desktop computers with CD-ROM drives, DVD drives, high-speed processors, and large memory capacity let you create business presentations using three-dimensional animated technology. Laptop and palmtop computers connect to the Internet using wireless technology in many public places, such as airports, hotels, and fast-food restaurants, worldwide. It is also coming to airplanes, such as Lufthansa's aircraft.[48] Tracking appointments, reading and sending e-mail, and connecting to the Web has never been easier.

Sweeping changes in communications technology have opened unusual opportunities. To better understand these changes, keep in mind that the first transatlantic telephone cable carried only 35 simultaneous calls.[49] Lucent Technologys' Bell Labs wave division multiplexing technology splits a single beam of light into multiple colors. Each color acts as a separate communication channel within an optical fiber, increasing the fiber's capacity.[50] New telephones let you send and receive e-mail, talk to a person by telephone, surf the Web, send and receive text messages, and take digital images … from anywhere.[51]

Electronically based measurement systems monitor manufacturing processes in modern factories and collect sales data at store checkouts. Microchip transmitters embedded in clothing let manufacturers track a garment from the factory to the end user.[52] Other computer technologies digitize information directly from voice interaction and handwriting on a digital tablet. Handheld computers help retailers track inventories and send orders electronically. Navigation satellites let trucking and shipping firms track entire fleets. Communication satellites allow managers to talk to drivers and ship captains anywhere in the world.

E-mail, voice mail, videoconferencing, and teleconferencing that are now widely used will increase in use in the future. Videoconferencing adds a two-way video connection to the now common teleconference. Many organizations have replaced or supplemented their e-mail systems with voice-mail systems. Oral messages, not written ones, appear in a person's electronic mailbox.

Social networking sites such as Facebook and MySpace link people in widely dispersed locations. Twitter also helps people interact worldwide, although with shorter messages. AOL's Instant Messenger features quick links to people with whom you wish to link. Such sites have an almost addictive quality, bonding people to the site and to each other.[53]

The revolution in materials technology and engineering that is now unfolding will continue into the future. Some materials already in use are carbon fiber composites and optical fibers, the basis of tennis rackets and communication cable, respectively. Others, such as super polymers, amorphous metal alloys, and superconductors, add to a growing list of human-created materials. Innovations in product ideas and technological solutions no longer depend on naturally existing materials.[54]

New materials have replaced steel and aluminum, making it possible to build lighter cars and trucks that can carry heavier loads. New ceramics technology allows designing jet engines with more thrust. The new engines weigh less than aluminum engines, letting larger planes go longer distances with more people and cargo.

Increasingly, organizations will create internal networks called intranets and connect to the Internet. These networks have changed the way people interact and have changed the ways managers should think about their roles. Employees in any part of the organization, even one with wide-ranging global operations, can interact effortlessly.

Manufacturing features agile manufacturing processes that keep almost no inventory and use computer-based technology to directly link with customers or end users. These processes are cost-effective and competitive in producing both single custom-made items and large production runs, all within the same manufacturing plant. The products moving through these processes can differ from item to item.[55]

Further innovations in manufacturing will occur because of advances in computer-assisted manufacturing (CAM), computer-integrated manufacturing (CIM), modern materials, robotics, laser cutting and bonding methods, and the like. The list is almost endless. No one can predict all future manufacturing process technologies.

Internet technology will let suppliers receive parts orders as a manufacturer updates a manufacturing schedule in real time. Ford Motor Company, for example, has built an impressive intranet-Internet system that links 120,000 workstations worldwide.[56] The precision of the system lets a car seat supplier know the color sequence of the next shipment of seats. Workers uncrate the blue seats at the seat installation station as the blue cars reach the station.

Managerial roles have changed because managers have people in scattered places. Computer networks act as coordinating mechanisms, replacing face-to-face interaction. Many employees now telecommute, or work from their homes, using computing and communication technology.[57]

New management strategies have flexibility as a key feature. Such flexibility pervades the design and response of manufacturing and service operations. It includes a thorough understanding of customer needs and variations among markets. The latter are especially true for companies that compete globally. Markets in different countries feature high diversity even between countries that are not far apart. Management must respond to those differences by treating the customers of the different countries in the way they expect. For example, the giant insurance company AIG has local agents collect monthly premiums at each insured person's home in Taiwan, but uses electronic bank transfers in Hong Kong.[58]

With strategy that emphasizes flexibility and customer needs, a decentralized organizational design is needed to reach the organization's goals. This organizational design moves decisions down to the lowest level in the organization, where fast responses meet shifting markets and customer needs. The close ties to both suppliers and customers require cross-functional teams that tightly integrate many parts of the total business process. Local teams with broad decision-making and problem-solving authority will help even large organizations decentralize. The modern information technologies described earlier help the most globally dispersed organization reach decentralization on a scale previously not possible.

Organization-wide, self-managing teams are another management change produced by new technologies.[59] An organization forms such teams around a specific customer base or product. In the first case, such teams make all decisions in response to customer needs. In the second case, teams can conceive, design, build, and market a product or service. In both instances, the self-managing teams are involved in all parts of the business process affecting a product or customer. Such teams also become involved in the hiring process by doing much of the selection and early socialization of new employees.

Companies also can link to various partners over the Internet, creating the "virtual organizations" described in Chapter 17, "Organizational Design." Aditi Inc., for example, offers software users customer support with a twist.[60] Based in Seattle and Bangalore, India, the company provides 24-hour support. After U.S. workers go home, messages transfer over the Internet to Bangalore. The reverse happens at the end of the Indian workday. Customers get almost immediate response, no matter what their time zone.

The Internet is bringing fast changes to worldwide commerce. Forecasters predict multibillions of dollars in Internet commerce into the future. The biggest growth areas in such commerce are computers, catalogs, books, and software. Amazon.com Inc., the online bookseller, offers 3,000,000 titles, outstripping Barnes & Noble's 175,000 titles. Setting up commercial websites is now so simple that it has created a flood of upstarts that are a new generation of competitors in many industries. The ability to reach many more customers and to offer them many more products is a major distinction between Internet commerce and physical business.[61]

THE GLOBAL ENVIRONMENT OF ORGANIZATIONS

The **global environment** of organizations demands that modern managers have an international focus that was not required before. Modern managers must begin to think beyond the domestic environment of their organizations. Now, the world is their environment, and will become more so in the future. For some organizations, thinking internationally means finding new markets outside the home country; for others, becoming a multinational organization operating in many countries; and, for yet others, becoming a transnational organization whose decisions are not limited by country boundaries. Modern managers must think of the entire planet as a source of labor and materials, places of production, and markets.[62] The world economy of the twenty-first century is so highly interconnected that positive or negative shifts in a major economy can echo throughout the world.[63]

Modern technology both enables and compels a global view.[64] Thanks to modern aircraft, international travel is common and fast. Telecommunication satellites let information in all forms move quickly from country to country. Managers of the same company working in different countries can easily hold videoconferences. Communication technologies such as the Internet smash country boundaries, letting people in different organizations interact with little concern for place and time.[65]

Advances in technology are not the only reasons modern managers are taking a global view. Regional trade agreements are opening vast new markets,[66] possibly increasing the competition faced by a firm. The North American Free Trade Agreement (NAFTA) opened the borders of Mexico, Canada, and the United States to easy movement of goods, capital, and services.[67] Europe took similar steps to encourage free trade among its countries. The movement of many European countries to a single currency (the euro) should enhance freer trade among its users.[68]

Many countries have dropped or plan to drop trade barriers that have prevented easy access to their markets. Many Latin American countries are moving toward freer trade.[69] South Korea is letting outside companies operate within its borders. The growing Korean middle class wants quality foreign-made goods, presenting rich new markets to managers with a global view.[70] Several Southeast Asian countries want Western products and are eager to form joint ventures with foreign firms.[71]

The combination of sweeping technological and market changes presents major opportunities to managers with a global orientation. Large California winemakers increasingly look to world markets for their products. The strategic reason is simple. Domestic consumption has increased by about 5 percent a year. Japanese consumption has jumped a startling 83 percent.[72]

Global opportunities are not limited to large organizations. For example, Blue Sky Natural Beverage Co. of Santa Fe, New Mexico, has successfully entered markets in Japan, Singapore, and the United Kingdom. Although Blue Sky is a small company without the resources of a multinational giant, its founders saw a new market for their products, worked toward it, and successfully entered it.[73]

Thinking globally raises many issues for managers. An obvious difficulty is the language difference among countries. Words carry many meanings in different cultures and contexts. *Profit* and *market* likely do not suggest negative images for many Westerners. These same words, whether spoken in English or Russian, remind many Russian managers of chaos and social injustice, a mindset inherited from the earlier Soviet era.[74] Managers who form partnerships with local businesspeople or learn the language themselves can help solve the language problem.

More difficult are the issues that stem from the cultural differences among countries. Understanding these differences can be difficult because outsiders are often not even aware of them. Modern managers need to develop a global mindset—an inclination and ability to understand cultural differences and synthesize those differences across cultures.[75]

Cultural differences affect how a company enters markets, the way it markets goods or services, how it deals with labor laws, and how it builds a loyal customer base. McDonald's restaurants outside the United States serve their traditional line of hamburgers, but tailor their menu to local tastes. Consumers can get vegetable McNuggets in New Delhi, India, or a McHuevo (hamburger with fried egg) in Montevideo, Uruguay.[76]

Many cultural differences appear in people's orientation to space and time.[77] North Americans ordinarily stand 5 to 8 feet apart while speaking. In Latin American cultures, people stand much closer. When a North American speaks to a Latin American in that person's home country, the Latin American moves close to the North American, who then feels uncomfortable and backs away. The Latin American might perceive the North American as cold and distant, an unintended communication of the nonverbal behavior.

Orientations to time and the meaning of time differ among cultures. Latin Americans view time more casually than North Americans. The latter value promptness in keeping appointments, a nonverbal behavior that is even more strongly emphasized by the Swiss. A North American or a Swiss might feel insulted if people were late for an appointment, although no insult was intended.

Egyptians usually do not look to the future, a state they define as anything more than a week away. South Asians think of the long term as centuries, not the typical five- or 10-year view of North Americans. The Sioux Indians of the United States do not have words for "time," "wait," or "waiting" in their native language. You can readily see that misunderstandings about time could arise in a face-to-face business meeting of people from different countries or among people in a culturally diverse workforce.

A major issue faced by managers of multinational organizations is the set of values they want globally dispersed operations to have. Do they want the values of the home country to dominate, or do they want to adopt those of the local culture? Managers who want their international units to hold the values of the home country place people from the home country in charge of those units. Organizations that hire local people for management positions often first socialize them to the major values of the home country organization. Hewlett-Packard has followed this practice for its worldwide operations. Managers know the "HP Way," whatever their national origins or the country in which they work.[78]

Cultural differences also define acceptable management behavior and preferences for organizational forms. One large cross-cultural research program found five **cultural dimensions** that imply management and organizational differences in different countries.[79] Although the research program had some methodological problems, these cultural dimensions are useful for an initial understanding of cultural differences in management behavior.[80] The five dimensions are:

■ **Power distance:** Degree of inequality among people that a culture considers normal.

■ **Uncertainty avoidance:** Value placed on predictability, structure, and stability.

■ **Individualism:** Value placed on individual behavior, acting alone and not as part of a group.

■ **Masculinity:** Value placed on decisiveness, assertiveness, independence, and individual achievement.

■ **Long-term orientation:** Value placed on persistence, status, and thrift.[81]

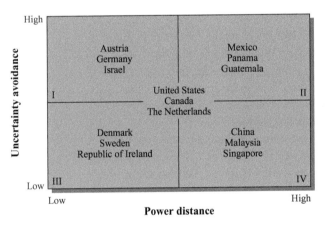

Figure 2.2:   Cultural Differences in Uncertainty Avoidance and Power Distance

Variations along the power distance and uncertainty avoidance dimensions have especially strong implications for management and organizations. Figure 2.2 shows the position of several countries on these dimensions. The countries in each quadrant scored toward the low or high ends of the dimensions. Those in the center of the figure had midlevel scores.

People in quadrant I countries prefer well-defined procedures and clear organizational structure. Rules and procedures guide daily behavior, with managers settling only exceptional matters. Quadrant II countries tend to use formal authority for coordination and simple structures that emphasize senior management's role. People in quadrant III countries rely less on formal rules and organizational form and more on direct interpersonal interactions to coordinate work activities. Quadrant IV countries rely on simple organizational forms and direct supervision. The countries in the center of the figure rely on middle management to coordinate activities and to specify the desired results.

The country positions shown in Figure 2.2, and discussed previously, can change as a country's external environment brings forces of change to a society. Managers should assess current values of a country's culture before concluding about preferred management behavior and organizational forms.[82]

Because preferences for management behavior and organizational forms differ among cultures,[83] each remaining chapter of this book has a separate part focused on the international issues surrounding the chapter's topics. Chapters 7 and 8 on motivation, for example, discuss the international implications of motivation. Chapter 12 on leadership discusses leadership issues raised in various countries. Those parts of each chapter are important sources of information as you begin to think more globally about managing behavior in an organization.

SUMMARY

This chapter introduced you to four topics that are at the center of managing modern organizations: workforce diversity, quality management, technology, and the global environment of organizations.

The Bureau of Labor Statistics' projections show the workforce becoming increasingly diverse. A diverse workforce presents managers with major opportunities to harness diverse talents in the pursuit of organizational goals. That same diverse workforce presents managers with the challenge of managing conflict that can come from diversity in a functional way.

Quality management (QM) is a system of management built upon work dating to the 1920s. QM has its roots in manufacturing, but it can help bring major improvements to any organization. It applies to managing all types of organizations and their internal processes. Those with QM training have a strong customer focus and a passion for continuous improvement in meeting customer wants and needs.

Massive changes in computing power and computer features, combined with communication – technology, have revolutionized much of what organizations and managers now do and will continue to do into the future. People in organizations often interact using computer and Internet technology. The combined effects of all technologies have changed managers' roles and the design of many organizations.

Modern technology and increasingly freer trade areas demand an unprecedented international view from modern managers. Organizations that want to expand their markets and profitability require managers with a global view. Managers can now regard the entire world as a source of labor, materials, customers, and places of production. Such a global view implies the need to understand different cultures, different views, and different ways of doing an organization's work.

REVIEW AND DISCUSSION QUESTIONS

1 Discuss the predicted future changes in the composition of the U.S. workforce. Compare that workforce profile to your work experiences. What issues have you or will you face in a highly diverse organization?

2 Workforce diversity has its roots in affirmative action and EEO. Discuss whether managing for diversity is the same as those programs. Does managing for diversity require a different view of people with varying characteristics and backgrounds?

3 Discuss the major features of quality management. How does it differ from an inspection-based, quality control system? What values does quality management ask all employees of an organization to accept?

4 Moving to quality management is a major organizational change for most organizations. Discuss some factors that could impede such a move. Would organizations that do not move to quality management suffer competitively in the global marketplace?

5 Reflect on the technological changes discussed earlier. Discuss the specific technological changes that will affect you in your work role.

6 Discuss the issues that a global orientation raises for managers. Are those issues problems or opportunities for modern managers? How do you expect those issues to affect you in your work career?

7 Reflect on the types of businesses that are prominent in your area. Would any of them benefit from having a global view of their markets? Is it realistic for managers in those companies to look beyond domestic borders to find opportunities elsewhere?

TAKE FIVE: OB ALIVE: *THE SECOND BEST EXOTIC MARIGOLD HOTEL* (2015)

Sonny Kapoor's (Dev Patel) original Marigold Hotel led him to secure a newer one. His challenge is to manage both properties and plan for his upcoming wedding. His resident friends add to the challenge and help as much as they can.

This scene appears late in the film. It starts with Sonny dancing on the stage surrounded by many people (DVD Chapter 26, 01:49:42). The scene ends at the end of the performance (DVD Chapter 26, 01:51:55). The film cuts to a shot of Muriel Donnelly (Maggie Smith) walking and holding an envelope.

Consider the following questions and observations while watching the scene. What aspects of this culture do you notice? Does the dancing and music appear to be unique to Indian culture? Notice the highly varied attire of the women as compared to the men.

REFERENCES AND NOTES

1. Prahalad, C. K., and V. Ramaswamy. 2004. *The Future of Competition: Co-Creating Unique Value with Customers*. Boston: Harvard Business School Press. Other citations throughout this chapter support the summary opening statements.

2. Developed from the following and other citations throughout this part.
   Barak, E. M. M. 2005. *Managing Diversity: Toward a Globally Inclusive Workplace*. Thousand Oaks: Sage Publications.

Bond, M. A., and J. L. Pyle. 1998. Diversity Dilemmas at Work. *Journal of Management Inquiry* 7: 252–69.

Fernandez, J. P. 1991. *Managing a Diverse Workforce*. New York: Lexington Books.

Frey, W. H. 2015. *Diversity Explosion: How New Racial Demographics are Remaking America*. Washington, DC: Brookings Institution Press.

Gebert, D., S. Boerner, E. Kearney, J. E. King, Jr., K. Zhang, and L. J. Song. 2014. Expressing Religious Identities in the Workplace: Analyzing a Neglected Diversity Dimension. *Human Relations* 67: 543–63.

Hayles, V. R., and A. M. Russell. 1997. *The Diversity Directive: Why Some Initiatives Fail & What to Do About It*. Chicago: Irwin Professional Publishing.

Jackson, S. E., K. E. May, and K. Whitney. 1995. Understanding the Dynamics of Diversity in Decision-Making Teams. In *Team Effectiveness and Decision Making in Organizations*, ed. R. Guzzo, E. Salas, and Associates. San Francisco: Jossey-Bass, pp. 205–61.

Jamieson, D., and J. O'Mara. 1991. *Managing Workforce 2000: Gaining the Diversity Advantage*. San Francisco: Jossey-Bass.

Jehn, K. A., L. L. Greer, and J. Rupert. 2008. Diversity, Conflict, and Their Consequences. In *Diversity at Work*, ed. A. P. Brief. Cambridge: Cambridge University Press, Chap. 5.

Ragins, B. R., and J. A. Gonzalez. 2003. Understanding Diversity in Organizations: Getting a Grip on a Slippery Construct. In *Organizational Behavior: The State of the Science*, 2nd edn, ed. J. Greenberg. Mahwah: Lawrence Erlbaum Associates, Inc., Chap. 4.

Rosener, J. B. 1995. *America's Competitive Secret: Utilizing Women as a Management Strategy*. New York: Oxford University Press.

Scott, C. L. 2014. Historical Perspectives for Studying Diversity in the Workforce. In *Diversity in the Workforce: Current Issues and Emerging Trends*, ed. M. Y. Byrd and C. L. Scott. New York: Routledge, Chap. 1. The chapters in "Part III: Diversity in the Workforce: Emerging Trends" discuss contemporary issues such as spirituality, linguistics, profiling, and racial harassment.

Thomas, R. R., Jr. 1991. *Beyond Race and Gender: Unleashing the Power of Your Total Work Force by Managing Diversity*. New York: AMACOM.

3. Jackson, S. E., and Associates, eds. 1992. *Diversity in the Workplace: Human Resources Initiatives*. New York: Guilford Press.

Jamieson and O'Mara, *Managing Workforce 2000*, Chaps. 1 and 2.

Milliken, F. J., and L. L. Martins. 1996. Searching for Common Threads: Understanding the Multiple Effects of Diversity in Organizational Groups. *Academy of Management Review* 21: 402–33.

4. Toossi, M. 2013. Labor Force Projections to 2022: The Labor Force Participation Rate Continues to Fall. *Monthly Labor Review* 136. http://go.galegroup.com/ps/i.do?id=GALE%7CA358849447&v=2.1&u=albu7848 4&it=r&p=AONE&sw=w&asid=994b74395a3938c397bc4955adba8298.

5. Toossi, M. 2006. New Look at Long-term Labor Force Projections to 2050. *Monthly Labor Review* 129: 19–39.

6. Fernandez, *Managing a Diverse Workforce*.

7. Bond, M. A., and J. L. Pyle. 1998. The Ecology of Diversity in Organizational Settings: Lessons from a Case Study. *Human Relations* 51: 589–623.

Knouse, S. B., P. Rosenfeld, and A. L. Culberston. 1992. Hispanics and Work: An Overview. In *Hispanics in the Workplace*, ed. S. B. Knouse, P. Rosenfeld, and A. L. Culberston. Newbury Park: Sage Publications, pp. 1–5.

Williams, K. Y., and C. A. O'Reilly III. 1998. Demography and Diversity in Organizations: A Review of 40 Years of Research. In *Research in Organizational Behavior*, Vol. 20, ed. B. M. Staw and L. L. Cummings. Greenwich, CT: JAI Press, pp. 77–140.

8. Alderfer, C. P., and A. D. Sims. 2003. Diversity in Organizations. In *Handbook of Psychology: Industrial and Organizational Psychology*, ed. W. C. Borman, D. R. Ilgen, and R. J. Klimoski. Hoboken: John Wiley and Sons, Chap. 23.

   De Dreu, C. K. W., F. Harinck, and A. E. M. Van Vianen. 1999. Conflict and Performance in Groups and Organizations. In *International Review of Industrial and Organizational Psychology*, ed. C. L. Cooper and I. T. Robertson. Chichester: John Wiley & Sons, pp. 369–414. The review of diversity and conflict potential appears on p. 377.

   Donnellon, A., and D. Kolb. 1997. Constructive for Whom? The Fate of Diversity Disputes in Organizations. In *Using Conflict in Organizations*, ed. C. K. W. De Dreu and E. Van de Vliert. London: Sage Publications, pp. 161–76.

   Horowitz, S. V., and S. K. Boardman. 1994. Managing Conflict: Policy and Research Implications. *Journal of Social Issues* 50: 197–211.

   Mannix, E., and M. Neale. 2005. What Differences Make a Difference? The Promise and Reality of Diverse Teams in Organizations. *Psychological Science in the Public Interest* 6: 31–55.

   Williams and O'Reilly, Demography and Diversity in Organizations.

9. Ferris, G. R., D. D. Frink, and M. C. McGalang. 1993. Diversity in the Workplace: The Human Resources Management Challenges. *Human Resource Planning* 16: 41–51.

10. Thomas, R. R., Jr. Managing Diversity: A Conceptual Framework. In *Diversity in the Workplace*, ed. S. E. Jackson and Associates. New York: Guilford Press, pp. 306–17.

11. Loden, M., and J. B. Rosener. 1991. *Workforce America! Managing Employee Diversity as a Vital Resource*. Homewood: Business One Irwin. Part III.

12. Herring, C. 2009. Does Diversity Pay? Race, Gender, and the Business Case for Diversity. *American Sociological Review* 74: 208–24.

   Jackson, S. E., and E. B. Alvarez. 1992. Working through Diversity as a Strategic Imperative. In *Diversity in the Workplace: Human Resources Initiatives*, ed. S. E. Jackson and Associates. New York: Guilford Press.

   Wolf, D. 1992. Whither the Work Force? In *In Diversity Is Strength: Capitalizing on the New Work Force*, ed. J. Alster, T. Brothers, and H. Gallo. New York: Conference Board, pp. 9–10.

13. Ely, R. J., and D. A. Thomas. 2001. Cultural Diversity at Work: The Effects of Diversity Perspectives on Work Group Processes and Outcomes. *Administrative Science Quarterly* 46: 229–73.

   Polzer, J. T., L. P. Milton, and W. B. Swann, Jr. 2002. Capitalizing on Diversity: Interpersonal Congruence in Small Work Groups. *Administrative Science Quarterly* 47: 296–324.

   Swann, W. B., Jr., J. T. Polzer, D. C. Seyle, and S. J. Ko. 2004. Finding Value in Diversity: Verification of Personal and Social Self-Views in Diverse Groups. *Academy of Management Review* 29: 9–27.

14. Thomas, D. A., and R. J. Ely. 1996. Making Differences Matter: A New Paradigm for Managing Diversity. *Harvard Business Review* (September–October): 79–90.

15. Alster, Brothers, and Gallo. *In Diversity Is Strength*.

Jackson and Associates, *Diversity in the Workplace*.

Thomas, R. R., Jr. 1990. From Affirmative Action to Affirming Diversity. *Harvard Business Review* 90 (March–April): 107–17.

16. Jackson and Alvarez, Working through Diversity, pp. 13–29.

    Richard, O. C. 2000. Racial Diversity, Business Strategy, and Firm Performance: A Resources-Based View. *Academy of Management Journal* 43: 164–77.

    Thomas, From Affirmative Action.

17. Roth, K. 1998. God on the Job. *Working Woman* (February): 65–66.

18. Jackson and Alvarez, Working through Diversity, pp. 26–27.

    Mor Barak, M. E., D. A. Cherin, and S. Berkman. 1998. Organizational and Personal Dimensions in Diversity Climate: Ethnic and Gender Differences in Employee Perceptions. *Human Relations* 34: 82–104.

19. Bond and Pyle, Diversity Dilemmas at Work.

    Gottfredson, L. S. 1992. Dilemmas in Developing Diversity Programs. In *Diversity in the Workplace: Human Resources Initiatives*, ed. S. E. Jackson and Associates. New York: Guilford Press, pp. 279–305.

20. Rosener, J. B. 1990. Ways Women Lead. *Harvard Business Review* 68 (November–December): 119–25.

21. Part of this section originally appeared in J. E. Champoux. 1999. Management Context of Not-for-Profit Organizations in the Next Millennium: Diversity, Quality, Technology, Global Environment, and Ethics. In *The Nonprofit Handbook, Management*. 2nd edn., 1999 Supplement, ed. T. D. Conners. New York: John Wiley & Sons, pp. 7–9. (Copyright © 1999 by John Wiley & Sons, Inc. This material is used by permission of John Wiley & Sons, Inc.)

    Space restrictions do not allow a detailed description of quality management history and research. See C. Noronha. 2002. Quality and TQM. In *The Theory of Culture-Specific Total Quality Management: Quality Management in Chinese Regions*. New York: Palgrave, Chap. 2, for a more extensive discussion.

22. Dale, B. G. 1999. *Managing Quality*. Oxford: Blackwell.

    Garvin, D. A. 1988. History and Evolution. In *Managing Quality: The Strategic and Competitive Edge*. New York: Free Press, Chap. 1.

    Gehani, R. R. 1993. Quality Value-Chain: A Meta-Synthesis of Frontiers of Quality Movement. *Academy of Management Executive* 7: 29–42.

23. 1993. A Cure for IBM's Blues? Retiring Exec Prescribes a Continuing Focus on Quality. *Information Week* (January 4): 48–49.

    Rickard, N. E., Jr. 1991. The Quest for Quality: A Race without a Finish Line. *Industrial Engineering* 23: 25–27.

    Saylor, J. H. 1992. *QM Field Manual*. New York: McGraw-Hill, p. xix.

24. Benner, M. J., and M. L. Tushman. 2003. Exploitation, Exploration, and Process Management: The Productivity Dilemma Revisited. *Academy of Management Review* 28: 238–56. This source has an excellent review of quality management and its effects on organizations.

    Harrington, H. J., and D. D. Mathers. 1997. *ISO 9000 and Beyond: From Compliance to Performance Improvement*. New York: McGraw-Hill.

    Harry, M., and R. Schroeder. 2000. *Six Sigma: The Breakthrough Management Strategy Revolutionizing the World's Top Corporations*. New York: Currency.

25. Daniels, S. E. 2002. The Little Hot Dog Stand That Could. *Quality Progress* 36 (September): 66–71.

    Kearns, D. T., and D. A. Nadler. 1992. *Prophets in the Dark: How Xerox Reinvented Itself and Beat Back the Japanese*. New York: HarperBusiness.

26. Garvin, *Managing Quality*.

Harry, M., and R. Schroeder. 1999. *Six Sigma: The Breakthrough Management Strategy Revolutionizing the World's Top Corporations*. New York: Doubleday Broadway.

McCabe, D., D. Knights, D. Kerfoot, G. Morgan, and H. Willmott. 1998. Making Sense of "Quality"? Toward a Review and Critique of Quality Initiatives in Financial Services. *Human Relations* 51: 389–411.

Radford, G. S. 1922. *The Control of Quality in Manufacturing*. New York: Ronald Press.

27. Shewhart, W. A. 1931. *Economic Control of Quality of Manufactured Product*. New York: D. Van Nostrand Company.

28. Feigenbaum, A. V. 1956. Total Quality Control. *Harvard Business Review* 34: 93–101. See A. V. Feigenbaum and D. S. Feigenbaum. 2003. *The Power of Management Capital: Utilizing the New Drivers of Innovation, Profitability, and Growth in a Demanding Global Economy*. New York: McGraw-Hill Trade, for his most recent thinking about quality management.

29. Juran, J. M. 1951. *Quality Control Handbook*. New York: McGraw-Hill.

Wren, D. A., and R. G. Greenwood. 1998. *Management Innovators: The People and Ideas That Have Shaped Modern Business*. New York: Oxford University Press, pp. 213–17.

30 Crosby, P. B. 1979. *Quality Is Free*. New York: Mentor/New American Library.

Crosby, P. B. 1996. *Quality Is Still Free*. New York: McGraw-Hill.

31. Garvin, *Managing Quality*, Chap. 10.

Wren and Greenwood, *Management Innovators*, pp. 204–13.

32. Noronha, Quality and TQM, pp. 21–24 gives an excellent description of the Japanese contributions.

33. Ishikawa, K. 1990. *Introduction to Quality Control*. Tokyo: 3A Corporation.

34. Taguchi, G. 1986. *Introduction to Quality Engineering: Designing Quality into Processes*. Tokyo: Asian Productivity Organization.

35. Noronha, Quality and TQM, pp. 28–31.

36. Deming, W. E. 1985. *Out of the Crisis*. Cambridge, MA: MIT Center for Advanced Engineering Study, p. 4.

37. Lengnick-Hall, C. A. 1996. Customer Contributions to Quality: A Different View of the – Customer-Oriented Firm. *Academy of Management Review* 21: 791–824.

38. Aikens, C. H. 2006. *Quality: A Corporate Force, Managing for Excellence*. Upper Saddle River: Prentice Hall. This source gives a comprehensive review of quality management.

Cameron, K. S., and C. K. Barnett. 2000. Organization Quality as a Cultural Variable: An Empirical Investigation of Quality Culture, Processes, and Outcomes. In *The Quality Movement & Organization Theory*, ed. R. E. Cole and W. R. Scott. Thousand Oaks: Sage Publications, Chap. 11.

Cole, R. E. 1998. *Managing Quality Fads: How American Business Learned to Play the Quality Game*. New York: Oxford University Press.

Coyle-Shapiro, J. A. M. 1999. Employee Participation and Assessment of an Organizational Change Intervention: A Three-Wave Study of Total Quality Management. *The Journal of Applied Behavioral Science* 35: 439–56.

Eaton, G. S., and S. L. Jarrell. 2000. Patterns in the Deployment of Total Quality Management. In *The Quality Movement & Organization Theory*, ed. R. E. Cole and W. R. Scott. Thousand Oaks: Sage Publications, Chap. 5.

Grant, R. M., R. Shani, and R. Krishnan. 1994. TQM's Challenge to Management Theory and Practice. *Sloan Management Review* 35 (Winter): 25–35.

Hackman, J. R., and R. Wageman. 1995. Total Quality Management: Empirical, Conceptual, and Practical Issues. *Administrative Science Quarterly* 40: 309–42.

Reger, R. K., L. T. Gustafson, S. M. DeMarie, and J. V. Mullane. 1994. Reframing the Organization: Why Implementing Total Quality Is Easier Said Than Done. *Academy of Management Review* 19: 565–84.

Zbaracki, M. J. 1998. The Rhetoric and Reality of Total Quality Management. *Administrative Science Quarterly* 43: 602–36.

39. An excellent practical discussion of the implications of this point appears in J. McGregor. 2009. When Service Means Survival. *Business Week* (March 2): 26–30.

Reed, R., D. J. Lemak, and J. C. Montgomery. 1996. Beyond Process: TQM Content and Firm Performance. *Academy of Management Review* 21: 173–202.

40. Carr, L. P. 1992. Applying Cost of Quality to a Service Business. *Sloan Management Review* 2: 72–77.

41. Rust, R. T., A. J. Zahorik, and T. L. Keiningham. 1994. Quality: What Went Wrong. *Return on Quality: Measuring the Financial Impact of Your Company's Quest for Quality*. Chicago: Probus Publishing Company, Chap. 1.

42. Barrett, A. 2001. At Honeywell, It's Larry the Knife. *Business Week* (November 26): 98, 100.

Hendricks, K. B., and V. R. Singhal. 2001. The Long-Run Stock Price Performance of Firms with Effective TQM Programs. *Management Science* 47: 359–68.

43. Douglas, T. J., and W. Q. Judge, Jr. 2001. Total Quality Management Implementation and Competitive Advantage: The Role of Structural Control and Exploration. *Academy of Management Journal* 41: 158–69.

44. Mathews, J. 1992. The Cost of Quality. *Newsweek* (September 7): 48–49.

45. Ivey, N. 1991. The Ecstasy and the Agony. *Business Week* (October 21): 40.

46. Benner and Tushman, Exploitation, Exploration, and Process Management. Rust, Zahorik, and Keiningham, *Return on Quality*.

47. Eaton and Jarrell, Patterns in the Deployment of Total Quality Management.

48. Quain, J. R. 1998. How to Shop for a Palmtop. *Fast Company* (September): 196–98, 202–3.

Tapscott, D., D. Ticoll, and A. Lowy. 2000. *Digital Capital: Harnessing the Power of Business Webs*. Boston: Harvard Business School Press.

Vogelstein, F. 2004. 10 Tech Trends to Bet on. *Fortune* (February 23): 74–78, 82, 86, 88.

Wright, R. T. 2008. *Technology*. Tinley Park: Goodheart-Willcox Company, Inc.

49. Cairncross, F. 2001. *The Death of Distance: How the Communications Revolution Is Changing Our Lives*. Boston: Harvard Business School Press.

50. Gross, N., and O. Port. 1998. The Next WAVE. *Business Week* (August 31): 80, 82–83.

51. See NTT DoCoMo advertisement, *Fortune*, February 23, 2004, pp. S1–S2 for some product examples.

52. Krane, J. 2003. *The Associated Press* as reported in *Business Outlook, The Albuquerque Journal* (March 13): 5.

53. Brynjolfsson, E., and A. McAfee. 2014. *The Second Machine Age: Work, Progress, and Prosperity in a Time of Brilliant Technologies*. New York: W. W. Norton & Company.

Cairncross, *The Death of Distance*, Chaps. 3 and 4.

Comm, J. 2009. *Twitter Power: How to Dominate Your Market One Tweet at a Time*. Hoboken: John Wiley & Sons.

Evans, D. 2008. *Social Media Marketing: An Hour a Day*. Indianapolis: Wiley Publishing.

Hempel, J. 2009. How Facebook Is Taking Over Our Lives. *Fortune* (March 2): 48–56.

Tapscott, D., and A. D. Williams. 2007. *Wikinomics: How Mass Collaboration Changes Everything*. New York: Penguin Group (USA).

54. Gross and Port, The Next WAVE.

55. Bylinsky, G. 1998. How to Bring Out Better Products Faster. *Fortune* (November 23): 238[B]–238[E], 238[J], 238[N], 238[R], 238[T].

Schonfeld, E. 1998. The Customized, Digitized, Have-It-Your-Way Economy. *Fortune* (September 28): 114–17, 120–21, 124.

56. Cronin, M. J. 1998. Ford's Intranet Success. *Fortune* (March 30): 158.

57. Davenport, T. H., and K. Pearlson. 1998. Two Cheers for the Virtual Office. *Sloan Management Review* 39 (Summer): 51–65.

Fitzpatrick, D., and S. Fishman. 2008. *The Work from Home Handbook: Flex Your Time, Improve Your Life*. Berkeley: Nalo. This easy-to-read source has excellent observations on working from home, especially for the first time experience.

Lister, K., and T. Harnish. 2009. *Undress for Success: The Naked Truth about Making Money at Home*. Hoboken: John Wiley & Sons.

Nilles, J. M. 1994. *Making Telecommuting Happen: A Guide for Telemanagers and Telecommuters*. New York: Van Nostrand Reinhold.

Saad, L. 2008. Telecommuting Still a Rare Perk: No Increase since 2006 in Percentage Punching in From Home. *The Gallup Poll Briefing* (August 15): 54–55.

58. Kraar, L. 1991. How Americans Win in Asia. *Fortune* (October 7): 133–34, 136, 140.

59. Yeatts, D. E., and C. Hyten. 1998. *High-Performing Self-Managed Work Teams: A Comparison of Theory and Practice*. Thousand Oaks: Sage Publications.

60. Vedantam, S. 1996. Indian Programmers Pick Up for U.S. Counterparts. *Albuquerque Journal* (August 27): B2.

61. 2004. A Perfect Market: A Survey of E-commerce. *The Economist* (May 15): 1–20.

Evans, P., and T. S. Wurster. 1999. *Blown to Bits: How the New Economics of Information Transforms Strategy*. Boston: Harvard Business School Press.

Hof, R. D. 1998. The Net Is Open for Business—Big Time. *Business Week* (August 31): 108–9.

62. Boudreau, M.-C., K. D. Loch, D. Robey, and D. Straud. 1998. Going Global: Using Information Technology to Advance the Competitiveness of the Virtual Transnational Organization. *Academy of Management Executive* 12: 120–28.

Gelfand, M. J., Z. Aycan, M. Erez, and K. Leung. Cross-Cultural Industrial Organizational Psychology and Organizational Behavior: A Hundred-Year Journey. *Journal of Applied Psychology* 102: 514–29.

Johnston, W. B. 1991. Global Workforce 2000: The New Labor Market. *Harvard Business Review* 69 (March–April): 115–29.

Kanter, R. M., and T. D. Dretler. 1998. "Global Strategy" and Its Impact on Local Operations: Lessons from Gillette Singapore. *Academy of Management Executive* 12: 60–68.

Miroshnik, V. 2002. Culture and International Management: A Review. *Journal of Management Development* 21: 521–44.

Porter, M. E. 1986. Changing Patterns of International Competition. *California Management Review* 28 (Winter): 9–40.

63. 1998. The 21st Century Economy. *Business Week* (August 31). This special issue details many aspects of the interconnected economies of the world.

64. Boudreau, Loch, Robey, and Straud, Going Global.
   Nulty, P. 1990. How the World WILL CHANGE. *Fortune* (January 15): 44–46, 50–54.

65. Boudreau, Loch, Robey, and Straud. Going Global.

66. Aho, C. M., and S. Ostry. 1990. Regional Trading Blocs: Pragmatic or Problematic Policy? In *The Global Economy: America's Role in the Decade Ahead*, ed. W. E. Brock and R. D. Hormats. New York: W. W. Norton, pp. 147–73.
   Ostry, S. 1990. Governments and Corporations in a Shrinking World: Trade and Innovation Policies in the United States, Europe and Japan. *Columbia Journal of World Business* 25: 10–16.

67. Davis, B., and J. Calmes. 1993. The House Passes Nafta—Trade Win: House Approves Nafta, Providing President with Crucial Victory. *The Wall Street Journal* (November 18): A1.

68. Fairlamb, D. 2001. Ready, Set, Euros! *Business Week* (July 2): 48–50.
   Fairlamb, D. 2001. Where the Euro Is a "Buy" Signal. *Business Week* (September 10): 130E2–E3.

69. Main, J. 1991. How Latin America Is Opening Up. *Fortune* (April 9): 84–87, 89.

70. Nakarmi, L. 1991. Korea Throws Open Its Doors. *Business Week* (July 29): 46.

71. Kraar, L. 1990. The Rising Power of the Pacific. *Fortune* (Pacific Rim): 8–9, 12.

72. Dorgan, M. 2000. Wine Goes Global to Cut Costs. *Albuquerque Journal* (December 10): C1, C6.

73. Chavez, B. 1995. Clear Sky Ahead for Blue Sky Co. *Albuquerque Journal* (June 19): 8–9.

74. Michailova, S. 2000. Contrasts in Culture: Russian and Western Perspectives on Organizational Change. *Academy of Management Executive* 14: 99–112.

75. Gupta, A. K., and V. Govindarajan. 2002. Cultivating a Global Mindset. *Academy of Management Executive* 16: 116–26.

76. Kanter and Dretler, "Global Strategy."
   Watson, J. L. 2000. China's Big Mac Attack. *Foreign Affairs* 79 (3): 120–34.

77. Hall, E. T. 1981. *The Silent Language*. New York: Anchor Books.
   Hall, E. T. 1982. *The Hidden Dimension*. New York: Anchor Books.

78. Schein, E. H. 1992. *Organizational Culture and Leadership*. San Francisco: Jossey-Bass, pp. 259–60.

79. Hofstede, G. 1990. The Cultural Relativity of Organizational Practices and Theories. In *Managing Organizations: Text, Readings and Cases*, ed. D. Wilson and R. Rosenfeld. London: McGraw-Hill, pp. 392–405.
   Hofstede, G. 1991. *Cultures and Organizations: Software of the Mind*. New York: McGraw-Hill.
   Hofstede, G. 2001. *Culture's Consequences: Comparing Values, Behaviors, Institutions, and Organizations across Nations*, 2nd edn. Thousand Oaks: Sage Publishing.

80. Ailon, G. 2008. Mirror, Mirror on the Wall: *Culture's Consequences* in a Value Test of Its Own Design. *Academy of Management Review* 33: 885–904.
   Fernandez, D. R., D. S. Carlson, X. X. Stepino, and N. Nicholson. 1997. Hofstede's Country Classification 25 Years Later. *Journal of Social Psychology* 137: 43–54.

McSweeney, B. 2002. Hofstede's Model of National Cultural Differences and Their Consequences: A Triumph of Faith—A Failure of Analysis. *Human Relations* 55: 89–118. This source has a detailed analysis of weaknesses in Hofstede's research.

Spector, P. E., C. L. Cooper, and K. Sparks. 2001. An International Study of the Psychometric Properties of the Hofstede Values Survey Module 1994: A Comparison of Individual and Country/Province Level Results. *Applied Psychology: An International Review* 50: 269–81.

Taras, V., B. L. Kirkman, and P. Steel. 2010. Examining the Impact of *Culture's Consequences: A Three-Decade, Multilevel,* Meta-Analytic Review of Hofstede's Cultural Value Dimensions. *Journal of Applied Psychology* 95: 405–39.

81. Ibid.

82. Fernandez, Carlson, Stepino, and Nicholson, Hofstede's Country Classification.

83. Adler, N. J., with A. Gundersen. 2008. *International Dimensions of Organizational Behavior*, 5th edn. Mason: Thomson South-Western.

Boyacigiller, N. A., and N. J. Adler. 1991. The Parochial Dinosaur: Organizational Science in a Global Context. *Academy of Management Review* 16: 262–90.

Chapter 3

ETHICS AND BEHAVIOR IN ORGANIZATIONS

After reading this chapter, you should be able to:

- Define ethical and unethical behavior.
- Discuss why some scholars believe "It's Good Business" to do business ethically.
- Know the functions of ethical values and standards for individuals and societies.
- Describe the various ethics theories and the guidelines each offers.
- Explain how to manage for ethical behavior in an organization.
- Identify some international aspects of ethical behavior in organizations.

Managers will feel growing pressure from the public and government to behave ethically in all business transactions. This pressure will affect employees of all types of organizations, whether public or private.

Ethical behavior is behavior viewed as right and honorable; unethical behavior is behavior viewed as wrong and dishonorable.[1] These straightforward definitions raise tough questions for managers and their organizations. First, what standards should they use to judge behavior as ethical or unethical? Second, how should the adjectives used to distinguish ethical from unethical behavior be defined? *Right* and *wrong* have different meanings to different people. Standards of ethical behavior also vary from one country to another. When issues of ethics combine with the growing opportunities for global business, the complexity of ethical questions in organizational behavior becomes clear.

Questions of ethics and ethical dilemmas abound in organizations and affect management decisions. Is it ethical for an organization to withhold product safety information? Is it ethical for a person to use knowledge about human perception to affect the perception of an organization's customers or employees? Is it ethical for an organization to refuse to improve the quality of its products or services when customers do not demand it? Those are only three ethical questions from an almost endless list that managers face.

Only a few in-depth studies of managers and ethical behavior exist. This type of research requires the cooperation of organizations and their managers, which is often hard to get.[2] Robert Jackall's *Moral Mazes* documents the complex and perplexing world of management decision making, where ethics often are not specific decision criteria.[3] Instead, managers find their decisions bound by context, leading to a situational form of ethics. Veteran managers navigate such moral mazes in ways that let them survive and succeed in their organizations.

Barbara Toffler's study of ethics and management reinforces this view of ethical ambiguity in management decisions.[4] Her extensive interview data showed that ethical dilemmas are common in management decision making and that the choices between right and wrong are not always clear. Although ethical concerns pervaded management decisions and actions, managers rarely used explicit ethical criteria during the decision process.[5]

ETHICAL AND UNETHICAL BEHAVIOR

Ethical behavior is behavior judged as good, right, just, honorable, and praiseworthy. **Unethical behavior** is behavior judged as wrong, unjust, dishonorable, or failing to meet an obligation.[6] The judgment of behavior as ethical or unethical is based on principles, rules, or guides that come from a specific ethics theory, character traits, or social values.[7] A later section of this chapter describes several ethics theories that you can consider for guidelines in behaving ethically.

The definitions of ethical and unethical behavior pose two nagging issues: the difficulty of finding a standard for judgment on which all reasonable people can agree, and the problem that *good* and *bad* or *right* and *wrong* have different meanings to different people and different societies.

More confusion and controversy come from the distinction between what is subjectively and objectively ethical.[8] A person's action is **subjectively ethical** if that person believes he acted ethically. A person's action is **objectively ethical** if that person acted according to a rule or law. The same distinction applies to unethical behavior that the person intended (subjectively unethical) and unethical behavior that violates an established rule or law (objectively unethical).

Conflict can arise when a person believes he behaved ethically and others who observed the behavior believe that person broke a law or rule. For example, doing business efficiently in some countries requires paying bribes. Some firms prohibit such bribes. A manager who pays bribes because he believes it is ethical in a particular country (subjectively ethical) violates his employer's policies (objectively unethical). Conflict can then arise between the employee and the employer over such behavior.[9]

"IT'S GOOD BUSINESS"

A basic assumption underlying this chapter is that doing business ethically is *good for business*. That is the position of Robert C. Solomon, a philosophy professor at the University of Texas, Austin, and Kristine Hanson, a New York businessperson. Together, they have written about business ethics and presented ethics workshops around the country.[10]

Solomon and Hanson argue that ethics is the keystone for smooth, effective, and efficient operation of business organizations. If we cannot trust another person's word or feel confident that a person will keep contractual agreements, business as we now understand it would stop. Although some businesspeople behave unethically and are not caught, unethical behavior can have long-term negative effects on a business. Customers who feel cheated will not return, will sue, or will report the business to law enforcement agencies. Ethical businesses develop a reputation of fair business dealings and concern for the effects of their decisions on society. They likely will face fewer punitive or regulatory efforts.

Solomon and Hanson take a long-term view of ethical management. They note that behaving ethically can be more costly in the short term than behaving unethically. For example, when a business adds safety equipment not required by law to a manufacturing operation, and another business in the same industry does not, the first company has higher manufacturing costs than the second company. Although such ethical concerns can enhance the reputation of the first firm, its higher costs could make it less competitive.

ETHICAL ISSUES IN ORGANIZATIONAL BEHAVIOR

The organizational behavior topics discussed in this book raise many ethical issues and questions. Each chapter has a separate section that discusses the ethical issues suggested by the behavioral topics of the chapter. The material developed in this chapter plays a central role in those discussions. After reading this chapter, you might want to read ahead and sample the ethical discussions in later chapters.

People who have knowledge of organizational behavioral processes can strongly affect other people's behavior. Having such knowledge raises questions about whether it is ethical to affect the behavior of others without their consent and free will. For example, behavior shaping is a central topic in the motivation chapters. The ethical questions about behavior shaping center on having a person's explicit and free consent to use the shaping process. Discussions about stress in organizations raise ethical issues about the obligation of managers to reduce dysfunctional stress. The remaining chapters of this book treat those questions and many others like them.

ETHICS: THE STUDY OF MORAL PHILOSOPHY

Ethics is the branch of philosophy that tries to develop a logical and systematic set of principles that define what ethical behavior is and what it is not.[11] Some call ethics moral philosophy. An essential feature of ethics and moral philosophy is its reflective quality—sitting back, looking at the way things usually are done, and asking how they *ought* to be done.[12]

Ethicists have debated the extent to which an ethical system is absolute or relative.[13] **Ethical absolutism** holds that a system of ethics applies to all people, everywhere, and always. The absolutist refers to an authority such as a religion, custom, or written code for support. **Ethical relativism** says that ethical behavior is whatever a person or society says is ethical. An ethical relativist sees ethics as based on personal feelings or opinion and rejects the view that moral judgments have objective validity.

A position halfway between the absolutist and relativist extremes sees ethics and moral judgments as changing over the course of human history. What is right (or wrong) at one point in the development of a social system can be wrong (or right) at another point in its development. According to this view, ethical systems evolve with the requirements of a social system so people in that system can behave in ways they judge acceptable.

Only you can decide which position best defines your feelings and beliefs about ethics. You will find that variations in ethical systems around the world present modern managers with extraordinary conflicts about right and wrong in their business decisions.

ETHICAL VALUES OF SOCIETIES AND INDIVIDUALS

Both societies and individuals develop systems of ethical values that serve important functions for them. This section describes how ethical values develop, their functions, and the ways in which they change.

Ethical Values of Societies

All societies have ethical standards that define the behavior they see as right, desirable, and good. The language of all societies distinguishes between good and bad, right and wrong, and desirable and undesirable. Ethical standards can be unwritten, as in preliterate societies, or written, as in literate societies.[14]

Ethical systems serve important social functions. They encourage collaborative efforts of organized social forms providing rules that bring predictability to behavior and help settle clashes of interest. In a world of scarce resources, ethical systems set standards for the allocation of those resources to competing parties. In short, such systems provide "recipes for action"[15] that can reduce internal strife and help a society survive.

Ethical systems are dynamic, not static. Ethical standards must serve the basic needs of the members of a society, or they will be changed. Standards that members of society view as rewarding are kept; other standards might be discarded or revised. Such change is often slow and evolutionary as events unfold within and around a society.

Intercultural contact and the diffusion of ethical standards from one culture to another also can change a society's ethical system. If many people are frustrated by the existing standards, acceptance of the new standard can be quick. Similarly, a society might quickly adopt another country's standards if it perceives them as having high prestige. In a world of extensive personal, audio, and video contacts among societies, diffusion of ethical standards and conflicts among standards are especially likely to occur.

Ethical Values of Individuals

Individuals develop their ethical values from societal-level values that they learn from their family, religious training, peers, education, and life experiences.[16] The earliest source of ethical values is one's family. The young child learns acceptable behaviors during early family socialization processes, developing an internal ethical standard both by instruction from others and by observation. As a person goes from infancy to adulthood, he develops more complex thinking

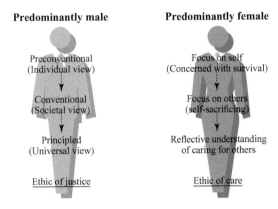

Predominantly male   **Predominantly female**

Preconventional
(Individual view)

Conventional
(Societal view)

Principled
(Universal view)

Ethic of justice

Focus on self
(Concerned with survival)

Focus on others
(self-sacrificing)

Reflective understanding
of caring for others

Ethic of care

■ **Figure 3.1:**   Stages of Moral Development

patterns with which to assess life experiences.[17] Those patterns include the person's ethical values. Although people from the same society will have similar systems of ethical values, differences will exist, and those systems can change over time.[18]

People go through three **stages of moral development**. Some theorists believe that men and women have different experiences at each stage and can end up with different views of morality.

The left side of Figure 3.1 shows the stages attributed mainly to men. The stages move from an individually based understanding of morality, to a societal one, and then to a universal moral view. That moral view is labeled an **ethic of justice** because it applies moral rules to determine what actions are fair. Each stage has different characteristics during its early and later periods.[19]

Preconventional is the first stage of moral development. This stage characterizes most children under age nine, some adolescents, and many criminal offenders. In the early period of this stage, the person is self-centered, does not consider anyone else's viewpoint, and obeys rules because authority backs them. Moral behavior is almost entirely a function of avoiding punishment. In the later period of this stage, the person becomes aware of the interests of others and the conflicts that arise among multiple interests. Moral behavior, though, stays focused on meeting one's personal interests.

Conventional is the second stage of moral development. This stage characterizes most adolescents and adults. It features a growing awareness of the expectations important to other people. A person at this stage has learned the importance of trust and loyalty in interpersonal relationships and accepts that mutual agreements take precedence over self-interest. This stage also features the internalization of the moral norms of the person's group or society. The latter part of the conventional stage features an awareness of the surrounding social system. A person fully developed at this stage believes moral behavior strengthens the social system.

Principled is the final stage of moral development. A person usually does not reach this stage until age 20 to 25, and many adults never reach it at all. This stage is called principled because it features the development of moral principles that guide the behavior of those who reach this stage. These moral principles emerge after the person critically assesses the norms accepted at the conventional stage and concludes that universal moral principles exist, such as the right to liberty. People at the latter part of this stage have a fully developed moral point of view centering on two beliefs: (1) a person's actions must always be guided by freely chosen moral principles; and (2) each person must be treated as a free and autonomous individual. Those principles might conflict with existing law. When they do, the person must follow the moral principle.

The right side of Figure 3.1 shows the three stages of moral development that lead to an ethic of care. A person with this moral view judges actions based on empathy for others and the person's relationships with them. Some theorists believe an ethic of care and its stages of development are more characteristic of women than men.[20]

The first stage features a strong focus on self with the intent of ensuring survival. This stage is similar to what men usually experience in the preconventional stage, but women often engage in self-criticism for being selfish. The transition to the second stage features moving from a self-focus to a focus on others. People who focus on others and on personal relationships consider actions moral that take into account other people involved in the situation. They focus on feelings, emotions, and the unique qualities of the situation in which the act happens.

In the third stage, the person enters the most mature stage, characterized by reflective understanding of caring for others. This stage features not only a strong focus on caring for others as the basis of moral action, but also a balanced view of the self in moral decisions. When choosing an ethical course of action, people in this stage consider the context of behavior, the people in that context, emotions, and feelings.

An ethic of justice refers to abstract rules with little reference to feelings, emotions, and relationships with people. It uses rules to mediate conflicts that often arise when emotions enter the arena of moral decisions. An ethic of care integrates feelings, emotions, and personal relationships. It is based on the notion that self is interdependent with others, an interdependence that cannot be ignored in moral actions.

The idea that differences in moral development and moral point of view might be gender-based sparked heated debate between moral philosophers and moral psychologists.[21] An analysis of data from 20,000 people in 66 samples found slight differences between the ethical perceptions of men and women. Women tended to have a slightly higher ethic than men. Other quantitative statistical analyses found small differences between men and women. One nonquantitative, or what academic researchers call qualitative research, found differences consistent with an ethic of care.[22]

A conservative interpretation of all empirical evidence says people do not have a single moral view that they bring to moral dilemmas. Both men and women use a justice or care view, although they can prefer one to the other. The choice of moral view can vary with the specific moral dilemma. Both men and women may apply a justice view to rights and justice problems and a care view to moral dilemmas involving social relationships.

ETHICS THEORIES

Four major ethics theories have evolved in the Western world.[23] This section describes each theory, its expected results, and objections to each theory. Figure 3.2 summarizes the main features of each theory.

Utilitarianism

An action is morally right if the total net benefit of the action exceeds the total net benefit of any other action.

Act utilitarianism ⟶ Utilitarianism ⟵ Rule utilitarianism

Rights-Based Ethics

A right is a person's just claim or entitlement.

Negative rights: Do not interfere with another person's rights.
Positive rights: A person has a duty to help others pursue their rights.

Justice-Based Ethics

Theory of distributive justice
(Rawls)

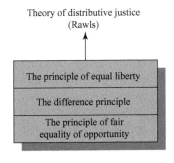

The principle of equal liberty

The difference principle

The principle of fair
equality of opportunity

Egoism

Individual ethical egoism asks a person to judge his actions only by their effects on his interests.

Universal ethical egoism asks a person to weigh the effects of his actions on his interests; some universal ethical egoists also consider the interests of others.

▪ **Figure 3.2:**   Main Features of Each Ethics Theory

Utilitarianism

Utilitarianism asks a person to examine the effects of an action to decide whether the action is morally correct under utilitarian guidelines. An action is morally right if its total net benefit exceeds the total net benefit of any other action. Utilitarianism assumes a person can know and assess all costs and benefits of his actions. The assessment of all future net benefits includes any significant indirect effects. An action is right if it yields the most benefit for everyone affected by the action, including the person doing the action. Utilitarianism forces a single actor to view the effects of an action on many others. Utilitarianism has two forms. **Act utilitarianism** asks a person to assess the effects of all actions according to their greatest net benefit to all affected. Under **rule utilitarianism**, a person assesses actions according to a set of rules designed to yield the greatest net benefit to all affected.

Act utilitarians hold that lying is right if it produces more good than bad. Because they always assess the effects of actions, they reject the view that one can judge actions as right or wrong in themselves.

Rule utilitarianism offers moral rules that should yield the most utility if everyone follows them. A person does not weigh the utility of each action. Instead, he compares the action to the rules to see whether it is moral according to those rules. Two principles are central to rule utilitarianism:

■ An action is morally right if it is required by correct moral rules.
■ A rule is correct if the total utility from everyone following the rule is more than the total utility of an alternate rule.

Unlike an act utilitarian, a rule utilitarian does not accept an action as right if it maximizes net benefits only once. Rule utilitarians assess the morality of their actions by referring to a set of absolute rules about what is right or wrong.

Moral philosophers have raised objections to utilitarianism based on the limits they see in its approach to ethics. One objection is that utility can have many different meanings, making it hard to measure for different people. Utilitarianism requires an assessment from the position of the actor because it is not possible to measure objectively the costs and benefits for all people affected by an action. A second objection is that some benefits or costs, such as life and health, are hard or impossible to measure. The costs and benefits of uncertain future results of an action are also difficult to assess. Lastly, what should a person count as a cost or a benefit of an action? This objection focuses on the difficulty of identifying all costs or benefits of an action and on the different ways various social groups value the effects of an action.

Utilitarians reply that the costs and benefits of many decisions can be assessed from their monetary equivalents. The benefits of safety equipment in automobiles, for example, can be assessed from the dollars saved in physical damage to people and property. Utilitarians also say precise measurement and full specification of all possible effects of an action are not required by utilitarianism. They ask only for an explicit statement and analysis of effects, recognizing that some measurements will be less accurate than quantitative measures.

Other objections have focused on utilitarianism's approach to moral issues of rights and justice. These objectors say an action that is morally right by utilitarian rules can also violate people's rights or lead to injustice. For example, a company that is deceptive during contract negotiations might win the contract to the benefit of its employees. In doing so, however, the company violated the other party's right to full disclosure.

Some moral philosophers have drawn two main conclusions about the limits of utilitarianism: (1) it is difficult to use when an action involves hard-to-quantify values such as life, death, or health; and (2) it does not deal adequately with rights and justice. The following sections describe other ethics theories that meet those objections.

Rights

A **right** is a person's just claim or entitlement. The right can focus on what that person does or on the actions of other people toward him. Rights can exist because a legal system defines them (**legal right**) or because of ethical standards (**moral right**). Rights let a person do something that is morally or legally correct or entitle a person to have something that is morally or legally correct for that person. The purpose of rights is to let a person freely pursue certain actions without interference from others. Moral rights are universal. They apply to all people, everywhere, under any legal system.

Rights have three features. First, other people, groups, and society have a moral duty to respect the rights of others. Second, rights let people pursue their interests as autonomous equals. The areas protected by rights exist despite any presumed social benefits that might come from restricting those rights. Third, rights provide moral justification for one's actions (i.e., people are not justified in interfering with another person's rights, but they are justified in helping that person pursue a right). For example, although the right to a fair trial is a basic human right in the United States, employees do not always have a right to due process within their organizations.

A rights-based ethic rejects the view that the results of actions should be used to assess those actions or to develop rules for guiding behavior. Rights-based ethics express moral rights from the individual's view, not society's view. Such ethics do not look to the number of people who benefit from limiting another person's rights. For example, the right to free speech in the United States stands even if a person expresses a dissenting view. At times, however, utilitarian concerns can override rights. A society can restrict pollution by an organization because of its effects on the health of many other people.

Moral philosophers distinguish between negative and positive rights.[24] **Negative rights** refer to the duty not to interfere with another's rights. Some writers have proposed such rights for employees. A right to free speech within an organization is an example of a basic employee right.[25] Such a right would let people speak out about actions they feel are wrong. **Positive rights** refer to the duty to help others freely pursue an interest to which they have a right. Such rights give people something they cannot provide for themselves, such as a right to proper health care.

Justice

Justice ethics theories use a comparative process that looks at the balance of benefits and burdens that are distributed among members of a group or that result from the application of laws, rules, and policies. Moral philosophers who propose justice-based ethics argue that just results of actions override utilitarian results. Justice-based ethicists usually do not consider an action just if it results in injustice to some members of society, although others benefit from the action.

The late philosopher John Rawls proposed a **theory of distributive justice** in the early 1970s.[26] He built his theory on the following three principles:

▪   **The principle of equal liberty:** Each person's basic liberties must equal those of others. Those liberties must also be protected from attack by others.

■ **The difference principle:** Societies will have inequalities, but must help the disadvantaged (sick, disabled, etc.).

■ **The principle of fair equality of opportunity:** Everyone must have the same chance to gain the best positions offered by society.

The **principle of equal liberty** includes the basic liberties of many Western societies, such as freedom of speech, the right to vote, and the right to hold personal property. The same principle also says organizations cannot invade employee privacy, use bribes to get contracts, or engage in any deceptive practices. Bribery and deception, for example, restrict a person's basic liberty of free choice.

The **difference principle** clearly implies that a society should care for its most needy. It also implies that managers of organizations should use resources efficiently in operating their firms. If they do not, the argument goes, society is less productive than it otherwise can be. If society is less productive, it cannot provide as many benefits to the disadvantaged as it could if it were more productive.

The **principle of fair equality of opportunity** says people must be allowed to advance in society based on their effort, contribution, and ability. Organizations must select people for jobs based on their ability to do the job. People who do not have the needed skills and abilities must have equal access to education and training to let them develop those skills.

Egoism

Ethical **egoism** is among the oldest and simplest of Western ethical systems. Moral philosophers distinguish two forms of ethical egoism: individual ethical egoism and universal ethical egoism. **Individual ethical egoism** asks a person to judge his actions only by their effects on his interests. Because this form of egoism never considers other people's interests, moral philosophers usually reject it as a defensible basis of ethics.[27]

Universal ethical egoism, although controversial, can include the interests of others when assessing one's actions. **Universal ethical egoism** asks a person to weigh the effects of his actions on his interests. The assessment is based on pursuing pleasure and avoiding pain. Although an ethical egoist pursues self-interest, some egoists consider others' interests as a way of reaching their ends. Such egoists consider the interests of others because they want other people to do the same toward them. Some moral philosophers refer to the latter view as "enlightened self-interest."

The objections raised by moral philosophers about ethical egoism focus on its inability to resolve conflicts between one person's self-interest and the interests of another.[28] If each person pursues his own interests, and those interests conflict with those of another person, that party is prevented from pursuing his interests. Moral philosophers argue that ethical egoism cannot resolve such conflicts independently of the interests of the involved parties.

MANAGING FOR ETHICAL BEHAVIOR

The demand for ethical behavior in organizations is forcing managers to find ways of **managing for ethical behavior**. In managing for ethical behavior, managers face a dilemma. Moral philosophers agree that ethical behavior happens because a person freely believes it is the right way to behave. Managers cannot impose ethical behavior by force. Although they can develop an organizational culture (see Chapter 4) that supports ethical behavior, the decision to behave ethically always rests with each person.[29]

Organizations and their managers have several methods available for managing for ethical behavior. These methods include codes of ethics, policy guidelines, decision procedures, standards of ethical performance, ethics training, and peer reporting of unethical behavior.

Codes of ethics are written statements describing behavior prohibited by an organization because it believes the behavior is unethical.[30] Such codes can be based on the ethics theories described earlier. Codes can come from industry associations, professional associations, or individual organizations. Behaviors most commonly prohibited include kickbacks, illegal political payments, extortion, inappropriate gifts, and conflicts of interest.[31]

Managers can also develop or change policies to improve the ethical culture of their organizations. **Policies** are written and usually available to all employees. Some typical areas covered by organizational policies are the organization's ethical responsibilities, employee rights, and work environment quality. Some writers have suggested that such policies amount to "constitutionalizing the corporation."[32] They can make an organization's culture more ethical if the policies are accepted, followed, and enforced.

Decision procedures specify the composition of a decision-making group and the scope of information the group will use for decision making. Such procedures aim to change an organization's decision processes to include more information about a decision's ethical effects. A decision-making group for locating a new plant could include community members and employees affected by the plant's design. Information procedures for new product decisions could require a fresh review of negative test results before a final decision.

Some writers have suggested that organizations develop **ethics performance standards**, which then become part of the organization's performance appraisal process.[33] Such standards prescribe required behavior consistent with existing law and discretionary behavior according to the organization's ethics policies. For example, an ethical standard for sexual harassment might say that all employees shall accept the mandate against sexual harassment in Title VII of the Civil Rights Act.

Since the late 1980s, interest in ethics training for employees has grown.[34] The goal of **ethics training** is to help the organization avoid governmental and societal sanctions by preventing unethical and illegal behavior. During training, employees discuss a code of ethics, organizational procedures for reporting unethical behavior, ethical frameworks based on ethics theories, and case studies showing ethical and unethical decisions. Another view of ethics training and education assumes it can change a person's basic character.[35] The dimensions of character important for ethical behavior are the person's capacities for ethical sensitivity, ethical reasoning, ethical conduct, and ethical leadership. Such capacities should be the target of development in both university education and organizational training programs.

A more subtle approach relies on peer reporting of unethical behavior to persuade employees to comply with an organization's ethical guidelines.[36] **Peer reporting** refers to coworkers' reports of perceived unethical behavior, a form of whistle blowing directed at someone with whom a person works. A whistle blower can often experience strong social pressure to overlook the unethical behavior. Management support for whistle blowers can offset such social pressure.

Managers can encourage peer reporting by specifying it as a desired behavior in the organization's code of ethics. Another way to encourage peer reporting is to ensure that unethical behavior by one person will have a negative effect on many others. For example, an organization might punish an entire group of workers for one member's unethical act.

INTERNATIONAL ASPECTS OF ETHICS

A sharp contrast exists between U.S. attitudes toward business ethics and those of other countries.[37] Of the major capitalist nations, the United States has the highest frequency of reporting ethical violations, the toughest laws, and the greatest prevalence of organizational codes of ethics. Concern for business ethics has been more episodic and viewed as faddish in many other countries.[38]

Codes of ethics are much less prevalent in Britain, Europe, and Japan than in the United States. U.S. organizations rely heavily on rules applied equally to all people. Organizations in other countries rely more on shared values and a sense of obligation to other people or organizations.[39] The perceived U.S. preoccupation with correct behavior prompted the British publication *The Economist* to observe, "America must lighten up a bit."[40]

As many organizations become multinational firms, they face additional ethical questions and issues. Multinational firms operate in many countries and are subject to the laws of those countries. The legal and social context of globally oriented organizations can present their managers with ethical dilemmas.[41]

Legal Views

Some legal views exist to guide ethical behavior in the international environment: (1) the Convention on Combating Bribery of Foreign Public Officials in International Business Transactions and related conventions; and (2) the Foreign Corrupt Practices Act. Note that these are legal views that describe the legality of actions in the international arena. A separate section discusses some ethical views.

Late 1998 saw a change in the international community toward ethical behavior. Twenty-nine members and five nonmembers of the Organization for

Economic Cooperation and Development signed an ethics treaty. The **Convention on Combating Bribery of Foreign Public Officials in International Business Transactions (OECD Convention)** has strong sanctions for bribery. The signatories represented economies in the major world regions. China and India were notable exceptions.[42]

Another convention that affects U.S. organizations is the Inter-American Convention Against Corruption covering activities in the Western hemisphere. Other conventions focus on corruption in Europe and the Pacific Basin, which also can affect U.S. organizations. See the citation for details of the various conventions.[43]

The **Foreign Corrupt Practices Act** of 1977 (FCPA) focuses on U.S. organizations doing business outside the United States. It prohibits a company from using bribes to get business in another country or to prevent the restriction of its business.[44] Foreign officials, foreign political parties, and foreign political candidates are the usual targets of bribes. An organization that violates the FCPA faces a fine between $1,000,000 and $2,500,000, depending on the provisions violated. Individuals who willfully violate the act face jail terms of five to ten years and fines ranging from $10,000 to $1,000,000, depending of the provisions violated.

The FCPA defines a payment as anything of value, including gifts. Under the act, a practice is corrupt if it tries to induce a person in another country to misuse his official position for the benefit of a company. A practice is also defined as corrupt by its motive. It is not necessary to complete the practice nor must it be illegal in the other country.

The FCPA excludes small payments to foreign officials that are required in the ordinary course of business in many countries. It allows such payments if they are a usual way of doing business in a country, although they would be bribes according to U.S. values. The act also allows entertainment and gifts if they are customary. The need to make small payments to help business along in some countries has presented many organizations with an ethical dilemma.

Ethical Views

Two ethical views apply to international affairs and multinational organizations: cultural relativism and ethical realism. Each takes a different approach to right and wrong in the international arena.

Cultural Relativism

Cultural relativism refers to ethical value differences among different cultures. It takes a normative ethical view based on the premise that each society's predominant ethical values decide right and wrong.[45]

A cultural relativist bases his argument on three points. First, moral judgments are statements of feelings and opinions and are not right or wrong. Second, moral judgments are based on applicable ethical systems and cannot be judged right or wrong across cultures. Third, because no way exists to prove whether an action is right or wrong, the prudent approach is not to claim that it is either right or wrong. Cultural relativism says managers should behave according to the ethics system of the countries in which they do business, even if their behavior violates their home country's ethics system.

Both classical and contemporary philosophers have rejected cultural relativism as an argument that codes of ethics cannot cross national boundaries.[46] They agree, however, that countries vary in what they define as right and wrong.

Ethical Realism

Ethical realism says that morality does not apply to international activities, behavior, and transactions. The realist arrives at this conclusion by way of some premises about people's moral behavior in the international arena. Because no power rules over international events, people will not behave morally. Because others will not behave morally, one is not morally required to behave according to ethical tenets.[47]

The realist view just described is the traditional view dating to the philosopher Thomas Hobbes. A revised view considers the effects of modern international transactions on people's behavior. The ethicist Manuel Velasquez has offered two revised premises setting out his view:

■ When other agents do not follow certain tenets of morality, it is not immoral for one to do the same when one would otherwise be putting oneself at a significant competitive disadvantage.[48]
■ Without an international sovereign, all rational agents will choose not to follow tenets of ordinary morality, when doing so will put one at a serious competitive disadvantage, if interactions are not repeated and agents are not able to signal their reliability to each other.[49]

Velasquez's second premise marks a major change from the traditional realist view. The revision substitutes interactions among agents in international markets for the third-party enforcer (international sovereign) of ethical rules. Many market interactions are repeated, letting people know whether they can trust each other in those interactions. It is in those repeated interactions that people must behave morally in the international arena.

The global environmental effects of certain decisions illustrate the application of the two principles. The use of chlorofluorocarbons adversely affects the global environment. The Montreal Protocol Treaty prohibits its signatories from manufacturing and using such chemicals.[50] Because countries that did not sign the treaty are not bound by it, a multinational firm could decide to move its chlorofluorocarbon manufacturing operations from a signatory country to a nonsignatory one. Any other decision would put the firm at a serious competitive disadvantage compared to a company that moved and continued manufacturing chlorofluorocarbons. The ethical realist concludes that the decision to move the manufacture of chlorofluorocarbons is not subject to ethical analysis.

SUMMARY

SUMMARY

3

Ethical behavior is behavior judged as good, right, just, honorable, and praise-worthy. Unethical behavior is behavior judged as wrong, dishonorable, or failing to meet an obligation. The judgment of behavior as ethical or unethical is based on principles, rules, or guides that come from an ethics theory, character traits, or social values. Some ethics scholars have argued that doing business ethically is simply good business.

The four ethics theories that can act as guides to ethical behavior are utilitarianism, rights, justice, and egoism. Utilitarianism asks a person to examine the effects of his actions to decide whether these actions are morally correct under utilitarian guidelines. An action is morally right if its total net benefit exceeds the total net benefit of any other action. A right is a person's just claim or entitlement. The right can focus on what that person does or on the action of other people toward him. Justice-based ethics theories use a comparative process, which looks at the balance of benefits and burdens among members of a group or resulting from the application of laws, rules, and policies. Egoism focuses on a person's self-interests, but can also include the interests of others.

Modern managers are feeling increasing pressure to promote ethical behavior in their organizations, causing them to look for ways of managing for ethical behavior. Managers can follow three steps to manage for ethical behavior in their organizations:

1. Understand the composition of the present ethical culture of their organizations.
2. Improve that ethical culture.
3. Sustain ethical behavior so that it becomes embedded in their organizations.

The section on international aspects of ethics described some legal views, including the Foreign Corrupt Practices Act (FCPA) and its implications for managers of multinational organizations. Besides the legal views, ethical views exist, such as cultural relativism and ethical realism.

REVIEW AND DISCUSSION QUESTIONS

REVIEW
AND
DISCUSSION
QUESTIONS

3

1   Review the discussion of ethical issues in organizational behavior. Discuss the areas of organizational behavior in which ethical issues have occurred in your work experiences.

2   Review the ethics theories described in the chapter. What are the implications for managing behavior in an organization of people having different ethical systems?

3   Discuss the implications of the argument that behaving ethically makes good business sense. How common is that view in contemporary organizations? Reflect on your work experience. Are there instances of ethical behavior having the positive effects noted in the chapter?

4 Review the discussion about ethical absolutism and ethical relativism. Discuss the views of each position. Which position applies to modern ethical issues?

5 Review the sections describing ethical values of individuals and societies. Discuss the ways both societies and individuals form those values. Which view best fits your moral development?

6 The chapter had an extended discussion about managing for ethical behavior in organizations. Discuss the implications of managing for ethical behavior. What effects do you expect for yourself in the future?

7 The chapter discussed two ethical views that apply to international affairs and multinational organizations. Which of those views do you hold? What are the implications of the different views for behavior in a multinational organization?

TAKE FIVE: OB ALIVE: *PRIME* (2005)

Rafi (Rafael) Gardet (Uma Thurman) tries to bounce back from a nasty divorce by seeking the help of her therapist Dr. Lisa Metzger (Meryl Streep). Young, aspiring painter David Bloomberg (Bryan Greenberg) enters her life, leading to a fast developing romantic and intimate relationship. Rafi's therapy sessions include detailed descriptions of her relationship with David. Unknown to Rafi, David is Metzger's only son.

This scene begins DVD Chapter 13, "Need to Talk." Rafi's voice-over says, "I was married to a man who couldn't love me." The scene ends after Metzger says, "Up until a few weeks ago, I didn't even think my son had a penis." She sighs. The film cuts to Rafi and David discussing these incidents.

Assess the ethical implications of Lisa Metzger's justification for her behavior. Do those reasons change the ethical or unethical quality of her behavior? Why or why not? This chapter described four ethics theories. What does each ethics theory reveal about the behavior?

REFERENCES AND NOTES

1. Brandt, R. B. 1959. *Ethical Theory: The Problems of Normative and Critical Ethics.* Englewood Cliffs: Prentice Hall, Chap. 1.
Brandt, R. B. 1996. *Facts, Value, and Morality.* New York: Cambridge University Press.
Brenkert, G. G., and T. L. Beauchamp. 2010. *The Oxford Handbook of Business Ethics.* New York: Oxford University Press.
Davis, P. E., ed. 1973. *Introduction to Moral Philosophy.* Columbus: Charles E. Merrill Publishing Company, pp. 1–8.

2. Phillips, N. 1992. Understanding Ethics in Practice: An Ethnomethodological Approach to the Study of Business Ethics. *Business Ethics Quarterly* 2: 223–44.

3. Jackall, R. 1988. *Moral Mazes: The World of Corporate Managers*. New York: Oxford University Press.

4. Toffler, B. L. 1986. *Tough Choices: Managers Talk Ethics*. New York: John Wiley & Sons.

5. For a review of these issues, see C. Anderson. 1997. Values-Based Management. *Academy of Management Executive* 11: 25–45.

6. Brandt, *Ethical Theory*, Chap. 1.
   Brandt, *Facts, Value, and Morality*.
   Davis, *Introduction to Moral Philosophy*, pp. 1–8.
   1997 Ethics. *The New Encyclopædia Britannica*, Vol. 18. Chicago: Encyclopædia Britannica, pp. 492–521.
   Frankena, W. K. 1973. *Ethics*. Englewood Cliffs: Prentice Hall.

7. Buchholz, R. A., and S. B. Rosenthal. 1997. The Nature of Business Ethics. In *Business Ethics: The Pragmatic Path beyond Principles to Process*. Englewood Cliffs: Prentice Hall, Chap. 1.
   Kish-Gephart, J. J., D. A. Harrison, and L. K. Treviño. 2010. Bad Apples, Bad Cases, and Bad Barrels: Meta-Analytic Evidence about Sources of Unethical Decisions at Work. *Journal of Applied Psychology* 95: 1–31.
   Rosenthal, S. B., and R. A. Buchholz. 2000. *Rethinking Business Ethics: A Pragmatic Approach*. New York: Oxford University Press.

8. DeGeorge, R. T. 2009. *Business Ethics*, 7th edn. Upper Saddle River: Prentice Hall.

9. Donaldson, T. 1996. Values in Tension: Ethics away from Home. *Harvard Business Review* (September–October): 48–49, 52–56, 58, 60, 62.

10. Solomon, R. C. 1992. *Ethics and Excellence: Cooperation and Integrity in Business*. New York: Oxford University Press.
    Solomon, R. C. 1997. *It's Good Business: Ethics and Free Enterprise for the New Millennium*. Lanham: Rowman & Littlefield.
    Solomon, R. C., and K. R. Hanson. 1985. *It's Good Business*. New York: Atheneum.

11. Brandt, *Ethical Theory*.
    Brandt, *Facts, Value, and Morality*.
    Ethics, *The New Encyclopædia Britannica*.
    Frankena, *Ethics*.

12. Williams, B. 1985. *Ethics and the Limits of Philosophy*. Cambridge, MA: Harvard University Press, Chap. 1.

13. Davis, *Introduction to Moral Philosophy*, pp. 140–41.
    DeGeorge, *Business Ethics*, pp. 28–35.
    Stace, W. T. 1937. *The Concept of Morals*. New York: Macmillan.
    Titus, H. H. 1959. *Living Issues in Philosophy*. New York: American Book Company, pp. 377–79.

14. Brandt, *Ethical Theory*, Chap. 5.

15. Ibid., p. 91.

16. Ibid., Chap. 6.

17. Piaget, J. 1970. Piaget's Theory. In *Carmichael's Manual of Child Psychology*, Vol. 1, ed. P. H. Mussen. New York: John Wiley & Sons.

18. Broad, C. D. 1985. The Subject Matter of Ethics. In *Ethics*, ed. C. L. Levy. Dordrecht: Martinus Nijhoff Publishers, Chap. 1.

19. Developed from Kohlberg's theory of moral judgment as described in A. Colby and L. Kohlberg. 1987. Theoretical Foundations and Research Validation. In *The*

Measurement of Moral Judgment, Vol. 1. Cambridge: Cambridge University Press, Chap. 1.

20. Gilligan, C. 1982. *In a Different Voice: Psychological Theory and Women's Development*. Cambridge, MA: Harvard University Press.
Gilligan, C., J. Ward, and J. M. Taylor, eds. 1988. *Mapping the Moral Domain*. Cambridge, MA: Harvard University Press.

21. Flanagan, O. 1991. *Varieties of Moral Personality: Ethics and Psychological Realism*. Cambridge, MA: Harvard University Press, Chap. 10.

22. Franke, G. R., D. F. Crown, and D. P. Spake. 1997. Gender Differences in Ethical Perceptions of Business Practices: A Social Role Theory Perspective. *Journal of Applied Psychology* 82: 920–34.
Jaffee, S., and J. S. Hyde, 2000. Gender Differences in Moral Orientation: A Meta-Analysis. *Psychological Bulletin* 126: 703–26.
Mitchell, K. 2002. Women's Morality: A Test of Carol Gilligan's Theory. *Journal of Social Distress and the Homeless* 11: 81–110. This study used a qualitative research approach. The article includes an excellent summary of Gilligan's approach and citations to works critical of her approach.

23. Developed from the following and other references cited throughout this section:
Beauchamp, T. L., and N. E. Bowie, eds. 1979. *Ethical Theory and Business*. Englewood Cliffs: Prentice Hall, Chap. 1.
Brandt, *Fact, Values, and Morality*.
DeGeorge, *Business Ethics*, Chaps. 2–4.
Ethics, *The New Encyclopædia Britannica*.
Mill, J. S. 1979. *Utilitarianism*. G. Sher, ed. Indianapolis: Hackett Publishing Company. (Originally published in 1861.)
Urmson, J. O. 1953. The Interpretation of the Moral Philosophy of J. S. Mill. *Philosophical Quarterly* 3: 33–39.
Velasquez, M. G. 1992. *Business Ethics: Concepts and Cases*. Englewood Cliffs: Prentice Hall, Chaps. 1–2.

24. Feinberg, J. 1973. *Social Philosophy*. Englewood Cliffs: Prentice Hall, pp. 59–61.

25. Ewing, D. W. 1978. Civil Liberties in the Corporation. *New York State Bar Journal* 50: 188–229.

26. Rawls, J. 1971. *A Theory of Justice*. Cambridge, MA: Harvard University Press, pp. 342–50.
Rawls, J. 1993. *Political Liberalism*. New York: Columbia University Press.

27. Baier, K. 1958. *The Moral Point of View: A Rational Basis of Ethics*. Ithaca, NY: Cornell University Press, pp. 173–204.
Beauchamp and Bowie, *Ethical Theory*, pp. 10–11.
Davis, *Introduction to Moral Philosophy*, pp. 140–44.
Sidgwick, H. 1907. Egoism. *The Methods of Ethics*, 7th edn (Book I and Book II). Chicago: University of Chicago Press. (Reprint 1966.)

28. Baier, *The Moral Point of View*, pp. 173–204.
Davis, *Introduction to Moral Philosophy*, pp. 140–44.
Sidgwick, Egoism.

29. This section developed from R. D. Gatewood and A. B. Carroll. 1991. Assessment of Ethical Performance of Organization Members: A Conceptual Framework. *Academy of Management Review* 16: 667–90.
Goodpaster, K. E. 1991. Ethical Imperatives and Corporate Leadership. In *Business Ethics: The State of the Art*, ed. R. E. Freeman. New York: Oxford University Press, Chap. 6.

Guy, M. E. 1990. *Ethical Decision Making in Everyday Work Situations*. Westport: Quorum Books.

Kanungo, R. N., and M. Mendonca. 1995. *The Ethical Dimensions of Leadership*. Thousand Oaks: Sage Publications.

Kaptein, M. 2011. Understanding Unethical Behavior by Unraveling Ethical Culture. *Human Relations* 64: 843–69.

Stone, C. D. 1975. *Where the Law Ends: The Social Control of Corporate Behavior*. New York: Harper & Row.

Thomas, T., J. R. Schermerhorn, Jr., and J. W. Dienhart. 2004. Strategic Leadership of Ethical Behavior in Business. *Academy of Management Executive* 18: 56–66.

Victor, B., and J. B. Cullen. 1987. A Theory and Measure of Ethical Climate in Organizations. In *Research in Corporate Social Performance and Policy*, ed. W. C. Frederick. Greenwich: JAI Press, pp. 51–71.

Waters, J. A., and F. Bird. 1987. The Moral Dimension of Organizational Culture. *Journal of Business Ethics* 6: 15–22.

Weaver, G. R., L. K. Treviño, and P. L. Cochran. 1999. Corporate Ethics Practices in the Mid-1990s. *Journal of Business Ethics* 18: 283–94.

30. Murphy, P. E. 1989. Creating Ethical Corporate Structures. *Sloan Management Review* 30: 73–79.

31. Chatov, R. 1980. What Corporate Ethics Statements Say. *California Management Review* 22 (Summer): 20–29.

32. Ewing, D. W. 1981. Constitutionalizing the Corporation. In *Corporations and Their Culture*, ed. T. Bradshaw and D. Vogel. New York: McGraw-Hill, pp. 253–68.

33. Gatewood and Carroll, Assessment of Ethical Performance.
Goodpaster, Ethical Imperatives.

34. Harrington, S. J. 1991. What Corporate America Is Teaching about Ethics. *Academy of Management Executive* 5 (February): 21–30.

35. Paine, L. S. 1991. Ethics as Character Development: Reflections on the Objective of Ethics Education. In *Business Ethics: The State of the Art*, ed. R. E. Freeman. New York: Oxford University Press, pp. 67–86.

36. Bouville, M. 2008. Whistle-Blowing and Morality. *Journals of Business Ethics* 81: 579–85.

Gundlach, M. J., S. C. Douglas, and M. J. Martinko. 2003. The Decision to Blow the Whistle: A Social Information Processing Framework. *Academy of Management Review* 28: 107–23.

Mesmer-Magnus, J. R., and C. Viswesvaran. 2005. Whistleblowing in Organizations: An Examination of Correlates of Whistleblowing Intentions, Actions, and Retaliation. *Journal of Business Ethics* 62: 277–97.

Miceli, M. P., and J. P. Near. 1994. Whistleblowing: Reaping the Benefits. *Academy of Management Executive* 8: 65–72.

Miceli, M. P., J. P. Near, and T. M. Dworkin. 2008. *Whistle-Blowing in Organizations*. New York: Routledge.

Near, J. P., and M. P. Miceli. 1996. Whistle-Blowing: Myth and Reality. *Journal of Management* 22: 507–26.

Treviño, L. K., and B. Victor. 1992. Peer Reporting of Unethical Behavior: A Social Context Perspective. *Academy of Management Journal* 35: 38–64.

37. Martin, K. D., J. B. Cullen, J. L. Johnson, and K. P. Parboteeah. 2007. Deciding to Bribe: A Cross-Level Analysis of Firm and Home Country Influences on Bribery Activity. *Academy of Management Journal* 50: 1401–22.

Small, M. W. 1992. Attitudes towards Business Ethics Held by Western Australian Students: A Comparative Study. *Journal of Business Ethics* 11: 745–52.

Whipple, T. W., and D. F. Swords. 1992. Business Ethics Judgments: A Cross-Cultural Comparison. *Journal of Business Ethics* 11: 671–78.

38. Vogel, D. 1992. The Globalization of Business Ethics: Why America Remains Distinctive. *California Management Review* 35 (Fall): 30–49.

39. Ibid., pp. 44–46.

40. 1990. America's Decadent Puritans. *Economist* 316 (July 28): 11–12. Quotation from p. 12.

41. Bowie, N. 1996. Relativism, Cultural and Moral. In *Ethical Issues in Business*, ed. T. Donaldson and P. R. Werhane. Upper Saddle River: Prentice Hall.

DeGeorge, R. 1993. *Competing with Integrity in International Business*. New York: Oxford University Press.

Donaldson, Values in Tension.

Küng, H. 1998. *A Global Ethic for Global Politics and Economics*. Translated by J. Bowden. New York: Oxford University Press, pp. 91–113, 250–76.

Werhane, P. H., and R. E. Freeman. 1999. Business Ethics: The State of the Art. *International Journal of Management Reviews* 1: 1–16.

42. Kaltenhauser, K. 1999. A Little Dab Will Do You? *World Trade* (January): 58–62.

43. Colton, N. 2001. Foreign Corrupt Practices Act. *American Criminal Law Review* 38: 891–912. The discussion of the OECD Convention appears on pp. 905–7.

44. Baruch, H. 1979. The Foreign Corrupt Practices Act. *Harvard Business Review* 57 (January–February): 32–34, 38, 44, 46, 48, 50.

Chesanow, N. 1985. *The World Class Executive: How to Do Business Like a Pro Around the World*. New York: Rawson Associates. This author suggests wrapping gifts so they do not look like bribes.

Colton, Foreign Corrupt Practices Act. This source has extensive citations for the FCPA.

See M. C. Piturro. 1992. Just Say … Maybe. *World Trade* (June): 87, 88, 90, 91 for a readable summary of the FCPA and recommendations of what is legal under the act.

45. Bowie, Relativism, Cultural and Moral.

Brandt, *Ethical Theory*, Chap. 5.

Davis, *Introduction to Moral Philosophy*, pp. 140–41.

DeGeorge, *Business Ethics*, pp. 28–34.

Donaldson, T. 1989. *The Ethics of International Business*. New York: Oxford University Press.

46. Donaldson, *The Ethics of International Business*, pp. 17–19.

47. Ibid., Chap. 2.

Velasquez, M. G. 1992. International Business, Morality, and the Common Good. *Business Ethics Quarterly* 2: 27–40.

48. Velasquez, International Business, Morality, and the Common Good, p. 33.

49. Ibid., p. 36.

50. Davis, B., B. Rosewicz, and D. Stipp. 1989. Scientists Track Earth's Urgent Global Warming. *The Wall Street Journal* (June 23): A24.

Freeman, A. 1987. Pact to Protect Ozone Is Signed by 24 Countries. *Wall Street Journal* (September 17): 38.

Chapter 4

ORGANIZATIONAL CULTURE

After reading this chapter, you should be able to:

- Discuss the concept of organizational culture.
- Analyze organizational culture effects on you as an individual.
- Distinguish different dimensions of organizational culture.
- Describe the different levels at which we experience an organization's culture.
- Analyze organizational culture from three perspectives.
- Understand cultural symbolism.
- Discuss the functions and dysfunctions of organizational culture.
- Diagnose an organization's culture.
- Describe the relationship between organizational culture and organizational performance.
- Explain the issues involved in creating, maintaining, and changing organizational culture.
- Appreciate some international and ethical issues raised by organizational cultures.

Organizational culture is a complex and deep aspect of organizations that can strongly affect organization members. It includes the values, norms, rites, rituals, ceremonies, heroes, and scoundrels in the organization's history. An organization's culture defines the content of what a new employee needs to learn to become an accepted organization member.[1]

Key aspects of organizational culture include value sharing and a structuring of experiences in an organization. Different sets of values can coexist among different groups of people throughout an organization. Although values differ among groups, members can share a common set of values. Not all people in an organization will fully agree about the dominant values and norms.[2]

If you have traveled abroad, you have already experienced what it is like to enter a new, different, and "foreign" culture. The architecture you saw was different from that at home. The food was not what you commonly ate. The language might have been different, possibly causing you some difficulty in communication. People in the new culture behaved differently toward each other. You probably felt some anxiety about learning your way around the new culture so you would not stand out as a foreigner. Organizational cultures are similar to cultures of different countries. Your entry into a new organizational culture is like entering the culture of another country.

■ Chapter Overview

Dimensions of Organizational Culture

Levels of Organizational Culture

Perspectives on Organizational Culture

Cultural Symbolism

Functions of Organizational Culture

Dysfunctions of Organizational Culture

Diagnosing Organizational Culture
As an Outsider
As an Insider

Organizational Culture and Organizational Performance

Creating, Maintaining, and Changing Organizational Culture

International Aspects of Organizational Culture

Ethical Issues in Organizational Culture

All human systems that have endured for some time and whose members have a shared history develop a culture. The specific content of an organization's culture develops from the experiences of a group adapting to its external environment and building a system of internal coordination.[3] Each system within which you interact has a culture. Your family, your college or university, your employer, and any leisure-time organizations such as sororities, fraternities, or social organizations all have their own cultures. These cultures can make different—and sometimes conflicting—demands on you.

Organizational cultures divide into multiple subcultures. An organization's design creates varying substructures and processes within the organization. Subcultures grow within these differentiated parts of an organization. They also form within an organization's departments, divisions, and operating locations.[4]

Different occupational groups within an organization often form different subcultures. Specialists in finance, accounting, information systems, and manufacturing often have their own jargon that helps them talk to each other. That jargon becomes an integral part of an occupational subculture which people from outside that subculture often cannot understand. An information systems specialist easily understands terms such as *upload*, *download*, and *token-ring networks*, which often are a foreign language to people outside that occupation.

Workforce diversity and the global environment of organizations, discussed in Chapter 2, "The Context of Modern Organizations (Diversity, Quality, Technology, International)," also help build subcultures in organizations. People from different social backgrounds and who have different values infuse organizations with a variety of values and viewpoints.[5] Global operations can require organizations to hire people from the host country. Those employees often bring values into the organization that differ from those of the organization's home country.

DIMENSIONS OF ORGANIZATIONAL CULTURE

Seven **dimensions of organizational culture** emphasize different aspects of culture and suggest different ways to understand an organization's culture.[6] The following paragraphs describe the seven dimensions.

The **levels** dimension describes organizational culture as having different degrees of visibility. Physical qualities of an organizational culture such as logos and other symbols are easy to see. Core values are the least visible.

The **pervasiveness** dimension views culture as widely dispersed in an organization. Culture affects people, their beliefs, their relationships inside and outside the organization, their views of the organization's product or service, their views of competitors, and much more. The list is almost endless and differs from one organizational culture to another.

The **implicitness** dimension refers to how veteran employees often take the core values of the organization's culture for granted, behaving according to certain core values without consciously thinking about them. Those values also are hard for a newcomer to discover because veteran employees assume everyone knows them.

The **imprinting** dimension suggests organizational cultures often have deep roots in the organization's history. This dimension applies to well-established cultures with an identifiable history. It also suggests the strong effects organizational cultures can have on their members. Cultures can imprint their values and beliefs on the culture's members so strongly that people find it hard to shift to new values and beliefs.

The **political** dimension sees culture as connected to systems of power in an organization. Coalitions, cliques, and alliances can have vested interests in the values that play key roles at different points in the organization's history. Their attachments to those values can make these groups either major sources of resistance to culture change or key resources in bringing culture change.

The **plurality** dimension emphasizes the existence of subcultures in most organizational cultures. Subcultures can develop vested interests over issues and beliefs. Power struggles in organizations often erupt over such vested interests, especially when managers try to change an organization's culture.

The **interdependency** dimension suggests the interconnections within an organization's culture and the ways cultures relate to other parts of an organization.

Complex connections can exist among subcultures, beliefs, and symbols. The culture also can form connections to other organization systems. For example, the values of an organization's culture often affect the development of the organization's reward system. Some cultures value associating rewards with performance; other cultures do not. Cultures also are interdependent with the external environment of the organization. Employees often behave toward customers and clients according to valued beliefs. Such behavior obviously can affect an important part of an organization's environment.

LEVELS OF ORGANIZATIONAL CULTURE

You can see organizational cultures at three different, but related, levels: arti-facts, values, and basic assumptions. These levels vary in visibility to an outsider. The first is the easiest to see and the last is the most difficult. Figure 4.1 shows the three **levels of organizational culture** and their visibility to an outsider.[7]

Artifacts are the most visible parts of an organization's culture. They are the obvious features of an organization that are immediately visible to a new employee. Artifacts include sounds, architecture, smells, behavior, attire, stories, language, products, and ceremonies.

Organizations differ in interior space layout and the formality of working relationships. Do people work in an open office space or behind closed doors? Do people dress formally or infor-mally? Does the interior design give the impres-sion of a cheerful or a somber work environment? Do people refer to each other by first names or do they use formal titles such as Doctor, Mr.,

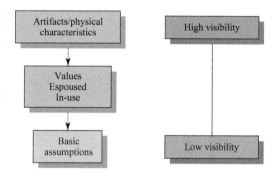

■ Figure 4.1: Levels of Organizational Culture

Ms., or Lieutenant? These factors are clues to an organization's culture. You can infer some values, norms, and required behavior from such factors. A new employee must first attend to messages from the physical characteristics of the organization and then watch the behavior of veteran organization members.

The next level of awareness is the values embedded in the culture. **Values** tell organization members what they "ought" to do in various situations. Values are hard for the newcomer to see, but she can discover and learn them. The newcomer must be wary of **espoused values** that guide what organization members say in a given situation. More important are the **in-use values** that guide what organization members do in a specific situation.[8] For example, a new employee learns from talking to superiors that equal promotion opportunity for women and men is the organization's policy. The person then finds that only men were promoted to management positions in the past five years.

The last level of discovery is almost invisible to a new employee. Even veteran organization members are not consciously aware of the basic assumptions of the organization's culture. Like values, these assumptions guide behavior in organizations. As a culture matures, many values become basic assumptions. **Basic assumptions** deal with many aspects of human behavior, human relationships within the organization, and relationships with elements in the organization's external environment. These assumptions develop over the history of the organization and from its ways of dealing with various events.

Because the assumptions are unconscious, veteran members find it hard to describe them to a new employee. People learn about them from trial-and-error behavior and by watching how veteran employees behave in different situations.

PERSPECTIVES ON ORGANIZATIONAL CULTURE

You can view organizational culture from three perspectives. One perspective says organizational cultures consist of shared values and basic assumptions among organization members. A second perspective says subcultures form within an organization's culture. A third perspective implies that ambiguity in organizations prevents pervasive agreement on values and basic assumptions. Figure 4.2 shows each perspective's view of an organization's culture. Each perspective lets you see an organization's culture from a different viewpoint, suggesting what you should look for when examining a culture. You will more fully understand an organization's culture if you use the perspectives together.[9]

Integration perspective   Differentiation perspective

Organizational culture

Fragmentation perspective

▨ **Figure 4.2:** Perspectives on Organizational Culture

The **integration perspective** emphasizes consensus among people about values and basic assumptions, consistent actions in accord with those values, and the absence of ambiguity. The consensus in values and basic assumptions is the organization's culture. Consistency appears in the culture's artifacts and its members' behavior. For example, if an organization's values stress the equal status of all employees, then there will be a single employee cafeteria and no designated parking. Culture, for the integration perspective, brings unity, predictability, and clarity to work experiences.

The **differentiation perspective** shows subcultures dispersed throughout an organization's culture. Though these subcultures can have an internal consensus about values and basic assumptions, they differ widely from each other. This perspective lets you uncover inconsistencies between values and artifacts. For example, an organization's management might say all employees are equal in status, but have special perquisites for senior executives.

The **fragmentation perspective** focuses on the presence of ambiguity in organizations. It finds that multiple interpretations of values and artifacts are common, making any search for consistency futile. One must note and accept the basic ambiguity of modern organization life.[10]

Ambiguity arises from fast changes both inside and outside organizations, growing workforce diversity, and the increasingly global environment organizations must face. Some ambiguity comes from the fleeting quality of many interactions. For example, people might communicate through direct computer interaction, without ever having face-to-face contact. The different viewpoints among members of a diverse or international workforce impose multiple interpretations on the same events. Such differences will not let a consensus about an organization's values and basic assumptions emerge.

CULTURAL SYMBOLISM

Organizational cultures have systems of symbols, objects that stand for something else. Some aspects of cultural symbols can have meaning for a wide group of people—organizational members, customers, and potential employees. Other aspects of cultural symbols are significant for only a small number of employees. This view of organizational cultures looks at artifacts as described earlier, but also examines anything within the culture that has symbolic meaning to its members.[11]

Cultural symbols have several characteristics. They represent more than the symbol alone by capturing emotional, cognitive, ethical, and aesthetic meanings. Symbols efficiently summarize those meanings. They serve the important cultural function of bringing order to otherwise complex events and processes, especially those that are repeated.

Symbols can be action, verbal, or material.[12] **Action symbols** are behaviors that have meaning beyond the obvious aspects of the behavior. For example, all managers dine together, but the female managers eat separately from the males, sending the added message of not valuing diversity. **Verbal symbols** are stories, slogans, sagas, legends, and jargon that both distinguish people in a culture and carry special meanings for them. **Material symbols** are found in the physical features of an organization's culture, including architecture, interior decor, and types of clothing.

Managers can create and use a cultural symbol to signal a need for large-scale organizational change. James McNerney Jr. felt he needed to emphasize the unacceptable ethics scandals that had plagued Boeing Co. He introduced General Counsel Douglas G. Bain to his top managers at the company's January 2006 annual retreat. Bain recited the federal prison numbers of two former Boeing employees. "Those are not Zip Codes," said Bain. He followed by noting that many prosecutors felt Boeing's organizational culture was "rotten to the core." The prison numbers became a symbolic anchor for the extensive changes McNerney wants to bring to Boeing.[13]

FUNCTIONS OF ORGANIZATIONAL CULTURE

Organizational cultures can have many **functional effects** on organizations and their management. The various functions help the organization adapt to its external environment and coordinate its internal systems and processes.[14]

An organization that has adapted successfully to its external environment can develop a culture with a consensus among members about the organization's mission. Specific goals derived from the mission and the means to reach those goals will be part of the culture. A consensus about a mission among veteran members lets the organization move forward smoothly toward those goals. Members agree about what needs to be done and how it will be done. In short, an organization's culture can help its members develop a sense of identity with the organization and a clear vision of the organization's direction.[15]

An organizational culture that gives its members a clear vision of the organization's mission also presents a consistent image to its markets, customers, and clients.[16] Over time, that image can give an organization a competitive advantage by building commitment to its products or services.

Members of developed organizational cultures agree about how to measure results and what remedial action to take if something goes wrong. Veteran members know almost automatically when things are not going right and how to take corrective action. If there were no consensus about those matters, conflict levels could be dysfunctionally high. With so much conflict among its members, the organization would have difficulty responding rapidly in situations requiring fast action.

Organizational cultures define the rewards and sanctions that managers can use. Rules develop about rewards for good performance and sanctions for poor performance. Some cultures respond to poor performance by saying the individual is not properly matched to the task. Those organizations reassign the person to a new task and let him try again. Other cultures develop specific sanctions that include demotions and terminations.

Organizational cultures differ in the way they use reward systems.[17] Some reward systems emphasize total organization performance, leading to a feeling that members are part of a fraternal group. Other cultures reward individual performance, ignoring the larger system. Members of the latter cultures develop a strong sense of individuality and independence. Later chapters about human motivation discuss the role of reward systems in organizations in more detail (Chapter 7, "Motivation: Need Theories" and Chapter 8, "Motivation: Cognitive and Behavioral Theories and Techniques").

Culture also helps integrate an organization's subsystems and processes, which lets the organization effectively coordinate its various actions. Common language develops within a culture, helping communication. Conceptual categories develop that filter unimportant detail and focus attention on important matters. Perceptual filtration reduces the likelihood that an individual will become overloaded by stimuli defined as unimportant by the culture.

The culture defines group boundaries and criteria for inclusion in the group. Well-defined group boundaries enhance member identification with the group and the group's work. Strong groups support and help members get their work done.

Organizational cultures define rules for power, rules for social stratification, and the ways in which social status is determined. Some accord social status and power to people of high achievement. Others base status and power on seniority.

The nature and quality of peer relationships and interpersonal interactions are defined by the organization's culture. Are interactions characterized by cooperation among peers at any cost or by confrontation and debate? Chapter 11, "Conflict in Organizations," describes conflict-management processes.

Organizational cultures develop and communicate an ideology that defines what the organization is all about. An ideology is a set of overarching values that hold the basic assumptions embedded in the organization's culture. The ideology appears in stories about past successes or descriptions of organization heroes.[18] The heroes might still be with the organization or might have left it long ago. In either case, what each hero represents stays in the ideology and becomes part of the organization's folklore. The ideology is a strong and sometimes overwhelming guide to action. As such, the ideology is an important element of an organization's culture that must be communicated to and discovered by the newcomer.

All the organizational culture functions come together to serve an overarching function—reduction of anxiety and uncertainty in human relationships. Rules of conduct and ways of viewing the world inside and outside the organization help members distinguish important stimuli from unimportant. Ignoring some stimuli reduces the chance of overloading the human organism.

DYSFUNCTIONS OF ORGANIZATIONAL CULTURE

The same functional features of an organization's culture can create **dysfunctions**.[19] Changes in an organization's external environment often require changes in an organization's strategy. However, the existing organizational culture developed from a particular strategy, and organizational members who are accustomed to that culture might resist changing the strategy. They might feel that such change will require changes in existing values and basic assumptions. When considering a change in strategy, managers must either dramatically change the existing culture or learn how to manage within its constraints.[20]

The existing organizational culture can lead to dysfunctional results when the organization tries product or market diversification, acquires a new company, or merges with another company. Analyses of these changes ordinarily include financial, physical, and technical aspects of the proposed action, but rarely consider the culture of the target organization. A merger can bring incompatible or opposing cultures together, producing conflicts and inefficiencies.[21] Moving into new markets brings the organization into new subcultures that might not respond in the usual ways to its product or service.

Organizations that introduce technologies to gain efficiency in manufacturing or providing service often experience latent dysfunctions. New technology can change familiar ways of acting that have become an accepted part of the existing organizational culture. Power and status can shift to those who know, understand, and use the new technology. Such shifts undermine the position of those who had power and status in the culture before the new technology arrived. All these factors can lead to conflict, inefficiency, and possible sabotage of the new technology.

Cultures produce different ways of looking at the world and interpreting language and events. People from one subculture might distrust those from other subcultures because of their different worldviews.[22] Conflict can erupt between people from different subcultures, especially when they passionately hold to different views.

Cultural differences can lead to communication failures between individuals even when they are expressing their thoughts clearly. For example, consider what the following words mean to you:

> tonic   braces   bubbler   ladder

Tonic is a soft drink in Boston; braces are suspenders in London; and a bubbler is a water fountain in Milwaukee. You might have trouble communicating with people from those cities if you do not know the meaning of those words.

Individuals from different subcultures within an organization have similar problems in communication. "Ladder," for example, is printers' jargon for the arrangement of the same words in successive lines at the edges of a paragraph. People in the accounting department might not know that meaning of the word.

DIAGNOSING ORGANIZATIONAL CULTURE

Diagnosing organizational culture is a systematic assessment of an organization's culture. You can diagnose an organization's culture from two perspectives: (1) as an outsider considering a job with a certain organization; and (2) as an insider after you have joined an organization. Table 4.1 shows an organizational culture diagnosis worksheet that you can use to guide a diagnosis. Other culture diagnosis tools exist. The Organizational Culture Assessment Instrument (OCAI) measures other aspects of an organization's culture than those shown in the worksheet.[23]

As an Outsider

Diagnosing an organization's culture as a potential employee can help you decide whether that organization is where you can do well, thrive, and grow, or whether the culture will make demands that you are unwilling or unable to meet. Although you will not learn all the inner secrets of a culture you have not yet joined, you can find clues about what it would be like to work for that organization.[24]

Study the organization's physical characteristics.[25] What does the external architecture look like? Does it convey an image of a robust, durable, dependable organization? Are the buildings of the same quality for all employees, or are modern buildings reserved for senior executives? Visits to the headquarters or other work sites of an organization can give you valuable insights. Short of a physical visit, photographs in annual reports or press accounts are good approximations.

■ **Table 4.1: Organizational Culture Diagnosis Worksheet**

Visible Artifacts
I. Physical Characteristics
(Architecture, office layout, decor, attire)

_____

_____

_____

_____

II. Behavior (Interpersonal and Oral)
(Interpersonal orientation, use of titles, rites, rituals,
ceremonies, language, stories, anecdotes, heroines, heroes)

_____

_____

_____

_____

III. Public Documents
(Annual reports, press accounts, Web sites,
internal newspapers, newsletters)

_____

_____

_____

_____

Invisible Artifacts
IV. Values
(Espoused values, in-use values)

_____

_____

_____

_____

V. Basic Assumptions
(Aspects of behavior, perceptions of internal
and external relationships, thoughts, feelings)

_____

_____

_____

_____

Sources: Suggested by the analysis in Schein, E. H. 2010. Chap. 18, "Assessing Cultural Dimensions: A Ten-Step Intervention." In *Organizational Culture and Leadership*. 4th edn. San Francisco: Jossey-Bass.

Deal, T. E., and A. A. Kennedy. 1982. *Corporate Cultures*. Reading, Massachusetts: Addison-Wesley, Chap. 7.

Read about the company. Examine annual reports, press accounts, and the organization's website. What do they describe? Do the reports emphasize the people who work for the organization and what they do or the financial performance of the organization? Each emphasis reflects a different culture. The first cares about the people who make up the company. The second might care only about the "bottom line." The choice is yours. Which culture do you prefer?

If you visit the organization as part of a recruiting interview, note how you are treated. You are an outsider. Are you treated as one or are you treated as a person about whom the company cares?

Lastly, talk to people who already work for the company. If graduates of your college or university work for the organization, try to contact them. Ask about the history of the company, the criteria of success, and what it is like to work there every day.

You have now compiled much information about the visible artifacts of an organization's culture. Typically, this is the easy step for an outsider. A much more difficult step is assessing the invisible artifacts as an outsider. Review all the visible artifacts material you have collected to infer the important values of the organization's culture. Likely you will not infer the basic assumptions, because these are often hidden to outsiders.

You can develop many clues about an organization's culture by following these suggestions. Only an insider, however, can get to the culture's inner secrets.

As an Insider

After you join an organization, you can begin to dig deeper into its culture. Stories and anecdotes are a strong source of evidence about the important qualities of the culture. Watch for similarities among stories told by different people. The subjects emphasized in recurring stories are what is important to the organization's culture. They might include satisfied customers, getting ahead on your merits, or the politics of the organization. Stories often describe organization heroes. What did those heroes do? Pay close attention because a hero's actions likely imply important values in the organization's culture.[26]

Find out the basis of promotions and pay increases. Are promotions based on competence and accomplishment or on tenure and loyalty to the organization? Such differences are clues to different types of organizational culture.

Observations of meetings are also useful sources of information about an organization's culture. Who does the talking? To whom do they talk? Such observations will tell you much about the status structure of the organization. Do participants defer to those with higher status, or are all considered equal contributors? What is the focus of meetings? How much time is spent on various topics? The topics discussed repeatedly and at length are clues about the culture's important values.

All these activities as an insider can lead to some conclusions about important values in the organization's culture. A more difficult step is to infer its basic assumption. Often, these assumptions emerge over time as you gain experience with the organization.

ORGANIZATIONAL CULTURE AND ORGANIZATIONAL PERFORMANCE

Several lines of theoretical and empirical research show a relationship between characteristics of an organization's culture and organizational performance. The theories vary in their explanations, but all point to a link between culture and performance.

One theory says organizations have a **competitive advantage** when their culture is valuable, rare, and not easily imitated.[27] The **value** of an organization's culture derives from the guidance it gives to direct people's behavior toward higher performance. **Rarity** refers to the features of a culture that are not common among competing organizations. Such rarity can come from the unique personalities of the organization's founders and the unique history underlying the culture. Cultures that are **not easily imitated** make it hard for competitors to change their cultures to get the same advantages. Difficulty of imitation follows from the rare features of some cultures and the difficulties managers have when trying to change a culture.

A second theoretical view focuses on **environment–culture congruence.**[28] Organizations facing high complexity and high ambiguity require a cohesive culture for effective performance. They feature widely shared values and basic assumptions that guide people's behavior. For organizations facing low uncertainty and low complexity, building a cohesive culture could be costly. Those organizations will reach high performance with more formal control processes such as organizational policies, rules, and procedures.

A third theory describes organizational cultures as having four distinct traits: involvement, consistency, adaptability, and mission.[29] **Involvement** is the degree of employee participation in organizational decisions. **Consistency** is the degree of agreement among organization members about important values and basic assumptions. **Adaptability** is the organization's capability to respond to external changes with internal changes. **Mission** describes the core purposes of the organization that keep members focused on what is important to the organization. Empirical research has found that involvement and adaptability are related to organizational growth. The consistency and mission traits are related to profitability.

Several empirical studies allow other observations about the culture–performance link. The following points summarize this research:

■ Organizations with strong cultural values that emphasize customers, employees, and shareholders, and value leadership at all levels outperform organizations without those cultural characteristics.[30]

■ Organizations with cultures featuring well-dispersed, participatory decision-making practices have higher returns on investment and sales than those that are not as well dispersed. The differences in financial performance become even greater over time.[31]

■ Organizations with cultures that have well-organized and adaptable work procedures and present clear goals to employees outperform organizations that do not. These cultural characteristics are stronger predictors of long-term financial performance than short-term performance.[32]

■ A strong, widely dispersed culture helps high-risk organizations, such as nuclear submarines and nuclear aircraft carriers, maintain high reliability.[33] People in these cultures perform with a "collective mind," a cognitive interdependence that helps them know how to act and know how others will act.[34]

■ Within accounting organizations with cultures emphasizing accuracy of work, predictability, and risk taking, poorly performing employees quit at a higher rate than higher performing employees.[35] No difference exists in the rate of quitting in organizations with cultures valuing collaboration and teamwork. Although the researcher did not directly assess organizational performance, these results imply potentially higher performance for low-turnover organizations.

■ Culture characteristics of widely shared values and a value of adaptability correlated well with performance in later years in 11 life insurance companies.[36]

These diverse results from empirical research show some culture–performance links. One comprehensive and critical review of the organizational culture performance literature suggests that this area needs much more work and with more consistent measures.[37]

CREATING, MAINTAINING, AND CHANGING ORGANIZATIONAL CULTURE

Managers of modern organizations face three decisions about their organization's culture. They can decide to create a completely new culture, usually in a separate work unit or in a new organization. They can maintain their existing organizational culture because they believe it is right for their environment. They can decide to change their culture to a new set of values, basic assumptions, and ideologies.[38]

Creating organizational culture is a deliberate effort to build a specific type of organizational culture. It happens when an entrepreneur forms an organization to pursue a vision or when managers of an existing organization form a new operating unit. The new culture needs an ideology that is understandable, convincing, and widely discussed. The ideology is a key tool for getting organizational members' commitment to the vision.

Building the culture around that ideology is easier if managers can recruit and select people who already share key parts of the ideology or who can easily develop commitment to it. Formal socialization practices (Chapter 6, "Organizational Socialization") play major roles in building an identity with the ideology. Forging that identity is easier when people's values on entry are close to the values and beliefs of the ideology. Cultural symbols must also be consistent with the ideology. For example, if the ideology has egalitarian values, the organization should have few physical status symbols distinguishing senior managers from other employees.

Maintaining organizational culture does not mean that managers passively and uncritically accept the values and basic assumptions of the present culture. Maintenance of a culture presents managers with a dilemma. They want to hold on to the values that were successful in the past, but they also need to question whether those values are right for the organization's environment.

Culture maintenance requires managers to be aware of what organizational culture is and how it manifests itself in their organization. It requires knowing the existing organizational culture's artifacts, values, and ideologies. A key way managers can become familiar with their culture is by doing a culture diagnosis, as described in an earlier section.

By maintaining their culture, managers want to maintain commitment of organization members to key parts of that culture.[39] They also want to strengthen key values so that they are widely held throughout the organization. In short, managers want to hold on to the good part of the organization's culture while helping the organization adapt to its newest challenges.

Culture maintenance also requires managers to carefully examine new practices for consistency with their culture's ideology. Introducing drug testing for employment screening in an organization with a culture built on trust might be a contradiction. Such testing might not appear contradictory in an organization that strongly values safety when working in hazardous areas.

Changing organizational culture requires breaking from some features of the old culture and creating new features.[40] The size and depth of the change varies depending on the degree of difference between the desired new culture and the old. For example, changing the culture of an organization that has a homogeneous workforce to one that values diversity will require an extended effort. The change reaches deep into the cultural fabric of the organization over many years.

Successfully managing the change process requires managers to attend to several issues. One is choosing the correct time for change. Managers are advised to act when the time seems right for culture change or when the situation clearly demands it. An opportune time for culture change might be when the organization wants to pursue new markets. IBM, for example, changed its culture when it shifted emphasis away from its historical roots in mainframe computers to small personal computers and workstations.[41] Change also might be required when the organization is performing poorly and faces clear threats to its viability.

Managers should not assume that everyone in the organization shares their view of the need to change. The senior executives of the organization will need to play leadership roles, convincing others in the organization that a cultural change is needed by offering a vision of that new culture. Managers will need to move forward with confidence, persistence, and optimism about the new culture. The change effort can focus on many aspects of the organization's culture, such as ideology, values, and symbols, although it is not realistic to expect that all parts of the prior culture will be removed.

Managers should know the roots of their organization's culture and maintain some continuity with the past by keeping elements that are valued widely in the organization.[42] This approach also lets managers say what will not change as a way of offering familiarity and security to veteran employees.

INTERNATIONAL ASPECTS OF ORGANIZATIONAL CULTURE

An organization operating in a global or international environment will face some special issues. The most obvious issues are the effects of national cultures on multinational organizations operating in different countries. Local cultures can shape the subcultures of globally dispersed units. National culture, local business norms, and the needs of local customers can affect the subcultures of such units.[43] The Gillette Company has a global focus that adjusts to local cultures. Performance goals are the same everywhere. Rules of interpersonal behavior, however, honor local cultural differences.[44]

Multinational organizations typically have employees from many countries working side by side. Those employees do not shed their national cultural values when they come to work. The heterogeneity of values in such organizations is extremely high, as is the chance of subcultures forming along national lines. Some research evidence suggests that instead of masking local differences with organizational culture, multinational cultures can increase ties people have to their native cultures.[45] Managing a multinationally diverse workforce presents all the challenges of managing a domestic diverse workforce described in Chapter 2.

Organizational cultures also differ in the value they place on multinational cultural diversity.[46] Managers might refuse to recognize cultural differences and insist that the home culture's way of doing business is the only correct way. Another view suggests recognizing cultural differences among people from different countries and using combinations of those differences for the strategic advantage of the organization. This "cultural synergy" view urges managers to view multinational cultural diversity as a resource.[47] That diversity could lead to better product ideas for culturally diverse markets and better communication with culturally diverse customers.

ETHICAL ISSUES IN ORGANIZATIONAL CULTURE

Does creating, maintaining, and changing organizational cultures manipulate and exploit human behavior in organizations?[48] Organizational culture scholars agree that an organization's culture affects the behavior of people in that culture. The ethical issue is what moral action managers should take in managing the cultures of their organizations.

An analysis with different ethical theories gives different answers. A utilitarian analysis says the moral action is the one that gives the greatest net benefit to the greatest number of people affected by the action. This view concludes that cultural values supporting such action are morally correct. Managers also are morally correct in changing or creating cultures in that direction.

A rights-based analysis suggests people must have the right to make free and informed choices about what affects them. This view argues, for example, for full disclosure to new employees about the values and basic assumptions of the organization's culture. It also argues for fully informing employees about proposed changes to the organization's culture.[49] Managers can have difficulty honoring a rights-based ethic because of the usual lack of conscious awareness of basic assumptions among veteran employees.

A justice analysis, using the principle of equal liberty, judges a culture as unethical if it prevents employees from freely voicing their opinions. It also judges a culture as unethical (principle of fair equality of opportunity) if all employee groups do not have an equal chance for advancement.

Diagnosing organizational cultures carries two major risks with ethical implications.[50] One risk is that a superficial analysis would accept only culture symbols or espoused values as representing the core ideology of the organization's culture. This form of diagnosis could yield observations that are misleading or wrong, if in-use values and basic assumptions differed.

The second risk centers on whether organization members are ready to receive feedback about its culture. Organizational cultures often give people protective interpretations about information from the organization's environment. Veteran employees may also hold ideals and basic assumption that have comfortably guided their behavior. The diagnosis could show those basic assumptions are myths held by veteran employees, not the values expressed in actions.

Some writers have pressed for the development of a moral dimension of organizational culture.[51] This dimension holds values and basic assumptions about including ethical dialogues in management decision processes. The importance of ethical dialogue must be an explicit part of the organization's ideology and be expressed repeatedly until it becomes a basic assumption. The goal of the moral dimension is to make the discussion of moral issues in decisions a comfortable, desired, and required part of every manager's job. The ethical scandals of the early part of the twenty-first century likely happened because of the lack of a moral dimension in those organizations' cultures.[52]

SUMMARY

SUMMARY
4

Organizational cultures include the values, norms, rites, rituals, symbols, ceremonies, heroes, and scoundrels in the history of the organization. Organizational cultures define what a new employee needs to learn for acceptance as an organizational member. Cultures are functional when they help an organization adapt to its external environment and coordinate internal activities. They are dysfunctional when they are the basis of resistance to change or create culture clashes when two different cultures merge.

Organizational cultures are pervasive in organizations, but are often taken for granted by veteran employees. Cultures have strong imprints from their historical roots, become highly interdependent with other organization processes, and can have many subcultures. Organizational cultures also have a political dimension and are often interlocked with the organization's power systems.

The levels at which you see organizational cultures vary from visible to almost invisible. Artifacts and other cultural symbols usually are visible to even the newest employee. Basic assumptions—a set of implicit values—are almost invisible to new employees and are learned only after a period of socialization and acceptance. Espoused values and in-use values have midlevel visibility.

Three perspectives view an organizational culture in different ways. An integration perspective sees organizational cultures as widely shared values among organization members. The differentiation perspective says subcultures form within an organization's culture. A fragmentation perspective sees ambiguity in organizations that prevents agreement on values.

Organizational cultures have systems of symbols that have meaning only to members of that culture. This view of organizational cultures looks at artifacts and examines anything with symbolic meaning to its members. Symbols can be action, verbal, or material.

Diagnosing an organization's culture is an important way for a potential employee to get information about the organization. It also is an important way for a manager to learn about the culture of the organization. An outsider's diagnosis usually cannot go beyond artifacts and values. The insider not only sees artifacts and values but, with much work, can also uncover basic assumptions.

Managers maintain an existing organizational culture because they believe it is right for the environments they face. They also can try to change their culture to a new set of values, basic assumptions, and ideologies. Those new values can focus on diversity, quality, global competitiveness, or ethical behavior in the organization. Managers can try to create a new culture, usually in a separate work unit or in a new organization. The new culture needs a core ideology that is understandable, convincing, and widely discussed.

International cultural diversity can lead to subcultures forming around national heritage. The "culture synergy" view argued for embracing this cultural diversity to give the organization a strategic advantage.

The major ethical issues center on free and informed choice by employees and freedom to express their views. An organization's culture can have a conscious moral dimension to guide management decision-making.

REVIEW AND DISCUSSION QUESTIONS

REVIEW
AND
DISCUSSION
QUESTIONS
4

1   Why do subcultures form within organizational cultures? What implications do subcultures have for new employees? Give some examples from your employment experience. What effects would you expect the increasingly more global environment of modern organizations to have on subcultures?

2 Review the sections "Perspectives on Organizational Culture" and "Cultural Symbolism." What parts of organizational culture do these views emphasize? Discuss the insights each view gives about an organization's culture. Use examples from your experience in the discussion.

3 What are the functions and dysfunctions of organizational culture? What role do basic assumptions play in those functions and dysfunctions?

4 Discuss the procedures for diagnosing an organization's culture. What are the major ethical issues you need to consider when making such a diagnosis?

5 Review the discussion of organizational culture and organizational performance. Discuss the three theoretical views of this link. What can you now conclude about organizational culture and organizational performance?

6 Review the expected effects on organizational culture of workforce diversity, quality management, a global environment, and an increasing emphasis on ethical behavior. Discuss the ways in which those effects could change the cultures of modern organizations.

7 Continue with the preceding question, but consider the discussion in the section "Creating, Maintaining, and Changing Organizational Culture." Discuss the implications for the observations in that section that follow from the effects mentioned in Question 6.

TAKE FIVE: OB ALIVE: THE GODFATHER (1972)

Don Vito Corleone (Marlon Brando) leads a powerful Mafia family. This intense film, based on Mario Puzo's novel, shows organized crime's violent side. It offers stunning parallels between managing any type of organization and managing a gangster organization.

This scene begins the film and follows some opening titles (DVD Chapter 1, "I Believe In America," Start: 0:00:49). It starts with Bonasera (Salvatore Corsitto) the undertaker's voice-over, "I believe in America." He continues to speak as the film opens on his face. The scene ends after Don Corleone says "I mean, we're not murderers ... in spite of what this undertaker says."

Consider the following questions while watching this scene: What organizational culture levels does the scene show? Does it show any basic assumptions or values that guide behavior? Do you perceive this culture as functional or dysfunctional for Don Corleone's organization?

REFERENCES AND NOTES

1. Alvesson, M., and P. O. Berg. 1992. *Corporate Culture and Organizational Symbolism*. Hawthorne: Walter de Gruyter, p. 123.
Ashkanasy N. M., C. P. M. Wilderom, and M. F. Peterson, eds. 2010. *The Handbook of Organizational Culture and Climate*. Thousand Oaks: Sage Publications.
Deal, T. E., and A. A. Kennedy. 1982. *Corporate Cultures: The Rites and Rituals of Corporate Life*. Reading, MA: Addison-Wesley, pp. 13–15.
Ehrhart, M. G., B. Schneider, and W. H. Macey. 2014. *Organizational Climate and Culture: An Introduction to Theory, Research, and Practice*. New York: Routledge.
Felsman, D. C., and O. A. O'Neill. 2014. The Role of Socialization, Orientation, and Training Programs in Transmitting Culture and Climate and Enhancing Performance. In *The Oxford Handbook of Organizational Climate and Culture*, ed. B. Schneider and K. M. Barbera. New York: Oxford University Press, Chap. 3.
Martin, J. 2002. *Organizational Culture: Mapping the Terrain*. Thousand Oaks: Sage Publications.
Ostroff, C., A. J. Kinicki, and M. M. Tamkins. 2003. Organizational Culture and Climate. In *Handbook of Psychology: Industrial and Organizational Psychology*, Vol. 12, ed. W. C. Borman, D. R. Ilgen, and R. J. Klimoski. Hoboken: John Wiley & Sons, Chap. 22. This citation has a thorough literature review and critique of organizational culture and climate research.
Schein, E. H. 1984. Coming to a New Awareness of Organizational Culture. *Sloan Management Review* 25 (Winter): 3–16.
Schein, E. H. 2010. *Organizational Culture and Leadership*. 4th edn. San Francisco: Jossey-Bass.
Schneider, B., M. G. Ehrhart, and W. H. Macey. 2011. Perspectives on Organizational Climate and Culture. In *APA Handbook of Industrial and Organizational Psychology*, Vol. 1, ed. S. Zedeck. Washington, DC: American Psychological Association, Chap. 12.
Trice, H. M., and J. M. Beyer. 1993. *The Cultures of Work Organizations*. Englewood Cliffs: Prentice Hall.
Wilkins, A. L. 1983. Organizational Stories as Symbols Which Control the Organization. In *Organizational Symbolism*, ed. L. R. Pondy, P. J. Frost, G. Morgan, and T. C. Dandridge. Greenwich, CT: JAI Press, pp. 81–92.

2. Martin, J. 1992. *Cultures in Organizations: Three Perspectives*. New York: Oxford University Press.
Organizational cultures are also more alike among organizations within a specific industry than among organizations in different industries. See Chatman, J. A., and K. A. Jehn. 1994. Assessing the Relationship between Industry Characteristics and Organizational Culture: How Different Can You Be? *Academy of Management Journal* 37: 522–53.

3. Schein, *Organizational Culture*, Chap. 1.

4. Sackmann, S. A. 1992. Culture and Subcultures: An Analysis of Organizational Knowledge. *Administrative Science Quarterly* 37: 140–61.

5. Loden, M., and J. B. Rosener. 1991. *Workforce America! Managing Employee Diversity as a Vital Resource*. Homewood: Business One Irwin.

6. Pettigrew, A. M. 1990. Organizational Climate and Culture: Two Constructs in Search of a Role. In *Organizational Climate and Culture*, ed. B. Schneider. San Francisco: Jossey-Bass, pp. 413–33.

7. Pratt, M. G., and A. Rafaeli. 1997. Organizational Dress as a Symbol of Multilayered Social Identities. *Academy of Management Journal* 40: 862–98.

   Schein, *Organizational Culture*, Chap. 2.

   Wilkins, Organizational Stories.

8. Argyris, C., and D. A. Schön. 1978. *Organizational Learning*. Reading, MA: Addison-Wesley. Argyris and Schön use the concept of "theory in use." I use a slightly modified label for the concept to allow parallel structure in this context.

9. Martin, *Cultures in Organizations*.

10. Alvesson and Berg, *Corporate Culture*, pp. 194–95, 210–13.

11. Developed from Alvesson and Berg, *Corporate Culture*.

   Frost, P., and G. Morgan. 1983. Symbols and Sensemaking: The Realization of a Framework. In *Organizational Symbolism*, ed. L. R. Pondy, P. J. Frost, G. Morgan, and T. C. Dandridge. Greenwich, CT: JAI Press, pp. 207–36.

   Jones, M. O. 1996. *Studying Organizational Symbolism*. Thousand Oaks: Sage Publications.

   Martin, *Cultures in Organizations*.

   Rafaeli, A., and M. Worline. 2000. Symbols in Organizational Culture. In *Handbook of Organizational Culture and Climate*, ed. N. M. Ashkanasy, C. P. M. Wilderom, and M. F. Peterson. Thousand Oaks: Sage Publications, Chap. 4.

   Strati, A. 1998. Organizational Symbolism as a Social Construction: A Perspective from the Sociology of Knowledge. *Human Relations* 51: 1379–1402.

   Trice and Beyer, *The Cultures of Work Organizations*, pp. 86–89.

   Turner, B., ed. 1990. *Organizational Symbolism*. Berlin: Walter de Gruyter.

   Wilkins, Organizational Stories.

12. Dandridge, T. C., I. I. Mitroff, and W. F. Joyce. 1980. Organizational Symbolism: A Topic to Expand Organizational Analysis. *Academy of Management Review* 5: 77–82.

13. Holmes, S. 2006. Cleaning Up Boeing. *Business Week* (March 13): 62–64, 66, 68. Quotations taken from p. 64.

14. Schein, *Organizational Culture*, Part Two: The Dimensions of Culture.

   Trice and Beyer, *The Cultures of Work Organizations*, Chap. 1.

15. Alvesson and Berg, *Corporate Culture*, Chap. 7.

16. Ibid.

17. Kerr, J., and J. W. Slocum, Jr. 1987. Managing Corporate Culture through Reward Systems. *Academy of Management Executive* 1: 99–108.

18. Deal and Kennedy, *Corporate Cultures*, Chap. 3.

19. Schein, *Organizational Culture*.

   Trice and Beyer, *The Cultures of Work Organizations*, Chap. 1.

20. Schein, *Organizational Culture*.

21. Cartwright, S., and C. L. Cooper. 1993. The Role of Culture Compatibility in Successful Organizational Marriage. *Academy of Management Review* 7: 57–70.

   Nahavandi, A., and A. R. Malekzadeh. 1988. Acculturation in Mergers and Acquisitions. *Academy of Management Review* 13: 79–90.

   Trice and Beyer, *The Cultures in Organizations*, pp. 323–31.

   Walter, G. 1985. Culture Collisions in Mergers and Acquisitions. In *Organizational Culture*, ed. P. Frost, L. Moore, M. Louis, C. Lundberg, and J. Martin. Beverly Hills: Sage Publications, pp. 301–14.

   Weber, Y. 2000. Measuring Cultural Fit in Mergers and Acquisitions. In *Handbook of Organizational Culture and Climate*, ed. N. M. Ashkanasy, C. P. M. Wilderom, and M. F. Peterson. Thousand Oaks: Sage Publications, Chap. 19.

22. Trice and Beyer, *The Cultures of Work Organizations*, pp. 10–11.
23. Developed from the following and other sources cited in this section:
    Cameron, K. S., and R. E. Quinn. 1999. *Diagnosing and Changing Organizational Culture*. Reading, MA: Addison-Wesley. See this citation for the Organizational Culture Assessment Instrument (OCAI) and methods of using it.
    Driskill, G. W., and A. L. Brenton. 2005. *Organizational Culture in Action: A Cultural Analysis Workbook*. Thousand Oaks: Sage Publications. This workbook offers a highly detailed approach to organizational culture diagnosis.
    Schein, *Organizational Culture*, Chap. 18.
24. Deal and Kennedy, *Corporate Cultures*, pp. 129–33.
25. Gagliardi, P., ed. 1990. *Symbols and Artifacts: Views of the Corporate Landscape*. Hawthorne: Walter de Gruyter.
26. Deal and Kennedy, *Corporate Cultures*, pp. 133–35.
27. Barney, J. B. 1986. Organizational Culture: Can It Be a Source of Sustained Competitive Advantage? *Academy of Management Review* 11: 656–65.
28. Wilkins, A. L., and W. G. Ouchi. 1983. Efficient Cultures: Exploring the Relationship between Culture and Organizational Performance. *Administrative Science Quarterly* 28: 468–81.
29. Denison, D. R. 1990. *Corporate Culture and Organizational Effectiveness*. New York: John Wiley & Sons.
    Denison, D. R., and A. K. Mishra. 1995. Toward a Theory of Organizational Culture and Effectiveness. *Organization Science* 6: 203–23.
    Kotrba, L. M., M. A. Gillespie, A. M. Schmidt, R. E. Smerek, S. A. Ritchie, and D. R. Denison. 2012. Do Consistent Corporate Cultures Have Better Business Performance? Exploring the Interaction Effects. *Human Relations* 65: 241–62.
30. Kotter, J. P., and J. L. Heskett. 1992. *Corporate Culture and Performance*. New York: Free Press.
31. Denison, *Corporate Culture*, Chap. 4.
32. Ibid.
33. Bierly, P. E., III, and J. C. Spender. 1995. Culture and High Reliability Organizations: The Case of the Nuclear Submarine. *Journal of Management* 21: 639–56.
    Weick, K. 1987. Organizational Culture as a Source of High Reliability. *California Management Review* 3 (Winter): 112–27.
34. Weick, K., and K. Roberts. 1993. Collective Mind in Organizations: Heedful Interrelating on Flight Decks. *Administrative Science Quarterly* 38: 357–81.
35. Sheriden, J. E. 1992. Organizational Culture and Employee Retention. *Academy of Management Journal* 35: 1036–56.
36. Gordon, G. G., and N. DiTomaso. 1992. Predicting Corporate Performance from Organizational Culture. *The Journal of Management Studies* 29: 783–98.
37. Wilderom, C. P. M., U. Glunk, and R. Maslowski. 2000. Organizational Culture as a Predictor of Organizational Performance. In *Handbook of Organizational Culture & Climate*, ed. N. M. Ashkanasy, C. P. M. Wilderom, and M. F. Peterson. Thousand Oaks: Sage Publications, Chap. 12.
38. Trice and Beyer, *The Cultures of Work Organizations*, Chaps. 9 and 10.
39. Van Maanen, J., and G. Kunda. 1989. "Real Feelings": Emotional Expression and Organizational Culture. In *Research in Organizational Behavior*, Vol. 2, ed. B. M. Staw and L. L. Cummings. Greenwich, CT: JAI Press, pp. 43–103.
40. Champoux, J. E., and L. D. Goldman. 1993. Building a Total Quality Culture. In *Nonprofit Organizations Policy and Procedures Handbook*, ed. T. D. Connors. New York: John Wiley & Sons, Chap. 3.

Day, D. V., M. A. Griffin, and K. R. Lauw. 2014. The Climate and Culture of Leadership in Organizations. In *The Oxford Handbook of Organizational Climate and Culture*, ed. B. Schneider and K. M Barbera. New York: Oxford University Press, Chap. 6.

Kotter and Heskett, *Corporate Culture and Performance*, Part III.

Sathe, V., and E. J. Davidson. 2000. Toward a New Conceptualization of Culture Change. In *Handbook of Organizational Culture and Climate*, ed. N. M. Ashkanasy, C. P. M. Wilderom, and M. F. Peterson. Thousand Oaks: Sage Publications, Chap. 17.

Trice and Beyer, *The Cultures of Work Organizations*, Chap. 10.

41. Verity, J. M. 1992. Does IBM Get It Now? *Business Week* (December 28): 32–33.

42. Schein, E. H. 2000. Sense and Nonsense about Culture and Climate. In *Handbook of Organizational Culture & Climate*, ed. N. M. Ashkanasy, C. P. M. Wilderom, and M. F. Peterson. Thousand Oaks: Sage Publications, pp. xxiii–xxx.

Watkins, A. L., and N. J. Bristow. 1987. For Successful Organizational Culture, Honor Your Past. *Academy of Management Executive* 1: 221–29.

43. Schein, *Organizational Culture*, Chap. 15.

44. Kanter, R. M., and T. D. Dretler. 1998. Global Strategy and Its Impact on Local Operations: Lessons from Gillette Singapore. *Academy of Management Executive* 12: 60–68.

45. Hofstede, G., B. Neuijen, D. D. Ohayv, and G. Sanders. 1990. Measuring Organizational Cultures: A Qualitative and Quantitative Study Across Twenty Cases. *Administrative Science Quarterly* 35: 286–316.

Laurent, A. 1983. The Cultural Diversity of Western Conceptions of Management. *International Studies of Management and Organizations* 13: 75–96.

46. Adler, N. J. 1980. Cultural Synergy: The Management of Cross-Cultural Organizations. In *Trends and Issues in OD: Current Theory and Practice*, ed. W. W. Burke and L. D. Goodstein. San Diego: University Associates, pp. 163–84.

Adler, N. J. (with Gundersen, A.). 2008. *International Dimensions of Organizational Behavior*, 5th edn. Mason: Thomson South-Western, Chap. 4.

47. Moran, R. T., and P. R. Harris. 1981. *Managing Cultural Synergy*. Houston: Gulf Publishing Company.

48. Trice and Beyer, *The Cultures of Work Organizations*, pp. 370–72.

49. Alvesson and Berg, *Corporate Culture*, p. 150.

50. Schein, E. H. 2004. *Organizational Culture and Leadership*, 3rd edn. San Francisco: Jossey-Bass, Chap. 10.

51. Waters, J. A., and F. Bird. 1987. The Moral Dimension of Organizational Culture. *Journal of Business Ethics* 6: 15–22.

52. Some prominent examples are Enron, Arthur Andersen, and the New York Stock Exchange executive pay scandal. For details, see Hamburger, T. 2002. Enron Official Tells of "Arrogant" Culture: Energy Firm Discouraged Staff Whistle-Blowing, House Panel Is Informed. *The Wall Street Journal* (February 15): A3, A4; B. L. Toffler with J. Reingold. 2003. *Final Accounting: Ambition, Greed, and the Fall of Arthur Andersen*. New York: Broadway Books; G. Weiss. 2003. The $140,000,000 Man: What Dick Grasso's Excessive Payout Reveals About How He Runs the New York Stock Exchange. *Fortune* (September 15): 84–88, 90, 92.

Part 1 Case[1]

Abstract

George Stein, a college student employed for the summer by Eastern Dairy, must decide if he is going to remove the filters from the plant's piping and, thus, allow the current production run of milkshake mix to be contaminated with maggots. This course of action will save the company money, at least in the short run, and allow George's shift to go home on time. George is disturbed, however, by the thought of children drinking those milkshakes. The workforce is unionized and George is feeling pressure from some of his co-workers to cut corners. The night shift is staffed by a self-managed team and no members of management are on duty.

DOES THIS MILKSHAKE TASTE FUNNY?*

George Stein, a college student working for Eastern Dairy during the summer, was suddenly faced with an ethical dilemma. George had very little time to think about his choices, less than a minute. On the one hand, he could do what Paul told him to do, and his shift could go home on time. However, he found it tough to shake the gross mental image of all those innocent kids drinking milkshakes contaminated with pulverized maggots. If he chose instead to go against Paul, what would the guys say? He could almost hear their derisive comments already: "wimp … wus … college kid …"

Background

George Stein had lived his entire life in various suburbs of a major city on the east coast. His father's salary as a manager provided the family with a solid middle-class lifestyle. His mother was a homemaker. George's major interests in life were the local teenage gathering place—a drive-in restaurant—hot rod cars, and his girlfriend, Cathy. He had not really wanted to attend college, but relentless pressure by his parents convinced him to try it for a year. He chose mechanical engineering as his major, hoping there might be some similarity between being a mechanical engineer and being a mechanic. After one year at engineering school, however, he had not seen any similarity yet. Once again this summer, his parents had to prod and cajole him to agree to return to school in the fall. They only succeeded by promising to give their blessing to his marriage to Cathy following his sophomore year.

---

* **Source:** Reprinted by permission from the *Case Research Journal*. Copyright 2001 by Anne Lawrence; Rebecca Morris, and the North American Case Research Association. All rights reserved.

George worked at menial jobs each of the last four summers to satisfy his immediate need for dating and car money. He did manage to put away a bit to be used for spending money during the school year. He had saved very little for the day that he and Cathy would start their life together, but they planned for Cathy to support them with her earnings as a secretary until George either finished or quit school.

The day after George returned home this summer, he heard that Eastern Dairy might hire summer help. He applied at the local plant the next day. Eastern Dairy was unionized, and the wages paid were over twice the minimum wage George had been paid on previous jobs, so he was quite interested in a position.

Eastern Dairy manufactured milkshake and ice cream mix for a number of customers in the metropolitan area. It sold the ice cream mix in 5- and 10-gallon containers to other firms, which then added flavoring ingredients (e.g., strawberries or blueberries), packaged and froze the mix, and sold the ice cream under their own brand names. Eastern Dairy sold the milkshake mix in 5-gallon cardboard cartons, which contained a plastic liner. These packages were delivered to many restaurants in the area. The packaging was designed to fit into automatic milkshake machines used in many types of restaurants, including most fast-food restaurants and drive-ins.

George was elated when he received the call asking him to come to the plant on June 8. After a brief visit with the human resources director, at which time George filled out the necessary employment forms, he was instructed to report for work at 11:00 p.m. that night. He was assigned to the night shift, working from 11:00 p.m. until 7:00 a.m., six nights per week—Sunday through Friday. With the regular wages paid at Eastern Dairy, supplemented by time and one-half for eight hours of guaranteed overtime each week, George thought he could save a tidy sum before he had to return to school at the end of the first week of September.

When George reported to work, he discovered that there were no managers assigned to the night shift. The entire plant was operated by a six-person crew of operators. One member of this crew, a young man named Paul Burnham, received each night's production orders from the day shift superintendent as the superintendent left for the day. Although Paul's status was no different from that of his five colleagues, the other crew members looked to him for direction. Paul passed the production orders to the mixer (who was the first stage of the production process) and kept the production records for the shift.

The production process was really quite simple. Mixes moved between various pieces of equipment (including mixing vats, pasteurizers, coolers, homogenizers, and filling machines) through stainless steel pipes suspended from the ceiling. All of the pipes had to be disassembled, thoroughly cleaned, and reinstalled by the conclusion of the night shift. This process took approximately one hour, so all the mix had to be run by 6:00 a.m. in order to complete the cleanup by the 7:00 a.m. quitting time. Paul and one other worker, Fred (the mixer), cleaned the giant mixing vats while the other four on the shift, including George, cleaned and reinstalled the pipes and filters.

George soon learned that Paul felt a sense of responsibility for completing all of the assigned work before the end of the shift. However, as long as that objective was achieved, he did not seem to care about what else went on during the shift. A great deal of storytelling and horseplay was the norm, but the work was always completed by quitting time. George was soon enjoying the easy camaraderie of the work group, the outrageous pranks they pulled on one another, and even the work itself.

George's position required that he station himself beside a conveyor in a large freezer room. He removed containers of mix as they came down the line and stacked them in the appropriate places. Periodically, Paul would decide that they had all worked hard enough and would shut down the line for a while so that they all could engage in some non-work activity like joke telling, hiding each other's lunch boxes, or "balloon" fights. The balloons were actually the five-gallon, flexible liners for the cardboard boxes in which the mix was sold.

While George did not relish being hit by an exploding bag containing five gallons of heavy mix, he found it great fun to lob one at one of his co-workers. The loss of 10 to 40 gallons of mix on a shift did not seem to concern anyone, and these fights were never curtailed.

George quickly learned that management had only two expectations of the night shift. First, the shift was expected to complete the production orders each night. Second, management expected the equipment, including the pipes, to be spotlessly cleaned at the conclusion of the shift. Paul told George that inspectors from the county health department would occasionally drop by unannounced at the end of the shift to inspect the vats and pipes after they had been disassembled and scrubbed. Paul also told George that management would be very upset if the inspectors registered any complaints about cleanliness.

George did join the union but saw very little evidence of their involvement in the day-to-day operations of the plant. Labor relations seemed quite amicable, and George only thought of the union when he looked at a pay stub and noticed that union dues had been deducted from his gross pay. The difference George noticed in working for Eastern Dairy compared to his previous employers was not the presence of the union but the absence of management.

The Current Situation

Things seemed to be going quite well for George on the job—until a few minutes ago. The problem first surfaced when the milkshake mix that was being run started spewing out of one of the joints in the overhead pipe network. The pumps were shut down while George disassembled the joint to see what the problem was. George removed the filter screen from the pipe at the leaking joint and saw that it was completely packed with solid matter. Closer inspection revealed that maggots were the culprits. George hurriedly took the filter to Paul to show him the blockage. Paul did not seem too concerned and told George to clean the filter and reassemble the joint. When George asked how this could have happened, Paul said maggots occasionally got into the bags of certain ingredients that were stored in a warehouse at the back of the lot. "But you do not have to worry," said Paul. "The filters will catch any solid matter."

Feeling somewhat reassured, George cleaned the filter and reassembled the pipe. But still, the image of maggots floating in a milkshake was hard to shake. And, unfortunately for George, this was not the end of it.

Shortly after the pumps were re-started, the mix began to flow out of another joint. Once again, a filter plugged with maggots was found to be the cause.

For the second time, George cleaned the filter and reassembled the connection. This time Paul had seemed a bit more concerned as he noted that they barely had enough time to run the last 500 gallons remaining in the vats before they needed to clean up in preparation for the end of the shift.

Moments after the equipment was again re-started, another joint started to spew. When maggots were found to be clogging this filter too, Paul called George over and told him to remove all five filters from the line so the last 500 gallons could be run without any filters. Paul laughed when he saw the shocked look on George's face.

"George," he said, "don't forget that all of this stuff goes through the homogenizer, so any solid matter will be completely pulverized. And when it's heated in the pasteurization process, any bacteria will be killed. No one will ever know about this, the company can save a lot of mix—that's money—and, most important, we can run this through and go home on time."

George knew that they would never get this lot packaged if they had to shut down every minute to clean filters, and there was no reason to believe it would not be this way for the rest of the run. The product had been thoroughly mixed in the mixing vats at the beginning of the process, which meant that contaminants would be distributed uniformly throughout the 500 gallons. George also knew that 500 gallons of milkshake was very expensive. He did not think management would just want it dumped down the drain. Finally, Paul was definitely right about one thing, removing all of the filters, a 10-minute job at most, would assure that they could get everything cleaned up and be out on time.

As George walked to the first filter joint, he felt a knot forming in his stomach as he thought of kids drinking all of the milkshakes they were about to produce. He had already decided he would not have another milkshake for at least a month, in order to be absolutely sure that this batch was no longer being served at restaurants. After all, he did not know exactly which restaurants would receive this mix. As he picked up his wrench and approached the first pipe joint that contained a filter, he still could not help wondering if he should not do or say something more.

NOTE

1. This case was prepared by Roland B. Cousins, LaGrange College, and Linda E. Benitz, InterCel, Inc., as a basis for class discussion and not to illustrate either effective or ineffective handling of an administrative situation. The names of the firm, individuals, and the location involved have been disguised to preserve anonymity.

The situation reported is factual. The authors thank Anne T. Lawrence for her assistance in the development of this case.

Part 2

INDIVIDUAL PROCESSES IN ORGANIZATIONS

Part 2 introduces you to some major individual processes in organizations. The main topics are perception, attitudes, and personality; organizational socialization; motivation and rewards; and the effects of job design on motivation. Each chapter discusses international aspects of the topics and the ethical issues they raise.

Chapter 5, "Perception, Attitudes, and Personality," starts with a description of human perceptual processes and distinguishes between self-perception (a view of self) and social perception (a view of others). The chapter next addresses such topics as how attitudes form, change, and affect behavior. Finally, personality and its development are discussed from a social and a biological perspective. The chapter describes several personality characteristics and types that are of interest to organizations and management. It also discusses the role of emotions in human behavior and emotional intelligence as a personality-like quality.

Chapter 6, "Organizational Socialization," describes an organizational process you experience after joining a new organization. The chapter opens with a description of roles, role behavior, and the transitions people make as they move through organizational roles. It then focuses on the three stages of organizational socialization: anticipatory socialization, entry/encounter, and metamorphosis.

Chapter 7, "Motivation: Need Theories," and Chapter 8, "Motivation: Cognitive and Behavioral Theories and Techniques," focus on major theories of human motivation. Chapter 7 describes the major need theories, the hierarchy of needs theory, existence-relatedness-growth theory, and McClelland's achievement motivation theory.

Chapter 8 describes cognitive and behavioral theories of motivation. The three cognitive theories are expectancy theory, equity theory, and goal setting theory. Expectancy theory and equity theory combine to form an analytical tool for understanding motivational issues in organizations. Goal setting theory describes how specific, challenging, reachable goals, which are accepted by a person, lead to higher performance than goals that are "fuzzy," unchallenging, not reachable, or not accepted. The chapter then describes behavior modification, a theory that shows how to shape people's behavior.

Chapter 9, "Job Design and Intrinsic Rewards," explains how job design affects people's experience of internal rewards. The chapter develops the job characteristics theory of work motivation, a well-researched theory that can guide the design of motivating jobs.

Chapter 5

PERCEPTION, ATTITUDES, AND PERSONALITY

After reading this chapter, you should be able to:

- Assess human perceptual processes and how people form impressions of others.
- Distinguish types of perceptual error and their effects on the information people get from their environment.
- Explain attribution processes and their effects on perceptions and attitudes.
- Discuss the nature of attitudes, how they form, and how they change.
- List the different parts of an attitude.
- Contrast different views of human personality development.
- Understand emotions and their role in human behavior.
- Discuss some dimensions of personality and several personality types.
- Recognize the effects of different cultures on perception, attitudes, and personality.
- Compare ethical issues that follow from stereotypes, attribution processes, and self-presentation.

Three related aspects of human psychology can strongly affect behavior in organizations. This chapter begins with a description of the human perceptual process. It then discusses attitudes, how they develop, and how they change. The chapter closes with a description of human personality, personality development, and personality types. Understanding these basic aspects of human psychology should help you understand behavior in organizations. They underlie all remaining chapters of this book.

PERCEPTION

Research on human perception is among the oldest psychological research, dating to the work of German psychologist Von Helmholtz in 1868. The research since then helps us understand this important basic human process that strongly affects behavior.[1]

Perception is a cognitive process that lets a person make sense of stimuli from the environment. These stimuli affect all senses: sight, touch, taste, smell, and hearing. The stimuli can come from other people, events, physical objects, or ideas.

The perceptual process includes both the inputs to the person and the selection of inputs to which the person attends. A person's perceptual process learns from repeated exposure to stimuli and stores recallable images, which process future inputs faster. The perceptual process is a mechanism that helps people adapt to changing environments.[2]

Figure 5.1 shows the major parts of the perceptual process. The **target** is the object of a person's perceptual process, such as another person, a physical object, an event, a sound, an idea, or a concept. **Threshold** is the minimum amount of information about, or stimulus from, the target for a person to notice its presence. The **detection threshold** is the point at which a person notices that something has changed in the environment. The **recognition threshold** is the point at which a person can identify the target or changes in the target's attributes.[3]

The target of perception emerges from its surrounding context, sometimes slowly and sometimes quickly. People quickly discriminate a high-contrast target from its background, but an ambiguous target takes time to see. The degree of contrast can come from the target's size, color, loudness, or smell. Personal aspects also affect

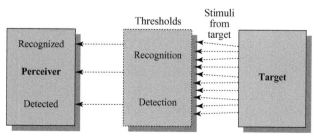

■ **Figure 5.1:** The Perceptual Process

the speed of emergence. People differ in their degree of motivation to attend to stimuli coming from their environment. They attend more quickly to positively valued stimuli than to negatively valued stimuli. For example, an achievement-oriented employee might notice announcements about promotion opportunities faster than an employee with less achievement motivation.

People also can use **perceptual defense** to shield themselves from negative stimuli. People can block out annoying sounds or disturbing and anxiety-provoking feedback. The latter ability is a particular concern in organizations that conduct performance appraisals. A person who finds a supervisor's observations unnerving does not hear all the content of the performance review.

Individuals can make two major **perceptual errors**: perceptual set and stereotyping. **Perceptual set** is beliefs based on previous experience with a target. These beliefs act like a set of instructions that process information a person gets about the target. The beliefs could have developed from prior association with the target, or the person might have learned them during early family socialization.[4] A person with a perceptual set about a target expects to find certain attributes or qualities associated with the target.

A **stereotype** is a perceptual set that holds beliefs and perceived attributes of a target person based on the group to which the target person belongs.[5] For example, a study of samples of Russian and American university students found that they held certain images of each other. The Russian students perceived Americans as independent, energetic, and spontaneous. The American students perceived Russians as conservative, orderly, restrained, and obedient.[6]

People's perceptions and stereotypes have many effects on behavior in organizations. The research literature shows their importance to several contemporary issues. Some research found that sexual harassment training increases a person's perception of sexual harassment in the workplace.[7] Other research has shown that the more people perceive political behavior in an organization, the more likely they will have negative work attitudes.[8] Another study assessed the stereotypes held by white men and women of white people, black people, and successful middle managers.[9] The descriptions of managers more closely matched the descriptions of white people than the descriptions of black people. If people widely hold these stereotypes, they have implications for management aspirations of blacks in an increasingly diverse workforce.

Self-Perception: A View of Self

Self-perception is the process by which people develop a view of themselves. This self-view develops from social interaction within different groups, and includes groups encountered on the Internet.[10] Self-perception has three parts: self-concept, self-esteem, and self-presentation.

Self-concept is the set of beliefs people have about themselves. It is the view people hold of their personal qualities and attributes. Several factors affect a person's self-concept, including the person's observations of his behavior, his recall of past significant events, and the effect of the surrounding social context.

People see their behavior, and the situation in which they behave, in much the same way that they see the behavior of other people.[11] If a person believes that his behavior occurred voluntarily and was not the result of a reward or sanction, he usually concludes the behavior happened because of some personal quality or attribute.

People learn about themselves by comparing themselves to other people with similar qualities.[12] They make such comparisons when they lack clear reasons for their behavior or are otherwise uncertain about themselves. In trying to assess your athletic abilities, you might compare yourself to other people of the same sex, size, and weight. In the work setting, to assess your abilities to hold a supervisory position, you might compare yourself to people with backgrounds similar to yours who have had recent promotions.

The ability to recall important events affects self-concept, but that recall often has errors.[13] People tend to recall events they attribute to themselves and not to a situation or other people. They often overestimate their role in past events.[14] They place more weight on the effects of their behavior and less on the surrounding situation or other people.

Self-esteem is the emotional dimension of self-perception. It refers to the positive and negative judgments people have of themselves. Self-concept is perceptual and cognitive; self-esteem is the feeling a person holds about his self-perception.[15] One's degree of self-esteem plays an important role in behavior. People with low self-esteem tend to be unsuccessful and do not adapt well to stressful events. Those with high self-esteem have the opposite experiences.[16]

Self-presentation, the third part of self-perception, includes the behavioral strategies people use to affect how others see them and how they think about themselves.[17] Self-presentations have three goals: to try to affect other people's impressions to win their approval, to increase the person's influence in a situation, or to ensure that others have an accurate impression of the person. Many people feel strongly motivated to have others perceive them accurately, whether positively or negatively.[18]

People tend to pursue some goals more than others with their self-presentations.[19] Those who are highly conscious of their public image change their behavior from situation to situation. They are conscious of situational norms and readily conform to them. People who want others to perceive them in a particular way behave consistently in different situations. They act in ways they perceive as true to themselves with little regard for situational norms.

Social Perception: A View of Others

Social perception is the process by which people come to know and understand each other.[20] When forming an impression of a person, a perceiver first observes the person, the situation, and the person's behavior. The perceiver might form a quick impression by making a snap judgment about that person, or make attributions and integrate the attributions to form a final impression.

Elements of Social Perception

People use three sets of clues when forming their impression of another person. These clues come from the person, the situation surrounding the person, and the observed behavior of the person.

In developing their first impressions, people use different physical aspects of the person, such as height, weight, hair color, and eyeglasses. Sometimes those impressions are stereotypes based on physical features. For example, some research suggests people perceive thin men as tense, suspicious, and stubborn; blond women as fun loving; and neatly dressed people as responsible.[21] Such stereotypes result from attributing qualities to people based on previously formed perceptions, despite what is true for the specific person.

We all have preconceptions about the situations in which we see the behavior of other people. Preconceptions develop from our experiences with the same or similar situations. Seeing another person in a given situation raises expectations about the behavior that the situation should cause. For example, when two people are introduced, we expect both parties to acknowledge the other and probably to shake hands.

Attribution Processes

People see, analyze, and explain the behavior of other people. They seek causes of behavior just as scientists search for an explanation of some phenomenon.[22] People use attribution processes to explain the causes of behavior they see in others. The **attribution process** begins with a quick personal attribution followed by some adjustment based on the characteristics of the situation.[23] Figure 5.2 shows an overview of the process.

Through the attribution process, people explain observed behavior by describing the characteristics of the person observed or the situation surrounding that person.[24] When people make a **personal attribution**, they say that some characteristic of the person, such as beliefs, disposition, or personality, and not the situation, caused the person's behavior. For example, when you conclude that another student or coworker spends many hours completing a project because he likes to work hard or values hard work, you are making a personal attribution.

Situational attributions turn to the context of the person's behavior to find its causes. You assume that aspects of the situation, not qualities of the person, cause the person's behavior. A situational attribution of a person's hard work would explain the person's behavior by a desire for good grades or other rewards, such as a promotion.

A perceiver uses three types of information when forming a personal or situational attribution: consensus information, distinctiveness information, and consistency information.[25] A perceiver gathers **consensus**

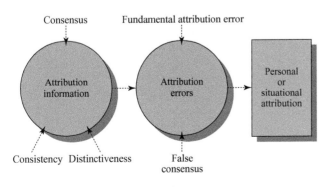

■ **Figure 5.2:** Overview of the Attribution Process

information by observing other people in the same or a similar situation. If other people show the same behavior as the target person, then the situation, not the person, caused the behavior. If other people behave differently from the target person, then the person caused his behavior.

Distinctiveness information comes from observing the target person in a different situation. If the person responds differently to the new situation, the perceiver attributes the cause of the original behavior to the situation. If the response is the same, the perceiver attributes the cause to the person.

Consistency information comes from observing the person in a similar situation, but at a different time. Consistency is high if the person's behavior is the same at both times and low if the behavior is different.

People combine consensus, distinctiveness, and consistency information to decide whether to attribute the causes of observed behavior to the person or to the situation. The perceiver attributes the cause of behavior to the person (personal attribution) when behavior is high in consistency and low in consensus and distinctiveness. The perceiver attributes the cause of behavior to the situation (situational attribution) when consensus and distinctiveness are high and consistency is low.

Here is an example of attribution processes in a work setting. Assume that you and a coworker are both candidates for a promotion. You believe you are more qualified, but your coworker gets the promotion. Now you try to explain why the promotion went to your coworker.

Attribution theory says you have two choices: the characteristics of the coworker or the characteristics of the situation. You have observed your coworker in different situations and noted wide variations in performance (high distinctiveness, low consistency). You also know your coworker rides a Harley-Davidson motorcycle, as does your supervisor (high consensus). You are disappointed, but do not feel you lost the promotion because of your skills and abilities. The information you have could easily let you conclude that your coworker's promotion resulted from the situation (interest same as supervisor), not from the coworker's skills and abilities.

This example illustrates one of several attribution errors. The **fundamental attribution error** occurs when the observer underestimates the situation as a cause of another person's behavior and overestimates the person's characteristics as the cause.[26] When explaining their own behavior, people tend to ascribe its causes to the situation, not to their personal qualities.[27] When explaining other people's behavior, people tend to ascribe its causes to personal qualities, not the situation. Such errors affect the accuracy of the view of the person that emerges from the attribution process. No matter how accurate or inaccurate their position might be, people tend to overestimate the degree to which others agree with their view. This belief in a **false consensus** reinforces the view the perceiver has of another person.[28]

A person takes the collection of attributions and integrates them to form an impression of the other person. Both the disposition of the perceiver and the way he weighs the individual attributed traits affect the perceiver's final impression. Recent experiences can affect one's interpretation of another person.[29] A positive or negative event just before meeting someone for the first time can affect the resulting impression of the person.[30] One's mood at the time of a first meeting affects that impression. People tend to form positive impressions of others when they are in a good mood and negative impressions when they are in a bad mood.[31]

ATTITUDES

Attitudes play a key role in social psychology because of the presumed connection between people's perceptions of their world and their behavior in it. Managers also consider attitudes important. They commonly attribute an employee's poor work performance to a bad attitude about work.[32]

An **attitude** is "a learned predisposition to respond in a consistently favorable or unfavorable manner with respect to a given object."[33] An attitude object can be anything in a person's environment, including physical objects, issues, ideas, events, and people. The evaluative or affective part of the definition is central to the concept of attitude. It conceptually distinguishes an attitude from other psychological concepts such as need, motive, and trait.[34]

An attitude has three separate, but related, parts:[35]

▪ **Cognitive:** Perceptions and beliefs about the attitude object; the person's perception of the distinguishing features of the object.
▪ **Affective:** Evaluation and feelings about the attitude object; a person's feeling of like or dislike for the object; includes neutral feelings about the object.
▪ **Behavioral intentions:** How the person wants to behave and what the person says about his behavior toward the object. It is not always the same as the behavior observed following the expression of the attitude.[36]

As an illustration, consider a person's positive attitude about his supervisor. The cognitive part of that attitude is the person's belief that his supervisor has high technical ability. The affective part includes his positive feelings and general liking of his supervisor. The behavioral intention part includes accepting his supervisor's directions and task assignments.

The most common work attitudes studied by researchers are organizational commitment, satisfaction, and job involvement. These attitudes are important aspects of work experiences and play a role in employee turnover.[37] Some research shows a consistent negative relationship between job satisfaction and intentions to leave an organization.[38] Reflect on your present work situation. How would you rate your feelings of satisfaction with your job, your pay, and your supervisor?

There is a connection between attitudes and behavior, although it is not strong.[39] Many other aspects of organizations and the people in them also affect behavior. For example, strong social norms or rules about a right way of behaving can affect behavior despite a person's attitude.

A person with strong attitudes about an object, issue, idea, or another person will usually behave in accord with that attitude. You have undoubtedly seen such strong attitudes in action. People who have a strong, positive attitude about Macintosh computers are more likely to buy a Macintosh than an IBM-compatible personal computer. People who abhor smoking are not likely to behave in a friendly way toward smokers. Ardent followers of Jesse Jackson will likely vote for him if he runs for an office.

Attitude Formation

A person's beliefs about an object and the amount and type of information the person has about the object contribute to the **attitude formation** about the object.[40] If a person has positive beliefs about an object, the person forms a positive attitude about it. If the person believes the object has negative attributes, the emerging attitude will be negative.

People form their beliefs by several different routes. The earliest influence on a person's beliefs and resultant attitudes is family upbringing. Each family holds a set of norms and values about what is right and wrong, good and bad. For example, French-Canadian families hold strong beliefs and attitudes about speaking French as their primary language. The children of such families develop positive attitudes about speaking French and negative attitudes about speaking English. As adults, their attitudes about speaking French spill over into attitudes about political candidates' positions on French as the primary language. Similar social influences on attitude formation come from the person's peer groups, work groups, and other social experiences.

Attitude Change

Attitudes are dynamic and change over time. The sources of change are within the person and in the person's social environment. **Attitude change** happens because (1) something persuades the person to shift his attitudes, (2) the norms of a social group important to the person affect his attitudes, or (3) the person becomes uncomfortable with some aspects of his beliefs about certain matters.

Common sources of attitude change are the **persuasive communications** designed to affect our beliefs, such as those found in radio, television, news-paper, and magazine advertising. Persuasive communication tries to change the cognitive part of an attitude and assumes the affective part will change in either a positive or a negative direction.[41]

Persuasive communication changes attitudes through four separate, but related, processes. First, the communication must win the target's attention. Television advertising, for example, often plays at a higher volume than the main program to get the attention of the viewer. Second, the target of the attitude change must comprehend the message. A persuasive communication must be presented in a language and format understandable by the target. The third process is acceptance. No matter how logical and persuasive a communication, if the target does not accept it, attitude change will not follow. The last process is retention. If the message is not memorable, attitude change will not last. The latter, of course, is central to the effectiveness of advertising. Shopping behavior is little affected by easily forgotten advertising.

The second major approach to attitude change (**social group norms**) views people as embedded in a social context and affected by the norms or standards held by the social groups a person experiences.[42] People who hold attitudes different from those of a group important to them will feel social pressures to conform to the norms of the group. Such pressures come from the tendency of social groups to reject people who do not conform to their norms. If a person with a differing attitude values membership in the group, that person will likely bring the attitude into alignment with the group norm.

People can have multiple beliefs or cognitions about an attitude object. The multiple cognitions can result from persuasive communications or social influence. If discrepancies (**cognitive dissonance**) develop among cognitions, the person feels internal tension and becomes motivated to reduce that tension. The person can reduce the dissonance by changing one or more cognitions. Such change in the cognitive part of an attitude can lead to change in the attitude itself.[43] The following is an example.

Assume that you believe in excelling at whatever you do. You are being transferred and want to learn more about your new boss. You check with several people and hear that your new boss is not well liked, leading you to develop a negative attitude about her. After starting your new job, you find that your boss demands high performance and rewards it with praise and pay increases. You should now feel tension from the dissonance between your prior negative attitude and your discovery that the boss's performance demands are consistent with your beliefs about yourself. You likely will dismiss your earlier negative attitude as based on the feelings of people who do not care to excel at their job. By doing so, you bring your cognitions about your new boss into a state of balance or consonance.

PERSONALITY

Undoubtedly, you have used or heard phrases such as "that person has an outgoing personality" or "that person has a pleasant personality." The word personality carries many meanings for both lay people and psychologists.[44] This chapter views **personality** as a set of traits, characteristics, and predispositions of a person. Personality usually matures and stabilizes by age 30.[45]

The complex factors that make up an individual's personality affect how the person adjusts to different environments. Think of personality as dynamically interconnected parts that act as multiple determinants of complex human behavior.[46]

Personality Theories

Psychologists have developed several personality theories since the early twentieth century. Each theory makes different assumptions about human personality and offers a different perspective of how personality develops.

Cognitive theory describes people as developing their thinking patterns as their lives unfold.[47] A person's patterns of thinking affect how the person interprets and internalizes life's events. People move through a series of cognitive development stages.[48] The stages begin shortly after birth with the reflexive behavior of the infant and proceed through increasingly more complex modes of perception and interpretation of events in the child's environment. This class of personality theory views a child as neither driven by instincts nor unwittingly shaped by environmental influences. Children are curious and actively explore their social world to understand it. They respond to their environments according to how they understand and interpret their environment's features. Two children in the same environment could interpret and react to it differently.

Learning theories of personality have appeared in several forms since the early 1900s.[49] The earliest versions assumed a child was a blank sheet of paper, shaped almost entirely by the social environment. Instincts played no role in these theories.[50] A need to satisfy a set of internal states, or drives, motivated a person's behavior.[51]

A person learns behavior from social interaction with other people. The young child learns acceptable behaviors during early family socialization. Adults continuously interact in different social environments and with different people. As behavior stabilizes, it forms the basic qualities of an individual's personality. Some learning theories view personality development as a continuous process from birth to death. The uniqueness of each personality follows from the variability in each person's social experiences.[52]

Operant-learning theory offers another view of social learning.[53] People learn behavior because external stimuli reinforce the behavior. Reinforcement increases the likelihood of the behavior in the future. The proper application of reinforcers develops complete behavior patterns, which form an individual's personality.[54]

Cognitive social-learning theory accepts the role of reinforcement, but sees behavior as largely learned by observation.[55] People learn by observing behavior and its consequences, not by directly responding to reinforcers. They learn by observation and try to imitate the behavior they see.

Biological theories of personality development have developed from two different sets of research. Ethological theory describes the ways in which the members of a given species, say, human beings, develop common characteristics because of evolution. Behavior genetics describe how an individual's unique gene structure affects personality development.[56] The accumulated research evidence points to strong genetic effects on human personality.[57]

Ethological theory has deep roots in an evolutionary perspective of human behavior.[58] This theory says that behavioral characteristics that have helped humans survive through successive generations become the inborn characteristics of all humans. The simplest example is the distress-like cry of an infant and the response of a person responsible for the infant's care. The infant cries because of hunger or other pain. The caregiver responds to the cry by caring for the infant. Ethologists view both behavioral responses as inborn characteristics common to all humans. Ethologists also believe humans learn from their social experiences. A child who cries, but does not consistently get a warm and nurturing response from a caregiver, might develop a personality characterized by distrust of others.[59]

Behavior genetics describes personality development as a process of behaviorally expressing a person's genotype or set of inherited genes. Modern gene-based personality research links specific genes to specific personality characteristics. For example, the novelty-seeking personality dimension describes people who are impulsive, excitable, and extravagant. Some research has linked this personality dimension to a specific genetic marker, suggesting a genetic basis for novelty-seeking behavior.[60]

Behavior geneticists do not view emerging behaviors, abilities, predispositions, and other characteristics of the personality as solely a function of genes. They see personality development as an involved series of interactions between a person's genetically based predispositions and influences from the person's social environment.

Although some aspects of personality can come from inborn qualities, others are learned. Modern personality researchers largely agree that personality develops from an interaction of internal qualities and the external environment.[61]

Emotions and Emotional Intelligence

Emotions, a key part of human personality, have engaged the research interests of psychologists since Freud's groundbreaking work more than one hundred years ago.[62] Emotions play a central role in people's behavior, underscoring a need for people to understand their emotional structure. Emotional intelligence is a contemporary parallel area of interest directed at discovering ways people can manage their emotions, and the emotions of others, to reach their goals.

Emotion is a feeling, psychological state, and biological state that inclines a person to act in a certain way. One's emotions quickly trigger behavior aimed at the emotion's stimulus. A person's collection of emotions defines the individual's temperament, a key part of personality.[63]

Psychologists largely agree that the following basic emotions define much of the emotional side of people's behavior:[64]

anger	hostility, annoyance, outrage, fury
disgust	aversion, distaste, contempt
fear	fright, anxiety, concern, terror
joy	thrill, enjoyment, contentment, delight, amusement
love	adoration, affinity, friendliness
sadness	dejection, self-pity, despair, grief, gloom
shame	remorse, guilt, regret, embarrassment
surprise	wonder, shock, amazement, astonishment, disbelief

Contempt, embarrassment, excitement, and guilt are other emotions that future research might add to the list of those viewed as basic to human behavior.

Behavior triggered by emotions happens fast, with little thought about why one behaves in a particular way. Quick behavioral reaction has its roots in the original primitive behavioral sources that extend back millions of years according to evolutionary theory. One reacts quickly to a threat to ensure survival. The fear emotion serves a person well in the presence of danger.[65]

The lack of careful, conscious thought underscores the difference between behavior driven by one's emotional mind ("heart brain") and behavior driven by one's rational mind ("head brain"). One's emotional mind ignores logic and analysis; one's rational mind savors logic and analysis and is mostly emotion free. Both forms of thinking—emotional and rational—exist. Psychological research points to a vital link between the two. Emotions quickly point a person in the right direction. The rational mind logically assesses a situation to arrive at a good decision. Here is an example.

Margot is an adopted child in the middle of three brilliant children.[66] Margot's brothers, Ritchie the oldest and Charles the youngest, all were as brilliant and accomplished as her. Margot's father, however, gave more attention to his sons' accomplishments than he gave to Margot's accomplishments. Margot developed intense feelings of unfair treatment from her father that she carried into her adult years. Many years later while employed by a well-known advertising agency, her creative director, Royal, passed over her for a promotion. After learning of Royal's decision, Margot stormed into Royal's office in a rage. She screamed at the advertising director about how unfairly he treated her. Royal urged Margot to stop acting like a child and calm down. He would explain his decision.

Margot's anger emotion sparked her behavioral reaction to a situation she perceived as unfair. She learned her association of anger with unfairness during her childhood upbringing by her father. Margot ignored Royal's suggestion to listen to his explanation and stormed out of his office. She eventually left the agency for a better position with a competitor. This example underscores the need for managers to understand the role of emotions in human behavior and how their decisions can have unintended, explosive effects.

Emotional intelligence is a mental process that includes (1) appraising and expressing emotions in self and others, (2) managing emotion in self and others, and (3) adaptively using emotions to guide behavior and solve problems.[67] The following four dimensions define emotional intelligence:

- Self-awareness: Knowing one's weaknesses, strengths, and limits; recognizing the effects of one's emotions.
- Self-management: Showing integrity, and flexibility; controlling one's emotions.
- Social awareness: Sensing and understanding other's emotions, having empathy and an active interest in other people's concerns.
- Relationship management: Developing others through guidance and feedback, building relationships, cooperating, and managing conflict.

Accurate assessment of emotions contributes to their useful expression. Verbal and nonverbal communication (see Chapter 13 "Communication Processes") play important roles in such emotional assessment. A person who has learned how to assess internal emotional information can more accurately express those emotions to others. Accurately assessing others' emotions also helps smooth interpersonal interactions and lets both parties express emotions without disrupting their interactions.

Managing emotions in self requires a high level of self-understanding to know why one's emotions spring to life in the presence of certain stimuli. An emotionally intelligent person also knows how to affect other people's emotions. Emotionally intelligent college students who go to a job interview with a campus recruiter know how to behave in the presence of the recruiter to create a positive impression.

The Big Five Personality Dimensions

After almost a century of research, personality psychologists largely agree that five dimensions can describe human personality.[68] Figure 5.3 shows the five dimensions and some traits associated with each dimension. These dimensions have appeared in many studies, across many samples, and in studies done in many countries outside the United States. Although some psychologists feel the dimensions are not precisely specified, less than five dimensions exist, or a different set of five dimensions exists, these dimensions are widely used in personality psychology.[69]

The following are typical traits associated with the high and low characteristics of each **Big Five personality** dimension.[70] Reflect on your personality as you read the descriptions and traits. Do any of these dimensions describe your personality?

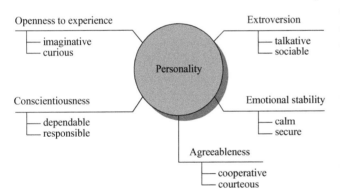

▨ **Figure 5.3:**   The Big Five Personality Dimensions

Extroversion	*High*: Talkative, active, sociable, assertive, gregarious
	Low: Reserved, quiet, introverted
Emotional stability	*High*: Calm, relaxed, secure
	Low: Worried, depressed, anxious, insecure, angry, embarrassed
Agreeableness	*High*: Cooperative, tolerant, good-natured, trusting, courteous, caring
	Low: Rude, cold, unkind
Conscientiousness	*High*: Dependable, thorough, organized, responsible, planful, achievement-oriented, hard-working

> *Low*: Sloppy, careless, inefficient
>
> **Openness to experience**   *High*: Curious, intelligent, broad-minded, creative, imaginative, cultured
>
> *Low*: Simple, unimaginative, conventional

Some dimensions have practical implications for organizations and management. For example, some research found extroversion is positively related to positive affect or attitudes. Other research found conscientiousness is negatively related to absenteeism and tardiness.[71]

Personality Types

Psychologists also describe human personality characteristics and dispositions as personality types. Many types are useful for understanding and managing behavior in organizations. The following paragraphs describe some personality types that can give you insight into that behavior.

Locus of Control

People differ in whether they feel they control the consequences of their actions or are controlled by external factors. External control personality types believe that luck, fate, or powerful external forces control their destiny. Internal control personality types believe they control what happens to them.[72]

Machiavellianism

A Machiavellian personality holds cynical views of other people's motives, places little value on honesty, and approaches the world with manipulative intent. Machiavellians maintain distance between themselves and others and are emotionally detached from other people in their lives. Their suspicious interpersonal orientation can contribute to high interpersonal conflict. Machiavellian personalities focus on personal goals, even if reaching them requires unethical behavior, deception, or manipulation of other people. Their suspicious orientation also leads them to view their organizational world as a web of political processes wherein they use their political strategies and tactics (see Chapter 15, "Power and Political Behavior").[73]

Type A and B Personalities

During the 1960s and 1970s, much research focused on personality patterns associated with coronary heart disease. The Type A personality emerged as a significant risk factor for that disease. Type A personalities also showed behavior patterns of interest in understanding the behavior of managers and supervisors in organizations.[74]

The Type A personality is aggressive, can quickly become hostile, has a keen sense of time urgency, and focuses excessively on achievement. Such people continuously create new and more difficult goals or engage in more activities than time allows. They do things fast and engage in multiple activities so they can get as much as possible done in a day. They have strong desires to dominate other people and quickly explode in anger over what others consider trivial events. For example, lines at a bank or a stalled vehicle in an intersection can throw a Type A personality into a rage.

Later research showed that some parts of the Type A personality predicted coronary heart disease and other parts were associated with high performance. Hostility was associated with coronary heart disease;[75] striving for achievement was associated with performance.[76]

The contrasting personality type is the Type B personality. Such people have no sense of time urgency and often stop to review their achievements and think about where they are headed in the future. They have high self-esteem, a characteristic that distinguishes them from Type A personalities. Type B personalities are even-tempered, are not bothered by common everyday events, and approach the world more calmly than Type A personalities.

Myers-Briggs Type Indicator (MBTI)

The Myers-Briggs Type Indicator (MBTI) is a popular personality assessment device based on Jung's personality theory.[77] This device assigns people to one of 16 personality types based on four bipolar dimensions: Extroverted (E)–introverted (I); sensing (S)–intuitive (I); thinking (T)–feeling (F); and perceiving (P)–judging (J). Extroverts look outward; introverts turn inward. Sensers use data; intuitives use hunches. Thinkers are objective; feelers are subjective. Perceivers are flexible; judgers want closure. The letters in parentheses form type indicators. An ESTJ, for example, is an extroverted, sensing, thinking, and judging type.

INTERNATIONAL ASPECTS OF PERCEPTION, ATTITUDES, AND PERSONALITY

A person's perceptual process has strong ties to the person's culture.[78] Some examples of culturally based stereotypes are that the Swiss are punctual, Germans are task-oriented, and Americans are energetic. Individuals who hold these stereotypes experience many surprises when they meet people from these countries who do not fit the stereotypes. A second form of stereotyping occurs when people project aspects from their culture onto people and situations in a different culture. People who travel to another country sometimes assume that the new culture mirrors their own.[79] For example, a male Korean manager visiting Sweden assumes all women seated behind desks are secretaries. The Korean's behavior, of course, is partly based on an assumption carried from the home culture. Such behavior would be inappropriate and possibly dysfunctional in Sweden, where many women hold management positions.

Attitudes and beliefs about organizational design, management, and decision-making vary widely across cultures.[80] U.S. managers feel a hierarchical organizational design helps solve problems and guides the division of labor in the organization. French and Italian managers feel a hierarchical design shows people the authority relationships in the organization. Italian managers, in contrast to those from Sweden, believe that bypassing a manager to reach a subordinate employee is equal to insubordination. Lastly, decision making is less centralized in Swedish and Austrian organizations than it is in organizations in the Philippines and India.[81] As you can see, an organization that crosses national borders and draws its managers from many different countries has high conflict potential.

Different cultures emphasize different personality characteristics.[82] People in individualistic cultures such as the United States have a stronger need for autonomy than people in more group-oriented cultures, such as Japan. Individuals in cultures that emphasize avoiding uncertainty have a stronger need for security than people in cultures that are less concerned about avoiding uncertainty. Belgium, Peru, Russia, and Spain are examples of cultures that stress uncertainty avoidance. Singapore, Ireland, and India are examples of cultures with lower avoidance tendencies.[83]

ETHICAL ISSUES IN PERCEPTION, ATTITUDES, AND PERSONALITY

Several ethical issues emerge directly from this chapter's discussions of perception, attitudes, and personality. Because almost no empirical research has focused on these issues, much of this section is speculative. The ethical issues that follow from perceptual processes[84] center on stereotypes, attribution processes, and self-presentation.

A stereotype can filter information about a target person's behavior. This perceptual error should be of special concern as the U.S. workforce becomes more diverse. Many people carry inaccurate stereotypes about the ethics of people with different social, racial, and ethnic backgrounds. These stereotypes can affect the opinions they develop about the behavior of such people in the workplace.

Self-presentations affect the images other people develop of a person.[85] Some people deliberately manage their presentations so their decisions and behavior appear ethical. Limited experimental evidence suggests some people can favorably manage other people's impressions of their ethical attitudes.[86]

The well-understood attribution errors that ascribe causes of behavior to the person or the situation raise questions about accountability for ethical behavior.[87] Individual responsibility is central to ethical behavior. If an observer attributes responsibility for a decision or action to a person, that person could be judged as behaving ethically or unethically. If an observer attributes the cause of the behavior to the situation, the individual is not held accountable. The latter could happen, for example, if an observer believed the person had behaved unethically because of a directive from the person's boss. Attribution errors also could lead a decision-maker to conclude that he was not responsible for an unethical act.

Little reliable and valid information about ethical attitudes exists.[88] Some evidence points to the absence of a fixed set of ethical attitudes among managers. Instead, attitudes about ethics in organizations and decision making are situational and varying. The social context determines the morality of behavior and decisions, not abstract and absolute rules.[89]

SUMMARY
5

SUMMARY

Perception is a selective cognitive process that lets a person make sense of stimuli from his environment. Perceptual errors include perceptual set and stereotyping. Self-perception (how you see yourself) has three parts: self-concept, self-esteem, and self-presentation. Social perception is the process of understanding another person using information from the person, from the situation, and from observed behavior. Social perception includes attribution processes, which explain the cause of other people's behavior. People make attribution errors that can lead to inaccurate perceptions and conclusions about another person.

Attitudes are favorable or unfavorable dispositions about an object. The three related parts of an attitude are cognitive, affective, and behavioral intention. Attitudes can change because something persuades the person to shift his attitudes, the norms of a social group affect his attitudes, or the person becomes cognitively uncomfortable with some aspects of his beliefs compared to others.

Personality is a set of traits, characteristics, and predispositions of a person. Three views of personality development came from cognitive theory, learning theories, and biological explanations of personality development. The Big Five personality dimensions are extroversion, emotional stability, agreeableness, conscientiousness, and openness to experience. Some personality types of interest are locus of control, Machiavellian, and Type A and B.

Emotions play a key role in human behavior, often without a person understanding why an emotion triggered a behavior. People with high emotional intelligence understand their emotions, those of others, and the role of emotions in determining behavior.

People often hold stereotypes about those from other cultures. These stereotypes can be inaccurate, leading to difficulties in interactions in other countries. Cultures also vary in the attitudes held about organizations, their management, and the types of personality characteristics considered important.

Several issues emerged in the ethics discussion earlier in this chapter. Stereotypes can affect one's perception of the ethical behavior of another person. People can also manage their self-presentations so that others perceive them as behaving ethically. Attribution processes can change whether one perceives the situation as causing unethical behavior or the person being responsible for the behavior.

REVIEW
AND
DISCUSSION
QUESTIONS
5

REVIEW AND DISCUSSION QUESTIONS

1   Self-concept, self-esteem, and self-presentation are the three parts of self-perception. How do you see yourself in each of these three areas? Compare your self-view with how some close friends see you. Be prepared for some surprises!

2   Review the description of social perception given earlier in this chapter. What do you consider most when forming an impression of a person you have just met? What types of attribution error are you most likely to

make? Discuss potential differences in attribution error among different people.

3   Review the earlier description of the sources of attitude change. Which of the three causes you to change your attitudes about some object most quickly?

4   Which personality development theory is the most realistic explanation of this important process? Why?

5   Review the personality dimensions and types discussed earlier in this chapter. Do you know people who fit these personality descriptions? Discuss your interactions with people of the different personality types.

6   Review the stereotypes of people from different cultures in the chapter's "International Aspects" section. Are those stereotypes shared by other students in your class? If students from other countries are in your class, ask them about the stereotypes they hold about U.S. and Canadian people.

7   The ethical issues section strongly implied that human perceptual processes can filter the information one gets about other people's actions. Such filtration affects the accuracy of one's judgment about ethical and unethical behavior. Fully discuss the implications of perceptual processes for ethical behavior in organizations.

TAKE FIVE: OB ALIVE: *THE BREAKFAST CLUB* (1985)

Strong characters emerge in director John Hugh's study of teen high school culture. Strong personalities emerge: the Criminal, the Brain, the Princess, the Kook, and the Jock. They had not met before their Saturday detention, but quickly develop strong associations with each other.

This scene starts DVD Chapter 8, "Lunchtime." Claire Standish (Molly Ringwald) assembles her lunch on the table. It ends after John Bender (Judd Nelson) mocks Brian Johnson (Anthony Michael Hall) and his family (Stop: 0:41:04).

The scene shows five characters: Claire Standish, John Bender, Andrew Clark (Emilio Estevez), Allison Reynolds (Ally Sheedy), and Brian Johnson. Assess these five personalities using the personality theories and types described in this chapter.

REFERENCES AND NOTES

1. Ballesteros, S. 1994. Cognitive Approaches to Human Perception: Introduction. In *Cognitive Approaches to Human Perception*, ed. S. Ballesteros. Hillsdale: Lawrence Erlbaum Associates, Chap. 1.
    Von Helmholtz, H. 1962. *Treatise on Physiological Optics*. Translated and edited by J. P. C. Southall. New York: Dover Publications. (Originally published in 1866.)

2. Dember, W. N. 1960. *The Psychology of Perception.* New York: Holt, Rinehart, and Winston.

   Goldstone, R. L. 1998. Perceptual Learning. In *Annual Review of Psychology,* Vol. 49, ed. J. T. Spence., J. Darley, and D. J. Foss. Palo Alto: Annual Reviews, pp. 585–612.

3. Dember, *Psychology of Perception,* Chap. 1.

4. Davidoff, J. B. 1975. *Differences in Visual Perception: The Individual Eye.* London: Crosby Lockwood Stapes, pp. 167–77.

5. Fiske, S. T., and T. L. Lee. 2008. Stereotypes and Prejudice Create Workplace Discrimination. In *Diversity at Work,* ed. A. P. Brief. New York: Cambridge University Press, Chap. 2.

6. Stephan, W. G., V. Ageyev, C. W. Stephan, M. Abalakina, T. Stefanenko, and L. Coates-Shrider. 1993. Measuring Stereotypes: A Comparison of Methods Using Russian and American Samples. *Social Psychology Quarterly* 56: 54–64.

7. Blakely, G. L., E. H. Blakely, and R. H. Moorman. 1998. The Effects of Training on Perceptions of Sexual Harassment Allegations. *Journal of Applied Social Psychology* 28: 71–83.

   Moyer, R. S., and A. Nath. 1998. Some Effects of Brief Training Interventions on Perceptions of Sexual Harassment. *Journal of Applied Social Psychology* 28: 333–56.

8. Zhou, J., and G. R. Ferris. 1995. The Dimensions and Consequences of Organizational Politics Perceptions: A Confirmatory Analysis. *Journal of Applied Social Psychology* 25: 1747–64.

9. Tomkiewicz, J., O. C. Brenner, and T. Adeyemi-Bello. 1998. The Impact of Perceptions and Stereotypes on the Managerial Mobility of African Americans. *The Journal of Social Psychology* 138: 88–92.

10. Cerulo, K. A. 1997. Identity Construction: New Issues, New Directions. In *Annual Review of Sociology,* Vol. 23, ed. J Hagan and K. S. Cook. Palo Alto: Annual Reviews, pp. 385–409.

11. Bem, D. J. 1967. Self-Perception: An Alternative Interpretation of Cognitive Dissonance Phenomena. *Psychological Review* 74: 183–200.

    Bem, D. J. 1972. Self-Perception Theory. In *Advances in Experimental Social Psychology,* Vol. 6, ed. L. Berkowitz. New York: Academic Press.

12. Festinger, L. 1954. A Theory of Social Comparison Processes. *Human Relations* 7: 117–40.

13. Rubin, D. C., ed. 1986. *Autobiographical Memory.* New York: Cambridge University Press.

14. Greenwald, A. G. 1980. The Totalitarian Ego: Fabrication and Revision of Personal History. *American Psychologist* 35: 603–18.

15. Coopersmith, S. 1967. *The Antecedents of Self-Esteem.* San Francisco: Freeman.

16. Brockner, J. 1983. Low Self-Esteem and Behavioral Plasticity: Some Implications. In *Review of Personality and Social Psychology,* Vol. 4, ed. L. Wheeler and P. Shaver. Beverly Hills: Sage Publications, pp. 237–71.

17. Baumeister, R. F. 1982. A Self-Presentational View of Social Phenomena. *Psychological Bulletin* 91: 3–26.

    Tedeschi, J. T., ed. 1981. *Impression Management Theory and Social Psychological Research.* New York: Academic Press.

    Tetlock, P. E., and S. R. Manstead. 1985. Impression Management versus Intrapsychic Explanations in Social Psychology: A Useful Dichotomy? *Psychological Review* 92: 59–77.

18. Swan, W. B., Jr. 1984. Quest for Accuracy in Person Perception: A Matter of Pragmatics. *Psychological Review* 91: 457–77.
    Swan, W. B., Jr. 1987. Identity Negotiation: Where Two Roads Meet. *Journal of Personality and Social Psychology* 53: 1038–51.
19. Snider, M. 1987. *Public Appearances/Private Realities: The Psychology of Self-Monitoring.* New York: Academic Press.
20. Developed from the following and other sources cited in this section: Brehm, S. S., and S. M. Kassin. 1996. *Social Psychology.* Boston: Houghton Mifflin, Chap. 3.
    Fiske, S. T. 1994. Social Cognition and Social Perception. In *Annual Review of Psychology*, Vol. 44, ed. L. W. Porter and M. R. Rosenzweig. Palo Alto: Annual Reviews, pp. 115–94.
21. Herman, C. P., M. P. Zanna, and E. T. Higgins. 1986. *Physical Appearance, Stigma, and Social Behavior: The Ontario Symposium I*, Vol. 3. Hillsdale: Erlbaum.
    Laborite, L., D. A. Kenya, and T. E. Mallow. 1988. Consensus in Personality Judgments at Zero Acquaintance. *Journal of Personality and Social Psychology* 55: 387–95.
22. Heider, F. 1958. *The Psychology of Interpersonal Relations.* New York: John Wiley & Sons.
23. Gilbert, D. T. 1989. Thinking Lightly About Others: Automatic Components of the Social Inference Process. In *Unintended Thought: Limits of Awareness, Intention, and Control*, ed. J. S. Uleman and J. A. Bargh. New York: Guilford, pp. 189–211.
24. Heider, *The Psychology of Interpersonal Relations.*
    Kelley, H. H. 1967. Attribution Theory in Social Psychology. In *Nebraska Symposium on Motivation*, ed. D. Levine. Lincoln: University of Nebraska Press.
25. Kelley, Attribution Theory.
    Kelley, H. H. 1973. The Processes of Causal Attribution. *American Psychologist* 28: 107–28.
26. Ross, L. 1977. The Intuitive Psychologist and His Shortcomings: Distortions in the Attribution Process. In *Advances in Experimental Social Psychology*, Vol. 10, ed. L. Berkowitz. New York: Academic Press.
27. Watson, D. 1982. The Actor and the Observer: How Are Their Perceptions of Causality Divergent? *Psychological Bulletin* 92: 682–700.
28. Mullen, B., J. L. Atkins, D. S. Champion, C. Edwards, D. Hardy, J. E. Story, and M. Vanderklok. 1985. The False Consensus Effect: A Meta-Analysis of 115 Hypothesis Tests. *Journal of Experimental Social Psychology* 21: 262–83.
    Ross, L., D. Greene, and P. House. 1977. The False Consensus Phenomenon: An Attributional Bias in Self-Perception and Social-Perception Processes. *Journal of Experimental Social Psychology* 13: 279–301.
29. Higgins, E. T., G. A. King, and G. H. Mavin. 1982. Individual Construct Accessibility and Subjective Impressions and Recall. *Journal of Personality and Social Psychology* 43: 35–47.
    Sears, D. O. 1983. The Person-Positivity Bias. *Journal of Personality and Social Psychology* 44: 233–50.
30. Erdley, C. A., and P. R. D'Agostino. 1988. Cognitive and Affective Components of Automatic Priming Effects. *Journal of Personality and Social Psychology* 54: 741–47.
31. Forgas, J. P., and G. H. Bower. 1987. Mood Effects on Person-Perception Judgments. *Journal of Personality and Social Psychology* 53: 53–60.
32. Ajzen, I. 1984. Attitudes. In *Wiley Encyclopedia of Psychology*, Vol. 1, ed. R. J. Corsini. New York: John Wiley & Sons, pp. 99–100.

Schleicher, D. J., S. D. Hansen, and K. E. Fox. 2011. Job Attitudes and Work Values. In *APA Handbook of Industrial and Organizational Psychology*, Vol. 3, ed. S. Zedeck. Washington, DC: American Psychological Association, Chap. 4.

33. Fishbein, M., and I. Ajzen. 1975. *Belief, Attitude, Intention and Behavior: An Introduction to Theory and Research*. Reading, MA: Addison-Wesley, p. 6. (Emphasis added.)

34. Ibid., pp. 6–11.

Judge, T. A., H. M. Weiss, J. D. Kammeyer-Mueller, and C. L. Hulin. 2017. Job Attitudes, Job Satisfaction, and Job Affect: A Century of Continuity and Change. *Journal of Applied Psychology* 102: 356–74.

35. Breckler, S. J. 1984. Empirical Validation of Affect, Behavior, and Cognition as Distinct Components of Attitude. *Journal of Personality and Social Psychology* 47: 1191–1205.

Eagley, A. H., and S. Chaiken. 1993. *The Psychology of Attitudes*. Fort Worth: Harcourt Brace Jovanovich.

Eagley, A. H., and S. Chaiken. 1998. Attitude Structure and Function. In *The Handbook of Social Psychology*, Vol. 1, ed. D. T. Gilbert, S. T. Fiske, and G. Lindsey. Boston: McGraw-Hill, Chap. 7.

McGuire, W. J. 1985. Attitudes and Attitude Change. In *Handbook of Social Psychology*, Vol. II, ed. G. Lindzey and E. Aronson. New York: Random House, pp. 233–346. (Definitions taken from p. 242.)

Rosenberg, J. J., and C. I. Hovland. 1960. Cognitive, Affective, and Behavioral Components of Attitudes. In *Attitude Organization and Change*, ed. C. I. Hovland and M. J. Rosenberg. New Haven: Yale University Press, pp. 1–14.

36. McGuire, Attitudes, p. 242.

37. George, J. M., and G. R. Jones. 1997. Experiencing Work: Values, Attitudes, and Moods. *Human Relations* 50: 393–416.

Harrison, D. A., D. A. Newman, and P. L. Roth. 2006. How Important are Job Attitudes? Meta-Analytic Comparisons of Integrative Behavioral Outcomes and Time Sequences. *Academy of Management Journal* 49: 305–25.

Steel, R. P., and J. R. Rentsch. 1995. Influence of Cumulation Strategies on the Long-Range Prediction of Absenteeism. *Academy of Management Journal* 38: 1616–34.

38. Hellman, C. M. 1997. Job Satisfaction and Intent to Leave. *The Journal of Social Psychology* 137: 677–89.

39. Ajzen, I. 1987. Attitudes, Traits, and Actions: Dispositional Prediction of Behavior in Personality and Social Psychology. In *Advances in Experimental Social Psychology*, Vol. 20, ed. L. Berkowitz. New York: Academic Press, pp. 1–63.

Hulin, C. L., and T. A. Judge. 2003. Job Attitudes. In *Handbook of Psychology: Industrial and Organizational Psychology*, ed. W. C. Borman, D. R. Ilgen, and R. J. Klimoski. Hoboken: John Wiley & Sons, Chap. 11.

Iaffaldano, M. T., and P. M. Muchinsky. 1985. Job Stisfaction and Job Performance: A Meta-Analysis. *Psychological Bulletin* 97: 251–73.

Judge, T. A., C. J. Thoresen, J. E. Bono, and G. K. Patton. 2001. The Job Satisfaction–Job Performance Relationship: A Qualitative and Quantitative Review. *Psychological Bulletin* 127: 376–407.

Kraus, S. J. 1995. Attitudes and the Prediction of Behavior: A Meta-Analysis of the Empirical Literature. *Personality and Social Psychology Bulletin* 21: 58–75.

McGuire, Attitudes, pp. 252–53.

40. Fishbein and Ajzen, *Belief, Attitude, Intention and Behavior*, Chaps. 5, 6.

Thompson, M. M., M. P. Zanna, and D. W. Griffin. 1995. Let's Not Be Indifferent about (Attitudinal) Ambivalence. In *Attitude Strength: Antecedents and Consequences*, ed. R. E. Petty and J. A. Krosnick. Mahwah: Lawrence Erlbaum Associates, pp. 361–86.

41. Berscheid, E., and E. Walster. 1969. Attitude Change. In *Experimental Social Psychology*, ed. J. Mills. New York: Macmillan, pp. 121–231.

Hovland, C. I., I. L. Janis, and H. H. Kelly. 1953. *Communication and Persuasion*. New Haven: Yale University Press.

Petty, R. E., and D. T. Wegener. 1998. Attitude Change: Multiple Roles for Persuasion Variables. In *The Handbook of Social Psychology*, Vol. 1, ed. D. T. Gilbert, S. T. Fiske, and G. Lindsey. Boston: McGraw-Hill, Chap. 8.

Zimbardo, P. G., E. B. Ebbesen, and C. Maslach. 1977. *Influencing Attitudes and Changing Behavior*. Reading, MA: Addison-Wesley.

42. Lewin, K. 1947. Group Decision and Social Change. In *Readings in Social Psychology*, ed. T. Newcomb and E. Hartley. New York: Henry Holt and Company, Inc.

43. Festinger, L. 1957. *A Theory of Cognitive Dissonance*. Palo Alto: Stanford University Press.

Petty and Wegener, Attitude Change, pp. 335–37.

44. Allport, G. W. 1937. *Personality: A Psychological Interpretation*. New York: Henry Holt and Company, Inc., pp. 24–25.

45. Costa, P. T., Jr., and R. R. McCrae. 1994. Set Like Plaster? Evidence for the Stability of Adult Personality. In *Can Personality Change?*, ed. T. Heatherton and I. Weinberger. Washington, DC: American Psychological Association, pp. 21–40.

McCrae, R. R., and P. T. Costa, Jr. 1994. The Stability of Personality: Observations and Evaluations. *Current Directions in Psychological Science* 3: 173–75.

46. James, L. R., and M. D. Mazerolle. 2002. *Personality in Work Organizations*. Thousand Oaks: Sage Publications. See Chaps. 1–3 of this readable source for a useful summary of personality and behavior in organizations.

Pervin, L. A. 1999. Epilogue: Constancy and Change in Personality Theory and Research. In *Handbook of Personality: Theory and Research*, 2nd edn, ed. L. A. Pervin and O. P. John. New York: Guilford Press, Chap. 28, pp. 693–94. This prominent personality psychologist discusses a systems view of personality.

Snyder, M., and W. Ickes. 1985. Personality and Social Behavior. In *Handbook of Social Psychology*, Vol. 2, ed. G. Lindzey and E. Aronson. New York: Random House, pp. 883–947.

47. Kenrick, D. T., D. R. Montello, and S. MacFarlane. 1985. Personality: Social Learning, Social Cognition, or Sociobiology? In *Perspectives in Personality: A Research Annual*, Vol. 1, ed. R. Hogan and W. H. Jones. Greenwich, CT: JAI Press, pp. 215–19.

Piaget, J. 1952. *The Origins of Intelligence in Children*. New York: International Universities Press.

Piaget, J. 1954. *The Construction of Reality in the Child*. New York: Basic Books.

Piaget, J. 1977. The Role of Action in the Development of Thinking. In *Knowledge and Development*, Vol. 1, ed. W. F. Overton and J. M. Gallagher. New York: Plenum Press.

48. Detailed description of the stages is beyond the purpose of this chapter. For a readable description of the stages, see D. R. Shaffer. 1988. *Social and Personality Development*. Pacific Grove: Brooks/Cole, Chap. 4.

49. Developed from the following and other sources cited in this section: Kenrick, Montello, and MacFarlane, Personality, pp. 211–15.
Shaffer, *Social and Personality Development*, Chap. 3.

50. Watson, J. B. 1913. Psychology as the Behaviorist Views It. *Psychological Review* 20: 158–77.
Watson, J. B. 1928. *Psychological Care of the Infant and Child*. New York: Norton.

51. Dollard, J., and N. E. Miller. 1950. *Personality and Psychotherapy: An Analysis in Terms of Learning, Thinking, and Culture*. New York: McGraw-Hill.

52. Ibid.

53. Skinner, B. F. 1953. *Science and Human Behavior*. New York: The Free Press.
Skinner, B. F. 1971. *Beyond Freedom and Dignity*. New York: Bantam.

54. Chapter 8 of this book has a more detailed explanation of Skinner's theory as it applies to motivation.

55. Bandura, A. 1977. *Social Learning Theory*. Englewood Cliffs: Prentice Hall.

56. Developed from the following and other sources cited in this section: Kenrick, Montello, and MacFarlane, Personality, pp. 211–15.
Shaffer, *Social and Personality Development*, pp. 38–51.

57. Bouchard, T. J., Jr. 1994. Genes, Environment and Personality. *Science* 264: 1700–1.
Bouchard, T. J., Jr. 1997. Genetic Influence on Mental Abilities, Personality, Vocational Interests and Work Attitudes. In *International Review of Industrial and Organizational Psychology*, Vol. 12, ed. C. L. Cooper and I. T. Robertson. Chichester: John Wiley & Sons, Ltd., pp. 373–95.
Bouchard, T. J., Jr. 1997. The Genetics of Personality. In *Psychiatric Genetics*, ed. K. Blum and E. P. Noble. Boca Raton: CRC Press, pp. 273–96.
Bouchard, T. J., Jr., and J. C. Loehlin. 2001. Genes, Evolution, and Personality. *Behavior Genetics* 31: 243–73.
Plomin, R., and A. Caspi. 1999. Behavioral Genetics and Personality. In *Handbook of Personality: Theory and Research*, 2nd edn, ed. L. A. Pervin and O. P. John. New York: The Guilford Press, Chap. 9.
Segal, N. I., and T. J. Bouchard, Jr. 2000. *Entwined Lives: Twins and What They Tell Us about Human Behavior*. New York: E. P. Dutton.

58. Cairns, R. B. 1979. *Social Development: The Origins of Plasticity of Interchanges*. New York: W. H. Freeman.
Jones, N. B. 1972. Characteristics of Ethological Studies of Human Behavior. In *Ethological Studies of Child Behavior*, ed. N. B. Jones. London: Cambridge University Press, pp. 3–33.

59. Sroufe, L. A., N. E. Fox, and V. R. Pancake. 1983. Attachment and Dependency in Developmental Perspective. *Child Development* 54: 1615–27.

60. Plomin and Caspi, Behavioral Genetics and Personality, pp. 262–64.

61. Kenrick, Montello, and MacFarlane, Personality, pp. 209–11.

62. Developed from P. Ekman. 1992. An Argument for Basic Emotions. *Cognition and Emotion* 6: 169–200.
Ekman, P. 1994. All Emotions Are Basic. In *The Nature of Emotion: Fundamental Questions*, ed. P. Ekman and R. J. Davidson. New York: Oxford University Press, pp. 15–19.
Epstein, S. 1994. Integration of the Cognitive and the Psychodynamic Unconscious. *American Psychologist* 49: 709–24.
Epstein, S. 1998. *Constructive Thinking: The Key to Emotional Intelligence*. Westport: Praeger, Part I.

Johnson-Laird, P. N., and K. Oatley. 1992. Basic Emotions, Rationality, and Folk Theory. *Cognition and Emotion* 6: 201–23.

LeDoux, J. 1996. *The Emotional Brain*. New York: Simon & Schuster.

The psychological and neuroscience research literature about emotions is filled with complex jargon. For a readable summary of this research, see N. M. Ashkanasy and C. S. Daus. 2002. Emotion in the Workplace: The New Challenge for Managers. *Academy of Management Executive* 16: 76–86.

63. Ekman, P. 1994. Moods, Emotions, and Traits. In *The Nature of Emotion: Fundamental Questions*, ed. P. Ekman and R. J. Davidson. New York: Oxford University Press, pp. 56–58.

Ekman, P. 2003. *Emotions Revealed: Recognizing Faces and Feelings to Improve Communication and Emotional Life*. New York: Times Books.

Pervin, L. A. 1993. Affect and Personality. In *Handbook of Emotions*, ed. M. Lewis and J. M. Haviland. New York: The Guilford Press, Chap. 21.

64. Eckman, An Argument for Basic Emotions, pp. 192–93.

Goleman, D. 1995. *Emotional Intelligence*. New York: Bantam Books, Appendix A.

Johnson-Laird and Oatley, Basic Emotions, Rationality, and Folk Theory.

65. Kandel, E. R., and R. D. Hawkins. 1992. The Biological Basis of Learning and Individuality. *Scientific American* (September): 79–86.

LeDoux, J. E. 1992. Brain Mechanisms of Emotion and Emotional Learning. *Current Opinion in Neurobiology* 2: 191–97.

LeDoux, J. E. 1993. Emotional Networks in the Brain. In *Handbook of Emotions*, ed. M. Lewis and J. M. Haviland. New York: The Guilford Press, Chap. 8.

LeDoux, J. E. 1994. Emotion, Memory and the Brain. *Scientific American* (June): 50–57.

LeDoux, *The Emotional Brain*.

LeDoux, J. E. 2002. *Synaptic Self: How Our Brains Become Who We Are*. New York: Viking Penguin.

Lindebaum, D., D. Geddes, and P. J. Jordan. 2018. *Social Functions of Emotion and Talking About Emotion at Work*. North Hampton, MA: Edward Egan Publishing, Inc.

MacLean, P. D. 1993. Cerebral Evolution of Emotion. In *Handbook of Emotions*, ed. M. Lewis and J. M. Haviland. New York: The Guilford Press, Chap. 6.

66. My apologies to Wes Anderson, co-screenwriter and director of the film *The Royal Tenenbaums* (2001) for liberally adapting this film's characters to this example.

67. Epstein, *Constructive Thinking*.

See Goleman, *Emotional Intelligence*, a popular, readable treatment of emotional intelligence. Goleman popularized the emotional intelligence concept. See Epstein, *Constructive Thinking*, pp. 3–4 for some critical comments that suggest caution in accepting all of Goleman's observations.

Goleman, D. 1998. *Working with Emotional Intelligence*. New York: Bantam Books.

Goleman, D., R. Boyatzis, and A. McKee. 2002. The Neuroanatomy of Leadership. In *Primal Leadership: Realizing the Power of Emotional Intelligence*. Boston: Harvard Business School Press, Chap. 3.

Salovey, P., and J. D. Mayer. 1990. Emotional Intelligence. *Imagination, Cognition, and Personality* 9: 185–211.

68. Digman, J. M. 1990. Personality Structure: Emergence of the Five-Factor Model. In *Annual Review of Psychology*, Vol. 41, ed. M. R. Rosenzweig and L. W. Porter. Palo Alto: Annual Reviews, pp. 417–40.

Goldberg, L. R. 1993. The Structure of Phenotypic Personality Traits. *American Psychologist* 48: 26–34.

Heaven, P. C. L., and A. Pretorius. 1998. Personality Structure among Black and White South Africans. *Journal of Social Psychology* 138: 664–66.

John, O. P., and S. Srivastava. 1999. The Big Five Trait Taxonomy: History, Measurement, and Theoretical Perspectives. In *Handbook of Personality: Theory and Research*, 2nd edn, ed. L. A. Pervin and O. P. John. New York: The Guilford Press, Chap. 4.

McCrae, R. R., and P. T. Costa, Jr. 1999. A Five-Factor Theory of Personality. In. *Handbook of Personality: Theory and Research*, 2nd edn, ed. L. A. Pervin and O. P. John. New York: The Guilford Press, Chap. 5.

Salgado, J. F. 1997. The Five Factor Model of Personality and Job Performance in the European Community. *Journal of Applied Psychology* 82: 30–43.

Wiggins, J. S., and A. L. Pincus. 1992. Personality: Structure and Assessment. In *Annual Review of Psychology*, Vol. 43, ed. M. R. Rosenzweig and L. W. Porter. Palo Alto: Annual Reviews, 473–504.

69. Chiaburu, D. S., I.-S. Oh, C. M. Berry, L. Ning, and R. G. Gardner. 2011. The Five-Factor Model of Personality Traits and Organizational Citizenship Behaviors: A Meta-Analysis. *Journal of Applied Psychology* 96: 1140–66.

Hurtz, G. M., and J. J. Donovan. 2000. Personality and Job Performance: The Big Five Revisited. *Journal of Applied Psychology* 85: 869–79.

Waller, N. G., and Y. S. Ben-Porath. 1987. Is It Time for Clinical Psychology to Embrace the Five-Factor Model of Personality? *American Psychologist* 42: 887–89.

Zuckerman, M. 1994. An Alternative Five-Factor Model for Personality. In *The Developing Structure of Temperament and Personality from Infancy to Adulthood*, ed. C. F. Halverson, Jr., G. A. Kohnstamm, and R. P. Martin. Hillsdale: Lawrence Erlbaum Associates, pp. 53–68.

70. Barrick, M. R., and M. K. Mount. 1991. The Big Five Personality Dimensions and Job Performance: A Meta-Analysis. *Personnel Psychology* 44: 1–26.

Digman, Personality Structure.

Mount, M. K., M. R. Barrick, and J. P. Strauss. 1994. Validity of Observer Ratings of the Big Five Personality Factors. *Journal of Applied Psychology* 72: 272–80.

71. Ashton, M. C. 1998. Personality and Job Performance: The Importance of Narrow Traits. *Journal of Organizational Behavior* 19: 289–303.

DeNeve, K. M., and H. Cooper. 1998. The Happy Personality: A Meta-Analysis of 137 Personality Traits and Subjective Well-Being. *Psychological Bulletin* 124: 197–229.

72. Rotter, J. B. 1966. Generalized Expectancies for Internal and External Control of Reinforcement. *Psychological Monographs* 80: 1–28.

Rotter, J. B. 1971. External and Internal Control. *Psychology Today* 5 (June): 37–39.

73. Christie, R., and F. L. Geis. 1970. *Studies in Machiavellianism*. New York: Academic Press.

Guterman, S. S. 1970. *The Machiavellians: A Social Psychological Study of Moral Character and Organizational Milieu*. Lincoln: University of Nebraska Press.

Wilson, D. S., D. Near, and R. R. Miller. 1996. Machiavellianism: A Synthesis of the Evolutionary and Psychological Literatures. *Psychological Bulletin* 119: 285–99.

74. Friedman, M., and R. Rosenman. 1974. *Type A Behavior and Your Heart*. New York: Alfred A. Knopf.

Friedman, M., and D. Ulmer. 1984. *Treating Type A Behavior—and Your Heart*. New York: Alfred A. Knopf.

75. Booth-Kewley, S., and H. S. Friedman. 1987. Psychological Predictors of Heart Disease: A Quantitative Review. *Psychological Bulletin* 101: 343–62.

Friedman, H. S., and S. Booth-Kewley. 1988. Validity of the Type A Construct: A Reprise. *Psychological Bulletin* 104: 381–84.

Mathews, K. A. 1988. Coronary Heart Disease and Type A Behaviors: Update on and Alternative to the Booth-Kewley and Friedman (1987) Quantitative Review. *Psychological Bulletin* 104: 373–80.

76. Mathews, K. A. 1982. Psychological Perspectives on the Type A Behavior Pattern. *Psychological Bulletin* 91: 292–323.

Mathews, K. A., R. L. Helmreich, W. E. Beanne, and G. W. Lucker. 1980. Pattern A, Achievement-Striving, and Scientific Merit: Does Pattern A Help or Hinder. *Journal of Personality and Social Psychology* 39: 962–67.

77. Gardner, W. L., and M. J. Martinko. 1996. Using the Myers-Briggs Type Indicator to Study Managers: A Literature Review and Research Agenda. *Journal of Management* 22: 45–83.

Jung, C. J. 1971. *The Collected Works of C. G. Jung*, Vol. 6: *Psychological Types*. Translated by H. G. Baynes; revised by R. F. Hull. Princeton: Princeton University Press. (Originally published 1921.)

78. Adler, N. J., with A. Gundersen. 2008. *International Dimensions of Organizational Behavior*, 5th edn. Mason: Thomson South-Western, Chap. 3.

79. Burger, P., and B. M. Bass. 1979. *Assessment of Managers: An International Comparison*. New York: The Free Press.

80. Laurent, A. 1983. The Cultural Diversity of Western Conceptions of Management. *International Studies of Management and Organization* 13: 75–96.

81. Hofstede, G. 1991. *Cultures and Organizations: Software of the Mind*. New York: McGraw-Hill.

Hofstede, G. 2001. *Culture's Consequences: Comparing Values, Behaviors, Institutions, and Organizations across Nations*, 2nd edn. Thousand Oaks: Sage Publications, Chap. 3.

82. Adler, *International Dimensions*.

83. Hofstede, G. 1993. Cultural Constraints in Management Theories. *Academy of Management Executive* 7: 81–94.

Hofstede, *Culture's Consequences*, Chap. 4.

84. Payne, S. L., and R. A. Giacolone. 1990. Social Psychological Approaches to the Perception of Ethical Dilemmas. *Human Relations* 43: 649–65.

85. Ibid., pp. 655–58.

86. Meehan, K. A., S. B. Woll, and R. D. Abbott. 1979. The Role of Dissimulation and Social Desirability in the Measurement of Moral Reasoning. *Journal of Research in Personality* 13: 25–38.

87. Payne and Giacolone, Social Psychological Approaches, pp. 653–54.

88. Randall, D. M., and A. M. Gibson. 1990. Methodology in Business Ethics Research: A Review and Critical Assessment. *Journal of Business Ethics* 9: 457–71.

89. Jackall, R. 1988. *Moral Mazes: The World of Corporate Managers*. New York: Oxford University Press, Chap. 5.

Chapter 6

ORGANIZATIONAL SOCIALIZATION

After reading this chapter, you should be able to:

- Explain organizational socialization as a process that communicates an organization's culture.
- Distinguish among roles, role behaviors, and boundary transitions.
- Discuss role episodes and their importance in organizational socialization.
- Describe each boundary transition and its role in the socialization process.
- Explain the stages of organizational socialization and how they repeat during a work career.
- Discuss individual differences in organizational socialization.
- Compare the socialization issues in expatriate and repatriate adjustment.
- Analyze ethical issues in organizational socialization.

Organizational socialization is a powerful process by which people learn the culture of an organization.[1] It affects individual behavior and helps shape and maintain the organization's culture. One scholar has defined organizational socialization as the "process by which a new member learns the value system, the norms, and the required behavior patterns of the … organization or group … [the person] is entering."[2] Organizations almost inevitably leave their imprint on individual members through their socialization processes.[3]

The preceding definition offers two ideas about organizational socialization. First, the definition tells us what an individual must do to participate as a successful member of an organization. The social-ization process is one way an organization tries to affect its members' desire to stay with the organiza-tion. Second, the values, norms, and required behav-iors are the contributions the organization expects from its successful members. Those contributions should nearly equal the inducements from the organ-ization if the person is to join and stay in the organization.

Values, norms, and required behaviors are all part of the culture of an organization.[4] As described in Chapter 4, "Organizational Culture," organizational culture includes the values, norms, rites, rituals, ceremonies, heroes, and scoundrels in the history of the organization.[5] It defines the content of what a new employee needs to learn to become an accepted organization member.

Organizational socialization is usually the first behavioral process a person experiences after joining an organization. Accordingly, this chapter starts by describing how the process affects a new employee trying to learn a new culture. It then describes how the socialization process unfolds through different stages in an employee's relationship with the organization. You will eventually see that people are socialized into multiple cultures throughout their careers.

This chapter examines organizational socialization from the perspective of an individual affected by the process and a manager using the process. The information that you gain here will increase your understanding of the socializa-tion process as it affects you. Such understanding will help you make choices about the organizations you might want to join after graduation. You also will gain insights into what will happen to you shortly after you join the organization and throughout your career.

Managers use the organization's socialization process to affect the behavior of the people they hire or who move into their work unit. Understanding the dynamics and content of the process helps managers use it more effectively.

Organizational socialization in the broadest sense is a process by which people adjust to new organizations, new jobs, and new groups of people. It focuses on getting employees to acquire the values, attitudes, and role behaviors defined as important by the culture.[6] It also is concerned with work skill development and adjustment to the norms and values of the immediate workgroup.[7] In short, organizational socialization deals with the basic question of individual–organization fit.[8]

ROLES AND ROLE BEHAVIOR

Organizations ask employees to take on roles with certain behavioral require-ments. The roles develop from the organization's division of labor and its organ-izational design. Other aspects of roles are defined by the organization's culture.

A **role** is a set of activities, duties, responsibilities, and required behaviors that the organization wants a person to accept. The behaviors that are part of a role are the contributions the organization wants in exchange for the inducements it is willing to give (pay, fringe benefits, and the like). The two must roughly balance for the individual to agree to the role.

Each role has role behaviors that vary according to what the organization requires of a person.[9] Three types of role behaviors exist: pivotal, relevant, and peripheral. **Pivotal role behaviors** are behaviors a person must accept to remain a member of the organization. Such behaviors are tied to an organization's core values. The organization requires these behaviors of all employees despite their background.[10] These behaviors are "the price of membership," the basic contri-butions the organization expects in exchange for its inducements. Examples of pivotal role behaviors include valuing a job well done, wearing proper attire, believing in a hierarchy of authority, viewing conflict as constructive, and accepting the profit motive.

Relevant role behaviors are behaviors the organization considers desirable and good, but not essential to membership. These behaviors can include appear-ance, extra work efforts such as committee work, and lifestyle.

Peripheral role behaviors are behaviors that are neither necessary nor desir-able, but allowed by an organization. An example of a peripheral role behavior is occasional chatting and visiting with coworkers during the workday. Management tolerates such behavior if it is not excessive and does not interfere with work performance. If management eventually decides that the behavior is unacceptable, it can then become either pivotal or relevant.

Role behavior that is pivotal in one organization might only be relevant in another and vice versa. Variations in what is pivotal and relevant can also occur in the same organization.

ROLE EPISODES

Role episodes communicate pivotal and relevant role behaviors, especially to those taking on new roles in an organization. These episodes start when an organization recruits a new employee and continue during the early employment period. Role episodes repeat when a person takes a new job in the organization. Figure 6.1 shows the content and dynamics of a role episode.[11]

One or more persons are **role senders**, the person or persons who define a role during a role episode. Before a person joins the organization, the role sender is often the company's recruiter. After the person joins the organization, the role sender is the person who hired or will supervise the new employee. Other role senders are coworkers and other managers throughout the organization.

The role sender defines a **sent role's** pivotal and relevant role behaviors by giving information about the role either orally or in writing. Job descriptions, company policies, and the employee handbook often communicate pivotal role behaviors. A role sender often communicates relevant role behaviors orally and less formally than pivotal role behaviors.

The **focal person** receives the role behavior sent by the role sender. The person then enacts the role behavior according to the way she perceives it. The focal person's perception forms the received role. The focal person either complies with the role sender's request or resists it.

The role sender perceives the focal person's behavior and assesses how closely it matches the sender's perception of the role's content. The role sender can react to the focal person's behavior in three ways: reinforcement, sanctions, or nonreinforcement (ignoring). If the behavior is acceptable, the focal person might receive some reinforcement, such as a compliment for doing a good job. If the focal person has not complied with the requested role behavior, the role sender might apply sanctions, such as a reprimand. Reinforcement and sanctions are most often used for pivotal and relevant role behaviors. Role senders often ignore (nonreinforcement) peripheral role behavior, at least until they decide whether the behavior is pivotal or relevant.

The role episode repeats with the same role sender. The episode ends when compliance is obtained, noncompliance is accepted, or the focal person is terminated by the organization. Alternatively, a new employee can leave the

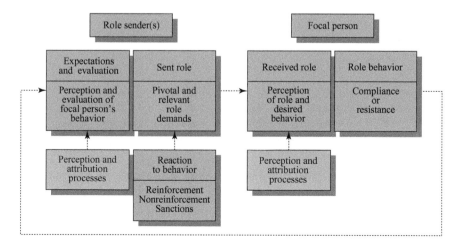

■ **Figure 6.1:** A Role Episode

organization. A person might quit if the required behavior is unacceptable or if inducements from the organization no longer equal contributions.

The role episode can repeat with other managers or coworkers as role senders. Often managers and coworkers send conflicting role behaviors to a new employee. The employee likely will comply with the role sender believed to have the most control over her future in the organization.

Managers find themselves behaving as role senders and focal persons simultaneously. As role senders, they try to affect the behavior of those who report to them, especially new employees. At the same time, the managers to whom they report view them as focal persons and try to shape their behavior, especially if they are considered good candidates for promotion.

BOUNDARY TRANSITIONS

The socialization process is continuous throughout a person's association with an organization, but is most intense before and after boundary transitions.[12] **Boundary transitions** occur when a new employee crosses the organization's boundary upon joining the organization. They also occur as the person's career unfolds and she crosses other organization boundaries. The employee is most susceptible to organizational influences just before and just after those transitions.[13]

Boundary transitions have three dimensions: functional, hierarchical, and inclusionary.[14] Each dimension presents different features of an organization's socialization process.

When you first join an organization, you cross its functional boundary. Most likely, you will take a job in a single department such as accounting, finance, marketing, or human resources. These departments perform many major work functions of the organization. You can cross other functional boundaries in the same organization if it has a program of employee development emphasizing experience in several functional areas.

The socialization process of the **functional** dimension emphasizes the development and use of skills and abilities in doing a particular task. The process also emphasizes "how we do things around here," which might or might not be what you learned in college. Basic values of an organization's culture are communicated following a functional boundary transition.

If you successfully master the requirements following a functional boundary transition, you might be promoted to a higher position. At this point, you experience the **hierarchical** dimension of a boundary transition. Now you are moving upward in the organization into a position with more authority. It might be a supervisory or management position or a more senior staff position within a functional area. The socialization process following the hierarchical boundary transition might emphasize rewards for good performance, taking on more responsibilities, and becoming more involved in organization affairs. If you were promoted into a different functional area, you also will experience the socialization processes for the functional dimension of the boundary transition.

The hierarchical dimension also features inward movement. Such transitions bring you closer to the center of the organization. The socialization process at a hierarchical transition includes many things about the heart of the organization's culture.

The last dimension of boundary transitions is the **inclusionary** dimension, which usually operates along with the first two dimensions. The inward movement on this boundary transition dimension emphasizes that you are a newcomer to an existing system. You will be expected to prove yourself before you will be accepted by veteran members of the organization.

The socialization process of the inclusionary dimension heavily emphasizes values, norms, and required behaviors. Acceptance of those values and norms will be critical to your acceptance by others already in the system. Over time, it could mean acceptance into the heart of the organization and admission into its "inner circle."

The early period following a boundary transition is highly important from both the individual's and the organization's perspective. During this time, you learn the performance expectations of the organization. Your success in the organization depends partly on getting a job assignment that fits your skills, needs, and values.

INDIVIDUAL AND ORGANIZATIONAL PERSPECTIVES ON SOCIALIZATION

Socialization is a two-way process. While the organization is trying to affect your values and behavior, you are trying to keep certain aspects of your individuality.[15] The organization wants to put its mark on you, and you want to put your mark on the organization. You presumably value who you are, and you want the organization to recognize and use what you value in yourself. Constant interplay happens between the organization's efforts at socialization and your bid for individualization.

As an individual, you have a unique set of skills and talents and want to satisfy a unique set of needs. You feel a desire to preserve your individual identity. Simultaneously, you feel a need for acceptance by your employing organization and its members so they will use your talents and abilities.

Members of an existing organizational culture feel they must require some degree of conformity to the values and behaviors the culture considers necessary for its survival. Uniform values and behaviors among an organization's members can decrease the potential for conflict. The organization also needs innovative behavior if it is to remain viable and survive in a changing environment. Organizations face the problem of getting what they need for effective role performance without over-specifying behavior for the role.[16]

Now you can see the basic dilemma of organizational socialization for both the individual and the organization. The process is a tug-of-war between an individual's need to be who she is and the organization's need to mold the individual to its image.

STAGES OF ORGANIZATIONAL SOCIALIZATION

Organizational socialization happens in three stages: "getting in" (choice: anticipatory socialization); "breaking in" (entry/encounter); and "settling in" (change: metamorphosis). The product of one stage becomes the input to the next stage. Understanding the stages of socialization is important from your perspective as an individual because of the experiences you are likely to have at each stage. It also is important from a management perspective because each stage helps the socialization process achieve what the organization wants it to achieve.[17]

Figure 6.2 shows the three stages of socialization. You experience the stages of socialization in your first job, in successive positions within the same organization, or in a new position in a different organization. The first two stages include several processes of socialization. These **socialization processes** are methods organizations use to shape the values and behavior they want you to have.

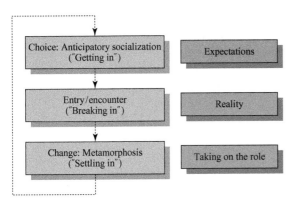

▨ **Figure 6.2:** Stages of Organizational Socialization

Choice: Anticipatory Socialization ("Getting In")

Choice: anticipatory socialization is the first socialization stage a person experiences.[18] This stage happens before a person joins an organization or takes a new job in the same organization. It prepares the individual for entry into an organization as a new employee.

Although the person is outside the organization, the events during the anticipatory stage are a first glimpse of the organization's culture. The person's **expectations** or beliefs about becoming an organization member develop during this stage. In short, when you consider a new position or a new organization, you predict what life will be like in the new situation.

The individual and the organization face two important issues at the anticipatory stage.[19] One issue involves the question of realism. Does the potential new employee have a realistic idea of the organization's culture? Does the individual understand the job requirements? Organizations present images of themselves and the jobs they offer potential employees. Individuals develop expectations about working in the organization from that image. The basic question is whether that image accurately portrays organizational life.

Realism is the responsibility of both the organization and the individual. The organization should present both the positive and negative side of what it is like to work for the company. As a potential employee, you should also present an accurate picture of yourself.[20] You must know what you can do and not oversell or undersell yourself to the organization.

An image of life in the organization is the basic product of the anticipatory stage of socialization. A new employee develops an image of the organization, and the organization develops an image of the employee. The degree of congruence in those images will prove critical to the mutual adaptation of the two parties.[21]

The second issue focuses on congruence between the individual and the organization. You have a set of skills and abilities. Are those skills and abilities congruent with the needs of the organization? You also have a set of needs and values. Can the organization satisfy those needs and offer you a congruent set of values?

These two sets of issues are important for both parties, because lack of realism and congruence are associated with high turnover, low satisfaction, low organizational commitment, and poor job performance. Errors at the anticipatory stage have negative effects for both the individual and the organization.[22]

Developing accurate expectations in the anticipatory stage suggests that you should get as much information as you can about the organizations that interest you. Examine existing documents for clues about the organization's culture. Materials, such as annual reports, Web pages, and press accounts about what the organization does, are useful sources. If possible, contact existing employees of the organization to get some idea about the organization's culture from an informed insider. The accuracy of your image of the organization and its culture will make your adaptation to the organization much easier.

Socialization Processes

Organizations use several socialization processes in the anticipatory stage. Although the processes are available to any organization, different organizations use them in varying degrees.

Recruitment activities are important processes within the anticipatory socialization stage. As you approach graduation, you will begin your job search by reading **recruitment advertising** or brochures. **Company recruiters** will come to campus to interview students. You might talk to former students who are now working for a company in which you are interested. The recruiting activities create a set of expectations about working for the organization. Although you have not yet joined the company, you develop a set of beliefs about working in the firm. The recruitment process—and choosing a company—socializes you to a set of beliefs or expectations about that organization before you even join it.[23]

Internships are a special type of socialization experience available to college students. Many companies offer internships as a way for students to get a glimpse of organizational life. Some limited research shows that internships can build realistic expectations about an organization, easing the intern's transition to full-time employment.[24]

Some companies use **screening and selection devices** to make hiring decisions. Screening and selection devices can be used with potential new employees and existing employees who are seeking promotion. Such devices include written tests, oral interviews, and job simulations. Written tests can assess skills, interests, and psychological characteristics. Oral interviews add information to an employment application and any written tests. Job simulations test a person's strengths and weaknesses in new and unfamiliar situations.[25] Some research shows positive retention effects of selection procedures that result in a good fit of the recruit and the organization.[26]

Companies vary widely in their selection and screening criteria. Southwest Airlines emphasizes character and personality. Barclay Enterprises, Inc., a telephone equipment remanufacturer, wants a positive work attitude. Microsoft emphasizes intelligence. These companies assume they can train people for their job duties.[27]

During these recruitment activities, the organization and the potential new employee should both consider whether the images they project are realistic. Lack of realism in the anticipatory stage creates problems for both parties after a person enters the organization.

Realistic Job Preview

Many organizations have recognized the importance of creating realistic expectations during the anticipatory stage of socialization. These organizations use many ways to give a realistic job preview to potential new employees. This employee recruiting approach sharply contrasts with approaches that describe an organization's positive qualities only.

A **realistic job preview** is a balanced description of important characteristics of the job and the organization. This description includes important sources of both satisfaction and dissatisfaction.[28] The preview is given to a potential employee before the applicant has accepted a job offer. Research evidence shows that a realistic job preview can help build realistic expectations about the organization, increase satisfaction after joining the organization, and reduce turnover.[29]

Organizations use several approaches to a realistic job preview. Some organizations use recruiting brochures that give an accurate description of what it is like to work for the organization. Others use videotapes and films lasting 25 to 80 minutes. The films show many aspects of the work situation that the recruit could face. They include descriptions by present employees of what they like and do not like about their jobs. Some organizations are starting to use work site visits for applicants for nonmanagerial, entry-level jobs.[30] Site visits have not been commonly used in the past for applicants to such positions.

A realistic job preview is a deliberate effort by an organization to set expectations. The intention is to create expectations that are neither unrealistically high nor unrealistically low.[31] By creating realistic expectations, the organization avoids the negative results that could occur if a new employee's image of the organization sharply differs from reality.

Entry/Encounter ("Breaking In")

Assume a person has accepted a job with an organization. That person crosses the organization's boundary on the first workday and starts the second socialization stage—**entry/encounter**. The anticipatory stage of socialization built expectations about what it is like to work for the organization. Now the new employee will learn whether those expectations match the reality of organizational life.[32]

A new employee who was highly motivated to join the organization is eager to be socialized by the organization.[33] Being new to the organization, the employee will want to "learn the ropes" from knowledgeable insiders by actively seeking information from many sources and forming social relationships to reduce feelings of uncertainty.[34] In the entry/encounter stage, the new employee will learn the role she is to play and the organization's culture, among other things.

During the entry/encounter stage, the organization wants to give the employee a new self-image. The pivotal and relevant role behaviors are the basis of the new self-image. Some organizations require many pivotal role behaviors. These organizations ask for a large change in self-image, similar to military organizations during basic military training. Others require only a few pivotal role behaviors and ask for a small self-image change. Various parts of the same organization will ask for different degrees of change in self-image. Whatever the degree of change required by the organization, the basic change process is the same.

The entry/encounter stage serves several purposes and raises some issues for both the individual and the organization. The issues and purposes are intertwined and are not independent of each other.[35]

Clarification of the new employee's role in the organization is a major purpose of the entry/encounter stage. Role clarification includes the definition of the person's role by both the organization and the immediate workgroup. An issue for the individual at this point is whether the two role definitions are the same.

A second purpose of the entry/encounter stage is to teach the new employee about tasks, duties, and responsibilities, including conflicting work assignment priorities. The supervisor's evaluation of the new person's performance plays a key role in the new employee's socialization. From these evaluative interactions, the new employee learns the nuances of the organization's culture.

A third purpose of the entry/encounter stage is to teach the new employee the immediate workgroup norms. Norms are rules of behavior that govern social interactions within the group. They include rules about social status and the bases of power and influence in the group. New employees learn who the informal leaders are and where power rests within the group. Performance norms often exist, and they are not always congruent with what either the organization or the new employee values.[36]

Workgroup socialization occurs not only from the group to the new employee, but also from the new employee to the group. An existing group could change with the addition of a star performer or a person hired because of her reputation.[37] Chapter 10, "Groups and Intergroup Processes" discusses workgroup socialization in detail.

The purposes of the entry/encounter stage can make different and conflicting demands on a person. The new employee might receive conflicting messages about job performance within the immediate workgroup. The norm of the workgroup might be either higher or lower than the performance desired by the organization and the employee's immediate supervisor. A new employee must resolve the conflicting behavioral demands to adjust successfully to the new role in the organization.

The new employee's job might require a high degree of interaction with other groups in the organization. These groups might place different and conflicting behavioral demands on the person. Successful adjustment to the new organizational role requires managing such intergroup role conflicts. New employees can experience much pressure and stress when adapting to these various sources of role conflict.[38]

Another major set of roles involved in the entry/encounter stage is the individual's nonwork roles—the roles played by the person outside the employing organization. Roles such as mother, father, spouse, partner, or student all place demands on the person. Adaptation to new organizational roles, with their multiple sources of conflict, can put stress on roles outside work. Successful adaptation to the organization's demands involves successful management of all the individual's roles, both at work and away from work.

Organizations can use several socialization processes to give new employees a new self-image. The formality and structure of socialization processes vary among organizations. Large bureaucracies often use formal, structured processes more than small, less bureaucratic organizations.[39]

Three steps are involved in creating a new **self-image**.[40] The first step is **unfreezing** the old self-image. The organization wants the new employee to discard some or all aspects of her old self-image. The second step is **changing** to the new self-image. The organization uses a series of role episodes to communicate pivotal and relevant role behaviors to the new employee. These behaviors and associated values will become part of the new self-image. The last step is **refreezing**, which puts the new self-image solidly in place. The new employee now has acquired the norms, values, and required behaviors that the organization considers important.

The socialization processes organizations use in the entry/encounter stage produce different degrees of change in self-image. Not only do the processes communicate different types of role behavior, but also they communicate it with different intensity. Empirical research continues to show the effects on the new employee of such socialization processes.[41]

Indoctrination programs teach the organization's formal rules and procedures. Organizations use such programs when they view rules and procedures as pivotal role behavior. Organizations dealing with classified or sensitive materials often use an indoctrination program to show how to handle such materials. The programs are presented in classroom-like settings or on videotape. As a result, the rules and procedures are presented uniformly to many different new employees.

Apprenticeship or **mentoring** socialization processes assign a new employee to a veteran employee as an apprentice. The mentor shows the new employee how to do the technical parts of the job and the nature of social relationships in the organization. A veteran employee also can tell the new employee about the formal rules and procedures of the organization and informal ways of doing work. Mentor relationships can now occur in the Internet environment. Known as "e-mentoring," they allow mentor relationships to develop over long distances.[42] Research shows that mentoring has many positive effects, especially for women moving into managerial roles.[43]

Organizations have less control over apprenticeship or mentoring process content than they do over an indoctrination program's content. This lack of control can produce highly varied results.[44] It also can negatively affect the apprentice if the mentoring relationship decays over time. For example, a manager could feel threatened by a recent college graduate who has a greater degree of knowledge of computer technology. The manager then withholds promotion information from the apprentice to sabotage the apprentice's career.[45]

Workforce diversity adds another dimension of complexity to apprenticeship socialization. Diverse mentoring pairs and groups bring different worldviews to mentor relationships. Mixtures of gender, ethnicity, and race bring possible pitfalls to the relationship. Stereotypes held by either party can introduce hostility to a relationship.[46]

Many organizations use formal **training programs** to develop skills considered important to a given job. The major accounting firms have extensive training programs for new accounting graduates. Although the new graduate has received academic training in accounting, the firm now wants to show how it does an audit. Such training programs usually communicate much more than just skills and formal job duties. They also often convey the values and norms of the firm. The new accounting graduate quickly learns what it means to be a "KPMG auditor."

Organizations can quickly unfreeze a new member from her old self-image with **debasement** or **upending experiences**.[47] Some organizations give a new employee an extremely easy or extremely difficult task to do in the early employment period. An easy task assignment for a recent college graduate can be humiliating, causing the new employee to question who she is and what she is doing. A difficult task can be humiliating for different reasons—it is beyond what the graduate can do now. The effect of both task assignments is the same. The college graduate questions her self-image, making her ready for change by the organization.

Change: Metamorphosis ("Settling In")

> When Gregor Samsa woke up one morning from unsettling dreams, he found himself changed in his bed into a monstrous vermin. He was lying on his back as hard as armor plate, and when he lifted his head a little, he saw his vaulted brown belly, sectioned by arch-shaped ribs ... His many legs, pitifully thin compared with the size of the rest of him, were waving helplessly before his eyes.[48]

The change new employees undergo in most organizations is usually not as dramatic as Gregor Samsa's change into a beetle-like insect. Change takes place during the entry/encounter stage, as it flows and blends into the **metamorphosis** stage. The word *metamorphosis* emphasizes the extraordinary changes that can happen to people from organizational socialization processes.[49]

If a new employee has successfully resolved the demands from the multiple sources of socialization, she now begins to feel comfortable in her new role. She has achieved some degree of mastery of job requirements and responsibilities. She has accepted the more obvious values of the organization's culture. She has adjusted to the norms of her immediate workgroup and now feels accepted by peers. Her self-confidence increases, and the anxiety of the early employment period decreases.

Some socialization processes clearly separate the metamorphosis stage from the entry/encounter stage with rights and rituals. Examples of rights and rituals include graduation ceremonies at universities, some management training programs, and the ceremonies that mark the end of basic military training or graduation from a military academy. Other organizations do not have such ceremonies, so this stage is not clearly separated from the encounter stage.

Individuals can have three socialization responses in the metamorphosis stage: a rebellious response, a custodial response, or an innovative response.[50] Figure 6.3 shows each response.

A **rebellious response** is a possible result if a new employee does not accept the socialization demands of different sources. Failure to accept the demands might cause the employee to leave the organization or to be terminated. Rebellion, from the organization's perspective, is a clear case of a socialization failure.[51]

A **custodial response** occurs when the employee conforms to role requirements, accepting all aspects of its content and process. Such a response can happen because it makes sense to a new employee. If the organization has been successful in the past doing things this way, there is no need to change it now.

A new employee might decide not to accept things the way they are and might choose an innovative response instead. Such a response comes in two different forms: content innovation and role innovation. **Content innovation** changes and improves the role's knowledge base and process characteristics. The

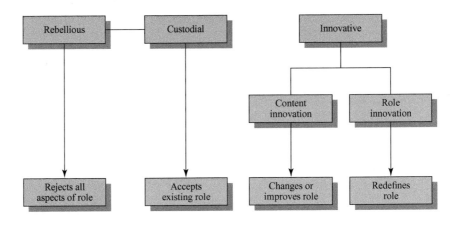

▨ **Figure 6.3:** Responses to Organizational Socialization

employee might decide that the way decisions were made in the past or the data upon which certain reports were based are not good enough for the job that needs to be done now. **Role innovation** is a more startling form of innovation. This response rejects most parts of the role and the norms associated with it. Role innovation is a form of rebellion. Unlike the rebellious response described earlier, if the organization and groups within it accept this response, the organization keeps the innovations.

INDIVIDUAL DIFFERENCES AND ORGANIZATIONAL SOCIALIZATION

People do not react uniformly to socialization experiences. Reactions vary depending on a person's characteristics—factors known as **individual differences**.[52] An individual's skills and abilities play a role in the speed with which a person learns job duties during the socialization process.[53] People with high levels of job-related skills and abilities learn job duties more quickly than people with few such skills and abilities. Success in learning job duties can be perceived positively by those watching the newcomer's reactions to the organization.

People vary in their beliefs about how successfully they can deal with this new, ambiguous, and possibly threatening experience. Such **self-efficacy beliefs** are associated with different responses to the socialization process. People with low self-efficacy adopt a custodial response. People high in self-efficacy adopt innovative responses.[54]

Recall the discussion about perception and attribution processes in Chapter 5, "Perception, Attitudes, and Personality." It argued that people have strong perceptual filters that alter or impart meaning to information they get from their environment. Selective perception affects how accurately they perceive information from socialization agents. A newcomer might not perceive information in the way the socialization agent intended. Conflict can develop between the newcomer and the agent because of those perceptual differences.

Attribution processes work in much the same way.[55] The newcomer interprets information sent by a socialization agent based on the newcomer's experience with situations perceived as similar. The socialization agent and the newcomer usually do not have a common set of experiences and therefore do not give the same meaning to a set of information. The different meanings might lead to conflict. Such inappropriate attributions can make it difficult for the newcomer to adapt. Adaptation is more successful, of course, when the newcomer and the socialization agent give the same meaning to information.

The last individual difference comes from the different needs people try to satisfy from their work experiences.[56] A newcomer with a strong need to associate with other people might be highly influenced by members of the workgroup. A newcomer with a strong need to achieve might aggressively pursue new job duties while trying to show the socialization agent(s) that she can quickly master a demanding job. You will learn much more about needs and motivation in later chapters.

INTERNATIONAL ASPECTS OF ORGANIZATIONAL SOCIALIZATION

The increasingly global environment of many organizations will present opportunities to work in different countries to more people than ever before. Each time a person moves to and from an international assignment, she experiences an international role transition.[57] As in domestic job changes, she also experiences the stages of socialization. At the same time, the international context creates some special issues for each part of the socialization process.

A person going to an assignment outside the home country is an **expatriate**; a person returning from an assignment is a **repatriate**. Both movements have elements of **culture shock**, a psychological and physiological disorientation caused by large differences between a home country culture and a foreign country culture.[58] The potential culture shock for the expatriate is easy to understand because the person moves from the home country to another country. The repatriate also can experience culture shock upon returning home. During a typical international assignment of three to four years, the home country could have changed in ways unknown to the repatriate. On return, the person enters a culture with many new features.

Expatriates and repatriates both go through a period of cross-cultural adjustment that occurs along three related dimensions: adjustment to a new job and work environment, adjustment to interacting with local nationals, and adjustment to the general culture of the country.[59] An organization's socialization process can help adjustment along those dimensions. Making cross-cultural training part of the socialization process can give people information that can smooth international role transitions.[60]

Issues in Expatriate Adjustment

Expatriate adjustment has aroused much interest because of the high incidence of failures and the costs associated with those failures.[61] Between 16 and 40 percent of U.S. employees sent to other countries return before their assignments end. One estimate puts the direct cost of expatriate failures for U.S. multinational organizations at more than several billion dollars a year. That figure does not include unmeasured costs such as lost business, damage to the organization's reputation, and loss of employee self-esteem.[62]

Expatriates face some special difficulties during the early part of socialization to their new assignment.[63] Their lack of knowledge about the local norms and rules of behavior important to insiders can lead to difficulty in entering international assignments. Expatriates can also experience dramatic changes and contrasts, depending on the differences between the expatriate's home culture and the other country's culture. Both difficulties argue for more preparation for international job transitions than for domestic job changes.

Multinational organizations typically choose people for international assignments based almost solely on successful performance in domestic roles. The underlying assumption is that success in domestic operations automatically means success abroad. Several researchers recommend selection criteria other than successful domestic performance. Those criteria include experience from an earlier international assignment, openness to differences among people, and willingness to learn about and adjust to another culture. Researchers also recommend using the same criteria in assessing the adjustment potential of a spouse or domestic partner, and other family members.[64]

Expatriate socialization should include cross-cultural training. Although research evidence shows that cross-cultural training helps smooth expatriate adjustment, only about 30 percent of expatriates receive such training before leaving their home country.[65] The training offered usually is not comprehensive. It typically includes an orientation to the other country's culture and its physical environment. Spouses and other family members often are not included in such training, although it is becoming clear that their adaptation plays a key role in successful expatriate adjustment.[66]

Some countries are harder to adjust to than others; the greater the differences between the other country's culture and the home culture, the harder the adjustment. Some research shows that India, Liberia, and some Southeast Asian countries are especially difficult for U.S. employees. Women face a special issue in cultures with male-dominated norms and values. Female expatriates—and female partners of male expatriates—find adjustment to such cultures especially difficult.[67]

Career-development programs and policies of multinational organizations have been suggested as ways of smoothing expatriate transitions.[68] Such programs and policies can show the career connections among the expatriate assignment, a repatriate assignment, and long-term career progress within the company. Multinational organizations can also assign at-home mentors to help guide the expatriate while abroad.

Issues in Repatriate Adjustment

Repatriate adjustment happens upon return to the home country. A repatriate who has been gone for several years may not have an accurate image of the home culture. During the anticipatory stage before leaving the international assignment, a repatriate can develop inaccurate expectations of life back home.[69]

Home leave or required visits to the home office can help maintain accurate expectations. Required interactions with people in the home office because of task interdependence also increase information flow. Such interactions can happen by any communication medium, including telephone, facsimile, international teleconference, e-mail, and direct computer connection.

A repatriate's adjustment will be easier if the organization provides a mentor in the home office. The mentor can keep the repatriate informed of major policy and strategic changes back home. In short, maintaining a flow of accurate information about changes in the home organization and culture gives the repatriate accurate expectations about returning.

The degree of adaptation to the other country's culture can affect adaptation to the home culture. Although such adaptation is functional for working in the international assignment, it is dysfunctional for adaptation on return. To have a successful repatriation adaptation, repatriates need to unlearn much of what made them successful abroad.

Many benefits that go with an international assignment can be dysfunctional to repatriation adjustment. Such assignments often have salary differentials and housing allowances that have high social status in the host country. Repatriation removes those differentials, possibly leading to a downward shift in perceived status and poorer housing conditions.

Few multinational organizations offer predeparture training to employees preparing to return to the home organization. Such training could parallel that of expatriates by including information on cultural shifts in the home culture and major changes in the home organization. Training on return could also help repatriation adjustment. Such training could become part of the organization's formal socialization program for its repatriates.

ETHICAL ISSUES IN ORGANIZATIONAL SOCIALIZATION

Organizational socialization processes pose ethical questions to potential employees, present employees, and the organization's managers. Because socialization processes can shape a person's values and behavior to those wanted by the organization, several ethical issues center on informed consent. Should the organization tell potential new employees that it will deliberately try to change some of their values and behavior? Should present employees be told that each time they change positions in the organization, their values and behavior will also change to some degree? A related issue centers on an organization's training programs. Such programs often have both socialization and training goals. Should an organization reveal those goals to employees before they enter the programs?

Debasement experiences are an effective way of forcing a person to shed an old self-image. Most organizations use mild forms of debasement of the type described earlier. Sororities, fraternities, basic military training, and military academies use stronger forms of debasement that can create feelings of fear and intimidation. Debasement experiences pose a clear ethical dilemma for organizations and their managers.

The discussions of anticipatory socialization emphasized the importance of having accurate expectations about working for a particular organization. An ethical issue occurs when an organization knowingly withholds negative information from potential employees. Some organizations use a realistic job preview to give potential employees a balanced view of the organization. At what point does an organization behave unethically by not giving a balanced view of itself? The same issues occur when potential employees knowingly withhold information about themselves that could affect their performance or retention by an organization. At what point do they behave unethically by not giving a balanced view of themselves?

SUMMARY

Organizational socialization is a powerful process that affects an individual's behavior and helps shape and maintain an organization's culture. It usually is the first behavioral process a person experiences after joining an organization. Part of the socialization process happens before joining an organization. Other parts happen after joining.

Organizations ask employees to take on specific roles that have behavioral requirements. The three types of role behavior are pivotal (required), relevant (desired), and peripheral (tolerated). Those role behaviors are learned in a series of role episodes that unfold during socialization. The socialization process is continuous throughout a person's association with an organization, but it is most intense before and after boundary transitions. Boundary transitions have three dimensions: functional (job), hierarchical (promotion), and inclusionary (inward movement).

The anticipatory stage of socialization creates expectations about life in the organization before a person enters the organization. The person compares those expectations to the reality experienced in the entry/encounter stage. The entry/encounter stage happens after the person crosses the organization's boundary and begins the first day of employment. After successful adaptation to socialization demands, the employee passes through the metamorphosis stage. In this stage, the employee experiences the final adaptation to the organization's demands.

Organizations operating in an international context face special socialization issues. People moving to other countries (expatriates) experience the same stages of socialization as they do in domestic job changes. On return to their home country, repatriates can experience culture shock while readapting to their home culture.

Several ethical issues center on whether there is a need for informed consent about an organization's goal of shaping a person's values and behavior by its socialization processes. The broad ethical question is: "Should the organization tell potential and existing employees about the goals of its socialization process?"

REVIEW AND DISCUSSION QUESTIONS

1 Which of the three types of role behavior is the most important for an organization? Why?

2 Describe the three stages of organizational socialization. What are the relationships among the stages? Which socialization processes happen within each stage?

3 What dysfunctions likely happen in the anticipatory stage of socialization? How can an organization reduce those dysfunctions?

4 Discuss the responses people can have to organizational socialization. Which of those responses is most likely to be yours?

5 Discuss the responsibilities of both the individual and the organization to present an accurate image of themselves. Why is accuracy important to both parties? What ethical issues surround the presentation of an accurate image?

6 Discuss the socialization issues that surround international job changes. Which of these is likely to have its strongest effects on you if you take an international assignment?

7 Discuss the ethical issues raised by organizational socialization. Are they real issues that managers should address, or are organizations justified in proceeding as they have in the past?

TAKE FIVE: OB ALIVE: *TOWER HEIST* (2011)

Josh Kovaks (Ben Stiller) manages a luxurious condominium that houses its wealthy owner Arthur Shaw (Alan Alda). Shaw's suite also houses his solid gold Ferrari and $20 million in cash. After their termination, Josh and several of his former employees launch a plan to remove the Ferrari and melt it down for the gold.

The selected scene starts with a shot of the front of Josh's house (DVD Chapter 9, 0:38:14). It ends in DVD Chapter 10, 0:47:59. The film cuts to a wide shot of New York City.

Consider these questions while viewing the scenes: Does everyone appear motivated to immediately join with Josh? If not, why not? What factors play in the scenes to motivate them to join?

REFERENCES AND NOTES

1. Allen, T. D., L. T. Eby, G. T. Chao, and T. N. Bauer. 2017. Taking Stock of Two Relational Aspects of Organizational Life: Tracing the History and Shaping the Future of Socialization and Mentoring Research. *Journal of Applied Research* 102: 324–37.
   Ott, J. S. 1989. *The Organizational Culture Perspective*. Pacific Grove: Brooks/Cole.
   Schein, E. H. 1992. *Organizational Culture and Leadership*. San Francisco: Jossey-Bass.
   Trice, H. M., and J. M. Beyer. 1993. Cultural Forms. In *The Cultures of Work Organizations*. Englewood Cliffs: Prentice Hall, Chap. 4.
2. Schein, E. H. 1968. Organizational Socialization and the Profession of Management. *Industrial Management Review* 9: 1–16. (The quoted material appears on p. 3.)
3. Van Maanen, J., and E. H. Schein. 1979. Toward a Theory of Organizational Socialization. In *Research in Organizational Behavior*, ed. B. M. Staw, Vol. 1, pp. 209–64. Greenwich, CT: JAI Press.
4. Schein, *Organizational Culture and Leadership*.
5. Deal, T. E., and A. A. Kennedy. 1982. *Corporate Cultures: The Rites and Rituals of Corporate Life*. Reading, MA: Addison-Wesley, pp. 13–15.

6. Bauer, T. N., and B. Erdogan. 2011. Organizational Socialization: The Effective Onboarding of New Employees. In *APA Handbook of Industrial and Organizational Psychology*, Vol. 3, ed. S. Zedeck. Washington, DC: American Psychological Association, Chap. 2.

Cooper-Thomas, H. D., and N. Anderson. 2006. Organizational Socialization: A New Theoretical Model and Recommendations for Future Research and HRM Practices in Organizations. *Journal of Management Psychology* 21: 492–516.

Liu, S., M. Wang, P. Bamberger, J. Shi, and S. B. Bacharach. 2015. The Dark Side of Socialization: A Longitudinal Investigation of Newcomer Alcohol Use. *Academy of Management Journal* 58: 334–55.

Van Maanen, J. 1976. Breaking-In: Socialization to Work. In *Handbook of Work, Organization, and Society*, ed. R. Dubin. Chicago: Rand McNally, pp. 67–130.

Van Maanen and Schein, Toward a Theory of Organizational Socialization.

7. Allen, Eby, Chao, and Bauer, Taking Stock of Two Relational Aspects of Organizational Life.

Argote, L., and J. E. McGrath. 1993. Group Processes in Organizations: Continuity and Change. In *International Review of Industrial and Organizational Psychology*, Vol. 8, ed. C. L. Cooper and I. T. Robertson. Chichester: John Wiley & Sons, pp. 333–89.

Chao, G. T., A. M. O'Leary-Kelly, S. Wolf, H. J. Klein, and P. D. Gardner. 1994. Organizational Socialization: Its Content and Consequences. *Journal of Applied Psychology* 79: 730–43.

Cooper-Thomas and Anderson, Organizational Socialization.

Feldman, D. C. 1976. A Contingency Theory of Socialization. *Administrative Science Quarterly* 21: 433–52.

Feldman, D. C. 1980. A Socialization Process That Helps Recruits Succeed. *Personnel* 57: 11–23.

Feldman, D. C. 1981. The Multiple Socialization of Organization Members. *Academy of Management Review* 6: 309–18.

8. The following citations have thorough reviews and discussions of individual–organization fit concepts and issues:

Hoffman, B. J., and D. J. Woehr. 2006. A Quantitative Review of the Relationship between Person-Organization Fit and Behavioral Outcomes. *Journal of Vocational Behavior* 68: 389–99.

Kristof, A. L. 1996. Person-Organization Fit: An Integrative Review of Its Conceptualizations, Measurement, and Implications. *Personnel Psychology* 49: 1–49.

Verquer, M. L., T. A. Beehr, and S. H. Wagner. 2003. A Meta-Analysis of the Relations between Person-Organization Fit and Work Attitudes. *Journal of Vocational Behavior* 63: 473–89.

9. Schein, *Organizational Culture and Leadership*.

10. Powell, G. N. 1998. Reinforcing and Extending Today's Organizations: The Simultaneous Pursuit of Person-Organization Fit and Diversity. *Organizational Dynamics* 26 (Winter): 50–61.

11. Katz, D., and R. Kahn. 1966. *The Social Psychology of Organizations*. New York: John Wiley & Sons, p. 187.

12. Van Maanen and Schein, Toward a Theory of Organizational Socialization.

13. Feldman, D. C., and J. M. Brett. 1983. Coping with New Jobs: A Comparative Study of New Hires and Job Changers. *Academy of Management Journal* 26: 258–72.

Van Maanen, J. 1978. People Processing: Strategies for Organizational Socialization. *Organizational Dynamics* 7 (Summer): 19–36.

14. Schein, E. H. 1971. The Individual, the Organization, and the Career: A Conceptual Scheme. *Journal of Applied Behavioral Science* 7: 401–26.
Van Maanen and Schein, Toward a Theory of Organizational Socialization, pp. 218–22.

15. Van Maanen and Schein, Toward a Theory of Organizational Socialization, pp. 224–25.

16. Schein, *Organizational Culture and Leadership*, p. 43.

17. Fisher, C. 1986. Organizational Socialization: An Integrative Review. In *Research in Personnel and Human Resource Management*, Vol. 4, ed. K. M. Rowland and G. R. Ferris. Greenwich, CT: JAI Press, pp. 101–45.
Trice, H. M., and J. M. Beyer. 1993. *The Cultures of Work Organizations*. Englewood Cliffs: Prentice Hall, pp. 150–55.
Van Maanen, Breaking-In.
Van Maanen, J., and E. H. Schein. 1977. Career Development. In *Improving Life at Work: Behavioral Science Approaches to Organizational Change*, ed. J. R. Hackman and J. L. Suttle. Santa Monica: Goodyear Publishing Company, Chap. 2.

18. Feldman, D. C. 1976. A Practical Program for Employee Socialization. *Organizational Dynamics* 5 (Autumn): 64–80.
Merton, R. K. 1968. *Social Theory and Social Structure*. New York: The Free Press, pp. 319–22.
Van Maanen, Breaking-In.
Van Maanen and Schein, Career Development.

19. Feldman, A Contingency Theory of Socialization.
Feldman, A Practical Program for Employee Socialization.
Feldman, The Multiple Socialization of Organization Members.

20. Feldman, A Practical Program for Employee Socialization.
Feldman, The Multiple Socialization of Organization Members.

21. Bauer, T. N., and S. G. Green. 1994. Effect of Newcomer Involvement in Work-Related Activities: A Longitudinal Study of Socialization. *Journal of Applied Psychology* 79: 211–23.

22. Allen, N. J., and J. P. Meyer. 1990. Organizational Socialization Tactics: A Longitudinal Analysis of Links to Newcomer's Commitment and Role Orientation. *Academy of Management Journal* 33: 847–58.
Nicholson, N., and J. Arnold. 1991. From Expectation to Experience: Graduates Entering a Large Corporation. *Journal of Organizational Behavior* 12: 413–29.
Wanous, J. P. 1977. Organizational Entry: The Individual's Viewpoint. In *Perspectives on Behavior in Organizations*, ed. J. R. Hackman, E. E. Lawler III, and L. W. Porter. New York: McGraw-Hill, pp. 126–35.

23. Stevens, C. K. 1997. Effects of Preinterview Beliefs on Applicant's Reactions to Campus Interviews. *Academy of Management Journal* 40: 947–66.

24. Bauer, T. N., E. W. Morrison, and R. R. Callister. 1998. Organizational Socialization: A Review and Directions for Future Research. In *Research in Personnel and Human Resources Management*, Vol. 16, ed. G. R. Ferris. Stamford: JAI Press, pp. 149–214. (See p. 166 for a summary.)

25. Anderson, N., and C. Ostroff. 1997. Selection as Socialization. In *International Handbook of Selection and Assessment*, ed. N. Anderson and P. Herriot. Chichester: John Wiley & Sons, pp. 413–40.

26. Shaw, J. D., J. E. Delery, G. D. Jenkins, Jr., and N. Gupta. 1998. An Organizational-Level Analysis of Voluntary and Involuntary Turnover. *Academy of Management Journal* 41: 511–25.

27. Behling, O. 1998. Employee Selection: Will Intelligence and Conscientiousness Do the Job. *Academy of Management Executive* 12: 77–86.

28. Bauer, Morrison, and Callister, Organizational Socialization.
Fisher, Organizational Socialization.
Wanous, J. P. 1992. *Organizational Entry: Recruitment, Selection, and Socialization of Newcomers.* Reading, MA: Addison-Wesley.

29. Breaugh, J. A. 1983. Realistic Job Previews: A Critical Appraisal and Future Research Directions. *Academy of Management Review* 8: 612–19.
Hom, P. W., R. W. Griffeth, L. E. Palich, and J. S. Bracker. 1998. An Exploratory Investigation into Theoretical Mechanisms Underlying Realistic Job Previews. *Personnel Psychology* 51: 421–51.
Phillips, J. M. 1998. Effects of Realistic Job Previews on Multiple Organizational Outcomes: A Meta-Analysis. *Academy of Management Journal* 41: 673–90.
Premack, S. L., and J. P. Wanous. 1985. A Meta-Analysis of Realistic Job Preview Experiments. *Journal of Applied Psychology* 70: 706–19.
Reilly, R. R., B. Brown, M. R. Blood, and C. Malatesta. 1981. The Effects of Realistic Job Previews: A Study and Discussion of the Literature. *Personnel Psychology* 34: 823–34.
Wanous, *Organizational Entry.*
Wanous, J. P., and A. Colella. 1989. Organizational Entry Research: Current Status and Future Directions. In *Research in Personnel and Human Resources Management,* Vol. 7, ed. G. R. Ferris and K. M. Rowland. Greenwich, CT: JAI Press, pp. 59–120.
Wanous, J. P., T. D. Poland, S. L. Premack, and K. S. Davis. 1992. The Effects of Met Expectations on Newcomer Attitudes and Behaviors: A Review and Meta-Analysis. *Journal of Applied Psychology* 77: 288–97.
Some research has found no relationship between realistic expectations and organizational commitment after entry. See C. L. Adkins, 1995. Previous Work Experience and Organizational Socialization: A Longitudinal Examination. *Academy of Management Journal* 38: 839–62.

30. Reilly, Brown, Blood, and Malatesta, The Effects of Realistic Job Previews, p. 832.
Wanous, *Organizational Entry.*

31. Breaugh, Realistic Job Previews.

32. Feldman, A Contingency Theory of Socialization.
Feldman, The Multiple Socialization of Organization Members.
Feldman, A Practical Program for Employee Socialization.
Van Maanen, Breaking-In.
Van Maanen and Schein, Career Development.

33. Schein, Organizational Socialization and the Profession of Management.

34. Ashford, S. J., and J. S. Black. 1996. Proactivity during Organizational Entry: The Role of Desire for Control. *Journal of Applied Psychology* 81: 199–214.
Miller, V. D., and F. M. Jablin. 1991. Information Seeking during Organizational Entry: Influences, Tactics, and a Model of the Process. *Academy of Management Review* 16: 92–120.

35. Bauer, T. N., T. Bodner, B. Erdogan, D. M. Truxillo, and J. S. Tucher. 2007. Newcomer Adjustment During Organizational Socialization: A Meta-Analytic Review of Antecedents, Outcomes, and Methods. *Journal of Applied Psychology* 92: 707–21.

Feldman, A Contingency Theory of Socialization.

Feldman, The Multiple Socialization of Organization Members.

36. Anderson, N. R., and H. D. C. Thomas. 1996. Work Group Socialization. In *Handbook of Work Group Psychology*, ed. M. A. West. Chichester: John Wiley & Sons, pp. 423–50.

Argote and McGrath, Group Processes, pp. 347–48.

Kozlowski, S. W. J., and B. S. Bell. 2003. Work Groups and Teams in Organizations. In *Handbook of Psychology*, Vol. 12, *Industrial and Organizational Psychology*, ed. W. C. Borman, D. R. Ilgen, and R. J. Klimoski. New York: John Wiley and Sons, Chap. 14. A discussion of workgroup socialization appears on pp. 341–43.

37. Ibid.

Levine, J. M., and R. L. Moreland. 1994. Group Socialization: Theory and Research. In *European Review of Social Psychology*, Vol. 5, ed. W. Stroebe and M. Hewstone. Chichester: John Wiley & Sons, pp. 305–36.

38. Ibid.

39. Ashforth, B. E., A. M. Saks, and R. T. Lee. 1998. Socialization and Newcomer Adjustment: The Role of Organizational Context. *Human Relations* 51: 897–926.

40. Lewin, K. 1951. *Field Theory in Social Science*. New York: Harper & Row.

Schein, Organizational Socialization and the Profession of Management.

41. Ashforth, B. E., and A. M. Saks. 1996. Socialization Tactics: Longitudinal Effects on Newcomer Adjustment. *Academy of Management Journal* 39: 149–78.

Bauer, Morrison, and Callister, Organizational Socialization.

Saks, A. M. 1996. The Relationship Between the Amount and Helpfulness of Entry Training and Work Outcomes. *Human Relations* 49: 429–51.

42. Ensher, E. A., and S. E. Murphy. 2007. E-mentoring: Next-Generation Research Strategies and Suggestions. In *The Handbook of Mentoring at Work: Theory, Research & Practice*, ed. B. R. Ragins and K. E. Kram. Thousand Oaks: Sage Publications, Chap. 12.

Johnson, W. B., and C. R. Ridley. 2008. *The Elements of Mentoring*. New York: Palgrave Macmillan.

Kram, K. E. 1985. *Mentoring at Work: Development Relationships in Organizational Life*. Glenview: Scott, Foresman.

Ragins, B. R., and K. E. Kram. 2007. The Roots and Meaning of Mentoring. In *The Handbook of Mentoring at Work: Theory, Research and Practice*, ed. B. R. Ragins and K. E. Kram. Thousand Oaks: Sage Publications, Chap. 1.

43. Allen, T. D., L. T. Eby, M. L. Poteet, E. Lentz, and L. Lima. 2004. Career Benefits Associated with Mentoring for Protégés: A Meta-Analysis. *Journal of Applied Psychology* 89: 127–36.

Langan-Fox, J. 1998. Women's Careers and Occupational Stress. In *International Review of Industrial and Organizational Psychology*, Vol. 13, ed. C. L. Cooper and I. T. Robertson. Chichester: John Wiley & Sons, Chap. 8.

Scandura, T. A., and B. A. Hamilton. 2002. Enhancing Performance through Mentoring. In *Psychological Management of Individual Performance*, ed. S. Sonnentag. Chichester: John Wiley & Sons, Chap. 14.

Weinberg, F. J., and M. J. Lankau. 2011. Formal Mentoring Programs: A Mentor-Centric and Longitudinal Analysis. *Journal of Management* 37: 1527–57.

44. Bauer, Morrison, and Callister, Organizational Socialization, p. 168.

Van Maanen and Schein, Career Development.

45. Scandura, T. A. 1998. Dysfunctional Mentoring Relationships and Outcomes. *Journal of Management* 24: 449–67.

46. Clutterbuck, D., and B. R. Ragins. 2002. *Mentoring and Diversity: An International Perspective*. Oxford: Butterworth-Heinemann.

Davis, J., and E. S. Rodela. 1992. Mentoring for the Hispanic: Mapping Emotional Support. In *Hispanics in the Workplace*, ed. S. B. Knouse, P. Rosenfeld, and A. L. Culberston. Newbury Park: Sage Publications, pp. 151–69.

Knouse, S. B. 1992. The Mentoring Process for Hispanics. In *Hispanics in the Workplace*, ed. S. B. Knouse, P. Rosenfeld, and A. L. Culberston. Newbury Park: Sage Publications, pp. 137–50.

Ragins, B. R. 1997. Diversified Mentoring Relationships in Organizations: A Power Perspective. *Academy of Management Review* 22: 482–521.

Thomas, D. A. 2001. The Truth About Mentoring Minorities: Race Matters. *Harvard Business Review* 79 (April): 99–107.

These readable citations have more detail about diversity and mentoring processes.

47. Schein, Organizational Socialization and the Profession of Management.

48. Kafka, F. 1981. *The Metamorphosis*. Translated and edited by S. Corngold. New York: Bantam Books, p. 3. (Originally published in 1915.)

49. Feldman, The Multiple Socialization of Organization Members.

Van Maanen and Schein, Career Development, pp. 61–62.

50. Schein, Organizational Socialization and the Profession of Management.

Van Maanen and Schein, Toward a Theory of Organizational Socialization, pp. 228–30.

51. Schein, Organizational Socialization and the Profession of Management.

52. See Cooper-Thomas and Anderson, Organizational Socialization, pp. 495–96 for a summary of the individual differences research.

53. Feldman, The Multiple Socialization of Organization Members.

54. Jones, G. R. 1983. Psychological Orientation and the Process of Organizational Socialization: An Interactionist Perspective. *Academy of Management Review* 8: 464–74.

Jones, G. R. 1986. Socialization Tactics, Self-Efficacy, and Newcomers' Adjustments to Organizations. *Academy of Management Journal* 29: 262–79.

55. Jones, Psychological Orientation and the Process of Organizational Socialization.

56. This section is speculative because no empirical research has yet been done. It is partly suggested by Jones, Psychological Orientation and the Process of Organizational Socialization and Chap. 7 of this book.

57. Black, J. S., M. Mendenhall, and G. Oddou. 1991. Toward a Comprehensive Model of International Adjustment: An Integration of Multiple Theoretical Perspectives. *Academy of Management Review* 16: 291–317.

Feldman, D. C., and H. B. Thompson. 1993. Entry Shock, Culture Shock: Socializing the New Breed of Global Managers. *Human Resource Management* 31: 345–62.

58. See the following for readable discussions of culture shock:

Ferraro, G. P. 1998. *The Cultural Dimension of International Business*. Upper Saddle River: Prentice Hall, Chap. 7.

Funham, A., and S. Bochner. 1986. *Culture Shock: Psychological Reactions to Unfamiliar Environments*. London: Methuen & Co.

Oberg, K. 1960. Culture Shock: Adjustment to New Cultural Environments. *Practical Anthropology* 7: 177–82.

Pedersen, P. 1995. *The Five Stages of Culture Shock: Critical Incidents Around the World*. Westport: Greenwood Press. This source reports the experiences of undergraduate students visiting different countries.

59. Black, J. S., and H. B. Gregersen. 1991. When Yankee Comes Home: Factors Related to Expatriate and Spouse Repatriation Adjustment. *Journal of International Business Studies* 22: 671–94.

60. Mendenhall, M., E. Dunbar, and G. Oddou. 1987. Expatriate Selection, Training, and Career-Pathing: A Review and Critique. *Human Resource Management* 26: 331–45.

61. Developed from the following and other citations throughout this part:
Black, J. S., H. B. Gregersen, and M. E. Mendenhall. 1992. *Global Assignments: Successfully Expatriating and Repatriating International Managers*. San Francisco: Jossey-Bass.
Black, Mendenhall, and Oddou, Toward a Comprehensive Model of International Adjustment.
Feldman, D. C., and D. C. Thomas. 1992. Career Management Issues Facing Expatriates. *Journal of International Business Studies* 23: 271–93.
Kraimer, M. L., S. J. Wayne, and R. A. Jaworski. 2001. Sources of Support and Expatriate Performance: The Mediating Role of Expatriate Adjustment. *Personnel Psychology* 54: 71–100.
Shaffer, M. A., D. A. Harrison, K. M. Gilley, and D. M. Luk. 2001. Struggling for Balance Amid Turbulence on International Assignments: Work-Family Conflict, Support and Commitment. *Journal of Management* 27: 99–121.

62. Copeland, L., and L. Griggs. 1985. *Going International*. New York: Random House.

63. Developed from the following and other citations throughout this part:
Bauer, T. N., and S. Taylor. 2001. A Globalized Conceptualization of Organizational Socialization. In *Handbook of Industrial, Work, and Organizational Psychology*, Vol. 1, ed. N. Anderson, D. S. Ones, H. K. Sinangil, and C. Viswesvaran. Thousand Oaks: Sage Publications, Chap. 19.
Black, Mendenhall, and Oddou, Toward a Comprehensive Model of International Adjustment.
Feldman and Thomas, Career Management Issues Facing Expatriates, pp. 271–93.
Van Vianen, A. E. M., I. E. De Pater, A. L. Kristof-Brown, and E. C. Johnson. 2004. Fitting In: Surface- and Deep-Level Cultural Differences and Expatriates' Adjustment. *Academy of Management Journal* 47: 697–709.

64. Bhaskar-Shrinivas, P., D. A. Harrison, M. A. Shaffer, and D. M. Luk. 2005. Input-Based and Time-Based Models of International Adjustment: Meta-Analytic Evidence and Theoretical Extensions. *Academy of Management Journal* 48: 257–81.
Mendenhall, Dunbar, and Oddou, Expatriate Selection, Training, and Career-Pathing.
Mendenhall, M., and G. Oddou. 1985. The Dimensions of Expatriate Acculturation: A Review. *Academy of Management Review* 10: 39–48.

65. Black, J. S., and H. B. Gregersen. 1999. The Right Way to Manage Expats. *Harvard Business Review* 77 (March–April): 52–54, 56, 58, 60, 62, 63.
Black J. S., and M. Mendenhall. 1990. Cross-Cultural Training Effectiveness: A Review and a Theoretical Framework for Future Research. *Academy of Management Review* 15: 113–36.

66. Caligiuri, P. M., M. M. Hyland, A. Joshi, and A. S. Bross. 1998. Testing a Theoretical Model for Examining the Relationship between Family Adjustment and Expatriate's Work Adjustment. *Journal of Applied Psychology* 83: 598–614.
Mendenhall, Dunbar, and Oddou, Expatriate Selection, Training, and Career-Pathing.

Shaffer, M. A., and D. A. Harrison. 1998. Expatriates' Psychological Withdrawal from International Assignments: Work, Nonwork, and Family Influences. *Personnel Psychology* 51: 87–118.

67. Mendenhall and Oddou, The Dimensions of Expatriate Acculturation, p. 43.
68. Feldman and Thomas, Career Management Issues Facing Expatriates, pp. 273–75. Naumann, E. 1992. A Conceptual Model of Expatriate Turnover. *Journal of International Business Studies* 23: 499–531.
69. Black and Gregersen, When Yankee Comes Home. Black, J. S., H. B. Gregersen, and M. E. Mendenhall. 1992. Toward a Theoretical Framework of Repatriation Adjustment. *Journal of International Business Studies* 23: 737–60.

Chapter 7

MOTIVATION: NEED THEORIES

After reading this chapter, you should be able to:

- Discuss the role of needs in behavior in organizations.
- Describe the major need theories of motivation.
- Appreciate that the importance of individual needs varies from person to person.
- Outline how a person can learn some needs.
- Distinguish between motivator and hygiene factors in a person's environment.
- Discuss the international and ethical issues in motivation.

The amount of space devoted to motivation in this book is based on the conviction that enhancing and sustaining employee motivation is a manager's major function. Psychologists have developed many theories of motivation to explain why people behave one way and not another.[1]

The theories share several assumptions.[2] First, they assume that behavior has a starting point, a direction, and a stopping point. Second, the behavior is voluntary and under a person's control. These theories try to explain why a person chooses to read one book over another or shop at one grocery store rather than another. They do not deal with involuntary or automatic responses such as breathing or eye blinking. Third, the theories assume that behavior is not random, but has a specific purpose and direction. Based on those assumptions, the chapter uses the following definition of motivation:

> Motivation ... [refers to] those psychological processes that cause the arousal, direction, and persistence of voluntary actions that are goal directed.[3]

Knowing the different theories helps you understand some aspects of your behavior and the behavior of others. These theories also suggest ways in which managers can affect and direct behavior. From a management perspective, understanding these theories helps a manager build and manage a system of motivation. These theories also provide the conceptual base for analyzing and diagnosing motivation problems in organizations.[4]

Organizations intentionally or unintentionally build "motivation systems." These systems hold assumptions about what affects behaviors and which behaviors are important for job performance.[5] The three motivation chapters give you information that will help you understand how an organization should build a motivation system. Motivation theories give you the tools you need to analyze an organization's existing motivation system. These theories also help you understand why an employee is or is not performing as needed.[6]

OVERVIEW OF WHERE WE ARE HEADED

Motivation theories fall into two groups: need theories, discussed in this chapter, and cognitive and behavioral theories, discussed in Chapter 8, "Motivation: Cognitive and Behavioral Theories and Techniques." Each motivation theory uses different mechanisms to explain why people behave in certain ways.

Need theories of motivation use personal characteristics or attributes to explain motivation. These theories apply to healthy personalities and do not try to explain disorders such as psychoses. This chapter describes four need theories. Murray's theory of human personality gives a basic understanding of the role of needs in deciding human behavior. Maslow's hierarchy of needs theory and E.R.G. theory help explain even more about the role of needs. McClelland's achievement motivation theory describes the way needs develop and the role of three needs in shaping and directing behavior.

Herzberg's motivator-hygiene theory does not fit cleanly into either of the theory groups. It gives useful observations about motivation and is a transition between the need theories of this chapter and the cognitive and behavioral theories in Chapter 8.

The three cognitive theories are expectancy theory, equity theory, and goal setting theory. Expectancy theory describes the decision process people use to choose among several courses of action. This theory introduces the role of various types of rewards or outcomes people get for their behavior. Equity theory complements expectancy theory by explaining comparisons people make with others and why people might or might not feel fairly treated. A feeling of unfairness motivates the person to behave in ways that reduce the unfairness. Goal setting theory explains how goals affect people's behavior and performance.

The one behavior theory is behavior modification. This technique is built on concepts that emphasize the role of external consequences in shaping and directing human behavior.

MURRAY'S THEORY OF HUMAN PERSONALITY: THE CONCEPT OF NEEDS

Henry Murray and his colleagues at Harvard University spent many years studying human personality. Their research program used interviews, questionnaires, and in-depth clinical studies of selected people to develop a pioneering theory of human needs and behavior.[7]

Murray's theory of human personality makes some assumptions about human beings and their behavior. This theory views people as adaptive when facing a dynamic and changing environment. Human behavior is goal directed and purposeful. Factors internal to the person (needs) and in the person's external environment govern behavior.[8] Human beings learn from their interactions with their external environment and from previous experiences. They also hold preconceptions about what the future will be like. In Murray's view, a college student would have some notion of what college life would be like, based on earlier experiences in the educational system. As you experience college life, you develop new preconceptions about future college experiences.

The concept of need is basic to Murray's explanations of human behavior. Need is a hypothetical concept used to explain observable differences in behavior among different individuals or of the same person over time. In Murray's words:

■ **Table 7.1: Some Needs in Murray's Theory of Human Personality**

Need*	Desire To
n Achievement	Attain difficult goals; perform as well as possible.
n Acquisition	Gather property, belongings, and objects.
n Affiliation	Associate with others, have friends, and join groups.
n Autonomy	Be independent and not be influenced by others.
n Deference	Respect authority; admire a person with authority.
n Dominance	Command, control, and influence others; affect a group's direction.
n Exhibition	Draw attention to oneself.
n Nurturance	Help others, give aid, improve the condition of other people.
n Order	Organize and systematically arrange objects; be clean, neat, and tidy.
n Recognition	Receive credit for actions; seek honors and recognition.

*The small "n" in front of each need's name is the psychologist's abbreviation for the word "need."
Source: Murray, H. A. 1938. *Explorations in Personality*. New York: John Wiley & Sons, pp. 80–83.

> Between what we can directly observe—the stimulus and the resulting action—a need is an invisible link, which may be imagined to have the properties that an understanding of the observed phenomena demand[9] ... [It is a] hypothetical process within ... [the person which over time] "points" activity and co-ordinates it.[10]

The theory puts needs into two classes. **Physical needs** are concerned with the satisfaction of the basic physical processes of the human body, such as the needs for food, air, and water. **Psychological needs** focus on emotional and mental satisfaction.[11] Some examples include a need for social interaction and a need to reach difficult goals. Table 7.1 lists and defines some psychological needs identified by Murray and his colleagues.

Characteristics of Needs

Needs are latent internal characteristics activated by stimuli or objects a person experiences. A person tends to behave in a way that satisfies an activated need. If you have a high need for affiliation and meet someone you know and like while walking around the campus, you will probably start a conversation with that person.

Needs, especially those that are opposites, can show rhythmic patterns over time. Managers are good examples of people whose behavior can be directed at satisfying needs that are opposites. A manager could satisfy a need for dominance in his relationships with subordinates. Yet the same manager is subordinate to someone else in the organization and might engage in behavior directed at the need for deference. Although these needs are distinct opposites, a healthy person has little difficulty displaying the different behaviors required.

Needs that are opposites can also be useful for understanding contradictory or puzzling behavior. A person can satisfy a need for dominance in work activities, especially if he has a management or supervisory position. The same person can abandon a leadership role in his nonwork life by choosing to follow others (need for deference).

Multiple needs often decide a person's behavior. One need can be the primary basis of behavior, and other needs serve this primary need. If you choose to join a sorority or fraternity on your campus, you might be seeking to satisfy a need for affiliation. You also might believe that a record of extracurricular activities in college is important for getting a desirable job after graduation, which shows a primary need for achievement. Your need for affiliation is serving it by moving you to join a student organization.

Implications of Murray's Theory for Behavior in Organizations

Murray's theory offers a general explanation of human behavior. This book is, of course, mainly interested in helping you understand your behavior and the behavior of others in organizations. How can you use this theory in that context?

Note that many needs have the potential to shape and direct behavior. Not all people have equal amounts of the needs in Murray's list. As will become clear, needs vary in importance among different people.

Needs can direct behavior toward some objects and away from others. Managers in organizations often control the objects toward which behavior is directed. Understanding how need structures affect individuals' reactions helps managers effectively influence the behavior of people in their organizations. A person with a strong need for recognition, for example, should respond favorably to praise from a supervisor.

You might be puzzled by another's behavior because of the stereotype you have about that person. You might be working with someone you consider to be a "loner," a person who does not associate much with a wide range of people. The same person, however, regularly associates with people who can give him technical help at work. The person probably has a high need for achievement and some need for affiliation. The latter need acts in the service of the achievement need. Murray's theory helps you understand behavior that otherwise is puzzling.

MASLOW'S HIERARCHY OF NEEDS THEORY

Murray's theory showed that needs are an essential and powerful force directing human behavior. In contrast with Murray's long list of needs, Abraham H. Maslow felt that needs could be put into five groups of basic human needs that all healthy adults try to satisfy. Maslow felt those needs are so basic that they motivate the behavior of people in many different cultures. Chronic frustration of those needs could produce psychopathological results.[12]

The following are the five need categories in Maslow's hierarchy of needs theory:

- **Physiological needs** are the basic requirements of the human body: food, water, and sleep.
- **Safety needs** are the desires of a person to be protected from physical or economic harm. Healthy adults normally avoid harm and seek safety.
- **Belongingness and love needs** include the desire to give and receive affection and to be in the company of others. This is also called a social or affiliation need. This need, described early in this chapter, helps people work in teams.
- **Esteem needs** deal with a person's self-confidence and sense of self-worth. Esteem needs are of two types. Esteem from others is the valuation of worth that a person gets from others. Self-esteem is the feeling a person has about himself, a feeling of self-confidence and self-respect.
- **Self-actualization needs** describe the desire for self-fulfillment. According to Maslow, self-actualization is "the desire to become more and more what one is, to become everything that one is capable of becoming."[13]

Maslow felt the five needs formed a **need hierarchy** according to their prepotency (see Figure 7.1). By **prepotency**, Maslow meant that the needs at the bottom of the hierarchy dominate human behavior if all needs are unsatisfied. A person living in poverty concentrates on satisfying physiological needs and does not try to satisfy the needs at the top of the hierarchy.

According to the theory, people must satisfy the needs at the bottom of the hierarchy before higher-level needs emerge as important or prepotent. An unsatisfied need is a potential motivator of behavior. After a person satisfies a need at one level, the need at the next level in the hierarchy becomes the focus of behavior. Physiological needs are satisfied first, followed by safety, belongingness and love, esteem, and finally self-actualization. A satisfied need no longer motivates behavior.

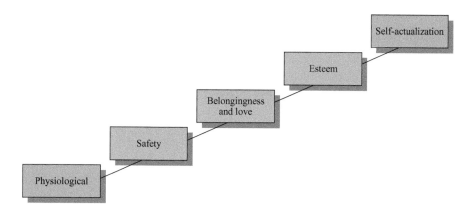

■ **Figure 7.1:**   Maslow's Hierarchy of Needs

Most people who are working have almost completely satisfied their physiological and safety needs, but they usually still have some unsatisfied belongingness and love, esteem, and self-actualization needs. Although you might eat periodically during the day when you are hungry, balanced, regular meals satisfy this part of your physiological needs. Your behavior, then, focuses more continually on the satisfaction of the higher-order needs, which happen throughout daily living.

As with Murray's theory, behavior can focus on more than one need. For example, a person actively seeks a promotion at work because he sees the promotion leading to more money (physiological and safety needs). The person might also feel the promotion will be an important satisfier of his esteem and self-actualization needs.

Maslow felt most people satisfy the needs in roughly the order shown by the hierarchy, although the hierarchy is not rigid. A strongly creative person might pursue the expression of creativity (self-actualization) at the expense of more basic needs such as maintaining an adequate diet (physiological needs). A chronically unemployed person is so concerned with staying alive (physiological) that esteem and self-actualization needs simply are not important. Lastly, people obsessed with seeking affection (love needs) or receiving feedback from others (esteem needs) will not see other needs in the hierarchy as important.[14]

Maslow did not think that needs were the only basis of human behavior. The context or environment within which the person behaves also is important. Although needs are useful explanatory concepts of people's behavior, you must also consider the person's situation and how it affects behavior.

"Maslow's need hierarchy theory ... presents the student of work motivation with an interesting paradox: The theory is widely accepted, but there is little research evidence to support it."[15] That gloomy quotation is the first sentence in a comprehensive review of research directed at the theory. Although research has occasionally given some support to Maslow's theory,[16] most parts of the theory have not been consistently supported when empirically tested.[17]

Maslow derived the theory clinically as a dynamic explanation for changes and development in human personality, especially its role in neurotic behavior. The theory was not always specific enough to let investigators develop testable hypotheses and studies that used the proper tests.[18] Two studies that used good tests of progression through the hierarchy did not empirically support that part of the theory.[19] Although Maslow found the theory useful in his clinical work, he was well aware of the tentative nature of his conclusions.[20]

E.R.G. THEORY

E.R.G. theory extends Maslow's theory. Many aspects of the theory are similar to Maslow's theory, but other aspects are unique and insightful about the effects of needs on human behavior.[21]

E.R.G. theory describes three groups of basic human needs: existence, relatedness, and growth. **Existence needs** are a person's physical and material

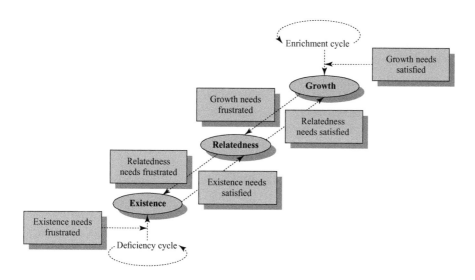

■ **Figure 7.2:**   The Existence, Relatedness, and Growth Need Hierarchy (E.R.G. Theory)

wants. Relatedness needs are the same as belongingness and love needs. Growth needs are the desires to be creative and productive, to use skills, and to develop additional capabilities. These three groups of needs form a hierarchy: existence, relatedness, growth. All people have these needs, although in varying degrees. Figure 7.2 shows the structure of E.R.G. theory.

Note the similarities between E.R.G. theory and the hierarchy of needs theory. Existence needs are the same as physiological and safety needs. Relatedness needs are the same as belongingness and love needs. Growth needs include both esteem and self-actualization needs.

In E.R.G. theory, needs affect an individual's behavior in much the same way as described by Maslow. An unsatisfied need is a motivator. If both lower-order and higher-order needs are unsatisfied, the lower-order needs will be the most important motivators of behavior.

Movement through the need hierarchy is both similar to and different from Maslow's description. Satisfaction of a need leads to upward movement in the hierarchy. Frustration of a need leads to downward movement in the hierarchy.

The first form of movement is satisfaction–progression, which is the same as described for Maslow's hierarchy of needs theory. The second form of movement is frustration–regression, a concept introduced by E.R.G. theory that gives additional insight about motivation and human behavior. Here is an illustration of the two forms of movement.

Assume you are seeking a promotion at work and apply for a new position. Many others have applied, but only one person will be selected. The people who work with you strongly support you for the promotion. Working hard for the promotion implies you have strong growth needs that you are trying to satisfy by getting the promotion. After a prolonged wait, you learn you have not been selected. Your growth needs are now frustrated. E.R.G. theory predicts you will move down the hierarchy and focus on relatedness needs. In this situation, you will turn to your coworkers for further support while adjusting to the disappoint-ment of not being promoted. If your growth needs are strong, however, sometime in the future, you will turn to satisfying them again.

Two other concepts in E.R.G. theory extend beyond Maslow's hierarchy of needs theory. A person can become locked into a **deficiency cycle** at the bottom of the hierarchy. An individual who cannot satisfy his existence needs will more strongly desire to satisfy those needs. Under conditions of scarcity, a person could become obsessed with satisfying existence needs.

A different cycle operates at the top of the hierarchy. A person who success-fully satisfies growth needs desires them even more. This **enrichment cycle** leads a person to want to continually grow and develop. The individual will also seek multiple environments to satisfy his needs for growth. For example, an individual who is successful in a challenging and demanding job should experi-ence the enrichment cycle. He will continue to seek challenges in activities away from work such as leading a community group or playing competitive sports.[22]

Empirical research supports many parts of the E.R.G. theory, but not all. The elements of the theory that have the most important implications for manage-ment received the most support.[23] Progression and regression were supported, but movement through the hierarchy was not as simple and clear-cut as originally thought. The research showed some thresholds in need satisfaction levels are related to movements in either direction. The enrichment cycle had empirical support, especially in settings that offered challenge and discretion. A person with an intensified desire for growth could also seek growth satisfaction in more than one setting.

McCLELLAND'S ACHIEVEMENT MOTIVATION THEORY

David McClelland and his colleagues studied the role of the need for achieve-ment, the need for power, and the need for affiliation in deciding human behavior. McClelland and some colleagues thoroughly studied the need for achievement, although they investigated all three needs.[24] **McClelland's achievement moti-vation theory**, and other directly related theories of personality such as Murray's, is the product of an impressive, long-running research program.[25] Controversy has surrounded the measurement methods of such theories, although some studies show the validity of different measures.[26] Atkinson and his colleagues have successfully rebutted this criticism, allowing some confidence in the research results.[27] Other critics describe the research activity as chaotic and not allowing definitive conclusions.[28]

The three needs are each associated with different behavior. As you read the following descriptions of a person's behavior with high need strengths in each need, think about your behavior. Possibly one of McClelland's needs is most characteristic of you.

People with a strong **need for achievement** take responsibility for the results of their behavior and want to solve problems.[29] Such people like to find the means for overcoming obstacles. They want to succeed, but they are willing to take calculated risks. High need for achievement people analyze situations, try to understand the chances of success, and set moderate achievement goals for themselves. Such goals are neither too easy nor too difficult to reach. These people prefer to set performance standards for themselves and do not respond well to externally applied incentives. They seek situations that allow achievement satisfaction and prefer nonroutine tasks to routine assignments. They look for and welcome feedback about how well they are doing. Skills, abilities, training, and experience all add to the performance of an achievement-motivated person.[30] A highly motivated person who also has high ability will outperform an equally motivated person with lower ability.

McClelland felt people acquired the need for achievement through socialization to the values of their culture. He based this conclusion on the results of his extensive studies of the presence of need for achievement concepts and themes in the folklore, mythology, and art of various societies. His research showed that societies emphasizing the need for achievement from generation to generation had higher levels of economic development than societies that did not.[31]

A person with a strong **need for power** focuses on "controlling the means of influencing the behavior of another person"[32] and having a strong effect on other people. Note the emphasis in the definition on influence and controlling the means of influence. The means of influence can be anything available to the person to control the behavior of another. A high need for power person actively searches for the means of influence. He could use a superior–subordinate relationship or external rewards, for example, to control the behavior of another.[33]

McClelland distinguished between two different ways of expressing the need for power.[34] One form of expression uses personal dominance, physical aggression, and exploitation. People who have learned to express the need for power in this way view situations from a win–lose perspective. They must win and the other party must lose. McClelland did not feel such power behavior resulted in the type of leadership required by organizations.

The second form of expression focuses on persuasion and interpersonal influence. The person tries to arouse confidence in those he wants to influence. If, for example, a person who expresses a need for power in this way is the head of a group, he will clarify the group's goals and persuade members to reach those goals. His influence efforts will emphasize the ability of group members to reach goals, and he will try to develop in those members a belief in their competence. Of the two types of power, McClelland felt the second one characterized effective leaders in organizations.[35]

A person with a strong **need for affiliation** focuses on "establishing, maintaining, and restoring positive affective relations with others."[36] He wants close, warm relationships with other people. Such people seek the approval of others, especially from those about whom they care. Strong need for affiliation people like other people, want to be liked, and want to be in the company of others.[37] They also are the people who will likely enjoy working in teams as noted previously.

What does McClelland's theory tell us about behavior in organizations, both your behavior and the behavior of others? The answer to this question requires us to consider all three needs that McClelland and his colleagues studied.

Money plays an important role for both high and low achievers, but for different reasons.[38] The high need for achievement person wants concrete feedback about performance. Making a profit, receiving a bonus, or earning a large salary is a statement about success or failure. The high achiever will not value the money as an end in itself. The monetary reward is a symbol of success and feedback about job performance.[39] The low achiever, on the other hand, views the monetary reward as an end in itself. An organization could get increased performance from a low need for achievement person by rewarding improved performance with more money.

More money alone does not get high performance from high need for achievement people. The job must be challenging, and the person must be responsible for what is done. Such people want to feel successful at doing something over which they have control. As you will see in Chapter 9, "Job Design and Intrinsic Rewards," the design of a person's job can be an important element in job performance for these reasons.

McClelland's research found that managers and executives usually had higher need for achievement scores than people in other occupations.[40] Considerable evidence points to strong need for achievement as a key characteristic of entrepreneurs.[41] This does not mean that people in many other achievement-oriented occupations such as scientists, professors, and artists are low achievers. It simply means that the nature of need for achievement behavior as previously described fits well with the role demands of managers, executives, and entrepreneurs. McClelland summarized his view as follows:

> The achievement motive should lead individuals to seek out situations which provide moderate challenge to their skills, to perform better in such situations, and to have greater confidence in the likelihood of their success. It should make them conservative where things are completely beyond their control, as in games of chance, and happier where they have some opportunity of influencing the outcome of a series of events by their own actions and of knowing concretely what those actions have accomplished.[42]

The need for achievement and the need for power relate in important ways with implications for behavior in organizations.[43] Both needs lead to task-focused, assertive behaviors. The strong need for achievement person is task centered, future oriented, and performs to an internal standard of excellence. The strong need for power person engages in behavior that draws attention to the person to achieve the desired effect. Such people are risk takers, present oriented, and assess situations for their change potential. Both types of people are important for successful organizations. High need for achievement managers are important to keep an organization going, but high need for power people can bring dramatic changes and innovations.[44] McClelland's research also found high need for power and low need for affiliation in more totalitarian-oriented countries.[45] We can speculate that this pattern of needs is associated with an authoritarian management style that uses close supervision.[46]

HERZBERG'S MOTIVATOR-HYGIENE THEORY

Frederick Herzberg's motivator-hygiene theory is not based directly on needs. It also does not fit neatly with the cognitive and behavioral theories described in the next chapter. It is useful as a transition between purely need-based theories and those based on cognitive and behavioral processes.

In developing his theory, Herzberg did his early research using samples of accountants and engineers. Each person was interviewed and asked to recall a past work event that was especially positive or negative. The interview responses were content analyzed to decide whether any relationships existed between positive and negative events and aspects of the job or work organization.[47]

Herzberg found that reports of negative events had items that mostly involved a person's job context. Negative reports described company policy, its administration, working conditions, and supervision more often than reports of positive events. The positive reports described aspects of the job itself, a feeling of achievement, and a feeling of responsibility. The person's salary was mentioned about the same proportion of time in both negative and positive reports.

Herzberg called the items predominantly found in descriptions of negative events dissatisfiers. He called those found in descriptions of positive events satisfiers. Dissatisfiers could lead to high levels of employee dissatisfaction. If management improved the dissatisfiers, employees would feel a reduction in dissatisfaction, but not higher satisfaction. Satisfiers could lead to high levels of employee satisfaction, but their absence or a person's failure to experience them would not produce dissatisfaction.

Herzberg's observations on satisfaction and dissatisfaction differed from commonly held views. The traditional view saw a single continuum with satisfaction at one end and dissatisfaction at the other. Herzberg's research suggested two distinct continua, one for satisfaction and one for dissatisfaction. In short, different aspects of an employee's experiences contributed separately to satisfaction and dissatisfaction.

Herzberg eventually called the satisfiers motivators and the dissatisfiers hygiene factors.[48] The motivators included achievement, recognition, and the work itself.[49] Hygiene factors included company policies and their administration, quality of supervision, and working conditions. Managers first must improve the hygienic conditions of work (e.g., before trying to increase motivation). Negative hygienic conditions distract employees from experiencing the motivators. After the work context is improved, the manager can try to provide the motivators by redesigning jobs using a process Herzberg called job enrichment. By adding more responsibility and autonomy to the job, the manager creates the opportunity for an employee to experience the motivators.

Empirical research designed to test the motivator-hygiene theory has had mixed results. The work of Herzberg and his colleagues, using the retrospective interview technique, has supported the distinction between motivators and hygiene factors. Work by other researchers using other research methods, however, has not produced confirming evidence.[50] Some also have questioned the basic validity of retrospective interviews.[51] As Chapter 5, "Perception, Attitudes, and Personality," explained, people can attribute positive work experiences to themselves and negative experiences to external factors.

There are, of course, two sides to this critique. Herzberg responded to the question of attribution by arguing that more conventional methods of measurement produce bias. His use of retrospective interviews was a deliberate effort to avoid such bias.[52]

INTERNATIONAL ASPECTS OF THE NEED THEORIES OF MOTIVATION

The need theories described in this chapter were the work of U.S. scholars. Early empirical research also often used U.S. samples. A major issue centers on whether those theories are culture bound.[53] Although the concept of needs holds across cultures, people with different cultural backgrounds might express and satisfy those needs differently.[54]

The accumulated research evidence shows Maslow's hierarchy of needs theory does not hold in many countries in the form proposed. Different needs appear as driving forces in different countries.[55] Many U.S. workers respond to self-actualization. Security and affiliation needs are the strongest needs among Latin American workers. French and German workers have a strong need for security. The strong cooperative and affiliation orientation of New Zealanders suggest that the belongingness and love needs are central in that country.

The results of one large study of the central values of different countries imply differences in saliency of needs among different countries. Different needs apparently are at the top of the hierarchy for workers in different cultures.[56] The study showed that self-actualization needs are most important in the United States, Great Britain, Ireland, India, the Philippines, New Zealand, Canada, South Africa, and Australia. Security needs are dominant in Italy, Japan, Greece, Colombia, and several other countries. Belongingness and love (social) needs are at the top in the Scandinavian countries, the Netherlands, and Singapore. Both security, belongingness and love (social) needs are the most important in many Latin American countries, Thailand, Taiwan, Israel, Turkey, and several other countries.

Some cross-cultural research suggests McClelland's achievement motivation theory is robust across different cultures,[57] although the author of the multi-country study just described strongly questions that view.[58] He sees the need for achievement as tied to U.S. values of desire for action and accomplishment. An emphasis on the need for achievement assumes cultural values of risk taking and performance, which are not found in all cultures. He also argued that the word "achievement" is almost untranslatable into languages other than English. Self-actualization, which is closely related to the need for achievement, was strongly held only in Anglo-American countries, their former colonies, or closely associated countries. Another study found some differences in need for achievement strengths in samples from four countries outside the United States.[59]

As more organizations develop global operations, there is an increasing likelihood that you could work as a manager outside your home country. Use caution when applying the need theories of motivation in different countries. There is strong evidence that they are culture bound and do not apply universally.

ETHICAL ISSUES AND THE NEED THEORIES OF MOTIVATION

The discussion of ethical issues surrounding the need theories of motivation begins with a set of broad ethical issues created by our knowledge of human motivation. Those issues will crystallize in the next two motivation chapters as your knowledge of motivation expands.

A general question involving motivation centers on the ethics of directly affecting the behavior of employees without their informed consent. Managers could consider the ethics of their actions to affect employee motivation from the views of the different ethical theories in Chapter 3, "Ethics and Behavior in Organizations." A utilitarian analysis would ask about the total effects of the manager's efforts and whether they produce a widespread net positive benefit for the organization. An analysis of rights and justice would question employees' rights to know in advance that their managers will try to shape their behavior with knowledge of human motivation. A manager working from ethical egoism would say it is right for him to have that effect because it meets his interests in his work unit's performance and his career.

Are organizations ethically obliged to create work experiences and environments that let people satisfy their needs? Such an argument was the centerpiece of much early normative management theory[60] and the Quality of Working Life efforts started in the 1970s.[61] The question persists today as you will see in the job design discussion of Chapter 9. As that chapter shows, existing research evidence does not clearly point to higher performance and satisfaction from work designs that align with people's needs. The ethical answer for now must rest on the philosophy of each organization and its managers.

The evidence presented for cultural differences in people's needs raises the ethical question of whether managers must consider such differences in designing work experiences in multinational operations. Should they take cultural differences into account and manage those operations according to the needs of people in the host culture, or should they manage the operations as if they were in their home culture? Both utilitarian and rights-based analyses answer *yes* to the first question and *no* to the second. If people's needs affect their motivation and job performance, then managing a multinational operation congruent with local people's needs could lead to high performance (utilitarian view). A rights-based view suggests people simply have the right of congruence with their needs in their work experiences. Anecdotal evidence reports that U.S. managers make many blunders when working abroad, suggesting that these issues have important implications for managers.[62]

SUMMARY

Murray's theory of human personality is a broad and complex picture of needs and behavior. His theory allowed for a complex collection of needs that often served as multiple bases of behavior.

Maslow's hierarchy of needs theory and the changes made to it by E.R.G. theory suggest that some needs that can be a source of motivation are stronger than others. Those needs can dominate the attention of the person for some time.

McClelland's achievement motivation theory gave much detail about the behavior associated with three needs, especially the need for achievement. The behaviors associated with the needs for achievement and power were both important for success in organizations, although for different reasons.

Herzberg's motivator-hygiene theory distinguished factors in the job itself from those in the work context. Factors in the job were the motivators; those in the work context were the hygiene factors. The motivators directly added to motivation. Hygiene factors could lead to dissatisfaction, but improving them would not lead to motivation.

The international aspects of the need theories suggested that these theories are culture bound. Although the concept of needs holds across cultures, people with different cultural backgrounds can have different patterns of needs, motivators, and hygiene factors.

The discussion of ethical issues surrounding the need theories of motivation focused on broad ethical issues created by a manager's knowledge of human motivation. Those issues will crystallize in the next two motivation chapters as we build more detailed theories of human motivation.

REVIEW AND DISCUSSION QUESTIONS

1 Discuss the similarities and differences between Maslow's hierarchy of needs theory and E.R.G. theory. What insights do you gain from each theory?

2 Discuss the satisfaction–progression and frustration–regression principles from E.R.G. theory. Give examples of the functioning of each principle.

3 Discuss the different ways of expressing the need for power as described in McClelland's achievement motivation theory. Which of the two types of power do you respond to best? Why?

4 Which parts of Herzberg's motivator-hygiene theory made useful contributions to understanding motivation in organizations?

5 What is the relationship between monetary rewards and different needs? How should managers view money as a motivator for people with different needs?

6 Discuss the international aspects of the need theories described in this chapter.

7 Review the discussion of ethical issues and the need theories of motivation. Discuss those issues with the goal of taking a strong position on them.

TAKE FIVE: OB ALIVE: *THE ODD COUPLE* (1968)

7
TAKE FIVE

Mismatched Oscar Madison (Walter Matthau) and Felix Ungar (Jack Lemmon) share Oscar's apartment. Sloppy and disorganized Oscar must contend with the tidy and controlled Felix. Many funny moments unfold as Oscar desires to live alone and Felix continues his controlling behavior.

These scenes start with DVD Chapter 4, "Impossible to Live With." Oscar enters the room while saying, "Oh, Felix, Felix, Felix, Felix." They end as Felix and Oscar leave a park bench (Stop: DVD Chapter 5, "Oscar's Proposal," 0:40:28).

The following questions can guide your viewing of these scenes: Which needs discussed in this chapter best fit Oscar and Felix? Are their need patterns the same or do they differ?

REFERENCES AND NOTES

REFERENCES AND NOTES
7

1. See the following sources for summaries of much of the content of this book's three motivation chapters: Kanfer, R., M. Frese, and R. E. Johnson. 2017. Motivation Related to Work: A Century of Progress. *Journal of Applied Psychology* 102: 338–55.
   Steers, R. M., R. T. Mowday, and D. L. Shapiro. 2004. The Future of Work Motivation Theory. *Academy of Management Review* 28: 379–87.
2. Mitchell, T. R. 1982. Motivation: New Directions for Theory, Research, and Practice. *Academy of Management Review* 7: 80–88.
   Mitchell, T. R., and D. Daniels. 2003. Motivation. In *Handbook of Psychology: Industrial and Organizational Psychology*, ed. W. C. Borman, D. R. Ilgen, and R. J. Klimoski. Hoboken: John Wiley & Sons, Chap. 10.
3. Mitchell, Motivation, p. 81.
4. Evans, M. G. 1986. Organizational Behavior: The Central Role of Motivation. In *Yearly Review of Management of the Journal of Management*, ed. J. G. Hunt and J. D. Blair, 12: 203–22.
5. Mitchell, Motivation, p. 82.

6. Other reviews of motivation theories include the following:

   Ambrose, M. L., and C. T. Kulik. 1999. Old Friends, New Faces: Motivation Research in the 1990s. *Journal of Management* 25: 231–76.

   Mitchell and Daniels, Motivation.

   Pinder, C. C. 1998. *Work Motivation in Organizational Behavior*. Upper Saddle River: Prentice Hall.

   Rainey, H. G. 1993. Work Motivation. In *Handbook of Organizational Behavior*, ed. R. T. Golembiewski. New York: Marcel Dekker, pp. 19–39.

   Weimer, B. 1992. *Human Motivation: Metaphors, Theories, and Research*. Newbury Park: Sage Publications.

7. Murray, H. A. 1938. *Explorations in Personality*. New York: John Wiley & Sons.

   Murray, H. A. 1948. *Assessment of Men*. New York: Holt, Rinehart, and Winston.

8. Murray dealt with other factors internal to the person, the details of which do not change the essence of what is presented here. Factors external to the person were stimuli to which the person reacted. Murray's word for such stimuli was *press*.

9. Murray, *Explorations in Personality*, p. 60.

10. Ibid., p. 73.

11. Murray's original terms were *viscerogenic* and *psychogenic*, respectively.

12. Maslow, A. H. 1943. Preface to Motivation Theory. *Psychosomatic Medicine* 5: 85–92.

    Maslow, A. H. 1943. A Theory of Human Motivation. *Psychological Review* 50: 370–96.

    Maslow, A. H. 1999. *Toward a Psychology of Being*, 3rd edn. New York: John Wiley & Sons. See Chapter 11, "Psychological Data and Human Values" for a 1957 discussion of the hierarchy of needs theory.

    Maslow, A. H., with D. C. Stephens and G. Heil. 1998. *Maslow on Management*. New York: John Wiley & Sons.

13. Maslow, A Theory of Human Motivation, p. 382.

14. Ibid., p. 386.

15. Wahba, M. A., and L. Bridwell. 1976. Maslow Reconsidered: A Review of Research on the Need Hierarchy Theory. *Organizational Behavior and Human Performance* 15: 212–40.

16. Mitchell, V. F., and P. M. Mougdil. 1976. Measurement of Maslow's Need Hierarchy. *Organizational Behavior and Human Performance* 16: 334–49.

    Mitchell and Daniels, Motivation, p. 238.

17. Locke, E. A., and D. Henne. 1986. Work Motivation Theories. In *International Review of Industrial and Organizational Psychology*, ed. C. L. Cooper and I. T. Robertson. Chichester: John Wiley & Sons, Chap. 1, pp. 5–6.

18. Hall, D. T., and K. E. Nougaim. 1967. An Examination of Maslow's Need Hierarchy in an Organizational Setting. *Organizational Behavior and Human Performance* 3: 12–35.

    Wahba and Bridwell, Maslow Reconsidered.

19. Hall and Nougaim, An Examination of Maslow's Need Hierarchy.

    Lawler, E. E., III, and J. L. Suttle. 1972. A Causal Correlation Test of the Need Hierarchy Concept. *Organizational Behavior and Human Performance* 7: 265–87.

20. Maslow, A. H. 1965. *Eupsychian Management*. Homewood: Dorsey, pp. 55–56.

21. Alderfer, C. P. 1972. *Existence, Relatedness, and Growth: Human Needs in Organizational Settings*. New York: Free Press.

22. Champoux, J. E. 1981. A Sociological Perspective on Work Involvement. *International Review of Applied Psychology* 30: 65–86.

23. Alderfer, *Existence, Relatedness, and Growth.*
Kaplan, R. E., and K. A. Smith. 1974. The Effect of Variations in Relatedness Need Satisfaction on Relatedness Desire. *Administrative Science Quarterly* 19: 507–32.
Wanous, J. P., and A. A. Zwany. 1977. A Cross-Sectional Test of Need Hierarchy Theory. *Organizational Behavior and Human Performance* 18: 78–97.

24. McClelland, D. C. 1961. *The Achieving Society.* Princeton: D. Van Nostrand.
McClelland, D. C. 1962. Business Drive and National Achievement. *Harvard Business Review* 40 (July–August): 99–112.
McClelland, D. C. 1965. Toward a Theory of Motive Acquisition. *American Psychologist* 20: 321–33.

25. Two excellent volumes capture much of the important work of both McClelland and his colleague Atkinson:
Atkinson, J. W., ed. 1983. *Personality, Motivation, and Action: Selected Papers.* New York: Praeger.
Stewart, A. J., ed. 1982. *Motivation and Society.* San Francisco: Jossey-Bass.

26. Entwisle, D. R. 1972. To Dispel Fantasies about Fantasy-Based Measures of Achievement Motivation. *Psychological Bulletin* 77: 377–91.
Lilienfeld, S. O., J. M. Wood, and H. N. Garb. 2000. The Scientific Status of Projective Techniques. *Psychological Science in the Public Interest* 1: 27–66.
Spangler, W. D. 1992. Validity of Questionnaire and TAT Measures of Need for Achievement: Two Meta-Analyses. *Psychological Bulletin* 112: 140–54.
Tuerlinckx, F., P. De Boeck, and W. Lens. 2002. Measuring Needs with the Thematic Apperception Test: A Psychometric Study. *Journal of Personality and Social Psychology* 82: 448–61.

27. Atkinson, J. W. 1981. Studying Personality in the Context of an Advanced Motivational Psychology. *American Psychologist* 36: 117–28.
Atkinson, J. W., K. Bongort, and L. H. Price. 1977. Explorations Using Computer Simulation to Comprehend Thematic Apperceptive Measurement of Motivation. *Motivation and Emotion* 1: 1–26.

28. Locke and Henne, Work Motivation Theories, pp. 12–14.

29. McClelland, *The Achieving Society.*

30. Atkinson, J. W. 1974. Motivational Determinants of Intellective Performance and Cumulative Achievement. In *Motivation and Achievement*, ed. J. W. Atkinson and J. O. Raynor. Washington, DC: Winston.

31. McClelland, *The Achieving Society.*

32. Atkinson, J. W., and D. Birch. 1978. *An Introduction to Motivation*, 2nd edn. New York: Van Nostrand, p. 82.
Winter, D. G., and N. B. Barenbaum. 1985. Responsibility and the Power Motive in Women and Men. *Journal of Personality* 53: 335–55. This source has an extended discussion of power and its role in different social situations and social institutions.

33. McClelland, D. C. 1970. The Two Faces of Power. *Journal of International Affairs* 24: 29–47.
Veroff, J. 1957. Development and Validation of a Projective Measure of Power Motivation. *The Journal of Abnormal and Social Psychology* 54: 1–8.

34. McClelland, D. C. 1975. *Power: The Inner Experience.* New York: Irvington.
McClelland, D. C., and D. H. Burnham. 1976. Power Is the Great Motivator. *Harvard Business Review* 55 (March–April): 100–10.

35. McClelland and Burnham, Power Is the Great Motivator.

36. Atkinson and Birch, *An Introduction to Motivation*, p. 82.

37. Atkinson, J. W., R. W. Heyns, and J. Veroff. 1954. The Effect of Experimental Arousal of the Affiliation Motive on Thematic Apperception. *Journal of Abnormal and Social Psychology* 49: 405–10.
38. McClelland, Business Drive and National Achievement.
39. McClelland, *The Achieving Society*, pp. 233–37.
    McClelland, D. C., and C. E. Franz. 1992. Motivational and Other Sources of Work Accomplishments in Mid-Life: A Longitudinal Study. *Journal of Personality* 60: 697–707.
    Mitchell, T. R., and A. E. Mickel. 1999. The Meaning of Money: An Individual Difference Perspective. *Academy of Management Review* 24: 568–78.
40. McClelland, Business Drive and National Achievement.
    McClelland, D. C., and R. E. Boyatzis. 1982. Leadership Motive Pattern and Long-Term Success in Management. *Journal of Applied Psychology* 67: 737–43.
    See Locke and Henne, Work Motivation Theories, pp. 12–14 for some contrary results.
41. Johnson, B. R. 1990. Toward a Multidimensional Model of Entrepreneurship: The Case of Achievement Motivation and the Entrepreneur. *Entrepreneurship Theory and Practice* 14: 39–54.
42. McClelland, *The Achieving Society*, pp. 238–39.
43. Veroff, J. 1982. Assertive Motivations: Achievement Versus Power. In *Motivation and Society*, ed. A. J. Stewart. San Francisco: Jossey-Bass, Chap. 4.
44. McClelland, D. C., and D. G. Winter. 1969. *Motivating Economic Achievement*. New York: Free Press.
45. McClelland, *The Achieving Society*, pp. 168–69.
46. McClelland had much the same speculation, although at a societal level. See ibid., p. 394.
47. Herzberg, F. 1966. *Work and the Nature of Man*. Cleveland: World Publishing Company.
    Herzberg, F., B. Mausner, and B. Snyderman. 1959. *The Motivation to Work*. New York: John Wiley & Sons.
48. Herzberg, *Work and the Nature of Man*.
49. Herzberg, F. 1968. One More Time: How Do You Motivate Employees? *Harvard Business Review* 46 (January–February): 54–62.
50. House, R. J., and L. A. Wigdor. 1967. Herzberg's Dual-Factor Theory of Job Satisfaction and Motivation: A Review of the Evidence and a Criticism. *Personnel Psychology* 20: 369–89.
    King, N. 1970. Clarification and Evaluation of the Two-Factor Theory of Job Satisfaction. *Psychological Bulletin* 74: 18–31.
51. Vroom, V. H. 1964. *Work and Motivation*. New York: John Wiley & Sons, p. 129.
52. Herzberg, *Work and the Nature of Man*, Chap. 8.
53. Hofstede, G. 1980. Motivation, Leadership, and Organization: Do American Theories Apply Abroad? *Organizational Dynamics* 9 (Summer): 42–63.
    Hofstede, G. 2001. *Culture's Consequences: Comparing Values, Behaviors, Institutions, and Organizations across Nations*, 2nd edn. Thousand Oaks: Sage Publications.
54. Adler, N. J., with A. Gundersen. 2008. *International Dimensions of Organizational Behavior*, 5th edn. Mason: Thomson South-Western, Chap. 7.
55. Bourgeois, L. J., III, and M. Boltvinik. 1981. OD in Cross-Cultural Settings: Latin America. *California Management Review* 23 (Spring): 75–81.

Hines, G. H. 1976. Cultural Influences on Work Motivation. In *Personal Goals and Work Design*, ed. P. Warr. London: John Wiley & Sons, Chap. 2.

Sirota, D., and J. M. Greenwood. 1971. Understand Your Overseas Work Force. *Harvard Business Review* 49 (January–February): 53–60.

56. Hofstede, Motivation, Leadership, and Organization.
    Hofstede, *Culture's Consequences*.

57. Adler, *International Dimensions*.

58. Hofstede, Motivation, Leadership, and Organization, pp. 126–28.
    Hofstede, *Culture's Consequences*.

59. Sagie, A., D. Elizur, and H. Yamauchi. 1996. The Structure and Strength of Achievement Motivation: A Cross-Culture Comparison. *Journal of Organizational Behavior* 17: 431–44.

60. Argyris, C. 1957. *Personality and Organization: The Conflict Between System and the Individual*. New York: Harper & Row.
    Likert, R. 1961. *New Patterns of Management*. New York: McGraw-Hill.
    McGregor, D. 1960. *The Human Side of Enterprise*. New York: McGraw-Hill.

61. Davis, L. E., and A. B. Cherns, eds. 1975. *The Quality of Working Life: Problems, Prospects, and the State of the Art*, Vol. 1. New York: Free Press.

62. Adler, *International Dimensions*.

Chapter 8

MOTIVATION: COGNITIVE AND BEHAVIORAL THEORIES AND TECHNIQUES

After reading this chapter, you should be able to:

- Describe how people develop expectations about what will happen to them.
- Analyze differences in the values people place on the results of their behavior.
- Distinguish the differences between extrinsic and intrinsic outcomes.
- Discuss the role of equity in human motivation and behavior.
- Use the techniques of goal setting.
- Describe the powerful technique of behavior modification.
- Discuss some international aspects of motivation.
- Contrast some ethical issues that surround motivation and behavior in organizations.

This chapter describes four motivation theories that differ from the theories in Chapter 7, "Motivation: Need Theories."[1] The first three theories use cognitive processes to explain human behavior.[2] The fourth theory focuses on observable behavior, rather than cognitive processes.

The three cognitive process theories are expectancy theory, equity theory, and goal setting theory. Expectancy theory describes internal processes of choice among different behaviors. Equity theory describes how people react when they feel unfairly treated by a manager. Goal setting theory emphasizes setting external goals that a person tries to reach.

Behavior modification is a fourth motivation theory that focuses on observable behavior. This theory does not use internal psychological processes to explain human behavior, which is sometimes a controversial feature of behavior modification.

EXPECTANCY THEORY

Expectancy theory is a useful tool for analyzing motivation issues and problems.[3] A review of the research literature shows some support for the theory, although it has had its share of criticism.[4] Despite the mixed support, the theory has intuitive appeal and works well as an analytical tool.

Expectancy theory makes certain assumptions about what people do when deciding how to behave. Some assumptions will be familiar to you, because they are similar to the assumptions described for need theories in Chapter 7. The following four assumptions underlie expectancy theory:

■ Forces in the environment and the individual interact to affect behavior.
■ People choose among different courses of action.
■ People make those choices based on preferences for the outcomes of those actions.
■ The choices among alternatives are rational and based on a person's perceptions of the value of the results of various actions. An individual moves toward outcomes valued positively and avoids outcomes valued negatively.

The first assumption is similar to Murray's theory of human personality. People have certain characteristics (needs) that they are trying to satisfy. The immediate environment can present opportunities for the satisfaction of those needs. People choose behavior directed at satisfying those needs in that particular environment.

People have different preferences for different outcomes. You have specific preferences for various course grades, and your preferences might differ from those of other students. Some students will be satisfied with an "A" or a "B." Others are determined to earn an "A." Still others simply want to avoid receiving a "C," "D," or "F."

The expectancy theory assumptions suggest that if you value receiving an "A" more than receiving any other grade, you will behave in a way that lets you earn that grade. Of course, you also will need to believe that receiving an "A" is possible. If you believe an "A" is possible, you will take notes in class, record class lectures, and spend considerable time studying. You will avoid behavior that will not lead to receiving the "A," such as socializing instead of studying.

Basic Concepts of Expectancy Theory

Three concepts form the basic structure of expectancy theory. The first two concepts deal with a person's expectancy that actions will lead to certain outcomes. The third concept deals with a person's preference among these outcomes.

Expectancy is a person's belief that "a particular act will lead to a particular outcome."[5] It is a subjective probability that a person's action will lead to some outcome. If the person believes the outcome is certain to happen, the expectancy is 1. If the person believes the action will not lead to that outcome, the expectancy is 0. Expectancy can have any value between 0 and 1. An expectancy of .50 means that a person believes there is a 50–50 chance that an act will be followed by a given outcome.

The first expectancy concept is a person's belief that effort leads to a desired or required performance level.[6] Effort is the extent to which a person tries to perform as desired. Because many factors affect whether a person can perform as desired, expectancy theory formulates this uncertainty as the **effort–performance expectancy (E→P)**. For example, a person works hard and meets an important deadline.

A second expectancy concept describes a person's belief that performance will be followed by some outcome. The **performance–outcome expectancy (P→O)** (also called **instrumentality**) describes the perceived connection between a person's performance and any outcomes for that performance. Those outcomes can include a pay increase, promotion, quality award, or a supervisor's praise.[7] Continuing the deadline example, the person receives a bonus for meeting the deadline.

The third concept in expectancy theory is valence. **Valence (V)** is the preference people have among outcomes. Outcomes an individual wants to receive have positive valence. Outcomes a person wants to avoid have negative valence. If the person is indifferent to an outcome, the valence is 0. Valences have a range of positive and negative values expressing the degree of attraction or avoidance a person associates with the outcome.

Relationships between Expectancies and Valences

Expectancy theory describes specific relationships between expectancies and valences in explaining how and why people choose among behaviors. Figure 8.1 shows a simplified version of expectancy theory and the relationships among the three concepts.

Expectancy theory states that people perceive a connection between effort and a desired or required performance level. People also perceive a link between that performance level and an outcome. Lastly, people have different preferences for different outcomes.

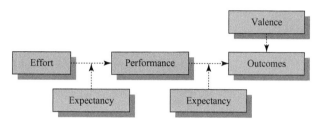

■ **Figure 8.1:** Expectancy Theory of Motivation

The following formula shows the relationships among the three concepts more directly:

$$\text{Motivation} = f \sum_{i=1}^{n} (E \rightarrow P)_i \times (P \rightarrow O)_i \times V_i$$

The formula shows two important expectancy theory features. First, multiple outcomes are possible for behavior. Those outcomes may be something positively valued (a raise) or something negatively valued (being fired). People's perception of the valence of all outcomes for a behavior decides their choice of behavior. People move toward positively valent outcomes and avoid negatively valent outcomes. They might need to consider several possible outcomes at once in their evaluation.

Second, the expectancies and valences are expected to combine multiplicatively when a person assesses different courses of action. Here, you can see the importance of a value of 0 for an expectancy or a valence. If an outcome has positive valence, but you know you cannot get it (expectancy = 0), the theory predicts you will not be highly motivated. Similarly, if you are indifferent to an outcome (valence = 0), you also will not be highly motivated although you believe you can get the outcome.

Types of Outcomes

The outcomes people receive for performance divide into two types: extrinsic and intrinsic. **Extrinsic outcomes** are rewards that people receive from someone else for their performance. **Intrinsic outcomes** are rewards that people give to themselves.[8] Figure 8.2 is an expanded version of the theory showing both extrinsic and intrinsic outcomes.

Extrinsic outcomes include pay increases, promotions, supervisor's praise, quality awards, and larger office space. Managers can give or withhold extrinsic outcomes for an employee's performance. The employee has control over the performance she is willing to give, but the employee does not directly control the outcome received. A time delay also exists between the employee's

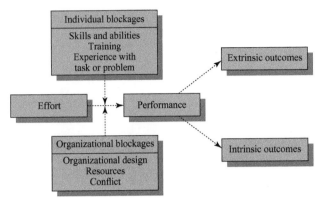

■ **Figure 8.2:** Expanded Expectancy Theory Model

performance and the extrinsic outcome. For example, organizations usually give pay increases annually or semiannually. The time lag of many extrinsic outcomes can reduce their motivational effect. Managers can increase the motivational effects of extrinsic outcomes by giving them publicly. CompUSA's salespeople who earn large commissions receive them in public meetings, making incentives a significant part of the company's culture.[9]

Employees have much more control over the intrinsic outcomes they experience. Because the individual controls intrinsic outcomes, there is little time delay between the performance and the outcome. The absence of a time lag increases the motivation effect of intrinsic outcomes.

Managers and organizations do not directly deliver intrinsic outcomes, nor can they require a person to experience such outcomes. People experience intrinsic outcomes from doing work they consider challenging and that uses many different skills and abilities.[10] Managers can affect the design of jobs and assign tasks that people will find challenging. In this way, managers can provide opportunities for people to experience intrinsic outcomes.

Intrinsic outcomes are believed to be associated mainly with higher-order needs, such as self-actualization.[11] Extrinsic outcomes can be related to many different needs, including physiological, esteem, and self-actualization needs. The amount of money a person makes clearly helps satisfy physiological needs by providing food and shelter. An individual's salary and merit pay increases also are signs of accomplishment. They give the individual feedback about how the organization feels about the person's performance.

Individual and Organizational Blockages

The link between effort and performance is not always direct or free of obstacles. Individual or organizational blockages can cause a person to perceive a low effort–performance expectancy.

Individual blockages derive from a person's perceived skills and abilities, real skills and abilities, and task experience, as well as from the difficulty of the task itself.[12] If a person believes she has the skills to do the job and has had similar task experiences, she should perceive a high effort–performance expectancy. Her motivation to do the job will then be high. If the task assignment is beyond the person's present skills and abilities, or she has had no experience with the task, she will perceive a low effort–performance expectancy. Her motivation also will be low.

Organizational blockages include the lack of resources to do a task, inadequate training to do a job, high conflict levels within the organization, and organizational design. If the organization does not give an individual enough resources, such as tools and equipment needed to do the job, the person will perceive a low expectancy between effort and performance. If the organization has not adequately trained the person to do the job, expectancy will also be low. When the job requires a level of cooperation among individuals that is impossible due to conflict levels in the organization, the effort–performance expectancy will again be low. The conflict can be high because the organization is complex and is not well coordinated. Organizations can also be designed so that a manager has little direct authority over the person the manager is trying to motivate.[13] In each case, expectancy theory predicts low motivation.

EQUITY THEORY

Equity theory tries to explain the behavioral dynamics of human exchange relationships. Any social relationship in which one person gives something to get something in return is an exchange relationship. Because one party is giving to the exchange, and another party is receiving, either party can perceive the exchange as inequitable or unfair. Many exchange relationships exist, such as marriage, parent–child relationships, teacher–student relationships, team members' relationships, and employer–employee relationships.[14]

Fairness in exchange relationships within organizations is part of a larger concern about organizational justice. Researchers view organizational justice as having at least two forms: distributive justice and procedural justice. Distributive justice focuses on fairness or equity in the distribution of costs and benefits. Procedural justice focuses on equity in decision-making processes that decide the distribution. For example, common organizational rewards such as pay increases and promotions have both distributive and procedural justice elements. Distributive justice plays a role when people receive these rewards. Procedural justice plays a role when managers decide the reward distribution. Because equity theory largely focuses on fairness in reward distribution, it is a distributive justice theory.[15]

Although equity theory research has been criticized on methodological grounds, research evidence points more toward accepting than rejecting the theory's overall structure and predictions.[16] The elements of the theory most useful to managers are those that have stood the test of empirical research.

Equity theory explains motivation and behavior differently from expectancy theory. The latter theory suggests people try to maximize the outcomes of behavior and choose among behavioral outcomes based on this maximization. Equity theory says people try to balance their ratios of inputs to outcomes from an exchange relationship.[17] You will see later that strong relationships exist between the two theories.[18]

Equity in the employer–employee exchange should be familiar to you from your job experiences. You have likely experienced times when you have felt unfairly treated. Perhaps you did not receive the pay raise you felt you deserved, or you received the same pay raise as a coworker, but felt you worked harder than she did. Both instances are examples of possible inequity. Equity theory explains why you felt inequitably treated and suggests several responses to that feeling.

Inputs are personal characteristics and behaviors a person brings to the employment exchange. These characteristics include the person's training, education, skills, experience, gender, age, and ethnic background, among other attributes. People also contribute some level of effort and individual performance.

The person contributing the inputs decides their importance or relevance to that exchange. If the contributor perceives the inputs as relevant, then they are relevant, even though the other party in the exchange might not see the inputs that way. For example, you might feel your pay increases each year should be based on your performance. Your employer, however, bases pay increases on the length of time an employee has been with the company. You feel your performance is a relevant input to the employment exchange. The company does not treat this input as relevant for pay increases and ignores individual performance when making pay decisions. You might feel inequitably treated in this exchange, if other events happen as described in the following paragraph.

An individual can receive many positive and negative outcomes from the employment exchange. Positive outcomes include pay, fringe benefits, pleasant working conditions, friendly coworkers, competent supervision, and intrinsic outcomes from the job itself. Negative outcomes include unpleasant or hazardous working conditions, a monotonous job, quarrelsome coworkers, and close, controlling supervision. The individual alone decides whether an outcome is positive or negative.

People assess the ratio between their relevant outcomes and their relevant inputs. Each person compares this ratio to the perceived ratio of another person or group of people. The ratios can also be compared to similar ratios in the past or to some absolute standard of fairness. Let's call the person making the comparison *person* (you) and the object of comparison *other* (say, a coworker).

A feeling of equity results when an individual perceives the ratios as roughly balanced:

$$\text{Person} \quad : \quad \text{Other}$$
$$\frac{\text{Outcomes}_P}{\text{Inputs}_P} \approx \frac{\text{Outcomes}_O}{\text{Inputs}_O}$$

The ratios are approximately equal when *person* perceives the outcomes and inputs of both *person* and *other* as about the same. This situation happens in a work environment when an individual believes she and a coworker are paid the same amount and that their relevant inputs are about the same.

A feeling of equity also can occur when *other's* outcomes are higher (or lower) than *person's* and when *other's* inputs also are higher (or lower). This form of equity is common in organizations. You should not feel inequitably treated if your supervisor receives a higher salary than you. More responsibility, seniority, and experience often accompany the higher salary. Of course, if you do not perceive those inputs as relevant, then you will feel a state of inequity.

Inequity exists for *person* if either of the following conditions result from the comparison:

$$\text{Person} \quad : \quad \text{Other}$$

$$\frac{\text{Outcomes}_P}{\text{Inputs}_P} < \frac{\text{Outcomes}_O}{\text{Inputs}_O} \quad \text{Negative inequity (``underpayment'')}$$

$$\frac{\text{Outcomes}_P}{\text{Inputs}_P} > \frac{\text{Outcomes}_O}{\text{Inputs}_O} \quad \text{Positive inequity (``overpayment'')}$$

As these formulas show, people can experience two types of inequity. People can feel underpaid for what they give the organization (**negative inequity**). They also can feel they are paid more than their work is worth (**positive inequity**). The amount of inequity experienced is proportional to the size of the perceived discrepancy in the two ratios. The point at which a person experiences inequity is higher for positive inequity than for negative inequity. People might attribute some amount of overpayment to "good fortune" or see it as their just reward for high levels of effort in the past.

The perception of inequity creates an internal state of psychological tension (anger and guilt, for example). The state of tension motivates the individual to reduce the tension by trying to alter directly or cognitively any of the four elements in the formulas presented earlier. People's **inequity responses** include the following actions:

■ **Change inputs:** People can change their inputs in different directions depending on whether the perceived inequity is positive or negative. Under a condition of negative inequity, an individual might reduce effort, productivity, or quality of work. Under a condition of positive inequity, the individual might increase those inputs.

■ **Change outcomes:** A person might try to improve outcomes by asking for a pay increase or more status symbols, such as a larger office.

■ **Cognitively distort own inputs and outcomes:** People can change their perceptions of their inputs or outcomes.[19] If they feel overpaid, they might begin to "see" more responsibility and duties in their job. If they feel underpaid, they might reduce the perceived importance of the job by suggesting to themselves that "it is just another job."

■ **Withdrawal:** A person might withdraw from the situation that produced the feeling of inequity.[20] The withdrawal can be permanent, such as leaving the company for another organization, or it can be temporary, such as increased absences or tardiness.

■ **Acting on *other*:** A person who feels inequitably treated might take action against the comparison person.

▨ **Cognitively distort inputs and outcomes of** *other*: People can change their perceptions of the inputs or outcomes of the comparison other. A person who feels overpaid might assign more importance to the task of the other party than in the past.

▨ **Change reference groups or the comparison** *person*: A person who feels underpaid compared to someone else in the organization might shift to a different comparison person.

Equity theory gives some strong warnings about what can happen when managers use extrinsic outcomes to reward performance. Low levels of satisfaction can result if the person perceives an unfair distribution of extrinsic outcomes.

People's responses to a state of inequity can differ. Some researchers have proposed three types of **equity sensitivity**: equity sensitives, benevolents, and entitleds.[21]

Equity sensitives react to felt inequity as described by equity theory. **Benevolents** accept fewer outcomes for their inputs than other people would accept. They accept negative inequity and do not try to reduce the feeling, as described by the theory. They can have altruistic tendencies and freely give more than they get. **Entitleds** have high inequity thresholds and accept positive inequity with no guilty feelings. They might feel the world owes them their due, and they might think whatever outcomes they get are their just reward. Think about yourself. Which type best describes you?

Empirical research of reactions of people in the three equity sensitivity groups shows several patterns. Benevolents tend to give more than they get, report higher levels of satisfaction, and more highly rate intrinsic outcomes than members of the other two groups. Entitleds have low satisfaction when they perceive themselves as under-rewarded and tend to rate pay high in importance. Although not consistently found in all studies, equity sensitives tended to hold a middle position between the other two groups.[22]

GOAL SETTING THEORY

Edwin A. Locke and his colleagues spent many years studying the effects of goals on human behavior and performance. Their research led to the development and continued testing of **goal setting theory**. Empirical research from diverse sources strongly supports the theory.[23]

Goals that are specific, challenging, reachable, and accepted by a person lead to higher performance than goals that are fuzzy, unchallenging, not reachable, or not accepted. Goal specificity includes what needs to be done, how much needs to be done, and the performance period. High performance is partly the result of clear expectations about what to do and when. People told to "do their best" do not perform as well as those who have specific task goals to reach. Goal setting affects behavior through the psychological processes of directing attention, stimulating effort, persisting in the effort, and finding ways to do the task well.[24]

Acceptance of the goal is important, but how one gets acceptance is unimportant. People do about the same, whether goals are set unilaterally by supervisors or are set jointly by themselves and their supervisors. Some research suggests that participation in goal setting is important when employees have high task involvement.[25] Participation increases information about the way a goal can be reached. This information can let employees discover better ways of doing the job.

People also need feedback about their performance and rewards while they are performing. Goal setting without feedback is not effective in improving performance.[26] Monetary rewards while working toward a goal can result in higher goal commitment and then increased performance.[27] Some evidence exists, however, that using rewards with difficult goals decreases commitment and then performance.[28]

Goal setting theory recommends the following steps to set goals:[29]

1. Specify the employee's tasks, duties, and responsibilities.
2. Specify how the employee's performance will be assessed. Be specific about the way job performance will be assessed and the behaviors that will be part of the assessment.
3. Specify the goal or target to reach. If employee performance can be quantified, then a specific amount of output can be stated. If performance cannot be quantified, then the goal or target should be specified clearly. The goal must be clear and high enough to be challenging, but not so high as to be reachable.
4. Specify the time span of employee performance. Here the employee learns about deadlines, the time within which the employee must reach the goal. That time can be short or long—one week, one month, or two years, for example.
5. Set priorities among goals. When several goals are set, distinguish the more important goals from the less important. A simple ranking of goals tells the employee which are the most important.
6. Specify goal difficulty and goal priority. If goals vary in difficulty of achievement, then reaching all or part of a difficult goal is a better performance than reaching a simple goal. Achieving goals of low priority is not as high a level of performance as achieving goals of high priority. Making distinctions at this step lets both the employee and the supervisor understand variations in the difficulty and importance of goals.
7. Review goals for coordination and cooperation with others. If an employee's goals cannot be reached without the cooperation of others, then the goals of many employees might have to be coordinated. This step is necessary to reduce conflict among goals in situations where employees are interdependent.

The goal setting steps can produce goals that are specific about the task and the time to finish the task. Stating how performance will be measured and stating the priorities among multiple goals makes the task even more specific. The challenge of the goal follows from its degree of difficulty.

Goal setting theory does not view goals as static. Goals often are based on the past and some predictions about the future. As circumstances change, goals might need to change. An important element is the ability to change goals after they have been set because the circumstances surrounding employee performance have changed. For example, a sales quota can be set for a salesperson based on a prediction about the economy over a one-year period. If economic conditions change sharply, the sales quota should also be changed. If the goal is not adjusted downward when the economy turns down, the goal becomes unreachable and employee performance will drop. If the economy turns up and the goal is not revised upward, the goal becomes too easy and the employee will not perform up to her capabilities.

The supervisor and the organization play important roles in goal accomplishment. The organization should train employees to increase their skills and let them reach increasingly more difficult goals. Management must also provide resources such as money, equipment, and time to get the job done. Lastly, it is especially critical that employees know how well they are doing while trying to reach a goal.

There are some connections between goal setting and expectancy theory discussed earlier. The effort–performance expectancy increases because of employee training and resources. Feedback and rewards for performance enhance the performance–outcome expectancy. If goals are sufficiently challenging, intrinsic outcomes also should result. The elements of goal setting theory and the steps in setting goals should all contribute directly to improved employee motivation.

BEHAVIOR MODIFICATION

Behavior modification is an approach to human motivation and behavior that differs in many ways from expectancy theory and equity theory.[30] The theory underlying **behavior modification** does not use cognitive processes to explain a person's actions.[31] Instead, the theory relies on observed behavior both to explain existing behavior and to change its direction. The theory assumes that people engage in behavior that has positive outcomes[32] and avoid behavior that fails to produce positive outcomes. Empirical research shows impressive performance increases from using a behavior modification approach to human motivation.[33]

The following four principles guide the application of the theory to the management of behavior in organizations:

- ▦ **Principle of contingent reinforcement:** A consequence has its strongest effect on behavior only if delivered when the desired behavior occurs.
- ▦ **Principle of immediate reinforcement:** A consequence has its strongest effect on behavior if it occurs immediately after the behavior happens.
- ▦ **Principle of reinforcement size:** Large consequences have stronger effects on behavior than small consequences.

■ **Principle of reinforcement deprivation:** The longer a person is deprived of a reinforcer, the stronger its effect on behavior in the future.

A Method of Behavior Modification

Behavior modification in organizations combines four approaches to affecting behavior with different schedules of controlling the consequences of behavior. This method also uses the technique of shaping to change behavior gradually when a single, big change is not possible.

Approaches to Affecting Behavior

Managers try to shape behavior by applying or withdrawing consequences of the behavior. Those consequences are either positive or negative for the target person. Managers use four approaches to affect the nature and direction of behavior: positive reinforcement, punishment, extinction, and negative reinforcement. Figure 8.3 shows each approach and the expected effect on the target person.

Positive reinforcement applies a positive event to increase the frequency or strength of desirable behavior. For example, a manager who receives a quality improvement suggestion from an employee could praise and give recognition to the employee. Positive reinforcement of that behavior increases the likelihood the person will repeat the behavior in the future.

Punishment applies a negative event to decrease the frequency of undesirable behavior. When the undesirable behavior appears, the manager applies some sanction to the employee's behavior. The sanction could be a reprimand or time off without pay. Punishment stops behavior, but does not change its direction. Because it does not prescribe desired behavior, punishment cannot produce new behavior. Punishment also has side effects that can be undesirable. Those side effects are discussed later in the chapter.

Extinction withdraws something the employee values to decrease the frequency of an undesirable behavior. Note that punishment and extinction have the same target—undesirable behavior—but the two differ sharply in other respects.

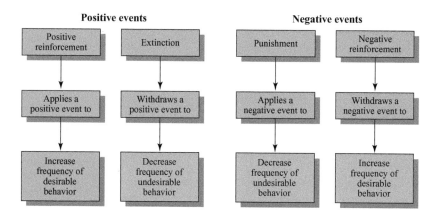

■ **Figure 8.3:** Applying and Withdrawing Positive and Negative Events

Punishment applies a negative event to a behavior, whereas extinction withdraws a positive event from a behavior. An example should make the difference clear.

Assume you are a manager who holds regular staff meetings each Monday morning. One member of your staff often disrupts meetings by telling jokes. Other staff members usually laugh at the person's behavior, giving the joke-teller positive reinforcement. The behavior continues because of this reinforcement. You decide that you have had enough and want to stop the behavior.

You could use punishment and orally reprimand the disruptive employee during the staff meeting. The behavior will stop, but the negative side effects could be strong, as you will see later. Extinction is an indirect approach to get the same result as punishment. You first encourage the others in the meeting to cooperate by not laughing at, or otherwise reinforcing, the employee's behavior at the next meeting. You are asking them to withhold something the disruptive employee values. If the other employees consistently withhold laughter from meeting to meeting, the disruptive employee's behavior will eventually stop. The frequency of the disruptions will gradually decline until they are completely gone or extinguished.

Negative reinforcement increases the frequency of desirable behavior by withdrawing or withholding a negative event. Although both negative reinforcement and punishment use a negative event, they use these methods in different ways. Punishment applies a negative event, whereas negative reinforcement withdraws or withholds a negative event.

Negative reinforcement causes the person to whom it is applied to try to escape from or avoid a negative event. An example of this effect can be seen when a supervisor scolds a person for being late for work. The person being scolded "escapes" from the negative event by showing up for work on time in the future. Coworkers see the interaction between the late employee and the supervisor. Those coworkers avoid any future scolding by coming to work on time. In both cases, the result is an increase in desired behavior following the negative reinforcement.[34]

Schedules of Reinforcement

Reinforcement of behavior can follow schedules based on the time between behaviors or the number of behaviors. Because the spacing of consequences has different effects on behavior, choosing a reinforcement schedule depends on the goal of the person doing the reinforcement.[35]

Continuous reinforcement applies a consequence after each behavior. Thanking employees each time they do something for you is an example of continuous reinforcement. The behavior will occur at a steady, high rate as long as the reinforcement continues. If the consequence is withheld deliberately or accidentally, the behavior will quickly vanish.

Intermittent reinforcement applies a consequence based on the time between behaviors or the number of behaviors. Intermittent reinforcement produces more enduring changes in behavior than continuous schedules. Four intermittent reinforcement schedules exist. Ratio schedules use the number of behaviors, whereas interval schedules use the time between behaviors.

With a fixed ratio schedule, a consequence is applied after a fixed number of behaviors. A sales commission system is an example of a fixed ratio schedule. The behavioral response under a fixed ratio schedule is high and steady, but stops quickly when the consequence is withheld.

With a variable ratio schedule, the consequence follows a varying number of behaviors. An example is complimenting employees for good performance, but not praising each occurrence of good performance. The behavioral response is high, steady, and enduring. The uncertainty of a variable ratio schedule can contribute to the lasting quality of the behavior.

With a fixed interval schedule, a consequence is applied after a constant time between behaviors. The most common example is receiving a paycheck at the end of a pay period. The behavioral response is strongest just before the consequence. A fixed interval paycheck will not have much effect on job performance, but will strongly reinforce organization membership.

With a variable interval schedule, a consequence is applied after different periods between behaviors. A manager who walks around the organization at random times, and praises employee performance when warranted, is using a variable interval schedule. The effect on behavioral response is strong and steady. Behavior endures and is not extinguished easily. Note again that the uncertainty of the reinforcement can contribute to the enduring quality of the behavior.

Shaping

Shaping gradually changes a person's behavior while aiming for a target behavior. Managers often face situations where the desired change in a person's behavior cannot happen in one step. Shaping can move a person's behavior toward the target, one step at a time.

Here is an example: An employee needs to learn a new job or a new procedure. A manager gives positive reinforcement on a continuous schedule as the employee gradually learns the new job or procedure. Behavior that does not move toward the target is treated with extinction. After the target is reached, the manager uses an intermittent reinforcement schedule. When the behavior is well in place, the manager can give reinforcement less often.

Side Effects of Punishment

The continual use of punishment can lead to undesirable side effects of punishment.[36] People might also perceive extinction as punishment, possibly resulting in side effects.[37] The side effects of extinction should be less strong than those of punishment.

Punishment stops behavior temporarily, but does not cause the person to adopt a more desirable behavior. Undesirable behavior often returns when the source of punishment is not present. Because punishment does not lead to learning new behavior, it is a less potent shaping tool than positive reinforcement.

A person who is punished continually might react emotionally. Anger, hostile behavior toward the source of punishment, and sabotage of equipment and the work process are all possible reactions. Punishment can also lead to inflexible behavior, particularly when it is applied during the early employment period. New employees are especially attentive to cues about the right type of behavior.[38] A new employee who is reprimanded after challenging the boss's decisions is unlikely to engage in that behavior later.

Some research evidence also indicates that the person receiving punishment develops negative feelings toward the source of punishment.[39] A climate of distrust—and even hate—can develop between a manager and subordinates, undermining the manager's ability to effectively shape behavior.

INTERNATIONAL ASPECTS OF THE COGNITIVE AND BEHAVIORAL THEORIES OF MOTIVATION

The theories described in this chapter have two underlying assumptions that could restrict their application in countries outside the United States. The first assumption states that the individual controls decisions about future actions. The second assumption states that a manager can deliberately shape the behavior of employees. Both assumptions reflect U.S. values of free will and individualism. All the theories described in this chapter were developed by U.S. scholars.[40] Are they so culture bound that they have limited application elsewhere in the world?

Some observers believe that because expectancy theory has such strong roots in U.S. values, it likely does not apply to other cultures. The U.S. value of individualism leads to the need to explain actions as a way of receiving something or for satisfying some need.[41] Expectancy theory also emphasizes individual control of one's destiny—another strong U.S. value that is not characteristic of all cultures.[42] For example, most Muslim managers believe something happens mainly because of Allah's will. Hong Kong Chinese believe that luck plays a role in all events. Both concepts are examples of attributing control to external factors, not internal factors.[43]

Only two studies offer evidence of expectancy theory's validity in other cultures. One study focused on female life insurance sales representatives in Japan who worked under a complex commission system tied to their performance. The study's results accorded well with U.S. findings of the same period.[44] Two studies done among Russian textile workers linked valued extrinsic rewards, praise, and recognition directly to worker performance.[45] Workers received those outcomes when they increased output. Productivity increased, as the theory predicts.

Empirical research is showing complex, cross-cultural effects on equity theory. Some studies imply that reward allocation decisions follow equity theory premises in U.S., Russian, and Chinese samples.[46] Other studies found that the Chinese emphasized seniority or personal needs in reward decisions more than Americans did and had a benevolent equity sensitivity orientation.[47] Still another study found that student subjects in the Eastern European transition economies of the Czech Republic, Croatia, Poland, Romania, and Slovenia endorsed positive inequity more than U.S. students did.[48]

Research on goal setting theory has been done in Australia, Canada, Israel, the former West Germany, Japan, and the Caribbean.[49] Results of those fourteen studies were consistent with the U.S. work that formulated the theory, as described earlier. One study of U.S. and Israeli students found that the U.S. students were not affected by how goals were set.[50] The Israeli students, however, performed better when goals were set participatively. Such collaboration in setting goals is consistent with features of Israeli culture that value cooperation between managers and subordinates.[51]

ETHICAL ISSUES AND THE COGNITIVE AND BEHAVIORAL THEORIES OF MOTIVATION

Using knowledge about human motivation to shape behavior in an organization raises some ethical questions. Consider the following questions; your personal ethical system will guide your answers.

- Should managers tell employees that they will try to affect their behavior by using specific motivational approaches?
- Is it ethical to deliberately create a condition of perceived negative inequity with the purpose of forcing an employee out of the organization?
- Should managers use their knowledge of human motivation to influence people's behavior in an ethical direction?
- Should that effort include punishment? Some limited evidence suggests that punishment can deter others from behaving unethically.[52]

Some empirical research suggests that a person's ethical system is related to responses to felt inequity. Act utilitarians (see Chapter 3, "Ethics and Behavior in Organizations") likely will respond to perceived negative inequity more strongly than others. Their ethical views increase their sensitivity to inequitable reward distribution.[53]

The ethical debates about behavior modification focus on three questions. First, should humans be subjected to the type of control offered by behavior modification? Second, who will control the people doing the controlling? Third, what are the ends (or purposes) of the control?

Is it right for managers to use behavior modification to shape and direct (control) the subordinates' behavior? The critics have said no.[54] B. F. Skinner, the primary researcher of behavior modification, responded to this issue by noting that the idea of no control is an illusion. Aspects of people's environments have always controlled their behavior. Behavior modification offers a positive alternative (positive reinforcement) to the widespread use of negative forms of control (punishment).[55]

Skinner also raised the notion of "counter control."[56] The use of behavior modification is not unilateral. If the target person does not respond to the arrangement of consequences by the "controller," the consequences must be rearranged and tried again. In this sense, the controller and the person being controlled interact. The target of the control can actually control the behavior of the person doing the controlling.

Who will control those doing the controlling?[57] This difficult issue does not have a foolproof answer. All managers in organizations, including senior executives, are subject to control by stockholders or government legislation. Counter control, as described earlier, also dampens the direct effects of behavior modification.

Few doubt that behavior modification can be used for evil or good ends. If you use behavior modification, you must decide, based on your values, whether you have ethical goals. A strong supporter of behavior modification addressed this issue as follows:

> From an ethical standpoint, it is imperative that every prospective user of [behavior modification] consider the ultimate ends of its use in terms of the general well-being of society rather than from solely the myopic standpoint of "will it sell?"[58]

SUMMARY

SUMMARY 8

This chapter focused on motivation from two perspectives: one perspective was external to the individual, and the other was internal. Expectancy theory explains different internal states of the process of motivation. The effort–performance expectancy is the perceived connection between an individual's effort and performance. Both individual and organizational blockages reduce the belief that a person's effort will lead to a given level of performance. A second expectancy describes the perceived connection between performance and the outcomes for performance. The performance–outcome expectancy is a person's belief that performance will be followed by one or more extrinsic or intrinsic outcomes. Of great importance is the valence, or value, put on those outcomes. Managers need to focus on what subordinates value for their performance and then reward good performance with valued outcomes.

Equity theory showed us that a manager must be careful when using extrinsic outcomes for job performance. If a person feels inequitably treated in comparison to someone else, the individual might decrease performance or leave the organization.

Goal setting theory describes other ways of directing and shaping a person's behavior. Goals that are specific, challenging, reachable, and accepted by a person lead to higher performance than goals that do not have those characteristics. Managers can follow the goal setting steps to improve a subordinate's performance.

Behavior modification does not use cognitive processes to describe human motivation and behavior; rather it looks outside the individual at the consequences of a person's behavior. The techniques of behavior modification center on controlling those consequences to direct and shape behavior.

U.S. scholars developed the motivation theories described in this chapter. Those theories have some underlying assumptions that reflect U.S. values of free will and individualism. The "International Aspects" section discussed whether the assumptions limit the application of these theories in countries outside the United States.

Several ethical issues emerge from the motivation theories in this chapter. The most basic issue is whether managers should tell employees that they will try to affect their behavior by various motivational approaches. Other issues derive from behavior modification because a manager, or any person, can clearly use it for good or evil ends.

REVIEW AND DISCUSSION QUESTIONS

1 What is your experience with the connection between job performance and outcomes? Were positive outcomes used more often than negative outcomes?

2 Have you experienced blockages between your effort and performance? Were they individual or organizational blockages? What form did the blockages take? What did you or your manager or supervisor do about the blockages?

3 Review the various reactions to inequity described earlier. How have you reacted to inequity in the past?

4 To whom have you compared yourself in the past when making equity comparisons? Under what circumstances have you changed your comparison *other*?

5 Discuss goal setting theory and its several steps for setting goals. Would you expect such activities to have a positive effect on your work performance?

6 Review the criticisms raised about behavior modification. Discuss those criticisms. Do those criticisms limit the use of behavior modification in organizations?

7 Review the discussion of the international aspects of the motivational theories described in this chapter.

TAKE FIVE: OB ALIVE: *MR. HOLLAND'S OPUS* (1995)

Glen Holland (Richard Dreyfuss) must set aside his passion for music composition and take a high school music teacher's position. He stays for 30 years during which time he discovers his teaching gifts and ability to motivate students.

These scenes begin with DVD Chapter 10, "New Assignment." They begin on the John F. Kennedy High School's football field with Mr. Holland trying to focus his marching band. The scenes end after

Lou Russ (Terrence Howard) successfully plays the bass drum (Stop: DVD Chapter 11, "Challenged," 0:53:54).

Use the following questions as guides while viewing the scenes: How does Mr. Holland motivate Lou Russ to play the drum? Does he make gradual or large changes in Lou Russ' behavior? Assess Lou Russ' self-esteem at the beginning and end of these scenes.

REFERENCES AND NOTES

REFERENCES
AND NOTES
8

1. See the following sources for summaries of much of the content of this book's three motivation chapters: Kanfer, R., M. Frese, and R. E. Johnson. 2017. Motivation Related to Work: A Century of Progress. *Journal of Applied Psychology* 102: 338–55. Steers, R. M., R. T. Mowday, and D. L. Shapiro. 2004. The Future of Work Motivation Theory. *Academy of Management Review* 28: 379–87.

2. See Bartol, K. M., and C. C. Durham. 2000. Incentives: Theory and Practice. In *Industrial and Organizational Psychology: Linking Theory with Practice*, ed. C. L. Copper and E. A. Locke. Malden, MA: Blackwell Business, Chap. 1. This reference has an excellent summary of the three theories introduced at the opening of this chapter. It includes a discussion of incentives and rewards in the context of those theories.

3. Lawler, E. E., III. 1970. Job Attitudes and Employee Motivation: Theory, Research, and Practice. *Personnel Psychology* 23: 223–37.
Porter, L. W., and E. E. Lawler, III. 1968. *Managerial Attitudes and Performance*. Homewood: Richard D. Irwin.
Vroom, V. H. 1964. *Work and Motivation*. New York: John Wiley & Sons.

4. Ambrose, M. L., and C. T. Kulik. 1999. Old Friends, New Faces: Motivation Research in the 1990s. *Journal of Management* 25: 231–76.
Garland, H. 1984. Relation of Effort-Performance Expectancy to Performance in Goal Setting Experiments. *Journal of Applied Psychology* 69: 79–84.
Garland, H. 1985. A Cognitive Mediation Theory of Task Goals and Human Performance. *Motivation and Emotion* 9: 345–67.
Heneman, H. G., III, and D. P. Schwab. 1972. Evaluation of Research on Expectancy Theory Predictions of Employee Performance. *Psychological Bulletin* 78: 1–9.
House, R. J., H. J. Shapiro, and M. A. Wahba. 1974. Expectancy Theory as a Predictor of Work Behavior and Attitudes: A Reevaluation of Empirical Evidence. *Decision Sciences* 5: 481–506.
Jenkins, G. D., Jr., A. Mitra, N. Gupta, and J. D. Shaw. 1998. Are Financial Incentives Related to Performance: A Meta-Analytic Review of Empirical Research. *Journal of Applied Psychology* 83: 777–87.
Kennedy, C. W., J. A. Fossum, and B. J. White. 1983. An Empirical Comparison of Within-Subjects and Between-Subjects Expectancy Theory Models. *Organizational Behavior and Human Performance* 32: 124–43.
Locke, E. A., and D. Henne. 1986. Work Motivation Theories. In *International Review of Industrial and Organizational Psychology*, ed. C. L. Cooper and I. T. Robertson. Chichester: John Wiley & Sons, Chap. 1, pp. 15–17.
Mitchell, T. R. 1974. Expectancy Models of Job Satisfaction, Occupational Preference, and Effort: A Theoretical, Methodological, and Empirical Appraisal. *Psychological Bulletin* 81: 1053–77.

Mitchell, T. R., and D. Daniels. 2003. Motivation. In *Handbook of Psychology: Industrial and Organizational Psychology*, ed. W. C. Borman, D. R. Ilgen, and R. J. Klimoski. Hoboken: John Wiley & Sons, pp. 228–29.

Murray, B., and B. Gerhart. 1998. An Empirical Analysis of a Skill-Based Pay Program and Plant Performance Outcomes. *Academy of Management Journal* 41: 68–78.

Schwab, D. P., J. D. Olian-Gottlieb, and H. G. Heneman III. 1979. Between-Subjects Expectancy Theory Research: A Statistical Review of Studies Predicting Effort and Performance. *Psychological Bulletin* 86: 139–47.

Thierry, H. 2002. Enhancing Performance through Pay and Reward Systems. In *Psychological Management of Individual Performance*, ed. S. Sonnentag. Chichester: John Wiley & Sons, Chap. 16.

Van Eerde, W., and H. Thierry. 1996. Vroom's Expectancy Models and Work-Related Criteria: A Meta-Analysis. *Journal of Applied Psychology* 81: 575–86.

5. Vroom, *Work and Motivation*, p. 17.

6. The word *performance* appears throughout the explanation of expectancy theory. You can substitute the word *behavior* if you like. The description of the theory focuses on a single class of behavior for this explanation, but this does not restrict the application of the theory.

7. Some descriptions of expectancy theory add the concept of *instrumentality* and use a different numerical notation than used here (Vroom, *Work and Motivation*). This chapter uses the modification to expectancy theory given by Porter and Lawler (*Managerial Attitudes and Performance*). No harm is done to this chapter's explanation of the theory by omitting *instrumentality*.

8. Deci, E. L. 1975. *Intrinsic Motivation*. New York: Plenum Press.
   Deci, E. L., and R. M. Ryan. 1985. *Intrinsic Motivation and Self-Determination in Human Behavior*. New York: Plenum Press, pp. 32–35.
   Pittman, T. S. 1998. Motivation. In *The Handbook of Social Psychology*, Vol. 1, ed. D. T. Gilbert, S. T. Fiske, and G. Lindzey. Boston: McGraw-Hill, pp. 566–70.
   Thomas, K. W. 2009. *Intrinsic Motivation at Work: What Really Drives Employee Engagement*. San Francisco: Berrett-Koehler Publishers.

9. Puffer, S. M. 1999. CompUSA's CEO James Halpin on Technology, Rewards, and Commitment. *Academy of Management Executive* 13: 29–36.

10. Hackman, J. R., and G. R. Oldham. 1976. Motivation through the Design of Work: Test of a Theory. *Organizational Behavior and Human Performance* 16: 250–79.
    Hackman, J. R., and G. R. Oldham. 1980. *Work Redesign*. Reading, MA: Addison-Wesley.

11. Porter and Lawler, *Managerial Attitudes and Performance*, Chap. 8.

12. Nadler, D. A., and E. E. Lawler III. 1977. Motivation: A Diagnostic Approach. In *Perspectives on Behavior in Organizations*, ed. J. R. Hackman, E. E. Lawler III, and L. W. Porter. New York: McGraw-Hill, pp. 26–38.
    Porter and Lawler, *Managerial Attitudes and Performance*, Chaps. 8, 9.

13. Chapter 17 of this text, "Organizational Design," discusses the organizational design concepts just mentioned.

14. Adams, J. S. 1963. Toward an Understanding of Inequity. *Journal of Abnormal Social Psychology* 67: 422–36.
    Adams, J. S. 1965. Inequity in Social Exchange. In *Advances in Experimental Social Psychology*, Vol. 2, ed. L. Berkowitz. New York: Academic Press, pp. 276–99.
    Cropanzano, R., and J. Greenberg. 1997. Progress in Organizational Justice: Tunneling through the Maze. In *International Review of Industrial and Organizational*

Psychology, Vol. 12, ed. C. L. Cooper and I. T. Robertson. Chichester: John Wiley & Sons, pp. 317–72.

Homans, G. C. 1958. Social Behavior as Exchange. *American Journal of Sociology* 63: 597–606.

Homans, G. C. 1961. *Social Behavior: Its Elementary Forms*. New York: Harcourt, Brace & World. Chaps. 3 and 4 give Homan's early basic argument about exchange relationships.

Kollack, P., P. Blumstein, and P. Schwartz. 1994. The Judgment of Equity in Intimate Relationships. *Social Psychology Quarterly* 57: 340–51.

Merton, R. K., and A. S. Kitt. 1950. Contributions to the Theory of Reference Group Behavior. In *Continuities in Social Research*, ed. R. K. Merton and P. F. Lazarsfeld. Glencoe, IL: Free Press, pp. 40–105. This source has an early discussion of a predecessor to equity theory. See "The Concept of Relative Deprivation," pp. 42–51.

Walster, E., G. W. Walster, and E. Berscheid. 1978. *Equity Theory and Research*. Boston: Allyn & Bacon.

15. Colquitt, J. A., D. E. Conlon, M. J. Wesson, C. O. L. H. Porter, and K. Y. Ng. 2001. Justice at the Millennium: A Meta-Analytic Review of 25 Years of Organizational Justice Research. *Journal of Applied Psychology* 86: 425–45. This review gives an excellent description of the development of thinking and research in distinguishing distributive and procedural justice.

Colquitt, J. A., and J. Greenberg. 2003. Organizational Justice: A Fair Assessment of the State of the Literature. In *Organizational Behavior: The State of the Science*, 2nd edn, ed. J. Greenberg. Mahwah: Lawrence Erlbaum Associates, Inc., Chap. 5. This source has an excellent review of the research literature on organizational justice.

Furby, L. 1986. Psychology and Justice. In *Justice: Views from the Social Sciences*, ed. R. L. Cohen. New York: Plenum Press, Chap. 6.

Leventhal, G. S. 1976. *Fairness in Social Relationships*. Morristown: General Learning Press.

Leventhal, G. S. 1980. What Should Be Done with Equity Theory? In *Social Exchanges: Advances in Theory and Research*, ed. K. J. Gergen, M. S. Greenberg, and R. H. Willis. New York: Plenum, pp. 27–55.

Sheppard, B. H., R. J. Lewicki, and J. W. Minton, 1992. *Organizational Justice: The Search for Fairness in the Workplace*. New York: Lexington Books.

Sociologist George C. Homans is among the first to note the role of distributive justice in exchange relationships. See Homans, Social Behavior as Exchange.

16. Ambrose and Kulik, Old Friends, New Faces.

Brockner, J., J. Davy, and C. Carter. 1985. Layoffs, Self-Esteem, and Survivor Guilt: Motivational, Affective, and Attitudinal Consequences. *Organizational Behavior and Human Decision Processes* 36: 229–44.

Brockner, J., J. Greenberg, A. Brockner, J. Bortz, J. Davy, and C. Carter. 1986. Layoffs, Equity Theory, and Work Performance: Further Evidence of the Impact of Survivor Guilt. *Academy of Management Journal* 29: 373–84.

Cropanzano and Greenberg, Progress in Organizational Justice.

Harris, R. J. 1983. Pinning Down the Equity Formula. In *Equity Theory: Psychological and Sociological Perspectives*, ed. D. M. Messick and K. S. Cook. New York: Praeger, pp. 207–41.

Lawler, E. E., III. 1968. Equity Theory as a Predictor of Productivity and Work Quality. *Psychological Bulletin* 70: 596–610.

Locke and Henne, Work Motivation Theories, pp. 10–12.

Masterson, S. S., K. Lewis, B. M. Goldman, and M. S. Taylor. 2000. Integrating Justice and Social Exchange: The Differing Effects of Fair Procedures and Treatment on Work Relationships. *Academy of Management Journal* 43: 738–48.

Mitchell and Daniels, Motivation, pp. 242–44.

Mowday, R. T. 1979. Equity Theory Predictions of Behavior in Organizations. In *Motivation and Work Behavior*, ed. R. M. Steers and L. W. Porter. New York: McGraw-Hill, pp. 124–46.

Robbins, T. L., T. P. Summers, and J. L. Miller. 2000. Intra- and Inter-Justice Relationships: Assessing the Direction. *Human Relations* 53: 1329–55.

Torre, E. D., M. Pelagatti, and L. Solari. 2015. Internal and External Equity in Compensation Systems, Organizational Absenteeism and the Role of Explained Inequalities. *Human Relations* 68: 409–40.

Werner, S., and N. P. Mero. 1999. Fair or Foul? The Effects of External, Internal, and Employee Equity on Changes in Performance of Major League Baseball Players. *Human Relations* 52: 1291–311.

17. Barnard, C. I. 1938. *The Functions of the Executive*. Cambridge, MA: Harvard University Press. Strong similarity exists between some elements of equity theory and Chester Barnard's concept of the inducement–contributions balance discussed in Chapter 1. In both cases, some balance (equity) must exist for the individual to accept the inducements offered for the person's contributions.

18. Lawler, Equity Theory as a Predictor of Productivity and Work Quality.

19. Greenberg, J. 1989. Cognitive Reevaluation of Outcomes in Response to Underpayment Inequity. *Academy of Management Journal* 32: 174–84.

20. Aquino, K., R. W. Griffeth, D. G. Allen, and P. W. Hom. 1997. Integrating Justice Constructs into the Turnover Process: A Test of a Referent Cognitions Model. *Academy of Management Journal* 40: 1208–27.

21. Huseman, R. C., and J. D. Hatfield. 1989. *Managing the Equity Factor*. Boston: Houghton Mifflin.

Huseman, R. C., J. D. Hatfield, and E. W. Miles. 1987. A New Perspective on Equity Theory: The Equity Sensitivity Construct. *Academy of Management Review* 12: 222–34.

Miles, E. W., J. D. Hatfield, and R. C. Huseman. 1989. The Equity Sensitivity Construct: Potential Implications for Worker Performance. *Journal of Management* 15: 581–88.

Sanley, K. S., and A. G. Bedeian. 2000. Equity Sensitivity: Construction of a Measure and Examination of its Psychometric Properties. *Journal of Management* 26: 885–910.

22. King, W. C., Jr., E. W. Miles, and D. D. Day. 1993. A Test and Refinement of the Equity Sensitivity Construct. *Journal of Organizational Behavior* 14: 301–17.

Miles, Hatfield, and Huseman, The Equity Sensitivity Construct.

Miles, E. W., J. D. Hatfield, and R. C. Huseman. 1994. Equity Sensitivity and Outcome Importance. *Journal of Organizational Behavior* 15: 585–36.

23. Ambrose and Kulik, Old Friends, New Faces.

Austin, J. T., and J. B. Vancouver. 1993. Goal Constructs in Psychology: Structure, Process, and Content. *Psychological Bulletin* 120: 338–75.

DeShon, R. P., and R. A. Alexander. 1996. Goal Setting Effects on Implicit and Explicit Learning of Complex Tasks. *Organizational Behavior and Human Decision Processes* 65: 18–36.

Kleingeld, A., H. van Mierlo, and L. Arends. 2011. The Effect of Goal Setting on Group Performance: A Meta-Analysis. *Journal of Applied Psychology* 96: 1289–304.

Latham, G. P., and E. A. Locke. 2006. Enhancing the Benefits and Overcoming the Pitfalls of Goal Setting. *Organizational Dynamics* 35: 332–40.

Latham, G. P., E. A. Locke, and N. E. Fassina. 2002. The High Performance Cycle: Standing the Test of Time. In *Psychological Management of Individual Performance*, ed. S. Sonnentag. Chichester: John Wiley & Sons, Chap. 10.

Locke, E. A., D. B. Feren, V. M. McCaleb, K. N. Shaw, and A. T. Denny. 1980. The Relative Effectiveness of Four Methods of Motivating Employee Performance. In *Changes in Working Life*, ed. K. D. Duncan, M. M. Gruneberg, and D. Wallis. London: John Wiley & Sons, pp. 363–83.

Locke and Henne, Work Motivation Theories, pp. 17–20.

Locke, E. A., and G. P. Latham. 1990. *A Theory of Goal Setting and Task Performance*. Englewood Cliffs: Prentice Hall.

Locke, E. A., and G. P. Latham. 1994. Goal Setting Theory. In *Motivation: Theory and Research*, ed. H. F. O'Neil Jr. and M. Drillings. Hillsdale: Lawrence Erlbaum Associates, pp. 1–29.

Locke, E. A., K. N. Shaw, L. M. Saari, and G. P. Latham. 1981. Goal Setting and Task Performance: 1969–1980. *Psychological Bulletin* 90: 125–52.

Miller, K. I., and P. R. Monge. 1986. Participation, Satisfaction, and Productivity: A Meta-Analytic Review. *Academy of Management Journal* 29: 727–53.

Mitchell and Daniels, Motivation, pp. 231–36.

Mitchell, T. R., K. Thompson, and J. George-Falvy. 2000. Goal Setting: Theory and Practice. In *Industrial and Organizational Psychology: Linking Theory with Practice*, ed. C. L. Cooper and E. A. Locke. Oxford: Blackwell Business, Chap. 9.

O'Leary-Kelly, A. M., J. J. Martocchio, and D. D. Frink. 1994. A Review of the Influence of Group Goals on Group Performance. *Academy of Management Journal* 37: 1285–301.

Woodford, J. C., V. L. Goodwin, and S. Premack. 1992. Meta-Analysis of the Antecedents of Personal Goal Level and of the Antecedents and Consequences of Goal Commitment. *Journal of Management* 18: 595–615.

24. Locke, Shaw, Saari, and Latham, Goal Setting and Task Performance.

25. Woodford, Goodwin, and Premack, Meta-Analysis.

26. Locke, Feren, McCaleb, Shaw, and Denny, Relative Effectiveness, pp. 363–88.

27. Lee, T. W., E. A. Locke, and S. H. Phan. 1997. Explaining the Assigned Goal-Incentive Interaction: The Role of Self-Efficacy and Personal Goals. *Journal of Management* 23: 541–59.

    Wright, P. M. 1992. An Examination of the Relationships Among Monetary Incentives, Goal Level, Goal Commitment, and Performance. *Journal of Management* 18: 677–93.

28. Wright, An Examination of the Relationships.

29. Locke and Latham, *A Theory of Goal Setting and Task Performance*.

30. Other names for the concepts in this section include *operant conditioning* and *positive reinforcement*. The phrase *behavior modification* says more completely what is being tried, especially in a management context. Developed from other references cited in this section and F. Luthans and R. Kreitner. 1985. *Organizational Behavior Modification and Beyond: An Operant and Social Learning Approach*. Glenview, IL: Scott, Foresman.

    Hamner, W. C. 1974. Reinforcement Theory. In *Organizational Behavior and Management*, ed. H. L. Tosi and W. C. Hamner. Chicago: St. Clair Press, pp. 93–112.

31. Skinner, B. F. 1953. *Science and Human Behavior*. New York: Free Press.

    Skinner, B. F. 1971. *Beyond Freedom and Dignity*. New York: Bantam.

Skinner, B. F. 1974. *About Behaviorism*. New York: Knopf.

32. Thorndike, E. L. 1913. *Educational Psychology: The Psychology of Learning*, Vol. 2. New York: Columbia University, Teachers College.

33. Ambrose and Kulik, Old Friends, New Faces.

    Luthans, F., and A. D. Stajkovic. 1999. Reinforce for Performance: The Need to Go Beyond Pay and Even Rewards. *Academy of Management Executive* 13: 49–57.

    Mitchell and Daniels, Motivation, pp. 241–42.

    Stajkovic, A. D., and F. Luthans. 1997. A Meta-Analysis of the Effects of Organizational Behavior Modification on Task Performance, 1975–95. *Academy of Management Journal* 40: 1122–49.

    Thierry, Enhancing Performance through Pay and Reward Systems, Chap. 16, pp. 329–30.

34. Hamner, Reinforcement Theory, pp. 100–1.

35. Dowling, W. F. 1973. Conversation with B. F. Skinner. *Organizational Dynamics* 1 (Winter): 31–40.

    Ferster, C. B., and B. F. Skinner. 1957. *Schedules of Reinforcement*. New York: Appleton-Century-Crofts.

36. For more details about the side effects of punishment, see Skinner, *Science and Human Behavior*, and Bandura, A. 1969. *Principles of Behavior Modification*. New York: Holt, Rinehart and Winston.

37. Nord, W. R. 1969. Beyond the Teaching Machine: The Neglected Area of Operant Conditioning in the Theory and Practice of Management. *Organizational Behavior and Human Performance* 4: 375–401.

38. Katz, R. 1980. Time and Work: Toward an Integrative Perspective. In *Research in Organizational Behavior*, Vol. 2, ed. B. Staw and L. L. Cummings. Greenwich, CT: JAI Press, pp. 81–127.

39. Arvey, R. D., and A. P. Jones. 1985. The Use of Discipline in Organizational Settings: A Framework for Future Research. In *Research in Organizational Behavior*, Vol. 7, ed. L. L. Cummings and B. M. Staw. Greenwich, CT: JAI Press, pp. 367–408.

40. Gelfund, M. J., M. Erez, and Z. Aycan. 2007. Cross-Cultural Organizational Behavior. *Annual Review of Psychology* 58: 479–514.

    Staw, B. M. 1984. Organizational Behavior: A Review and Reformulation of the Field's Outcome Variables. *Annual Review of Psychology* 35: 627–66.

41. Hofstede, G. 1980. Motivation, Leadership, and Organization: Do American Theories Apply Abroad? *Organizational Dynamics* 9: 42–63.

    Hofstede, G. 1991. *Cultures and Organizations: Software of the Mind*. New York: McGraw-Hill.

    Hofstede, G. 2001. *Culture's Consequences: Comparing Values, Behaviors, Institutions, and Organizations across Nations*, 2nd edn. Thousand Oaks: Sage Publications.

42. Adler, N. J., and A. Gundersen. 2008. *International Dimensions of Organizational Behavior*, 5th edn. Mason: Thomson South-Western, p. 190.

43. Ibid.

44. Matsui, T., and I. Terai. 1979. A Cross-Cultural Study of the Validity of the Expectancy Theory of Motivation. *Journal of Applied Psychology* 60: 263–65.

45. Welsh, D. H. B., F. Luthans, and S. M. Sommer. 1993. Managing Russian Factor Workers: The Impact of U.S.-Based Behavioral and Participative Techniques. *Academy of Management Journal* 36: 58–79.

    Welsh, D. H. B., F. Luthans, and S. M. Sommer. 1993. Organizational Behavior Modification Goes to Russia: Replicating an Experimental Analysis across Cultures and Tasks. *Journal of Organizational Behavior Management* 13: 15–33.

46. Chen, C. C. 1995. New Trends in Rewards Allocation Preferences: A Sino-U.S. Comparison. *Academy of Management Journal* 38: 408–28.

Chen, C. C., J. R. Meindl, and H. Hui. 1998. Deciding on Equity or Parity: A Test of Situational, Cultural, and Individual Factors. *Journal of Organizational Behavior* 19: 115–29.

Giacobbe-Miller, J. K., D. J. Miller, and V. I. Victorov. 1998. A Comparison of Russian and U.S. Pay Allocation Decisions, Distributive Justice Judgments, and Productivity Under Different Payment Conditions. *Personnel Psychology* 51: 137–63.

47. Fok, L. Y., S. J., Hartman, M. F. Villere, and R. C. Freibert III. 1996. A Study of the Impact of Cross Cultural Differences on Perceptions of Equity and Organizational Citizenship Behavior. *International Journal of Management* 13: 3–14. This study has methodological limitations. Its results suggest the possibility that some Chinese people have a benevolent equity sensitivity orientation.

Rusbult, C. E., C. A. Insko, and Y.-H. W. Lin. 1995. Seniority-Based Reward Allocation in the United States and Taiwan. *Social Psychology Quarterly* 58: 13–30.

Zhou, J., and J. J. Martocchio. 2001. Chinese and American Managers' Compensation Award Decisions: A Comparative Policy Capturing Study. *Personnel Psychology* 54: 115–46.

48. Mueller, S. L., and L. D. Clarke. 1998. Political-Economic Context and Sensitivity to Equity: Differences Between the United States and the Transition Economies of Central and Eastern Europe. *Academy of Management Journal* 41: 319–29.

49. Locke and Latham, *A Theory of Goal Setting and Task Performance*, p. 43.

Locke and Latham, Goal Setting Theory, p. 16.

50. Erez, M., and P. C. Earley. 1987. Comparative Analysis of Goal Setting Strategies Across Cultures. *Journal of Applied Psychology* 72: 658–65.

51. Hofstede, Motivation, Leadership, and Organization, pp. 56–59.

52. Treviño, L. K. 1992. The Social Effects of Punishment in Organizations: A Justice Perspective. *Academy of Management Review* 17: 647–76.

Treviño, L. K., and G. A. Ball. 1992. The Social Implications of Punishing Unethical Behavior: Observer's Cognitive and Affective Reactions. *Journal of Management* 18: 751–68.

53. Schminke, M., M. L. Ambrose, and T. W. Noel. 1997. The Effect of Ethical Frameworks on Perceptions of Organizational Justice. *Academy of Management Journal* 40: 1190–207.

54. Locke, E. A. 1977. The Myths of Behavior Mod in Organizations. *Academy of Management Review* 2: 543–53.

Locke, E. A. 1979. Myths in "The Myths about Behavior Mod in Organizations." *Academy of Management Review* 4: 131–36.

55. Rogers, C. R., and B. F. Skinner. 1956. Some Issues Concerning the Control of Human Behavior: A Symposium. *Science* 124: 1057–66.

56. Kreitner, R. 1982. Controversy in OBM: History, Misconceptions, and Ethics. In *Handbook of Organizational Behavior Management*, ed. L. Frederiksen. New York: John Wiley & Sons, pp. 71–91.

57. Ibid., p. 89.

58. Ibid., p. 88.

Chapter 9

JOB DESIGN AND INTRINSIC REWARDS

After reading this chapter, you should be able to:

- Discuss the role of job design in giving people opportunities to experience intrinsic rewards.
- Describe the major job design theories.
- Analyze how the work context affects people's reaction to the design of their jobs.
- Explain the process of diagnosing and redesigning jobs.
- Compare individual job design to group job design.
- Identify some international aspects of job design and intrinsic rewards.
- Discuss ethical issues that surround job design and intrinsic rewards.

The design of a job can strongly affect a person's motivation and satisfaction.[1] The previous chapters on motivation spent much time discussing the role of extrinsic rewards in developing and guiding human behavior in organizations. Those theories of motivation suggested the importance of both extrinsic and intrinsic rewards in human motivation.[2] The conditions under which people experience the two types of rewards differ from each other.

This chapter also focuses on how organizations and managers can create a context within which employees experience intrinsic rewards. Although managers use extrinsic rewards directly, they have only indirect control over intrinsic rewards. A manager cannot tell an employee to experience intrinsic rewards such as self-esteem or self-actualization. The manager can only create a context or set of job experiences that lets the employee experience intrinsic rewards.

JOB DESIGN AND INTRINSIC REWARDS

The primary method of designing jobs well into the twentieth century used task specialization. People did small tasks repeatedly. Although such jobs could be done more efficiently, there also were many human costs (dysfunctions). Jobs that had small, repeated tasks created boredom and dissatisfaction among those doing the jobs.[3] By the early 1940s, different methods of work redesign emerged to reduce the negative effects of high specialization.[4]

Job rotation moved the same worker among different jobs. Each job often had few tasks or activities. Proponents believed a worker became less bored by doing many different activities in a day or week. **Job enlargement** added duties and tasks to a job. People did not move from one job to another as they did with job rotation. Instead, duties and tasks were repackaged to make an individual's job larger. Two or more jobs were combined into a single new job. The duties, tasks, or jobs usually were at the same level. **Job enrichment** also repackaged duties, but increased worker autonomy, responsibility, and decision-making involvement.[5]

The three approaches to job design had two major characteristics. All tried to enhance the content of a person's job to increase satisfaction and decrease boredom. Because job enrichment required the addition of the "motivators" described by Herzberg's motivator-hygiene theory (see Chapter 7, "Motivation:

Need Theories"),[6] employee motivation was expected to increase. The high motivation also should lead to higher job performance and productivity.

A second characteristic was the assumption of a positive linear relationship between job design and employee attitudes, motivation, and performance. By increasing the activities a person did (job rotation and job enlargement), or increasing the responsibility and autonomy of the worker (job enrichment), a positive response should follow. It became clear by the 1960s that such a universal, positive, linear response would not be the case for all people.[7] The next section describes a major theory of job design and motivation that does not include this assumption.

THE JOB CHARACTERISTICS THEORY OF WORK MOTIVATION

The job characteristics theory of work motivation is a well-developed and well-understood job design theory.[8] It is a cognitive theory with many similarities to the cognitive motivation theories described in Chapter 8. With some exceptions noted later, empirical research supports many parts of the theory.[9]

The theory says that the design of a person's job produces two major classes of outcomes. Affective outcomes are the individual's internal reactions to a job's design such as job satisfaction and motivation. Behavioral outcomes are observed employee behavior such as individual productivity and quality of work. The theory expects high levels of behavioral outcomes to follow high levels of affective outcomes, especially motivation.

People experience a set of critical psychological states that produce positive affective and behavioral outcomes. The characteristics of a job induce the critical psychological states. People have perceptions about the objective qualities of their jobs, such as tasks, duties, responsibilities, activities, and the like. The theory uses those perceptions to explain the presence and level of the critical psychological states.

The perceived job characteristics, critical psychological states, and affective outcomes are factors internal to a person. Both the objective job characteristics and the behavioral outcomes are external to a person. The theory is strongly cognitive in its explanation of people's reactions to their jobs. It includes direct connections, however, to aspects external to the person. Those external factors are important to fully understand people's responses to work design.

Figure 9.1 shows the structure of the job characteristics theory of work motivation. The following sections describe each group of variables in the figure.

Affective and Behavioral Outcomes

The theory predicts that the design of a person's job will produce several affective and behavioral outcomes.[10] The affective outcomes are internal work motivation, growth satisfaction, and general job satisfaction. The figure shows the behavioral outcomes as work effectiveness, which refers to the quality

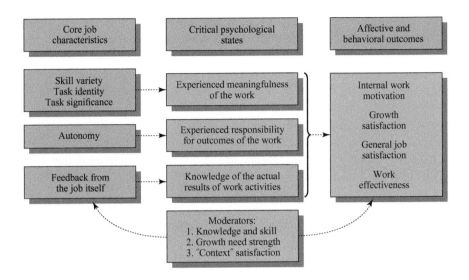

Figure 9.1: Job Characteristics Theory of Work Motivation

of a person's work performance and the quantity of work produced. Some research suggests adding lower absenteeism to work effectiveness.[11] The design of a person's job can add to or detract from work effectiveness. Other research notes the connection between job design, emotional exhaustion, and stress.[12]

Work effectiveness is the behavioral outcome most closely associated with internal work motivation. **Internal work motivation** is a feeling of self-reward from doing the job itself. Think of it as intrinsic motivation,[13] an idea closely tied to the intrinsic rewards you saw in the Chapter 8 discussion of expectancy theory. That chapter described how a person's job performance could lead to intrinsic rewards. Those intrinsic rewards are central to internal work motivation. A person who does a job well experiences intrinsic rewards, which then reinforce the work behavior. They act as a form of self-propulsion, causing the person to want to continue to do the job well. A person who experiences high internal work motivation should show high work effectiveness. The opposite also is true.

Growth satisfaction is associated with a person's chances of experiencing personal growth and development from the work itself. If the job design allows such opportunities, we expect a high degree of growth satisfaction. Jobs that produce feelings of high internal work motivation and result in high work effectiveness should also provide opportunities for personal growth and development and the resulting growth satisfaction.

The last affective outcome is **general job satisfaction**, or a person's overall feelings about work and the work organization. Although many other factors affect those feelings, the job is a basic connection between a person and the employing organization. Consequently, a person's job has some effect on feelings of overall job satisfaction.

Critical Psychological States

For a job to produce high levels of the affective and behavioral outcomes, the individual must experience three critical psychological states:

■ **Experienced meaningfulness of the work:** The person doing the job must experience the work as important. Work perceived as unimportant by the person doing the job is not likely to produce high levels of affective and behavioral response.

■ **Experienced responsibility for outcomes of the work:** A person must also control the outcomes of his work activities. If the employee believes external factors such as coworkers, equipment, or the supervisor were responsible for job outcomes, he likely will not feel particularly good about having done a good job or feel particularly bad about having done a poor job.

■ **Knowledge of the actual results of work activities:** The person must know how well or how poorly he is doing while doing the work itself. Neither positive nor negative feelings will result if the individual does not know the results of work activities.

A job where the employee controls the results of meaningful work and learns about how he is doing while doing the job should produce a positive response. The theory asserts that all three critical psychological states must be present to produce the highest level of positive affective and behavioral outcome. Some empirical research, however, has shown that all three do not need to be present to get the predicted effects.[14]

Perceived and Objective Job Characteristics

The following description divides job characteristics into two groups: perceived and objective. The job characteristics theory does not carefully distinguish perceived from objective job characteristics. There are good practical and theoretical reasons, however, to make the distinction.[15]

Five **core job characteristics** must be present to produce the critical psychological states. People have perceptions of the objective characteristics of their jobs that form their impressions of the core job characteristics. The following are the five core job characteristics used by the theory:[16]

■ **Skill variety:** The degree to which the job has many different activities using several of a person's skills, abilities, and talents.

■ **Task identity:** The degree to which the job lets a person do a whole piece of work from start to finish.

■ **Task significance:** The degree to which the person doing the job perceives it as important to others in the organization or clients of the organization.

■ **Autonomy:** The degree of a person's discretion in deciding how and when to do the job.

▪ **Feedback from the job itself:** The degree to which the person learns about the quality of his job performance while doing the task. Feedback comes from clients directly served by the job, but not from a supervisor or coworkers.

Objective job characteristics are associated with perceived job characteristics, although the association is not direct. A job that appears simple and routine to an outsider might not appear that way to the person doing the job. The chapter later discusses the factors affecting the connection between objective and perceived job characteristics.

The five core job characteristics are not equally related to the critical psychological states. Skill variety, task identity, and task significance are associated with experienced meaningfulness of the work. If these job characteristics are present, the person could experience the work as meaningful. All three characteristics do not need to be present to induce a state of meaningfulness. The three job characteristics associated with experienced meaningfulness can have offsetting effects among themselves. For example, a job that is not perceived as significant can be a whole job, using many skills and abilities. Such a job should be meaningful to the person doing the job.

The remaining two core job characteristics are related to different psychological states. Jobs high in autonomy should produce a feeling of personal responsibility for the outcomes of the work. Jobs that give feedback while doing the job should let the person know the actual results of work activities.

The concept of **motivating potential** summarizes the effect of the five core job characteristics on the critical psychological states. The following formula shows how the theory expects the job characteristics to combine to result in some level of motivating potential for a job:[17]

$$\begin{array}{c} \text{Motivating} \\ \text{Potential} \\ \text{Score} \\ \text{(MPS)} \end{array} = \left[\dfrac{\text{Skill variety} + \text{Task identity} + \text{Task significance}}{3} \right] \times \text{Autonomy} \times \begin{array}{c} \text{Feedback} \\ \text{from} \\ \text{the job} \\ \text{itself} \end{array}$$

The formula emphasizes the strong effect autonomy and feedback from the job itself can have on motivating potential. The theory does not expect a job low in autonomy or in job-related feedback to produce high levels of affective or behavioral response. Figure 9.1, shown earlier, shows the reasons for this effect. Autonomy and job feedback are related to two of the three psychological states, experienced responsibility and knowledge of results. Low levels of those psychological states are associated with low affective and behavioral response.

The results of some well-designed empirical research suggest this portion of the job characteristics theory might need modification in the future.[18] One study found interactions between the job characteristics. For example, the interaction between autonomy and variety in a complex job led to higher performance. Changing the pace and order of work in a complex job helps a person perform better. This was not true for simple tasks.[19] If future researchers duplicate these results, the theory likely will need modification.

Relationships Predicted by the Theory

Figure 9.2 shows the relationships predicted by the theory. On the left side of the figure is the positive relationship expected between motivating potential and internal work motivation. Jobs high in motivating potential should produce higher internal work motivation than jobs low in motivating potential.[20]

Note the use of the word *potential* in the preceding paragraph. Jobs high in motivating potential offer a person the likelihood of experiencing high levels of motivation and satisfaction. Incumbents of such jobs should also perceive the jobs as meaningful and important. There is always a chance that other factors within the person or within the work context will block the job's potential.

The theory includes the moderator variables shown earlier at the bottom of Figure 9.1 to accommodate blockages that can inhibit a job's motivating potential. Those variables are called moderators because they change or affect the relationships among parts of the theory. Some factors are in the person (individual moderators); others surround the person while doing the job (work context moderators). Each variable allows for differences in the way people respond to the motivating potential of their jobs. The theory, therefore, does not assume a universal, positive response to jobs high in motivating potential.

Figure 9.1 shows three moderator variables: knowledge and skill, growth need strength, and satisfaction with the context of the job. The right side of Figure 9.2 shows the change in the relationship between motivating potential and internal work motivation expected from these variables.

Assume a person is trying to do a job high in motivating potential. Because of its high motivating potential, the person could perceive the job as meaningful and important. A person with the needed skills and abilities should do that job successfully. High motivating potential combines with the person's knowledge and skill to produce high internal work motivation. A person without the required skills and abilities should not do the job as successfully as a person

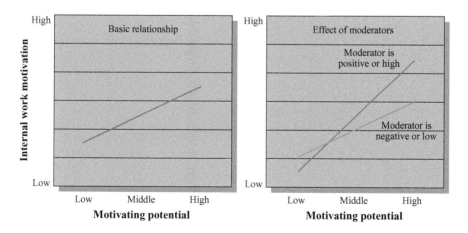

Figure 9.2: Relationships Predicted by the Job Characteristics Theory of Work Motivation

with the needed skills and abilities. In this case, the person is failing at a job perceived as meaningful and important. This combination produces a low level of internal work motivation.

People's needs can also affect their reaction to job design. Some people have strong needs for personal growth, development, and learning from the job.[21] Others have weak needs for such growth. Such desires for growth and development from the job are characteristic of people with strong needs for achievement or self-actualization as discussed in Chapter 7.

The concept of **growth need strength (GNS)** captures the variability in growth needs among different people. People with strong growth needs should respond more positively to jobs high in motivating potential than people with weak growth needs. Individuals with strong growth needs are more "ready" to respond to the motivating potential of a job than people with weak growth needs. Individuals with weak growth needs can be "stretched" by the demands of a job high in motivating potential. They would find such work experiences stressful and not do as well as someone with strong growth needs.

The last set of moderators focuses on the work context (**context satisfaction** as shown earlier in Figure 9.1), which includes quality of supervision, the compensation system, job security, and immediate coworkers. A negative work context distracts a person from experiencing the qualities of a high motivating potential job. A person working in a positive work context would perceive it as supportive, letting the person experience the job's motivating qualities.

The right side of Figure 9.2 summarizes the expected moderating effect of the three sets of variables. The relationship between motivating potential and internal work motivation (or performance and satisfaction) is still positive. If a moderator variable is positive, the theory predicts a more positive response to a level of motivating potential than when a moderator variable is negative. The line with the steeper slope shows the form of this moderating effect. When a moderator variable is negative, the theory predicts a less positive response to the motivating potential of the job. The line with the shallower slope shows the latter relationship.

The expected moderating effects have not had consistent empirical support.[22] The moderating effect of skill has not been studied. One study found that knowledge, as assessed by education level, has an opposite moderating effect. Managers with less education had more favorable affective responses than those with more education.[23] Various studies did not always find the moderating effects of GNS or failed to find them in the form the theory predicts.

Moderating effects of the context satisfactions also have not always appeared as predicted.[24] The theory expects a negative work context to distract a person from experiencing the intrinsic motivating qualities of a job with a high motivating potential score (MPS). Empirical research about this part of the theory has had mixed results.[25] Some research has supported the predictions of the theory.[26] Other research has suggested an opposite effect.[27] The research evidence suggests two different reactions to a negative work context: the distraction effect suggested by the theory and an escape effect where people turn to the job to escape a negative work context.[28]

The job characteristics theory carries direct implications for you, depending on your valence for extrinsic and intrinsic outcomes (Chapter 8). If you desire intrinsic outcomes, jobs designed according to the job characteristics theory should be a source of satisfaction and motivation for you. If you desire extrinsic outcomes, the opposite conclusion is true. The intrinsic motivational qualities are less important to you than the extrinsic outcomes you receive for good performance.

CONTEXTUAL FACTORS IN JOB DESIGN

Contextual factors such as organizational design, work process technologies, and management behavior can affect the designs of people's jobs and their reaction to them.[29] Figure 9.3 shows the context factors discussed in the following sections.

Organizational Design and Job Design

A major feature of organizational design that affects job design is the degree of specialization the organization has chosen for its division of labor. Highly specialized tasks tend to have low core job characteristics, resulting in low motivating potential. Less specialized tasks will be higher in the job characteristics and higher in motivating potential. You can easily see the differences between assembly-line work and a manager's job.

Organizations with centralized decision-making processes restrict the scope of decision making and responsibility of individuals lower in the organization. Centralized decision making yields jobs low in skill variety and autonomy. The person might also do only a small part of a larger task, reducing task identity. Lastly, if the individual does not make important decisions because they are made at a higher level, task significance can also be reduced. You probably can

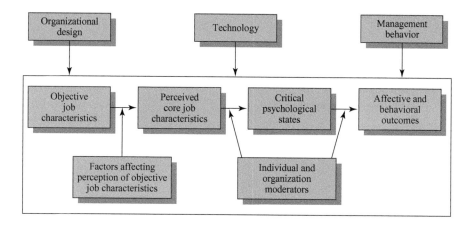

■ **Figure 9.3:** Context Factors and the Job Characteristics Theory of Work Motivation

see the effect those actions have on motivating potential and the resultant levels of motivation, performance, and satisfaction.

Organizations with decentralized decision-making processes have the opposite effect on job characteristics and motivating potential. Employees might perceive their jobs as being more significant, having more wholeness (task identity), and allowing more autonomy. Motivating potential could be higher than it is in a centralized organization.

Technical Process and Job Design

The **technical process** of an organization is the major way the organization's work gets done. The nature of the process affects the characteristics of a person's job[30] by either impeding or helping job design. Large capital investment in an existing technical process can limit job redesign. The cost of changing a physical facility or replacing an existing manufacturing process often prevents managers from considering new ways of designing jobs. On the other hand, adopting a particular technical process can help work redesign. A company that adopts a group-based technical process can redesign jobs to take advantage of that technology.[31]

Mass-production technical processes usually have highly standardized jobs. Such jobs are routine, not highly skilled, and individually are a small piece of a larger set of activities. Skill variety, task identity, task significance, autonomy, and feedback from the job could be low. In contrast, technologies that do custom-designed work have jobs that are nonstandard, not narrowly defined, and not repetitive. All core job characteristics and motivating potential could be high.

Many manufacturing companies have changed their manufacturing approaches by adopting flexible manufacturing techniques, robotics, group-based manufacturing, and just-in-time inventory management.[32] Each approach could require or induce changes in job design of those working in such systems.[33]

Flexible manufacturing techniques let companies respond quickly to changing customer requirements. Such technologies require worker flexibility, which can increase the skill variety and autonomy of their jobs.

Group-based manufacturing technologies need jobs designed around groups of people, not individuals. You will read about many aspects of group-based job design later in this chapter.

Just-in-time inventory management removes buffers from within the technical process. The tighter links among parts of the technical process require workers to respond quickly to any disruptions in the manufacturing process.[34] Such responses call for jobs designed with more skill variety, autonomy, and feedback from the job.

Management Behavior and Job Design

A **manager's behavior** can affect the design of a subordinate's job.[35] Managers using close control over subordinates (close supervision) narrow the scope of a subordinate's work. The subordinate's job becomes narrowly defined with little decision-making discretion. Under those circumstances, low skill variety, task identity, and autonomy are expected. Managers using general control and delegation of decision-making authority have the opposite effect on a subordinate's job. Skill variety, task identity, and autonomy should all increase under such circumstances.

Managers who involve their subordinates in the decision-making process will affect many job characteristics.[36] Involvement in decision making requires subordinates to use previously unused skills and abilities. Such involvement can show a person the importance of their role in the organization. Because involvement can increase the employees' commitment to the decision, the manager can allow employees more discretion in carrying out the decision. When a manager increases employees' participation in decisions, skill variety, task significance, and autonomy of subordinates' jobs can increase.

DIAGNOSING AND REDESIGNING JOBS

Jobs in organizations can be diagnosed to decide whether they should be redesigned. The safest approach to job redesign uses a theoretical orientation to guide the questions that need to be asked about jobs in any organization.[37] This chapter developed a conceptual framework that should prove useful in that task.

The first step in any redesign program is getting information about the existing state of jobs in the organization. The information should be collected by multiple measurement methods. Questionnaires can be used and supplemented with personal interviews and direct observations.

One questionnaire that can be used is the **job diagnostic survey (JDS)**.[38] Norms are available for many job types, allowing the results from one organization to be compared to the results for similar jobs in other organizations.

Data collected with the JDS will show the overall MPS of individual jobs, the job characteristics, and affective responses. The MPS can be compared to norms to decide whether a job has an excessively low score, and then the job characteristics that are responsible for that low MPS can be identified.

The JDS also gives information about employee GNS and levels of work context satisfaction. If a job is a target for a redesign activity, the GNS should be examined to decide whether employees in that job are ready to respond to a redesigned job (high GNS). The context satisfactions give important information about whether employees perceive a positive work context. Although the JDS does not measure employee knowledge and skills, any job redesign activity must consider whether employees have the needed knowledge and skills to do the redesigned work. If they do not, it may be necessary to include a training program with the job redesign program.

The employees who provide the data should see the results to verify their accuracy. Asking employees to suggest ways to redesign their jobs can also yield useful information.

GROUP-BASED JOB DESIGN

Up to this point, the discussion has focused on job design for individual employees of an organization. Some tasks, however, are better done by groups of people than by individuals. Such groups are known as self-managing workgroups or self-managing teams. Chapter 10, "Groups and Intergroup Processes," discusses such teams in more detail.

A **self-managing workgroup**[39] has three characteristics. First, it is an intact group, whether permanent or temporary, whose members are interdependent while doing the group's tasks. Both members and nonmembers perceive the group as real. Second, the group produces a defined product, service, or decision. Third, group members control the group's tasks and interpersonal processes. They have the authority to make task assignments within the group and decide how and when to do the work. This third characteristic of the group is the major source of its self-managing quality.

The problem for the organization is to design both the group's task and some aspects of the group. Chapter 10 gives you other information about groups important for group-based job design.

Design of the Task and the Group

Designing jobs for a group is done in much the same way as for individuals. Each core job characteristic is still necessary, but it is now defined for a group task, not an individual task. Skill variety requires the group to use many different skills in doing the task. The task must still be a whole task (task identity) that the members of the group perceive as important to others (task significance). The group task must give group members discretion in getting the work done (autonomy). This discretion includes task assignments within the group, the group's work processes, and the setting of priorities for the tasks of the group. The group's work should give feedback to members while doing the task (feedback from the job itself). As you can see, the elements used in designing a group task are much the same as the job characteristics of an individual task.

One important element to consider in designing the group is its composition. Members of the group must have the skills and abilities needed for task performance. The size of the group is important. If the group is too large, the group process becomes inefficient and productivity will be lower than desired.[40] There is no formula for finding the optimal size of the group. Careful analysis of the task requirements usually will show how many people the group needs.

The self-managing characteristic of the group and the degree of autonomy designed into the group's task require group members to have the interpersonal skills needed to manage the interpersonal processes in such activities. A balance also must be struck between the heterogeneity and homogeneity of group members. If the people in the group are different from each other, managing the interpersonal processes might be more difficult than if the members are similar to each other. A group whose members are similar in background and perspective, however, might be less likely to find creative solutions to work problems. Highly homogeneous, enduring groups often suffer from groupthink, a phenomenon that blocks the discovery of creative solutions by the group.[41]

People who work together in a group develop norms about how to do the work and how much work to do. Those norms are rules of conduct that can control the behavior of group members. The problem for management is to encourage norms consistent with the group's task and the desired level of productivity. The goal is to help build a climate that encourages open discussion of existing and developing group norms. From this process, members of the group can learn that it is all right to discuss and change the group's performance norms.

What Are the Expectations for Group-Based Jobs?

Properly designed groups and group-based jobs can produce several desirable results. The presence of the core job characteristics, adjusted for a group work process, can lead to high levels of effort, motivation, and performance. The composition of the group, its size, individual skills and abilities, and balance between heterogeneity and homogeneity can lead to a high level of knowledge and skill to do the group's work. Individual members of the group also can feel good about their membership in the group and feel satisfied with their experiences in the group. The accumulated research evidence shows sizable positive effects of group-based job design compared to individual job design.[42]

Self-managing workgroups can develop such strong norms that group members try to control each other's behavior.[43] Positive performance norms help focus members on successfully completing the group's tasks. Strong behavioral norms also focus group members on quickly discovering ways of successfully dealing with work problems the group might face.

Individual and Contextual Considerations

As with individual job design, the organization must consider several individual and contextual characteristics before trying group-based job design. If the individual and contextual characteristics do not support a group approach, success with group-based job design is unlikely.

Group-based job design makes more interpersonal demands on individuals than does individual job design. Chapter 7 described how the importance of people's social needs can vary. The most likely candidates for a group-based approach are people with strong needs for affiliation. Such people should enjoy the interpersonal processes found in a self-managing workgroup. The individuals in a group should also have strong growth needs. Such needs show a readiness to respond to the design of the group's task. Strongly affiliative people with weak growth needs can find the group attractive, more because of the social interaction than because of the intrinsic qualities of the group's tasks. For this reason, individuals who have both strong growth needs and strong social needs are highly desirable.

The organization's reward system is a contextual feature that can affect team performance. Research evidence suggests managers need to consider reward system design when moving toward group-based job design. An interdependent reward system, where each person's payoffs depend on the performance of other group members, is associated with significantly higher performance levels than less interdependent rewards.[44]

FACTORS AFFECTING PERCEPTIONS OF OBJECTIVE JOB CHARACTERISTICS

The job characteristics theory has not always been clear on whether the core job characteristics are the "objective" characteristics of the job or those perceived by the job incumbent.[45] The social context of a person doing a job affects his perception of the job's objective features. Therefore, a person's perceptions of job characteristics are not necessarily an accurate picture of the job's objective features. As Chapter 5, "Perception, Attitudes, and Personality," described, perceptions can strongly affect people's behavior.[46]

Social information processing theory is an alternative to the job characteristics theory.[47] This view holds that interactions with other people affect a person's perceptions of job characteristics. For example, social interactions with coworkers and supervisors can lead a person to cognitively develop a view of a job's characteristics. Informational cues about the task can come from either present or previous coworkers. They may describe the job in positive or negative terms, affecting the current incumbent's perception of the job.[48] This socially constructed view might not be the same as the "objective" features of the job.

The social information processing view of task design has the following implications for those considering job redesign:[49]

- ▦ Participation in the job design process might produce feelings of high satisfaction independent of any job design changes.
- ▦ Using the JDS, or any other questionnaire, before changing the design of jobs can sensitize people to certain job characteristics they had not previously noticed.
- ▦ Perceptions of job characteristics can be manipulated by the social information made available to employees by managers and coworkers in the organization.

Research focused on social information processing theory has produced mixed results. Some early studies supported the theory's predictions while others did not.[50] Other research shows that employee perceptions accurately represent objective job characteristics.[51]

A conservative conclusion points to social information processing theory as a complement to job characteristics theory.[52] The largest change in perceptions of job characteristics and satisfaction can occur in the presence of both changes in the objective job characteristics (job redesign) and oral cues by supervisors.[53]

Information given to employees about the design of their jobs, and the favorable effects of that information on their task perceptions, can be important elements in a job redesign activity.[54]

INTERNATIONAL ASPECTS OF JOB DESIGN

The "International Aspects" section of Chapter 7 emphasized differences in the motivational needs that are driving forces in different countries. For example, people in the United States emphasize self-actualization, people in France stress a need for security, and people in Scandinavian countries emphasize belonging-ness and love (social) needs.[55] Two implications follow from those cultural differences. Because all cultures do not view self-actualization from work experiences as important, striving for intrinsic rewards from job redesign does not apply to all cultures. Another implication is that cultural differences should guide the choice of individual-based or group-based approaches.

U.S. managers have mostly used individual-based approaches to job design, although that emphasis has shifted in the quest to manage for quality. Managers in other countries have mainly emphasized group-based job design. Swedish and Norwegian managers in particular have restructured their work systems around self-managing workgroups,[56] an approach consistent with their more socially oriented values, desire for quality interpersonal relationships, and little emphasis on competition among people.[57]

Changing specific job characteristics also is likely to lead to different reactions in different cultures. For example, efforts to increase autonomy and task identity are not likely to be accepted in countries such as Belgium, Mexico, Greece, Thailand, Turkey, and France. French managers in particular dislike recommendations to decentralize their decision authority and their subordinates do not expect them to do so.[58]

ETHICAL ISSUES IN JOB DESIGN

Self-managing workgroups raise some ethical questions for two reasons: (1) people with a low need for affiliation might have little desire for group-based work; and (2) some people might not want high involvement in their work roles, preferring high involvement in nonwork roles instead.[59] Those reasons imply at least two ethical questions. Should involvement in such groups be voluntary for those already employed by a company? Should job applicants be fully informed about the company's use of groups and teams and the likelihood of a team assignment if they are hired?

Multinational and transnational organizations face ethical issues that derive from the cultures in which they operate. As Chapter 7 described, people around the world differ in the needs they consider central to their personalities and lives. People in many countries do not readily accept decentralizing decision authority. They perceive decision making as the proper role of managers, not nonmanagers.

This orientation is especially true of Mexico, many South American countries, India, Hong Kong, and Singapore. Swedish and Austrian employees, however, expect high involvement in decision making.[60] Should managers honor the host national culture, or should they adhere to their home organization's emphasis on self-managing workgroups?

SUMMARY

SUMMARY

9

The job characteristics theory of work motivation describes how the design of jobs affects motivation, performance, and satisfaction. The theory specifies several core job characteristics that can affect three internal psychological states and induce high levels of motivation and performance.

The theory includes both individual and work context factors that can affect (moderate) the expected positive relationships between job characteristics and levels of motivation and performance. The strength of a person's need for growth on the job must be strong for a high positive response to the job's characteristics. Many other factors in the work context can help or hinder job design such as an organization's design, its technical process, and management behavior.

The diagnosis and redesign of jobs start by getting information about the present state of jobs using a questionnaire similar to the job diagnostic survey (JDS). Data collected with the JDS show the job's motivating potential score (MPS), the core job characteristics, and affective responses. The MPS can be compared to norms to decide whether a job has an excessively low score, and then the job characteristics that are responsible for that low MPS can be identified.

Jobs can be designed either for groups or for individuals. The basic approach is the same for each. Other factors considered in group-based job design include internal group dynamics and group norms. Countries differ in whether they emphasize individual-based or group-based job design. Scandinavian organizations have emphasized self-managing work teams more than individual-based approaches to work design.

An alternative to the job characteristics theory describes how perceptions of job characteristics develop and the factors that can affect those perceptions. Supervisors, coworkers, and the job redesign process all can positively or negatively affect perceptions, even when the job is not changed.

Two implications for intrinsic rewards and job design follow from cultural differences. Because all cultures do not view self-actualization from work experiences as important, striving for intrinsic rewards from job redesign does not always apply. Another implication is that cultural differences should guide the choice of individual-based or group-based approaches. U.S. managers have mostly used individual-based job design approaches. Managers in other countries such as Norway and Sweden have mainly emphasized group-based job design.

Some ethical implications derive from people's differences in the need for affiliation and designing group-based work. People with a low need for affiliation might have little desire for group-based work. Some people might not want high involvement in their work roles, preferring high involvement in nonwork roles instead. Those reasons imply at least two ethical questions. Should involvement in such groups be voluntary for those already employed by a company? Should job applicants be fully informed about the company's use of groups and the likelihood of a group assignment if they are hired?

REVIEW AND DISCUSSION QUESTIONS

1 Discuss examples of work contexts within which you have worked. Did your job's design take advantage of the work context or did it conflict with the work context? What were your reactions?

2 Discuss the factors that affect a person's perception of a job's objective characteristics. What implications do you see for a job redesign strategy? Discuss examples from your work experiences.

3 Jobs can be designed for groups or individuals. What individual needs should be strong in people who will work in a group or team setting? Which countries emphasize one approach instead of the other?

4 Discuss the role of individual moderators in job design. Which needs discussed in earlier chapters are closely tied to the concept of growth need strength? Will you find differences in important needs in different cultures around the world?

5 Which work context factors can affect a person's reaction to a job's design? Discuss how these factors affect such reactions. Include examples from your work experiences.

6 What are the steps in diagnosing and redesigning jobs? Discuss the role of job incumbents in the diagnosis and redesign of their jobs.

7 Review the discussion of ethics and job design. Are those real issues facing managers in modern organizations? Why?

TAKE FIVE: OB ALIVE: *MODERN TIMES* (1936)

Charlie Chaplin plays a factory worker while satirically showing 1930s American factory life. Chaplin's daily work involves tightening bolts on some nondescript parts. He cracks from the work stress and runs through the factory trying to sabotage its various parts.

These scenes start the film (DVD Chapter 01 through DVD Chapter 02). They begin with a dark screen followed by a close-up of a clock. The scenes end after Charlie Chaplin returns to work and continues to tighten bolts.

Consider the following questions while viewing the scenes: Predict a Motivating Potential Score (MPS) for the jobs of Chaplin and his coworkers. How do you assess the context of Chaplin's work—good or bad? Does the job characteristics theory of work motivation explain the behavior of Chaplin and his coworkers?

REFERENCES AND NOTES

REFERENCES AND NOTES 9

1. See the following sources for summaries of much of the content of this book's three motivation chapters: Kanfer, R., M. Frese, and R. E. Johnson. 2017. Motivation Related to Work: A Century of Progress. *Journal of Applied Psychology* 102: 338–55.
   Parker, S. K., F. P. Morgeson, and G. Johns. 2017. One Hundred Years of Work Design Research: Looking Back and Looking Forward. *Journal of Applied Research* 102: 403–20.
   Steers, R. M., R. T. Mowday, and D. L. Shapiro. 2004. The Future of Work Motivation Theory. *Academy of Management Review* 28: 379–87.
2. Pittman, T. S. 1998. Motivation. In *The Handbook of Social Psychology*, Vol. 1, ed. D. T. Gilbert, S. T. Fiske, and G. Lindzey. Boston: McGraw-Hill, pp. 566–70.
3. Sheppard, H. L., and N. Q. Herrick. 1972. *Where Have All the Robots Gone?* New York: The Free Press.
   Walker, C. R., and R. Guest. 1952. *The Man on the Assembly Line*. Cambridge, MA: Harvard University Press.
4. Grant, A. M., Y. Fried, and T. Juillerat. 2011. Work Matters: Job Design in Classic and Contemporary Perspectives. In *APA Handbook of Industrial and Organizational Psychology*, Vol. 1, ed. S. Zedeck. Washington, DC: American Psychological Association, Chap. 13.
   Griffin, R. W. 1982. *Task Design: An Integrative Approach*. Glenview, IL: Scott, Foresman, Chaps. 2, 3.
   Parker, S. K., T. D. Wall, and J. L. Cordery. 2001. Future Work Design Research and Practice: Towards an Elaborated Model of Work Design. *Journal of Occupational and Organizational Psychology* 74: 413–40. Pages 414–17 summarize the history of past job design research.
5. Herzberg, F. 1968. One More Time: How Do You Motivate Employees? *Harvard Business Review* (January–February): 53–62.
6. Herzberg, F. 1966. *Work and the Nature of Man*. Cleveland: World Publishing Company.
7. Blood, M. R., and C. L. Hulin. 1967. Alienation, Environmental Characteristics, and Worker Responses. *Journal of Applied Psychology* 51: 284–90.
   Griffin, R. W., and G. C. McMahan. 1994. Motivation through Work Design. In *Organizational Behavior: The State of the Science*, ed. J. Greenberg. Hillsdale: Lawrence Erlbaum Associates, pp. 23–43.
   Hulin, C. L., and M. R. Blood. 1968. Job Enlargement, Individual Differences, and Worker Responses. *Psychological Bulletin* 69: 41–55.
   Turner, A. N., and P. R. Lawrence. 1965. *Industrial Jobs and the Worker*. Boston: Harvard Graduate School of Business Administration.
   Wall, T. D., and R. Martin. 1994. Job and Work Design. In *Key Reviews in Managerial Psychology: Concepts and Research for Practice*, ed. C. L. Cooper and I. T. Robertson. Chichester: John Wiley & Sons, pp. 158–88.

8. Developed from the following and other citations throughout this section:

Hackman, J. R., and G. Oldham. 1976. Motivation through the Design of Work: Test of a Theory. *Organizational Behavior and Human Performance* 16: 250–79.

Hackman, J. R., and G. Oldham. 1980. *Work Redesign*. Reading, MA: Addison-Wesley.

9. Algera, J. A. 1990. The Job Characteristics Model of Work Motivation Revisited. In *Work Motivation*, ed. U. Kleinbeck, H. Quast, H. Thierry, and H. Hacker. Hillsdale: Lawrence Erlbaum Associates, pp. 85–103.

Ambrose, M. L., and C. T. Kulik. 1999. Old Friends, New Faces: Motivation Research in the 1990s. *Journal of Management* 25: 231–76.

Baba, V. V., and M. Jamal. 1991. Routinization of Job Context and Job Content as Related to Employees' Quality of Working Life: A Study of Canadian Nurses. *Journal of Organizational Behavior* 12: 379–86.

Berlinger, L. R., W. H. Glick, and R. C. Rodgers. 1988. Job Enrichment and Performance Improvement. In *Productivity in Organizations: New Perspectives from Industrial and Organizational Psychology*, ed. J. P. Campbell and R. J. Campbell. San Francisco: Jossey-Bass, pp. 219–54.

Bond, F. W., P. E. Flaxman, and D. Bunce. 2008. The Influence of Psychological Flexibility on Work Redesign: Mediated Moderation of a Work Reorganization Intervention. *Journal of Applied Psychology* 93: 645–54.

Cunningham, J. B., and J. MacGregor. 2000. Trust and the Design of Work: Complementary Constructs in Satisfaction and Performance. *Human Relations* 53: 1575–91.

Dodd, N. G., and D. C. Ganster. 1996. The Interactive Effects of Variety, Autonomy, and Feedback on Attitudes and Performance. *Journal of Organizational Behavior* 17: 329–47.

Edwards, J. R., J. A. Scully, and M. D. Brtek. 2000. The Nature and Outcomes of Work: A Replication and Extension of Interdisciplinary Work-Design Research. *Journal of Applied Psychology* 85: 860–68.

Fried, Y., and G. R. Ferris. 1987. The Validity of the Job Characteristics Model: A Review and Meta-Analysis. *Personnel Psychology* 40: 287–322.

Griffin, R. W. 1991. Effects of Work Redesign on Employee Perceptions, Attitudes, and Behaviors: A Long-Term Investigation. *Academy of Management Journal* 34: 425–35.

Hackman and Oldham, *Work Redesign*, p. 97.

Humphrey, S. E., J. D. Nahrgang, and F. P. Morgeson. 2007. Integrating Motivational, Social, and Contextual Work Design Features: A Meta-Analytic Summary and Theoretical Extension of the Work Design Literature. *Journal of Applied Psychology* 92: 1332–56.

Locke, E. A., and D. Henne. 1986. Work Motivation Theories. In *International Review of Industrial and Organizational Psychology*, ed. C. L. Cooper, and I. T. Robertson. Chichester: John Wiley & Sons, Chap. 1.

Loher, B. T., R. A. Noe, N. L. Moeller, and M. P. Fitzgerald. 1985. A Meta-Analysis of the Relation of Job Characteristics to Job Satisfaction. *Journal of Applied Psychology* 70: 280–89.

Morgeson, F. P., and M. A. Campion. 2003. Work Design. In *Handbook of Psychology: Industrial and Organizational Psychology*, Vol. 12, ed. W. C. Borman, D. R. Ilgen, and R. J. Klimoski. Hoboken: John Wiley and Sons, pp. 423–52.

Morgeson, F. P., and S. E. Humphrey. 2006. The Work Design Questionnaire (WDQ): Developing and Validating a Comprehensive Measure for Assessing Job Design and the Nature of Work. *Journal of Applied Psychology* 91: 1321–29.

Oldham, G. R. 1996. Job Design. In *International Review of Industrial and Organizational Psychology*, Vol. 11, ed. C. L. Cooper, and I. T. Robertson. Chichester: John Wiley & Sons, Chap. 2.

Parker, S. K., and S. Ohly. 2008. Designing Motivating Jobs: An Expanded Framework for Linking Work Characteristics and Motivation. In *Work Motivation: Past, Present, and Future*, ed. R. Kanfer, G. Chen, and R. D. Pritchard. New York: Routledge, Chap. 7.

Parker, S. K., and N. Turner. 2002. Work Design and Individual Job Performance: Research Findings and an Agenda for Future Inquiry. In *The Psychological Management of Individual Performance: A Handbook in the Psychology of Management in Organizations*, ed. S. Sonnentag. Chichester: John Wiley & Sons, Chap. 4. This source summarizes some important, rigorous research showing a relationship between job design and individual work performance (see pp. 74–77).

Parker, Wall, and Cordery, Future Work Design Research and Practice.

Rentsch, J. R., and R. P. Steel. 1998. Testing the Durability of Job Characteristics as Predictors of Absenteeism Over a Six-Year Period. *Personnel Psychology* 51: 165–90.

Roberts, K. H., and W. Glick. 1981. The Job Characteristics Approach to Task Design: A Critical Review. *Journal of Applied Psychology* 66: 193–217.

Spector, P. E., and S. M. Jex. 1991. Relations of Job Characteristics from Multiple Data Sources with Employee Affect, Absence, Turnover Intentions, and Health. *Journal of Applied Psychology* 76: 46–53.

10. The original presentations of the theory did not describe the connections between affective and behavioral outcomes as is done here. The connections appear logical and allow clearer description of the theory.

11. Rentsch and Steel, Testing the Durability.

12. De Jonge, J., and W. B. Schaufeli. 1998. Job Characteristics and Employee Well-Being: A Test of Warr's Vitamin Model in Health Care Workers Using Structural Equation Modeling. *Journal of Organizational Behavior* 19: 387–407.

13. Deci, E. L. 1975. *Intrinsic Motivation*. New York: Plenum Press.

14. Oldham, Job Design, p. 41.
   Renn, R. W., and R. J. Vandenberg. 1995. The Critical Psychological States: An Underrepresented Component in Job Characteristics Model Research. *Journal of Management* 21: 279–303. Also see their summary of other research.

15. Griffin, *Task Design*.

16. Hackman and Oldham, *Work Redesign*, pp. 78–80.
   These five job characteristics derive from the research behind the Job Characteristics Theory of Work Motivation. Other research suggests there are many more job characteristics. See Morgeson and Humphrey, The Work Design Questionnaire, for more details.

17. Ibid., p. 81.

18. Summarized in Oldham, Job Design, p. 41.
   Morgeson and Campion, Work Design.

19. Dodd and Ganster, The Interactive Effects.

20. Jobs high in motivating potential should produce lower absenteeism.

21. Growth need strength is not always discussed as specific to the job itself. It is clear from the way it is measured that this was the authors' intent. See Hackman and Oldham, *Work Redesign*, pp. 287–93.

22. Algera, The Job Characteristics Model of Work Motivation Revisited.
Locke and Henne, Work Motivation Theories, pp. 7–8.
Oldham, Job Design, pp. 43–44.

23. Johns, G., J. L. Xie, and Y. Fang. 1992. Mediating and Moderating Effects in Job Design. *Journal of Management* 18: 657–76.

24. Fried and Ferris, The Validity of the Job Characteristics Model.
Griffin, *Task Design*.
Hackman and Oldham, *Work Redesign*.
Hogan, E. A., and D. A. Martell. 1987. A Confirmatory Structural Equations Analysis of the Job Characteristics Model. *Organizational Behavior and Human Decision Processes* 39: 242–63.
Loher, Noe, Moeller, and Fitzgerald, A Meta-Analysis.
Morgeson and Campion, Work Design.
Roberts and Glick, The Job Characteristics Approach to Task Design.
Spector, P. E. 1985. Higher-Order Need Strength as a Moderator of the Job Scope-Employee Outcome Relationship: A Meta-Analysis. *Journal of Occupational Psychology* 58: 119–27.
Tiegs, R. B., L. E. Tetrick, and Y. Fried. 1992. Growth Need Strength and Context Satisfactions as Moderators of the Relations of the Job Characteristics Model. *Journal of Management* 18: 575–93.

25. Oldham, Job Design, p. 44.

26. Oldham, G. R. 1976. Job Characteristics and Internal Motivation: The Moderating Effect of Interpersonal and Individual Variables. *Human Relations* 29: 559–69.

27. Abdil-Halim, A. A. 1979. Individual and Interpersonal Moderators of Employee Reactions to Job Characteristics: A Re-Examination. *Personnel Psychology* 32: 121–37.
Ferris, G. R., and D. C. Gilmore. 1984. The Moderating Role of Work Context in Job Design Research: A Test of Competing Models. *Academy of Management Journal* 27: 885–92.

28. Champoux, J. E. 1992. A Multivariate Test of the Moderating Effect of Work Context Satisfactions on the Curvilinear Relationship between Job Scope and Affective Outcomes. *Human Relations* 45: 87–111.

29. The material in this section draws from Griffin, *Task Design*. Other sources are noted in the appropriate places. Some material also is speculative because of little research in some areas discussed.

30. Brass, D. J. 1985. Technology and the Structuring of Jobs: Employee Satisfaction, Performance, and Influence. *Organizational Behavior and Human Decision Processes* 35: 216–40.
Buchanan, D. A., and D. Boddy. 1982. Advanced Technology and the Quality of Working Life: The Effects of Word Processing on Video Typists. *Journal of Occupational Psychology* 55: 1–11.

31. Safizadeh, M. H. 1991. The Case of Workgroups in Manufacturing Operations. *California Management Review* 33 (Summer): 61–82.

32. Cummings, T. G., and M. Blumberg. 1989. Advanced Manufacturing Technology and Work Design. In *The Human Side of Advanced Manufacturing Technology*, ed. T. D. Wall, C. W. Clegg, and N. Kemp. Chichester: John Wiley & Sons, pp. 37–60.

Kelley, M. R. 1990. New Process Technology, Job Design, and Work Organization. *American Sociological Review* 55: 191–208.

Nemetz, P. L., and L. W. Fry. 1988. Flexible Manufacturing Organizations: Implications for Strategy Formulation and Organization Design. *Academy of Management Review* 13: 627–38.

33. Dean, J. W., Jr., and S. A. Snell. 1991. Integrated Manufacturing and Job Design: Moderation Effects of Organizational Inertia. *Academy of Management Journal* 34: 776–804.

34. Davy, J. A., R. E. White, N. J. Merrit, and K. Gritzmacher. 1992. A Derivation of the Underlying Constructs of Just-in-Time Management Systems. *Academy of Management Journal* 35: 653–70.

Schonberger, R. J. 1982. The Transfer of Japanese Manufacturing Management Approaches to U.S. Industry. *Academy of Management Review* 7: 479–87.

35. Champoux, J. E. 1978. A Serendipitous Field Experiment in Job Design. *Journal of Vocational Behavior* 12: 364–70.

36. Vroom, V., and P. Yetton. 1973. *Leadership and Decision Making*. Pittsburgh: University of Pittsburgh Press.

37. Griffin, *Task Design*.

Hackman and Oldham, *Work Redesign*, Chaps. 5, 6.

38. Griffin, *Task Design*.

Hackman and Oldham, *Work Redesign*.

Taber, T. D., and E. Taylor. 1990. A Review and Evaluation of the Psychometric Properties of the Job Diagnostic Survey. *Personnel Psychology* 43: 467–500.

The newer Work Design Questionnaire has more comprehensive coverage than the Job Diagnostic Survey discussed in this chapter. See Morgeson and Humphrey, The Work Design Questionnaire, for details on its development and measurement properties.

39. Griffin and McMahan, Motivation through Work Design, pp. 36–38.

Hackman, J. R. 1978. The Design of Self-Managing Work Groups. In *Managerial Control and Organizational Democracy*, ed. B. King, S. Streufert, and F. E. Fiedler. Washington, DC: Winston & Sons, Chap. 5.

Hackman and Oldham, *Work Redesign*, Chap. 7.

Sundstrom, E., K. P. De Meuse, and D. Futrell. 1990. Work Teams: Applications and Effectiveness. *American Psychologist* 45: 120–33.

Wall and Martin, Job and Work Design, pp. 162–63.

40. Steiner, I. D. 1972. *Group Process and Productivity*. New York: Academic Press.

41. Janis, I. L. 1982. *Groupthink*, 2nd edn. Boston: Houghton Mifflin.

Moorhead, G. 1982. Groupthink: Hypothesis in Need of Testing. *Group & Organization Studies* 7: 429–44.

Chapter 14, "Decision-Making and Problem-Solving Processes," examines the groupthink phenomenon in more detail.

42. Cordery, J. L., W. S. Mueller, and L. M. Smith. 1991. Attitudinal and Behavioral Effects of Autonomous Group Working: A Longitudinal Field Study. *Academy of Management Journal* 34: 464–76.

Cotton, J. L. 1993. *Employee Involvement: Methods for Improving Performance and Work Attitudes*. Newbury Park: Sage Publications.

Oldham, Job Design, pp. 49–53.

Pearce, J. A., and E. C. Ravlin. 1987. The Design and Activation of Self-Regulating Work Groups. *Human Relations* 40: 751–82.

43. Barker, J. 1993. Tightening the Iron Cage: Concertive Control in Self-Managing Teams. *Administrative Science Quarterly* 38: 408–37.

44. Wageman, R., and G. Baker. 1997. Incentives and Cooperation: The Joint Effects of Task and Reward Interdependence on Group Performance. *Journal of Organizational Behavior* 18: 139–58.

45. Roberts and Glick, The Job Characteristics Approach to Task Design, p. 196.

46. Griffin, R. W., M. A. Welsh, and G. Moorhead. 1981. Perceived Task Characteristics and Employee Performance: A Literature Review. *Academy of Management Review* 6: 655–64.
    Salancik, G., and J. Pfeffer. 1977. An Examination of Need-Satisfaction Models of Job Attitudes. *Administrative Science Quarterly* 22: 427–56.
    Salancik, G., and J. Pfeffer. 1978. A Social Information Processing Approach to Job Attitudes and Task Design. *Administrative Science Quarterly* 23: 224–53.
    Thomas, J., and R. W. Griffin. 1983. The Social Information Processing Model of Task Design: A Review of the Literature. *Academy of Management Review* 8: 672–82.

47. Salancik and Pfeffer, An Examination of Need-Satisfaction Models.
    Salancik and Pfeffer, A Social Information Processing Approach.

48. O'Reilly, C. A., and D. F. Caldwell. 1979. Informational Influence as a Determinant of Perceived Task Characteristics and Job Satisfaction. *Journal of Applied Psychology* 64: 157–65.
    White, S. E., and T. R. Mitchell. 1979. Job Enrichment versus Social Cues: A Comparison and Competitive Test. *Journal of Applied Psychology* 64: 1–9.

49. Salancik and Pfeffer, A Social Information Processing Approach.

50. Berlinger, Glick, and Rodgers, Job Enrichment and Performance Improvement.
    Caldwell, D. F., and C. A. O'Reilly. 1982. Task Perception and Job Satisfaction: A Question of Causality. *Journal of Applied Psychology* 67: 361–69.
    Griffin, R. W. 1983. Objective and Social Sources of Information in Task Redesign: A Field Experiment. *Administrative Science Quarterly* 28: 184–200.
    Kilduff, M., and D. T. Regan. 1988. What People Say and What They Do: The Differential Effects of Informational Cues and Task Design. *Organizational Behavior and Human Decision Processes* 41: 83–97.
    Thomas and Griffin, The Social Information Processing Model of Task Design.

51. Oldham, Job Design, pp. 38–40.
    Spector, P. E. 1992. A Consideration of the Validity and Meaning of Self-Report Measures of Job Conditions. In *International Review of Industrial and Organizational Psychology*, Vol. 7, ed. C. L. Cooper and I. T. Robertson. Chichester: John Wiley & Sons, Chap. 4.
    Taber, T. D., and E. Taylor. 1990. A Review and Evaluation of the Psychometric Properties of the Job Diagnostic Survey. *Personnel Psychology* 43: 467–500.

52. Griffin, *Task Design*, pp. 169–71.

53. Griffin, Objective and Social Sources of Information in Task Redesign.

54. Griffin, *Task Design*, p. 171.

55. Hofstede, G. 2001. *Culture's Consequences: Comparing Values, Behaviors, Institutions, and Organizations across Nations*, 2nd edn. Thousand Oaks: Sage Publications.

56. Berggren, C. 1992. *Alternatives to Lean Production: Work Organization in the Swedish Auto Industry*. Cornell International Industrial and Labor Relations Report No. 22 (December).

57. Hofstede, G. 1980. Motivation, Leadership, and Organization: Do American Theories Apply Abroad? *Organizational Dynamics* 9: 42–63.
   Hofstede, *Culture's Consequences*, Chap. 6.
58. Hofstede, Motivation, Leadership, and Organization, pp. 56–59.
59. Champoux, J. E. 1980. A Three Sample Test of Some Extensions to the Job Characteristics Model of Work Motivation. *Academy of Management Journal* 23: 466–78.
60. Hofstede, *Culture's Consequences*.

Part 2 Case

Abstract

Nordstrom has been one of the most successful retailers in recent years based on its tradition of outstanding customer service. This case describes the management practices that have shaped the customer-oriented culture of Nordstrom and contributed to its success. The human resource management activities that produce its highly motivated sales force are particularly emphasized. Yet, not all employees at Nordstrom have reacted positively to its management practices. A number of employees have viewed the company as being unfair and unethical in its dealings with them. Dissatisfied employees have even organized a unionization campaign. An interesting feature of the case is the positive and negative perceptions of current and former employees to "The Nordstrom Way."

NORDSTROM*

In 1880, John W. Nordstrom left Sweden and sailed to the United States. Twenty-one years later, with a $13,000 fortune struck in Klondike gold, he opened up a shoe store in Seattle. Today that small downtown store is a shoe and apparel empire with almost 100 outlets in more than 10 states.

Nordstrom is one of the most successful department stores with 1995 sales of $3.9 billion and net earnings of $203 million.[1] During the 1980s and 1990s, the company doubled its size from 29 to 89 stores, opening outlets across California and eastward, in Virginia, Washington, DC and, most recently, in Paramus, New Jersey. Sales and net earnings grew comparably. In 1995 profits were up 45% and same store sales were up 4.4%.[2] The number of Nordstrom employees has grown to 35,000.

Despite its recent expansion, Nordstrom has remained a family operation. Grandsons John, Bruce, and Jim are all co-chairmen and Jack McMillan, a Nordstrom by marriage, is the company's president. Nordstrom has no chief executive. The company prides itself on having cultivated a family orientation among its workers. All employees are made to feel like members of a family sharing in "the Nordstrom Way."[3]

The Nordstrom Way is perhaps what has set the department store apart from its competition. It is customer service like no one else offers, service above and beyond the call of duty. At Nordstrom, service is an art form. The store hosts gala dinners and fashion shows, has valet parking, concierges for special requests stationed near every store's entrance, and soothing ballads played on Steinways

* **Source:** This case was prepared by Richard D. Freedman Distinguished Service Professor of Management Emeritus and Jill Vohr, Leonard N. Stern School of Business, New York University. Copyright © 1991 by Professor Richard D. Freedman. Reprinted with the permission of Richard D. Freedman.

at every store accompanying eager smiles from salespeople ready and willing to go to great lengths to please the Nordstrom customer. Such amenities have won Nordstrom customer loyalty and affection. In Seattle, it is common to see bumper stickers that proclaim: "I'd rather be shopping at Nordstrom's." Bruce Nordstrom says of the company's customer service tradition: "We were raised sitting on a shoe stool on our knees in front of a customer. And that is both a literal and figurative posture ... a born servant, if you will. There's nothing wrong with that. We're proud of it ... and I think our people know that that's what we do."[4] Nordstrom employees, "Nordies," all have similar characteristics. They are upbeat, ambitious but, at the same time, selfless. The Nordstrom store directory describes the Nordie service expectation:

> Our staff is genuinely interested in seeing that all your needs are met. They are professionals—will help you with everything from gift suggestions to wardrobe planning. They will even accompany you from department to department until you find exactly what you're looking for.[5]

Nordies keep personal books listing each of their customers and record every activity and correspondence. Thank-you letters are sent to customers for purchases regardless of how small. One man was sent a thank-you note for buying only a pair of socks.[6] Nordies will personally deliver purchases as well, outside of work time and even on holidays, all to cultivate that special relationship and trust that has resulted in Nordstrom's faithful customer base and glowing sales record.

Thank-you letters and personal deliveries only barely suggest what the Nordstrom Way entails. One employee spent over three hours on Easter Sunday finding a customer's house so he could deliver a stuffed rabbit to the customer's wife in person.[7] Another employee searched every store in the company to find a blue shirt with a white cuff and white collar that a customer had seen in an ad. Although the employee never found the shirt in his size, she personally delivered one to him at work the next morning. She had sewn a blue and white shirt together.[8]

What motivates Nordstrom employees to go to such personal trouble for their customers? High salaries for one. Nordstrom employees earn some of the highest salaries in the retail business. Pat McCarthy, a longtime Nordie, is one of them. Twenty years at Nordstrom has enabled him to cultivate a strong, loyal customer base that has brought him commissions of $80,000 plus a year.[9] "It's really a people job, which I love," says McCarthy. "Every year my sales have gotten progressively better."[10] Base pay rates are also high—between $5 and $11 an hour, which is well above the industry standard of $6 to $7.[11] High salaries have given Nordstrom a reputation that attracts good salespeople. Company officials say as many as 2,000 employment applications are received when 100 new entry-level openings are announced.[12]

All salespeople start "on the floor," and the company has a strict policy of promoting only from within. Potential managers are required to have at least two years' experience selling, and are promoted after less time only under special circumstances. Promotions for all Nordies are based on three criteria: customer service, productivity, and teamwork. If a salesperson has good team spirit, a solid record of fine customer service, and high sales per hour (SPH), after an appropriate length of time with the company, that employee will likely be promoted to department manager. Similarly, a manager whose department goals have been successively reached or surpassed over his or her length of employment, has fine customer service skills, and good relations with employees will rise to buyer or store manager positions.

Employees receive little formal training when they are hired or promoted to a new position. Most of the training is informally provided through on-the-job communication. What formal training they do receive is of a practical nature (e.g., scheduling procedures, salary and commission determinations, and benefit opportunities). The three Nordstrom performance criteria (customer service, productivity, and teamwork) are emphasized, although trainees are not told how these criteria are evaluated. Trainees are encouraged to seek information from coworkers and superiors who are described as friendly and accessible. Personal books are provided for use in keeping records of customers, sales, thank-you letters, and letters from customers. New employees are also given their own set of business cards to emphasize entrepreneurial opportunities and to encourage them to develop a solid customer base.

Not long ago, Nordstrom replaced its 20-page rule book with a one-page sheet and a few words of wisdom: "Use your best judgment in all situations," and "Do whatever it takes to make the customer happy."[13] Nordstrom gives people the freedom to do whatever it takes to make the customer happy (as long as it's legal). The company has since continued to maintain a decentralized approach to management. Managers are given significant freedom to operate their departments in the Nordstrom way. Individual creativity is a by-product of freedom. They are responsible for hiring, scheduling, and evaluating their crew and receive little guidance in the form of written company policies. Nordstrom hires people that will create their own business, and strict policy might stifle ingenuity and creativity. Therefore, most of the information guiding salespeople is received from their managers and not dictated from above. As described by regional personnel director Molly Goe, each department manager runs his or her department like an individual boutique.[14]

Managers are solely responsible for evaluating their employees. According to personnel manager Mary Kim Stuart, no specific, company-wide evaluation forms are used for salespeople and managers.[15] Rather, each manager designs his or her own evaluation system. If the manager considers an aspect of an employee's performance worth noting it is communicated to the store manager. The store manager, in turn, decides whether to note it in the employee's file.

Like their salespeople, managers are "on the floor" selling and receive a commission. However, their base salaries are much higher. Consequently, although commissions provide managers with an incentive to sell, they are less critical for their income than for salespeople.

All Nordstrom salespeople are on a commission system called a draw. Hourly rates are determined based on the salesperson's abilities and length of employment with the company. Commission percentages for salespeople are strictly based on SPH. Employees receive either their commission percentage times their total sales for that pay period or their hourly rate times their total work hours depending on which is higher. For example, Joe Demarte, Nordstrom's vice president of personnel, explains that a salesperson with a 6.75% commission who works 40 hours for $10 an hour and sells $10,000 worth would earn $675 rather than $400. If he sold $1,000 worth, he would earn his hourly wage and no commission.[16] Consequently, only if an employee's sales are high relative to the hours they have worked, will they receive a commission. The higher the total dollar sales, the higher the commission. The incentive is to generate high pace and high-dollar sales.

Although most of the training is implicit, Nordstrom's expectations of its employees are explicit. "The life of a Nordstrom salesperson is defined by goals. Daily, monthly, quarterly, and annual goals; departmental, storewide and company goals; qualitative and quantitative."[17] These goals are formulated at the top by senior managers and trickle down through the hierarchy to departmental managers who are responsible for meeting designated sales quotas for their departments. Managers' salaries, commissions, and bonuses depend on whether or not they attain these goals. Successive failure to reach targets can lead to dismissal. The same is true for salespeople. Managers encourage salespeople to reach high SPH levels. Some even set specific targets for their employees to ensure the attainment of their departments' sales quotas. Managers are free to implement their own approach to productivity as long as it achieves set targets and is consistent with the Nordstrom Way.

SPHs must be kept above a specified minimum level or a salesperson will not receive commission. Low SPHs reflect poor performance and can therefore be grounds for dismissal. Charts are displayed on bulletin boards in back rooms that rank employees by SPH. Ranking reflects an employee's sales ability on the floor. A red line across the chart designates the minimum SPH level necessary to receive a commission. Employees use these charts to keep tabs on their performance and see themselves in relation to their coworkers.

Everyone is formally and informally aware of their sales performance. In addition to the SPH chart, employees can keep track of their performance on computer printouts available in back offices that list their sales by employee identification number. Salespeople often know each other's number and can see how they stand in relation to one another. To keep it that way, some store managers broadcast the prior day's top 20 salespeople over a loudspeaker each morning. Numerous sales contests operate as incentives. For example, free dinners are given to employees who make the most multiple-item sales to individual customers. Often, within a department, a $20 bill is passed around throughout the day to the salesperson who has rung up the highest single sale. At the end of the day, the winner gets to keep the $20 bill. Top salespeople are named "Pacesetters," which carries with it roughly the status of a varsity letter on a high school athlete's jacket. Motivational skits are used to generate sales enthusiasm. Managers dress up as Kermit the Frog to get employees whipped into a selling frenzy, or a department's staff performs the Michael Jackson song

"Beat it" with the words, "Charge it."[18] Nordstrom also offers a course on self-motivation encouraging salespeople to ask themselves what they want to accomplish each day to spur them to take responsibility for their own future. Many do, especially the successful ones. Employees seem to know precisely what they want and need to achieve. One top salesperson stated, "The first year I consciously set quarterly goals to achieve the Pacesetter requirement. My second year my personal goal was $500,000, and I paced myself accordingly. My third year I wanted to achieve $1 million in total sales. To accomplish this I set monthly and quarterly quotas and closely monitored my progress."[19] Clearly, the best salespeople are entrepreneurial self-starters.

Managers are also encouraged to be self-motivated. "Every year the company's managers gather in meetings where they publicly state their store or departmental goals for the next 12 months. Then their bosses will reveal their own goals for the same manager, sometimes with a dramatic flourish."[20] Working at Nordstrom is not for everybody. The company has very high expectations. If you don't meet them, you're gone.

Good customer relations the Nordstrom Way are also important. Employees buzz with tales of extraordinary efforts made by salespeople. Peer competition and pressures to be a member of "the Nordstrom family" keep salespeople striving for a popularity that is based on their sales ability. Rewards for customer satisfaction are high. Bonuses up to $100 are awarded to salespeople with the best customer relations. Managers read letters received from pleased customers aloud at company meetings and over the loudspeaker. Whoops and cheers are heard from listeners. The salespeople who received the letters are honored as "Customer Service All Stars."[21] Their pictures are hung on the wall next to the customer service desk. They receive extra discounts on store merchandise and commendations on their personal records.

To check on the customer service provided by their employees, Nordstrom periodically dispatches "secret shoppers," people who pretend to be shoppers.[22] Salespeople are encouraged to be friendly and warm. Nordstrom does not tolerate rude behavior towards its customers. Smile contests are conducted to motivate courteous behavior. Pictures of smiling employees are taken and displayed in the lunchroom. Those that smile the most on the job receive the highest praise. "Recognition is the number one motivation," says Demarte with respect to Nordstrom contests. "We recognize our top performers constantly, as well as our customer service heroics."[23]

Most Nordstrom employees strongly uphold the Nordstrom philosophy of service. Some are almost religious about it, happily dedicating their lives to master "The Nordstrom Way." Yet, other employees feel the customers are catered to at the expense of their own working conditions, that systems meant to encourage employees actually oppress them, placing them in an environment of constant pressure, harassment, and competition. Some employees began to accuse Nordstrom of unfair labor practices. The United Food and Commercial Workers Union, of which only 2,000 of the 30,000 Nordstrom work force are members, became involved.[24] Accusations of "off-the-clock" work and overbearing work pressures dominated complaints.

All employees are expected to contribute to stocking, delivering, and picking up merchandise. Much of this work is done off the clock, past the end of a shift, on the weekends, or through breaks and lunches. Also employees are expected to maintain close relations with their customers, which implicitly entails thank-you notes and sometimes personal deliveries. The Nordstrom practice is not to include the hours spent at these activities in the total hours worked for each employee's pay period. Union leader, Joe Peterson, in his fight against Nordstrom and what he feels is grossly unfair treatment of employees, continues to search for and encourage employees to hop on the bandwagon. Over 500 complaints were filed with the workers' union and as more complaints poured in, the union set up an 800 hotline to handle them. An article in The Wall Street Journal included several stories told by Nordstrom employees themselves.

Taking Out the Trash

A divorced California homemaker who returned to the job market at 40, Patty Bemis joined Nordstrom in 1981, lured by the promise of a bigger income and the "status" of induction in the Nordie elite. She stayed for eight years. "They came to me," she recalls of the Nordstrom recruiters. "I was working at The Broadway as Estee Lauder's counter manager and they said they had heard I had wonderful sales figures." Ms. Bemis was thrilled. "We'd all heard Nordstrom was the place to work. They painted a great picture and I fell right into it." She found herself working progressively harder—for less money and amid more fear. "The managers were these little tin gods, always grilling you about your sales," she recalls. "You feel like your job was constantly in jeopardy. They'd write you up for anything, being sick, the way you dressed." Once, she had to get a doctor's note so she wouldn't get in trouble for wearing low-heel shoes to work. Sufficiently cowed, she reported to work even when she had strep throat. Worn down by pressure, "the girls around me were dropping like flies," she says. "Everyone was always in tears. You feel like an absolute nothing working for them."

Ms. Bemis was consistently one of her department's top sellers, but some years she only made $18,000, far below what she had expected she would earn. She won a company-wide sales contest, and received "a pair of PJs," she recalls. "Whoopiedoo!" And she logged many unpaid hours delivering cosmetics to customers and unpacking hundreds of boxes of makeup. "Working off the clock was standard," crucial to elevating sales per hour. "In the end, really serving the customer, being an All-Star, meant nothing; if you had low sales per hour, you were forced out."

During a big Clinique sale, Ms. Bemis says she worked 12- to 15-hour shifts for a number of days without overtime pay or a day off. On the drive home at 10:30 on the tenth night, she passed out at the wheel and slammed into the freeway's center divider, she says. While she was at home recovering from head injuries, she recalls, "The manager kept calling me and saying, 'Patty, we can't hold your job much longer.'" Her doctor told her she should stay out a few weeks but she didn't dare. "Now, I know I have all these rights. But at the time all I knew was I had to have that job."

She finally left last spring. "I just couldn't take it anymore—the constant demands, the grueling hours. I just said one day, life's too short." She took a sales post at Scandia Down Shops, where she says she makes $400 more a month than at Nordstrom. "And I can sleep at night."[25]

A Broken Clock

The first time Lori Lucas came to one of the many "mandatory" Saturday morning department meetings and saw the sign—"Do Not Punch the Clock." She assumed the managers were telling the truth when they said the clock was temporarily out of order. But as weeks went by, she discovered the clock was always "broken" or the timecards were just missing.

Finally she and several other employees just marked the hours down on their timecard manually. She and another employee recall that their manager whited-out the hours and accused the two of not being "team players."

The department meetings "were unbelievable," Ms. Lucas recalls. "There you'd be at seven in the morning and they had all these security guards dressed up like the California Raisins, with plastic garbage bags stuffed with M&Ms around their midriffs. And all you can hear is people chanting, 'We're number one!' and 'You want to do it for Nordstrom.' Finally I went up to the store manager and said, 'What is this all about?' and she said, 'You are here to learn the Nordstrom Way.'"

The Nordstrom Way involved an endless round of contests ("Who Looks More Nordstrom" was a popular one, intended to encourage employees to shop at the stores) and the daily recital of "affirmations" ("I only sell multiples," was one chanted by salespeople).

And the Nordstrom Way, Ms. Lucas discovered, meant working for free. "My manager would say, 'You go clock out and come down and we'll talk.' That was her little trick way of saying there's nonsell work to do."

Like most salesclerks at Nordstrom, Ms. Lucas also had daily quotas of thank-you letters to write, and monthly customer service "books" to generate photo albums that are supposed to be filled with letters from grateful customers. ("People would get so desperate they would have their friends and relatives write fake letters for them," Petra Rousu, a 10-year salesclerk veteran, recalls.) Such duties, Ms. Lucas says, were supposed to be tackled only after hours. "I'd be up till 3 a.m., doing my letters, and doing my manager's books," she says. "Before you know it, your whole life is Nordstrom. But you couldn't complain, because then your manager would schedule you for the bad hours, your sales per hour would fall, and next thing you know, you're out the door."

The pressure eventually gave Ms. Lucas an ulcer, she says. One day after working 22 days without a day off, she demanded a lunch break. On her hour off, she applied for and got a new job elsewhere and gave notice as soon as she returned. "I remember thinking, I'm making less than $20,000 a year. Why am I killing myself? Nordstrom was the most unfair place I ever worked."[26]

Staying on Top

For nearly two years, Cindy Nelson had stayed on top of the chart in one of the Bellevue, Washington, stores. She was on her way to making "Pacesetter" again … A clique of salesclerks on the floor—led by numbers two and three on the charts—held a pow-wow one day, decided that Ms. Nelson must be stealing their sales, and vowed to have her "watched," according to court depositions that later became part of a suit filed by Ms. Nelson against Nordstrom in Bellevue, Washington.

On September 29, 1986, Cindy Nelson reported for work and was immediately whisked into the personnel office. The department manager had before her five notes of complaint from the salesclerks, all unsigned, which claimed Ms. Nelson had been stealing sales.

Ms. Nelson asked to inspect the sales receipts in question and confront her accusers, but the manager, Rhonda Eakes, refused. "I just didn't feel that it was any of her business," Ms. Eakes explained later in her deposition. Then she told Ms. Nelson that she was fired. (All of the managers and employees involved in Ms. Nelson's firing declined comment, referring queries to Mr. Nordstrom, who said, "That gal wasn't a good employee.")

"I was totally stunned," recalls Ms. Nelson, who had a stack of customer service citations in her file and had been told she was about to make manager. She was also, up until then, "your 100-percent gung-ho Nordie. This whole time I thought I was going to be this great Nordstrom person and now I was nothing, a nobody. I became an emotional wreck."[27]

Other criticisms were made of Nordstrom. Allegedly employees were required to purchase and wear Nordstrom clothing while on the job.[28] The company was also accused of having discriminatory practices.[29] Part of becoming a Nordie, employees say, involves acquiring a certain look. Lupe Sakagawa, a top salesperson, recalls that on her first day on the job, her manager strong-armed her into buying $1,400 of the "right" clothes—all from the department. But that wasn't enough: The store manager then called her in and told her, "Correct your accent." Ms. Sakagawa is Mexican. "It was very hard for me to prove myself," she says, "because of that image of the Nordstrom Girl—blond hair, young, and cute."[30] Nordstrom has since hired a black human resources officer and the company reports that 25.6% of all its employees are minorities.[31]

Other sentiments were brought to the attention of the media through Peterson, who felt employees are being exploited. Peterson specifically criticized the SPH incentive. He believed that in order to keep SPH up, employees were encouraged to keep their work hours down. Consequently, they could not record hours spent doing certain nonselling chores (stock taking, personal deliveries, thank-you notes) on their time sheets. Nordstrom's position was that the employees are compensated by commissions that actually pay them for doing extra tasks. Employees willingly donate their time. It is not explicitly required of them. Peterson argued that "If one employee is donating a lot of time, it forces others to do the same or it creates an atmosphere where everyone is playing on an unequal playing field."[32] Because employees who log only sales times have higher SPH than coworkers who clock in all other business and support activities, employees are motivated to decrease their nonsales hours. They work off the clock to be awarded better shifts and more hours. In response, Demarte insisted that because "SPH is the objective performance evaluation factor … that's what people focus on."[33] Evaluation is not based just on SPH. People who perform the best are also best in giving the customer service and working as a team. Yet, Demarte does admit there is pressure. "People who perform the most effectively are the ones we need to have on the floor. Therefore, there's this pressure to be better."[34] Middle management encourages workers to get jobs done within certain time frames and if they can't meet the deadlines, exert "implied pressures" on their salespeople to get the job done after work hours. President Jack McMillan insists that "the system is as level a playing field as you can find for people to rise up quickly on their own merit. Everybody starts on the selling floor and the ones that show initiative, creativity, and desire rise up in the system and become department managers. Those department managers that show the ability to make things happen rise up to be buyers or store managers or vice presidents. We think it's a great system, but it's obvious there are some glitches in it. One way to control selling costs—not the right way—is to encourage people to get the work done in a certain time frame. If they can't get it done, then there is implied pressure to work off the clock. We are responsible for the pressure from middle managers. There was no plan or scheme, but it happened. I guess you could say we were negligent for not knowing, but we are responsible for it."[35] Recently Nordstrom set aside $15 million to pay back employees who had performed off-the-clock services.[36]

Despite Nordstrom's promises of back pay the union still fought them, pointing a finger at Nordstrom's high turnover rates, even for the retail industry. Nordstrom replied that although salespeople who regularly had trouble meeting sales quotas or coping with pressure to improve their performance were dismissed, these employees usually leave of their own volition. Having been made to feel uncomfortable or inadequate in the Nordstrom culture that celebrates accomplishment, they recognize that they do not belong. They leave before the company has cause to dismiss them. Nordstrom compensates by attempting to hire people who are innate Nordies. The company's hiring philosophy supports their decentralized management style. Bruce Nordstrom is quoted as saying, "All we do is hire nice, motivated, hardworking people and then we leave them alone to do what they do best. The system is to have self-empowered people who have an entrepreneurial spirit, who feel that they're in this to better themselves and to feel good about themselves and to make more money and to be successful."[37] Jim Nordstrom adds, "There's expectations on our people. And when people apply for a job any place, they want to work hard and they want to do a good job. That's their intention. And our intention is to allow them the freedom to work as hard as they want to work."[38] However, miss your quota three months in a row, and you're out. "If you don't like to win, it's hard to be successful in this company," says Midwestern regional manager Bob Middlemas.[39]

Although there were several complaints, it seemed that most Nordstrom employees also did not support their union leader's accusations. In December 1990, more than half of the 1,850 employees left the union after membership became optional.[40] With continued pressure by Peterson, a former Nordstrom shoe salesperson, Nordstrom responded with an anti-union campaign. And in July of 1991, employees consisting of salespeople, office workers, clerks, and display workers at five stores in Seattle voted by more than a 2-to-1 ratio to end union representation altogether.[41] Indeed, several employees speak in favor of Nordstrom stating that they love working for the company and do not want anything changed.[42]

"It's a feeling, it's family," Ms. Sargent says enthusiastically. "Sure, during the busy seasons, you do work six to seven days a week, but being in the store with the Christmas tree here, you create your own memories." Ms. Sargent, who has worked for Nordstrom in Seattle for seven years, says she doesn't mind working for free. "When I go home and do follow-ups or write thank yous, I think it's inappropriate to be charging the company for that."

At the San Francisco store, another set of employees testify to the company's virtues. "Here at Nordstrom, I feel I can be the best that I can be," says Doris Quiros, a salesperson in the women's sportswear department. While other retailers "give you a big book of rules, when I came here, Nordstrom gave me one with only one rule: Use your best judgment. That's because they want me to be my own boss." In the women's shoe department, Tim Snow, a former waiter, says people are impressed now when they learn where he works. "You can be at the grocery store and you show them your ID card and they'll start right off on how much they love to shop there."[43]

If happy employees are not enough to justify the existing Nordstrom system, the company's success and their numerous satisfied customers are. "They treat you with the most reverence you can imagine," one customer said after a salesperson offered her the option of either wearing a Nordstrom dress that had a run in it and returning it at her convenience for a full refund or taking $100 off the price. "It's so darn easy to go in there."[44] Betsy Sanders, the head of the company's Southern California division, sometimes stands at the store exit at night as the store closes and says good night to departing customers. One evening, as she bade some shoppers farewell, she heard one say: "What kind of drugs are these people on? Even the doormen are nice."[45]

Looking for ways to attract more customers, Nordstrom introduced a mail-order catalog. In its first year, 1994, it attracted 300,000 shoppers. At the same time Nordstrom introduced a proprietary Visa credit card and went online with its Nordstrom Personal Touch America on market place MCI (www.internetmci.com/marketplace, 6870401@mcimail.com, or http://www.nordstrom-pta.com).

REFERENCES AND NOTES

REFERENCES AND NOTES
PART 2 CASE

1. *Hoover's Company Profile Database*, 1996. Austin, TX: The Reference Press, Inc.
2. Ibid.
3. Robert Spector and Patrick D. McCarthy, *The Nordstrom Way* (New York: John Wiley & Sons, Inc., 1995). Charlene Marrner Solomon, "Nightmare At Nordstrom," *Personnel Journal* (September 1990): 77.
4. Marti Galovic Palmer, Producer, "The Nordstrom Boys," *60 Minutes*, Vol. XXII, Num. 33 (May 6, 1990): 8.

5. "How Nordstrom Got There," *Stores* (January 1990): 68.

6. Mary Kim Stuart, Nordstrom Personnel Director (Paramus, New Jersey) telephone conversation with author, November 9, 1990.

7. "The Nordstrom Boys," *60 Minutes*: 8.

8. Ibid.

9. Susan C. Faludi, "At Nordstrom Stores, Service Comes First—But at a Big Price," *The Wall Street Journal* (February 20, 1990).

10. Ibid.

11. Seth Lubove, "Don't Listen to the Boss, Listen to the Customer," *Forbes* (December 4, 1995): 45–46; Dori Jones Yang, "Will 'The Nordstrom Way' Travel Well?" *Business Week* (September 3, 1990): 83.

12. Joyce Anne Oliver and Eric J. Johnson, "People Motive Redefines Customer Service," *HR Magazine*, Vol. 35, Iss. 6 (June 1990): 120.

13. Mary Kim Stuart interview, November 9, 1990.

14. Solomon, "Nightmare At Nordstrom," p. 77.

15. Mary Kim Stuart interview, November 9, 1990.

16. Solomon, "Nightmare At Nordstrom," p. 79.

17. Richard W. Stevenson, "Watch Out Macy's, Here Comes Nordstrom," *New York Times* – (August 27, 1989): 39.

18. Ibid.

19. Ibid.

20. Ibid.

21. Solomon, "Nightmare At Nordstrom," p. 83.

22. Faludi, "At Nordstrom Stores, Service Comes First—But at a Big Price."

23. Solomon, "Nightmare At Nordstrom," p. 77.

24. Ibid., 78.

25. Faludi, "At Nordstrom Stores, Service Comes First—But at a Big Price"; Spector and McCarthy, *The Nordstrom Way*.

26. Ibid.

27. Ibid.

28. Solomon, "Nightmare At Nordstrom," p. 78.

29. Faludi, "At Nordstrom Stores, Service Comes First—But at a Big Price."

30. Ibid.

31. Solomon, "Nightmare At Nordstrom," p. 78.

32. Ibid., 80.

33. Ibid., 81.

34. Ibid.

35. Robert Spector, "Nordstrom Discusses Its Problems," *Women's Wear Daily* (March 27, 1990): 18.

36. Solomon, "Nightmare At Nordstrom," p. 80.

37. "The Nordstrom Boys," *60 Minutes*: 10.

38. Ibid.

39. Lubove, "Don't Listen to the Boss, Listen to the Customer," p. 46.

40. "Nordstrom Workers in Seattle Reject Union," *New York Times* (July 20, 1991).

41. Ibid.

42. Solomon, "Nightmare At Nordstrom," p. 77.

43. Faludi, "At Nordstrom Stores, Service Comes First—But at a Big Price."

44. Stevenson, "Watch Out Macy's, Here Comes Nordstrom."

45. Ibid., 40.

Part 3

GROUP AND INTERPERSONAL PROCESSES IN ORGANIZATIONS

Part 3 introduces you to group dynamics and interpersonal processes in organizations. The main topics include behavior in and between groups, conflict in organizations, and leadership and management. Each chapter discusses international aspects of the topics and the ethical issues they raise.

The first chapter in this part, Chapter 10, "Groups and Intergroup Processes," describes groups and intergroup processes in organizations. It begins by distinguishing between formal and informal groups in organizations and then lays a basic conceptual foundation. The chapter offers various perspectives on groups in organizations. It builds a model of group formation that should help you understand how and why cohesive groups form in organizations. Chapter 10 features sections on virtual groups, self-managing teams, workgroup socialization, the effects of workforce diversity on group dynamics, and factors that affect group effectiveness. The chapter also examines the functions and dysfunctions of groups.

Chapter 11, "Conflict in Organizations," focuses on conflict and conflict management in organizations. It begins by defining conflict and discussing functional conflict, dysfunctional conflict, and different levels of conflict. Conflict episodes and the dynamics of conflict behavior are then discussed. The episodic feature of conflict in organizations is a key point. A section on conflict frames and orientations notes their effects on a conflict episode. The chapter develops a model of conflict management that can guide you in choosing when to reduce conflict and when to increase conflict. The model can also help you diagnose conflict in an organization.

The third chapter in this part, Chapter 12, "Leadership and Management," describes leadership processes and organizations. It views leadership as an influence process that affects other people's behavior. Several approaches to the study of leadership have evolved over the years. Trait approaches looked for personal qualities that distinguished effective from ineffective leaders or leaders from followers. Behavioral approaches focused on leader behavior and leader effectiveness. Contingency approaches studied the effects of different behaviors in different situations. The chapter also describes several alternative views of leadership.

Chapter 10

GROUPS AND INTERGROUP PROCESSES

Groups, group dynamics, and intergroup processes are inevitable and critical aspects of organizations and their management. This chapter builds upon premises that emphasize the inevitability of groups in organizations. Those premises view groups as having both good and bad effects for organizations and their members. The chapter also examines the growing use of virtual groups and self-managing teams.[1]

A **group** is an interdependent set of people doing a task or trying to reach a common goal. Group members regularly interact with each other and depend on each other to do their tasks. Job and organizational design can affect the degree of mutual dependence. A group is a complex, adaptive system that can change its membership, goals, and structure over time.[2]

Groups can powerfully affect people's behavior. Knowledge of how and why groups form, and an understanding of their dynamics, can help you function better within a group or manage group activities. The following classic statement captures this chapter's orientation toward groups in organizations:

> [G]roups exist; they are inevitable and ubiquitous; they mobilize powerful forces having profound effects upon individuals; these effects may be good or bad; and through a knowledge of group dynamics there lies the possibility of maximizing their good value.[3]

FORMAL AND INFORMAL GROUPS

Formal groups are either functional groups within an organization or task groups.[4] Functional groups are clusters of people formed by the organization's design, such as divisions, departments, sections, and work units. They are a product of the organization's division of labor, the way the organization has divided its total work to reach its goals. Such groups are often permanent, but can change if the organization redesigns its structure.

Organizations form task groups as temporary groups to carry out specific duties, usually special projects.[5] Committees, project teams, and task forces are examples of task groups. Other examples from quality management are process-action teams and continuous-improvement teams. Temporary task groups do not have the enduring qualities of permanent groups because they usually disband when they finish their assignment.

Virtual groups and self-managing teams are emerging types of formal groups.[6] Networked computers and workstations link members of virtual groups. Self-managing teams typically have high internal autonomy and decision authority about work scheduling, team member assignments, and the choice of a team leader. Later sections examine both virtual groups and self-managing teams in detail.

Interaction patterns within organizations can affect the formation of informal groups within and across formal groups.[7] **Informal groups** can form along interest lines, such as the task specialization of individuals, hobbies, or other concerns. They might be friendship groups whose members associate with each other both at work and away from work. Outsiders and newcomers cannot readily see informal groups, which are part of an organization's background. These informal groups form a "shadow organization" that applies good and bad powerful forces to the organization.[8]

BASIC CONCEPTS FOR UNDERSTANDING GROUPS IN ORGANIZATIONS

Several basic concepts will help you understand the dynamics of groups in organizations.[9] Group members take on specific roles within the group. A **role** is a set of activities, duties, responsibilities, and required behaviors. It is also a set of shared expectations about how a person ought to behave in a group. Both the organization and the group help define a person's role.

Group **norms** are unwritten rules that define acceptable role behavior of group members. Norms include performance levels valued by the group, teamwork within the group, and relationships with managers and other aspects of the formal organization.[10] New members learn a group's norms from its socialization process, a process described in the later section, "Workgroup Socialization."

A **cohesive group** has members who are attracted to the group's task, to its prestige, and to other members of the group. Members of cohesive groups like to be together, care about each other, and typically know each other well. A cohesive group can also pressure a new member to conform to its norms. Some research suggests that cohesive groups can perform better than noncohesive groups.[11]

Two types of **conformity** to group norms are possible: compliance and personal acceptance.[12] **Compliance** means a person goes along with the group's norms but does not accept them. A person might comply to help the group appear united to outsiders or to prevent conflict within the group. **Personal acceptance** means an individual's beliefs and attitudes are congruent with group norms. Personal acceptance is the more powerful of the two types of conformity. A person might strongly defend the group's norms and try to socialize new members to them, because she has internalized those norms. Conformity to group norms is not necessarily bad; it can bring order to a group's activities.[13] Because members know what to expect from each other and share performance expectations, conformity often leads to more effective group performance. A later section in the chapter discusses the dysfunctions of excessive conformity.

Behavior in groups falls into two major classes: required and emergent. Required behavior is what a person must do because of organization membership and as part of the person's role in the formal group. Required behaviors include being at work at a specific time, performing job duties in a certain way, and interacting with specific people in another department to complete a task.[14] Emergent behavior grows out of the interactions among group members. Such behavior can focus on work tasks or be purely social.[15] The norms of a group can define emergent behavior. Organizations do not prescribe emergent behaviors and often do not formally acknowledge that such behavior happens. The newcomer to an existing cohesive group will not immediately understand the function and meaning of many emergent behaviors.

FUNCTIONS OF GROUPS IN ORGANIZATIONS

Groups have several functional effects on organizations. As described in Chapter 6, "Organizational Socialization," groups can be an important source of socialization of organization members. Whether the result of the socialization will be functional for the organization depends on the group's orientation to management.

Groups can be a source of rewards for members, serving as an important motivational system. Praise and other rewards offered by the group can reinforce member behavior. Groups also provide support for their members while they work. This function of groups is especially important to those doing hazardous work, where the cooperation of all members of the group is necessary to do a job safely.

Cohesive groups with norms supportive of management can have several other functional results.[16] If tasks are interdependent, the cooperative behavior of cohesive group members helps them complete tasks. A cohesive group can produce innovative work behavior that has value for the organization. Cohesive groups are self-policing and can stamp out deviant behavior. Control over individual behavior in cohesive groups is more immediate than controls used by managers.[17]

DYSFUNCTIONS OF GROUPS IN ORGANIZATIONS

Groups sometimes have dysfunctional consequences for either the group member or the organization.[18] Groups can take more time to do some tasks than individuals. The group structure takes time to develop. Conflict in the early stages of group development takes time to settle.

People who are members of cohesive groups often experience some loss of their individual identity. Groups give individuals a degree of anonymity, causing some people to behave in atypical ways. Responsibility for negative results of the group's actions can become diffused among group members. Because no single person takes responsibility for a bad decision, people in groups can escape accountability for their behavior.

Virtual groups (discussed more fully in the later section "Virtual Groups") can experience negative effects that are unique to such groups.[19] The absence of social cues because of little or no face-to-face interaction removes important communication information that humans use. Nonverbal communication such as eye contact and emotional gestures can tell people in the group that the speaker feels passionately about her views. Their absence in electronic communication can reduce the effect of minority positions (see the section, "Majority and Minority Influences in Groups") on group results, perhaps leading to poor decisions or ineffective problem solving.[20]

Virtual groups can take longer to make decisions than other types of groups. If the decision or problem has a time-critical element, then a virtual group is not a likely optimal approach.

Other dysfunctional consequences can appear in all types of groups. **Social loafing**, or the free-rider effect, can develop when a person perceives her effort in the group as unimportant or as not easily seen by others.[21] **Sucker effects** happen when other group members perceive a member as a free rider, someone not pulling her weight, and reduce their efforts to remedy feelings of inequity. In both cases, group members reduce their efforts toward the group's goals, often lowering overall group performance.

A cohesive group can put strong pressure on its members to conform to its norms. Such **conformity** can lead to high levels of uniformity of behavior within the group. It also can lead to close monitoring of member behavior to ensure compliance with the group's norms. The amount of control a group exerts over its members can exceed the control of individual managers or supervisors.[22] The almost continual interaction among group members keeps them under the watchful "eye of the norm."[23]

Uniformity in decision-making groups can also lead to groupthink.[24] **Groupthink** is a major dysfunction of cohesive decision-making groups. Groups suffering from groupthink strive for consensus, typically consider only a few alternatives before making a decision, and do not periodically reexamine the assumptions underlying their decisions. The obvious results for an organization are a less effective decision-making process and poor-quality decisions. Chapter 14, "Decision-Making and Problem-Solving Processes," has a more extended discussion of groupthink.

MODEL OF COHESIVE GROUP FORMATION

This section builds a conceptual model that you can use to analyze how and why cohesive groups form in an organization. The model applies to both formal and informal groups. Central to the model are the concepts of activities, interactions, and sentiments.[25]

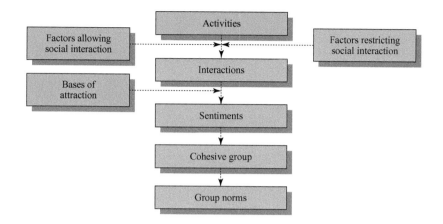

■ **Figure 10.1:** Model of Cohesive Group Formation

Figure 10.1 shows a model of cohesive group formation. Required work activities lead to social interaction when the factors allowing it exceed those restricting it. The bases of attraction affect the formation of sentiments during the interactions. If individuals are attracted to each other, mutually positive sentiments can develop. A cohesive group then forms with norms governing group member behavior.

Activities, Interactions, and Sentiments

Activities are the formal organizational requirements, such as job duties and responsibilities. Activities follow from formal group membership and the division of labor of the organization. The physical layout of the work area and the technical process of the organization can also demand certain activities. Activities are the same as required behaviors. They are behaviors a person must do because of organizational membership.

Interaction refers to social interaction between two or more people. The interaction can be face-to-face with two people talking to each other or interaction through memoranda and reports. Interaction can also occur using telecommunications devices, televideo devices, personal computers (PCs), e-mail, and the World Wide Web.[26]

Sentiments are attitudes, beliefs, and feelings about the person or persons with whom an individual interacts. Sentiments develop from social interactions and are feelings of like or dislike for one another.

Required behavior can lead to social interaction. People are required to do certain things as employees of the organization (activities). Those required activities bring a person into contact with other people (interaction). The following is an example of an activities, interactions, and sentiments pattern:

Valerie has just joined a cross-functional team that has the task of analyzing the complex procurement processes of her company. The team is large with 15 members. Valerie comes from the Human Resources function; other team members come from Accounting, Finance, Marketing, and Manufacturing.

During the team's discussions (activities), Valerie must interact with Jessica from Manufacturing. She learns from their conversations that she and Jessica share a common interest in restoring older Vespa motor scooters.

Notice that the interactions are part of required work behavior. During the interaction, Valerie and Jessica learn about each other's background and interests and discover they have a common interest. From this information, they can develop positive or negative feelings (sentiments) about each other.

Work activities lead to patterns of social interaction that let people sort out their sentiments. If they find they share similar interests, likes, and dislikes, they can be attracted to each other. A cohesive group can form if the interactions involve several people.

Organizational Factors that Affect Cohesive Group Formation

Several **factors** in the physical layout of work areas, work processes, organizational design, and job design affect the **formation of cohesive groups**.[27] Those factors will either allow social interaction or restrict it. If the factors allowing social interaction exceed those that restrict it and positive sentiments emerge among those who interact, a cohesive group should form. A manager who understands those factors can use them to encourage the formation of a cohesive group or to build barriers against its formation.

The proximity of people affects social interaction. If people are physically close together, the potential for social interaction is high. If they are widely separated, the potential is low. The physical separation of formal groups forms clear boundaries between groups. A clearly defined boundary increases the potential for social interaction within the formal group. A less well-defined boundary decreases that potential. Fuzzy boundaries can also increase social interaction among members of different groups, decreasing the possibility of a cohesive group forming. The ambient noise level affects whether people can talk easily to each other while working. A high noise level decreases the chance of oral communication; a low noise level increases that chance.

Job activities requiring interaction among workers, as in the payroll clerk example, increase the potential of cohesive group formation. Similarly, incomplete job descriptions can require an individual to go to a coworker for help. The presence of complete job descriptions decreases the likelihood of such social interaction.

Free time at work during rest periods and the ability to move around while working increase the probability of social interaction. A job that does not require close attention lets the worker interact with other nearby workers. The opposite characteristics decrease the potential for social interaction.

Absenteeism and turnover within a formal group also affect social interaction. High absenteeism decreases the chance of the same group of people interacting with each other. Low absenteeism has the opposite effect. High turnover increases the instability of group membership. The continual presence of new people causes the group to focus on socializing the new people, decreasing the likelihood of a stable pattern of social interaction.

Bases of Attraction

Physical factors alone do not fully explain cohesive group formation. **Bases of attraction** explain why people who can potentially interact are sufficiently attracted to each other to form a cohesive group.[28]

Similarities in attitudes, beliefs, gender, ethnic background, age, social status, and education can be the bases of people's attraction to each other. Individuals are attracted to each other because they share common experiences. Membership in a group can also satisfy a person's desire for social interaction, causing the person to be attracted to group members. Individuals might perceive group memberships as helping them to reach a goal. For example, you might join a college sorority or fraternity because you believe that companies like to hire college graduates who have been involved in such organizations.

When people form mutually positive sentiments about each other, they move toward the formation of a cohesive group. Such groups have norms that guide the behavior of group members.

STAGES OF GROUP DEVELOPMENT

All types of groups (face-to-face, virtual, and self-managing teams) can develop in a series of stages with each stage emphasizing something different.[29] Early aspects of development focus on the social structure of the group: norms, social status, roles, and role relationships.[30] Each stage has different implications for member behavior and group performance. The stages are not discrete, clearly identifiable states. They are plateaus in the group's evolution from beginning to end. Groups of strangers that have not done the group's task before are most likely to experience all stages of development.[31]

The **stages of group development** are a controversial area of group and group dynamics research. Little research has examined the stages in organizational settings.[32] A conservative conclusion from the research evidence says the stages apply only to newly formed groups.[33] That conclusion suggests that knowledge about group development could be especially important in an organization that deliberately uses groups to do work.

During the **group formation stage (forming)**,[34] group members meet each other for the first time and learn about the group's tasks. The group defines its social and task boundaries. People who have never been together before introduce themselves to each other. They reveal their characteristics and abilities to other group members, sometimes slowly. The members also discuss preliminary ideas about how to do the group's task.

The **intragroup conflict stage (storming)** begins to evolve. Discussions focus on behavior, roles, and social relationships that are right for doing the group's task. Informal leaders begin to emerge, even if a formal leader exists, as is often true for a formal task group. Power struggles might erupt between competing informal leaders. Conflict arises about how the group should do its tasks. People often struggle to keep their identity and autonomy as the group tries to give an identity to the individual. New members entering an existing cohesive group experience the power and force of the group's socialization process at this stage.[35]

By the **group cohesion stage (norming)**, the group has defined its roles and role relationships. The group agrees about correct member behavior. Members accept each other, and an identifiable group culture emerges. Conflict is less intense at this stage than during the preceding stage. If conflict is accepted as part of the group's norms, the group defines acceptable conflict behavior. The conflict at this stage focuses less on the social structure of the group than on different ways of doing the group's task.[36] The way group members perform their tasks might be evaluated. Conflict can arise if an individual sharply deviates from the group's norm about task behavior.

Group members become comfortable with each other at the **task orientation stage (performing)** and have accepted the group's norms. Members have settled upon their goals and worked out their division of labor. The task or tasks are now defined, and energy focuses on doing the group's work.

Some groups reach their goals, disband, and end their existence as an identifiable group (**termination or adjourning stage**). Other groups redefine their task and membership. If either event happens, the group returns to the first stage of development and restarts the process.

Functional groups and cohesive informal groups reach the task orientation stage of development and plateau there. Under certain conditions, such groups repeat the stages and experience redevelopment.[37] When newcomers join an established group, the group's social structure and ways of doing its task often are altered. Established members of the group, especially formal or informal leaders, socialize the new member to the group's norms. All the forces and dynamics of socialization processes come into play for the newcomer.

Organizations that undergo a major redesign often redistribute existing organization members into new formal groups. The people are not new to the organization, but they are new to the groups in which they find themselves. The stages of group development repeat as groups affected by the reorganization try to redevelop.

SOCIAL STRUCTURE OF GROUPS

All mature groups have a **social structure** with several dimensions.[38] These dimensions include group member roles, role relationships, the communication network of the group, and influence patterns within the group. Knowing the social structure of a group will help you understand its members' behavior and your behavior.

Each role within a group is a major dimension of its structure. Group norms partly define each member's role and expected behavior. Individuals can change their roles, adding to and taking away from them. Each member learns a role in a group during early socialization to the group's norms. Each role has a specific position within the group's status structure. The **status** structure defines the relative position of each role and the relationships among the roles.

Table 10.1 describes some typical roles found in groups.[39] The roles cluster into the broad classes of task roles, maintenance roles, and individual roles. Task roles focus on the group's tasks, issues, or problems. Maintenance roles focus on behavioral processes within the group with the intent of reaching the group's goals. Individual roles focus on member needs and behavior that often have little to do with the group's task.

Each group member holds a position in the group's communication network. Some members have a central position in the network with connections to all group members. They play a central role in the group because of their connections to other group members. Other people play peripheral roles; they are distant from other group members and are not highly involved in its communication network. The degree of centrality or marginality of an individual varies from one group to another. Another possible position in a group's communication network is between two other members. Communication must go through a

■ **Table 10.1: Typical Roles Found in Groups**

Task Roles

Initiator	Offers new ideas about how to do the group's task or resolve its problems.
Information seeker/giver	Seeks clarifying information or adds new information to the group's discussions.
Elaborator	Extends the information used by the group by offering examples or trying to show the expected results of the group's effort.
Coordinator	Helps pull together the activities of group members.
Recorder	Keeps a written record of the group's activities.

Maintenance Roles

Encourager	Motivates other members to contribute ideas to the group.
Harmonizer	Referees conflict among group members.
Compromiser	Reduces conflict within the group by finding ways of splitting differences.
Gatekeeper	Tries to keep communication links open with important parties outside the group.
Follower	Accepts the direction of the group, usually passively.

Individual Roles

Aggressor	Acts hostilely toward other group members.
Blocker	Resists the group's direction and opposes the views of others.
Joker	Engages in horseplay; tells stories and jokes unrelated to group activities.
Dominator	Tries to give direction to other group members and assert own higher status over others.

Source: Benne, K., and P. Sheats. 1948. Functional Roles of Group Members. *Journal of Social Issues 2*: 43–46. This classic source also describes other roles in groups.

person who has such a connecting role. That person can impede or enhance communication within the group depending on how well she handles the communication requirements of this role.

Power and influence patterns within a group follow from a person's role in the group. Formal groups often have appointed leaders with authority over other members of the group. Informal leaders develop within informal and formal groups. Those individuals take on the social power other group members give them.

A group's structure can affect its members and the performance of the group.[40] A person's position and role in a group can lead to the satisfaction or frustration of the person's needs. An individual with a strong need for dominance or power can satisfy that need by assuming a leadership role within a group. If forced into a subordinate role, that person's needs will be frustrated.

People often are members of many groups in an organization and play different roles in different groups. A person can hold a leadership position in one group and a subordinate position in another. The different roles require the person to behave differently in the two groups. Such differences can lead to conflict among the roles people play within an organization.

FACTORS THAT AFFECT GROUP EFFECTIVENESS

Many factors can affect a group's effectiveness.[41] **Effectiveness** includes member satisfaction and reaching group and organization goals. These factors are important considerations when managers and organizations deliberately use groups to get work done.

A group's **physical environment** affects interaction within the group. People at the ends of a rectangular table participate more in group activities than those in other positions. People who know each other well often sit next to each other. People interact more with those seated across from them than with those in different seats. Leaders often emerge from the head of a rectangular table, but it is more difficult to predict the emergence of leaders in a circular arrangement.

The **size and type of area** in which a group works can affect its effectiveness. Large groups feel crowded when they do not have enough space to work comfortably. Groups with physical boundaries can become more cohesive than groups whose boundaries are diffused or blurred.

Compatibility of group members in both needs and personality can lead to higher group productivity.[42] Individuals who have a high need for dominance, for example, are more compatible with people who can play a subordinate role. Conflict within a group increases when members are not compatible with each other.

Although compatibility can lead to high performance, groups with members of diverse abilities who apply those abilities to the group's task also are effective. Group tasks requiring variations in people's performance call for differences in member characteristics. If the tasks require similarities in people's performance, similarities in member characteristics lead to higher performance. Members with special skills who apply those skills to the group's task will often actively participate and can strongly affect the group's decisions.

Group goals have strong effects on group performance. Groups with specific, clear goals outperformed those with less specific goals. The research evidence is unclear about whether involvement in goal setting has positive effects. Feedback also likely plays an important role in group performance.[43] Other evidence suggests that interdependent groups should receive group, not individual, rewards.[44]

Productivity typically is lower in large groups than in small ones.[45] Group size has several specific effects, including the following:

■ Satisfaction with the group's activities decreases as size increases.
■ Participation of members drops as size increases.
■ The strength of bonds among group members decreases as group size increases.
■ Large groups have more resources such as information for doing the group's task.
■ Reaching agreement about a group's activities or making decisions is more difficult in large groups than in small ones.
■ A leader more likely emerges as group size increases.
■ Large groups make communication and coordination of group members more difficult.
■ People in large groups have difficulty learning about each other. For example, in a three-person group, the number of possible relationships is 6; in a four-person group, 25; and in a six-person group, 301!

Small groups work well for tasks with high cooperation requirements.[46] People working on difficult tasks do better when the group allows feedback while doing the task. A group norm of letting people know how they are doing will help such feedback. Keeping the group size small enough also can encourage feedback so that people will know the performance of other group members.

VIRTUAL GROUPS

Virtual groups are human groups using computer systems to link group members. They feature an information technology environment using PCs or workstations connected over a network. The network can be in a single room, over an organization's intranet, or over the Internet. Such connections allow different temporal and physical patterns ranging from meeting in a single room simultaneously or at dispersed locations asynchronously. Figure 10.2 shows one virtual group configuration. Software within the system supports problem-solving and decision-making groups. The system's goal is to support group processes that increase decision effectiveness and quality.[47]

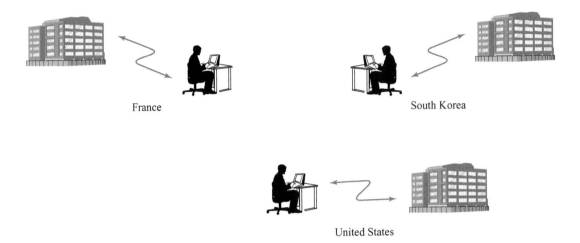

France

South Korea

United States

▨ **Figure 10.2:**   A Virtual Group Configuration

A single room layout has individuals or small groups seated at individual PCs. Some physical interaction is possible within this pattern. Another pattern lets people work from their offices either within the same building or at scattered locations. This design typically does not allow direct physical interaction. Another design links people over the Internet either within rooms equipped for virtual groups or at individual computers. The people in this pattern can be at scattered locations anywhere in the world. This type of group becomes part of the virtual organization described in Chapter 17, "Organizational Design."

Electronic meeting systems or **group decision support systems** are underlying technologies for virtual groups. Several such systems exist from different sources. Two examples are GroupSystems ThinkTank (www.group systems.com) and Cisco Systems WebEx (www.webex.com).

Virtual group technologies have the following features and characteristics:

▨ Decision tools software supports a problem-solving or decision-making task.

▨ Process tools software supports a particular approach to a group's task. Example: electronic brainstorming tool (see Chapter 14, "Decision-Making and Problem-Solving Processes" for more details).

▨ Parallel communication allows group members to communicate with everyone in the group. Members input ideas and observations and simultaneously receive other members' ideas and observations, with little domination by a few people.

▨ Anonymous communication attaches no identification to a person's message. Some virtual groups allow identification of the person who originated a message.

▨ Shared software is available equally to all group members. Such sharing lets group members work on joint tasks.

■ Shared view gives all group members the same view of the group's work.
■ Communication within the virtual group is either synchronous (real time) or asynchronous (any time). Synchronous communication happens in chat rooms, with e-mail, and with other direct computer conferencing. The latter can include videoconferencing on a PC or workstation. Asynchronous communication uses e-mail or bulletin boards for threaded discussions.

Virtual groups present organizations and managers with the following challenges:[48]

■ Building trust among group members.
■ Building group cohesiveness.
■ Reducing feelings of member isolation and detachment from the group.
■ Balancing interpersonal and technical skill requirements of group members.
■ Managing potential conflict among geographically dispersed group members.
■ Recognizing the performance of groups and group members.

Some research has given guidelines on how to meet these challenges. Timeliness and consistency of interactions among members brings trust to the group. Training in conflict management, meeting management, and virtual group leadership helps build cohesiveness. Periodic face-to-face meetings of group members help reduce feelings of isolation. Selecting people with the right interpersonal and technical skills helps ensure a balance in these skills among members. Fair performance assessments come from peer reviews and using interaction information available from virtual group software. All these factors help reduce the challenges and increase virtual group effectiveness.[49]

SELF-MANAGING TEAMS

Self-managing teams are increasingly part of modern organizational life. These teams also are called self-directed teams, self-leading teams, self-regulating teams, or empowered teams. If properly designed, such groups adopt the good features of face-to-face workgroups and use knowledge about groups and their dynamics. Modern technology lets people work at remote locations connected to each other over the Internet or over an organization's intranet.[50]

A self-managing team is a group of people doing interdependent tasks to produce a product or deliver a service. Team members manage most aspects of their work, including making member work assignments, choosing a leader, and assessing their work quality. Managers should not use self-managing teams when people should work independently or when they want to work independently.

Sports teams have many examples of task independence and task interdependence in team success.[51] Swimming, track, and gymnastics rely on individual athletic performance, not a group of them in an interdependent relationship. Hockey, soccer, and basketball depend on closely coordinated interdependent athletes for success. Successful self-managing work teams in organizations depend on these same factors.

An organization that relies on self-managing teams moves decisions to the teams. Managers authorize the teams to decide about product design, process design, and customer service. Decentralization and self-managing teams flatten organizations by removing one or more layers of management. The result is often a nimble organization poised to meet changing opportunities and constraints in the external environment.

Managers assume team members have more knowledge about the technical aspects of their work and specific tasks than do other people. Team members share their technical knowledge among themselves and help train new members. Teams usually have specific quantity and quality goals to reach. Managers hold the team accountable for reaching these goals, but let the team decide how to reach them.

Team size and composition can affect team performance.[52] Large groups typically perform worse than smaller groups. Some experts recommend teams of five to seven members. Managers need to balance the heterogeneity and homogeneity of the team and select team members based on skills and abilities required by technical tasks. Teams with members who have experience in many functional areas of an organization can perform higher than teams with members from few functional areas. Managers also need to consider the social skills of team members. They should choose those who are comfortable interacting with other people and who believe they can perform effectively in a team environment.[53]

Team processes include cooperative behavior, interdependence, and conflict management.[54] The interaction, activities, and sentiments view described earlier applies to self-managing teams. Organizations use self-managing teams to maximize the benefit of the technical and social abilities of team members. Well-managed teams guide themselves through the inevitable conflict and emerge as cohesive teams with widely shared goals of quality work performance.

Team leader selection varies widely among self-managing teams.[55] Some teams choose their leader without management approval. In other cases, management appoints the leader or approves a team's recommendation. In still other situations, a team will not have an appointed leader. Leadership responsibilities and duties rotate among team members.

Organizations that use self-managing teams often use group-based performance rewards. They base the rewards on team performance, not individual performance. The reward goes to the team and is distributed to team members either as a percentage of base pay or a fixed amount. Research evidence shows positive performance effects of such rewards.[56]

Self-managing teams can directly interact with suppliers and customers inside and outside the organization.[57] Direct interaction with customers gives teams quick, accurate feedback. Such feedback can play an important role in sustaining member motivation, as noted in Chapter 9, "Job Design and Intrinsic Rewards."

Interactions with suppliers let information flow quickly in both directions. Suppliers can inform a team of any changes in what they supply; the team can inform suppliers about quality or scheduling problems so the supplier can quickly correct the problem.

Managers in organizations using self-managing teams have many roles that can help team performance.[58] Typically, several teams report to a manager. The manager plays a supportive role for the teams by getting needed resources and managing conflict between teams and other parts of the organization. She also plays an informative role, getting critical information to the team. Such information can focus on team performance, the team's contribution to the larger organization, or about the organization's direction.

Several empirical studies show the positive effects of properly designed self-managing teams that have the management support described earlier.[59] Such teams have higher work performance and higher levels of customer service than either individuals or other types of workgroups. Team members report higher job satisfaction and higher team and organizational commitment than people working under other systems. Research results also show decreased absenteeism and turnover.

Other research shows the failure of poorly designed or poorly supported teams. Managers who want to move their organizations toward self-managing teams face difficult tasks. The use of such teams often requires large-scale organizational change and many changes in management behavior.[60] Employees also can respond to such changes with resistance to the change effort. Some research shows that employee belief of possible unfair treatment within the new teams was associated with resistance to the change effort. The unfair treatment included perceptions of undesirable task assignments and conflicts with other team members over preferred days off.[61]

WORKGROUP SOCIALIZATION

Chapter 6, "Organizational Socialization," discussed socialization at the organizational level. This section discusses socialization at the group level. The two processes have similar features and dynamics, but also differ in some significant ways.

Most past empirical socialization research focused on socialization processes and effects at the organization or individual level. Little empirical research focused on workgroup socialization. This section presents current conceptual and theoretical thinking about workgroup socialization and its probable effects on you.[62]

Workgroup socialization processes likely unfold in the following three related phases:

■ **Phase I: Anticipation:** A potential newcomer to a group develops an image of participation in the group. That image includes expectations about a work role in the group and the character of interactions with group members.

Existing group members develop expectations about the newcomer's behavior and conformity to group norms.

■ **Phase II: Encounter:** The new group member enters the group, learns her role in it, and meets the reality of the workgroup's social processes. Both the newcomer and group members experience simultaneous processes of acceptance.

■ **Phase III: Adjustment:** The new group member has successfully adapted to the workgroup's requirements and the workgroup has successfully adapted to the new member.

The phase names and process descriptions might look familiar. They are similar to the socialization phases described in Chapter 6. Workgroup socialization phases, however, have a distinctly reciprocal quality in the interaction between the newcomer and group members.

Some workgroup socialization dynamics distinguish it from organizational socialization processes. A new member's entry into an existing group can strongly affect its processes and structure. Because workgroups are smaller than the organization to which they belong, newcomers come into closer contact with workgroup processes than organizational processes. For example, a gifted athlete joins an existing team and profoundly affects the team's dynamics and playing ability. A major distinguishing characteristic of workgroup socialization from organizational socialization is this process of mutual adjustment and adaptation.

Another distinguishing feature of workgroup socialization occurs in the formation of new workgroups, whether they are face-to-face groups, virtual groups, or self-managing teams. Forming new groups starts the process of socializing the entire workgroup. Note the wording of the last phrase. It implies that an entire group of people concurrently passes through the workgroup socialization phases described in the previous list. This process features complex interactions during a frenzied mutual adjustment period.

Any group member can want to leave a group or a group can decide it wants an individual to leave. In either case, a withdrawal process starts with the person becoming a marginal group member. Other group members might try to reattract or resocialize the person. If unsuccessful, the person leaves, keeping a memory of group membership and becoming part of the group's history.

Empirical and theoretical research continues on workgroup socialization. You will likely experience many dynamics discussed in this section as you enter and leave workgroups during your work career.

MAJORITY AND MINORITY INFLUENCES IN GROUPS

Cohesive groups feature an attachment to a group's norm or position by most group members. **Majority group members** can pressure minority or deviant members to conform to a group's norm or position. Majority group members outnumber minority group members and often hold negative views of minority or deviant members.[63]

Although outnumbered in groups, research shows positive group performance effects of minority group member influence. A group could perform at a low level because members ignore information from one or more nonconforming members. Minority group members do not accept prevailing group opinion on an issue, problem, or decision. Minority members bring alternative views to a problem or decision faced by the group. They actively increase conflict within the group (see Chapter 11, "Conflict in Organizations") to promote broad-ranging discussion. Minority members promote divergent thinking among majority members. The result is new information that can lead to better decisions or problem solutions.

Minority group members affect majority opinion by three methods. They present consistent, confident statements of their position. They repeat statements of opinion showing persistence and commitment to their position. Minority members also can time their statements for maximum effect. For example, a minority member notices an increase in workplace accidents and pushes for better health insurance coverage.

EFFECTS OF WORKFORCE DIVERSITY

Workforce diversity has both positive and negative effects on group development and functioning.[64] People of different backgrounds and orientations view problems and issues differently. Potentially, their diverse outlooks can help them create more solutions to problems and find better ways of doing the group's work. This feature of diverse groups is especially useful to organizations that use teams to analyze work processes to achieve continuous improvement. Successful management of diverse groups requires knowledge of group dynamics and conflict management (see Chapter 11) and an understanding and acceptance of differences among people.

Workforce diversity can also have negative effects on groups. Group members' intentions can be misinterpreted because of their different ways of viewing the world. Such problems are especially likely when members hold stereotypes about other members. Communication difficulties can arise if group members do not have a common first language or do not speak English in a smooth, polished way. Distrust might exist because group members fear the new and unknown. Diversity can also create high conflict potential, leading to inefficiencies in the group's processes.

These aspects of workforce diversity can introduce confusion and complexity to a group's processes. Diverse groups will take longer to pass through the early stages of group formation and become cohesive. Recall that some bases of attraction are people's personal qualities. Workforce diversity introduces wide variation in those qualities, making the process of becoming cohesive longer, more complex, and more difficult.

Empirical research directed at the effects of workforce diversity and group dynamics has shown mixed results.[65] Heterogeneous groups can take longer to match the performance of homogeneous groups. The emerging evidence from continued research points to positive effects within groups that effectively manage their differences.[66]

INTERGROUP PROCESSES IN ORGANIZATIONS

Intergroup processes happen when members of two or more groups must interact to complete a task.[67] Such processes feature interactions among members of different groups in an organization, such as manufacturing, quality assurance, finance, marketing, and design engineering. Although behavior at group interfaces is called intergroup behavior, groups do not interact directly. Members of groups interact with each other, representing their group's interests. The basic management issue is the effective coordination of activities that require contributions of people from different groups.

People from different groups can have different task, time, and goal orientations. Marketing people might have a strong customer focus; manufacturing people usually are cost- and schedule-conscious; research and development people often take a long-term view. These different orientations can affect the quality of social interaction among members of different groups.

Several forces affect intergroup interactions. People typically view their group as composed of members with differing characteristics and other groups as having homogeneous members. People also tend to favor people from their own group and to place positive value on its purpose. Groups with poor interpersonal relations (low cohesiveness) often experience high intergroup conflict.[68] Such social psychological responses can lead to categorization, stereotyping, and perceptual distortion of members from other groups.

Intergroup behavior often leads to conflict between groups, partly because of these social psychological forces. That conflict must be managed to keep it at a functional level so people can reach their work goals.[69] Conflict management, discussed in Chapter 11, is an almost inevitable and key part of managing intergroup processes.

The intergroup processes described here apply to both formal and informal groups. As organizations become increasingly affected by workforce diversity, formal groups likely will have more diverse members. Not only will diversity have positive and negative effects on intragroup processes, it can have similar effects on intergroup processes.

Workforce diversity could have important effects on the behavior between members of informal groups. Because informal groups form around bases of attraction, cohesive informal groups could form based on workforce demography. Characteristics such as gender, race, country of origin, and age could be the basis of such groups. Stereotyping and perceptual distortion of people from such informal groups can affect the quality of intergroup behavior among group members.

INTERNATIONAL ASPECTS OF GROUPS IN ORGANIZATIONS

Cross-cultural factors affect groups, group dynamics, and intergroup processes in several ways. Although forming and participating in groups are natural human characteristics, their functions vary in different cultures.[70]

The tendency to accept group pressure for conformity to a group's norms, for example, varies among cultures. The Japanese encourage high conformity to the norms of a group, which has the person's primary loyalty. Experimental research with German students showed a low tendency to conform. Conformity was moderate among people in Hong Kong, Brazil, Lebanon, and the United States. Such evidence suggests caution in carrying your home country view of conformity into other cultures.[71]

All societies pressure deviates to conform to norms, but the strength of the pressure and the intensity with which deviates are rejected vary from culture to culture. Some limited experimental evidence showed that French, Swedish, and Norwegian groups were highest in pressuring members to conform and in the intensity with which they rejected deviates. German and British groups were much lower in those pressures. Other research suggests that collectivistic cultures usually have higher levels of conformity than individualistic cultures.[72] These research results imply that understanding cultural differences in conformity is important for managers in organizations operating in different countries.

Acceptance of self-managing teams and some of their features likely varies across cultures.[73] Such teams fit the low power distance, high individualistic cultures of Australia and the United States. Countries that emphasize collectivism and strongly emphasize social status (high power distance) would accept teams, but possibly resist their self-managing feature. Group-oriented work activities likely will work, but supervisors should continue with their authority for hiring and firing and other areas of customary decision making.

Some research shows that team effectiveness is high in collectivistic systems.[74] One possible reason is the likely absence of social loafing, the group dysfunction discussed earlier. It appears more strongly within groups in individualistic cultures than within groups in collectivistic cultures. Collectivistic cultures also expect little expression of conflict during intergroup interactions. They favor suppressing conflict with little discussion about the feelings of different group members.[75]

ETHICAL ISSUES ABOUT GROUPS IN ORGANIZATIONS

The major ethical issues about groups in organizations center on conformity to group norms and the question of informed free choice. Cohesive groups develop powerful forces of socialization to their norms. If their socialization efforts are unsuccessful, such groups reject deviant members. A person can expect assignment to a formal group as a regular part of an employment contract, but can have little knowledge of the presence of informal groups and their norms before joining the organization. The ethical question becomes: Are managers required to inform recruits about all cohesive groups in the organization?

A second ethical issue centers on the selection of members for self-managing teams. People with weak affiliation needs usually do not enjoy high levels of interpersonal interaction. Self-managing teams require extensive interaction among members for success. Do managers have an ethical duty to screen people for membership based on the strength of their social needs? Should managers make membership on such teams voluntary, so people can choose whether to join a team?

Conflict levels within groups, especially heterogeneous groups, can be high and continuous. Such heterogeneity can come from the deliberate selection of members or can mirror the diversity of an organization's workforce. Some people find high conflict stressful. Do managers have an ethical duty to screen people for group membership based on the amount of conflict they can tolerate?

SUMMARY

SUMMARY
10

A group is a collection of people doing a task or trying to reach a goal. Formal groups are either task groups or functional groups, such as departments and work units. Informal groups form within and across formal groups. The basic concepts for understanding groups in organizations are norms, cohesiveness, required behavior, and emergent behavior. People join informal groups for many reasons, such as satisfying social needs. People with strong dominance or power needs can satisfy those needs through leadership roles in groups.

Many factors in the physical layout of work areas and work processes, organizational design, and job design affect the formation of a cohesive group. If such factors allow social interaction and positive feelings emerge among those who interact, a cohesive group should form.

The stages of group development each emphasize something different for group members. Conflict levels typically are high during the early stages of group development. Later stages focus on the group's tasks.

Several factors affect a group's effectiveness. The physical environment, social environment, group size (number of group members), and type of task all influence group effectiveness in different ways. Each factor has implications for designing groups in organizations to get work done.

Virtual groups are human groups using computer systems to link members. They feature an information technology environment using PCs or workstations connected over a network. Such connections allow different temporal and physical patterns ranging from meeting in a single room simultaneously or at dispersed locations asynchronously. The system's goal is to support group processes that increase decision effectiveness and quality.

Self-managing teams are an emerging, important type of formal group. These teams typically have high internal autonomy. They usually have decision authority on work scheduling, team member assignments, and the choice of a team leader. Empirical research focused on self-managing teams shows that such teams have consistent positive effects.

Workgroup socialization happens in a series of related phases, similar to the organizational socialization phases described in Chapter 6. A major distinguishing characteristic of workgroup socialization from organizational socialization is a process of mutual adjustment and adaptation for newcomers and group members.

Cohesive groups feature an attachment to a group's norm or position by most group members. Majority group members can pressure minority or deviant members to conform to a group's norm or position. Majority group members outnumber minority group members and often hold negative views of minority or deviant members. Although outnumbered in groups, research shows positive group performance effects of minority group member influence.

Cultural differences in group dynamics suggest one should learn about those differences before taking an assignment in another country. The pressure to conform to group norms and the value placed on conformity to those norms vary from culture to culture. Cultures also differ in how much conflict between groups they will accept.

The major ethical issues about groups in organizations center on conformity to group norms and informed free choice. Cohesive groups develop powerful forces of socialization to their norms. Such groups reject deviant members after unsuccessful efforts to get conformity to norms. Are managers ethically required to tell recruits about all cohesive informal groups in the organization?

REVIEW AND DISCUSSION QUESTIONS

REVIEW AND DISCUSSION QUESTIONS 10

1   Why are cohesive groups important to us as individuals? What are some reasons managers should care about the presence of groups and group cohesiveness?

2   What factors help or impede cohesive group formation? Reflect on your work experiences to find examples of these factors.

3   Discuss the model of cohesive group formation. Apply it to your experiences. Discuss instances where you have experienced the formation of a group.

4   Discuss the stages of group development. What behavior or events does each stage emphasize? Reflect on your work experiences. Discuss examples of each stage.

5   Review the section on "Virtual Groups." Discuss your experiences with electronic communication such as e-mail, threaded discussion bulletin boards, and chat rooms. What are some positive effects of virtual groups? What are some negative effects of such groups?

6   Discuss self-managing teams. Have you experienced such teams? Discuss your experiences from both a positive and negative perspective.

7 How should managers reward group performance? You might want to review the earlier motivation chapters (Chapter 7, "Motivation: Need Theories" and Chapter 8, "Motivation: Cognitive and Behavioral Theories and Techniques") for some hints.

TAKE FIVE: OB ALIVE: *HOOSIERS* (1986)

Norman Dale (Gene Hackman) takes on his new high school basketball coaching job with a high degree of focus and energy. A basketball-loving Indiana small town does not support him immediately but grows with him as the team has successive victories.

These scenes show Norman Dale's first day as the new basketball coach. George (Chelcie Ross), the Assistant Coach, is guiding a practice session when Coach Dale arrives. The scenes are DVD Chapter 5, "First Practice."

Consider the following questions while viewing these scenes: Did the team act as a cohesive group on the first day? Does it begin to develop into a cohesive group by the end of the first day of practice? If it does, what factors helped the team in that direction?

REFERENCES AND NOTES

1. Major sources for this chapter include:

Argote, L., and J. E. McGrath. 1993. Group Processes in Organizations: Continuity and Change. In *International Review of Industrial and Organizational Psychology*, Vol. 8, ed. C. L. Cooper and I. T. Robertson. Chichester: John Wiley & Sons, pp. 333–89.

Arrow, H., J. E. McGrath, and J. L. Berdahl. 2000. *Small Groups as Complex Systems: Formation, Coordination, Development, and Adaptation*. Thousand Oaks: Sage Publications.

Bettenhausen, K. L. 1991. Five Years of Group Research: What Have We Learned and What Needs to be Addressed. *Journal of Management* 17: 345–81.

Cartwright, D., and R. Lippitt. 1957. Group Dynamics and the Individual. *International Journal of Group Psychotherapy* 7: 86–102.

Kozlowski, S. W. J., and B. S. Bell. 2003. Work Groups and Teams in Organizations. In *Comprehensive Handbook of Psychology*, Vol. 12: *Industrial and Organizational Psychology*, ed. W. C. Borman, D. R. Ilgen, and R. J. Klimoski. New York: John Wiley & Sons, Chap. 14.

Levine, J. M., and R. L. Moreland. 1990. Progress in Small Group Research. In *Annual Review of Psychology*, Vol. 41, ed. M. R. Rosenzweig, and L. W. Porter. Palo Alto: Annual Reviews, pp. 585–634.

Levine, J. M., and R. L. Moreland. 1998. Small Groups. In *Handbook of Social Psychology*, Vol. 2, ed. D. T. Gilbert, S. T. Fiske, and G. Lindzey. New York: McGraw-Hill, Chap. 26.

Mathieu, J. E., J. R. Hollenbeck, D. van Knippenberg, and D. R. Ligen. 2017. *Journal of Applied Psychology* 102: 452–67.

McChrystal, S., T. Collins, D. Silverman, and C. Fussell. 2015. *Team of Teams: New Rules of Engagement for a Complex World*. New York: Penguin.

McGrath, J. E. 1984. *Groups: Interaction and Performance*. Englewood Cliffs: Prentice Hall.

McGrath, J. E., and L. Argote. 2003. Group Processes in Organizational Contexts. In *Blackwell Handbook of Social Psychology: Group Processes*, ed. M. A. Hogg and R. S. Tindale. London: Blackwell, pp. 603–27.

Moreland, R. L., and J. M. Levine. 1992. The Composition of Small Groups. In *Advances in Group Processes: A Research Annual*, ed. E. J. Lawler, B. Markovsky, C. Ridgeway, and H. A. Walker. Greenwich, CT: JAI Press, pp. 237–80.

Shaw, M. E. 1981. *Group Dynamics: The Psychology of Small Group Behavior*, 3rd edn. New York: McGraw-Hill.

Thibaut, J. W., and H. H. Kelley. 1959. *The Social Psychology of Groups*. New York: Wiley.

2. McGrath, J. E., H. Arrow, and J. L. Berdahl. 2000. The Study of Groups: Past, Present, and Future. *Personality and Social Psychology Review* 4: 95–105.

3. Cartwright and Lippitt, Group Dynamics and the Individual, p. 90.

4. Cartwright, D., and A. Zander. 1960. *Group Dynamics: Research and Theory*. New York: Harper & Row, pp. 36–38.

Hare, A. P. 1992. *Groups, Teams, and Social Interaction: Theories and Applications*. New York: Praeger.

5. Argote and McGrath, Group Processes in Organizations, pp. 339–40.

6. McLeod, P. L. 1999. A Literary Examination of Electronic Meeting System Use in Everyday Organizational Life. *The Journal of Applied Behavioral Science* 35: 188–206.

Stewart, G. L., C. C. Manz, and H. P. Sims, Jr. 1999. *Team Work and Group Dynamics*. New York: John Wiley & Sons.

Yeatts, D. E., and C. Hyten. 1998. *High-Performing Self-Managed Work Teams: A Comparison of Theory and Practice*. Thousand Oaks: Sage Publications.

7. Krackhardt, D., and J. R. Hanson. 1993. Informal Networks: The Company Behind the Chart. *Harvard Business Review* 71 (July–August): 104–11.

8. Allen, R. F., and S. Pilnick. 1973. Confronting the Shadow Organization: How to Detect and Defeat Negative Norms. *Organizational Dynamics* 1 (Spring): 6–10.

9. Developed from Bettenhausen, Five Years of Group Research, pp. 361–64.

Homans, G. C. 1950. *The Human Group*. New York: Harcourt, Brace & World.

Homans, G. C. 1961. *Social Behavior: Its Elementary Forms*. New York: Harcourt, Brace & World.

Lembke, S., and M. G. Wilson. 1998. Putting the "Team" into Teamwork: Alternative Theoretical Contributions for Contemporary Management Practice. *Human Relations* 51: 927–44.

Levine and Moreland, Progress in Small Group Research, pp. 600–1, 603–5.

10. Allen and Pilnick, Confronting the Shadow Organization.

11. Casey-Campbell, M., and M. L. Martens. 2009. Sticking It All Together: A Critical Assessment of the Group Cohesion–Performance Literature. *International Journal of Management Reviews* 11: 223–46.

Evans, C. R., and K. L. Dion. 1991. Group Cohesion and Performance: A Meta-Analysis. *Small Group Research* 22: 175–86.

Friedkin, N. E. 2004. Social Cohesion. *Annual Review of Sociology* 30: 409–25.

Kerr, N. L., and R. S. Tindale. 2004. Group Performance and Decision Making. *Annual Review of Psychology* 55: 623–55. See pp. 625–27 for a discussion of group cohesiveness and performance.

Kozlowski, S. W. J., and D. R. Ilgen. 2006. Enhancing the Effectiveness of Work Groups and Teams. *Psychological Science in the Public Interest* 7: 77–124. The discussion of group cohesiveness appears on pp. 87–89.

Mullen, B., and C. Copper. 1994. The Relation Between Group Cohesiveness and Performance: An Integration. *Psychological Bulletin* 115: 220–27.

12. Kent, M. V. 1994. Conformity. In *Small Group Research: A Handbook*, ed. A. P. Hare, H. H. Blumberg, M. F. Davies, and M. V. Kent. Norwood: Ablex Publishing Corporation, Chap. 4.

Kiesler, C. A., and S. B. Kiesler. 1969. *Conformity*. Reading, MA: Addison-Wesley.

13. Shaw, *Group Dynamics*, pp. 289–90.

14. Dubin, R. 1958. *The World of Work*. New York: Prentice Hall, Chap. 4.

15. Ibid., pp. 61–76.

16. Ibid., Chap. 6.

17. Barker, J. 1993. Tightening the Iron Cage: Concertive Control in Self-Managing Teams. *Administrative Science Quarterly* 38: 408–37.

18. Shaw, *Group Dynamics*, pp. 397–99.

19. McLeod, A Literary Examination of Electronic Meeting System Use.

Sillince, J. A. A., and M. H. Saeedi. 1999. Computer-Mediated Communication: Problems and Potentials of Argumentation Support Systems. *Decision Support Systems* 26: 287–306.

20. McLeod, P. L., R. S. Baron, M. W. Marti, and K. Yoon. 1997. The Eyes Have It: Minority Influence in Face-to-Face and Computer-Mediated Group Discussion. *Journal of Applied Psychology* 82: 706–18.

21. George, J. M. 1992. Extrinsic and Intrinsic Origins of Perceived Social Loafing in Organizations. *Academy of Management Journal* 35: 191–202.

Karau, S. J., and K. D. Williams. 1993. Social Loafing: A Meta-Analytic Review and Theoretical Integration. *Journal of Personality and Social Psychology* 65: 681–706.

Latané, B., K. Williams, and S. Harkins. 1979. Many Hands Make Light the Work: The Causes and Consequences of Social Loafing. *Journal of Personality and Social Psychology* 37: 822–32. This source first used the term *social loafing*.

Liden, R. C., S. J. Wayne, R. A Jaworski, and N. Bennett. 2004. Social Loafing: A Field Investigation. *Journal of Management* 30: 285–304.

Shepperd, J. A. 1993. Productivity Loss in Performance Groups: A Motivation Analysis. *Psychological Bulletin* 113: 67–81.

Social psychology researchers have traced the origins of social loafing research to Max Ringelmann, a French agricultural engineer. He collected his data between 1882 and 1887 and published his experiment's results in 1913. (Ringelmann, M. 1913. Recherches sur les Moteurs Animés: Travail de l'Homme [Research on Animated Sources of Power: The Work of Man]. *Annales de l'Institut National Agronomique, 2e série, tome XII*, 1–40.) See D. A. Kravitz and B. Martin. 1986. Ringelmann Rediscovered: The Original Article. *Journal of Personality and Social Psychology* 50: 936–41 for a readable review of this intellectual history.

22. Barker, Tightening the Iron Cage.

23. Ibid., p. 432.

24. Janis, I. L. 1973. *Victims of Group Think*. Boston: Houghton Mifflin.

25. Homans, *The Human Group*.
Homans, *Social Behavior*.

26. Good reviews appear in the introduction of A. R. Dennis and J. S. Valacich. 1994. Group, Sub-Group, and Nominal Group Idea Generation: New Rules for a New Media? *Journal of Management* 20: 723–36.
Kahai, S. S., J. J. Sosik, and B. J. Avolio. 1997. Effects of Leadership Style and Problem Structure on Work Group Process and Outcomes in an Electronic Meeting System Environment. *Personnel Psychology* 50: 121–46.

27. Developed from Davies, M. F. 1994. Physical Situation. In *Small Group Research: A Handbook*, ed. A. P. Hare, H. H. Blumberg, M. F. Davies, and M. V. Kent. Norwood: Ablex Publishing Corporation, Chap. 1.
Hare, A. P. 1976. *Handbook of Small Group Research*. New York: Free Press.
Hare, *Groups, Teams, and Social Interaction*.
Shaw, *Group Dynamics*, Chap. 4.

28. Berscheid, E., and E. H. Walster. 1969. *Interpersonal Attraction*. Reading, MA: Addison-Wesley.
Bramel, D. 1969. Interpersonal Attraction, Hostility and Perception. In *Experimental Social Psychology*, ed. J. Mills. New York: Macmillan, pp. 1–120.
Shaw, *Group Dynamics*, pp. 83–93.

29. Hare, *Handbook of Small Group Research*, Chap. 4.
Shaw, *Group Dynamics*, Chap. 4.

30. Shaw, *Group Dynamics*, pp. 98–99.

31. Seeger, J. A. 1983. No Innate Phases in Group Problem Solving. *Academy of Management Review* 8: 683–89.

32. Maples, M. F. 1988. Group Development: Extending Tuckman's Theory. *Journal for Specialists in Group Work* 13: 17–23.
Tuckman, B. W. 1965. Developmental Sequence in Small Groups. *Psychological Bulletin* 64: 384–99.
Tuckman, B. W., and M. A. C. Jensen. 1977. Stages of Small Group Development Revisited. *Group and Organization Studies* 2: 419–27.

33. Seeger, No Innate Phases.

34. The names in parentheses are quick ways of remembering each stage.

35. Wanous, J. P., A. E. Reichers, and S. D. Malik. 1984. Organizational Socialization and Group Development: Toward an Integrative Perspective. *Academy of Management Review* 9: 670–83.

36. Chapter 11 has much more about the role of conflict in groups and organizations.

37. Wanous, Reichers, and Malik, Organizational Socialization and Group Development, p. 671.

38. Developed from Cartwright and Zander, *Group Dynamics*, Chap. 34.
Levine and Moreland, Progress in Small Group Research, pp. 600–3.
Shaw, *Group Dynamics*, Chap. 8.

39. Benne, K., and P. Sheats. 1948. Functional Roles of Group Members. *Journal of Social Issues* 2: 41–49.

40. Cartwright and Zander, *Group Dynamics*, pp. 655–64.

41. Developed from Hare, *Handbook of Small Group Research*.
Gist, M. E., E. A. Locke, and M. S. Taylor. 1987. Organizational Behavior: Group Structure, Process, and Effectiveness. *Journal of Management* 13: 237–57.
Kozlowski and Ilgen, Enhancing the Effectiveness of Work Groups and Teams.
Levine and Moreland, Small Groups.

Sundstrom, E., K. P. De Meuse, and D. Futrell. 1990. Work Teams: Applications and Effectiveness. *American Psychologist* 45: 120–33.

42. Bettenhausen, Five Years of Group Research.

43. O'Leary-Kelly, A. M. 1998. The Influence of Group Feedback on Individual Group Member Response. In *Research in Personnel and Human Resources Management*, ed. G. R. Ferris. Stamford: JAI Press, pp. 255–94.

    O'Leary-Kelly, A. M., J. J. Martocchio, and D. D. Frink. 1994. A Review of the Influence of Group Goals on Group Performance. *Academy of Management Journal* 37: 1285–301.

44. DeMatteo, J. S., L. T. Eby, and E. Sundstrom. 1998. Team-Based Rewards: Current Empirical Evidence and Directions for Future Research. *Research in Organizational Behavior* 20: 141–83.

    Wageman, R., and G. Baker. 1997. Incentives and Cooperation: The Joint Effects of Task and Reward Interdependence on Group Performance. *Journal of Organizational Behavior* 18: 139–58.

45. Gooding, R. Z., and J. A. Wagner, III. 1985. A Meta-Analytic Review of the Relationship Between Size and Performance: The Productivity and Efficiency of Organizations and Their Subunits. *Administrative Science Quarterly* 30: 462–81.

    Guzzo, R. A., and M. W. Dickson. 1996. Teams in Organizations: Recent Research on Performance and Effectiveness. In *Annual Review of Psychology*, Vol. 47, ed. J. T. Spence, J. M. Barley, and D. J. Foss. Palo Alto: Annual Reviews, pp. 307–38.

    Hare, *Handbook of Small Group Research*.

    Kozlowski and Bell, Work Groups and Teams in Organizations, p. 338.

    Mullen and Copper, The Relation Between Group Cohesiveness and Performance, p. 213.

46. Shaw, *Group Dynamics*, pp. 375–77.

47. Developed from Borges, M. R. S., J. A. Pino, D. A. Fuller, and A. Salgado. 1999. Key Issues in the Design of an Asynchronous System to Support Meeting Preparation. *Decision Support Systems* 27: 269–87.

    Caldwell, D. F. and J. L. Koch. 2000. The Impact of Mobile Computing on Work Groups. In *Technology*, ed. T. L. Griffith. Stamford: JAI Press, pp. 133–56.

    Dennis, A. R., J. F. George, L. M. Jessup, J. F. Nunamaker, Jr., and D. R. Vogel. 1988. Information Technology to Support Electronic Meetings. *MIS Quarterly* 12: 591–624.

    Dennis, A. R., and M. L. Williams. 2003. Electronic Brainstorming: Theory, Research, and Future Directions. In *Group Creativity: Innovation Through Collaboration*, ed. P. B. Paulus and B. A. Nijstad. New York: Oxford University Press, Chap. 8.

    Duarte, D. L., and N. T. Snyder. 2001. *Mastering Virtual Teams: Strategies, Tools, and Techniques That Succeed*, 2nd edn. San Francisco: Jossey-Bass.

    George, J. F., G. K. Easton, J. F. Nunamaker, Jr., and G. B. Northcraft. 1990. A Study of Collaborative Group Work With and Without Computer-Based Support. *Information Systems Research* 1: 394–415.

    Hollingshead, A. B., and J. E. McGrath. 1995. Computer-Assisted Groups: A Critical Review of the Empirical Research. In *Team Effectiveness and Decision Making in Organizations*, ed. R. A. Guzzo, E. Salas, and Associates. San Francisco: Jossey-Bass, Chap. 3.

    McLeod, P. L. 1992. An Assessment of the Experimental Literature on the Electronic Support of Group Work: Results of a Meta-Analysis. *Human Computer Interaction* 7: 257–80.

McLeod, A Literary Examination of Electronic Meeting System Use.

McLeod, P. L., and J. K. Liker. 1992. Electronic Meeting System: Evidence from a Low Structure Environment. *Information Systems Research* 3: 195–223.

Nunamaker, J. F., Jr., R. O. Briggs, and D. D. Mittleman. 1996. Lessons from a Decade of Group Support Systems Research. In *Information Systems: Decision Support and Knowledge-Based Systems*, Vol. III, ed. J. F. Nunamaker, Jr. and R. H. Sprague, Jr. Washington, DC: IEEE Computer Society Press, pp. 418–27.

Rosen, B., S. Furst, and R. Blackburn. 2007. Overcoming Barriers to Knowledge Sharing in Virtual Teams. *Organizational Dynamics* 36: 259–73.

Saunders, C. S. 2000. Virtual Teams: Piecing Together the Puzzle. In *Framing the Domains of IT Management: Projecting the Future ... through the Past*, ed. Robert W. Zmud. Cincinnati: Pinnaflex Educational Resources, pp. 29–50.

Townsend, A. M., S. M. DeMarie, and A. R. Hendrickson. 1998. Virtual Teams: Technology and the Workplace of the Future. *Academy of Management Executive* 12: 17–29.

48. Cascio, W. F., and S. Shurygailo. 2002. E-Leadership and Virtual Teams. *Organizational Dynamics* 31: 362–76.

Kirkman, B. L., B. Rosen, C. B. Gibson, P. E. Tesluk, and S. O. McPherson, 2002. Five Challenges to Virtual Team Success: Lessons from Sabre, Inc. *Academy of Management Executive* 16: 67–79. This source has an excellent summary of the growth in virtual team usage.

Malhotra, A., A. Majchrzak, and B. Rosen. 2007. Leading Virtual Teams. *Academy of Management Perspectives* 21: 60–69.

Townsend, DeMarie, and Hendrickson, Virtual Teams.

Von Glinow, M. A., D. L. Shapiro, and J. M. Brett. 2004. Can We Talk and Should We? Managing Emotional Conflict in Multicultural Teams. *Academy of Management Review* 29: 578–92.

49. Cramton, C. D. 2002. Finding Common Ground in Dispersed Collaboration. *Organizational Dynamics* 30: 356–67.

50. Developed from the following sources and others cited throughout this section:

Hackman, J. R. 2002. *Leading Teams: Setting the Stage for Great Performances*. Boston: Harvard Business School Press.

Hackman, J. R., R. Wageman, T. M. Ruddy, and C. R. Ray. 2000. Team Effectiveness in Theory and Practice. In *Industrial and Organizational Psychology: Theory and Practice*, ed. C. Cooper and E. A. Locke. Oxford: Blackwell, Chap. 5.

Ketchum, L. D., and E. Trist. 1992. Designing the New Plant. In *All Teams Are Not Created Equal*. Newbury Park: Sage Publications, Chap. 8.

Kozlowski and Bell, Work Groups and Teams in Organizations, pp. 358–59.

Lipnack, J., and J. Stamps. 1997. *Virtual Teams: Reaching Across Space, Time, and Organizations with Technology*. New York: John Wiley & Sons.

Mohrman, S., S. Cohen, and A. Mohrman. 1995. *Designing Team-Based Organizations*. San Francisco: Jossey-Bass.

Ray, D., and H. Bronstein. 1995. *Teaming Up: Making the Transition to a Self-Directed, Team-Based Organization*. New York: McGraw-Hill.

Stewart, Manz, and Sims, Jr., *Team Work and Group Dynamics*.

Yeatts and Hyten, *High-Performing Self-Managed Work Teams*.

51. Katz, N. 2001. Sports Teams as a Model for Workplace Teams: Lessons and Liabilities. *Academy of Management Executive* 15: 56–69.

52. Bunderson, J. S., and K. M. Sutcliffe. 2002. Comparing Alternative Conceptualizations of Functional Diversity in Management Teams: Process and Performance Effects. *Academy of Management Journal* 45: 875–93.

    Hackman, Wageman, Ruddy, and Ray, Team Effectiveness in Theory and Practice, p. 115.

    Yeatts and Hyten, *High-Performing Self-Managed Work Teams*, Chap. 24.

53. Thomas, P., K. S. Moore, and K. S. Scott. 1996. The Relationship between Self-Efficacy for Participating in Self-Managed Work Groups and the Big Five Personality Dimensions. *Journal of Organizational Behavior* 17: 349–62.

54. Alper, S., D. Tjosvold, and K. S. Law. 1998. Interdependence and Controversy in Group Decision Making: Antecedents to Effective Self-Managing Teams. *Organizational Behavior and Human Decision Processes* 74: 33–52.

55. Yeatts and Hyten, *High-Performing Self-Managed Work Teams*, Chap. 27.

56. Batt, R. 1999. Work Organization, Technology, and Performance in Customer Service and Sales. *Industrial and Labor Relations Review* 52: 539–64.

    DeMatteo, Eby, and Sundstrom, Team-Based Rewards.

    Guthrie, J. P., and E. C. Hollensbe. 2004. Group Incentives and Performance: A Study of Spontaneous Goal Setting, Goal Choice, and Commitment. *Journal of Management* 30: 263–84.

    Wageman and Baker, Incentives and Cooperation.

57. Yeatts and Hyten, *High-Performing Self-Managed Work Teams*, Chaps. 19, 20.

58. Ibid., Chap. 18.

    Hackman, *Leading Teams*.

    Hogan, R., G. J. Curphy, and J. Hogan. 1994. What We Know About Leadership. *American Psychologist* 49: 493–505. Their team discussion appears on pp. 499–500.

59. Bettenhausen, Five Years of Group Research, pp. 368–69.

    Cohen, S. G., G. E. Ledford, Jr., and G. M. Spreitzer. 1996. A Predictive Model of Self-Managing Work Team Effectiveness. *Human Relations* 49: 643–76.

    Cotton, J. L. 1993. *Employee Involvement: Methods for Improving Performance and Work Attitudes*. Newbury Park: Sage Publications, Chap. 8.

    Ilgen, D., J. R. Hollenbeck, D. J. Sego, and D. A. Major. 1993. Team Research in the 1990s. In *Leadership Theory and Research: Perspectives and Directions*, ed. M. M. Chemers and R. Ayman. San Diego: Academic Press, Chap. 10.

    Kirkman, B. L., and B. Rosen. 1999. Beyond Self-Management: Antecedents and Consequences of Team Empowerment. *Academy of Management Journal* 42: 58–74.

    Levine and Moreland, Progress in Small Group Research, pp. 614–17.

    Oldham, G. R. 1996. Job Design. In *International Review of Industrial and Organizational Psychology*, Vol. 11, ed. C. L. Cooper and I. T. Robertson. Chichester: John Wiley & Sons, Chap. 2.

    Wageman, R. 2001. How Leaders Foster Self-Managing Team Effectiveness: Design Choices versus Hands-on Coaching. *Organization Science* 12: 559–77.

60. Hackman, J. R., ed. 1990. *Groups That Work (and Those That Don't)*. San Francisco: Jossey-Bass.

    Hackman, *Leading Teams*. Professor Hackman's wonderfully readable concluding chapter summarizes this view with many good examples. See Chapter 8, "Thinking Differently about Teams."

61. Shapiro, D. L., and B. L. Kirkman. 1999. Employees' Reaction to the Change to Work Teams: The Influence of "Anticipatory" Injustice. *Journal of Organizational Change Management* 12: 51–66.

62. Developed from Anderson, N., and H. D. C. Thomas. 1996. Work Group Socialization. In *Handbook of Work Group Psychology*, ed. M. A. West. Chichester: John Wiley & Sons, Chap. 17, pp. 423–48.

Kozlowski and Bell, Work Groups and Teams in Organizations, pp. 340–45.

Levine, J. M., and R. L. Moreland. 1994. Group Socialization: Theory & Research. In *European Review of Social Psychology*, Vol. 5, ed. W. Stroebe and M. Hewstone. Chichester: John Wiley & Sons, pp. 305–36.

Moreland, R. L., and J. M. Levine. 1982. Socialization in Small Groups: Temporal Changes in Individual-Group Relations, ed. L. Berkowitz. *Advances in Experimental Social Psychology* 15: 137–92.

Moreland, R. L., and J. M. Levine. 1984. Role Transitions in Small Groups. In *Role Transitions: Explorations and Explanations*, ed. V. L. Allen and E. Van de Vleirt. New York: Plenum Press, pp. 181–95.

63. De Dreu, C. K. W., and N. K. De Vries. 1997. Minority Dissent in Organizations. In *Using Conflict in Organizations*, ed. C. K. W. De Dreu and E. Van de Vliert. London: Sage Publications, Chap. 5.

De Dreu, C. K. W., F. Harinck, and A. E. M. Van Vianen. 1999. Conflict and Performance in Groups and Organizations. In *International Review of Industrial and Organizational Psychology*, Vol. 14, ed. C. L. Cooper and I. T. Robertson. Chichester: John Wiley & Sons, pp. 391–94.

McLeod, Baron, Marti, and Yoon, The Eyes Have It.

Nemeth, C. J. 1986. Differential Contributions of Majority and Minority Influence. *Psychological Review* 93: 22–32.

Nemeth, C., and P. Owens. 1996. Making Work Groups More Effective: The Value of Minority Dissent. In *Handbook of Work Group Psychology*, ed. M. West. Chichester: John Wiley & Sons, Chap. 6.

Wood, W., S. Lundgren, J. A. Ouellette, S. Busceme, and T. Blackstone. 1994. Minority Influence: A Meta-Analytic Review of Social Influence Processes. *Psychological Bulletin* 115: 323–45.

64. Adler, N. J., with A. Gundersen. 2008. *International Dimensions of Organizational Behavior*, 5th edn. Mason: Thomson South-Western, Chap. 5.

Jackson, S. E. 1992. Team Composition in Organizational Settings: Issues in Managing an Increasingly Diverse Work Force. In *Group Process and Productivity*, ed. S. Worchel, W. Wood, and J. A. Simpson. Newbury Park: Sage Publications, pp. 138–73.

Jackson, S. E., K. E. May, and K. Whitney. 1995. Understanding the Dynamics of Diversity in Decision-Making Teams. In *Team Effectiveness and Decision Making in Organizations*, ed. R. Guzzo, E. Salas, and Associates. San Francisco: Jossey-Bass, pp. 204–61.

Larkey, L. K. 1996. Toward a Theory of Communicative Interactions in Culturally Diverse Workgroups. *Academy of Management Review* 21: 463–91.

Lau, D. C., and J. K. Murnighan. 1998. Demographic Diversity and Faultlines: The Compositional Dynamics of Organizational Groups. *Academy of Management Review* 23: 325–40.

Levi, D. 2011. *Group Dynamics for Teams*. Los Angeles: SAGE.

Philips, K. W. 2008. *Diversity and Groups*. Bingley: Emerald Group.

Polzer, J. T., C. B. Crisp., S. L. Jarvenpaa, and J. W. Kim. 2006. Extending the Faultline Model to Geographically Dispersed Teams: How Colocated Subgroups Can Impair Group Functioning. *Academy of Management Journal* 49: 679–92.

Shaw, J. B., and E. Barrett-Power. 1998. The Effects of Diversity on Small Work Group Processes and Performance. *Human Relations* 51: 1307–25.

Williams, K. Y., and C. A. O'Reilly III. 1998. Demography and Diversity in Organizations: A Review of 40 Years of Research. In *Research in Organizational Behavior*, Vol. 20, ed. B. M. Staw and L. L. Cummings. Greenwich, CT: JAI Press, pp. 77–140.

Ziller, R. C. 1972. Homogeneity and Heterogeneity of Group Membership. In *Experimental Social Psychology*, ed. C. G. McClintock. New York: Holt, Rinehart & Winston. pp. 385–411.

65. Chatman, J. A., and F. J. Flynn. 2001. The Influence of Demographic Heterogeneity on the Emergence and Consequence of Cooperative Norms in Work Teams. *Academy of Management Journal* 44: 956–74.

Cox, T. H., S. A. Lobel, and P. L. McLeod. 1991. Effects of Ethnic Group Cultural Differences on Cooperative and Competitive Behavior on a Group Task. *Academy of Management Journal* 34: 827–47.

Gist, Locke, and Taylor, Organizational Behavior.

Harrison, D. A., K. H. Price, and M. P. Bell. 1998. Beyond Relational Demography: Time and the Effects of Surface- and Deep-Level Diversity on Work Group Cohesion. *Academy of Management Journal* 41: 96–107.

Keller, R. T. 2001. Cross-Functional Project Groups in Research and New Product Development: Diversity, Communications, Job Stress, and Outcomes. *Academy of Management Journal* 44: 547–55.

Levi, *Group Dynamics for Teams*.

Milliken, F. J., and L. L. Martins. 1996. Searching for Common Threads: Understanding the Multiple Effects of Diversity in Organizational Groups. *Academy of Management Review* 21: 402–33.

Phillips, *Diversity and Groups*.

Randel, A. E., and K. S. Jaussi. 2003. Functional Background Identity, Diversity, and Individual Performance in Cross-Functional Teams. *Academy of Management Journal* 46: 763–74.

Riordan, C. M., and L. M. Shore. 1997. Demographic Diversity and Employee Attitudes: An Empirical Examination of Relational Demography within Work Units. *Journal of Applied Psychology* 82: 342–58.

Watson, W. E., K. Kumar, and L. K. Michaelsen. 1993. Cultural Diversity's Impact on Interaction Process and Performance: Comparing Homogeneous and Diverse Task Groups. *Academy of Management Journal* 36: 590–602.

66. Earley, P. C., and E. Mosakowski. 2000. Creating Hybrid Team Cultures: An Empirical Test of Transnational Team Functioning. *Academy of Management Journal* 43: 26–49.

Ely, R. J., and D. A. Thomas. 2001. Cultural Diversity at Work: The Effects of Diversity Perspectives on Work Group Processes and Outcomes. *Administrative Science Quarterly* 46: 229–73.

Guzzo and Dickson, Teams in Organizations. See pp. 331–32 for the diversity discussion.

Jackson, S. E. 1996. The Consequences of Diversity in Multidisciplinary Work Teams. In *Handbook of Work Group Psychology*, ed. M. West. Chichester: John Wiley & Sons, Chap. 3.

McLeod, P. L., S. A. Lobel, and T. H. Cox, Jr. 1996. Ethnic Diversity and Creativity in Small Groups. *Small Group Research* 27: 246–64.

Polzer, J. T., L. P. Milton, and W. B. Swann, Jr. 2002. Capitalizing on Diversity: Interpersonal Congruence in Small Work Groups. *Administrative Science Quarterly* 47: 296–324.

Richard, O. C. 2000. Racial Diversity, Business Strategy, and Firm Performance: A Resource-Based View. *Academy of Management Journal* 43: 164–77.

Watson, Kumar, and Michaelsen, Cultural Diversity's Impact.

67. Developed from J. M. Brett and J. K. Rognes. 1986. Intergroup Relations in Organizations. In *Designing Effective Work Groups*, ed. P. S. Goodman and Associates. San Francisco: Jossey-Bass, pp. 202–36.

Brewer, M. B., and R. J. Brown. 1998. Intergroup Relations. In *Handbook of Social Psychology*, Vol. 2, ed. D. T. Gilbert, S. T. Fiske, and G. Lindzey. New York: McGraw-Hill, Chap. 29.

Fisher, R. J. 1990. *The Social Psychology of Intergroup and International Conflict Resolution*. New York: Springer-Verlag.

Hartley, J. F. 1996. Intergroup Relations in Organizations. In *Handbook of Work Group Psychology*, ed. M. West. Chichester: John Wiley & Sons, Chap. 16.

Messick, D. M., and D. M. Mackie. 1989. Intergroup Relations. In *Annual Review of Psychology*, Vol. 40, ed. M. R. Rosenzweig and L. W. Porter. Palo Alto: Annual Reviews, pp. 45–81.

68. Keenan, P. A., and P. J. D. Carnevale. 1989. Positive Effects of Within-Group Cooperation on Between-Group Negotiation. *Journal of Applied Psychology* 19: 977–92.

Labianca, G., D. J. Brass, and B. Gray. 1998. Social Networks and Perceptions of Intergroup Conflict: The Role of Negative Relationships and Third Parties. *Academy of Management Journal* 41: 55–67.

69. Neilsen, E. H. 1972. Understanding and Managing Intergroup Conflict. In *Managing Group and Intergroup Relations*, ed. J. W. Lorsch and P. R. Lawrence. Homewood: Irwin.

70. Coon, C. S. 1946. The Universality of Natural Groupings in Human Societies. *Journal of Educational Sociology* 20: 163–68.

Triandis, H. C. 1989. Cross-Cultural Studies of Individualism and Collectivism. *Nebraska Symposium on Motivation* 37: 41–133. This source has an excellent discussion of the intellectual history of individualism and collectivism. It also discusses the complexity of these cultural differences that is not developed in this text's brief discussion.

Triandis, H. C. 1995. *Individualism and Collectivism*. Boulder: Westview Press.

71. Mann, L. 1980. Cross-Cultural Studies of Small Groups. In *Handbook of Cross-Cultural Psychology, Social Psychology*, Vol. 5, ed. H. C. Triandis and R. W. Brislin. Boston: Allyn & Bacon, pp. 155–209.

Mann, L. 1988. Cultural Influences on Group Processes. In *The Cross-Cultural Challenge to Social Psychology*, ed. M. H. Bond. Newbury Park: Sage Publications, pp. 182–95.

72. Bond, R., and P. B. Smith. 1996. Culture and Conformity: A Meta-Analysis of Studies Using Asch's (1952b, 1956) Line Judgment Task. *Psychological Bulletin* 119: 111–37. (Note: The date references to Asch's publications refer to Asch, S. E. 1952. *Social Psychology*. Englewood Cliffs: Prentice Hall and Asch, S. E. 1956. Studies of Independence and Conformity: A Minority of One Against a Unanimous Majority. *Psychological Monographs* 70 (9, Whole No. 416).)

Coon, The Universality of Natural Groupings.

73. Gelfund, M. J., M. Erez, and Z. Aycan. 2007. Cross-Cultural Organizational Behavior. *Annual Review of Psychology* 58: 479–514.

Kirkman, B. L., and D. L. Shapiro. 1997. The Impact of Cultural Values on Employee Resistance to Teams: Toward a Model of Globalized Self-Managing Work Team Effectiveness. *Academy of Management Review* 22: 730–57.

Kirkman, B. L., and D. L. Shapiro. 2001. The Impact of Cultural Values on Job Satisfaction and Organizational Commitment in Self-Managing Work Teams: The Mediating Role of Employee Resistance. *Academy of Management Journal* 44: 557–69.

74. Earley, P. C. 1989. Social Loafing and Collectivism: A Comparison of the United States and the People's Republic of China. *Administrative Science Quarterly* 34: 565–81.

Earley, P. C. 1993. East Meets West Meets Mid-East: Further Explorations of Collectivistic and Individualistic Work Groups. *Academy of Management Journal* 36: 319–48.

Gabrenya, W. K., Jr., B. Latané, and Y. Wang. 1983. Social Loafing in Cross-Cultural Perspective: Chinese in Taiwan. *Journal of Cross-Cultural Psychology* 14: 368–84.

Gabrenya, W. K., Jr., Y. Wang, and B. Latané. 1985. Social Loafing on an Optimizing Task: Cross-Cultural Differences Among Chinese and Americans. *Journal of Cross-Cultural Psychology* 16: 223–42.

Gibson, C. B. 1999. Do They Do What They Believe They Can? Group Efficacy and Group Effectiveness Across Tasks and Cultures. *Academy of Management Journal* 42: 138–52.

75. Gudykunst, W. B. 1988. Culture and Intergroup Processes. In *The Cross-Cultural Challenge to Social Psychology*, ed. M. H. Bond. Newbury Park: Sage Publications, pp. 165–81.

Chapter 11

CONFLICT IN ORGANIZATIONS

After reading this chapter, you should be able to:

- Define conflict and conflict behavior in organizations.
- Distinguish between functional and dysfunctional conflict.
- Compare different levels and types of conflict in organizations.
- Analyze conflict episodes and the linkages among them.
- Examine the role of latent conflict in a conflict episode and its sources in an organization.
- Describe different conflict frames and orientations.
- Discuss conflict management.
- List the sources of latent conflict in organizations.
- Use various techniques to reduce and increase conflict.
- Explain some international and ethical issues in conflict management.

Conflict is doubt or questioning, opposition, incompatible behavior, controversy, or antagonistic interaction.[1] Conflict in organizations includes interactions in which (1) one party opposes another party or (2) one party tries to block another party from reaching his goals. The range of events considered conflict is deliberately broad. It includes disagreements, debates, disputes, and active efforts to prevent a party from getting what he wants. Critical elements of conflict are interdependence with another party and the perception of incompatible goals.[2] The parties in conflict can be individuals, entire groups within the organization, or members of virtual teams at scattered locations.[3]

Conflict is a basic organizational process that needs managing.[4] Some conflict scholars argue that conflict is vital to continuous improvement in organizations and that conflict management is crucial to its successful use.[5] Many managers, however, believe they should eliminate conflict from their organizations.[6] Social scientists who have studied conflict have usually focused on its negative results.[7] Although this chapter's observations are supported by the results of much conflict research,[8] you will find parts of this chapter unsettling if you have a negative view of conflict. Conflict in organizations is a fascinating subject in its own right and something that any manager needs to understand thoroughly.

Later, this chapter describes conflict as happening in episodes. As the conflict episodes rise and fall, periods of cooperation might occur. Task groups where members must work together to reach their goals often display a common pattern. At some point, especially in the group's early stages of development,[9] the members can fiercely disagree about how to reach the group's goals. Conflict develops at this point as discussions and disagreements. If the members of the group eventually agree about how to reach the goals, the conflict recedes and cooperation returns.

The chapter's perspective does not view conflict as bad for an organization or suggest that managers should remove all conflict. This perspective views conflict as an inevitable part of organization life and as necessary for organizational growth and survival. The latter is especially true if the organization is in an environment requiring innovation and change.[10]

Conflict management, including both increasing and decreasing conflict, is a basic responsibility of any manager. The goals of this chapter are to: (1) help you develop an understanding about conflict processes in organizations; and

(2) show you how to diagnose conflict situations. This knowledge can help you do a better job of conflict management.

FUNCTIONAL AND DYSFUNCTIONAL CONFLICT

Functional conflict works toward the goals of an organization or a group. Dysfunctional conflict blocks an organization or a group from reaching its goals.[11] Conflict is dysfunctional when it is either higher than needed by a group to reach its goals or so low that a group is less effective than it could be in reaching its goals. Because the boundary between functional and dysfunctional conflict is often fuzzy, deciding what level of conflict is functional requires a manager to understand both the positive and negative results of conflict. A knowledgeable manager then tries to manage conflict to keep it within functional bounds.

Conflict that is functional in one group can be dysfunctional in another group. A process analysis team that is trying to solve a difficult quality problem, for example, might need more conflict than a group doing routine tasks. The conflict requirements of a group or an entire organization can also change with time. Conflict that is functional at one point can be dysfunctional at another point. Organizations or groups that have enjoyed an unchanging environment might need more conflict to help adapt to a turbulent environment.

Dysfunctionally high conflict can produce excessive levels of tension, anxiety, and stress. It can drive out people who could be valuable to the group but cannot tolerate such a high level of conflict. Dysfunctionally high conflict can also reduce trust, leading to continual antagonistic interactions. As a result, one or more parties to the conflict might withhold or distort information. Poor-quality decision making can result when conflict reaches a dysfunctional level.[12] The conflict can also absorb management's attention, diverting valuable resources from other tasks.

Dysfunctionally low conflict is the opposite of dysfunctionally high conflict. The organization or group does not encourage new ideas or tolerate different points of view. Decisions are made with poor information. The organization encourages traditional approaches, although the external environment requires innovation and change. This description of dysfunctional conflict might strike you as strange because of the widespread idea that conflict is bad for organizations.[13]

Conflict management involves maintaining conflict at a level that is functional for the group. If the conflict level is dysfunctionally high, managers should reduce the conflict. If the conflict level is dysfunctionally low, managers should increase the conflict. Much of the rest of this chapter will show you how to manage conflict to get functional results.

LEVELS AND TYPES OF CONFLICT IN ORGANIZATIONS

Organization conflict occurs at several levels and appears in different forms. The various levels and types of conflict often have different sources and roots.

Understanding the levels and types of conflict can help a person diagnose a conflict episode and effectively manage conflict.

Intraorganization Conflict

Intraorganization conflict includes all types of conflict occurring within an organization.[14] This type of conflict occurs at the interfaces of organization functions created by the design of the organization. Such conflict can occur along the vertical and horizontal dimensions of the organization. Vertical conflict develops between managers and subordinates.[15] Horizontal conflict occurs between departments and workgroups. Two department managers, for example, might be in conflict because the organization has not clearly defined their areas of authority. Their decision-making areas overlap and each wants the other to give up some authority.

Other types of intraorganization conflict are intragroup conflict and intergroup conflict. **Intragroup conflict** is conflict among members of a group. Conflict within a group is likely highest during the early stages of group development when there are strong differences among members. The conflict can be about ways of doing tasks or reaching the group's goals. Note that conflict within a group is also interpersonal conflict. **Intergroup conflict** is conflict between two or more groups in an organization.[16] This type of conflict often has its roots in the organization's design.[17]

Interpersonal conflict happens between two or more people, such as between a customer and a sales clerk or between two people within an organization.[18] Interpersonal conflict is the most basic form of conflict behavior in organizations. Although the previous discussions focused on the interfaces at which intraorganization conflict can happen, the conflict behavior actually occurs at the interpersonal level.[19]

Interpersonal conflict happens for many reasons, including basic differences in views about what should be done, efforts to get more resources to do a job, or differences in orientation to work and time in different parts of an organization. Interpersonal conflict can also arise because of intrapersonal conflict. A person might release the internal tension of intrapersonal conflict by lashing out at someone during an interpersonal interaction.

Intrapersonal Conflict

Intrapersonal conflict happens within an individual. The conflict arises because of a threat to the person's basic values, a feeling of unfair treatment by the organization, or from multiple and contradictory sources of socialization. Cognitive dissonance, discussed in Chapter 5, "Perception, Attitudes, and Personality," described how people react to intrapersonal conflict. People will feel internally uncomfortable and try to reduce the discomfort. Another form of intrapersonal conflict is negative inequity, described in Chapter 8, "Motivation: Cognitive and Behavioral Theories and Techniques." Individuals who perceive themselves as getting less for their contributions to the organization than they believe they deserve experience intrapersonal conflict.

Intrapersonal conflict can also arise when an employee sees actions within an organization that he considers illegal or unethical. Individuals base such judgments on their personal values and ethics. The tension created by the intrapersonal conflict can lead the individual to act directly against the organization. This act of "whistle blowing" pits the individual against other members of the organization in what can become extremely heated conflict behavior.[20]

Interorganization Conflict

Interorganization conflict is conflict between two or more organizations that results from relationships between them. For example, an organization might become highly dependent on its suppliers or distributors, increasing the potential for conflict over delivery times or other agreements. The hostile takeover of one organization by another is also a form of interorganization conflict.[21]

Interorganization conflict differs from competition between organizations. Two organizations can compete in the same market without engaging in conflict behavior. Burger King and McDonald's are competitors in the fast-food business, but neither organization tries to prevent the other from doing business.

CONFLICT EPISODES

Conflict processes in organizations occur as a series of **conflict episodes** that rise, fall, and vary in duration.[22] The episode model used in this chapter is one of several such models in the research literature. Although the models vary in specific features, they have common elements. Each sees antecedents to conflict (latent conflict) that lead to conflict behavior. An episode ends with an aftermath that links it to a later episode.[23] Figure 11.1 shows the stages of a conflict episode.

Latent Conflict

Latent conflict includes factors in the person, group, or organization that might lead to conflict behavior. These conditions are conflict antecedents and are a potential for conflict in an organization.

Think of latent conflict as lurking in the background waiting for the right conditions to emerge as conflict behavior. Just as a latent image on a piece of exposed film becomes visible in the presence of certain chemicals,

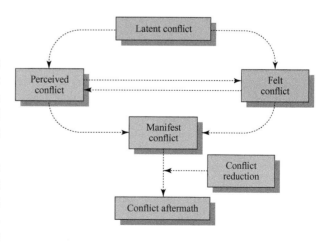

■ **Figure 11.1:**   Conflict Episode Model

latent conflict rises to the level of awareness under certain conditions. Some basic forms of latent conflict are scarce resources, such as limited budgets or equipment, and incompatible goals of both individuals and groups. More than one form of latent conflict can be present at the same time. A later section, "Latent Conflict: Sources of Conflict in Organizations," describes several types of latent conflict found in organizations.

Perceived Conflict

Even when latent conflict factors are present, conflict might not be perceived by those potentially in conflict. **Perceived conflict** is the moment when the parties to a conflict become aware of the conflict. Two mechanisms limit perceived conflict. People can block out mild conflict by suppressing their awareness of it. If many conflict conditions exist in an organization, individuals might focus selectively on them, letting them successfully manage the conflict. All the perceptual mechanisms discussed in Chapter 5 operate for perceived conflict.

Latent conflict does not always precede the perception of conflict. People can perceive themselves in conflict when no latent conditions exist. A common example is misunderstanding another person's position on an issue. The misperception substitutes for the antecedent.

Felt Conflict

Felt conflict is the emotional part of a conflict episode. At least one individual personalizes the conflict and focuses on the parties involved, losing sight of the underlying issues. Some conflict episodes never enter the felt conflict stage. Two individuals disagree, but neither feels any hostility toward the other. They treat the disagreement as an issue to settle that has nothing to do with them personally.

Other conflict episodes have a strong felt conflict element. Feelings between the two parties can become intense. They express hostility orally and in extreme cases physically. This type of conflict episode is what you likely recall if you have strong negative feelings about conflict. The arrow from perceived conflict to felt conflict in Figure 11.1 shows the possibility of personalizing conflict after the parties perceive the presence of the conditions for conflict. Conflict episodes with strong felt conflict are among the more difficult to manage well.

Felt conflict also includes the values and attitudes the parties to a conflict episode hold about each other. High levels of trust and a value orientation of interpersonal cooperation can lead to lower perceived conflict. The opposite attitudes and values can lead to high perceived conflict. The arrow from felt conflict to perceived conflict in Figure 11.1 shows that felt conflict can lead to perceived conflict.

Manifest Conflict

Manifest conflict is the actual conflict behavior between the parties to the conflict episode. It includes oral, written, or physical aggression. Oral manifestations are the arguments often seen either between one another or between other people. Written manifest conflict is the exchange of memoranda or other documents designed to make a point or win an argument. Physical aggression is strongly negative conflict behavior intended to injure an opponent.

Some research notes that any party in a conflict episode can involve others outside the episode.[24] The other people include coworkers or friends. The person who engages another person can share perceptions of the conflict, trying to make sense of an episode. Such sense-making behavior is likely to happen when a conflict episode continues for an extended period.

Conflict Aftermath

Conflict episodes end with a **conflict aftermath**. If the conflict episode is settled to the satisfaction of the parties involved, the conflict aftermath will be clear of any potential latent conflict for a new episode. When the conflict ends, but the basis of the conflict is still present, the aftermath holds the latent conflict for a new conflict episode. For example, disputes over the allocation of scarce resources often are settled by compromise. No one gets exactly what he or she wants, so the aftermath contains the latent desires for more resources. A new episode might start later because of the latent conflict left in the aftermath of a previous episode. As you will see later, each method of reducing conflict leaves a different conflict aftermath.

Relationships among Conflict Episodes

Figure 11.2 shows the relationships among conflict episodes. Each conflict episode links to the next by the connection between the conflict aftermath and the latent conflict. Breaking that connection is the challenge of effective conflict management. Effective long-term reduction of dysfunctionally high conflict requires discovering the latent conflict and removing it from the conflict aftermath. You

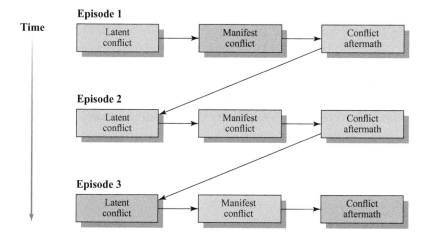

■ **Figure 11.2:** Relationships among Conflict Episodes

will discover that it is not always possible to completely clear the aftermath of a conflict episode. In this sense, conflict is a fact of organization life.

CONFLICT FRAMES AND ORIENTATIONS

People approach conflict episodes with different perceptual frames. They also have different conflict orientations that can affect their behavior during an episode. If you must manage conflict, understanding these frames and orientations can help you diagnose conflict.

Conflict frames are the perceptual sets that people bring to conflict episodes. They act as perceptual filters, removing some information from the episode and emphasizing other information. Research has identified conflict frames that vary along three dimensions:[25]

- **Relationship-Task:** A **relationship** emphasis focuses on the parties' interpersonal relationship. A **task** emphasis focuses on the material aspects of an episode, such as a budget.
- **Emotional-Intellectual:** An **emotional** emphasis focuses on feelings in the episode (felt conflict). An **intellectual** emphasis focuses on observed behavior (manifest conflict).
- **Cooperate-Win:** A **cooperation** focus emphasizes the role of all parties to the conflict. A party with a **winning** focus wants to maximize personal gain.

Some limited research shows the different frames' effects in conflict episodes.[26] People can start an episode with different conflict frames, but end the episode with the same frame. Those who end an episode with a relationship or intellectual frame feel good about their relationship with the other party. Cooperation-focused people end an episode with more positive results than those focused on winning.

Conflict orientations are different behavioral patterns that people bring to a conflict episode.[27] Understanding your orientation and the possible orientations of others can help you understand behavior in the episode. Some conflict orientations overlap with some conflict frames.

The five conflict orientations are dominance, collaborative, compromise, avoidance, and accommodative:

- **Dominance:** Person wants to win the conflict episode and overwhelm the other party; views conflict episodes as battles to fight and win.
- **Collaborative:** Person wants to satisfy the desires of all parties to the conflict and sincerely wants to find a solution that satisfies everyone.
- **Compromise:** Person splits the difference so each party gets part of what it wants.
- **Avoidance:** Person backs away from a conflict episode, possibly because of low tolerance for conflict.
- **Accommodative:** Person focuses on the other party's needs and desires, ignoring his own needs and desires.

A person's orientation toward conflict can change as the conflict episode unfolds. Whether a change in orientation occurs depends on how firmly the person holds to the orientation, the importance of the issues to the person, and his perception of an opponent's power. A dominance-oriented person presses to win important issues, but can shift to a compromise orientation. The shift can happen if the person perceives that the other party's power and potential to win the conflict episode is stronger.

Each orientation affects the conflict episode aftermath differently. Avoidance, accommodative, and dominance orientations leave well-defined aftermaths that can result in later conflict. A collaborative orientation can leave the cleanest aftermath when it successfully identifies and satisfies the desires of all parties to the conflict. A clean aftermath reduces the chance of future conflict over the same issues. Compromise is a middle ground, leaving some aftermath, but not as much as the first three orientations.

Research evidence strongly shows that a collaborative orientation to conflict yields more positive long-term benefits for organizations than the other four orientations. Benefits include better-quality decisions, increased trust, and increased satisfaction with the results of a conflict episode.[28]

LATENT CONFLICT: SOURCES OF CONFLICT IN ORGANIZATIONS

Recall that latent conflict is the antecedent to a conflict episode. Many natural conditions of organizations act as latent conflict. Such latencies lurk in the background and trigger conflict when the right conditions occur. The presence of latent conflict does not always lead to manifest conflict, although the latencies create high conflict potential. Latent conflict also is important to understand because the latencies provide clues about how to reduce dysfunctionally high conflict.

The types of latent conflict described in this section are major sources of organizational conflict.[29] They are representative, but not exhaustive, of conflict sources. Creative diagnosis of organizational conflict requires identifying conflict latencies. Any specific conflict episode can have variations in latent conflict.

Dependence on **scarce resources** is a common latent conflict in organizations. The scarce resources can be tangible—such as money, equipment, and facilities—or intangible—such as knowledge and expertise.[30] Individuals or groups often find themselves dependent on the same facility to do their work. The resource is finite and cannot be expanded quickly. The dependence on the single facility can bring individuals into conflict. A common example is a single copying machine within a department. Several people could want to use the machine simultaneously, and an argument could erupt between two potential users. The single machine as a scarce resource is the latency for the conflict episode.

Organizational differentiation[31] produces groups and work units with different goals, time horizons, views of the world, and languages. For example, research and development people typically think in the long term and have their own scientific jargon. Production people want to get tasks done now according to a specific schedule. The various orientations produced by this differentiation form a latency that can lead to a conflict episode when members of the different units must interact.

Organizations have many **rules, procedures, and policies** to guide decision making about recurring events. The rules, procedures, and policies that can help produce a smooth functioning organization also can act as a latent conflict.[32] This type of latent conflict could be lurking in your college or university. Each school usually has policies governing when a new section of a class can be opened. For example, your school might say one hundred students must be enrolled in a section of a course before the school opens a new section. A professor, however, might prefer that his classes not exceed 60 students. The professor closes the class at 60. Students complain to an administrator. The administrator and the professor begin a conflict episode, the latency for which was a previously existing policy.

Cohesive groups develop a culture of their own. The members of such groups strongly identify with the group and care about what it represents. Groups also can differ in what they value. Conflict can start when members of such groups interact with each other.[33]

High **interdependence** among people at work is another source of conflict in organizations. Interdependence can come from job design, with jobs linked to each other. It also can be found where work is designed around groups and not individuals. Whatever its source, interdependence in organizations forces people to interact with each other. The required interaction increases the potential for conflict within the organization.

Communication barriers are another source of latent conflict in organizations. If individuals or groups do not interact frequently with each other, misunderstandings can develop between the groups. This type of latent conflict is common in organizations with shift work. The day shift does not interact with the evening shift except briefly at a shift change. Members of each shift develop opinions about the quality of the other shift's work. As those opinions become diverse, the potential for conflict during the change in shifts increases.

Ambiguous jurisdictions occur when the organization has not clearly defined areas of decision authority. "Turf battles" erupt when two people or groups believe they have responsibility for the same activity. This type of latent conflict is common in a matrix organization, if the organization has not clearly defined the areas of jurisdiction.[34] Many people in such organizations work for more than one person. Conflict can arise when those people receive conflicting orders from their multiple bosses.

The reward system of the organization is another area of latent conflict. **Reward systems** that encourage different and incompatible behavior are a significant source of latent conflict. A common example is the design of reward systems for sales and manufacturing people. Salespeople receive a commission for selling. Manufacturing managers get rewards for keeping costs down. Salespeople can make more sales by offering early delivery dates, but those dates might not fit into manufacturing's production schedule. The conflict potential is high and can lead to a conflict episode when sales and manufacturing interact.

CONFLICT MANAGEMENT

Conflict management focuses on maintaining conflict at functional levels for a department, work unit, or an entire organization. Conflict management does not mean the complete elimination of conflict nor does it refer only to conflict reduction. It means maintaining conflict at the right level to help the department, work unit, or organization reach its goals.[35]

Basic to the process of conflict management is the choice of a desired conflict level. The desired conflict level varies according to the perceived conflict requirements of the unit. Several factors affect the choice of the desired conflict level. Organizational cultures place differing values on debate, disagreement, and conflict. Managers in organizational cultures that support debate, doubt, and questioning might perceive a higher desired conflict level than managers in cultures that do not. The nature of the organization's product or service also affects the desired conflict level. Creative and innovative products or services require a higher level of conflict than more routine and predictable products and services. Organizations facing fast-changing external environments require higher conflict levels for successful adaptation than organizations facing stable external environments.

Desired conflict levels for an organization, department, or work unit can vary from one group to another and for the same group over time.[36] If an organization's environment shifts from stable to turbulent, then the right level of conflict can become higher. A shift in the opposite direction can cause the right level of conflict to become lower.

The preceding paragraphs emphasized a manager's perception of the desired conflict level. The manager's tolerance for conflict affects his perception of a unit's conflict requirements. A manager who avoids conflict likely has a lower tolerance for conflict than a manager who actively engages in functional conflict behavior. Even when a work unit requires a specific conflict level, a manager's tolerance for conflict affects his perception of the desired level.

Figure 11.3 shows the conflict management process. The figure shows the process as a thermostat, emphasizing a manager's monitoring of conflict levels. If conflict levels are at a functional level, the manager (thermostat) does nothing. If the conflict level is dysfunctionally high, the manager tries to reduce the conflict. If the conflict level is dysfunctionally low, the manager tries to increase the conflict. In the same way that a thermostat maintains a desired room temperature, conflict management maintains a desired conflict level.

What are the symptoms that a manager can read to decide whether the conflict level is dysfunctionally high or low?[37] Low trust in a work unit, deliberate distortion of information, high levels of tension during interpersonal interactions, and antagonism between parties are all signs of dysfunctionally high conflict.

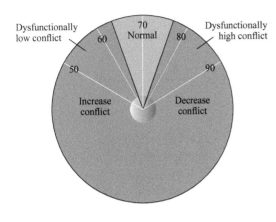

In extreme cases, dysfunctional conflict can take the form of sabotage of the organization's products or services or violence against other parties.

Suppression and withdrawal are two symptoms of dysfunctionally low conflict.[38] Suppression includes denial of differences and a desire to perceive similarities between parties that do not exist. Repressing controversial information and prohibiting disagreements about legitimate issues also are signs of suppression. Withdrawal includes reduced communication to avoid interactions that could lead to controversy, the belief in "peace at any price," and walking away from a disagreeable interaction.

▧ **Figure 11.3:**   Conflict Management

Reducing Conflict

Three types of approaches exist for **reducing conflict** in organizations: lose–lose, win–lose, and win–win. Although these approaches usually are called methods of conflict resolution, this chapter refers to them as methods of conflict reduction because many do not remove conflict.[39] Managers should use caution when reducing conflict to ensure it does not fall to a dysfunctionally low level.

U.S. organizations are increasingly convinced of the effectiveness of conflict reduction training. Training programs are now widely used. Some research points to their effectiveness in successfully reducing conflict.[40]

Lose–lose methods of conflict reduction do not try to deal directly with the conflict. None of the parties to the conflict episode get what they want. These methods of conflict reduction leave a conflict aftermath that can start a new conflict episode about the same issues. Sometimes the lose–lose approaches ignore the conflict and do not try to reduce it. Typical lose–lose methods include avoidance, compromise, and third-party intervention.

Avoidance is an obvious way to reduce conflict in the short run, but it does not permanently reduce the conflict. A conflict episode can recur when the parties meet again. Withdrawal can happen because one party to the conflict has a low tolerance for conflict or because one party has an avoidance orientation to conflict. The conflict episode is stressful, and the party simply wants to avoid the confrontation. Anyone trying to manage conflict must be aware of the prospect of avoidance. Although manifest conflict levels will not be high, the latent conflict is still there. Later conflict episodes can arise and surprise those managing conflict.

Compromise uses bargaining and negotiation to reduce conflict. Each party to the conflict gives up something to get something he values. Although manifest conflict drops, there is no clear conflict aftermath. The parties to the conflict have not completely resolved the underlying issues. When the latent conflict is scarce resources, compromise is a common reduction method because resources often cannot be expanded quickly. The conflict over the copying machine described earlier offers an opportunity for compromise. Let each party copy part of what he needs and return later to copy the rest. The manifest conflict behavior subsides, but the latent conflict stays.

Third-party intervention often asks a neutral person for a solution to a conflict episode. Arbitration of labor disputes is a common example of third-party intervention. The third party might try to reduce the conflict by giving something to each party in the conflict episode. In this respect, it is much like compromise, with the third party suggesting the compromise. Also, like compromise, a conflict aftermath follows the episode. The issues often are not satisfactorily settled for all concerned. A manager can also act as the third party, but managers are rarely neutral in their view of the conflict episode.[41]

Win–lose conflict-reduction methods make one party to the conflict a clear winner and the other party a clear loser. Such techniques leave a conflict aftermath that can result in a new conflict episode about the same issues. The techniques include dominance, authoritative command, and majority rule.

Dominance happens when one party to a conflict overwhelms the other. Dominance can occur because one party has higher organization status or more power. It can also happen when one party to the conflict has a low tolerance for conflict. You can think of dominance as the other side of avoidance. If one party has an appeasement or avoidance conflict orientation, the other party can easily dominate the episode. Dominance leaves a conflict aftermath because it does not try to discover why the conflict occurred.

Organizations widely use authoritative command for conflict reduction, partly because of the formal authority relationships found there. Two people in conflict refer their conflict to a common superior who decides the solution to the conflict. Manifest conflict stops, but the conflict episode ends with a conflict aftermath.

Decision-making groups faced with conflict over issues can use majority rule to reduce the conflict. Each issue is put to a vote, letting some members of the group win and others lose. If the alternatives are acceptable to all concerned, this method can work effectively. If the same people lose repeatedly and personalize the loss, majority rule leaves a potentially destructive aftermath.

With win–win conflict-reduction methods, parties to the conflict episode get what they want. These methods include problem solving, integration, and a superordinate goal. Win–win approaches do not leave a conflict aftermath because they directly address the causes of the conflict and try to remove them. Although these techniques do not strongly differ, they have some useful distinctions.

Problem solving tries to find the true basis of a conflict episode.[42] This method tries to fully expose all differences among the parties. All parties to the conflict encourage and support minority views to ensure they get full expression. As noted in Chapter 10, "Groups and Intergroup Processes," minority views often positively contribute to group performance. The parties view differences as important sources of information leading to creative solutions to the conflict. Organizations and managers that use problem solving do not view conflict negatively. They see conflict episodes as constructive opportunities for creative solutions to problems. Properly done, problem solving leaves little or no conflict aftermath.

Integration seeks solutions that are in the best interests of all parties.[43] It assumes that people's deeply held interests and desires are the basis of conflict. This approach tries to find a solution that fully meets the goals of each party.

A **superordinate goal** is a goal desired by all parties to the conflict but unattainable by any party alone.[44] Superordinate goals compel cooperation even if the parties otherwise do not want to cooperate. Organizations using group-based incentive programs are using a form of superordinate goal. Everyone in the group wants to get the reward, but no one can do it alone.

Superordinate goals should work well where the latent conflict is high inter-dependence. The superordinate goal operates in the background, forcing the members of the group to cooperate. Later conflict episodes are less likely in the presence of a continually operating superordinate goal.

Increasing Conflict

Conflict management includes **increasing conflict** when it is dysfunctionally low. The goal of increasing conflict is to get the functional qualities of conflict described earlier, such as more information for decisions and creative solutions to problems. Increasing conflict must be done skillfully and cautiously so conflict levels do not become dysfunctionally high. The manager's role is to structure situations as described in this section and not express opinions or take positions on issues. This role is especially important because it can encourage subordinates to express their views.[45]

Groups with members of different social backgrounds, education, expertise, organization positions, and opinions have high conflict potential. By deliberately forming **heterogeneous groups** to find creative solutions to problems, a manager tries to use the functional qualities of conflict. Organizations with a diverse workforce have an especially rich resource for forming groups with high conflict potential.

A manager of a decision-making group can ask one group member to play the **devil's advocate** role. This person deliberately criticizes a position that has emerged as dominant within the group. Alternatively, the manager can ask each person in the group to critique the alternatives under consideration. Each approach recognizes the information-generating function of conflict.

Dialectical inquiry is a structured debate of opposing views about solutions to a decision problem. Two people or groups prepare arguments and debate the question in the presence of the person who makes the final decision. One argument presents the prevailing opinion about a decision. The other argument presents a believable and plausible alternative. The decision-maker forms a final decision by drawing upon information presented by both sides.[46]

Managers can also try to **develop an organizational culture** with a set of values and norms that support openness about debate and opinions. They must devote time to building this type of culture. Searching for quick solutions to problems can lead to pressure to reduce differences and emphasize similarities.

INTERNATIONAL ASPECTS OF CONFLICT IN ORGANIZATIONS

The research and conceptual models underlying this chapter are mainly of North American origin. They likely require modification when considering cross-cultural differences in the meaning of conflict and its related concepts.[47] Cultures of various countries place differing values on conflict. Cultures that emphasize individualism and competition among people likely positively value conflict. English-speaking countries, the Netherlands, Italy, and Belgium are examples. Cultures that emphasize collaboration, cooperation, and conformity likely negatively value conflict. Examples include many Asian and Latin American countries, Portugal, Greece, and Turkey.[48] Although there is no direct research evidence, such cultural differences imply that different conflict levels are functional for organizations in different countries.

As noted in the previous chapter, cross-cultural research has studied intergroup processes, the processes within which intergroup conflict happens.[49] The research implies that collaborative and cooperative cultures expect little conflict during intergroup interactions. They favor suppression of conflict with little discussion about people's feelings during a conflict episode. Felt conflict will likely be part of some conflict episodes, but hidden from public view.

Managers from an individualistic country face some dilemmas when managing conflict in a less individualistic country. Because they believe that expression of feelings during a conflict episode is acceptable, the suppression of feelings could baffle them. The idea that increasing conflict in such countries can be good might confuse local people. A manager might believe that more conflict will produce more information, better ideas, and innovation, but the local culture might not support that behavior. The result could be almost immediate dysfunctional results.

ETHICAL ISSUES ABOUT CONFLICT IN ORGANIZATIONS

Potential differences in people's tolerance for conflict suggest some ethical issues. Experiencing conflict levels that are much higher than a person's tolerance level can lead to stress. A manager with a high tolerance for conflict might deliberately keep conflict levels higher than subordinates want. The ethical question pivots on whether such managers should reveal their intentions about desired conflict levels. Full disclosure would let subordinates leave the group if they found the conflict levels dysfunctionally stressful. Disclosure would be needed when new people are considered for employment or when a new manager takes over an existing group.

Managers can create conditions that increase conflict potential in an organization. Deliberately increasing conflict is an effort to guide behavior in a desired direction. Some methods, such as using a devil's advocate in a decision-making group, often are obvious to group members. Other methods, such as building a group with heterogeneous members, are less obvious. Subtle methods of increasing conflict connote manipulation of people's behavior, raising an ethical issue. Full disclosure by managers can help. Managers can openly state their intention to use conflict to generate ideas and innovation. If people are then free to join a group or not, the ethical issue likely subsides.

People in organizations might experience intrapersonal conflict from requests to act against their moral values, or from observing behavior they consider unethical. In both cases, the people might feel compelled to act, such as reporting unethical acts, seeking a transfer to another part of the organization, or quitting the organization altogether.

Optimal conflict levels can vary among countries. The ethical issue centers on whether managers should honor such values even if their home country values support higher conflict levels.

SUMMARY

11

SUMMARY

Conflict in organizations is opposition, incompatible behaviors, or antagonistic interaction. It includes interactions in which one party opposes another party, or one party tries to prevent or block another party from reaching his goals. Conflict can have both functional and dysfunctional effects on an organization.

Conflict behavior happens within interpersonal interactions, between groups (intergroup), within groups (intragroup), and between organizations (interorganization). Other conflict behavior starts because people experience strong conflicts within themselves (intrapersonal).

Conflict in organizations has an episodic quality. Many aspects of organizations act as the conflict latencies that can start an episode. Latent conflict lies dormant until conditions are right for the conflict to emerge as manifest conflict. The latter is the actual conflict behavior between the parties in a conflict episode. Managers can try to reduce the conflict by using a method of conflict reduction. Conflict episodes often end with a conflict aftermath that can become the latent conflict for a later episode.

There are many methods for reducing and increasing conflict. Most methods of conflict reduction leave a conflict aftermath. A few, such as integration and resource expansion, do not. Managers must carefully use the methods for increasing conflict so conflict levels do not become dysfunctionally high.

Countries differ in the levels of conflict that are functional. For example, collectivistic countries have a lower level of functional conflict than individualistic countries. Such differences raise an ethical question: Should managers honor the local country's values even if their home country values support higher levels of conflict?

REVIEW AND DISCUSSION QUESTIONS

REVIEW AND DISCUSSION QUESTIONS

11

1 Define conflict in organizations. Discuss the functions and dysfunctions of conflict. Do you view conflict as mainly functional or dysfunctional? Discuss examples of functional and dysfunctional conflict you have experienced.

2 Describe the parts of a conflict episode and the relationships among them. Discuss the role of perceived and felt conflict on the results of a conflict episode.

3 Discuss conflict frames and orientations. Which orientation best characterizes you? What do you tend to do when entering a conflict episode?

4 Discuss the methods of reducing conflict that are most likely and least likely to leave a conflict aftermath. Why do the different methods leave or not leave an aftermath?

5 Discuss the methods of increasing conflict. When should a manager increase conflict? What cautions should a manager observe when increasing conflict?

6 What is latent conflict? What are some organizational features that can be latent conflict? What is the relationship between latent conflict and conflict aftermath? Give examples from your work experiences.

7 Conflict management includes both reducing and increasing conflict. What major issues do you see for a manager trying to manage conflict in an organization?

TAKE FIVE: OB ALIVE: *BUTCH CASSIDY AND THE SUNDANCE KID* (1969)

11
TAKE FIVE

A distant posse endlessly pursues outlaws Butch Cassidy (Paul Newman) and the Sundance Kid (Robert Redford). They go to Bolivia expecting to outwit the posse and find a new life. Events do not turn out positively for them, leading to a dramatic shoot out in the end.

This sequence starts at the beginning of DVD Chapter 4, "The Hole in the Wall" and continues to the end of DVD Chapter 5, "How Harvey Sees it." Butch and Sundance ride to the gang's Hole-in-the-Wall, Wyoming hideout. The sequence ends after Butch says, "Harvey thought of that! Well I'll tell you something fellas, that's exactly what we're gonna do."

Consider the following questions and observations while viewing this film sequence: When does Butch perceive that a conflict episode might begin? Describe the latent conflict shown in this sequence. Which conflict-reduction method discussed in this chapter does Butch use to end the conflict episode?

REFERENCES AND NOTES

1. The following citations were the background sources for this chapter:
   De Dreu, C. K. W. 2011. Conflict at Work: Basic Principles and Applied Issues. In *APA Handbook of Industrial and Organizational Psychology*, Vol. 3, ed. S. Zedeck. Washington, DC: American Psychological Association, Chap. 13.
   Deutsch, M. 1980. Fifty Years of Conflict. In *Retrospections on Social Psychology*, ed. L. Festinger. New York: Oxford University Press, Chap. 3.
   Deutsch, M. 1990. Sixty Years of Conflict. *The International Journal of Conflict Management* 1: 237–63.
   Dirks, K. T., and J. M. Parks. 2003. Conflicting Stories: The State of the Science of Conflict. In *Organizational Behavior: The State of the Science*, 2nd edn, ed. J. Greenberg. Mahwah: Lawrence Erlbaum Associates, Chap. 8.
   Jehn, K. A., L. L. Greer, and J. Rupert. 2008. Diversity, Conflict, and Their Consequences. In *Diversity at Work*, ed. A. P. Brief. Cambridge: Cambridge University Press, Chap. 5.
   Pruitt, D. G. 1998. Social Conflict. In *Handbook of Social Psychology*, Vol. 2, ed. D. T. Gilbert, S. T. Fiske, and G. Lindzey. New York: McGraw-Hill, Chap. 27.
   Robbins, S. P. 1974. *Managing Organizational Conflict*. Englewood Cliffs: Prentice Hall, p. 23.
   Tjosvold, D. 1991. *The Conflict-Positive Organization: Stimulate Diversity and Create Unity*. Reading, MA: Addison-Wesley Longman, p. 33.
   For other introductions to conflict, see:
   Lewicki, R. J., S. E. Weiss, and D. Lewin. 1992. Models of Conflict, Negotiation and Third Party Intervention: A Review and Synthesis. *Journal of Organizational Behavior* 13: 209–52.
   Putnam, L. L., and M. S. Poole. 1987. Conflict and Negotiation. In *Handbook of Organizational Communication: An Interdisciplinary Perspective*, ed. F. M. Jablin, L. L. Putnam, K. H. Roberts, and L. W. Porter. Newbury Park: Sage Publications, pp. 549–99.
   Rubin, J. Z., D. G. Pruitt, and S. H. Kim. 1994. *Social Conflict: Escalation, Stalemate, and Settlement*. New York: McGraw-Hill.
   Wall, J. A., Jr., and T. T. Callister. 1995. Conflict and Its Management. *Journal of Management* 21: 515–58.
2. Schmidt, S. M., and T. A. Kochan. 1972. Conflict: Towards Conceptual Clarity. *Administrative Science Quarterly* 17: 359–70.
3. Brown, L. D. 1983. *Managing Conflict at Organizational Interfaces*. Reading, MA: Addison-Wesley.
   Schmidt and Kochan, Conflict.
   Shin, Y. 2005. Conflict Resolution in Virtual Teams. *Organizational Dynamics* 34: 331–45.
4. De Dreu, C. K. W., F. Harinck, and A. E. M. Van Vianen. 1999. Conflict and Performance in Groups and Organizations. In *International Review of Industrial and Organizational Psychology*, Vol. 14, ed. C. L. Cooper and I. T. Robertson. Chichester: John Wiley & Sons, Chap. 8.
   Thomas, K. W. 1992. Conflict and Negotiation Processes in Organizations. In *Handbook of Industrial and Organizational Behavior*, Vol. 3, 2nd edn, ed. M. D. Dunnette and L. M. Hough. Palo Alto: Consulting Psychologists Press, Chap. 11.
5. Tjosvold, *The Conflict-Positive Organization*.

Tjosvold, D. 1993. *Learning to Manage Conflict: Getting People to Work Together Productively*. New York: Lexington Books, Chap. 1.

6. Robbins, *Managing Organizational Conflict*, p. 18.
7. De Dreu, C. K. W., and L. R. Weingart. 2003. Task versus Relationship Conflict, Team Performance, and Team Member Satisfaction: A Meta-Analysis. *Journal of Applied Psychology* 88: 741–49.
   De Dreu, Harinck, and Van Vianen, Conflict and Performance.
   Thomas, K. 1976. Conflict and Conflict Management. In *Handbook of Industrial and Organizational Behavior*, ed. M. D. Dunnette. Chicago: Rand McNally, p. 889.
8. Rahim, M. A. 1986. *Managing Conflict in Organizations*. New York: Praeger.
9. Discussed in Chapter 10, "Groups and Intergroup Processes." See also K. Jehn and E. A. Mannix. 2001. The Dynamic Nature of Conflict: A Longitudinal Study of Intragroup Conflict and Group Performance. *Academy of Management Journal* 44: 238–51.
10. Tjosvold, *The Conflict-Positive Organization*.
11. Jehn and Mannix, The Dynamic Nature of Conflict.
    Pondy, L. R. 1967. Organizational Conflict: Concepts and Models. *Administrative Science Quarterly* 12: 296–320.
    Robbins, *Managing Organizational Conflict*, pp. 24–25.
12. Amason, A. C. 1996. Distinguishing the Effects of Functional and Dysfunctional Conflict on Strategic Decision Making: Resolving a Paradox for Top Management. *Academy of Management Journal* 39: 123–48.
    Amason, A. C., and H. J. Sapienza. 1997. The Effects of Top Management Team Size and Interaction Norms on Cognitive and Affective Conflict. *Journal of Management* 23: 494–516.
    Cosier, R. A., and D. R. Dalton. 1990. Positive Effects of Conflict: A Field Assessment. *The International Journal of Conflict Management* 1: 81–92.
13. Brown, *Managing Conflict*, p. 9.
14. Ibid.
15. Pondy, Organizational Conflict.
16. Neilsen, E. H. 1972. Understanding and Managing Intergroup Conflict. In *Managing Group and Intergroup Relations*, ed. J. W. Lorsch and P. R. Lawrence. Homewood: Irwin, pp. 329–43.
    de Wit, F., L. L. Greer, and K. A. Jehn. 2012. The Paradox of Intragroup Conflict: A Meta-Analysis. *Journal of Applied Psychology* 97: 360–90.
17. Dutton, J. M., and R. E. Walton. 1966. Inter-Departmental Conflict and Cooperation: Two Contrasting Studies. *Human Organization* 25: 207–20.
18. Walton, R. E. 1987. *Managing Conflict: Interpersonal Dialogue and Third-Party Roles*, 2nd edn. Reading, MA: Addison-Wesley.
19. Brown, *Managing Conflict*.
20. Miceli, M. P., and J. P. Near. 1984. The Relationships Among Beliefs Organizational Position and Whistle-Blowing Status: A Discriminant Analysis. *Academy of Management Journal* 27: 675–705.
    Miceli, M., and J. P. Near. 1992. *Blowing the Whistle: The Organizational and Legal Implications for Companies & Their Employees*. San Francisco: Jossey-Bass.
21. Dobrzynski, J. H. 1988. The Lessons of the RJR Free-for-All. *Business Week* (December 19): 30–31.
    Farrell, C. 1988. Learning to Live with Leverage. New Risks, New Rewards—and Bigger Failures? *Business Week* (November 7): 138–43.

22. Developed from Pondy, Organizational Conflict.
    Filley, A. C. 1975. *Interpersonal Conflict Resolution*. Glenview, IL: Scott, Foresman, Chap. 1.
    Jehn and Mannix, The Dynamic Nature of Conflict.
    Thomas, Conflict and Negotiation Processes in Organizations.
23. Thomas, Conflict and Negotiation Processes in Organizations.
    Van de Vliert, E. 1990. Small Group Conflicts. In *The Annual Review of Conflict Knowledge and Conflict Resolution*, Vol. 2, ed. J. B. Gittler. New York: Garland, pp. 83–118.
24. Volkema, R. J., K. Farquhar, and T. J. Bergmann. 1996. Third-Party Sensemaking in Interpersonal Conflicts at Work: A Theoretical Framework. *Human Relations* 49: 1437–54. This source also reviews the empirical research on sense-making.
25. Deutsch, Sixty Years of Conflict, pp. 257–58.
    Pinkley, R. L. 1990. Dimensions of Conflict Frame: Disputant Interpretations of Conflict. *Journal of Applied Psychology* 75: 117–26.
26. Pinkley, R. L., and G. B. Northcraft. 1994. Conflict Frames of Reference: Implications for Dispute Processes and Outcomes. *Academy of Management Journal* 37: 193–205.
27. Deutsch, Sixty Years of Conflict, pp. 257–58.
    Thomas, Conflict and Conflict Management, pp. 895–912.
28. Thomas, Conflict and Negotiation Processes in Organizations, pp. 667–68.
    Tjosvold, *The Conflict-Positive Organization*.
29. Filley, *Interpersonal Conflict Resolution*.
    Neilsen, Understanding and Managing Intergroup Conflict.
    Pondy, Organizational Conflict.
    Thompson, V. A. 1977. *Modern Organization*. Tuscaloosa: University of Alabama Press.
30. Neilsen, Understanding and Managing Intergroup Conflict, p. 333.
31. Lawrence, P. R., and J. W. Lorsch. 1967. *Organization and Environment*. Homewood: Richard D. Irwin.
32. Thomas, Conflict and Conflict Management.
33. Neilsen, Understanding and Managing Intergroup Conflict.
34. See Chapter 17, "Organizational Design," for a discussion of matrix organizations.
35. Brown, *Managing Conflict*.
    De Dreu, Conflict at Work, pp. 467–78.
    De Dreu, C. K. W. 1997. Productive Conflict: The Importance of Conflict Management and Conflict Issue. In *Using Conflict in Organizations*, ed. C. K. W. De Dreu and E. Van de Vliert. London: Sage Publications, Chap. 1.
    De Dreu, Harinck, and Van Vianen, Conflict and Performance.
    Jehn, K. 1995. A Multimethod Examination of the Benefits and Detriments of Intragroup Conflict. *Administrative Science Quarterly* 40: 256–82.
    Jehn, K. A., and C. Bendersky. 2003. Intragroup Conflict in Organizations: A Contingency Perspective on the Conflict-Outcome Relationship. In *Research in Organizational Behavior*, Vol. 25, ed. R. M. Kramer and B. M. Staw. Oxford: Elsevier, pp. 187–242.
    Robbins, *Managing Organizational Conflict*.
    Robbins, S. P. 1978. "Conflict Management" and "Conflict Resolution" Are Not Synonymous Terms. *California Management Review* 21 (Winter): 67–75.
36. Robbins, *Managing Organizational Conflict*.
37. Brown, *Managing Conflict*, Chap. 3.
38. Ibid.

39. De Dreu, Harinck, and Van Vianen, Conflict and Performance, pp. 396–99.

Deutsch, M. 1994. Constructive Conflict Management for the World Today. *International Journal of Conflict Management* 5: 111–29.

Filley, *Interpersonal Conflict Resolution.*

Neilsen, Understanding and Managing Intergroup Conflict, Chap. 2.

Pinkley, R. L., J. Brittain, M. A. Neale, and G. B. Northcraft. 1995. Managerial Third-Party Dispute Intervention: An Inductive Analysis of Intervenor Strategy Selection. *Journal of Applied Psychology* 80: 386–402.

Pruitt, D. G., and P. V. Olczak. 1995. Beyond Hope: Approaches to Resolving Seemingly Intractable Conflict. In *Conflict, Cooperation, and Justice: Essays Inspired by the Work of Morton Deutsch*, ed. B. B. Bunker, J. Z. Rubin, and Associates. San Francisco: Jossey-Bass, Chap. 3.

Robbins, *Managing Organizational Conflict*, Chaps. 7, 8.

Ross, W. H., and D. E. Conlon. 2000. Hybrid Forms of Third-Party Dispute Resolution: Theoretical Implications of Combining Mediation and Arbitration. *Academy of Management Review* 25: 415–27.

Thomas, Conflict and Conflict Management, pp. 911–12.

Thomas, Conflict and Negotiation Processes in Organizations, pp. 690–93.

40. Dudley, B. S., D. W. Johnson, and R. T. Johnson. 1996. Conflict-Resolution Training and Middle School Students' Integrative Negotiation Behavior. *Journal of Applied Social Psychology* 26: 2038–52.

Johnson, D. W., R. T. Johnson, B. Dudley, J. Mitchell, and J. Fredrickson. 1997. The Impact of Conflict Resolution Training on Middle School Students. *Journal of Social Psychology* 137: 1–21.

Raider, E. 1995. Conflict Resolution Training in Schools: Translating Theory into Applied Skills. In *Conflict, Cooperation, and Justice: Essays Inspired by the Work of Morton Deutsch*, ed. B. B. Bunker, J. Z. Rubin, and Associates. San Francisco: Jossey-Bass, Chap. 4.

41. Nugent, P. S. 2002. Managing Conflict: Third-Party Interventions for Managers. *Academy of Management Executive* 16: 139–55. This source has detailed observations on managers using third-party interventions in a conflict episode.

42. Likert, R., and J. B. Likert. 1976. *New Ways of Managing Conflict*. New York: McGraw-Hill.

43. Ibid.

Metcalf, H. C., and Urwick, L., eds. 1941. *Dynamic Administration: The Collected Papers of Mary Parker Follett*. New York: Harper & Row, pp. 30–49.

44. Sherif, M., and C. Sherif. 1966. *In Common Predicament: Social Psychology of Intergroup Conflict and Cooperation*. Boston: Houghton Mifflin.

45. Brown, *Managing Conflict.*

De Dreu, Productive Conflict.

Robbins, *Managing Organizational Conflict.*

Tjosvold, D. 1985. Implications of Controversy Research for Management. *Journal of Management* 11: 21–37.

Tjosvold, *The Conflict-Positive Organization.*

Turner, M. E., and A. R. Pratkanis. 1997. Mitigating Groupthink by Stimulating Constructive Conflict. In *Using Conflict in Organizations*, ed. C. K. W. De Dreu and E. Van de Vliert. London: Sage Publications, Chap. 4.

For a dissenting view to the observations in this section, see Wall and Callister, Conflict and Its Management, pp. 525–26, 545, and 549.

46. Cosier, R. A., and C. R. Schwenk. 1990. Agreement and Thinking Alike: Ingredients for Poor Decisions. *Academy of Management Executive* 4: 69–74.

Mason, R. O. 1969. A Dialectical Approach to Strategic Planning. *Management Science* 15: B-403–B-414.

47. Faure, G. O. 1995. Conflict Formulation: Going Beyond Culture-Bound Views of Conflict. In *Conflict, Cooperation, and Justice*, ed. B. B. Bunker, J. Z. Rubin, and Associates. San Francisco: Jossey-Bass, Chap. 2.

48. Hofstede, G. 2001. *Culture's Consequences: Comparing Values, Behaviors, Institutions, and Organizations across Nations*, 2nd edn. Thousand Oaks: Sage Publications, Chaps. 4, 5.

49. Gudykunst, W. B. 1988. Culture and Intergroup Processes. In *The Cross-Cultural Challenge to Social Psychology*, ed. M. H. Bond. Newbury Park: Sage Publications, pp. 165–81.

Von Glinow, M. A., D. L. Shapiro, and J. M. Brett. 2004. Can We Talk and Should We? Managing Emotional Conflict in Multicultural Teams. *Academy of Management Review* 29: 578–92.

Chapter 12

LEADERSHIP AND MANAGEMENT

After reading this chapter, you should be able to:

- Describe leadership as an influence process in organizations.
- Discuss the differences between leadership and management.
- Distinguish among the trait, behavioral, and contingency theories of leadership.
- List the traits that distinguish leaders from nonleaders.
- Compare some alternative views of leadership.
- Analyze the effects of self-managing teams on leadership.
- Explain the role of substitutes, neutralizers, and enhancers of leadership behavior.
- Contrast some aspects of women, men, and leadership.
- Describe how perceptual processes affect people's conclusions about who is a leader and who is not a leader.
- Appreciate some international and ethical issues that surround leadership and management.

Leadership is a social influence process involving two or more people: the leader and a follower (or a potential follower).[1] The influence process has two dimensions: (1) the leader's intention to affect the behavior of at least one other person, and (2) the extent to which the target of the influence effort perceives the behavior as acceptable. Perception and attribution, which Chapter 5, "Perception, Attitudes, and Personality" discusses, are important parts of the leadership process in organizations. The person who is the target of the influence effort must attribute the behavior to a specific person and consider that behavior acceptable.

Leaders can hold formal organization positions or emerge spontaneously within an organization.[2] The formal positions carry titles such as manager, supervisor, foreman, or vice president. Both the formal qualities of the position and the characteristics of the person holding it contribute to leadership. Other people who are not in formally appointed positions can also play leadership roles. Such leaders are **emergent leaders** and often found within formal and informal groups in organizations.[3]

This chapter begins with a discussion of the differences between management and leadership. The chapter then discusses some major leadership theories in the temporal order of their emergence since the early 1900s. This chapter closes with a discussion of: leadership and self-managing teams; substitutes, neutralizers, and enhancers of leadership; leadership perceptions; and women, men, and leadership.[4]

MANAGEMENT AND LEADERSHIP

Leadership theory suffers from a defect—it does not represent leadership—not as historians define it and as leaders themselves practice it … [T]he theorists have not rediscovered the essential difference between leadership and management and blindly perpetuate the myth that the two concepts are interchangeable. For centuries, man has endowed leadership with special meaning. The manager arrived relatively late on the scene of human debate and enterprise. The two ideas were never intended to be fused. Great leaders were seldom effective managers.[5]

Historians, scholars, and other observers have often distinguished between management and leadership. Managers and leaders play different roles in an organization. **Managers** sustain and control organizations; **leaders** try to change them.[6] Organizations also have different needs for those roles at different levels and at different times in their history.[7]

Leaders have a vision of how the organization can have a better future and can inspire followers to pursue that vision. Carefully crafted visions contain powerful imagery about the future.[8] An effective vision is "future oriented, compelling, bold, aspiring, and inspiring, yet believable and achievable."[9] Some writers emphasize the importance for a leader to fill a vision with emotion and express it so followers respond with equal emotion.[10] Research evidence is now showing the positive performance effects of an effective vision.[11]

Leaders take risks, especially if they perceive high payoffs from a course of action. They readily use power for influence, pulling people along instead of using punishment to coerce people into compliance. Leaders actively seek opposing views to identify options to a course of action. Because of their relentless pursuit of a vision, their risk-taking behavior, and their desire to use conflict, they often plunge an organization into chaos while pursuing that vision.

Managers follow an organization's present vision; they do not create a new vision. They solve problems and try to bring order to the workplace while building commitment to organization goals. Managers take fewer risks than leaders. They use available rewards and sanctions, coupled with their knowledge of human motivation, to get predictable behavior.

The supervisory, management, and executive positions in organizations can have different requirements for management and leadership. Some positions require only management. Other positions require large amounts of leadership with little need for management. Still others need a mixture of leadership and management.

An organization's management and leadership requirements will change as the factors affecting the organization change. Because leaders are important change agents, they play key roles in fast-changing external environments. Managers play key roles in stable external environments. An organization has little need for a strong change agent if little is changing around it.

Different organization levels might have different needs for managers and leaders. Management might be required at the top, with leadership needed at lower levels. Decentralized organizations are especially likely to have this pattern.

TRAIT APPROACHES TO LEADERSHIP

People often describe those in leadership and management positions as having certain traits, such as initiative and drive. Personality psychology also relies on traits to explain consistencies in people's behavior across situations.[12] Not surprisingly, the earliest studies of leadership in organizations focused on the psychological and personal characteristics that distinguished leaders from nonleaders.[13]

Much leadership research has focused on finding a set of leadership traits that a successful leader should have (or that distinguishes leaders from followers).[14] The traits investigated were physical factors, such as height and weight; social characteristics, such as interpersonal skills and status; and personality characteristics, such as self-confidence. Leaders were found to be intelligent, aware of their situations, and able public speakers. Leaders had higher intelligent quotients than their followers, but were not successful if they were much more intelligent than their followers. Leaders with knowledge that applied to their situation and who knew how to get things done could move people to high levels of achievement. Leaders carried out their responsibilities. They were self-confident, took the initiative, and persisted when rough times occurred. Leaders had high energy and showed a high level of physical and social activity. They were cooperative and were able to persuade group members to cooperate. Leaders were adaptable and were able to change with changing situations.[15]

Some reviews of past research have found the traits of intelligence, dominance, self-confidence, energy, and task-relevant knowledge consistently associated with leadership.[16] A later review of leadership research identified these six traits as consistently associated with leadership: "drive, the desire to lead, honesty/integrity, self-confidence, cognitive ability, and knowledge of the business."[17] The two trait lists overlap. Drive overlaps with energy and task-relevant knowledge is similar to knowledge of the business. A summary of a leader described by these traits could read: "Leaders are bright, honest, self-confident, high-energy people who know something about the situation they are trying to affect, and take control when they must."

Both reviews found three traits: self-confidence; cognitive ability, which includes intelligence; and knowledge of the business, which is similar to task-relevant knowledge. The desire to lead and honesty/integrity expanded the list of traits. Leaders want to affect the behavior of others. Effective leaders also are honest and have integrity, which helps gain their followers' trust.

The leadership research community is becoming increasingly aware that traits play an important role in leadership. Personality psychologists have argued that traits are associated with consistent behavior across situations. They also have shown that the relationship between traits and behavior is not as small as many had argued in the past.[18] Some studies have reported stable leadership in groups with varied tasks and membership. Leaders varied their behavior according to the group's needs and task requirements.[19]

BEHAVIORAL THEORIES OF LEADERSHIP

Leadership researchers eventually realized that traits alone did not fully explain leadership effectiveness. As a result, they turned to studying leader behavior in the late 1950s. Two complementary behavioral theories of leadership were developed to describe the behavior that distinguished leaders of effective and ineffective workgroups. One group of researchers was at the University of Michigan; the other group was at Ohio State University.

The University of Michigan Leadership Studies: Production-Centered and Employee-Centered Behavior

The University of Michigan leadership studies conceptualized two leadership behavior dimensions:[20] production-centered behavior and employee-centered behavior. Production-centered leader behavior focuses on tasks, not people. Although they do not set high-performance goals, production-centered leaders pressure subordinates to perform. Such leaders do not trust people to work on their own, and therefore they closely supervise others. Production-centered leaders have little understanding of their work unit's social system, a factor that is consistent with their lack of people focus.

Employee-centered leader behavior focuses on people, their personal success, and the quality of the social system that forms within the work unit. Such leaders have high-performance goals for their work units and communicate their performance expectations to their subordinates. Employee-centered leadership combines a strong concern for the social aspects of the work unit with high-performance expectations.

The Michigan researchers felt that their research showed employee-centered leadership more likely leads to higher work unit performance than production-centered leadership. They also felt that production-centered leadership could lead to high productivity, but had several latent dysfunctions. Those dysfunctions included poor employee attitudes with resulting high turnover or absenteeism, little group loyalty, and high levels of distrust between subordinates and their leaders.[21]

The Ohio State University Leadership Studies: Initiating Structure and Consideration

The Ohio State University leadership studies found two dimensions of leadership behavior: initiating structure and consideration. Initiating structure is the task-oriented dimension of leader behavior. Leaders high in initiating structure make individual task assignments, set deadlines, and clearly lay out what needs to be done. They act decisively without asking for their subordinates' suggestions and ideas. Leaders low in initiating structure tend not to take the initiative. These leaders practice "hands off" management, leaving people alone and letting them define the tasks and deadlines. Excessively high initiating structure, especially when combined with strong elements of coercion, is associated with high turnover, high grievance rates, and low satisfaction. A moderate amount of initiating structure can help get good task performance in situations where people are not trained or face high task ambiguity.[22] Initiating structure also had positive relationships with project quality and schedule in industrial development teams.[23]

Consideration is the people-oriented dimension of leadership behavior. Leaders high in consideration show concern for group members. They are empathic, interpersonally warm, and interested in developing relationships with their subordinates based on mutual trust. They actively seek their subordinates' suggestions and opinions and accept and carry out those suggestions. Leaders low in consideration often publicly criticize a subordinate's work. They lack concern for the feelings of others and have little interest in the quality of their interpersonal interactions.

High consideration is associated with high job satisfaction, low turnover, and group cohesiveness. The last two factors can help maintain a group's performance level.[24] Consideration also had positive relationships with project quality and schedule in industrial development teams.[25] Employees working for supervisors high on both dimensions had more positive work attitudes than employees working for supervisors with other combinations of the dimensions.[26]

CONTINGENCY THEORIES OF LEADERSHIP

Neither the trait nor behavioral approaches offered completely satisfactory explanations of leadership in organizations, causing researchers to develop contingency theories of leadership. Such theories viewed successful leadership as dependent upon the leader's situation. The two contingency theories described in this section strongly differ. The first contingency theory views the leader as unable to change behavior readily; the second theory sees the leader as able to choose from a repertoire of behaviors. Each theory offers different ways of thinking about how a leader fits the requirements of a situation.

Fiedler's Contingency Theory of Leadership

Fred E. Fiedler studied leadership in widely varying groups, such as manufacturing groups, boards of directors, managers, and military combat teams. His work built a **contingency theory** of leadership that considered the characteristics of the leader and the characteristics of the situation.[27]

Fiedler's theory assumes leaders are predisposed to a particular set of leader behaviors. Leaders are either task-oriented or relationship-oriented. **Task-oriented leaders** are directive, structure situations, set deadlines, and make task assignments. **Relationship-oriented leaders** are not strongly directive, focus on people, and desire positive social interaction. Although the two types of leaders are similar to the behavioral dimensions discussed earlier, an important distinction exists between Fiedler's contingency theory and the behavioral theories. Fiedler's theory assumes that it is hard to change a predisposition to a particular leadership style; the behavioral theories assume a leader has behavior choices.

Situations differ in how favorable they are for a leader to influence subordinates based on variations in the three dimensions of leader–member relations, task structure, and position power. **Leader–member relations** describe the quality of the relationship between subordinates and the leader. This dimension includes the amount of trust between the leader and subordinates and whether the leader is liked and respected by the subordinates. **Task structure** describes the extent to which the work is well defined and standardized or ambiguous and vague. When task structure is high, the work is predictable and can be planned. Low task structure creates an ambiguous situation with changing circumstances and unpredictable events. **Position power** refers to the leader's formal authority. A situation with high position power lets the leader hire people and directly reward or punish behavior. A leader with low position power does not have the authority for such actions. In the latter situation, policies might constrain the leader from using any rewards or punishments.

The three dimensions help classify situations according to how favorable the situation is for the leader's influence.[28] Figure 12.1 shows a classification based on a dichotomy of each dimension. Favorable situations allow high leader influence; unfavorable situations allow little leader influence. Fiedler's contingency theory makes two broad recommendations about leadership: Task-oriented leaders are more effective in highly favorable or highly unfavorable situations, and relationship-oriented leaders are more effective in situations between those two extremes. These recommendations have received strong empirical support.[29]

Fiedler did not think organizations could easily and reliably select leaders to match the situations in the organization. He also was not optimistic about the effectiveness of leadership training designed to change leaders. He argued strongly that the situation had to be changed to fit a leader's predispositions, that is, "'engineer' the job to fit the [leader]."[30] Alternatively, the leader can be trained to understand her approach to leadership. The leader learns ways to change the situation to be successful.[31]

The relationship between a successful leader type and the characteristics of the situation is logical and easy to understand in some situations, but is less clear in others. For example, in the first situation on the far left of the figure, the leader is well liked, and the task is clear. Focusing on the task in this situation might seem right. The situation on the far right also makes sense. The leader has nothing to lose by being task-oriented if everything in the situation already is unfavorable. What is less clear is why a relationship-oriented leader

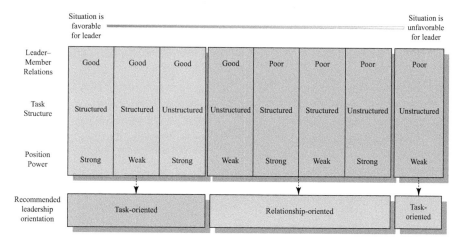

Figure 12.1: Fiedler's Contingency Theory: Situational Factors and Recommended Leadership Orientations

is right for some situations shown for that orientation. A relationship-oriented leader will have difficulty being effective in a group where she is disliked. This type of leader also is nondirective and possibly lets the structure of the task affect subordinate behavior.

House's Path-Goal Theory of Leadership

Robert J. House developed the path-goal theory of leadership to resolve inconsistencies in previous leadership research. A contingency theory says characteristics of the situation govern the choice of leader behavior. Although path-goal theory and Fiedler's theory are both contingency theories, they view the contingency relationship differently.[32] An extensive analysis of empirical studies showed partial support for the theory.[33] Reviewers of the research history of path-goal theory noted its complexity and lack of thorough testing.[34]

Path-goal theory sees the leader's role as affecting a subordinate's motivation to reach desired goals. The leader affects a subordinate's motivation by using rewards when the subordinate reaches desired goals, being supportive while the subordinate is trying to reach the goals, making intrinsically motivating task assignments, and clearing barriers to goal accomplishment. The theory's name summarizes what a leader does—clearing subordinates' paths so they can reach desired goals. A leader's behavior can enhance a subordinate's motivation and increase a subordinate's job satisfaction. Acceptance of the leader by the subordinate should also increase.

Path-goal theory proposes four leader behaviors:

- ▨ **Directive:** Directive leader behavior focuses on what must be done, when it must be done, and how it must be done. This behavior clarifies performance expectations and the role of each subordinate in the workgroup.
- ▨ **Supportive:** Supportive leader behavior includes concern for subordinates as people and the needs they are trying to satisfy. Supportive leaders are open, warm, friendly, and approachable.
- ▨ **Participative:** Participative leader behavior includes consultation with subordinates and serious consideration of subordinates' ideas before making decisions.
- ▨ **Achievement-oriented:** Achievement-oriented leader behavior emphasizes excellence in subordinate performance and improvements in performance. An achievement-oriented leader sets high-performance goals and shows confidence in people's abilities to reach those goals.

The four behaviors of path-goal theory have several important qualities. Directive and supportive behavior are the same as initiating structure and consideration. These two behaviors have been a consistent part of leadership research and are basic to the functioning of leaders in organizations. Participative leader behavior emphasizes the decision-making function of leaders. Note that subordinate participation emerges as an important part of decision making.

Achievement-oriented leader behavior is the heart of subordinate motivation. Chapter 8, "Motivation: Cognitive and Behavioral Theories and Techniques," showed how high and achievable performance goals are part of high work performance. The leader's expressed confidence also emerges as an important contributor to motivation.

The path-goal theory describes two sets of contingency factors that play important roles in the choice of leader behavior: (1) personal factors of subordinates and (2) work environment factors.

Personal factors are subordinates' perceptions of their ability, their perceptions of the source of control (locus of control) over what happens to them, and their views about people in authority positions (authoritarianism). **Work environment factors** include tasks, the nature of the system of authority in the organization, and the primary workgroup.

Figure 12.2 shows the structure of path-goal theory. The four leader behaviors are described as a "repertoire" to emphasize that the leader chooses among the behaviors. The theory does not suggest that leaders should use all behaviors. The choice of behavior is based on the skills and personality of the leader and on the circumstances facing the leader. Those circumstances include contingency factors from the person and from the work environment.

Subordinates whose **ability** is less than that required by the task are likely to respond positively to directive leader behavior. They welcome clarification of their duties and tasks because their level of ability makes it difficult to complete the task. High-ability subordinates might feel such leader behavior is unnecessary and demeaning, because they already know what to do and do not need the boss telling them how to complete a task.

People can perceive the **locus of control** of their behavior as either internal or external to them. Subordinates who feel their behavior is responsible for the results they achieve (internal control) are likely to respond positively to participative behavior and less positively to directive behavior. Because they feel in control, they do not want the leader to direct them to task completion. Instead, they like to affect decisions that lead to task accomplishment. Low participative and directive leader behavior work better for subordinates who feel externally controlled.

People high in **authoritarianism** are strongly status-oriented. They readily accept the direction of people in an authority position and want to please them. People low in authoritarianism are flexible and tend not to defer to authority. People high in authoritarianism accept directive leader behavior, whereas people low in authoritarianism prefer participative behavior.

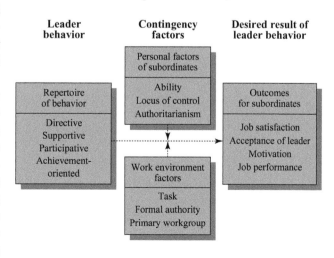

■ **Figure 12.2:** Path-Goal Theory of Leadership

The three work environment factors contribute to a work environment that varies in degree of ambiguity. Routine **tasks** done in a setting with clearly defined relationships among roles and standard operating procedures are less ambiguous than tasks done in a more fluid setting. **Formal authority** also contributes to the degree of ambiguity. Well-defined authority in a leader's role allows a leader to clearly define work roles and set clear goals.

Primary workgroups consisting of people strongly identified with each other often develop well-defined procedures for doing the group's work. The opposite is true of workgroups with people not strongly identified with each other. The first type of group presents an unambiguous environment to the subordinate, while the second type presents an ambiguous environment.

Path-goal theory suggests different leader behaviors for work environments low in ambiguity than for those high in ambiguity. Subordinates working in a low-ambiguity situation can clearly see the task and how to do it. Directive leader behavior is perceived as redundant and could reduce subordinate satisfaction and motivation. A better behavioral choice is supportive, because it can offset possible negative effects of routine tasks. Directive leader behavior, however, can bring structure to an ambiguous situation. Such behavior could clarify the task and reduce subordinate frustration with the uncertainty of the situation.[35]

House has reformulated and expanded the theory after 25 years of research by him and others.[36] The theory describes leader behaviors and relationships that not only affect subordinate performance, but also help work unit performance. Instead of four behaviors, the new version of the theory features eight behaviors. The new behaviors focus on path-goal clarification, social interaction within the workgroup, the political behavior necessary to increase the group's power, and the leader's charismatic behavior. These behaviors add to the behavior repertoire noted earlier. This expanded version of path-goal theory has not yet been empirically tested.

ALTERNATIVE VIEWS OF LEADERSHIP

The next sections describe some alternative views of leadership that differ from those described so far in this chapter. Look for similarities and differences in what has already been said about leadership in organizations.

The Leadership Mystique

E. E. Jennings' **leadership mystique** is a set of ideas, values, and beliefs that Jennings feels is the essence of leadership.[37] The leadership mystique has three dimensions:

▪ A sense of mission.
▪ A capacity for power.
▪ A will to survive and to persevere.

A leader has a **sense of mission**—a vision of some future state for the organization. The vision is more than a strategic plan; rather, it is a dream about something that the leader wants to create. The result does not exist now, but it will exist. The mission becomes part of the heart, soul, and ego of the leader and is the leader's heroic vision of the possible. A leader pursues that mission at great personal sacrifice and describes the mission with intense passion, trying to enlist others to pursue it also.

A **capacity for power** is the ability to get and use power to pursue the mission. Leaders have no fear of power, nor do they believe having power is undesirable. Power—and the capacity to get it—is basic to achieving the mission.

Leaders are often frustrated in their pursuit of their mission. They must have a **will to survive and to persevere** in reaching their mission. This third quality of the leadership mystique deals with impediments to achieving the mission— financial backers, competitors, government restrictions, and so on. A leader has "a will to persevere against a discourteous, unbelieving world of sometimes total opposition."[38]

Transformational Leadership

Transformational leadership emphasizes charisma, individualized consideration, and intellectual stimulation.[39] **Charisma** is the most important part of transformational leadership because of the power it gives a leader.[40] Followers of charismatic leaders trust them, identify with them, and have high confidence in them. Charismatic leaders often have high self-confidence, self-esteem, and self-determination.

Individualized consideration means the transformational leader recognizes variations in subordinates' skills, abilities, and desires for growth opportunities. The transformational leader knows her subordinates well. The transformational leader also gives individual counseling, guidance, and support, and constructively critiques a subordinate's performance. A key part of individualized consideration is the degree to which the leader shows genuine interest in subordinates.

Intellectual stimulation is the transformational leader's ability to build high awareness of problems and solutions. Such leaders induce changes in the values and beliefs of subordinates. They stimulate subordinates to imagine new and different future states for the group. Intellectual stimulation is more than a change in present direction—it demands a large leap in the values, beliefs, and problem focus of subordinates.

Transformational leaders get their intellectual stimulation from superior technical ability and personal brilliance. They also create and manage symbols and images that represent their vision for the group or the organization. Emotional stimulation can be part of intellectual stimulation. The transformational leader imbues followers with a consciousness about some future state and each follower's role in reaching that state.

Transformational leaders strive for major increases in performance beyond that needed to reach immediate organization goals. They bring excitement to the workplace and build strong emotional bonds between themselves and their followers. Transformational leaders work toward what they believe is right and good for the organization, not for its present direction. They often bring dramatic changes to an organization's culture and are remembered long after they are gone.

Empirical research has usually shown positive relationships between transformational leadership and organizational performance.[41] All three dimensions of transformational leadership had positive relationships with organizational performance. Charisma, however, evoked the strongest positive relationships.

Charismatic Leadership Theories

A major shift in leadership research in the mid-1970s led to the development of many charismatic leadership theories.[42] Transformational leadership, discussed in the previous section, was one such theory. Many others appeared through the 1990s. These theories sought answers to the same questions:

■ How do charismatic leaders lead their followers to outstanding performance?
■ Why do such leaders receive high levels of follower trust and loyalty?
■ What specific behaviors distinguish charismatic leaders from other types of leaders?

Charismatic leaders attract devoted followers who energetically pursue the leader's vision. The leaders move their followers to extraordinary heights of performance, profoundly affect their aspirations, build emotional attachment to the leader, and win commitment to the leader's vision. Charismatic leaders win the loyalty of their followers and inspire them to self-sacrifice in the pursuit of the vision.

Charismatic leaders see well beyond their organization's current situation and develop a view of the future that is different from the present.[43] They develop and widely communicate an inspirational vision—a vision they describe as better in specific ways from the present. Such leaders form bonds of trust between themselves and their followers. Charismatic leaders empower others in their organizations to carry out the vision.

Looking beyond the present situation includes scanning the environment for new market opportunities, predicting changes in markets and technologies, and looking for ways to keep the organization aligned with its outside environment. Charismatic leaders are impatient with present conditions and press their organizations to continuously improve. They push their organizations toward a new state by creating dissatisfaction with the present.

Creating and communicating an inspirational vision is a key behavior of charismatic leaders. They use all media with which they are comfortable, including written documents, speeches, conversations with individual employees, television, and electronic communications. Charismatic leaders are especially skilled at framing messages that clearly state and support their vision.

Building trust between the leader and followers is a key part of getting followers to commit to the leader's vision. Charismatic leaders behave in ways that are consistent with statements about the vision. The leader also tries to forge values supporting the vision into the cultural fabric of the organization.

Charismatic leaders are especially skilled at tapping unused motivational energy in their followers. They rely on empowerment, an approach that helps followers build self-confidence in their ability to reach the leader's vision. Such leaders often design experiences to stretch their followers to new levels of performance. By giving them feedback on their performance, charismatic leaders help steer followers in the desired direction and inspire them to higher performance levels.

Empirical research shows a positive relationship between charisma and organizational performance.[44] Other research suggests that such leaders emerge during periods of crisis.[45] As noted at the beginning of the chapter, a charismatic leader's vision is positively associated with employee performance and attitudes.[46]

Leader-Member Exchange (LMX) Theory

Leader-member exchange (LMX) theory proposes that the leadership process in organizations emerges from exchange relationships between each leader and each of the leader's followers.[47] It is not based on the degree of unilateral influence that a leader has over a follower because of the leader's organizational position. The relationship can mature into a partnership with each follower. Each leader and follower shapes the partnership according to the mutual desires of each party. The emerging LMX relationships can vary from one leader–follower pair to another.

LMX relationships vary in quality. High-quality exchange relationships feature high levels of mutual respect, trust, and obligation. A strong bond develops between the leader and follower, helping to build high job performance. Low quality exchange relationships feature low levels of mutual respect, trust, and obligation. The follower's job performance stays within the required behaviors described in a job description.

Workgroups can have variations among group members in the quality of their LMX relationship. Some members will have a strong tie to the group leader; others will have a weak tie. Teams with large differences in LMX relationship quality can have reduced member satisfaction and higher interpersonal conflict. This result appears especially true for teams with interdependent tasks and less true for teams with independent tasks.[48]

Self-Leadership, SuperLeadership, and Servant-Leadership

Self-leadership focuses on the individual and moves the person toward intrinsically motivating tasks. Self-leaders derive strength and resilience from difficult experiences. It also helps the person do required tasks that are not intrinsically motivating.[49]

SuperLeadership is a form of empowerment that focuses on getting followers to lead themselves. The effect for the SuperLeader is to have enhanced strength from the strength of followers. The effect for followers is the development of their self-leadership skills.[50]

Servant-leadership combines serving and leading. It also focuses on the environment to harmoniously reach its goals. A servant-leader has a strong ability to lead and a strong wish to serve. These characteristics combine to positively strengthen each other.[51]

LEADERSHIP AND SELF-MANAGING TEAMS

Managers in organizations are increasingly using self-managing teams to get work done. Chapter 10, "Groups and Intergroup Processes," described the characteristics of such teams. This section addresses the leadership issues raised by self-managing teams.

The use of self-managing teams changes the traditional distribution of decision authority in an organization. Teams take on much decision authority formerly exercised by managers and supervisors. In addition to doing their regular work of producing a product or providing a service, these teams often establish work schedules, set performance goals, assess team member performance, buy supplies, assess quality, and interact with vendors and internal or external customers.[52] Managers and supervisors had typically decided such matters. The redistribution of decision authority changes the roles of managers and supervisors outside the team and defines new roles for team members.

Each team typically has a team leader who is either selected by team members or is appointed by a manager or supervisor outside the team.[53] Some team leaders hold the job permanently. Other teams rotate members through the position. The growing popularity of self-managing teams increases the likelihood that you could become a member of such a team and rotate through the team leader position.

The role of traits in the leadership process and the different leader behaviors described earlier in this chapter also apply to team leaders. For example, a team member who rotates into the team leader role might not have leadership traits, or other team members might not attribute those traits to the person. Leaders of self-managing teams could benefit from viewing the team leader role from perspectives offered by the various theories.

Managers and supervisors outside the team do not cease to be leaders or managers. The nature of their work shifts from close, day-to-day supervision to long-range planning, team guidance, team development, resource support, and more senior management political support. Managers responsible for self-managing teams focus on encouraging various team behaviors such as goal-setting, self-criticism, and performance feedback. The behavior of external leaders and managers should focus on developing the self-managing part of self-managing teams.[54]

SUBSTITUTES, NEUTRALIZERS, AND ENHANCERS OF LEADERSHIP BEHAVIOR

Substitutes, neutralizers, and enhancers each operate differently in the relationship between a leader and a subordinate. Figure 12.3 shows the different relationships for substitutes, neutralizers, and enhancers.[55]

Substitutes for leadership act in place of the leader, making leader behavior unnecessary. The substitute, not the leader, affects subordinate attitudes and behavior. Some leadership theories described in this chapter have suggested that characteristics of the task, subordinate, organization, and workgroup can substitute for the leader. For example, path-goal theory suggests that people doing routine and predictable tasks would find directive leader behavior redundant. The nature of the task, not the leader, guides the person's behavior. Tasks allowing high levels of intrinsic motivation also substitute for motivational influences from the leader.

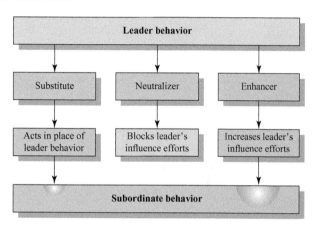

■ **Figure 12.3:** Substitutes, Neutralizers, and Enhancers of Leadership Behavior

Neutralizers prevent leader behavior from affecting the attitudes and behavior of subordinates. A neutralizer breaks the connection between leader behavior and subordinate response. A neutralizer has no direct effect on the subordinate. Instead, it is a block between the leader and the subordinate. For example, workgroups often develop norms or rules that control the behavior of group members. If those norms are not consistent with what the group leader wants, the norm neutralizes the leader's efforts to influence the group. Employees with a professional orientation, such as scientists and university professors, often turn to their professional peers for recognition and rewards. That orientation can neutralize supportive leader behavior and any efforts at recognition by the leader.

Enhancers strengthen the effects of leader behavior on subordinates. If a leader controls rewards for a subordinate's performance, and the subordinate perceives a direct connection between performance and getting the reward, the reward system enhances the leader's influence over the subordinate. Similarly, organization policies that let the leader hire and fire enhance the leader's influence over subordinates by increasing the leader's coercive power.

LEADERSHIP PERCEPTIONS: "WE KNOW A LEADER WHEN WE SEE ONE"

This chapter's discussions of leadership have focused on the traits and behavior of leaders. Human perceptual processes underlie people's observations of leader traits and behaviors. Researchers have developed two different, but related views of leadership perceptions. The first view builds on perceptual categories; the second view describes the process of leadership attribution.

Leadership Categorization

According to the **leadership categorization** view of leadership perception, people observe the behavior of another person and then quickly compare those observations to a cognitive category describing a leader.[56] The person compares perceived observations to a cognitive category that is either a leadership prototype or a leadership exemplar. A **leadership prototype** is a person's cognitive or mental image of the characteristics, qualities, behaviors, and traits that make up a leader. For example, some people might view leaders as intelligent and industrious whereas others think of leaders as honest and outgoing. A **leadership exemplar** is a specific person people regard as a leader, such as Mahatma Gandhi or Martin Luther King, Jr.

A key step in the leadership categorization process is deciding whether the perceived observations match the leadership prototype or exemplar. If they do not match, the observer decides that the observed person is not a leader. If they match, the observer decides the observed person is a leader.

Leadership Attributions

Leadership attribution follows the attribution processes described in Chapter 5.[57] Individuals observe the behavior of other people and the effects associated with the behavior. An observer can also infer other behaviors from the observed behavior. For example, an observer might conclude that a talkative person who interacts with many people in a group has much job-related information. The observer made the inference from the observed talkative and interactive behavior.

In the next step of the process, the observer assesses the observed and inferred information for evidence of leadership. A key factor in this step is whether the behavior is specific to one person or is widely shared by other people in a group. An observer accepts only distinctive behavior as evidence of leadership. The observer then compares the distinctive behavior to an **implicit leadership theory**. Such theories act as perceptual filters and standards of comparison for the leadership qualities a person believes are important for a leader to have. Some people think decisiveness is an important leadership quality. If a leader shows decisiveness, then the person is a leader. The observer now decides whether the behavior is consistent across situations and over time. If the observer sees similar behavior from the same person in different situations and at different times, she will build a strong attribution of leadership.

Some evidence exists suggesting that the observer's social network or group's leadership attributions can affect that person's leadership attribution. Other people in the network or group might share specific leadership attributions of an individual such as charisma. Membership in the group, and socialization to the group's norms about leadership (see Chapter 6 "Organizational Socialization"), affect a person's leadership attributions.[58]

WOMEN, MEN, AND LEADERSHIP

Do women and men exhibit different leadership behavior? That question has been the center of a continuing debate since the 1980s. Those who feel a difference exists base their argument on presumed differences in the socialization of women and men. Supposedly, the socialization of men leads to a competitive, aggressive leadership style whereas the socialization of women results in a nurturing, caring leadership style.[59]

One study showed some differences in the leadership behavior of women and men. Women described themselves as sharing power, sharing information, and encouraging their subordinates' self-worth. Men described themselves as using authority that came from their position and relying on rewards and punishments to shape subordinates' behaviors.[60] The design of this study, however, restricts generalizing its results. The sample was drawn from members of the International Women's Forum and male leaders nominated by the respondents. The 31 percent response rate also limits interpretation of these results.

Empirical evidence from other sources says little difference exists in leadership behavior of women and men in organization positions.[61] One study assessing the consideration and initiating structure dimensions found some differences. People who worked for men whose leadership was high on both dimensions had the most positive attitudes in the sample. The researchers expected men to be task-oriented, but were pleasantly surprised when they also showed consideration for employees.[62] A careful statistical analysis of a wide range of other studies showed that women behaved more democratically and participatively than men.

Other research showed differences in transformational leadership between women and men. Both male and female raters perceived female leaders as slightly higher in charisma and individualized consideration than male leaders.[63] A careful analysis of 45 studies found that female leaders showed more transformational leadership behavior than male leaders.[64]

INTERNATIONAL ASPECTS OF LEADERSHIP AND MANAGEMENT

The core values that define the relationships between leaders and followers or managers and subordinates vary from country to country. People in countries with values that specify strongly hierarchical relationships in organizations react more positively to directive approaches than to participative approaches. A directive approach is congruent with the values of many Latin American countries, India, Hong Kong, and France. More participative approaches fit the values of countries such as Austria, Sweden, Great Britain, Canada, the United States, and Germany. Variations in cultures suggest trying to match a leader or manager's behavior to the culture's expectations.[65]

Leader and manager behavior might not always vary for multinational organizations operating in different countries. Uniformity could occur because the company selects managers with behaviors and orientations valued by the firm. Socialization practices could also give people a consistent set of core values that do not vary from country to country.[66]

A long line of research shows cultural differences in response to directive leadership and management. Such leadership and management behavior includes initiating structure, production-centered, task-oriented, and directive behaviors discussed earlier in the chapter. Workers in countries with authoritarian values expect their leaders and managers to behave in an autocratic way.[67] Other cross-cultural leadership research is finding evidence that the positive effects of a supportive leadership and management style might not vary from culture to culture. Managers who tie positive rewards to people's performance apparently get positive results in whatever country they are a manager.[68]

Cross-cultural evidence for transformational leadership comes from research done on every continent except Antarctica. The results show uniformity in the underlying concepts across country cultures. Although the concepts appear in people's descriptions of great leaders, the specific behaviors vary. Individualized consideration in Japan is an assumed relationship between superior and subordinate. It tends to have more open expression in individualistic cultures of the West.[69]

The research results of the Global Leadership and Organizational Behavior Effectiveness Research Program (GLOBE) show many cultural effects of leadership behavior.[70] This unprecedented international research effort collected data from 951 organizations in 62 societies around the world. Seventeen thousand managers participated in the study. The results show that confidence building and encouraging attributes of transformational and charismatic leader behavior appear almost universally across cultures. Other attributes such as sensitivity and compassion are specific to certain cultures. Such behavior is highly valued in China and Malaysia and less so in the United States and Germany.

ETHICAL ISSUES IN LEADERSHIP AND MANAGEMENT

Leaders can also use much of the behavioral knowledge in this book to shape and direct others' behaviors. A major ethical issue focuses on whether such efforts are an unethical manipulation of other people's behavior.[71]

Behavior changes induced by leadership can also change a person's attitudes, values, and beliefs. For example, a leader's efforts to move an organization toward quality management might try to transform an organization's values to include an emphasis on customers, processes, and continuous improvement—not just on profits and costs. Individual employees can undergo similar changes.

That possibility has led some observers to suggest that leadership can have a brainwashing-like effect on people.[72]

These possible results of leadership have led some researchers to try to discover ethical and unethical leadership qualities. An ethical leader confronts moral dilemmas, rewards ethical behavior, and builds an ethical organizational culture.[73] Such qualities are especially important to consider when leaders have strong effects on their followers. Transformational leaders, with strong charismatic features, can get strong commitment from followers who accept the vision. This type of leadership can clearly have ethical or unethical results.

SUMMARY

Leadership is an influence process involving two or more people. The person who is the target of the influence effort must attribute that effort to a specific person and consider it acceptable.

Leaders and managers play different roles in organizations. Leaders try to change organizations, while managers sustain and control them. Organizations also have different needs for those roles at different levels and at different times in their history.

Trait theories describe traits consistently associated with leadership, such as intelligence, dominance, self-confidence, energy, the desire to lead, honesty, and task-relevant knowledge. Behavioral theories of leadership describe task- and people-oriented behavior as stable dimensions of leader behavior. Two contingency theories give different views of how situations affect leader behavior. Fiedler's contingency theory of leadership says that leaders have a predisposition to focus on people or on tasks. House's path-goal theory of leadership says that leaders can choose from four behaviors and combine them according to the needs of the situation. Those behaviors are directive, supportive, participative, and achievement-oriented.

The alternative leadership theories are the leadership mystique, transformational leadership, charismatic leadership, and LMX theory. Each of these theories emphasizes the role of charisma and vision in effective leadership. Self-leadership, SuperLeadership, and Servant-leadership were also part of the alternative theories.

The growing use of self-managing work teams in American and Canadian organizations is changing the role of leaders inside and outside the teams. Many observations in this chapter apply to such teams and can guide team leaders and those who coordinate activities of several teams.

Situations surrounding leaders have many factors that substitute for leader behavior, neutralize the behavior, or enhance the behavior. Understanding a situation's characteristics is an important step in being an effective leader in an organization.

The core values that define the relationships between leaders and followers or managers and subordinates vary across cultures. People in countries with values that specify hierarchical relationships in organizations react more positively to directive approaches than to participative approaches.

An ethical leader confronts moral dilemmas, rewards ethical behavior, and builds an ethical organizational culture. Such qualities are especially important to consider for leaders who have strong effects on their followers.

REVIEW AND DISCUSSION QUESTIONS

REVIEW AND DISCUSSION QUESTIONS 12

1 Discuss the difference between leadership and management. What roles do leaders and managers play in organizations?

2 Review the leadership traits described earlier. Are there any people, living or dead, who have those traits? To which traits do you respond most positively?

3 Review the two behavioral approaches to leadership. What are the similarities and differences in the two approaches?

4 Discuss the three dimensions in Fiedler's contingency theory of leadership. Try to identify an example from your experiences of one situation shown in Figure 12.1. Did the leader in that situation behave as predicted by the theory? If not, did you perceive the leader as effective or ineffective? Discuss how the theory explains why the leader was effective or ineffective.

5 The path-goal theory of leadership describes two sets of contingency factors—personal factors of subordinates and work environment factors. Discuss how these factors affect the choice of leader behavior. Give examples from your work experiences.

6 Review the alternative views of leadership. How do those views differ from the other leadership theories? Why?

7 Have you ever been in a situation where substitutes, neutralizers, or enhancers of leadership existed? What did the leader do in that situation? What was the effect of the substitutes, neutralizers, or enhancers?

TAKE FIVE: OB ALIVE: *NORMA RAE* (1979)

The reluctant workers of a Southern textile mill move slowly toward union membership. Norma Rae's (Sally Field) leadership and dedication move them toward that goal. Encouragement and guidance come from labor organizer Reuban (Ron Leibman).

The scenes are completely contained within DVD Chapter 26, "A Woman Alone." It begins with a shot of a sign on a door that reads, "Transfer Traffic Only." The scenes end after Sheriff Lamar Miller (Gregory Walcott) escorts Norma Rae out of the factory.

View the scene first and then answer the following questions: What are Norma Rae's leadership traits? Do the workers respond to her leadership efforts? Which leadership behaviors discussed in this chapter does Norma Rae show?

REFERENCES AND NOTES

1. House, R. J., and M. L. Baetz. 1979. Leadership: Some Empirical Generalizations and New Research Directions. In *Research in Organizational Behavior*, Vol. 1, ed. B. M. Staw. Greenwich, CT: JAI Press, pp. 342–46.
2. Ibid., pp. 341–423.
3. Ibid., p. 344.
   Hogan, R., G. J. Curphy, and J. Hogan. 1994. What We Know About Leadership. *American Psychologist* 49: 493–505. This article has a good summary of emergent leadership.
4. Aditya, R. N., R. J. House, and S. Kerr. 2000. Theory and Practice of Leadership: Into the New Millennium. In *Industrial and Organizational Psychology: Linking Theory with Practice*, ed. C. L. Copper and E. A. Locke. Oxford: Blackwell, Chap. 6. This reference has an excellent summary and discussion of the leadership research literature. It includes observations on the practical implications of the leadership theories (pp. 149–55).
   Barling, J., A. Christie, and C. Hoption. 2011. Leadership. In *APA Handbook of Industrial and Organizational Psychology*, Vol. 1, ed. S. Zedeck. Washington, DC: American Psychology Association, Chap. 7.
   House, R. J., and R. N. Aditya. 1997. The Social Scientific Study of Leadership: Quo Vadis? *Journal of Management* 23: 409–73.
   House, R. J. and P. M. Podsakoff. 1994. Leadership Effectiveness: Past Perspective and Future Directions for Research. In *Organizational Behavior: The State of the Science*, ed. Jerald Greenberg. Hillsdale: Lawrence Erlbaum Associates, pp. 45–83. This source also has an excellent discussion of the leadership research literature.
   Lord, R. G., D. V. Day, S. J. Zaccaro, B. J. Avolco, and A. H. Eagley. 2017. Leadership in Applied Psychology: Three Waves of Theory and Research. *Journal of Applied Psychology* 102: 434–51.
5. Jennings, E. E. 1974. On Rediscovering the Leader. In *Contemporary Management: Issues and Viewpoints*, ed. J. W. McGuire. Englewood Cliffs: Prentice Hall, p. 390.
6. Ibid., pp. 390–96.
7. House and Aditya, The Social Scientific Study of Leadership, pp. 444–45.
   Kotter, J. P. 1990. What Leaders Really Do. *Harvard Business Review* (May–June): 103–11.
   Zaleznik, A. 1977. Managers and Leaders: Are They Different? *Harvard Business Review* (May–June): 67–80. [Reprinted: *Harvard Business Review*, March–April 1992, pp. 126–35.] This classic source has an excellent, readable discussion of leadership and management.
   Zaleznik, A. 1990. The Leadership Gap. *Academy of Management Executive* 4: 7–22.
8. Collins, J. C., and J. I. Porras. 1996. Building Your Company's Vision. *Harvard Business Review* 76 (September–October): 65–77.

Nutt, P. C., and R. W. Backoff. 1997. Crafting Vision. *Journal of Management Inquiry* 6: 308–28.

9. Levin, I. M. 2000. Vision Revisited: Telling the Story of the Future. *The Journal of Applied Behavioral Science* 36: 91–107. (Quotation taken from p. 92.)

10. Goleman, D. 2000. Leadership That Gets Results. *Harvard Business Review* (March–April): 78–90.
Goleman, D., R. Boyatzis, and A. McKee. 2002. *Primal Leadership: Realizing the Power of Emotional Intelligence*. Boston: Harvard Business School Press. See especially pp. 48–49.

11. Baum, J. R., E. A. Locke, and S. A. Kirkpatrick. 1998. A Longitudinal Study of the Relation of Vision and Vision Communication to Venture Growth in Entrepreneurial Firms. *Journal of Applied Psychology* 83: 43–54.
Kirkpatrick, S. A., and E. A. Locke. 1996. Direct and Indirect Effects of Three Core Charismatic Leadership Components on Performance and Attitudes. *Journal of Applied Psychology* 81: 36–51.

12. Kenrick, D. T., and D. C. Funder. 1988. Profiting from Controversy: Lessons from the Person-Situation Debate. *American Psychologist* 43: 23–34.

13. Bartlett, F. C. 1926. The Social Psychology of Leadership. *The Journal of the National Institute of Industrial Psychology* 3: 188–93.
Bass, B. M. 1990. *Bass and Stogdill's Handbook of Leadership: Theory, Research, and Managerial Applications*. New York: Free Press, Chaps. 4, 5.
House and Aditya, The Social Scientific Study of Leadership, pp. 410–19.
Jenkins, W. O. 1947. A Review of Leadership Studies with Particular Reference to Military Problems. *Journal of Educational Psychology* 44: 54–79.
Mann, R. D. 1959. A Review of the Relationships between Personality and Performance in Small Groups. *Psychological Bulletin* 56: 241–70.
Smith, H. L., and L. M. Kreuger. 1933. A Brief Summary of Literature on Leadership. *Bulletin of the School of Education, Indiana University* 9: 1–80.
Stogdill, R. M. 1948. Personal Factors Associated with Leadership: A Survey of the Literature. *Journal of Psychology* 25: 35–71.

14. Jago, A. G. 1982. Leadership: Perspectives in Theory and Research. *Management Science* 28 (March): 315–36.

15. Lord, R. G., C. L. DeVader, and G. M. Alliger. 1986. A Meta-Analysis of the Relation between Personality Traits and Leadership Perceptions: An Application of Validity Generalization Procedures. *Journal of Applied Psychology* 71: 402–10.
Stogdill, Personal Factors Associated with Leadership, pp. 44–45.

16. Bass, *Bass and Stogdill's Handbook of Leadership*, Chaps. 4, 5.
Mann, A Review of the Relationships.
House and Baetz, Leadership, p. 349.

17. Kirkpatrick, S. A., and E. A. Locke. 1991. Leadership: Do Traits Matter? *Academy of Management Executive* 5: 48–60. (Quotation taken from p. 49; emphasis added.)

18. Kenrick and Funder, Profiting from Controversy.

19. Kenny, D. A., and S. J. Zaccaro. 1983. An Estimate of Variance Due to Traits in Leadership. *Journal of Applied Psychology* 68: 678–85.
Zaccaro, S. J., R. J. Foti, and D. A. Kenny. 1991. Self-Monitoring and Trait-Based Variance in Leadership: An Investigation of Leader Flexibility across Multiple Group Situations. *Journal of Applied Psychology* 76: 308–15.

20. Likert, R. 1961. *New Patterns of Management*. New York: McGraw-Hill.
Likert, R. 1967. *The Human Organization: Its Management and Value*. New York: McGraw-Hill.

21. Likert, *New Patterns of Management*, pp. 58–60.
22. Bass, *Bass and Stogdill's Handbook of Leadership*, Chap. 24.
    Howell, J. M., and P. J. Frost. 1989. A Laboratory Study of Charismatic Leadership. *Organizational Behavior and Human Decision Processes* 43: 243–69.
    Stogdill, R. M. 1959. *Individual Behavior and Group Achievement*. New York: Oxford University Press.
23. Keller, R. T. 1992. Transformational Leadership and the Performance of Research and Development Project Groups. *Journal of Management* 18: 489–502.
24. Bass, *Bass and Stogdill's Handbook of Leadership*, Chap. 24.
25. Keller, Transformational Leadership.
26. Hutchison, S., K. E. Valentino, and S. L. Kirkner. 1998. What Works for the Gander Does Not Work as Well for the Goose: The Effects of Leader Behavior. *Journal of Applied Social Psychology* 28: 171–82.
27. Fiedler, F. E. 1965. Engineer the Job to Fit the Manager. *Harvard Business Review* 43 (September–October): 115–22.
    Fiedler, F. E. 1967. *A Theory of Leadership Effectiveness*. New York: McGraw-Hill.
    Fiedler, F. E. 1971. Validation and Extension of the Contingency Model of Leadership Effectiveness: A Review of Empirical Findings. *Psychological Bulletin* 76: 128–48.
    Fiedler, F. E., and M. M. Chemers. 1974. Leadership and Management. In *Contemporary Management: Issues and Viewpoints*, ed. J. W. McGuire. Englewood Cliffs: Prentice Hall, pp. 362–89.
28. Developed from Fiedler, Validation and Extension of the Contingency Model.
29. See House and Aditya, The Social Scientific Study of Leadership, pp. 421–22 for a review of the empirical evidence.
30. Fiedler, Engineer the Job, p. 115.
31. Fiedler, F. E. 1976. The Leadership Game: Matching the Man to the Situation. *Organizational Dynamics* (Winter): 6–16.
32. House, R. J. 1971. A Path-Goal Theory of Leadership Effectiveness. *Administrative Science Quarterly* 16: 321–38.
    House, R. J. 1996. Path-Goal Theory of Leadership: Lessons, Legacy and a Reformulated Theory. *The Leadership Quarterly* 7: 323–52.
    Schriesheim, C. A., and L. L. Neider. 1996. Path-Goal Leadership: The Long and Winding Road. *Leadership Quarterly* 7: 317–21.
33. Wofford, J. C., and L. Z. Liska. 1993. Path-Goal Theories of Leadership: A Meta-Analysis. *Journal of Management* 19: 857–76.
34. Evans, M. G. 1996. R. J. House's "A Path-Goal Theory of Leader Effectiveness." *The Leadership Quarterly* 7: 305–9.
    House, Path-Goal Theory of Leadership.
    Yukl, G. A. 1994. A Retrospective on Robert House's 1976 Theory of Charismatic Leadership and Recent Revisions. *The Leadership Quarterly* 4: 367–73.
35. Keller, Transformational Leadership.
36. House, Path-Goal Theory of Leadership.
37. Jennings, E. E. 1960. *An Anatomy of Leadership*. New York: Harper & Row.
    Jennings, On Rediscovering the Leader, pp. 390–96.
38. Jennings, On Rediscovering the Leader, p. 391.
39. Bass, B. M. 1985. *Leadership and Performance beyond Expectations*. New York: Free Press.
    Bass, B. M. 1990. From Transactional to Transformational Leadership: Learning to Share the Vision. *Organizational Dynamics* 18: 19–31.

Burns first described transformational leadership in J. M. Burns. 1978. *Leadership.* New York: Harper & Row.

40. Bass, *Leadership and Performance*, pp. 42–43.

41. Keller, Transformational Leadership.

    Lowe, K. B., K. G. Kroeck, and N. Sivasubramanian. 1996. Effectiveness Correlates of Transformational and Transactional Leadership: A Meta-Analytic Review of the MLQ Literature. *Leadership Quarterly* 7: 385–425.

    Walumbwa, F. O., B. J. Avolioa, and W. Zhu. 2008. How Transformational Leadership Weaves Its Influence on Individual Job Performance: The Role of Identification and Efficacy Beliefs. *Personnel Psychology* 61: 793–825.

    For some negative findings, see R. Basu and S. G. Green. 1997. Leader-Member Exchange and Transformational Leadership: An Empirical Examination of Innovative Behaviors in Leader-Member Dyads. *Journal of Applied Social Psychology* 27: 477–99.

42. Developed from A. Bryman. 1993. Charismatic Leadership in Business Organizations: Some Neglected Issues. *The Leadership Quarterly* 4: 289–304.

    Gardner, W. L., and B. J. Avolio. 1998. The Charismatic Relationship: A Dramaturgical Perspective. *Academy of Management Review* 23: 32–58.

    Grabo, A., B. R. Spisak, and M. van Vugt. 2017. Charisma as Signal: An Evolutionary Perspective on Charismatic Leadership. *The Leadership Quarterly* 28: 473–85.

    House and Aditya, The Social Scientific Study of Leadership, pp. 439–43.

    Lowe, Kroeck, and Sivasubramanian, Effectiveness Correlates of Transformational and Transactional Leadership.

43. Conger, J. A. 1989. *The Charismatic Leader: Behind the Mystique of Exceptional Leadership*. San Francisco: Jossey-Bass, pp. 9–10.

44. Conger, J. A., R. N. Kanungo, and S. T. Menon. 2000. Charismatic Leadership and Follower Effects. *Journal of Organizational Behavior* 21: 747–67.

    Fuller, J. B., C. E. P. Patterson, K. Hester, and D. Y. Stringer. 1996. A Quantitative Review of Research on Charismatic Leadership. *Psychological Reports* 78: 271–87.

    House and Aditya, The Social Scientific Study of Leadership, pp. 439–43.

    Lowe, Kroeck, and Sivasubramanian, Effectiveness Correlates of Transformational and Transactional Leadership.

    Shamir, B., E. Zakay, E. Breinin, and M. Popper. 1998. Correlates of Charismatic Leader Behavior in Military Units: Subordinates' Attitudes, Unit Characteristics, and Superiors' Appraisals of Leader Performance. *Academy of Management Journal* 41: 387–409.

    van Knippenberg, D., and S. B. Sitkin. 2013. A Critical Assessment of Charismatic-Transformational Leadership Research: Back to the Drawing Board? *Academy of Management Annals* 7: 1–60. This source offers a detailed critique of this research.

45. Pillai, R. 1996. Crisis and the Emergence of Charismatic Leadership in Groups: An Experimental Investigation. *Journal of Applied Social Psychology* 26: 543–62.

46. Baum, Locke, and Kirkpatrick, A Longitudinal Study.

    Kirkpatrick and Locke, Direct and Indirect Effects.

47. Gerstner, C. R., and D. V. Day. 1997. Meta-Analytic Review of Leader-Member Exchange Theory: Correlates and Construct Issues. *Journal of Applied Psychology* 82: 827–44.

    Graen, G. B., and M. Uhl-Bien. 1995. Relationship-Based Approach to Leadership: Development of Leader-Member Exchange (LMX) Theory over 25 Years: Applying a Multi-Level, Multi-Domain Perspective. *Leadership Quarterly* 6: 219–47.

Howell, J. M., and B. Shamir. 2005. The Role of Followers in the Charismatic Leadership Process: Relationships and Their Consequences. *Academy of Management Review* 30: 96–112.

Liden, R. C., R. T. Sparrowe, R. T., and S. J. Wayne. 1997. Leader-Member Exchange Theory: The Past and Potential for the Future. In *Research in Personnel and Human Resource Management*, ed. G. R. Ferris. Greenwich, CT: JAI Press, pp. 47–119.

Schriesheim, C. A., S. L. Castro, and C. C. Cogliser. 1999. Leader-Member Exchange (LMX) Research: A Comprehensive Review of Theory, Measurement, and Data-Analytic Practices. *Leadership Quarterly* 10: 63–113.

48. Hooper, D. T., and R. Martin. 2008. Beyond Personal Leader-Member Exchange (LMX) Quality: The Effects of Perceived LMX Variability on Employee Reactions. *The Leadership Quarterly* 19: 20–30.

Van Breukelen, W., D. Konst, and R. Van Der Vlist. 2002. Effects of LMX and Differential Treatment on Work Unit Commitment. *Psychological Reports* 91: 220–30.

49. Bryant, A., and A. L. Kazan. 2013. *Self-Leadership: How to Become a More Successful, Efficient, and Effective Leader from the Inside Out*. New York: McGraw-Hill.

Manz, C. C. 1983. *The Art of Self-Leadership: Strategies for Personal Effectiveness in Your Life and Work*. Englewood Cliffs.

Manz, C. C. 1986. Self-Leadership: Toward an Expanded Theory of Self-Influence Processing Organizations. *Academy of Management Review* 11: 585–600.

Stewart, G. L., S. H. Courtright, and C. C. Manz. 2011. Self-Leadership: A Multilevel Review. *Journal of Management* 37: 185–222.

50. Manz, C. C., and H. P. Sims, Jr. 2001. *The New SuperLeadership: Leading Others to Lead Themselves*. San Francisco: Berrett-Koehler Publishers, Inc.

51. Greenleaf, R. K. 1977. *Servant Leadership: A Journey into the Nature of Legitimate Power and Greatness*. Mahwah: Paulist Press.

Keith, K. M. 2012. *The Case for Servant Leadership*, 2nd edn. Westfield: The Greenleaf Center for Servant Leadership.

Trompenaars, F., and E. Voerman. 2009. *Servant-Leadership across Cultures: Harnessing the Strength of the World's most Powerful Leeadership Philosophy*. Oxford: Infinite Ideas Limited.

52. Wellins, R. S., W. C. Byham, and J. M. Wilson. 1991. *Empowered Teams: Creating Self-Directed Work Groups that Improve Quality, Productivity, and Participation*. San Francisco: Jossey-Bass.

53. Ibid., Chap. 7.

Morgeson, F. P., D. S. DeRue, and E. P. Karam. 2010. Leadership in Teams: A Functional Approach to Understanding Leadership Structures and Processes. *Journal of Management* 36: 5–39.

54. Hogan, Curphy, and Hogan, What We Know About Leadership. See pp. 499–500 for their team discussion.

Manz, C., and H. P. Sims, Jr. 1987. Leading Workers to Lead Themselves: The External Leadership of Self-Managing Work Teams. *Administrative Science Quarterly* 12: 106–28.

Manz, C., and H. P. Sims, Jr. 1989. *Superleadership: Leading Workers to Lead Themselves*. Englewood Cliffs: Prentice Hall.

Manz, C., and H. P. Sims, Jr. 1993. *Business without Bosses: How Self-Managing Teams Are Building High-Performing Companies*. New York: John Wiley & Sons.

55. Drescher, M. A., M. A. Kirsgaard, I. M. Welpe, A. Picolt, and R. T. Wigand. 2014. The Dynamics of Shared Leadership: Building Trust and Enhancing Performance. *Journal of Applied Psychology* 99: 771–83.

Howell, J. P., D. E. Bowen, P. W. Dorfman, S. Kerr, and P. M. Podsakoff. 1990. Substitutes for Leadership: Effective Alternatives to Ineffective Leadership. *Organizational Dynamics* (Summer): 21–38.

Howell, J. P., P. W. Dorfman, and S. Kerr. 1986. Moderator Variables in Leadership Research. *Academy of Management Review* 11: 86–102.

Kerr, S. 1977. Substitutes for Leadership: Some Implications for Organizational Design. *Organization and Administrative Sciences* 8: 135–46.

Kerr, S., and J. M. Jermier. 1978. Substitutes for Leadership: Their Meaning and Measurement. *Organizational Behavior and Human Performance* 22: 375–403.

Podsakoff, P. M., S. B. MacKenzie, and R. Fetter. 1993. Substitutes for Leadership and the Management of Professionals. *Leadership Quarterly* 4: 1–44.

Podsakoff, P. M., B. P. Niehoff, S. B. MacKenzie, and M. L. Williams. 1993. Do Substitutes for Leadership Really Substitute for Leadership? An Empirical Examination of Kerr and Jermier's Situational Leadership Model. *Organizational Behavior and Human Decision Processes* 54: 1–44.

56. Hall, R. J., J. W. Workman, and C. A. Marchioro. 1998. Sex, Task, and Behavioral Flexibility Effects on Leadership Perceptions. *Organizational Behavior and Human Decision Processes* 74: 1–32.

House and Aditya, The Social Scientific Study of Leadership, pp. 437–39.

Lord, R. G., R. J. Foti, and C. DeVader. 1984. A Test of Leadership Categorization Theory: Internal Structure, Information Processing and Leadership Perceptions. *Organizational Behavior and Human Performance* 34: 343–78.

Lord, R. G., and K. J. Maher. 1993. *Leadership and Information Processing: Linking Perceptions and Performance*. New York: Routledge.

57. Developed from Calder, B. J. 1977. An Attribution Theory of Leadership. In *New Directions in Organizational Behavior*, ed. B. M. Staw and G. R. Salancik. Chicago: St. Clair Press, pp. 179–204.

58. Pastor, J.-C., J. R. Meindl, and M. C. Mayo. 2002. A Network Effects Model of Charisma Attributions. *Academy of Management Journal* 45: 410–20.

59. Loden, M. 1985. *Feminine Leadership or How to Succeed in Business without Being One of the Boys*. New York: Times Books.

60. Rosener, J. B. 1990. Ways Women Lead. *Harvard Business Review* 68 (November–December): 119–25.

61. Bass, *Bass and Stogdill's Handbook of Leadership*, Chap. 32.

Dobbins, G. H., and S. J. Platz. 1986. Sex Differences in Leadership: How Real Are They? *Academy of Management Review* 11: 118–27.

Eagly, A. H., and B. T. Johnson. 1990. Gender and Leadership Style: A Meta-Analysis. *Psychological Bulletin* 108: 233–56.

62. Hutchison, Valentino, and Kirkner, What Works for the Gander Does Not Work as Well for the Goose.

63. Bass, B. M., B. J. Avolio, and L. Atwater. 1996. The Transformational and Transactional Leadership of Men and Women. *Applied Psychology: An International Review* 45: 5–34.

64. Eagly, A. H., M. C. Johannesen-Schmidt, and M. L. van Engen. 2003. Transformational, Transactional, and Laissez-Faire Leadership Styles: A Meta-Analysis Comparing Women and Men. *Psychological Bulletin* 129: 569–91.

65. Gelfund, M. J., M. Erez, and Z. Aycan. 2007. Cross-Cultural Organizational Behavior. *Annual Review of Psychology* 58: 479–514.

Hofstede, G. 1980. Motivation, Leadership, and Organizations: Do American Theories Apply Abroad? *Organizational Dynamics* 9: 42–63.

Hofstede, G. 1993. Cultural Constraints in Management Theories. *Academy of Management Executive* 7: 81–94.

Hofstede, G. 2001. *Culture's Consequences: Comparing Values, Behaviors, Institutions, and Organizations across Nations*, 2nd edn. Thousand Oaks: Sage Publications.

Rockstuhl, T., J. H. Dulebohr, S. Ang, and L. M. Shore. 2012. Leader-Member Exchange (LMX) and Culture: A Meta-Analysis of Correlates of LMX across 23 Countries. *Journal of Applied Psychology* 97: 1097–130.

Vertinsky, I., D. K. Tse, D. A. Wehrung, and K. Lee. 1990. Organizational Design and Management Norms: A Comparative Study of Managers' Perceptions in the People's Republic of China, Hong Kong, and Canada. *Journal of Management* 16: 853–67.

66. Bass, *Bass and Stogdill's Handbook of Leadership*, p. 761.

67. Ibid., Chap. 34.

Mann, L. 1980. Cross-Cultural Studies of Small Groups. In *Handbook of Cross-Cultural Psychology*, Vol. 5, *Social Psychology*, ed. H. C. Triandis and R. W. Brislin. Boston: Allyn & Bacon, pp. 155–209.

68. Dorfman, P. W., and J. P. Howell. 1987. Dimensions of National Culture and Effective Leadership Patterns. In *Advances in International Comparative Management*, ed. E. G. McGoun. Greenwich, CT: JAI Press, pp. 127–50.

69. Bass, B. M. 1997. Does the Transactional-Transformational Leadership Paradigm Transcend Organizational and National Boundaries? *American Psychologist* 52: 130–39.

70. Brodbeck, F. C., M. Frese, and M. Javidan. 2002. Leadership Made in Germany: Low on Compassion, High on Performance. *Academy of Management Executive* 16: 16–29.

Den Hartog, D. N., R. J. House, P. J. Hanges, S. A. Ruiz-Quintanilla, and P. W. Dorfman. 1999. Culture Specific and Cross-Culturally Generalizable Implicit Leadership Theories: Are Attributes of Charismatic/Transformational Leadership Universally Endorsed? *Leadership Quarterly* 10: 219–56.

House and Aditya, The Social Scientific Study of Leadership, pp. 438, 465.

House, R. J., P. J. Hanges, M. Javidan, P. W. Dorfman, and V. Gupta, eds. 2004. *Culture, Leadership, and Organizations: The GLOBE Study of 62 Societies*. Thousand Oaks: Sage Publications.

House, R. J., P. J. Hanges, S. A. Ruiz-Quintanilla, P. W. Dorfman, M. Javidan, M. Dickson, V. Gupta, and GLOBE Country Co-Investigators. 1999. Cultural Influences on Leadership and Organizations: Project Globe. In *Advances in Global Leadership*, Vol. 1, ed. M. H. Mobley, M. J. Gessner, and V. Arnold. Stamford, CT: JAI Press, pp. 171–233.

Kennedy, J. C. 2002. Leadership in Malaysia: Traditional Values, International Outlook. *Academy of Management Executive* 16: 15–22.

71. Sims, H. P., Jr., and P. Lorenzi. 1992. *The New Leadership Paradigm: Social Learning and Cognition in Organizations*. Newbury Park: Sage Publications, Chap. 13.

72. Ibid., pp. 272–73.

73. Bird, F., and J. Gandz. 1991. *Good Management: Business Ethics in Action*. Toronto: Prentice Hall.

Howell, J. M., and B. J. Avolio. 1992. The Ethics of Charismatic Leadership: Submission or Liberation. *Academy of Management Executive* 6: 43–54.

Johnson, C. E. 2001. *Meeting the Ethical Challenges of Leadership*. Thousand Oaks: Sage Publications.

Kanungo, R. N., and M. Mendonca. 1995. *The Ethical Dimensions of Leadership*. Thousand Oaks: Sage Publications.

Murphy, P. E., and G. Enderle. 1995. Managerial Ethical Leadership: Examples Do Matter. *Business Ethics Quarterly* 5: 117–28.

Ng, T. W. H., and D. C. Feldman. 2015. Ethical Leadership: Meta-Analytic Evidence of Criterion Related and Incremental Validity. *Journal of Applied Psychology* 100: 948–65.

Ogunfowora, B. 2014. It's All a Matter of Consensus: Leader Role Modeling Strength as a Moderator of the Link Between Ethical Leadership and Employee Outcomes. *Human Relations* 67: 1467–90.

Part 3 Case

Abstract

This case presents a number of difficult situations encountered by a contract negotiating team in a West African country. The cultural differences between doing business in West Africa and Peter Janes' expectations are explored. In addition, the situation leads Mr. Janes to question his basic values and presuppositions about his identity and integrity, through a rather bizarre incident. Finally, the question of the effectiveness of company policy is raised, particularly in relation to the structure of the negotiating teams and the relationship between headquarters and the team.

CONTRACT NEGOTIATIONS IN WESTERN AFRICA: A CASE OF MISTAKEN IDENTITY

Peter Janes, a young member of Eurojet's Contracts Department, was on his way to Saheli in French-speaking West Africa to work on the complicated negotiations involved in selling a jet airliner to the Saheli government. He was not altogether thrilled with the assignment, and hoped it would be a quick deal, since financing seemed to be available for it. He had experience in contract negotiation in India, the Philippines, and Saudi Arabia, and most recently, Australia. At 27, he was one of the younger members of the department, but was seen as trustworthy with a high degree of motivation. If he succeeded, it would be the first deal he brought to closure on his own. But he had serious doubts about the project's feasibility or desirability. In addition, he had left behind what seemed to be the beginning of a great relationship in Australia, and he wanted to get back to his girlfriend. Furthermore, Janes had no desire to become a Francophone Africa expert within the company.

The Company

Eurojet was one of the larger diversified aircraft manufacturers. It had developed a particular jet for Third World operations, able to operate from hot and high airfields, including unprepared strips. Orders, however, were hard to come by because of the difficulties of Third World financing and the poor financial condition of regional airlines. The company was therefore delighted to learn that its regional sales executive in Saheli, Mr. Ali Osaju, had found a potential sale in the country's desire for a presidential aircraft, along with its need for reliable regional air transport.

The sale looked even more possible when it was discovered that the government Export Import Bank had a substantial budget available for Saheli, making financing of the multimillion-dollar aircraft feasible. It would be necessary to arrange an international commercial bank loan for Saheli as well. The potential of the airliner to earn revenue through regional transport was considered important in securing the loan.

The Negotiating Team

In December 1987, the Saheli government announced that they were ready to begin detailed negotiations. According to company policy, negotiations were conducted by the Contracts Department in close cooperation with sales and internal specialist functions. Mr. Janes, having just spent a hard-working three months—he had had four days off in the last six months based in Australia and working across Southeast Asia on specialist leasing packages—was assigned to the team because of his Third World experience, and his ability to speak French. He had been with the company for about two years. He had no experience in Africa.

Mr. Osaju was a highly placed African of Middle Eastern origin, educated in Europe, with a background in aviation. He had joined the company at about the same time as Mr. Janes. He had no previous experience in selling high-tech capital goods, but had many good connections, and was seen as invaluable to the company because of his African cultural background, combined with his European education. He had been developing local contacts in Saheli by spending a week there every two or three months over the past two years.

The Negotiating Policy

The company's negotiating policy inevitably led to what was referred to as the "two-headed monster approach." The sales representative was responsible for initial discussions and for overall relations with the customer. The contracts representative was responsible for negotiating concrete offers and signing contracts and finance agreements on behalf of the company. This double approach led to varying degrees of tension between the members of particular teams as well as between the departments in general. Sales were particularly aggrieved that contracts operated on a worldwide rather than a regional basis.

Working in a team where both have important roles to play required considerable sensitivity. In his two years of working at Eurojet, Peter Janes was looked on by the sales people as a considerate and skilled negotiating partner. He was not likely to lose a contract that they had spent years developing because of cultural clumsiness. Nevertheless, he walked a very narrow line, as it was his role to say no to all the wishes of the customer which were not feasible from the company's perspective. As this was to be his first solo contract negotiation, and Ali Osaju's first sale with the company, they shared a certain personal enthusiasm for closing the deal.

The Negotiation: The Early Days

Eurojet was not the only company trying to sell a jetliner to Saheli. The Russians, who had had considerable influence over the country since its independence 20 years earlier, were very present, trying to sell their aircraft and to sabotage the deal with Eurojet. Mr. Janes and Mr. Osaju frequently received strange phone calls in their hotel rooms and were aware that all their telephone calls were bugged. Once, Mr. Janes returned to his room to find that his briefcase had been tampered with. In addition, another European company with a number of contracts in surrounding countries was trying to arrange a deal.

The main negotiating point of the team to begin with was to have the Sahelis accept one airplane that could be converted from a regional airliner to a VIP presidential jet. The Sahelis originally wanted a specially designed VIP jet, which would have cost an extra 10 million dollars and would never have been used other than for the president. The negotiations moved extremely slowly. Mr. Janes and Mr. Osaju spent hours waiting to see officials, chasing papers from one office to another. They became aware that no one official wanted to be responsible for making the decision, in case he would be blamed for it should things go wrong.

They spent many hours debating strategy in the bar of the hotel. Mr. Janes objected to Mr. Osaju telling him what to do. Mr. Osaju objected to Mr. Janes making issues too complicated for the client. The relationship was a very tense one. They both felt they were getting little support from the head office and that the circumstances they were working in were very difficult.

Mr. Janes began to feel he was in a no-win situation. He realized that the negotiating process could go on for months, and he knew that his colleague had already begun to take over his activities with multi-order prospects in Australia. Conditions at the hotel were not that comfortable, and both he and Mr. Osaju were paid on a salary only basis. There were no overseas allowances.

The lack of support from headquarters was a problem for both the negotiators. Communications were difficult, as they felt they could not talk freely over the telephone because of being bugged. Furthermore, they did not feel their contacts at headquarters would begin to understand the finer points of the negotiation difficulties. They did learn from headquarters that they were considered to be moving too slowly in making the deal.

There were constant discussions on finance, spares, configuration, certification, and training. All the legal and technical documents had to be translated from English to French, causing many minor but significant misunderstandings. In one case, the standard contract at home called for the Saheli government to waive its "sovereign immunity" and "contract in its private rather than its public capacity." Saheli had adopted the Napoleonic Code from France, and had no equivalent legal concepts. The courts in the home country have a very limited right to hear actions against the Crown, and they assume this element of the law holds true for all countries. The Saheli negotiators listened with polite disbelief to these explanations and sent a telegram to the president saying, "Sahelian sovereignty is being threatened."

Mr. Janes and Mr. Osaju decided on a very basic strategy of patience and a friendly, open manner. Establishing trust and preserving individual and corporate credibility were recognized as being vital. They placed great emphasis on simplifying the bureaucratic process. Two months of negotiating passed with no commitment in sight.

Eurojet management was beginning to show their lack of confidence in the deal. Peter Janes had committed them to one million dollars of expenditure on completing an airline to the Sahelis' expectations, so that it could be delivered on time, yet they saw no formalization of the contract, nor had they received any of the loan money. On the Saheli side, there was considerable nervousness about the commercial sovereign loans from the international banks.

Mr. Janes continued to make his daily round of visits to offices and homes, establishing himself as open and trustworthy and using his skill in expressing complex legal and technical terms in a simple way. He began to be aware of a warming of perceptions toward him. Up until then he had felt that the Sahelian officials were always guarded, on the defense in the presence of Eurojet's legal commercial representative. He thought that this was because it was his role to say "no" in the negotiations. In the third month of the negotiations, he received an extremely encouraging sign. A source close to the president had recently been quoted as saying, "He (Janes) doesn't say 'yes' very often, but when he says 'yes,' he means 'yes.'" This was the sign that they had been waiting for, that his credibility had been established and they could now begin to deal with some of the more sensitive issues in the negotiation.

Mr. Janes had adapted himself to local culture as much as he could. Although his natural inclination would have been to get things done quickly, deal with business first, and make friends later, he was aware that this was not how business deals were made in Saheli. So he spent many hours making friends, going to people's houses, walking around their businesses and factories. On one such occasion, he was walking around a factory with one of his friends, holding his hand as was the custom for Sahelian male friends. To his horror, a group of foreign diplomats came toward them on their tour of the factory. Mr. Janes was aware of an almost super-human effort on his part not to let go of his friend's hand and keep it relaxed, even as he felt the rest of his body stiffen with tension.

On another occasion, one of Mr. Janes' acquaintances attributes to him the status of being a great football (soccer) player. Peter thinks this person is just kidding at first, so he just "plays along with it." Later, when Peter's friends begin introducing him around as an international soccer player, it begins to worry him. He was unwilling to embarrass people by saying they were wrong, but was equally uncomfortable not striking down the myth. Perhaps it served some purpose. His status as an international soccer player was apparently much greater than that of a young lawyer; perhaps he needed a little extra to justify his power in negotiating and signing the contract. It was relatively easy to give indirect answers to questions, thus saving his conscience and protecting his strangely acquired status. Nonetheless, alluding to his legal training, Mr. Janes had said to Mr. Osaju at this time, "I can put my hand on my heart and say, 'I have not told a lie,' but I don't feel comfortable. We have worked so hard for credibility, I would hate a silly issue like this to backfire on us." At the time, they agreed to laugh off the issue, because so far the people involved were not main players in the negotiations.

Mr. Janes continued to make noncommittal replies and managed to avoid any further serious problems. Although greatly disturbing to him personally, it was a nonissue in terms of the negotiations. Fortunately for Peter Janes, he could discuss his feelings about the situation with Ali Osaju, and so relieve some of his own tension by laughing about the absurdity of it.

After 10 months of intense negotiations, the deal was almost called off by the negotiating team at the last minute. They had spent days retranslating the French contract back into English, and then sitting by a Sahelian typist who did not speak English saying each word to her phonetically so that she could type it. They both had had very little sleep in order to get the contract finished on time. When they finally went with the attorney general to the president's office to sign the contract, they were as usual kept waiting for a few hours. During that time, the attorney general reread the French contract and discovered numerous spelling mistakes in it. He then declared that he could not give it to the president in its present condition, and that the signing would have to be delayed for another week.

Ali and Peter both hit the walls—literally. It was the last straw. While Ali threw books and papers at the walls, Peter strode around the room shouting that unless they signed immediately, he was withdrawing Eurojet's approval of the contract. The attorney general stood his ground, and Ali and Peter stormed off to the hotel. They could scarcely believe what they had done after almost a year's worth of friendly and meticulous negotiating. Peter went to sleep, exhausted after the last 10 days of work and the loss of the contract.

He was woken four hours later to be informed that the attorney general was waiting to see him. He was escorted to an office across the road, where he found the attorney general in his shirtsleeves, sitting at a typewriter, carefully changing all the spelling mistakes himself. He wanted Peter to initial all the changes so that he would feel confident that no substantial changes were being made in the contract. The contract was signed the next day.

Epilogue

Despite Eurojet's advice, the aircraft was not handled by the national airlines but kept under the president's control, and so, rarely used. Debt servicing soon became a problem, and one year later, the aircraft was quietly and informally repossessed. Eurojet has offered to resell the aircraft, but the Saheli government balked at authorizing the sale.

Mr. Osaju spent one more year in Africa, and then was promoted to the Far East where he was made regional sales director. Mr. Janes was promoted to another program in early 1983, where he continued to work for the next four years.

Part 4

ORGANIZATIONAL PROCESSES

Part 4 describes the organizational processes of communication, power, politics, decision making, and stress. Each chapter discusses international aspects of the topics and the ethical issues they raise.

Chapter 13, "Communication Processes," describes communication processes in organizations. The basic communication process has a sender, a receiver, and a message sent over a communication channel. Noise surrounding the process can distort messages. Communication in organizations occurs in networks of various forms. Verbal communication includes oral, written, electronic, and video communication. Nonverbal communication includes gestures, facial expressions, and the sender's voice. The meaning of nonverbal communication varies across cultures.

Chapter 14, "Decision-Making and Problem-Solving Processes," describes decision processes in organizations and presents several decision-making models that have different assumptions and limitations. The various models apply to different decision types and decision situations. Individuals do well with some types of decisions while groups are better for other types of decisions. Cohesive decision-making groups often suffer from a major dysfunction called groupthink. The chapter also discusses methods of improving decision making, some of which can help avoid groupthink.

Power and political behavior are major processes that can affect the behavior of all employees in organizations (see Chapter 15, "Power and Political Behavior"). People's sources of power include charisma, important work activities, and their political network. Attribution processes can affect a person's perception of someone else's power, even when the other party has little power. Political maneuvering in organizations includes political strategy and political tactics. Strategy is a person's political plan, which often focuses on career development or resource allocation decisions. Tactics are individual steps in carrying out a plan, such as controlling a meeting agenda or building coalitions with important people or groups. Doing a political diagnosis of an organization lets a person see her political position compared to others in the system. Sadly, political behavior has a dark side—deception, lying, and intimidation.

The part closes with Chapter 16, "Stress in Organizations," which presents an integrated model of stress. This model should help guide your understanding of how factors in a person's environment can lead to either positive or negative stress. Individuals and organizations can manage stress in several ways, including stress reduction, stress resilience, and stress recuperation.

Chapter 13

COMMUNICATION PROCESSES

After reading this chapter, you should be able to:

- Define communication in organizations.
- Explain the basic communication process.
- Discuss the effects of noise in communication processes.
- Describe verbal and nonverbal communication.
- Analyze the effects of verbal and nonverbal communication.
- Distinguish between the functions and dysfunctions of organizational communication.
- Discuss the features of listening, especially active listening.
- Compare ways to make communication processes more effective.
- Explain the effects of new technology on communication.
- Describe communication networks and the roles that can emerge within a network.
- Appreciate some international and ethical issues that surround communication processes in organizations.

The word communication will be used here in a very broad sense to include all of the procedures by which one mind may affect another. This, of course, involves not only written and oral speech, but also music, the pictorial arts, the theatre, the ballet, and in fact all human behavior.[1]

This quotation comes from the opening of a classic work describing a communication theory. The heart of the definition is in the first sentence. All communication tries to affect the behavior of at least one other person. Communication can change the way a person perceives his environment and lead to behavior change.[2]

Organizational communication includes the purpose, flow, and direction of messages and the media used for those messages. Such communication happens within the complex, interdependent social systems of organizations.[3] Think of organizational communication as another view of behavior in organizations. This chapter calls such behavior "message behavior"—behavior that includes sending, receiving, and giving meaning to messages.

Communication processes in organizations are continuous and constantly changing. They do not have a beginning or an end, nor do they follow a strict sequence. During communication, the sender creates messages from one or more symbols to which he attaches meaning. Messages can be oral, written, or nonverbal; they can also be intentional or unintentional. Messages deal with tasks to be done, maintenance of organizational policies, or information about some state of the organization. They can go to people inside the organization or outside the organization.

Organizational communication happens over a pathway called a network, a series of interconnected positions in an organization. The network can be formal as defined by organizational positions and relationships among them. It can also be informal as defined by informal patterns of social interaction and the informal groups described in Chapter 10, "Groups and Intergroup Processes." Communication over the network goes in any direction: downward, upward, or horizontally. Communication networks in organizations are interdependent, interlocking, and overlapping systems of human interaction. They involve relationships among individuals, within and among groups, or dispersed almost randomly throughout an organization.

■ **Chapter Overview**

The Basic Communication Process

Types of Communication
  Verbal Communication
  Nonverbal Communication

Functions of Organizational Communication

Dysfunctions of Organizational Communication

Listening

Active Listening

Improving Communication Effectiveness
  Sender
  Receiver
  Message
  Medium

Technology and Communication

Communication Roles in Organizations

Communication Networks

International Aspects of Organizational Communication

Ethical Issues in Organizational Communication

THE BASIC COMMUNICATION PROCESS

Figure 13.1[4] shows the basic communication process. The **sender** decides what message to send and encodes it using symbols that he assumes the receiver will understand. The sender converts the message to a signal and transmits the message over a communication channel to the receiver. The **channel** can be a person's voice, an electronic device, a written medium, or a video medium. The **receiver** decodes the received message and interprets its meaning. The receiver responds to the message by acting consistently with that interpretation. You use the basic communication process whenever you send an e-mail to a friend. You are the sender, your friend is the receiver, and the channel is the electronic method of transmission.

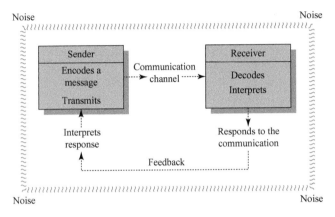

Figure 13.1: The Basic Communication Process

Modern **communication media** provide senders many choices. Senders can choose to use telephones, e-mail, letters or memoranda, videoconferencing, and face-to-face meetings. The criteria for choosing a medium vary. Senders can use written media for formality and a clear message and face-to-face meetings to convey a sense of teamwork. E-mail use, however, is largely based on availability and ease of use.[5]

The **feedback loop** at the bottom of the figure implies interdependence between the sender and receiver during the communication process. The sender interprets the receiver's response and can send an additional message for clarification.

Noise surrounds the entire communication process in organizations and can make communication less effective. Various distortions, errors, and foreign material often affect the quality of the signal. The noise shown in the model represents these distortions; they are additions to the signal not intended by the sender. You can illustrate this for yourself by tuning a radio to a distant station. The static you hear is noise in the communication channel. The static makes it hard for you to understand the radio message. A later section discusses communication dysfunctions that result from the presence of noise.

Workforce diversity introduces other forms of noise.[6] The different worldviews that come from the backgrounds of a diverse workforce can prove troublesome to some people. If the receiver stereotypes a sender as ignorant because of the way he speaks, the receiver likely will distort the message. Senders with English as a second language also might not speak like native speakers, causing some receivers to distort or ignore the message.

A person's accent can also add noise to a communication interaction. The large regional differences in accents throughout the United States can distort communication for some receivers. The same is true for people interacting with call center technicians that are outside the United States. Noise from accents also appears in languages other than English. Telemundo, the Spanish-language television network, trains its telenovela (soap opera) actors to speak an accent-free Spanish. The actors come from all over Latin America and normally speak Spanish with regional accents. Telemundo's accent-free approach reduces noise for its largely Mexico-born and Mexican American audience (receivers).[7]

International diversity can also add noise. Korean culture, for example, values a stern, strict demeanor. This cultural value makes it difficult for Koreans to smile when providing service. The Korean Air Service Academy in Seoul, South Korea, offers smile training to companies who want to present a warm, friendly service experience.[8]

TYPES OF COMMUNICATION

Verbal and nonverbal communication are the two major types of communication found in organizational communication processes. **Verbal communication** includes oral, written, and electronic forms of communication. **Nonverbal communication** includes eye movements, gestures, facial expressions, tone of voice, and the like.[9]

Both verbal and nonverbal communication can appear together in a communication process and interact to create meaning for a receiver. Nonverbal communication adds much of the feeling and emotion that a sender wants to give to a message.[10] Nonverbal communication often has more effect than verbal communication on the meaning receivers give a message.[11]

Verbal Communication

Oral and written messages are the two major forms of verbal communication. The following paragraphs discuss many characteristics of the different forms of verbal communication you will likely find in today's organizations.

Oral communication includes all forms of speech between a sender and receiver.[12] Oral communication can occur during face-to-face interaction or by telephone, radio, or television. Although oral communication usually has the immediate attention of the receiver, sometimes the message can be recorded and played later; cassette recordings, telephone answering devices, and computer-recorded voice mail are examples.

Unless the interaction is transcribed or recorded, oral communication leaves no retrievable record of the message and response. When the sender wants to affect the receiver's opinion on some matter, oral communication is more effective than written. Nonverbal communication by both the sender and the receiver, however, can affect the final interpretation of the message.

American Sign Language (ASL), the language that deaf and hearing-impaired people use, is a form of verbal communication.[13] Although it is a visual language, communication theorists classify it as mainly verbal.[14] Deaf and hearing-impaired people use ASL's patterns of hand and finger movements to communicate. ASL includes patterns of facial expression and body movements to express emotions and distinguish sentence types. The United States and Canada use ASL. French Canadians use a different form of signing. Country and regional differences in signing systems vary greatly.

Written communication is any form of handwriting, printed memo, report, or message sent over an electronic medium such as a computer network.[15] The receiver's response is more delayed in written communication than in oral communication because the receiver must first read the message before interpreting and responding to it.

Written communications compete with each other for the time and attention of the receiver. They also compete with oral communication, a form with the advantage of at least the sender's vocal presence. Written communication can interact with nonverbal communication. The way a sender gives a memo or report to a receiver, for example, can affect the receiver's perception of the message when he reads it.

Written communication has some advantages over oral communication. First, it is a retrievable and almost permanent recording of a message. Second, comprehension often is greater with written than with oral communication[16] because the receiver can reread a written communication to be sure he understands the sender's intended meaning. Therefore, managers commonly use memoranda to document agreements.

As modern technology develops, **electronic** and **video communications** are becoming increasingly important. Such communication includes the use of e-mail, computer networks, fax machines, computer conferencing, and video-conferencing. Those methods offer the advantages of speed, accuracy, easy dispersal to many locations, direct interaction, and quick feedback. Videoconferencing also allows people in different places to see each other while they talk. A later section discusses emerging technologies and their effects on communication in detail.[17]

Nonverbal Communication

Nonverbal communication is behavior that communicates without written or spoken words.[18] Examples include gestures, posture, seating position, voice tone and inflection, speed of speech, and the physical environment of the communication interaction. People use these nonverbal cues to communicate explicitly or implicitly with each other. Individuals combine verbal and nonverbal communications to create unique communication styles.

Nonverbal communication can contradict, amplify, or complement verbal communication. Subordinates might perceive a supervisor who does not maintain eye contact during a conversation as insincere. Some people might perceive a person with a relaxed facial expression as having more power than a person with a nervous facial expression.[19] A professor who tells you to ask questions when you do not understand something and then leaves time for questions reinforces your perception that he wants you to understand.

The rest of this section describes four aspects of nonverbal communication: (1) physical aspects of the person, (2) the physical environment of communication, (3) time, and (4) communication with signs and signals. The interpretations given here are North American. A later section, "International Aspects of Organizational Communication," gives interpretations from other cultures. See that section's citations for a description of the almost endless forms of nonverbal communication in different cultures.

Physical Aspects of the Person

Physical aspects of the person, such as voice, facial expressions, gestures, body movements, and posture, are all forms of nonverbal communication. Each can regulate, add to, or detract from the intended meaning of the sender.[20]

Receivers infer meaning from how a sender vocalizes a verbal message. Receivers often can sense that a sender has positive feelings about the receiver when the sender speaks fast, fluently, and with few references to himself. A sender who increases the volume and rate of his speech can also persuade a receiver to accept a message. A receiver might perceive deceit when the sender makes many speech errors and talks slowly.

Facial expressions tell much about feelings, especially when the person is unwilling or unable to express his feelings. A smile while speaking can show affection for the receiver. A frown can suggest disgust or despair, feelings the sender might not want to mention.

Senders can use gestures, such as punctuated hand and arm movements, to emphasize parts of their message. Senders who look away from the receiver imply uncertainty about their message. A shift in posture, such as leaning forward, implies the sender is about to make a new and possibly important point.

Physical Environment of Communication

The physical setting of a communication interaction is the second major type of nonverbal communication. The environment includes all aspects of using space, including the distance between the sender and the receiver.

A person who remains seated behind a desk puts a barrier between himself and a visitor.[21] Such an arrangement might unintentionally tell the visitor that the seated person is cold, distant, and even uninterested in the visitor. Increasingly, U.S. managers place tables and comfortable chairs in an open area of the office. Coming out from behind the desk makes a guest feel more comfortable, and the arrangement gives a feeling of openness.

North Americans normally hold business conversations with a distance of 5.5–8 feet between speakers.[22] Any closer distance can make the receiver uncomfortable and cause the person to move away. As a later section will explain, this North American custom does not hold in many other countries. The difference in the distance between speakers is an especially difficult cross-cultural issue in communication.

Time

The third type of nonverbal communication is a person's orientation to and use of time.[23] North American businesspeople consider it rude to arrive late for an appointment or a meeting. They interpret lateness as disrespect for themselves and for the organization they represent.

North Americans are also distinctly future oriented. They consider the long term to be about five to ten years. You will find later that time orientations and the meaning of time vary among cultures.

Communication with Signs and Signals

Communication with signs and signals is a pervasive part of our lives.[24] Turn signals on vehicles, traffic control signals, and caution flags used by highway workers are all common examples. A handshake is an important and almost everyday physical sign. Some people in North America believe a firm handshake suggests confidence and a weak handshake shows uncertainty.

FUNCTIONS OF ORGANIZATIONAL COMMUNICATION

The **functions of organizational communication** include sharing information, providing performance feedback, integrating and coordinating parts of the organization, persuading others, expressing emotion, and innovating.[25] Figure 13.2 summarizes these functions.

Communication processes help **share information** with people inside and outside the organization. The information includes descriptions of the organization's mission, strategy, policies, and tasks. Descriptions of the organization's mission go to organization members, stockholders, and, through advertising and other media, to people outside the organization. Information about task direction and feedback on task performance mainly goes to members of the organization.

The **performance feedback** function of organizational communication lets people know about the quality of their job performance.[26] Feedback can reduce uncertainty, give people important cues about levels of performance, and act as a motivational resource. Reducing uncertainty is especially important during the early stages of learning a task. Giving the right behavioral cues early lets people know which behaviors will lead to valued rewards and which will not. Feedback can be given orally face-to-face or provided more formally through the organization's performance appraisal system.

An organization's communication process helps **integrate and coordinate** the many parts of an organization. Communication among design engineering, manufacturing, and marketing departments helps coordinate successful new product development. The performance of project groups, for example, can benefit from cross-functional team members communicating with colleagues they know outside the group.[27]

A key part of the definition of communication is its role in affecting the behavior of someone else. People in organizations use communication processes to persuade other people to behave in a way the communicator desires. The

a) **Functions**

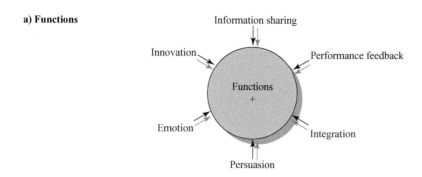

b) **Dysfunctions**

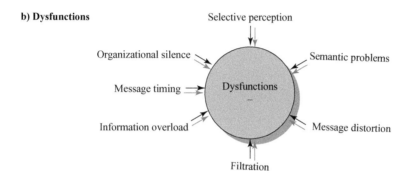

▪ **Figure 13.2:**   Functions and Dysfunctions of Organizational Communication

persuasion function of communication often plays a key role in large-scale organizational change.[28]

The **emotional** function of communication focuses on the human side of the organization. People often need to express their feelings of satisfaction or dissatisfaction with their tasks, supervision, and the context within which they work. An organization's communication process can play a useful function for its members by letting them express their feelings.

Modern organizations feel they must turn out a continuous stream of **innovative** services and products to compete in both domestic and world markets.[29] The communication process lets an organization gather information from its external environment and move it to key decision points within the organization. As managers make innovative decisions, they can move information about those decisions to people both inside and outside the organization. By supporting innovation, the communication process plays a major role in how the organization adapts to its ever-changing external environment.

DYSFUNCTIONS OF ORGANIZATIONAL COMMUNICATION

Figure 13.1 showed the basic model of communication surrounded by noise. Noise includes all forms of error that can happen during communication. Errors can come from the sender, the receiver, the message, and the medium of communication. Such noise or errors lead to **dysfunctions of organizational communication**.[30] Other dysfunctions come from powerful organizational processes that pressure employees to keep silent about events they see or experience. Figure 13.2 summarizes these dysfunctions. A later section, "Improving Communication Effectiveness," describes ways of decreasing these dysfunctions to improve communication effectiveness.

Selective perception lets receivers block out information they do not want to hear in a message.[31] Receivers might block out threatening information or information that disagrees with their beliefs. They might also block some information to reduce the amount they need to process. Despite the sender's intended meaning, the receiver "selectively listens" to the communication. The receiver then uses the perceived information in the message to develop his meaning of it. Selective perception can also affect the information the sender gets from the receiver about the receiver's interpretation of the sender's message. The sender's assessment of the accuracy of the receiver's interpretation can affect the sender's reaction to the receiver. For example, the sender might repeat the message several times if he believes the receiver did not understand it correctly.

Semantic problems are communication dysfunctions that occur when the receiver's interpretation of a message differs from the sender's intended message.[32] Some words have different meanings for different people. For example, words or phrases such as good, average, and do your best can have widely varying interpretations. Such words often are at the center of semantic problems in oral and written performance appraisals. Other semantic problems stem from the jargon used by professional or technical groups and the in-group language of different functional groups in an organization.[33] Accountants talk about "burden," manufacturing engineers discuss "metrology," computer specialists worry about "upload and download," and Harry Potter fans chant "expecto patronum, expecto patronum" just before a major business presentation.[34] Further semantic problems come from the international context of globally operating firms. One case study of five Russian companies with Western participation showed the immense difficulties in communication because of different meanings given to words. For example, the concept of feedback in an organization meant "top-down control" to the Russian managers and "continuous involvement of employees" to their Western counterparts.[35]

Message distortion can occur when the sender and receiver do not have the same frame of reference. We all have had different experiences that give different meanings to our present experiences. The attributes, background, organizational position, and culture of the sender and receiver might differ, causing them to interpret messages differently. Receivers can distort messages by making assumptions about the sender and what his message means. Such assumptions can cause the receiver to begin decoding and taking action before hearing the entire message. Both the meaning and the action might not be what the sender intended.

Senders can filter (subtract from) the content of a message either intentionally or unintentionally. **Message filtration** reduces a message's information content, possibly leading to misinterpretation by the receiver. The sender might intentionally filter a message because of fear of the receiver's reaction. The sender might unintentionally filter a message if he does not understand the problem or issue he wants to communicate. Both types of message filtration produce messages without enough information to let the receiver interpret them accurately.

Information overload is a communication dysfunction that happens when a person gets more information than he can process effectively.[36] Receivers can react to information overload in several ways. They might ignore or screen out some messages to prevent overwhelming themselves with incoming information. Sometimes, receivers delay their responses to incoming messages to a later, less busy time. An overloaded sender or receiver might not immediately pass on information needed to understand a message or he might duplicate a message already sent. In either case, the receiver asks questions to help understand the intended meaning. These are especially dangerous reactions because the duplication and questioning increases information overload throughout a communication system.[37]

Message timing affects whether communication dysfunctions will happen.[38] Messages with short deadlines do not leave enough time for accurate interpretation. The action taken by the receiver might not be the sender's intended action. Dysfunctions can also happen when a sender transmits a message well ahead of the time for action. Receivers do not always remember such messages, so no action takes place.

Senders get the action they want from a message only if the receiver accepts it.[39] The sender's credibility and power play a central role in the acceptance. Such factors are important in organizational communication because the sender's position often gives him power over the receiver. This relationship is a central feature of superior–subordinate communication. If the subordinate does not consider the sender to be a credible source of a message, he is unlikely to accept the message.

Organizational silence, the absence of communication, is a serious communication dysfunction proposed by some contemporary researchers.[40] Employees are unwilling to voice their views of organizational events. Organizational silence is not affected by noise, as are the other dysfunctions. Employees withhold their opinions about organizational matters because they believe it is futile or they will experience reprisal. The areas noted for organizational silence include pay inequity, decision procedures, unethical behavior, poor customer service, and the negative effects of organizational change.

LISTENING

Many communication professionals consider listening a primary skill for success in almost any activity. It is the first skill a person learns as a child, followed by speaking, reading, and writing. Listening is also a big part of human communication activities. Estimates suggest people spend about 50 percent of their time listening.[41]

Listening is different from hearing. Hearing is a physiological process of detecting and processing sounds. **Listening** is the mental process of assigning meaning to sounds. The **listening process** includes both intrapersonal and interpersonal activities.[42] A person receives a message from another person (interpersonal), tries to interpret it (intrapersonal), and responds to the other person to show the meaning given to the message (interpersonal). The process repeats during a communication interaction as both parties try to reach mutual understanding.

ACTIVE LISTENING

With **active listening**,[43] the listener is responsible for the completeness of a speaker's message. A listener's role in the communication process is not to passively absorb a spoken message and derive meaning from it. With active listening, the listener is responsible for hearing a speaker's message correctly by accurately hearing the facts in a message and understanding the speaker's feelings about the message. An active listener makes a deliberate effort to understand a message from the speaker's viewpoint.

A message's meaning includes its content and the sender's feelings. In active listening, a listener attends to all verbal and nonverbal cues to get the total meaning. Verbal cues include message content, speed of speech, body movements, and the like. A listener asks questions to get the speaker to clarify a point. A listener might also rephrase the message until the speaker is satisfied that the listener understands. A manager can use active listening to help positively manage conflict. Active listening helps the manager understand the true wants of the parties to the conflict episode (see Chapter 11, "Conflict in Organizations").

Active listening can have positive effects on the speaker because the speaker knows that an active listener cares about the message, respects the speaker's opinion, and wants to understand the speaker. Active listening gives speakers the sense that their message is important and that the listener is sincerely interested.

IMPROVING COMMUNICATION EFFECTIVENESS

Improving communication effectiveness is possible throughout the communication process. The previous discussion of communication dysfunctions implied many of the following improvements.

Sender

Senders who understand the receiver's background and culture are more effective than senders who do not understand. A receiver's background includes education, social status, and professional or technical training. The last is important because of the special meaning such training can give to many words. Senders avoid using jargon to avoid communication dysfunctions. What a sender knows about the receiver helps him send messages with enough content to communicate as intended.

Knowing the receiver's culture is important when communicating across national boundaries. Senders must take special care when communicating (oral, written, or nonverbal) with people from other cultures.

Asking for oral or written feedback to a message helps a sender improve his communication effectiveness. The feedback gives the sender some observations on how the receiver perceived and interpreted the message. The sender can then adjust the message as needed for clearer understanding.

Formal training in written and oral communication can improve a sender's effectiveness. Training in written communication skills can focus on basic writing skills such as sentence structure and the right level of complexity for various audiences. Senders can also use software tools such as WhiteSmoke™ and RightWriter® to analyze their written communication.[44] Although neither tool automatically makes a person a more effective writer, they offer observations on a person's writing that can improve effectiveness.

Receiver

A receiver can improve communication effectiveness by knowing and understanding the sender. If the sender is in an organization subunit that uses its own language, then the receiver needs to learn that language or ask the sender to clarify the message. The same suggestion applies to jargon used by senders with a professional or technical background. In both situations, the receiver is at a disadvantage in the communication process because he does not understand the sender's language.

The receiver's knowledge of himself can also improve communication effectiveness. If the receiver uses jargon or in-group language, he will interpret messages with that jargon in the background. The jargon introduces noise into the communication process and can distort the messages received. The receiver's perceptual process can also make the communication process less effective. Being aware of how jargon and his own perceptual process can alter the meaning of messages helps a receiver improve his communication effectiveness.

Receivers can use the feedback loop of the communication process to improve their role in that process. A receiver can ask a sender to clarify a message, especially if the sender typically uses jargon or in-group language. The receiver can also state his understanding of the message, so the sender can react to that interpretation. Both feedback activities require close interdependence between the sender and receiver to improve communication.

Message

The construction of the message can play a key role in communication effectiveness. Long messages with complex language are often difficult to understand.

Messages using language that is highly different from the receiver's language can also be misinterpreted. Differences in language include jargon, in-group language, and languages of different cultures. Simple, concise messages, in language shared by the sender and receiver, are more effective than long, complex messages riddled with jargon.

Electronic message systems such as e-mail, voice mail, local area networks, and computer conferencing systems let a sender transmit the same message quickly to many people.[45] Such computer-based messages lack the feelings and emotional information that can come from nonverbal communication. To add nonverbal communication, Internet users developed emoticons ("smileys") to put some emotion into their text messages.[46]

Medium

The message transmission medium should have little noise for the communication process to be effective. A sender can overcome or reduce noise in communication by using multiple channels. A manager can follow an oral message, such as instructions to a subordinate, with a written memo summarizing the conversation. The manager can also meet with a subordinate to discuss a memo sent earlier. In both cases, the manager is using multiple channels to improve communication effectiveness.[47]

An earlier chapter's discussion of perception emphasized that people perceive high-contrast objects faster than low-contrast objects (see Chapter 5, "Perception, Attitudes, and Personality"). A sender can introduce high contrast into messages by using a different color paper or ink than is normal for written communications. A sender can also change the setting in which he sends oral messages. Sitting behind a desk can imply formality and distance from the receiver. Sitting next to the receiver can imply informality and closeness.

TECHNOLOGY AND COMMUNICATION

Some forecasters predict that **technology and communication** will combine and lead to major changes in organizational communication processes in the future.[48] Although these technologies are available to almost any organization, if they are to improve an organization's communication processes, they must be used in various combinations. Existing and expected combinations of these technologies will cause nearly revolutionary changes in the way people will communicate in the future. These emerging technologies encourage the development of the "virtual groups" described in Chapter 10 and the "virtual organizations" described in Chapter 17, "Organizational Design."

The telephone will remain a major communication device in developed nations. Major changes will come from fiber optics and new satellites. Digital cellular telephones allow communication among cellular users in most parts of the world. Laptop, notepad, and tablet personal computers (PCs) will include digital cellular facsimile devices and wireless Internet connectors. Combine these devices with digital communication satellites,[49] and you can quickly see the flexibility and mobility of future communication.

Distributed computing technology exists now and will grow in use. An organization's members will continue to communicate directly on a computer network. Digital technology lets all forms of text, images, audio, video, and numeric data move over a network. Satellites and fiber optics allow high-speed connections among networks at any of an organization's locations. An organization with global operations, for example, could move all forms of information quickly to distant places. All of these factors combine to contribute to the growing phenomenon of "multicommunicating"—synchronous conversations that overlap.[50]

Distributed computing also affects communication among organizations. The Internet links millions of people in more than one hundred countries[51] and is a fast-growing source of commerce.[52] The Internet also lets students in different countries interact to complete their course work.[53]

Social networking sites can link people in widely dispersed locations. Facebook, Twitter, MySpace, and LinkedIn help people interact worldwide. The Instant Messenger feature of AOL allows quick links among people. Such sites have an almost addictive quality, bonding people to the site and to each other.[54]

A significant transformation of communication has happened, and will continue into the future, because of "social software."[55] This software features Internet-based applications that help people communicate from almost anywhere. The following are the prominent forms of social software:

- Blogs: web log; personal online journals.
- Wikis: collaborative websites that anyone can edit.
- Social Tagging: online services that let people bookmark Web content.
- Podcasting: Audio and video distributed over the Internet; can download to personal computers and iPods.

PCs will continue to grow in use as communication tools. PCs equipped with modems, faxes, and wireless communication cards let people in an organization quickly communicate with each other. Satellite and fiber optic links enable them to transmit media, such as text, numeric data, graphic images, audio, and video images. By communicating with their PCs, people in different countries can lessen the effects of time zone differences. For example, someone in Calgary, Canada, can send an e-mail or fax to someone in Bucharest, Romania, before the latter person arrives at work.

Videoconferencing allows face-to-face communication over almost any distance.[56] People in a videoconference can see each other, speak to each other, show graphic images, and send documents over the Internet. Such systems are a substitute for traveling to distant sites for meetings.

Existing technology also allows desktop videoconferencing[57] in which a small camera mounted on a computer monitor sends the video image to the receiving computer. The other party has the same configuration, making two-way video and audio interaction possible. A window containing the video image opens on each person's computer. Other parts of the screen can show the text of a report the two parties are revising or graphics for an upcoming joint business presentation. Fiber optics, wireless technology, and new satellite technology allow desktop videoconferencing between locations almost anywhere in the world.

Multimedia PCs help users manage any form of information media. Such computers feature scanners, soundboards, business presentation software, CD-ROMs, and, for advanced users, animation software. Business presentations can include full-color three-dimensional graphics, photographs, video images, background sound, and text. Properly designed, such presentations can have dramatic effects on an audience. The overhead projector with black-and-white celluloid slides is giving way to multimedia business presentations controlled by a presenter and his PC. Such presentations make large audience communication not only possible, but also dramatic.

COMMUNICATION ROLES IN ORGANIZATIONS

Individuals in organizations play different communication roles and serve different functions in the communication process. The five roles are initiator, relayer, liaison, terminator, and isolate. The following descriptions emphasize the relative frequency of communication behaviors of each role.[58]

Initiators start communications and send more messages than they receive or pass on to someone else. Relayers receive and pass on more messages than they start or end. The liaison role is more complicated than either the initiator or relayer. Liaisons connect two parts of an organization but are not a member of either part.[59] A liaison helps coordinate organizational functions by getting messages from one part of an organization to another.[60] Liaisons can hinder message flow, however, if they become bottlenecks in a communication network. Managers can have all of these roles in organizations. Nonmanagers will most typically have relayer and liaison roles. Highly specialized nonmanagement employees, such as an Internet specialist, can have an initiator role because of a need to send critical information to other employees.

The last two roles involve more passive communication behavior. Terminators are at the end of a communication network and mainly receive messages. They infrequently send messages or relay information to others in the organization. Isolates are usually outside the normal communication process. They send, receive, or relay only a few messages.

COMMUNICATION NETWORKS

Communication in organizations takes place within a structured system called a communication network. Some networks form from an organization's design. Others emerge from informal social interaction within organizations.

Figure 13.3 shows several possible communication networks using lines to show communication channels between nodes. Communication over a network is often bidirectional. The following discussion of communication networks applies to all communication forms whether face-to-face, by electronic media, or by video media.[61]

Pair-wise communication is any form of oral or written communication between two people. It occurs between superiors and subordinates, between individuals of different status with no direct reporting relationship, between peers, and between friends. Whenever you chat with a friend, for example, you are involved in pair-wise communication. Each person in a pair focuses attention on the other person. This feature distinguishes pair-wise communication from

a) Pair-Wise Communication

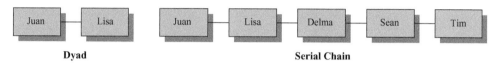

b) Small Group Communication (Centralized)

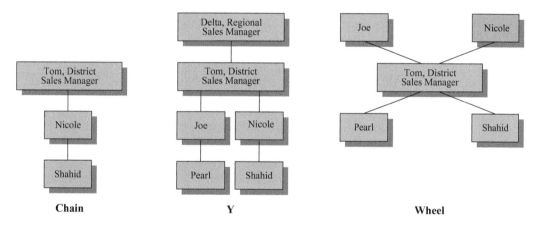

c) Small Group Communication (Decentralized)

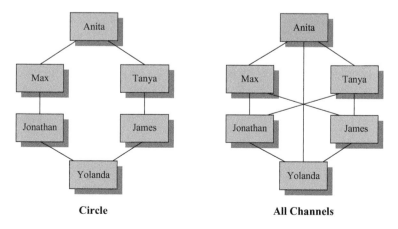

■ **Figure 13.3:** Communication Networks

the other forms of communication described in this section. The direction of pair-wise communication can be top-down, bottom-up, or lateral.

Small group communication networks involve three or more people directly interacting during the communication. The groups can be face-to-face or widely dispersed if the communication process uses an audio, video, or computer-based medium. Small group communication occurs within an organization's departments, work units, and teams, and within an organization's informal groups. Communication interaction within small groups rotates among group members in either a structured or a random pattern. Whether the group is in one location or dispersed, communication occurs within either a centralized or a decentralized communication network.

Centralized communication networks have a single person as a key figure in sending and receiving messages, no matter where they go in the network. In centralized networks, only one or a few parts of the network have the potential to get information. Branch managers of banks often have this communication role between their branch and other parts of the bank organization.

Decentralized communication networks feature freely flowing communication with no person playing a central or controlling role. Decentralized networks spread the potential to get information throughout the network, so that all parts have about equal information status. No person in the network depends exclusively on anyone else. For example, many insurance companies let their claims processors make almost all decisions about a claim without referring to anyone else in the company.

Centralized and decentralized communication networks have different advantages and disadvantages. Centralized networks are faster and have fewer errors when solving simple problems or tasks, but are less effective with complex problems or tasks. Decentralized networks are faster and more accurate with complex problems than with simple problems. They also process more messages and yield higher satisfaction among network members, whatever the type of problem or task.

Large audience communication gets a message from one person or a few people and delivers it to many people. The sender designs a message before sending it to the audience. Such messages usually are sent continuously with no interruption from the audience. The audience can include 20, hundreds, thousands, or, with the help of radio and television, millions of people. Some typical organization examples are department meetings, briefing sessions, training programs, orientation meetings, and new product or service introductions.

INTERNATIONAL ASPECTS OF ORGANIZATIONAL COMMUNICATION

This chapter alluded several times to cross-cultural issues in communication. Those issues go beyond the spoken and written language of another country. Although English is widely spoken when doing business in non-English-speaking countries, nonnative speakers will not always understand your message correctly due to nonverbal communication differences.[62]

Nonverbal communication often has different meanings in different countries.[63] North Americans ordinarily stand 5.5–8 feet apart while speaking. In Latin American cultures, people stand much closer. When a North American speaks to a Latin American in that person's home country, the Latin American moves close to the North American, who then feels uncomfortable and backs away. The Latin American might perceive the North American as cold and distant, an unintended communication of the nonverbal behavior.

Time orientation and the meaning of time differ widely among cultures as well. Latin Americans view time more casually than North Americans. North Americans value promptness in keeping appointments, a nonverbal behavior that the Swiss even more strongly emphasize. A North American or a Swiss might feel insulted if someone is late for an appointment, even though no insult was intended.

Egyptians usually do not look to the future, which they define as anything more than a week away. South Asians think of the long term as centuries, not the typical five- or ten-year view of North Americans. The Sioux Indians of the United States do not have words for "time," "wait," or "waiting" in their native language. You can readily see that misunderstandings about time could arise in a face-to-face business meeting of people from different countries or among people in a culturally diverse workforce.

ETHICAL ISSUES IN ORGANIZATIONAL COMMUNICATION

An organization's communication processes play an important role in presenting an ethical image to people inside and outside the organization. Internal processes include newsletters, satellite television broadcasts, direct mailings, mass e-mail, and bulletin board postings. External processes include annual reports, press releases, and public statements. What does the organization say or not say about ethical behavior and ethical decisions? Those statements—or their absence—form the ethical image of the organization.

Organizations manage external impressions of their behavior by giving their own accounts of behavior that protesters say is unethical. The protest might come from a special interest group that believes the organization has behaved unethically. An organization's response is a communication in any form designed to affect the perception of others inside or outside the organization. A response is designed to make the organization (or individual members) appear more ethical than the charges allege.[64]

Another ethical issue centers on how much an organization should disclose to employees, customers, suppliers, and the community in which it operates. The groups may raise several ethical questions, including the following:

■ Should an organization fully reveal negative information about its plans to employees? Such information includes planned layoffs, transfers, and other large changes that could disrupt people's lives.

▪ How much should an organization tell its customers or clients about product safety, service errors, and testing program results?

▪ The disclosure issue also extends to suppliers. Should an organization tell its suppliers how it chooses among them, its contracting process, and the basis of its commitment to a supplier?

A growing ethical issue surrounds communication privacy in organizations. Do employees have the right to private communications in the work setting that cannot be revealed to anyone without their consent? This ethical issue will grow in the future, as more employees using PCs become part of computer networks in organizations. Existing software lets both network managers and senior managers read employees' voice mail, e-mail, and other computer files. Keystroke logger software records every keystroke and lets managers monitor what employees enter into their computers. Such software separately records keystrokes, even if a person deletes a file. The underlying ethical issue is whether people's privacy rights extend to such computer surveillance.[65]

SUMMARY

SUMMARY
13

Communication processes in organizations involve a sender, a receiver, and a message flowing over a communication channel. The process includes feedback the sender gets from the receiver's response to the message. Noise surrounds the entire process, distorting the messages.

Communication has both verbal and nonverbal forms. Verbal communication includes oral, written, electronic, and video communication. Nonverbal communication includes gestures, facial expressions, and the sender's voice. Nonverbal communication can contradict, amplify, or complement verbal communication.

Organizational communication has several functions and dysfunctions. The functions include letting people share information and helping managers integrate or coordinate different parts of the organization. Dysfunctions include selective perception, semantic problems, and information overload. Communication effectiveness can be improved through training, asking for a receiver's feedback, and understanding cultural differences in communication.

Listening is the mental process of assigning meaning to sounds. Active listening is accurately hearing the facts in a message and understanding the speaker's feelings about the message. The active listener makes a deliberate effort to understand a message from the speaker's viewpoint.

Technology forecasters predict major changes in organizational communication processes because of emerging technologies such as digital cellular phones, satellites, and videoconferencing.

Individuals in organizations can play different communication roles: initiator, relayer, liaison, terminator, and isolate. Communication in organizations occurs within different communication networks. Some communication is pair-wise, involving only two people. Small group communication uses either centralized or decentralized networks. Large audience communication features a single sender and multiple receivers.

Large cultural variations in nonverbal communication can make cross-cultural transitions especially difficult for some people. Nonverbal communication in the international environment adds to any difficulties a person has with a language he does not understand.

The central ethical issues in communication are image management, full disclosure, and communication privacy. Managers can deftly use external communication to present an ethical image. Whether to fully disclose product safety information and planned layoffs, for example, are ethical questions that managers must consider. Modern communication technology helps an organization monitor employee electronic communication such as e-mail. Do employee's have privacy rights in such communications?

REVIEW AND DISCUSSION QUESTIONS

REVIEW AND DISCUSSION QUESTIONS 13

1   Review the description of the basic communication process presented earlier in this chapter. Discuss the effect of noise on the process. What forms of noise have you experienced?

2   What is the role of the feedback loop in the basic communication process? How can the sender and receiver use it to improve communication effectiveness?

3   Discuss the different types of communication. What is the role of nonverbal communication in the larger communication process?

4   Review the "Dysfunctions of Organizational Communication" section. Have you experienced any of those dysfunctions during your college education? Reflect on your work experiences. Discuss examples of communication dysfunction from those experiences.

5   Ask some close friends to describe your nonverbal behavior when you talk. Ask them whether such behavior adds to or detracts from the meaning of what you say.

6   Review the "Active Listening" section. Have you experienced any of the recommendations in that section? If yes, did active listening improve the communication processes where it was used?

7   Review the technologies that forecasters expect will change communication processes in the future. Which technologies does your college or university use? Which technologies have you seen in your work experiences?

TAKE FIVE: OB ALIVE: *MILK MONEY* (1994)

Frank Wheeler (Michael Patrick Carter) and his two friends pool their milk money until they have enough to hire a woman to show them her naked body. They get stranded in the city after they have their bicycles stolen. V (Melanie Griffith) drives them home. The car breaks down and Frank's dad, Tom Wheeler (Ed Harris), makes the repairs.

The selected scenes start at the beginning DVD Chapter 5, "The Math Tutor." They end after V walks away and Tom Wheeler dangles the jumper cables while looking bewildered (Stop: 0:32:46).

Use the following questions as guides to your viewing of the scene: Does any misperception occur between V and Tom? What is its basis? How does it affect the communication process? Did any nonverbal communication occur that could have improved communication between V and Tom?

REFERENCES AND NOTES

1. Shannon, C. E., and W. Weaver. 1949. *The Mathematical Theory of Communication.* Urbana: University of Illinois Press, p. 3. (Emphasis in original.)
2. Burke, P., and R. Porter, eds. 1995. *Languages and Jargons: Contributions to a Social History of Language.* Cambridge: Polity Press.
   Clampitt, P. G. 1991. *Communicating for Managerial Effectiveness.* Newbury Park: Sage Publications.
   Goldhaber, G. M. 1993. *Organizational Communication.* Madison: Brown & Benchmark.
   Poole, M. S. 2011. Communication. In *APA Handbook of Industrial and Organizational Psychology,* Vol. 3, ed. S. Zedeck. Washington, DC: American Psychological Association, Chap. 7.
   Porter, L. W., and K. H. Roberts. 1976. Communication in Organizations. In *Handbook of Industrial and Organizational Psychology,* ed. M. D. Dunnette. Chicago: Rand McNally, Chap. 35.
3. Porter and Roberts, Communication in Organizations, p. 1567.
4. Developed from Shannon and Weaver, *The Mathematical Theory.*
   Berlo, D. K. 1960. *The Process of Communication.* New York: Holt, Rinehart & Winston, pp. 102–3, 109–16.
5. Webster, J., and L. K. Treviño. 1995. Rational and Social Theories as Complementary Explanations of Communication Media Choices: Two Policy-Capturing Studies. *Academy of Management Journal* 38: 1544–72. This source reviews earlier research on media choice.
6. Bhappu, A. D., T. L. Griffith, and G. B. Northcraft. 1997. Media Effects and Communication Bias in Diverse Groups. *Organizational Behavior and Human Decision Processes* 70: 199–205.
   Larkey, L. K. 1996. Toward a Theory of Communicative Interactions in Culturally Diverse Workgroups. *Academy of Management Review* 21: 463–91.

7. Ahrens, F. 2004. Accent on Higher TV Ratings: Spanish-Language Network Telemundo Coaches Actors to Use Mexican Dialect. *The Washington Post* (August 2): A–1.

Harrison, C. 2002. New Challenges Arise as US Firms Move Call Centers Overseas. *The Dallas Morning News* (October 16): K4121.

8. Jelinek, P. 1998. Koreans Practice Service, Smiling. Associated Press, as published in *The Albuquerque Journal* (December 19): G3.

9. Andersen, P. A. 2008. *Nonverbal Communication: Forms and Functions*, 2nd edn. Long Grove: Waveland Press, Chap. 1.

Burgoon, J. K., D. B. Buller, and W. G. Woodall. 1996. *Nonverbal Behavior: The Unspoken Dialogue*. New York: McGraw-Hill.

DePaulo, B. M., and H. S. Friedman. 1998. Nonverbal Communication. In *Handbook of Social Psychology*, Vol. 2, ed. D. T. Gilbert, S. T. Fiske, and G. Lindzey. New York: McGraw-Hill, Chap. 18.

Knapp, M. L., and J. A. Hall. 1997. *Nonverbal Communication in Human Interaction*. Fort Worth: Harcourt Brace College Publishers, Chap. 1.

10. Porter, G. W. 1969. Nonverbal Communication. *Training and Development Journal* 23: 3–8.

11. Porter and Roberts, Communication in Organizations, p. 1564.

12. Guetzkow, H. 1965. Communications in Organizations. In *Handbook of Organizations*, ed. J. G. March. Chicago: Rand McNally, pp. 538–39.

13. Developed from H. W. Hoemann. 1986. *Introduction to American Sign Language*. Bowling Green: Bowling Green Press.

14. Knapp and Hall, *Nonverbal Communication*, p. 5.

15. Ibid.

16. Porter and Roberts, Communication in Organizations, p. 1563.

17. Huber, G. P. 1990. A Theory of the Effects of Advanced Information Technologies on Organizational Design, Intelligence, and Decision Making. *Academy of Management Review* 15: 47–71.

18. Andersen, *Nonverbal Communication*.

DePaulo and Friedman, Nonverbal Communication.

Ekman, P. 2003. *Emotions Revealed: Recognizing Faces and Feelings to Improve Communication and Emotional Life*. New York: Times Books. Chapters 5 through 9 of this source have a highly readable discussion of nonverbal communication.

Knapp and Hall, *Nonverbal Communication*.

Mahl, G. F. 1987. *Explorations in Nonverbal Behavior*. Hillsdale: Lawrence Erlbaum Associates.

Pentland, A. 2008. *Honest Signals: How They Shape Our World*. Cambridge, MA: The MIT Press.

Pentland, A., with T. Heibeck. 2008. Understanding "Honest Signals" in Business. *MIT Sloan Management Review* 50 (Fall): 70–75.

19. Aguinis, H., M. M. Simonsen, and C. A. Pierce. 1998. Effects of Nonverbal Behavior on Perceptions of Power Bases. *The Journal of Social Psychology* 138: 455–69.

20. DePaulo, B. M., J. I. Stone, and G. D. Lassiter. 1985. Deceiving and Detecting Deceit. In *The Self and Social Life*, ed. B. R. Schlenker. New York: McGraw-Hill, pp. 323–70.

Hostetter, A. B. 2011. When Do Gestures Communicate? A Meta-Analysis. *Psychological Bulletin* 137: 297–315.

Mehrabian, A. 1972. *Nonverbal Communication*. Piscataway: AldineTransaction, Chaps. 1, 2, 6.

21. Harrison, R. 1970. Nonverbal Communication: Explorations into Time, Space, Action, and Object. In *Dimensions in Communication*, ed. J. H. Campbell and H. W. Hepler. Belmont: Wadsworth, pp. 158–74.

22. Hall, E. T. 1959. *The Silent Language*. Garden City: Doubleday.

23. Ibid., Chap. 1.

24. Porter, Nonverbal Communication.

25. Goldhaber, *Organizational Communication*.
    Ilgen, D. R., C. D. Fisher, and M. S. Taylor. 1979. Consequences of Individual Feedback on Behavior in Organizations. *Journal of Applied Psychology* 64: 349–71.

26. Ilgen, Fisher, and Taylor, Consequences of Individual Feedback.

27. Keller, R. T. 2001. Cross-Functional Project Groups in Research and New Product Development: Diversity, Communications, Job Stress, and Outcomes. *Academy of Management Journal* 44: 547–55. This source summarizes much of the research on cross-functional teams and communication effects on performance.

28. Ford, J. D., and L. W. Ford. 1995. The Role of Conversations in Producing Intentional Change in Organizations. *Academy of Management Review* 20: 541–70.

29. Bylinsky, G. 1998. How to Bring Out Better Products Faster. *Fortune* (November 23): 238[B]–[E], 238[J], 238[N], 238[R], 238[T].

30. Developed from Guetzkow, Communications in Organizations, pp. 550–58, and other sources cited throughout this part.

31. Porter and Roberts, Communication in Organizations, p. 1564.

32. Shannon and Weaver, *The Mathematical Theory*, pp. 115–16.

33. Guetzkow, Communications in Organizations, p. 551.

34. Burden refers to overhead costs of organizations, such as the cost of operating a human resource management department; metrology is a system of weights and measures; upload means send data to another computer and download means receive data from another computer.
    "Expecto patronum" creates a spell that keeps dementors away. Dementors are prison guards who suck the joy out of people. See Rose, M., and E. Nelson. 2000. Potter Cognoscenti All Know When They See One: Coinages in the Kids' Books are Code, in Fans' Hands, to Realms of Daily Life. *The Wall Street Journal* (October 18): A1, A10.

35. Michailova, S. 2000. Contrasts in Culture: Russian and Western Perspectives on Organizational Change. *Academy of Management Executive* 14: 99–112.

36. Guetzkow, Communications in Organizations, pp. 551–53.
    O'Reilly, C. A. 1980. Individual and Information Overload in Organizations: Is More Necessarily Better? *Academy of Management Journal* 23: 684–96.

37. O'Reilly, Individual and Information Overload, p. 692.

38. Dilenschneider, R. L., and R. C. Hyde. 1985. Crises Communications: Planning for the Unplanned. *Business Horizons* 28 (January–February): 35–41.

39. Hovland, C. I., I. L. Janis, and H. H. Kelly. 1953. *Communication and Persuasion*. New Haven, CT: Yale University Press.
    Zimbardo, P. G., E. B. Ebbesen, and C. Maslach. 1977. *Influencing Attitudes and Changing Behavior*. Reading, MA: Addison-Wesley.

40. Morrison, E. W., and F. J. Milliken. 2000. Organizational Silence: A Barrier to Change and Development in a Pluralistic World. *Academy of Management Review* 25: 706–25.

41. Purdy, M. 1991. What Is Listening? In *Listening in Everyday Life: A Personal and Professional Approach*, ed. D. Borisoff and M. Purdy. Lanham: University Press of America, Chap. 1.

Seibert, J. H. 1990. Listening in the Organizational Context. In *Listening Behavior: Measurement and Application*, ed. R. N. Bostrom. New York: Guilford Press, Chap. 8.

42. Rhodes, S. C. 1993. Listening: A Relational Process. In *Perspectives on Listening*, ed. A. D. Wolvin and C. G. Coakley. Norwood: Ablex Publishing, Chap. 11.

43. Rogers, C. R., and R. E. Farson. 1976. *Active Listening*. Chicago: Industrial Relations Center of the University of Chicago.

44. WhiteSmoke Inc., Wilmington, Del., publishes WhiteSmoke™ and holds its trademark. RightSoft, Inc., Sarasota, Fla, publishes RightWriter® and holds its trademark.

45. Holtz, S. 2006. The Impact of Technology on Corporate Communication. In *The IABC Handbook of Organizational Communication*, ed. T. L. Gillis. San Francisco: Jossey-Bass, Chap. 40.

46. Angell, D., and B. Heslop. 1994. *The Elements of E-Mail Style: Communicate Effectively via Electronic Mail*. Reading, MA: Addison-Wesley, pp. 111–12.
Flynn, N., and T. Flynn. 1998. *Writing Effective E-Mail: Improving Your Electronic Communication*. Menlo Park: Crisp Publications.

47. Hsia, H. J. 1968. On Channel Effectiveness. *Audio-Visual Communication Review* 16: 245–61.

48. Developed from the following and other sources cited throughout this section:
Burrus, D. 1993. *Technotrends: How to Use Technology to Go Beyond Your Competition*. New York: Harper Business.
Fulk, J., and L. Collins-Jarvis. 2001. Wired Meetings: Technological Mediation of Organizational Gatherings. In *The New Handbook of Organizational Communication: Advances in Theory, Research, and Methods*, ed. F. M. Jablin and L. L. Putnam. Thousand Oaks: Sage Publications, pp. 624–63.
Gunn, A. 1993. Connecting Over the Airwaves. *PC Magazine* (August): 359–62, 360, 365, 376, 378, 384.
Sterling, B. 2002. *Tomorrow Now: Envisioning the Next Fifty Years*. New York: Random House.
Weil, M. M., and L. D. Rosen. 1997. *TechnoStress: Coping with Technology @Work @Home @Play*. New York: John Wiley & Sons.

49. Freund, J. 1998. A Global Calling. *Wired* (August): 144.
Green, H. 2003. Wi-Fi Means Business. *Business Week* (April 28): 86–92.
Wildstrom, S. H. 2004. Tablets: Waiting for More Smart Software. *Business Week* (September 27): 30.

50. Reinsch, N. L., Jr., J. W. Turner, and C. H. Tinsley. 2008. Multicommunicating: A Practice Whose Time Has Come? *Academy of Management Review* 33: 391–403.

51. Schatz, W. 1994. Internet: Open for Business? *Informationweek* (February 14): 34, 36, 39, 40.

52. 2004. A Perfect Market: A Survey of E-Commerce. *The Economist* (May 15): 2–6, 8, 11–12, 14–20.

53. Walther, J. B. 1997. Group and Interpersonal Effects in International Computer-Mediated Collaboration. *Human Communication Research* 23: 342–69.

54. Cairncross, F. 2001. *The Death of Distance: How the Communication Revolution Is Changing Our Lives*. Boston: Harvard Business School Press, Chaps. 3, 4.
Comm, J. 2009. *Twitter Power: How to Dominate Your Market One Tweet at a Time*. Hoboken: John Wiley & Sons.
Evans, D. 2008. *Social Media Marketing: An Hour a Day*. Indianapolis: Wiley.

Hempel, J. 2009. How Facebook Is Taking Over Our Lives. *Fortune* (March 2): 48–56.

Tapscott, D., and A. D. Williams. 2007. *Wikinomics: How Mass Collaboration Changes Everything*. New York: Penguin Group (USA).

55. Holtz, The Impact of Technology on Corporate Communication.

56. Kramer, M. 1990. Cost-Effective Videoconferencing Will Be Worth the Wait. *PC Week* (June 19): 61.

57. Fitzlof, E. 1999. 3M Hits Sweet Spot in Videoconferencing Pricing. *Infoworld* (April 19): 10.

58. Developed from P. R. Monge and E. M. Eisenberg. 1987. Emergent Communication Networks. In *Handbook of Organizational Communication: An Interdisciplinary Perspective*, ed. F. M. Jablin, L. L. Putnam, K. H. Roberts, and L. W. Porter. Newbury Park: Sage Publications, pp. 304–42.

Porter and Roberts, Communication in Organizations, p. 1569.

Rogers, E. M., and R. Agarwala-Rogers. 1976. *Communication in Organizations*. New York: Free Press, pp. 132–40.

Sutton, H., and L. W. Porter. 1968. A Study of the Grapevine in a Governmental Organization. *Personnel Psychology* 21: 223–30.

59. Rogers and Agarwala-Rogers, *Communication in Organizations*, pp. 135–38.

60. Jacobson, E., and S. Seashore. 1951. Communication Practices in Complex Organizations. *Journal of Social Issues* 7: 28–40.

Rogers and Agarwala-Rogers, *Communication in Organizations*, pp. 135–38.

61. Developed from B. Barry and J. M. Crant. 2000. Dyadic Communication Relationships in Organizations: An Attribution/Expectancy Approach. *Organization Science* 11: 648–64.

Monge and Eisenberg, Emergent Communication Networks.

Monge, P. R., and N. S. Contractor. 2001. Emergence of Communication Networks. In *The New Handbook of Organizational Communication: Advances in Theory, Research, and Methods*, ed. F. M. Jablin and L. L. Putnam. Thousand Oaks: Sage Publications, pp. 440–502.

Porter and Roberts, Communication in Organizations.

Shaw, M. E. 1964. Communication Networks. In *Advances in Experimental Social Psychology*, ed. L. Berkowitz. New York: Academic Press, pp. 111–47.

62. Adler, N. J., and A. Gundersen, 2008. *International Dimensions of Organizational Behavior*, 5th edn. Mason: Thomson South-Western, Chap. 3.

Andersen, *Nonverbal Communication*, Chap. 4.

63. Hall, *The Silent Language*.

Hall, E. T. 1966. *The Hidden Dimension*. Garden City: Doubleday.

64. Garrett, D. E., J. L. Bradford, R. A. Meyers, and J. Becker. 1989. Issues Management and Organizational Accounts: An Analysis of Corporate Responses to Accusations of Unethical Business Practices. *Journal of Business Ethics* 8: 507–20.

65. Jesdanun, A. 2001. Boss Is Watching 1 Out of 3: Study Says E-Monitor Costs Just $5.25 a Year. Associated Press, as reported in *The Albuquerque Journal* (July 11): B4.

McCarthy, M. J. 2000. You Assumed "Erase" Wiped Out That Rant Against the Boss? Nope. *The Wall Street Journal* (March 7): A1, A16.

Chapter 14

DECISION-MAKING AND PROBLEM-SOLVING PROCESSES

After reading this chapter, you should be able to:

- Describe decision-making and problem-solving processes in organizations.
- Discuss the relationship between problem solving and decision making in organizations.
- Compare the decision strategies that managers can use for decision making.
- Analyze several decision-making models and the perspectives they bring to the decision process.
- List the assets and liabilities of group decision making.
- Distinguish between individual and group decision making and identify the situations for which they are best suited.
- Discuss the sources of decision-making bias and error.
- Describe the process of escalation of commitment to a losing course of action.
- Recognize groupthink and how to avoid it during group decision making.
- Explain several methods of improving decision processes in organizations.
- Appreciate some international and ethical issues that surround decision making in organizations.

The **decision-making process** defines a decision problem, creates alternative courses of action, and chooses among them using decision criteria. The criteria for choosing among alternatives can include the cost, profit, danger, or pleasure of each alternative. Although decision making focuses on choice, it also intends to reach a goal.[1]

Decision making fits within the larger context of problem-solving activities in organizations. Individuals in organizations, especially managers, face problems, opportunities, and events that require action. The **problem-solving** process identifies the problem, tries to find root causes, and creates options that become input to a decision-making process. Decision making is the part of the problem-solving process that chooses a course of action.[2]

Both individuals and groups can make decisions. Individuals do a good job with well-structured problems that have several tightly coupled parts. Groups do a better job with ill-defined problems with loosely coupled parts. They work well with problems too complex for a single person to solve. Such decisions include those affecting multiple constituencies and decisions needing the commitment of those affected to get effective execution.[3]

Although decision making is a basic function of a manager's role, nonmanagers also make decisions.[4] Organizations that embrace quality management or use self-managing teams involve many nonmanagers in decision processes. Throughout this chapter, the term decision maker refers to a person at any organizational level who chooses a course of action when faced with a decision situation.

DECISION STRATEGIES

The two major **decision strategies** are programmed and unprogrammed.[5] Three dimensions define the characteristics of each strategy. The **routine–nonroutine dimension** describes whether the decision is common or unusual. The **recurring–nonrecurring dimension** describes whether the decision happens often or infrequently. The **certainty–uncertainty dimension** describes the degree of predictability of the decision. Risk embraces a large part of the certainty–uncertainty dimension. Situations with complete certainty or uncertainty are not as common as risky situations. When making decisions under risk, the decision maker assesses the probability of the alternatives during the decision process.[6]

Decision makers use a **programmed decision strategy** for routine, recurring, and predictable decisions. This strategy relies on existing rules and standard procedures, uses well-known decision criteria, and applies uniform processing to a decision problem.[7] Examples include handling exchanges and returns after Christmas and recording and processing accrued vacation and sick leave time.

Decision makers use an **unprogrammed decision strategy** for nonroutine, nonrecurring, and unpredictable decisions. Decision makers use this strategy when faced with novel or unusual events that they have not encountered in the past. Such unstructured events require creative problem solving for effective decision making.

THE DECISION-MAKING PROCESS

The decision-making process is much more than choosing from alternative courses of action. The process involves several interrelated phases, only one of which is choice. Figure 14.1 shows those phases.[8]

Decision processes are dynamic. They can unfold linearly or restart at an earlier phase. A decision maker can also repeat or restart the entire process, depending on the conditions that unfold during the process. Decision makers can move in both directions in the sequence and even stop for an extended time at one phase.[9]

The first phase is **problem identification and diagnosis**. The organization faces an issue or problem that needs a solution. The issue or problem could be as simple as a request by a customer or an employee to do something not covered by existing policies or as major as widespread unethical behavior in the organization. Whether the problem is simple or difficult, its presence starts the decision process.

The first phase includes **identification of criteria** that will show that the issue is resolved or the problem is solved. This element is important because it ties directly to the last phase, which is assessing the decision's effects. The criteria should be as explicit and as measurable as possible so managers can determine the success or failure of the decision.

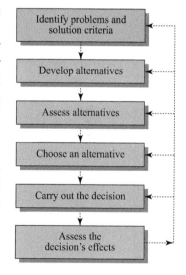

■ **Figure 14.1:** The Decision-Making Process

The second phase focuses on **developing alternatives** for dealing with the issue or solving the problem. The decision maker searches for alternatives and information about the alternatives. The search can be informal, such as a telephone call for advice on a simple but unusual issue, or formal, such as a marketing survey to find out why the company's product is losing market share.

When faced with a complex problem, the decision maker might look at many different alternatives and consider them simultaneously. During the search, the decision maker often faces time and cost constraints, which can lead to imperfect or incomplete information about each alternative.

Decision makers discard alternatives they view as unacceptable solutions to the problem or issue, based on the criteria developed in the first phase. Acceptability, of course, is a judgment based on the decision maker's perception of the alternatives. Acceptable alternatives then become part of the decision maker's set of possible alternatives that move to the assessment phase of the decision process.

The decision maker now **assesses the alternatives** in the feasible set. She examines each alternative to see what desirable and undesirable results it is likely to have. The decision maker considers whether those affected by an alternative are likely to accept it. How well the decision is accepted can affect its success. The decision maker also considers the amount of risk each alternative involves and the certainty of its results.

After the decision maker completes the assessment, she must **choose an alternative**. Although people commonly associate decision making only with this phase, the decisions are actually made by means of the entire dynamic and interdependent process just described.

Decision makers may face several dilemmas, including the following:

- ▪ Two or more alternatives appear equally good. If the decision maker is truly indifferent, a random process such as a coin toss can make the choice.
- ▪ No one alternative can solve the issue or problem. Here the decision maker can use a set of alternatives to solve the problem or restart the decision process to search for better alternatives.
- ▪ No alternatives offer enough positive results to offset expected negative effects. The decision maker can restart the process to see if better alternatives exist. Note that in both this and the previous dilemma, a decision has been made—the decision not to decide.[10]
- ▪ The decision maker perceives many alternatives as acceptable. The decision maker can go back to the previous phase to get more information about the alternatives and then try to make a choice.

The decision maker is ready to **carry out the decision**, after she has chosen an alternative. Moving the decision to action is often as complicated as making the decision. Those asked to carry out the decision may accept decisions about simple issues but resist tough decisions about complex problems. The major issues in this phase go beyond the quality of the decision. They focus squarely on managing a successful implementation.

The last phase in the decision process **assesses the decision's effects**. The criteria for assessing the decision come from the first phase. The people asked to carry out the decision measure the results and compare them to the criteria. If the results are not as desired, corrective action may be required. If it becomes clear that the criteria need revision, the entire process begins again.

DECISION-MAKING MODELS

Problem-solving and decision-making processes can follow several models. Each model describes variations in the decision process and includes different assumptions. These assumptions imply that the models apply to different types of decisions in modern organizations.

The Rational Model

The Rational Model of decision making has its roots in the classical economic theory of the firm and statistical decision making. According to this model, a decision maker approaches a decision problem in the following way:[11]

1. The decision maker has a goal she wants to maximize or minimize. That goal can be profit, revenue, market share, cost, and so on.
2. The decision maker knows all alternatives and their results. She has complete information about each alternative. The decision maker is also fully knowledgeable about the degree of risk and uncertainty associated with each alternative.
3. The decision maker uses some function to give a preference ordering to the alternatives under consideration. The decision maker knows that function at the beginning of the decision process.
4. The decision maker applies the preference ordering function to the set of alternatives and chooses the alternative that maximizes the goal.

The Rational Model sees decision making as proceeding sequentially from beginning to end. This model does not have dynamic properties such as revising the goal or extending the search for new alternatives.

The Bounded Rationality Model

The Bounded Rationality Model assumes decision makers have limitations that constrain rationality in the decision process. Those limits include the absence of complete information about alternatives and their results, cost constraints, time constraints, and limitations in dealing with complex problems.[12]

Because of these limitations, decision makers might not consider all possible alternatives and therefore might not choose the alternative that maximizes a goal. Instead, the decision maker picks an alternative that is good enough to reach the goal. Selecting a satisfactory, but not optimal, alternative is known as satisficing behavior, a term that emphasizes the decision maker's search for satisfactory, not optimal, solutions. The following classical analogy shows the distinction between optimizing and satisficing.

An example is the difference between searching a haystack to find the sharpest needle in it and searching the haystack to find a needle sharp enough to sew with.[13]

The Bounded Rationality Model is both open and dynamic. Decision makers attend to forces and constraints imposed by the environment of the decision. As new information comes into the decision process, they can change both the goal of the decision problem and the set of alternatives. If the decision maker does not find a satisficing alternative in the set under consideration, she broadens the search for more alternatives.

Unstructured Decision-Making Models

Unlike the two models just described, many decisions do not have a structure that allows orderly progression from identifying the decision problem to selecting an alternative. Unstructured decisions often are unprecedented, significant, and complex events that defy program-like decision processes.[14] To put it more dramatically, unstructured decision making is a "process characterized by novelty, complexity, and openendedness, by the fact that the organization usually begins with little understanding of the decision situation it faces or the route to its solution, and only a vague idea of what the solution might be and how it will be evaluated when it is developed."[15]

Decision makers solve such complex, unstructured, and ambiguous problems by breaking them into manageable parts to which they apply more structured decision-making approaches. The novelty of such problems usually does not allow an optimizing approach to selecting an alternative. Decision makers rely on satisficing approaches for finding solutions to unstructured problems.[16]

Unstructured decisions are especially vulnerable to factors that can disturb orderly movement through the decision process. The process can encounter political forces trying to stop a decision, make false starts because of inadequate information about the problem, or run into blank walls when an alternative does not solve the unstructured problem.[17] The decision maker assesses many alternatives simultaneously using a series of cycles for finding and assessing them.[18] During the process of finding and assessing alternatives, one alternative can emerge as the preferred choice. Such an "implicitly favored" alternative emerges during the decision process, not just at the end of the process. During the search for alternatives, the decision maker rejects those alternatives that are unacceptable and adds those that are acceptable to the set, even though she has already identified a preference.

The decision maker then moves to a stage of confirming the implicitly chosen alternative. During this stage, she tries to arrive at the belief that her implicit preference was the right choice. Many aspects of selective perception, distortion, and attribution discussed in Chapter 5, "Perception, Attitudes, and Personality," operate during this phase. The task for the decision maker is to believe that her implicit favorite is better than at least one alternative to which it is compared.

The Garbage Can Model of Decision Making

The Garbage Can Model of decision making was developed to explain decision making under highly ambiguous conditions. Ambiguous conditions arise in organizations when goals are not clear, organizational participants change fast, and the technologies of the organization are either poorly understood or swiftly change. The fast-changing global environments of many organizations also add ambiguity.[19]

Decision making under ambiguity does not lend itself to the more rational, structured approaches described earlier. In ambiguous situations, a decision maker might not know all the alternatives available and the results of each alternative. She also might not have a clear set of rules to guide her as she chooses from the alternatives.

The Garbage Can Model sees decision making under ambiguity as a time-sensitive process of four almost independent streams or flows: problem streams, solution streams, participant streams, and choice opportunity streams. These streams are constantly moving through an organization. The convergence of the streams at some point results in a decision.

Problem streams are the issues or problems facing the organization or part of the organization at a particular time. **Solution streams** are the solutions available to a decision maker, even though these solutions might have no direct connection to the problems. **Participant streams** are the decision makers and others who are available to decide. The **choice opportunity streams** are the chances to decide.

The garbage can metaphor was chosen deliberately and is not an attempt at humor. The contents of a real garbage can consist of whatever people have tossed into the can. A decision-making garbage can is much the same. The four streams flow toward the garbage can. Whatever is in the can when a decision is needed contributes to that decision. The Garbage Can Model sees decision making in organizations as chaotic: Solutions look for problems to solve, and decision makers make choices based on the arbitrary mix of the four streams in the garbage can.

Political Decision-Making Models

Political decision-making models assume that individuals and groups in organizations pursue their self-interests and try to reach decisions that serve those interests. These models see decision making as a power- and conflict-based process featuring bargaining and compromise as ways of reducing conflict. The decisions that emerge from this process usually do not satisfy everyone involved.[20]

Political decision-making models view power as a central feature of the decision process. Such models define power as the ability or capacity of an individual or group to overcome an opponent. According to the model, individuals or groups try to gain power and affect decisions by developing strategies such as controlling information that is critical to a decision and building coalitions within the organization to gain support for a position. Political forces within an organization are most likely to affect resource allocation decisions (see Chapter 15, "Power and Political Behavior") such as budget decisions.

ASSETS AND LIABILITIES OF GROUP DECISION MAKING

Group decision-making processes have both **assets and liabilities**.[21] Recognizing these assets and liabilities can help you understand what group decision making can and cannot do.

Assets

Groups of people can bring more knowledge, information, skills, and abilities to a problem than individuals working alone. The heterogeneity of a decision-making group can stimulate discussion and debate about how to solve the problem. Each person contributes a piece of information or knowledge to the decision process. Some research shows that groups with goals of cooperation manage their discussions more effectively than groups with goals of competition.[22]

When groups make decisions, everyone in the group understands more about the decision. Participants in the process know which alternatives were reviewed and why one was selected and others rejected.

Participation in a decision-making group can lead to increased acceptance of the decision. If they perceive their participation as legitimate, participants can develop a sense of ownership of decisions, reducing resistance while carrying out the decision.

Group decision making also helps the personal development of participants, letting them work on more complex problems in the future. Group decision making can improve collaborative problem-solving skills, develop trust among those who participate, enhance interpersonal skills, and increase job satisfaction.[23]

Liabilities

Group decision making also has liabilities. Individuals who participate in group decision making might feel strong social pressures to conform to an emerging norm. Pressure is placed on those who disagree to get them to accept the favored alternatives.

Often one person dominates a group, especially if the group had no appointed leader from the start. Such people become dominant by participating more, being particularly persuasive, or persisting in their position.

As the group uncovers alternatives, individuals can develop strong preferences for a particular alternative. Although that alternative might not be the best solution to the problem, attention may shift to converting those who do not agree with the favored alternative.

Group decision making takes time and is ill-suited for problems that require quick decisions. The time liability of group decision making includes not only the time of the principal decision maker, but also the time of everyone involved in the process.

CHOOSING BETWEEN INDIVIDUAL
AND GROUP DECISION MAKING

Managers can choose from several alternative social processes for decision making. This section describes the approaches and briefly discusses a normative model that guides choices among them.[24]

Alternative Social Processes for Decision Making

Table 14.1 shows several approaches to group decision making. The table identifies the approaches with a combination of letters and Roman numerals.

The letters represent the major characteristics of a process; the Roman numerals are variants of a process. The approaches labeled with an "A" are authoritative in character, which means the decision maker alone makes the decision. The "C" approaches are consultative with the decision maker getting information and

■ **Table 14.1: Different Approaches to Decisions Affecting Individuals and Groups**

Symbol	Definition
AI	You solve the problem or make the decision yourself using information available to you at the present time.
AII	You obtain any necessary information from subordinates, then decide on a solution to the problem yourself. You may or may not tell subordinates the purpose of your questions or give information about the problem or decision on which you are working. The input provided by them is clearly in response to your request for specific information. They do not play a role in the definition of the problem or in generating or evaluating alternative solutions.
CI	You share the problem with relevant subordinates individually, getting their ideas and suggestions without bringing them together as a group. Then you make the decision. This decision may or may not reflect your subordinates' influence.
CII	You share the problem with your subordinates in a group meeting in which you obtain their ideas and suggestions. You make the decision, which may or may not reflect your subordinates' influence.
GII	You share the problem with your subordinates as a group. Together you generate and evaluate alternatives and attempt to reach agreement (consensus) on a solution. Your role is much like that of [a] chairperson, coordinating the discussion, keeping it focused on the problem, and making sure that the critical issues are discussed. You can provide the group with information or ideas you have, but you do not try to "press" them to adopt "your" solution, and you are willing to accept and implement any solution that has the support of the entire group.

Source: Table 2.1. Decision Methods for Group and Individual Problems, Case I and Case IV from *Leadership and Decision-Making*, by Victor H. Vroom and Philip W. Yetton, © 1973. All rights are controlled by the University of Pittsburgh Press, Pittsburgh, PA 15260. Used by permission of the University of Pittsburgh Press. There is no GI approach for decisions affecting groups.

advice from others before deciding. The "G" approach uses **group** processes for decision making and tries to get consensus among group members.

You can view the approaches as social processes for decision making. These approaches have several characteristics as you move from the "A" approaches to the "G" approaches:

■ Social interaction increases between the decision maker and others involved in the decision.

■ Participants in the decision process have increased involvement that can lead to more influence on the decision and increased commitment to the decision. They also have a better understanding of the problem because of their involvement in making the decision.

■ The social processes for making a decision become increasingly complex and feature increased potential for conflict.

■ The time to make a decision increases.

The Vroom-Yetton Model

A normative decision-making model has been proposed that guides a person's choices among the alternative approaches to decision making just described. The **Vroom-Yetton Model** uses a set of rules that protects a decision's acceptance and quality. The model picks the approach indicated by the rules as best for the decision problem under consideration.

The Vroom-Yetton Model considers decision problems to have certain characteristics. The decision maker assesses the characteristics of the decision problem by asking some diagnostic questions. The answers to those questions guide the decision maker to the model's recommended approach for that decision problem. For example, if the decision maker has enough information to decide, the model selects AI. If high conflict about decision alternatives is likely, the model selects CII or GII.

The model has received broad general support from several research efforts.[25] No one suggests the model guarantees perfect decisions; however, research evidence says that decisions made by processes that the model selects are consistently higher quality than decisions made by processes the model does not select. The decision's effectiveness, quality, and acceptance decline as the number of rule violations increase.[26] One study focused on the model's prescription of group processes (CII and GII) when conflict is likely to occur among subordinates and acceptance of the decision is important. That study showed that subordinates were more likely to accept a decision from a group decision process than an individual one.[27]

JUDGMENT BIASES

The description of decision-making models started with models that see the process as rational and ended with models that have a less rational view. Those models see decision makers using less than optimal judgment. Many factors can affect human judgment during the decision-making process.

Heuristics

Decision makers use several heuristics or guidelines to simplify the task of processing an often bewildering array of information developed during decision making. These strategies let them move quickly through the process, but also limit the information to which they attend. Although heuristics can lead to accurate decisions, they often introduce biases in human judgment. People are not always aware that they use heuristics. The next paragraphs describe three heuristics. Which do you tend to use when faced with a decision?

The availability heuristic[28] is the tendency to recall and use information that is easily retrieved from memory. Such information usually is vivid, emotional, specific, and recent. Information without those characteristics might apply to the decision problem, but is less available to the decision maker. For example, managers who do performance appraisals often recall recent events better than earlier events. As a result, they do not have a continuous stream of information for the entire performance period. The result could be an unbalanced and possibly unfair performance appraisal.

The representativeness heuristic[29] leads a decision maker to compare a current event to past events about which the person has knowledge or beliefs. If the current and past events are not comparable or if the decision maker's beliefs are incorrect, the decision might not be accurate. This heuristic includes stereotypes. Using stereotypes with an increasingly diverse workforce can lead to inaccurate or discriminatory hiring and promotion decisions.

Anchoring and adjustment[30] is a heuristic decision makers use to get a starting point for a decision and then adjust beyond that point. This heuristic can play a big role in setting a person's hiring salary or developing a budget. For example, a manager might set a new employee's salary by increasing the person's present salary by some percentage. The salary offer will not necessarily reflect the new employee's true value to the organization. The anchoring and adjustment heuristic is tenacious, tying the decision maker to the original anchor even when other information indicates that the behavior is irrational.

Judgment Biases

When heuristics are right for the decision problem, they can help managers make good decisions. They help the person process information and simplify complex decisions. When the heuristic is not right for the decision, it can introduce systematic judgment biases that lead to wrong or irrational decisions. Heuristics can work alone or in combination to bias a person's judgment.[31]

The availability heuristic leads to judgment biases that adversely affect the accuracy of the information used in a decision process. Inaccuracies come from the recalled information, estimates of the frequencies of events, and errors in association. The **ease of recall bias** occurs when people recall vivid, recent events more easily than other events. A person perceives easily recalled events as happening more often than less easily recalled events. This bias can affect a supervisor's judgment in a performance appraisal. Recent, dramatic events can have more effect on a performance appraisal than older, less remarkable events.

The representativeness heuristic yields judgment biases that affect estimates of events that occur and misperceptions about whether a series of events is random or not. A **misconception of chance bias** occurs when people judge the randomness of a sequence of events from its appearance, although the number of events is statistically too small for that conclusion. A manufacturing manager could question the randomness of a sampling process that resulted in good, good, good, good, bad, good, bad, bad, bad, good. Statistical theory says that one sequence is equally likely as any other sequence when drawn randomly.[32]

The anchoring and adjustment heuristic affects a decision maker's ability to make accurate estimates that can affect project completions or budgets. An **overconfidence bias** can lead to inaccurate judgments when answering questions about which the person has little knowledge. For example, a manager firmly believes her sales estimate for Gillie's Hatch Valley Chile Company in Hatch, New Mexico, is accurate. Gillie's is a real, but little known, company that does not publish sales figures.

Some judgment biases stem from multiple heuristics. A **confirmation trap bias** can lead to behavior that avoids disconfirming and uncomfortable information. People tend to search for information that supports what they believe is true. They tend not to seek information that challenges their views. For example, a manager tentatively decides to introduce a product and seeks only confirming evidence to reach a decision.

Framing Effects

The presentation of a decision problem can lead to **framing effects**, a form of judgment bias that affects decision makers. Differences in presentation or framing of the problem affect their choices.[33] As an illustration, read Decision Problems 1 and 2 in Table 14.2 and choose an alternative for each.

Psychological research on decision making has consistently shown that people prefer Program A for Decision Problem 1 and Program D for Decision Problem 2. Perhaps you did the same. Now look closely at the problems. The only difference between them is the wording. The programs in Problem 1 are phrased as gains and those in Problem 2 as losses. People prefer to avoid risks (**risk-averse** behavior) when facing decisions involving gains. They prefer to take risks (**risk-seeking** behavior) in decisions involving losses.

Framing decisions as losses can contribute to excessively risky decision behavior. Hoping to regain losses through the risky alternative, decision makers might engage in excessive and possibly inappropriate risky decision behavior. Such decision behavior can be associated with high levels of decision failures.[34]

■ Table 14.2: Framing Effects and Decision Problems

Problem 1

Assume you are a plant manager faced with the prospect of laying off 600 workers. You are considering two programs to reduce the number of people laid off:

- ■ If you choose Program A, you will save 200 jobs.
- ■ If you choose Program B, a 33 percent chance exists to save the jobs of all 600 workers and a 67 percent chance exists to not save any workers' jobs.

Problem 2

Assume that you are a plant manager faced with the prospect of laying off 600 workers.

You are considering two alternative programs to reduce the number of people laid off:

- ■ If you choose Program C, you will lay off 400 workers.
- ■ If you choose Program D, you have a 33 percent chance of no layoffs and a 67 percent chance of laying off all 600 workers.

Source: Tversky, A., and D. Kahneman. 1981. The Framing of Decisions and the Psychology of Choice. *Science* 211: 453–58. Problems 1 and 2 are based on p. 453.

Decision makers also should view a decision problem from different frames to see whether they get contradictory results.[35] Some research points to success from reframing decision problems. Although such efforts add time to the decision process, better decisions can result.[36]

ESCALATION OF COMMITMENT

Decision makers face a common dilemma: Should they end a losing course of action or increase their commitment to it in the hope of getting future positive results and recovering past losses? Research evidence suggests they are likely to commit more resources, a process called **escalation of commitment**, to a losing course of action.[37] Some evidence suggests this result varies among cultures. Managers from low uncertainty avoidance cultures such as Singapore are less likely to follow a losing course of action.[38]

Commitment escalation typically happens when decisions can have strong effects on an organization. Such decisions include capital investments, major research and development investments, plant expansions, and the like. Decision makers watch the effects of their decisions to see whether intended results occur. Some decisions succeed and others fail—it is when they fail that irrational decision behavior happens.

Rational decision theory emphasizes using future costs and benefits, not past or sunk costs, to assess alternatives.[39] Economists argue that sunk costs should play no role in a present decision, but decision makers often do not see them as psychologically sunk. As a result, past decisions can have negative effects on present ones.

Several factors contribute to escalating commitment.[40] The decision maker might feel a need to justify past actions to self for ego protection or to others who assess her performance. Pressures for decision behavior consistency and the desire to appear as a rational decision maker can result in irrational escalation. Decision makers with confidence in their skills and abilities appear more likely to escalate commitment than those with less confidence.[41]

Recall from the framing effects discussion that decision makers tend to avoid risk for positively framed problems and seek risk for negatively framed problems. The latter tendency can contribute to commitment escalation, which leads to failure. A failing project appears to the decision maker as a choice between losses. The first choice is to stop the project and accept the sunk costs. That option has a 100 percent chance of happening if the action is taken. The second choice is to consider an option with some probability of loss and some probability of success. This is the risky choice a decision maker will likely take when she frames the problem as a loss.

GROUPTHINK

Groups can make bad, even disastrous, decisions. A major example is the space shuttle Challenger tragedy. Despite evidence of safety hazards, senior managers at the National Aeronautics and Space Administration (NASA) pressed for the launch.[42] Why do group decision processes go awry?

One prominent and popular explanation is the groupthink phenomenon, an ugly disease presumed to infect cohesive decision-making groups. Members of such groups have worked closely together for some time and share a common set of values. These groups often operate during times of crisis, putting stress on their members to reach a commonly agreed-upon decision.[43]

Groupthink involves excessive conformity to a group norm that supports agreement among group members. Decision-making groups with groupthink have lost their ability to critically assess alternative solutions to a problem. They also have lost the ability to examine the effects of past decisions critically, especially decisions that have become dysfunctional for the organization. Another major feature of groupthink is the absence of ethical concerns for the effects of the group's decisions.

Groupthink does not affect decision-making groups simply because they are cohesive. The nature of the norms of such groups is the key to groupthink. If those norms have the qualities just described, then the decision process becomes seriously dysfunctional. If those norms support continuously and critically examining alternatives, the decision-making group will not suffer from groupthink.

The group leader can head off the disastrously dysfunctional effects of groupthink in several ways. She can encourage critical appraisals of issues, ideas, and alternatives that are considered by the group. She should deliberately stimulate conflict during the decision process to get the information the group needs for a quality decision.[44] The group leader can assign one member to play devil's advocate for each group meeting. It also helps to invite knowledgeable outsiders to the group's meetings and to encourage them to analyze and comment on the group's deliberations.

Groupthink theory has received extensive research attention since its introduction in the early 1970s. Existing research evidence does not support all parts of the theory. Despite its lack of clear empirical research support, it remains an intuitive explanation of group decision-making failure.[45]

IMPROVING DECISION MAKING IN ORGANIZATIONS

Many methods exist to **improve decision making** in organizations. Some are human-based methods; others use computers and related technologies.

Human-Based Methods

The human-based methods for improving decision making are designed to generate more decision alternatives or to increase the criticism of the alternatives. Some methods also increase conflict in a decision-making group to offset the liabilities of such groups.

Brainstorming is a method of improving decision making that involves spontaneously generating ideas while deferring critical evaluation of those ideas. Its role in the decision process is to create a set of decision alternatives, not to pick the final alternative.

Four rules guide brainstorming. First, group members generate ideas in a freewheeling fashion. Wacky ideas are welcome. Second, at this stage there is no criticism of any idea, despite how bizarre or bland. Third, many ideas are desired. The assumption is that if people suggest many ideas, some will be good ones. Fourth, after ideas are presented, group members suggest ways to combine or improve them. At the end of a brainstorming session, decision makers should have many alternative solutions to a problem or issue.[46]

A new approach to brainstorming uses computer technology to improve the results of the process.[47] Some research has shown that face-to-face brainstorming does not always yield as many good alternatives as people working alone. The lack of anonymity in a face-to-face group inhibits some people from offering their ideas. **Electronic brainstorming** links people by computers so they do not interact directly. Participants behave anonymously in the process, letting them offer ideas without fear of social pressure from a dominant person. Electronic groups, described in detail in Chapter 10, "Groups and Intergroup Processes," are the broader example of using technology in decision-making groups.

The **nominal group technique (NGT)** is a procedure for generating large amounts of information about a decision problem. The NGT uses a structured approach to decision making that is useful for generating, evaluating, and choosing alternative courses of action. It is a special case of brainstorming that does not include direct interaction. Research evidence shows NGT as outperforming the interactive brainstorming just described. NGT usually creates more ideas of at least equal quality.[48]

During the early stages of the NGT, members of the decision-making group do not interact or talk with each other. Instead, they write their ideas about the decision problem on paper. After about 20 minutes, each person reads one idea from her list. Another person records each idea on a flip-chart in full view of all members of the group. The reading and recording continues with each member of the group presenting one idea at a time, until all ideas are recorded.

During the reading and recording phase, no discussion takes place. By the end of this phase, the group has generated its set of ideas for the decision problem. The group then discusses the ideas on the flip-chart. After the discussion, each member of the group votes privately on the ideas. Finally, the individual votes are pooled to arrive at a decision about the problem.

The **Delphi method** is a structured technique for making decisions that are surrounded by uncertainty or conflicting values laden. This method also is used when group members are geographically scattered. Forecasting future events and determining public policy are examples of the types of decisions that can use the Delphi method.[49]

Several people anonymously contribute to a group's decision when made by the Delphi method. Such people often are experts in their fields. They do not have any face-to-face contact. Members of a Delphi group interact through paper-and-pencil questionnaires or through computers.

The Delphi method follows a sequence of interrelated steps. The person managing the Delphi summarizes the outcomes of those steps using frequency distributions, the median, the quartile, or other appropriate statistics. The summary then becomes the input to the next step.

The Delphi method avoids some liabilities of group decision making. The lack of face-to-face interaction decreases the chance of one person becoming dominant. The controlled feedback from the summaries of each stage helps ensure the information accuracy passed from step to step.

The **devil's advocate technique** starts with one decision maker, or a group of decision makers, advocating and arguing forcefully for a decision alternative. Another person or group plays the role of critic, finding fault with the alternative and arguing for its rejection. The devil's advocate technique assumes a good decision alternative will withstand harsh criticism.[50] Research evidence suggests the technique helps reach high-quality decisions.[51]

Dialectical inquiry is a structured, logical, and analytical method of examining decision alternatives. The process begins by describing the favored decision alternative and the data used to select it. The process analyzes the assumptions held by the decision makers when choosing the alternative. Another decision alternative is then selected for consideration. That alternative could be a new one or one rejected earlier in the decision process. The assumptions underlying the choice of the counter alternative are also derived logically.[52] Research evidence suggests this technique can also help reach high-quality decisions.[53]

Other human-based methods exist for improving group decision making. These diverse methods have many names including "appreciative management" and "Technology of Participation." They recognize that decision-making groups are increasingly diverse with many different viewpoints. The goal of these methods is to harness differences, decrease dysfunctional conflict, and focus diverse members on the organization's goals.[54]

Computer-Based Methods

Computer-based methods of improving decisions in organizations include management information systems, decision support systems, and expert systems. The rapid spread of computer-based methods means you will likely encounter some of these systems in your work career.

Management information systems are information processing systems used by organizations to support their daily operating activities and decision-making functions. The systems can be manual, but are most powerful when they are computer based. Management information systems integrate different subsystems according to a general information management plan. Data within the subsystems conform to the specifications of the integrated system, allowing easy sharing throughout the system.[55] Multiple users reach the management information system with terminals or personal computers (PCs). Users get a wide range of data, decision models, and database querying methods. Management information systems strongly support the analytical, strategic planning, and decision activities of an organization.

Decision support systems are computer-based systems designed to aid human decision makers' judgment. These systems do not automate an organization's decision processes; instead, they support those processes and help decision makers arrive at better decisions. Decision support systems are dynamic systems that change and evolve as a decision maker uses them. They can also be tailored to a decision maker's way of making decisions. An organization could have several decision support systems for different decision makers and classes of decisions. Contemporary uses of such systems include sales forecasting, cargo aircraft flight schedules, and medical decisions.[56]

Expert systems support decision making by simulating an expert's knowledge and decision process. An expert system designed to help medical diagnosis, for example, has a database of symptoms and a set of decision rules that guide a user through a diagnosis. Users access the interactive systems through a terminal or a PC. The users do not need to be experts in the area covered by the expert system.[57]

INTERNATIONAL ASPECTS OF DECISION MAKING AND PROBLEM SOLVING

The earlier description of the decision process phases applies most directly to decision making in the United States, Canada, and some European countries.[58] The behavior of a single decision maker, or those participating in each phase, varies depending on the culture in which the decision process happens. Because behaviors vary, decision makers from different cultures who must interact to reach decisions often have difficulty understanding each other's behavior.

Decision makers from different cultures bring different orientations to the problem identification and diagnosis phase of decision making. Some cultures focus on solving problems. Other cultures accept their situation and rely on providence to take care of the future. U.S. decision makers, for example, often see problems as something to attack and solve. Malaysian, Thai, and Indonesian decision makers usually try to adjust to the problem and accept situations presented to them.

Evaluating and choosing alternatives differs dramatically across cultures. The person who makes the decision, the speed of the decision process, and the risk allowed in choosing alternatives all vary from culture to culture. Decision making is more centralized in Philippine and Indian organizations than in Swedish and Austrian organizations.[59] Decision making proceeds slowly in Egyptian organizations, but quickly in U.S. organizations. Decision makers in Singapore and Denmark are more likely to take bigger risks than decision makers in Portugal and Greece.[60] Cultures also vary in the order in which decision makers assess alternatives. Decision makers in Japan and China usually consider all alternatives before choosing. Decision makers in the United States, Germany, and Canada typically use a serial process, rejecting alternatives along the way to a final choice.

ETHICAL ISSUES IN DECISION MAKING AND PROBLEM SOLVING

Decision-making and problem-solving processes in organizations raise several ethical concerns.[61] Ethical questions can arise not only when choosing among alternatives, but also when setting the goal for a decision, creating a set of alternatives, and assessing them. Other ethical questions arise when carrying out the decision.

An ethical decision maker willingly engages in an open and fair dialogue with all parties potentially affected by the decision.[62] The decision maker's responsibilities include giving information freely without deceiving others involved. The moral decision maker likely does not know the right answer for every ethical issue, but freely discusses all issues with affected parties.

A model of decision making and ethics has been proposed that tries to explain why unethical decisions happen.[63] The model proposes that decision makers who face ethical issues in a decision proceed in two phases. The first phase applies a decision rule that states a minimum cutoff for each dimension. An ethical rule in this phase could state, "We reject any alternative that creates a conflict of interest." When an alternative passes that rule, the decision maker then assesses it further by considering its benefits or costs weighted by its importance.

Research underlying this model suggests decision makers consider the ethical dimension with other dimensions when assessing alternatives. Positive benefits of dimensions other than the ethical one can overwhelm an undesirable ethical dimension. The ethical dimension also can have negative effects with little likelihood of happening. For example, the penalty is a large fine, but the organization is unlikely to be caught, which might lead decision makers to an unethical decision.

SUMMARY

Decision making is the process of choosing among different courses of action using decision criteria. The criteria for choosing among alternatives can include cost, profit, danger, or pleasure.

Some decision-making models describe a process for problems with well-known alternatives, results, and decision rules (Rational Model). Another model describes a process for conditions of uncertainty and ambiguity (Garbage Can Model). Each model gives different insights into organizational decision processes.

Managers can choose from different social processes for individual and group decisions. These approaches include processes involving a single individual, consultation with one or more people, or groups designed to reach consensus.

Decision makers use several heuristics or guidelines to simplify information processing during decision making. Such information processing strategies let decision makers move quickly through the process, but also limit the information they use, resulting in several judgment biases.

Decision makers can frame a decision in two different ways with different effects on their decision behavior. People prefer to avoid risks in decisions framed as gains; they prefer to take risks in decisions framed as losses.

Decision makers often face a common dilemma: abandon a losing course of action or increase commitment to it. Evidence supports that most decision makers are more likely to commit more resources, a process called escalation of commitment to a losing course of action.

Cohesive decision-making groups often develop groupthink, a phenomenon featuring excessive conformity to group norms that support agreement about decisions. Decision groups with groupthink are unable to critically assess alternative solutions to a problem.

Several human-based methods and computer-based methods exist for improving decision making in organizations. Human-based methods include brainstorming and techniques for increasing the information available to a decision maker (for example, the nominal group technique and the Delphi method). Computer-based methods include management information systems, decision support systems, and expert systems.

The international context of organizations adds complexities to organizational decision processes. Cultural variations in decision-making behavior and decision orientations suggest potential difficulties for multicultural decision-making groups.

An ethical decision maker has an open dialogue with all parties potentially affected by a decision and does not engage in deceptive behavior. A proposed model of decision making and ethics uses an explicit ethics decision rule.

SUMMARY
14

REVIEW AND DISCUSSION QUESTIONS

1 Review the decision-making process. Discuss each step in the process and the relationships among them.

2 Review the decision-making models described in this chapter. Which model do you think is closest to what managers do when they make decisions? Why?

3 Review the assets and liabilities of group decision making. Which methods of improving decision making in organizations help offset the liabilities? How? Why?

4 Have you experienced groupthink? Discuss the conditions under which it happened and how it could have been prevented.

5 Discuss the different methods of improving decision making in organizations. Which of these methods do you expect to find widely used in organizations? Discuss differences in how easy it is to use each method of improvement.

6 Discuss the culturally based differences in decision making and problem solving described in this chapter with students from countries other than your own or with students who have visited other countries. Have any students experienced the differences described? Discuss their reactions to those differences.

7 Review the discussion of ethics in decision making and problem solving. Discuss the value of explicitly considering the ethics of a decision.

TAKE FIVE: OB ALIVE: *HORRIBLE BOSSES* (2011)

Dale (Charlie Day), Kurt (Jason Sudeikis), and Nick (Jason Bateman) each have a different boss but share a common feeling about them: they want to see them dead. The film shows the complex process the three use to focus on the death of their bosses.

This scene begins in DVD Chapter 3 (00:26:32) as Dale pulls up to Nick Hendricks' (Jason Bateman) house and runs through the front door. It ends in DVD Chapter 3 (00:28:21) after Dale says "Because I don't have it figured out. But I will." The film cuts to a panning shot of the city. This scene has some R-rated language.

Consider the following questions while viewing this scene: What factors do they consider in deciding their qualifications? Do they decide to find another party ("hit man") to carry out the killings?

REFERENCES AND NOTES

1. Bromiley, P., and D. Rau. 2011. Strategic Decision Making. In *APA Handbook of Industrail and Organizational Psychology*, Vol. 1, ed. S. Zedeck. Washington, DC: American Psychology Association, Chap. 6.
   Koopman, P. L., and J. Pool. 1990. Decision Making in Organizations. In *International Review of Industrial and Organizational Psychology*, Vol. 5. ed. C. L. Cooper and I. T. Robertson. Chichester: John Wiley & Sons, Chap. 4.
   Wilson, C. Z., and M. Alexis. 1962. Basic Frameworks for Decisions. *Academy of Management Journal* 5: 150–64.
2. Huber, G. P. 1980. *Managerial Decision Making*. Glenview, IL: Scott, Foresman, pp. 8–9.
3. Developed from ibid.
   March, J. G., and H. A. Simon. 1958. *Organizations*. New York: John Wiley & Sons, pp. 180–82.
   Vroom, V. H., and A. G. Jago. 1988. *The New Leadership: Managing Participation in Organizations*. Englewood Cliffs: Prentice Hall.
4. Barnard, C. I. 1938. *The Functions of the Executive*. Cambridge, MA: Harvard University Press.
5. Developed from E. F. Harrison. 1975. *The Managerial Decision Making Process*. Boston: Houghton Mifflin, pp. 13–15.
   Starke, K., and M. Brand. 2016. Effects of Stress on Decisions Under Uncertainty: A Meta-Analysis. *Psychological Bulletin* 142: 909–33.
6. March and Simon, *Organizations*, p. 137.
7. Simon, H. A. 1960. *The New Science of Management Decision*. New York: Harper & Row, pp. 5–6.
8. Developed from Koopman and Pool, Decision Making in Organizations.
   Harrison, *The Managerial Decision Making Process*, Chap. 2.
   Huber, *Managerial Decision Making*, Chap. 2.
9. Abelson, R. P., and A. Levi. 1985. Decision Making and Decision Theory. In *The Handbook of Social Psychology*, Vol. 1., ed. G. Lindzey and E. Aronson. Reading, MA: Addison-Wesley, Chap. 5.
10. Barnard, *The Functions of the Executive*.
11. Developed from March and Simon, *Organizations*.
    Simon, H. A. 1997. *Administrative Behavior: A Study of Decision-Making Processes in Administrative Organizations*, 4th edn. New York: Free Press.
12. Developed from March and Simon, *Organizations*, Chap. 6.
    Simon, *Administrative Behavior*.
13. March and Simon, *Organizations*, p. 141.
14. Koopman and Pool, Decision Making in Organizations.
    Newell, A., and H. A. Simon. 1972. *Human Problem Solving*. Englewood Cliffs: Prentice Hall.
    Mintzberg, H., D. Raisinghani, and A. Theoret. 1976. The Structure of "Unstructured" Decision Processes. *Administrative Science Quarterly* 21: 246–75.
    Simon, *The New Science*.
15. Mintzberg, Raisinghani, and Theoret, The Structure of "Unstructured" Decision Processes, pp. 250–51. (Emphasis in original.)
16. March and Simon, *Organizations*, pp. 140–41.
17. Mintzberg, Raisinghani, and Theoret, The Structure of "Unstructured" Decision Processes, pp. 263–66.

18. Soelberg, P. O. 1967. Unprogrammed Decision Making. *Industrial Management Review* 8: 19–29.

19. March, J. G., and J. P. Olsen, eds. 1976. *Ambiguity and Choice in Organizations*. Bergen: Universitetsforlaget.

    March, J. G., and J. P. Olsen. 1986. Garbage Can Models of Decision Making in Organizations. In *Ambiguity and Command: Organizational Perspectives on Military Decision Making*, ed. J. G. March and R. Weissinger-Baylon. Cambridge, MA: Ballinger, pp. 11–35.

    A recent summary of research appears in N. Takahashi. 1997. A Single Garbage Can Model and the Degree of Anarchy in Japanese Firms. *Human Relations* 50: 91–108.

20. Pfeffer, J. 1982. *Organizations and Organization Theory*. Marshfield: Pitman Publishing.

21. Developed from F. C. Brodbeck, R. Kerschreiter, A. Mojzisch, and S. Schhulz-Harqdt. 2007. Group Decision Making under Conditions of Distributed Knowledge: The Information Asymmetries Model. *Academy of Management Review* 32: 459–79.

    George, E., and P. Chattopadhyay. 2008. Group Composition and Decision Making. In *The Oxford Handbook of Organizational Decision Making*, ed. G. P. Hodgkinson and W. H. Starbuck. Oxford: Oxford University Press, Chap. 19.

    Gist, M. E., E. A. Locke, and M. S. Taylor. 1987. Organizational Behavior: Group Structure, Process, and Effectiveness. *Journal of Management* 13: 237–57.

    Hare, A. P. 1992. *Groups, Teams, and Social Interaction: Theories and Applications*. New York: Praeger, p. 4.

    Maier, N. R. F. 1967. Assets and Liabilities in Group Problem Solving: The Need for an Integrative Function. *Psychological Review* 74: 239–49.

    Nemeth, C. J., and B. Nemeth-Brown. 2003. Better than Individuals? The Potential Benefits of Dissent and Diversity for Group Creativity. In *Group Creativity: Innovation Through Collaboration*, ed. P. B. Paulus and B. A. Nijstad. New York: Oxford University Press, Chap. 4.

    Pate, S., W. E. Watson, and L. Johnson. 1998. The Effects of Competition on the Decision Quality of Diverse and Nondiverse Groups. *Journal of Applied Social Psychology* 28: 912–23.

    Vroom and Jago, *The New Leadership*, Chap. 3.

    Wagner, J. A., III, C. R. Leana, E. A. Locke, and D. M. Schweiger. 1997. Cognitive and Motivation Frameworks in U.S. Research on Participation: A Meta-Analysis of Primary Effects. *Journal of Organizational Behavior* 18: 49–65.

    West, M. A. 2003. Innovation Implementation in Work Teams. In *Group Creativity: Innovation Through Collaboration*, ed. P. B. Paulus and B. A. Nijstad. New York: Oxford University Press, Chap. 12.

22. Alper, S., D. Tjosvold, and K. S. Law. 1998. Interdependence and Controversy in Group Decision Making: Antecedents to Effective Self-Managing Teams. *Organizational Behavior and Human Decision Processes* 74: 33–52.

23. Black, J. S., and H. B. Gregersen. 1997. Participative Decision-Making: An Integration of Multiple Dimensions. *Human Relations* 50: 859–78.

24. Developed from V. H. Vroom and A. G. Jago. 1974. Decision Making as a Social Process: Normative and Descriptive Models of Leader Behavior. *Decision Sciences* 5: 743–69.

    Vroom and Jago, *The New Leadership*.

    Vroom, V. H., and P. Yetton. 1973. *Leadership and Decision-Making*. Pittsburgh: University of Pittsburgh Press.

25. Pasewark, W. R., and J. R. Strawser. 1994. Subordinate Participation in Audit Budgeting Decisions: A Comparison of Decisions Influenced by Organizational Factors to Decisions Conforming with the Vroom-Jago Model. *Decision Sciences* 25: 281–99.

   Vroom and Jago, *The New Leadership*, Chap. 6.

26. Field, R. H. G. 1982. A Test of the Vroom-Yetton Normative Model of Leadership. *Journal of Applied Psychology* 67: 523–32.

   Field, R. H. G., and R. J. House. 1990. A Test of the Vroom-Yetton Model Using Manager and Subordinate Reports. *Journal of Applied Psychology* 75: 362–66.

   Vroom, V. H., and A. G. Jago. 1978. On the Validity of the Vroom-Yetton Model. *Journal of Applied Psychology* 63: 151–62.

27. Ettling, J. T., and A. G. Jago. 1988. Participation under Conditions of Conflict: More on the Validity of the Vroom-Yetton Model. *Journal of Management Studies* 25: 73–83.

28. Tversky, A., and D. Kahneman. 1973. Availability: A Heuristic for Judging Frequency and Probability. *Cognitive Psychology* 5: 207–32.

29. Kahneman, D., and A. Tversky. 1972. Subjective Probability: A Judgment of Representativeness. *Cognitive Psychology* 3: 430–54.

   Kahneman, D., and A. Tversky. 1973. On the Psychology of Prediction. *Psychological Review* 80: 237–51.

30. Nisbett, R. E., and L. Ross. 1980. *Human Inference: Strategies and Shortcomings of Social Judgment*. Englewood Cliffs: Prentice Hall.

   Tversky, A., and D. Kahneman. 1974. Judgment under Uncertainty: Heuristics and Biases. *Science* 185: 1124–31.

31. Bazerman, M. H. 1994. Biases. *Judgment in Managerial Decision Making*. New York: John Wiley & Sons, Chap. 2.

   Tversky and Kahneman, Judgment Under Uncertainty.

32. Bazerman, *Judgment in Managerial Decision Making*, p. 24.

33. Kahneman, D., and A. Tversky. 1979. Prospect Theory: An Analysis of Decisions Under Risk. *Econometrica* 47: 263–91.

   Kuhberger, A. 1998. The Influence of Framing on Risky Decisions: A Meta-Analysis. *Organizational Behavior and Human Decision Processes* 75: 23–55.

   Levin, I. P., S. L. Schneider, and G. J. Gaeth. 1998. All Frames are Not Created Equal: A Typology and Critical Analysis of Framing Effects. *Organizational Behavior and Human Decision Processes* 76: 149–88.

   The classic treatment of framing effects appears in A. Tversky and D. Kahneman. 1981. The Framing of Decisions and the Psychology of Choice. *Science* 211: 453–58.

34. Kahneman, D., and A. Tversky. 1984. Choices, Values, and Frames. *American Psychologist* 39: 341–50.

   Whyte, G. 1991. Decision Failures: Why They Occur and How to Prevent Them. *Academy of Management Executive* 5: 23–31.

35. Whyte, Decision Failures.

36. Bazerman, *Judgment in Managerial Decision Making*, p. 61.

   Nutt, P. C. 1993. The Formulation Processes and Tactics Used in Organizational Decision Making. *Organization Science* 4: 226–51.

37. Sleesman, D. J., A. C. Lennard, G. McNamara, and D. E. Conlon. 2017. Putting Escalation of Commitment in Context: A Multilevel Review and Analysis. *Academy of Management Annals* 12: 178–207.

Staw, B. M. 1981. The Escalation of Commitment to a Course of Action. *Academy of Management Review* 6: 577–87.

Staw, B. M., and J. Ross. 1987. Behavior in Escalation Situations: Antecedents, Prototypes, and Solutions. In *Research in Organizational Behavior*, Vol. 9, ed. B. M. Staw and L. L. Cummings. Greenwich, CT: JAI Press, pp. 39–78.

38. Keil, M., B. C. Y. Tan, K.-K. Wei, T. Saarinen, V. Tuunainen, and A. Wassenaar. 2000. A Cross-Cultural Study on Escalation of Commitment Behavior in Software Projects. *MIS Quarterly* 24: 299–325.

39. Edwards, W. 1954. The Theory of Decision Making. *Psychological Bulletin* 51: 380–417.

40. Summarized in J. Ross and B. M. Staw. 1993. Organizational Escalation and Exit: Lessons from the Shoreham Nuclear Power Plant. *Academy of Management Journal* 36: 701–32.

Staw and Ross, Behavior in Escalation Situations.

Whyte, G. 1986. Escalating Commitment to a Course of Action: A Reinterpretation. *Academy of Management Review* 11: 311–21.

41. Whyte, G., A. M. Saks, and S. Hook. 1997. When Success Breeds Failure: The Role of Self-Efficacy in Escalating Commitment to a Losing Course of Action. *Journal of Organizational Behavior* 18: 415–32.

42. McConnell, M. 1987. *Challenger: A Major Malfunction*. New York: Doubleday.

43. Janis, I. L. 1971. Groupthink. *Psychology Today* (November), pp. 43–46, 74–76.

Janis, I. L. 1982. *Groupthink: Psychological Studies of Policy Decisions and Fiascoes*, 2nd edn. Boston: Houghton Mifflin.

Janis, I. L. 1989. *Crucial Decisions: Leadership in Policymaking and Crisis Management*. New York: Free Press.

Janis, I. L., and L. Mann. 1989. *Decision Making: A Psychological Analysis of Conflict, Choice, and Commitment*. New York: Free Press.

44. George and Chattopadhyay, Group Composition and Decision Making.

Turner, M. E., and A. R. Pratkanis. 1997. Mitigating Groupthink by Stimulating Constructive Conflict. In *Using Conflict in Organizations*, ed. C. K. W. De Dreau and E. V. de Vliert. London: Sage Publishing, Chap. 4.

45. Aldag, R. J., and S. R. Fuller. 1993. Beyond Fiasco: A Reappraisal of the Groupthink Phenomenon and a New Model of Group Decision Processes. *Psychological Bulletin* 113: 533–52.

Esser, J. K. 1998. Alive and Well After 25 Years: A Review of Groupthink Research. *Organizational Behavior and Human Decision Processes* 73: 116–41.

Kerr, N. L., and R. S. Tindale. 2004. Group Performance and Decision Making. *Annual Review of Psychology* 55: 623–65. See p. 640 for a summary of groupthink research.

Longley, J., and D. G. Pruitt. 1980. Groupthink: A Critique of Janis's Theory. In *Review of Personality and Social Psychology*, ed. L. Wheeler. Newbury Park: Sage Publishing, pp. 507–13.

Park, W. 1990. A Review of Research on Groupthink. *Journal of Behavioral Decision Making* 3: 229–45.

46. Bouchard, T. J. 1971. Whatever Happened to Brainstorming? *Journal of Creative Behavior* 5: 182–89.

Litchfield, R. C. 2008. Brainstorming Reconsidered: A Goal-Based View. *Academy of Management Review* 33: 649–68.

Osborn, A. F. 1963. *Applied Imagination: Principles and Procedures of Creative Thinking*, 3rd edn. New York: Charles Scribner's Sons.

Rickards, T. 1999. Brainstorming Revisited: A Question of Context. *International Journal of Management Reviews* 1: 91–110.

47. Dennis, A. R., and M. L. Williams. 2003. Electronic Brainstorming: Theory, Research, and Future Directions. In *Group Creativity: Innovation Through Collaboration*, ed. P. B. Paulus and B. A. Nijstad. New York: Oxford University Press, Chap. 8.

    Gallupe, R. B., and W. H. Cooper. 1993. Brainstorming Electronically. *Sloan Management Review* 35: 27–36.

    Gallupe, R. B., A. R. Dennis, W. H. Cooper, J. S. Valacich, L. M. Bastianutti, and J. F. Nunamaker, Jr. 1992. Electronic Brainstorming and Group Size. *Academy of Management Journal* 35: 350–69.

    Kerr and Tindale, Group Performance and Decision Making, pp. 627–28.

    Nunamaker, J. F., Jr., R. O. Briggs, and D. D. Mittleman. 1996. Lessons from a Decade of Group Support Systems Research. In *Information Systems: Decision Support and Knowledge-Based Systems*, Vol. 3, ed. J. F. Nunamaker, Jr. and R. H. Sprague, Jr. Washington, DC: IEEE Computer Society Press, pp. 418–27.

48. Bartunek, J. M., and J. K. Murninghan. 1984. The Nominal Group Technique: Expanding the Basic Procedure and Underlying Assumptions. *Groups and Organizational Studies* 9: 417–32.

    Cook, C. W. 1980. Nominal Group Methods Enrich Classroom Learning. *Exchange: The Organizational Behavior Teaching Journal* 5: 33–36.

    Delbecq, A. L., and A. H. Van deVen. 1971. A Group Process Model for Problem Identification and Program Planning. *Journal of Applied Behavioral Science* 7: 466–92.

    Rickards, Brainstorming Revisited.

    Van de Ven, A., and A. L. Delbecq. 1971. Nominal Versus Interacting Group Processes for Decision-Making Effectiveness. *Academy of Management Journal* 14: 203–12.

49. Dalkey, N. C. 1969. *The Delphi Method: An Experimental Study of Group Opinion.* Santa Monica: RAND Corporation.

    Dalkey, N. C., D. L. Rourke, R. Lewis, and D. Snyder, eds. 1972. *Studies in the Quality of Life: Delphi and Decision-Making.* Lexington: Lexington Books.

50. Cosier, R. A., and C. R. Schwenk. 1990. Agreement and Thinking Alike: Ingredients for Poor Decisions. *Academy of Management Executive* 4: 69–74.

    Mason, R. O. 1969. A Dialectical Approach to Strategic Planning. *Management Science* 15: B-403–B-414.

    Schwenk, C. R. 1984. Devil's Advocacy in Managerial Decision Making. *Journal of Management Studies* 21: 153–68.

51. Schweiger, D. M., W. R. Sandberg, and J. W. Ragan. 1986. Group Approaches for Improving Strategic Decision Making: Analysis of Dialectical Inquiry, Devil's Advocacy, and Consensus. *Academy of Management Journal* 29: 51–71.

    Schwenk, C. R. 1990. Effects of Devil's Advocacy and Dialectical Inquiry on Decision Making: A Meta-Analysis. *Organizational Behavior and Human Decision Processes* 47: 161–76.

52. Churchman, C. W. 1971. *The Design of Inquiring Systems: Basic Concepts of Systems and Organization.* New York: Basic Books.

    Cosier and Schwenk, Agreement and Thinking Alike.

53. Schweiger, Sandberg, and Ragan, Group Approaches.

    Schweiger, D. M., W. R. Sandberg, and P. L. Rechner. 1989. Experiential Effects of Dialectical Inquiry, Devil's Advocacy, and Consensus Approaches to Strategic Decision Making. *Academy of Management Journal* 32: 745–72.

54. Cooperider, D. L. 1990. Positive Image, Positive Action: The Affirmative Basis of Organizing. In *Appreciative Management and Leadership: The Power of Positive Thought and Action in Organizations*, ed. S. Srivasta, D. L. Cooperider, and Associates. San Francisco: Jossey-Bass, Chap. 4.

Spence, L. J. 1989. *Winning through Participation: Meeting the Challenge of Corporate Change with the Technology of Participation*. Dubuque, Iowa: Kendall/Hunt Publishing Co.

55. McLeod, R., Jr. 1993. *Management Information Systems: A Study of Computer-Based Information Systems*. New York: Macmillan.

56. Antes, J., L. Campen, U. Derigs, C. Titze, and G.-D. Wolle. 1998. SYNOPSE: A Model-Based Decision Support System for the Evaluation of Flight Schedules for Cargo Airlines. *Decision Support Systems* 22: 307–23.

Kuo, R. J., and K. C. Xue. 1998. A Decision Support System for Sales Forecasting Through Fuzzy Neural Networks with Asymmetric Fuzzy Weights. *Decision Support Systems* 24: 105–26.

McLeod, *Management Information Systems*, Chap. 13.

Rao, G. R., and M. Turoff. 2000. A Hypermedia-Based Group Decision Support System to Support Collaborative Medical Decision-Making. *Decision Support Systems* 30: 187–216.

Sprague, R. H., and E. D. Carlson. 1982. *Building Effective Decision Support Systems*. Englewood Cliffs: Prentice Hall.

57. McLeod, *Management Information Systems*, Chap. 15.

58. Developed from the following and other citations throughout: N. J. Adler, with A. Gundersen. 2008. *International Dimensions of Organizational Behavior*, 5th edn. Mason: Thomson South-Western, Chap. 8.

59. Hofstede, G. 2001. *Culture's Consequences: Comparing Values, Behaviors, Institutions, and Organizations across Nations*, 2nd edn. Thousand Oaks: Sage Publishing.

60. Ibid., Chap. 4.

61. Harrison, *The Managerial Decision Making Process*, pp. 131–37.

62. Bowen, M. G., and F. C. Power. 1993. The Moral Manager: Communicative Ethics and the Exxon Valdez Disaster. *Business Ethics Quarterly* 3: 97–115.

63. Fritzsche, D. J. 1991. A Model of Decision-Making Incorporating Ethical Values. *Journal of Business Ethics* 10: 841–52.

Chapter 15

POWER AND POLITICAL BEHAVIOR

After reading this chapter, you should be able to:

- Describe the nature of power in organizations.
- Discuss the relationship between power and politics in organizations.
- Analyze bases of power and ways of building power in organizations.
- Describe political behavior in organizations.
- Discuss political strategies and their role in organizations.
- Compare the political tactics a manager can use in a political strategy.
- Do a political diagnosis.
- Discuss each element of the dark side of organizational politics—lying, deception, and intimidation.
- Analyze international differences in political behavior in organizations.
- Distinguish the ethical issues surrounding organizational politics.

Power and political behavior pervade organizational life, affecting everyone, not only senior executives. Of these two constructs, political behavior has the more divisive intellectual history. Some researchers describe political behavior as an important way to understand and explain much of the behavior that occurs in organizations. Other researchers view political behavior as a necessary evil of organizational life. The formal organization often does not recognize this social influence process, but it is essential to much of managerial work. Political behavior processes can serve organizational goals for some managers and the self-interest of others.[1]

This chapter focuses on the development and use of power in organizations and the role political behavior plays in building and using that power. You can decide for yourself whether political behavior is a necessary or essential evil in organizations.

POWER

Power is a person's ability to get something done the way he wants it done.[2] Power lets a person affect other people's behavior, get people to do what they otherwise might not do, overcome resistance to changing direction, and overcome opposition. Someone with power also can prevent controversial issues from surfacing, especially during decision-making processes.[3] Power includes the ability to gather and use physical and human resources to reach the person's goals.[4] Although power has a negative meaning for many people,[5] it can have positive effects in organizations.

Power is essential to the functions of leadership and management.[6] More than simply dominance, power is the capacity to get things done in an organization. Powerful managers and leaders can achieve more, get more resources for their subordinates, and give their subordinates more chances to develop and grow. Power is also a necessary part of controlling your fate and building self-esteem.[7]

Power in organizations has the distinct facets of potential power, actual power, and the potential for power.[8] **Potential power** exists when one party perceives another party as having power and the ability to use it. **Actual power** is the presence and use of power. The use of power may or may not successfully reach desired results. Use of power, whether successful or unsuccessful, is actual power.[9] **Potential for power** is the chance that individuals or groups have to build a power base with resources they control. The facets of power imply a perceptual basis of power. Power exists when one party perceives that another party has potential power, actual power, or the ability to build a power base.

A **power relationship** is a moment of social interaction where power shows itself in organizations. Three dimensions define power relationships.[10] The **relational** dimension is the social interaction part of power. Power in organizations happens during social interactions between people and groups. The **dependence** dimension views power as how much one party relies on the actions of another. Dependence is high when valued results are unavailable from another source. High power follows from high dependence. The **sanctioning** dimension refers to one party's ability to affect the results of the other party by using rewards, penalties, or both. This power dimension has both actual and potential aspects. Actual sanctioning arises because of observations of sanctioning behavior. Potential sanctioning arises from expected sanctions or from the person's reputation for using sanctions.[11]

Power and authority are different concepts, although a person can have both power and authority.[12] Authority is the right to make decisions and to give direction to other people in an organization. Such authority comes to a person because of his position in the organization. It often is formally recognized in writing so people know their authority relationships. Look back at the definition of power given earlier. That definition associated power with a person's ability to get things done, not with the person's position in an organization. A person with power can be at any level in an organization, not just at the senior levels.

Power flows in all directions in organizations.[13] It flows along the vertical dimension of organizations within superior–subordinate relationships. Power can also flow upward within superior–subordinate relationships. Here the subordinate influences his superior, a process some call "managing the boss."[14] The third direction of power is lateral. Managers usually are highly dependent on others at the same level for cooperation and resources. A manager needs to influence people and groups outside his direct reporting relationships. Such influence extends to people and groups in other departments, in other work units, and outside the organization.[15]

Power is dynamic, not static.[16] As the organization's external environment changes, different subsystems of the organization, different individuals, and different coalitions may emerge as seats of power. Individuals, departments, and work units that are powerful at one point in the organization's history may not be powerful at another point. For example, individuals and units responsible for marketing a successful new product are likely to develop power, but if the product's market share drops, their power will likely subside.

Bases of Power

Much of a manager's success in an organization depends on the influence he has over others. A manager's power decides the amount of influence he has over a subordinate. A manager can draw on several sources or **bases of power** that come from both his formal management position and his personal characteristics.[17]

Figure 15.1 shows the organizational and personal bases of power as accumulating to a total power base. The amount of power a leader or manager has depends

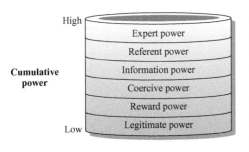

High

Cumulative power

Low

Expert power
Referent power
Information power
Coercive power
Reward power
Legitimate power

Figure 15.1: The Cumulative Effects of the Bases of Power

on the number of bases he has available. Some research is beginning to add to the bases shown in Figure 15.1.[18] The six shown remain the most common ones investigated in organizational research.[19]

Some managers have only the organizational bases of power to influence people. Other managers have both organizational and personal bases. These people are in the enviable position of having many bases of power at their disposal.

Organizational Bases of Power

The **organizational bases of power** are legitimate power, reward power, coercive power, and information power. **Legitimate power** derives from the manager's position. The organization gives the manager decision authority that he uses to affect the behavior of subordinates. Assigning tasks and setting goals for completing them are examples of legitimate power.

Reward power derives from the manager's ability to tie positive outcomes to a subordinate's behavior. A manager has high reward power if he can give positive outcomes for desirable behavior. Positive outcomes can include praise, pay increases, or time off. The use of reward power to provide positive outcomes makes the manager more attractive to the subordinate. You will see later in this chapter that understanding the subordinates' desires for various outcomes is an important part of leadership.

Coercive power derives from efforts to affect the behavior of another person through the fear of punishment. A manager has high coercive power if he has the authority to penalize subordinates. A manager has low coercive power if he has no such authority. The spoken or unspoken threat of a poor evaluation of a subordinate's performance is an example of coercive power.

Information power derives from the control and distribution of information in an organization.[20] Deliberately controlling the receipt and distribution of information increases a manager's information power. People who hold central positions in communication networks (for example, relayer and liaison; see Chapter 13, "Communication Processes") can often build this power base.[21] When information is scarce, others become more dependent on the manager for information.[22]

Each management position in an organization has certain amounts of organization-based power. The amount of power in a position varies, depending on the organization's policies about rewards and punishments. The person who takes that position has some organization-based power available to affect the behavior of subordinates. When the person leaves the position, the power stays behind and does not travel with the person to a new position.

Personal Bases of Power

The **personal bases of power** flow from the manager's qualities or attributes. Those bases also depend on how subordinates attribute those qualities to the manager. The personal bases of power available to a manager with one group of subordinates will not be available to the same manager with a different group of subordinates. The personal bases of power are referent power and expert power.

Referent power is based on the personal liking a subordinate has for a manager. The more the subordinate identifies with the manager, the stronger the referent power. A manager who is disliked by a subordinate has low referent power.

Expert power derives from the manager's technical knowledge and expertise. A manager with the knowledge and skills needed for group success has high expert power. A manager with little knowledge has low expert power. The source of the manager's influence is the subordinates' dependence on the manager for the information that they need to do their job successfully.

Power, Leadership, and Management

Powerful leaders and managers delegate decision authority to subordinates and view their subordinates' talents as a resource. Such leaders and managers can more easily change their subordinates' working conditions than powerless leaders and managers can. The powerful can get the resources and information that subordinates need to be effective. They take risks and press for innovations in their organizations. Subordinates of powerful leaders and managers can develop from the new experiences and increase their promotional opportunities. Powerful leaders and managers often share their power with their subordinates, creating more total power for the entire workgroup.[23] A leader who uses power fairly has stronger positive effects on subordinates than one who uses power unfairly.[24]

Because having and using power are key characteristics of a leader, power-lessness is more a feature of managers and supervisors than of leaders. Those with little or no power use close supervision and do not delegate authority to subordinates. They often distrust their subordinates and view talented subordinates as threatening. Such managers and supervisors stick to the rules and do not take risks. Subordinates who work for the powerless do not have the chance to develop from involvement in new activities. Powerless managers and supervisors strongly focus on the work of their group, protecting it from outside interference. Their workgroup becomes "their" territory, a symbol they use to try to increase their significance in the organization.

Building Power

The task of **building power** identifies the power sources shown in Figure 15.2. Leaders and managers can use these sources to build their power base. An important step in building power is a political diagnosis. A later section of this chapter describes how to do a diagnosis.[25]

A person can build power from his **knowledge, reputation, and professional credibility**. People with specialized knowledge have power if other people depend on that knowledge to do their jobs. A person's reputation builds from a series of successes. Power grows as a manager or leader develops a positive

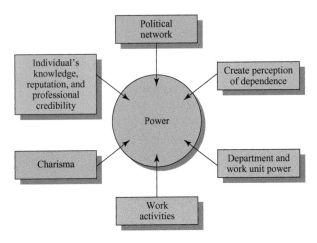

Figure 15.2: Sources of Power in Organizations

reputation. Giving talks at professional meetings and serving on committees of professional associations, for example, can increase a person's professional credibility, which can lead to influence both outside and inside the organization.

A person can create a strong power base by building a **political network** within an organization. A political network depends on the person's communication channels in the organization. The communication can follow the formal organizational design or be informal in character. Forming alliances with other peer leaders and managers adds to a person's power base in an organization.

Creating a perception of dependence is still another way to build power in an organization. The perception comes from the belief that the leader or manager controls scarce resources, including people, equipment, money, information, and rewards, and can use these resources to help or impede other people. Note that the leader or manager does not need to actually control the resources. The perception of control is the key to this method of building power.

The **power base of the work unit** headed by the manager or leader depends on the department's capability to cope with uncertainty, its unique functions, changes in the external environment, and its centrality to the organization's workflow. The movement of power among departments is part of its dynamic character.

Departments that reduce uncertainty for an organization can have high power. For example, human resource management departments that become expert in affirmative action, equal employment opportunity, and workforce diversity can increase their power in their organizations.[26] Departments offering a service available from few other sources in the organization have high power as well. Departments at key points in the workflow of an organization also enjoy considerable power. Managers or leaders whose departments hold a central position or perform a unique function in an organization can build a strong power base for themselves.

Work activities can also be another source of power. Work activities that are extraordinary, visible, and appropriate to the organization's goals are important sources of power. Extraordinary work activities usually are risky activities successfully done. Other people in the organization notice the results and develop positive feelings about the successful person. A person who is continuously successful at high-risk work activities may be regarded as charismatic.

Chapter 12, "Leadership and Management," discussed **charisma** as an important quality of leadership. Its importance comes from the power a charismatic person has over others. Those who attribute charisma to a manager or leader feel inspired by his ideas and become committed to carrying them out. Although charisma is mainly a personality quality, managers and leaders can learn to make effective and influential appeals to others. Charisma is especially important as a source of power in lateral relationships, where the manager or leader has no direct authority.

Attribution of Power

Chapter 5, "Perception, Attitudes, and Personality," described attribution processes of social perception. Attribution processes also operate when power is ascribed to people at all levels in an organization. The power a person assigns to another person may not be the same as the actual power of the other person.

Both personal characteristics and the context in which the person works can lead to the attribution of power. Personal characteristics include the person's formal position in the organization, technical knowledge, and position within a communication network. A person whose formal position has high status and authority will have high formal authority. Others who interact with that person will ascribe to him high power and potential influence. An attribution of power can flow to a person with high technical knowledge, especially in a technical organization. Holding a central position in a communication network might lead others to perceive the person as having high power because of his information access.[27]

The formal and informal contexts of the person also affect how people attribute power to the person. The formal context includes membership in a powerful group or project. A member of such a group can mirror the power of the group and have high power attributed to him. A similar attribution process works for members of informal coalitions and social networks, if an observer believes the coalition or network is powerful.

POLITICAL BEHAVIOR

Political behavior in organizations focuses on getting, developing, and using power to reach a desired result in ambiguous, uncertain, or conflict-filled situations. Such behavior often happens outside accepted channels of authority. You can view political behavior as unofficial, unsanctioned behavior to reach a goal. Such goals often are individual goals, not organizational.[28]

A person can use political behavior to build his bases of power. People also use political behavior to affect decisions, get scarce resources, and earn the cooperation of people outside their direct authority. Political behavior rises and falls with the dynamics of power. A person's need for power also can affect his willingness to become involved in an organization's inevitable political processes.

An organization's political processes have two characteristics that distinguish them from other organizational processes: power and influence.[29] Behavior that uses power, builds power, or tries to influence others is political. Such behavior tries to control a result and can feature high levels of conflict. Political behavior can be directed at reaching organizational goals or individual goals that do not benefit the organization. An example of the latter is a manager who drives his work unit to high-performance levels to enhance his reputation. His demands could increase the stress on people in the work unit and have long-term dysfunctional effects, such as damaged equipment.

People at different organizational levels hold different perceptions of political behavior and react differently to it. People's perceptions tend to focus on reward practices, the presence of dominant groups, and their coworkers' political behavior. Reward practices that are not performance based are associated with negative reactions to supervisors. Favoring influential groups can yield high levels of dissatisfaction. High levels of perceived coworker political behavior are related to high levels of dissatisfaction with coworkers. Nonsupervisory personnel perceive more political behavior, and have stronger negative reactions, than supervisory personnel.[30]

Political behavior is especially important in managing lateral relationships. Three lateral relationships in particular feature political behavior. Line-staff relationships put a staff person in a position of influencing someone else in the organization to approve an important project. Managers of human resources and finance departments usually do not have line authority over those who approve a project and carry it out. They often use their bases of power and political tactics to influence others to adopt the project.

The second type of lateral relationship is competition for resources. Managers use political behavior when competing for resources, such as money, people, equipment, and office space. They compete with other managers at the same organizational level for those resources, but none of the managers can decide the resource allocations directly.

The third type of lateral relationship is interdependence in the workflow. Managers of some work units are often dependent on other work units. Earlier stages in the workflow must be successfully completed for the success of the dependent work unit. Managers must negotiate with the managers of earlier work units to ensure an efficient workflow. Such interdependence is common in serially interdependent manufacturing (assembly lines) and service processes. Processing insurance claims is an example of a service process.

Political behavior and the political processes of organizations can institutionalize the current power holders. Political processes can become part of the organization's cultural fabric, forming a context for daily political behavior.[31] Institutionalization is the product of a mature political process. Those in power build an organizational structure, develop policies, and create information systems that support their power bases. Once in place, these structures prevent people with little power from gaining power against the established coalition.

Political Strategies

A **political strategy** is a written or unwritten plan to reach a goal using specific political tactics. The strategy specifies the goal to reach and the political means to reach that goal. A well-designed political strategy includes a plan for dealing with changes in the political context within which the person works. The plan explicitly recognizes that political events in organizations do not always happen as expected. A political strategy specifies political tactics in various combinations and sequences for dealing with different political events as the strategy unfolds.

Executives, managers, and supervisors are not the only ones who use political strategies. Strategies are available to people at all levels of an organization. This aspect of political strategies is one reason political behavior is so pervasive in organizations. It also helps explain the intrigue organizational politics brings to organizational life.

Researchers have documented political strategies in the following areas:

- Decisions about resource allocations, such as budgets, choice of senior executives, and the design of the organization.[32]
- Career development and enhancement.[33]
- Performance appraisals prepared by a supervisor or manager.[34]
- Pay increase decisions.[35]
- Major organizational change.[36]

Political Tactics

Political tactics are specific political influence behaviors used to reach a goal. The tactics involve either building power or using power unobtrusively. A political strategy can use a mix of tactics, moving from one to another as the political landscape changes.[37]

Decision-making processes can have a distinctly political dimension. Politically oriented decision makers can affect the choice of alternatives that favor themselves or their organizational units. A decision maker can use his power to affect the process by **selectively emphasizing a favored decision alternative**. The alternative he wants will enhance or increase the power of the decision maker or his unit.

A politically oriented decision maker can also call upon an **outside expert or consultant**. Because the consultant is an outsider, he can bring an aura of objectivity and legitimacy to the decision alternatives under consideration. Decision makers call in consultants when power within the decision-making process is about equally dispersed and the issue is critical to either the organization or the individual. When power is well balanced, the decision maker needs another lever to increase his power within the process.

An unobtrusive way of using power in an organization is to **control the decision-making agenda**. People who want matters to stay as they are often use this tactic. By controlling the agenda, they can decide both whether an issue or problem is considered at all and, if considered, where it will appear on the agenda. Items toward the end of an agenda may get less attention than those presented earlier. Decisions made about earlier issues on the agenda can affect later decisions.[38]

People **build coalitions** when they want to create a power base to reach the goals of their political strategy. The coalition can be internal, formed around people and groups within the organization, or external, formed around people and groups outside the organization. In both cases, the decision maker believes the individuals or groups are important to his position.

A person uses **co-optation** as a political tactic to persuade outsiders or insiders to favor his position. Through co-optation, he tries to lure people to his side. The targets of co-optation are potential opponents or people whose help can smooth the way to reaching his goals. Placing outsiders on boards of directors, advisory councils, or task forces can give them information that persuades them that a particular issue or position is important. A politically savvy person can use committees to co-opt insiders. Issues or problems that require information from many sources and the commitment of those sources to a decision can benefit from a committee approach.

Impression management is a highly manipulative political tactic. People use this tactic to control the image they project to another person. Behaviors such as looking busy and asking for more tasks and responsibilities can build positive impressions. Supervisors who want to convey an impression of impartiality during performance feedback can begin with positive commentary before moving to any negative feedback.[39]

Other political tactics include a repertoire of eight **influence tactics**.[40] People can use these tactics to influence others' behavior in the three power flow directions described earlier. The following summarizes the eight tactics:

- **Assertiveness:** Use threats, demands, and intimidation to affect behavior, especially with someone of lower status and power; similar to coercive power described earlier.
- **Ingratiation:** Use flattery and create goodwill with another person to affect his behavior; an element of impression management described earlier.
- **Rationality:** Use a logical argument, oral or written, to affect another person's behavior.
- **Sanctions:** Use organizationally based punishments to affect a person's behavior; coercive power described earlier in the chapter. Used more with subordinates than with coworkers or superiors.
- **Exchange of benefits:** Use favors and benefits to influence another person, especially a coworker.
- **Upward appeal:** Get support for a cause from higher levels in the organization.
- **Inspirational appeal:** Focus on a person's values to arouse emotional support for a proposal. Similar to transformational and charismatic leadership described in Chapter 12, "Leadership and Management."[41]
- **Consultation:** Involve the person you want to influence in the decision process.[42]

Recall that power flows in all directions: downward, laterally, and upward. Some research shows that managers often use consultation, rationality, inspirational appeal, and ingratiation in all three directions.[43] Because power most easily flows downward in organizations, supervisors can use all political tactics in supervisor–subordinate relationships. For example, a supervisor could use sanctions to change the direction of someone's behavior in his work unit. Tactics that can work in lateral relationships include coalitions and upward appeals. A marketing manager who is trying to influence peer managers to accept a marketing campaign could appeal to a higher authority for support. The higher authority could then coerce the peer managers to accept the campaign. Upward influence efforts call for tactics that do not directly use formal authority. Impression management and rationality can help a junior team member affect the thinking of the team leader about the team's direction.[44]

Political Skill

Political skill is a person's ability to interact effectively in various social situations to affect the behavior of another person or group.[45] A politically skilled person gives the impression of sincerity. He leaves a social interaction with the other party or parties feeling a sense of trust and confidence. Politically skilled people can work successfully within an organization's political system, influence others in the desired direction, and gain positive results for themselves and often the organization.

The social situations in which a person uses political skill can occur inside or outside an organization. Using political skill at a social event outside the organization can be as important as using the same skill inside the organization. Interactions also can occur over communication media such as voice mail, e-mail, discussion boards, and chat rooms.

Political skill has the following four dimensions:

- **Social astuteness:** Has high self-awareness; accurately perceives varying social situations; insightfully observes other people's social behavior.
- **Interpersonal influence:** Flexibly adapts behavior in varying social situations to reach desired goals; convincing, but subtle, personal style.
- **Networking ability:** Deliberately gains positions in alliances and coalitions; creates opportunities that help in social interactions; uses those opportunities to own advantage; knows the powerful assets that exist in political networks.
- **Apparent sincerity:** Leaves an impression of openness and honesty (or the person is open and honest); perceived by others as genuine and honest in a social interaction. Apparent sincerity is a key factor in successful social interactions.

Current research suggests that political skill is a personality-level quality that almost anyone can learn. Various forms of management training and coaching can develop political skill. The recommended training goes beyond content-oriented training such as reading the previous paragraphs about political skill. It includes experientially based training, in which a person develops heightened self-awareness and practices the behaviors required for political skill. The latter includes drama-based theatrical training, in which a person learns emotional control, emotional expression, and the use of effective nonverbal behavior.

Political Diagnosis

A political diagnosis assesses where power is located in an organization and what type of political behavior is likely to happen. It identifies politically active individuals and coalitions in the organization, the amount of power they have, and the likely ways they will use their power. The diagnosis also examines political networks in the organization.[46]

A political diagnosis helps an employee understand the political systems present in the organization. Some research shows that employees who understand the political systems have lower anxiety and greater job satisfaction. Members of minority groups in a diverse organization can use a political diagnosis to get political information that the majority group might try to withhold.[47]

Individuals

A political diagnosis focused on individuals:

▨ Identifies the powerful and politically active people in the organization.
▨ Learns the power base of each person.
▨ Assesses each person's skill in using his power base.
▨ Decides how each person is likely to use power.
▨ Identifies the goals each person is trying to reach through power and political behavior.

The political diagnosis collects information in each of those areas from organizational records and key informants inside and outside the organization.

Politically diagnosing individuals begins by identifying presumably powerful people in the organization from an organization chart and a description of titles and duties. This part of the diagnosis also includes identifying people external to the organization who play important roles in its political processes. External individuals might include union officials, regulatory agents, and key financial backers of the organization. Be careful when ascribing power to a person because of position and title. Some people with powerful-sounding titles might not have power.

You can interview a sample of people in the organization about the reputation of those initially identified as power holders. You can also identify major decisions and the people involved in those decisions. These steps test the conclusions from the first step.

After you identify the power holders, you need to assess their power base. The power base depends on both the resources available to the person and his political skill in using those resources. Resources include budget discretion, rewards, sanctions, and information. A power base is strong if the person has discretion in using resources that are important for major issues facing the organization. The power base becomes stronger when there is little substitute for the person's resources and when the resources apply to a wide range of situations.

A diagnosis assesses a person's ability to develop a general political strategy and use the political tactics described earlier. It also is necessary to assess the person's flexibility in using the resources available. This step in the diagnosis relies on both archival information, such as minutes of key decision-making groups and reports, and people in the organization familiar with the power holder's background. These sources can also give information about how the power holder is likely to use his power and the goals he wants to reach.

Coalitions

The political diagnosis then identifies and assesses coalitions in the organization. A **coalition** is an alliance of individuals who share a common goal. Coalitions are also interest groups that try to affect decisions in the organization. Coalitions can have members from widely scattered parts of the organization. The goals of a political diagnosis of coalitions are the same as those listed earlier for individuals.

Information from veteran informants inside and outside the organization can help identify coalitions. Reports of past major decisions are also a useful source of information. Any stable group of people that regularly affects major decisions is a coalition.

The power of a coalition depends on the power bases of its individual members. You can use the methods of assessing an individual's power base described earlier to do an initial assessment of a coalition's power. A coalition's power also depends on how stable its membership is and how effectively it manages group processes. An unstable, mismanaged coalition loses the advantages of its individual members' power. To assess the power of a coalition, you might need to observe the coalition in action. You can infer how a coalition is likely to use its power from the political styles of its high-status members. Often such members strongly affect the coalition's norms. The political goals of a coalition are most easily assessed from its public statements.

Political Networks

Diagnosing political networks gets at the heart of an organization's political processes. **Political networks** form from affiliations and alliances of individuals and coalitions. Political networks can control information and other resources throughout the organization. They also can give support to those in the network and provide a common ideological view.

The diagnosis of networks depends upon knowledge from informants and direct experience in the organization. The diagnosis should identify the people and coalitions that have major influence within the network. Information from the diagnosis helps identify those strategic positions and should identify the individuals with informal access to the organization's decision-making processes. Such people play key political roles in affecting the results of major decisions.

The Dark Side of Organizational Politics: Deception, Lying, and Intimidation

Organizational politics also has a dark side: deception, lying, and intimidation. Machiavellian personalities (see Chapter 5) are especially well adapted to the dark side of organizational politics. Their resistance to social influence, lack of ethical concerns, and use of deception and manipulative tactics make the dark side an attractive part of organizational politics.[48] These gloomy aspects of political behavior help explain why it has a negative image in the eyes of many people.

Deception

The following advice from Niccolò Machiavelli promotes the use of **deception** to build and hold power:

> A prince being thus obliged to know well how to act as a beast must imitate the fox and the lion, for the lion cannot protect himself from traps, and the fox cannot defend himself from wolves. One must therefore be a fox to recognize traps, and a lion to frighten wolves …
>
> [A] prudent ruler ought not to keep faith when by so doing it would be against his interest, and when the reasons which made him bind himself no longer exist … [M]en are so simple and so ready to obey present necessities, that one who deceives will always find those who allow themselves to be deceived.[49]

Today, hundreds of years after Machiavelli's observations, deceptive behavior is still a part of organizational life. Deception tricks another party into arriving at incorrect conclusions or picking the wrong alternative in a decision process. Deceptive behavior happens in organizations when an individual's personal goals become more important than the organization's goals. Here are some examples of deceptive behavior:[50]

- A manager does not want change, but never actually says he does not want change. Instead, he authorizes an endless series of studies that result in everyone forgetting the proposed change.
- An executive appears to select successors based on ability, but really selects them based on loyalty to his ideas.
- An Equal Employment Opportunity (EEO) manager proposes expanding his staff to develop a training program to improve job opportunities for underrepresented groups. Many judge the overt goal as the worthy pursuit of diversity. The EEO manager's covert goal is to increase his chances of a promotion to a higher level, something never discussed in the proposal.

The costs to organizations of the deceptive behavior in this list are clear: high economic costs of endless studies, selection of less-capable successors, and the higher cost of an otherwise worthy diversity-enhancement program.

Despite its costs, some argue that deceptive behavior is functional for organizations.[51] Deceptive behavior brings political intrigue and a sense of uneasiness to an organization. It lends an air of excitement to otherwise routine daily activities. No one knows upon arriving at work which "hidden agenda" will play out on a given day.

Lying

Lying intentionally misstates the truth to mislead another party. Lying helps the liar build power by distorting information in favor of the liar. A person lies to gain a political advantage. Although lying can help a person reach his political goals, the long-term effects include a loss of power, especially if others discover the lie.[52]

Intimidation

The third gloomy side to political behavior uses indirect and direct **intimidation** on someone who wants to reform organizational practices, but does not have the authority to cause such changes. Such people typically are in lower-level organizational positions. They may perceive middle management and upper management as incompetent or acting in illegal or immoral ways.[53]

Managers perceive the reformer as threatening their authority. They first react by trying to intimidate the reformer indirectly. If indirect intimidation does not silence the reformer, the intimidation escalates to a more direct form. Here are some management actions that can intimidate a reform-minded subordinate:

■ The manager assures the subordinate that he misperceives the situation, and his suggestions are not valid. If the reformer persists, the manager suggests an investigation to find the truth. The results of the investigation will show the reformer that the charges have no basis.

■ The next level of intimidation isolates the reformer from others in the organization. The manager first reduces or ends communication with the reformer and restricts his interactions with others. If the reformer persists, the manager physically can isolate the person by transferring him to a position that has low visibility or is physically distant from the part of the organization to which the reformer objects.

■ The third level of intimidation focuses on the character and motives of the reformer. The manager defames the reformer by suggesting to others that he is incompetent or even psychopathic.

These intimidation methods try to prevent the reformer from building support among others in the organization. The intimidation also tries to drive the reformer out of the organization. If none of these methods work, the manager can escalate to the last level—firing the reformer.

INTERNATIONAL ASPECTS OF POWER AND POLITICAL BEHAVIOR IN ORGANIZATIONS

This section presents some observations on the international aspects of political behavior in organizations. Some observations are speculative because little direct assessment of political behavior in organizations across cultures has been done. Several observations come from known cultural differences that can affect how power is attributed to a person and that person's political behavior.[54]

People from different cultures hold different beliefs about the proper relationship between individuals who have power and those who do not. Some cultures see a directive and autocratic use of power as correct. Other cultures define a consultative or democratic approach as correct. Such cultural differences affect reactions to the use of power and related political behavior. Different individuals within those cultures, of course, can have different beliefs about power relationships.

People in the Philippines, Mexico, many South American countries, India, Singapore, and Hong Kong value a directive use of power. A manager who gives clear directions and instructions to subordinates receives more respect than a manager who consults subordinates. Workers in those countries ascribe power to a directive manager and weakness to a consultative one. Status symbols also play important roles in defining who has power and who does not. The political processes within the organizations of those countries should also mirror the power orientation of the underlying culture. Consultative-oriented managers have a distinct disadvantage when trying to maneuver through the political systems of power-directive cultures.

People in Israel, Switzerland, Austria, New Zealand, and the Scandinavian countries have an opposite orientation. Workers in those countries expect their managers to involve them in the decision-making process. A directive manager from India or Singapore, for example, would not be well accepted by workers in Scandinavian organizations. Although such a manager enjoys high power in his home culture, the same manager would have little power in Scandinavian cultures.

Cultures vary widely in their orientation to uncertainty. Some cultures value the reduction of uncertainty. Other cultures see uncertainty as a manageable part of organizational life. Workers in Greece and France expect managers to maintain low levels of uncertainty. A manager who cannot keep uncertainty low has little power and influence over his workers. Workers in Denmark and the United States, however, have a higher tolerance for uncertainty. Nonmanagers in those countries expect managers to make risky decisions. Such workers could ascribe high power to risk-taking managers and low power to those who avoid risk. The degree of power ascribed to various managers affects their ability to influence others with political tactics.

Workers in the United States, Australia, Great Britain, Canada, and the Netherlands are more individualistic than workers from many South American countries. The latter value family ties and conformity to social norms. South American workers expect managers to look after them. Managers who show genuine interest in their subordinates' private lives enjoy higher power in South American organizations than they do in North American organizations.

ETHICAL ISSUES ABOUT POWER AND POLITICAL BEHAVIOR IN ORGANIZATIONS

Political behavior in organizations raises many questions about what is ethical and what is not. You may have sensed some ethical issues as you read this chapter.

If any of the discussions of power or political behavior caused you to ponder the "rightness" of the observations, you were thinking of implicit ethical questions.[55]

Using power and political behavior in an organization to serve self-interest is unethical, if you reject an egoistic view of ethics and accept a utilitarian view. Similarly, political behavior that uses excessive organizational resources to reach a personal goal is also unethical. These observations suggest that any political strategy and its associated tactics are unethical if they do not serve the organization's goals or the goals of a larger group of people than the single political actor. For example, an individual who ignores equipment maintenance to push products through a manufacturing process for personal gain is behaving unethically.

Using power and political behavior that violates another person's rights is also unethical. Political tactics such as blaming others, ingratiation, and co-optation violate others' rights. A co-opted individual, unless he understands the goal of the political actor, has not consented to be influenced. Making accusations against someone violates that individual's right to an impartial hearing of the charges.

A sense of justice strongly argues for fair treatment, fair pay, and the fair administration of rules and procedures. Treating someone preferentially to build a sense of obligation is unethical.

Does this discussion of ethics and political behavior mean political behavior is inherently unethical? No! If you accept the discussions of ethics in Chapter 3, "Ethics and Behavior in Organizations," any political behaviors, uses of power, and efforts to affect others that have the following characteristics are ethical:

■ The behavior should serve people outside the organization and beyond the single political actor.
■ Individuals should clearly know the person's intent and give their implicit or explicit consent to be influenced.
■ The right of due process should not be violated while the political behavior unfolds.
■ Administering the organization's resources, procedures, and policies should allow fair treatment of all affected people.

These guidelines should help you distinguish an organizational statesman from a person playing "dirty politics."[56]

SUMMARY

SUMMARY
15

Power is a person's ability to get something done the way the person wants it done, including the ability to gather physical and human resources and use them to reach the person's goals. Power has three facets: potential power, actual power, and potential for power. The power people have in organizations also has individual and organizational bases and comes from different sources.

Political behavior in organizations focuses on getting, developing, and using power to reach a desired result. Power and political behavior play key roles in lateral relationships in organizations.

Political strategies are broad plans for reaching some goal using political tactics. Political strategies usually focus on resource allocation decisions, career development, management succession, and the redesign of organizations.

Political tactics are political behaviors that become part of a political strategy. Five major political tactics exist: (1) selectively emphasize decision criteria, (2) use outside experts, (3) control the agenda, (4) build coalitions, and (5) co-optation. Other tactics include impression management, sanctions, and ingratiation.

Political skill is a person's ability to interact effectively in various social situations, intending to influence the behavior of another person or group. A person high in political skill gives the impression of sincerity. Four dimensions define political skill: social astuteness, interpersonal influence, networking ability, and apparent sincerity. Political skill is a personality-level quality that almost anyone can learn.

A political diagnosis helps explain the location of power in an organization and the type of political behavior that is likely to happen. A political diagnosis focuses on individuals, coalitions, and political networks.

People from different cultures hold different beliefs about the proper relationship between those who have power and those who do not. Some cultures see a directive and autocratic use of power as correct. Other cultures view a consultative or democratic approach as correct.

"Ethical Issues about Political Behavior in Organizations" took a distinctly normative position about political behavior. Using power and political behavior in an organization to serve only self-interest is unethical. Using political behavior and power to violate a person's rights is also unethical.

REVIEW AND DISCUSSION QUESTIONS

REVIEW AND DISCUSSION QUESTIONS
15

1   Review the discussion of power at the beginning of this chapter. Does power serve positive or negative functions for an organization? Discuss your experiences with power.

2   Power has the three facets of actual power, potential power, and potential for power. Discuss the implications of the three facets for all employees of an organization.

3   Review the ways managers can build power in organizations. Discuss your experiences with managers who build a power base.

4   Review the discussion of the difference between leadership and management in Chapter 12. Discuss the role of power in effective leader or manager behavior.

5   Discuss using political strategies and tactics in organizations. Are the strategies and tactics realistic elements of modern organizational life? What were your reactions to the descriptions of political strategy and tactics?

6 This chapter argued that organizational politics has a dark side. Discuss your experiences with the dark side of organizational politics.

7 Review the description of the ethical issues surrounding political behavior in organizations. Do you accept or reject the normative positions taken from the various ethics theories? Why or why not?

TAKE FIVE: OB ALIVE: *WORKING GIRL* (1988)

Ambitious Tess McGill (Melanie Griffith) wants to move to a management position from her present secretary position. She gets her chance after her boss Katherine Parker (Sigourney Weaver) has a skiing accident. Investment banker Jack Trainer (Harrison Ford) guides Tess through a proposal presentation to Trask Industries, which helps her to move into a management position.

These scenes start in DVD Chapter 18, "Taking A Stand" and end in DVD Chapter 19, "Another Chance," 1:45:08. They begin as Tess leaves the elevator while carrying a box. The scenes end after accepting Mr. Trask's job offer.

Consider the following questions while viewing these scenes: Which bases of power discussed in this chapter most likely apply to Tess McGill? Does power shift among the characters in the scenes? If so, who gains or loses power?

REFERENCES AND NOTES

1. Ferris, G. R., D. B. Fedor, J. G. Chachere, and L. R. Pondy. 1989. Myths and Politics in Organizational Contexts. *Group & Organization Studies* 14: 83–103.

    Ferris, G. R., and W. A. Hochwarter. 2011. Organizational Politics. In *APA Handbook of Industrial and Organizational Psychology*, Vol. 3, ed. S. Zedeck. Washington, DC: American Psychological Association, Chap. 12.

    Ferris, G. R., G. S. Russ, and P. M. Fandt. 1989. Politics in Organizations. In *Impression Management in the Organization*, ed. R. A. Giacalone and P. Rosenfeld. Hillsdale: Lawrence Erlbaum Associates, Chap. 9.

    Ferris, G. R., D. C. Gilmore, T. A. Beehr, and D. D. Frink. 1995. Political Fairness and Fair Politics: The Conceptual Integration of Divergent Constructs. In *Organizational Politics, Justice, and Support: Managing the Social Climate of the Workplace*, ed. R. S. Cropanzano and K. M. Kacmar. Westport: Quorum Books. This source compares the two views. See especially pp. 21–23.

    Mechanic, D. 1962. Sources of Power of Lower Participants in Complex Organizations. *Administrative Science Quarterly* 7: 349–64.

2. Frost, P. J. 1987. Power, Politics, and Influence. In *Handbook of Organizational Communication*, ed. F. M. Jablin, L. L. Putnam, K. H. Roberts, and L. W. Porter. Newbury Park: Sage Publishing, pp. 503–48.

    Pfeffer, J. 1992. *Managing with Power: Politics and Influence in Organizations*. Boston: Harvard Business School Press.

Raven, B. H., J. Schwarzwald, and M. Koslowsky. 1998. Conceptualizing and Measuring a Power/Interaction Model of Interpersonal Influence. *Journal of Applied Social Psychology* 28: 307–32.

Salancik, G. R., and J. Pfeffer. 1977. Who Gets Power and How They Hold Onto It: A Strategic Contingency Model of Power. *Organizational Dynamics* 5 (Winter): 3–21.

3. Bachrach, P., and M. Baratz. 1962. Two Faces of Power. *American Political Science Review* 56: 947–52.

4. Kanter, R. M. 1977. *Men and Women of the Corporation*. New York: Basic Books.

5. Hardy, C., and S. Clegg. 1999. Some Dare Call It Power. In *Studying Organization: Theory and Method*, ed. S. Clegg and C. Hardy. London: Sage Publications.

Kanter, R. M. 1979. Power Failures in Management Circuits. *Harvard Business Review* 57 (July–August): 65–75.

Kotter, J. P. 1977. Power, Dependence, and Effective Management. *Harvard Business Review* 55 (July–August): 125–36.

Martin, N. H., and J. H. Sims. 1956. Thinking Ahead: Power Tactics. *Harvard Business Review* 34 (November–December): 25, 26, 28, 30, 32, 34, 36, 40.

6. Kanter, *Men and Women of the Corporation*.
Kanter, Power Failures in Management Circuits.

7. May, R. 1972. *Power and Innocence*. New York: W. W. Norton.

8. Wrong, D. H. 1968. Some Problems in Defining Social Power. *American Journal of Sociology* 73: 673–78.

9. Bacharach, S. B., and E. J. Lawler. 1980. *Power and Politics in Organizations*. San Francisco: Jossey-Bass, p. 25.

10. Ibid., pp. 15–26.

11. Wrong, Some Problems in Defining Social Power.

12. Bacharach and Lawler, *Power and Politics in Organizations*, pp. 27–32.
Kotter, Power, Dependence, and Effective Management, pp. 217–18.
Pfeffer, J. 1981. *Power in Organizations*. Marshfield: Pitman, pp. 4–6.

13. Griener, L. E., and V. E. Schein. 1988. *Power and Organization Development*. Reading, MA: Addison-Wesley.
Phillips, N. 1997. Bringing the Organization Back In: A Comment on Conceptualizations of Power in Upward Influence Research. *Journal of Organizational Behavior* 18: 43–47.

14. Gabarro, J. J., and J. P. Kotter. 1980. Managing Your Boss. *Harvard Business Review* 58: 92–100.

15. Kaplan, R. E. 1984. Trade Routes: The Manager's Network of Relationships. *Organizational Dynamics* 2 (Spring): 37–52.

16. Griener and Schein, *Power and Organization Development*, pp. 35–37.
Salancik and Pfeffer, Who Gets Power, pp. 14–15.

17. French, J., and B. Raven. 1959. The Bases of Social Power. In *Studies in Social Power*, ed. D. Cartwright. Ann Arbor: Institute for Social Research, pp. 150–67.
Raven, Schwarzwald, and Koslowsky, Conceptualizing and Measuring a Power/Interaction Model of Interpersonal Influence.

18. Raven, Schwarzwald, and Koslowsky, Conceptualizing and Measuring a Power/Interaction Model of Interpersonal Influence.

19. See, for example, K. W. Mossholder, N. Bennett, E. R. Kemery, and M. A. Wesolowski. 1998. Relationships between Bases of Power and Work Reactions: The Mediational Role of Procedural Justice. *Journal of Management* 24: 533–52.

20. Raven, B. H., and A. W. Kruglanski. 1970. Conflict and Power. In *The Structure of Conflict*, ed. P. Swingle. New York: Academic Press, Chap. 3.
21. Monge, P. R., and E. M. Eisenberg. 1987. Emergent Communication Networks. In *Handbook of Organizational Communication: An Inter-disciplinary Perspective*, ed. F. M. Jablin, L. L. Putnam, K. H. Roberts, and L. W. Porter. Newbury Park: Sage Publishing, pp. 304–42. See pp. 323–25 for a summary.
22. Kotter, J. P. 1979. *Power in Management*. New York: AMACOM.
    Pettigrew, A. 1972. Information Control as a Power Resource. *Sociology* 6: 187–204.
23. Developed from Kanter, *Men and Women of the Corporation*.
    Salancik and Pfeffer, Who Gets Power.
24. Mossholder, Bennett, Kemery, and Wesolowski, Relationships between Bases of Power.
25. Developed from Griener and Schein, *Power and Organization Development*.
    Kanter, *Men and Women of the Corporation*.
    Kotter, Power, Dependence, and Effective Management.
    Salancik and Pfeffer, Who Gets Power.
26. Galang, M. G., and G. R. Ferris. 1997. Human Resource Department Power and Influence Through Symbolic Action. *Human Relations* 50: 1403–26.
    Griener and Schein, *Power and Organization Development*, p. 34.
27. Fombrun, C. J. 1983. Attributions of Power Across a Social Network. *Human Relations* 36: 493–508.
28. Ferris, Fedor, Chachere, and Pondy, Myths and Politics.
    Frost, Power, Politics, and Influence.
    Griener and Schein, *Power and Organization Development*.
    Madison, D. L., R. W. Allen, L. W. Porter, P. A. Renwick, and B. T. Mayes. 1980. Organizational Politics: An Exploration of Managers' Perceptions. *Human Relations* 33: 79–100.
    Mintzberg, H. 1983. *Power in and around Organizations*. Englewood Cliffs: Prentice Hall, p. 172.
    Mintzberg, H. 1985. The Organization as a Political Arena. *Journal of Management Studies* 22: 133–54.
    Pfeffer, *Power in Organizations*, p. 7.
    Salancik and Pfeffer, Who Gets Power.
29. Mayes, B. T., and R. W. Allen. 1977. Toward a Definition of Organizational Politics. *Academy of Management Journal* 2: 635–44.
30. Monge and Eisenberg, Emergent Communication Networks.
31. Frost, Power, Politics, and Influence.
    Salancik and Pfeffer, Who Gets Power.
32. Pfeffer, *Power in Organizations*, p. 2.
33. Ferris, G. R., and T. A. Judge. 1991. Personnel/Human Resources Management: A Political Influence Perspective. *Journal of Management* 17: 447–88.
    Judge, T. A., and R. D. Bretz, Jr., 1994. Political Influence Behavior and Career Success. *Journal of Management* 20: 43–65.
34. Ferris and Judge, Personnel/Human Resources Management.
    Ferris, G. R., T. A. Judge, K. M. Rowland, and D. E. Fitzgibbons. 1994. Subordinate Influence and the Performance Evaluation Process: Test of a Model. *Organizational Behavior and Human Decision Processes* 58: 101–35.
    Gioia, D. A., and C. O. Longenecker. 1994. Delving into the Dark Side: The Politics of Executive Appraisal. *Organizational Dynamics* 22 (3): 47–58.

35. Bartol, K. M., and D. C. Martin. 1990. When Politics Pays: Factors Influencing Managerial Compensation Decisions. *Personnel Psychology* 43: 599–614.
Ferris and Judge, Personnel/Human Resources Management.

36. Monge and Eisenberg, Emergent Communication Networks.

37. Developed from Allen, R. W., D. L. Madison, L. W. Porter, P. A. Renwick, and B. T. Mayes. 1979. Organizational Politics: Tactics and Characteristics of Its Actors. *California Management Review* 22: 77–83.
Bacharach and Lawler, *Power and Politics in Organizations*, pp. 120–29.
Kipnis, D., S. M. Schmidt, C. Swaffin-Smith, and I. Wilkinson. 1984. Patterns of Managerial Influence: Shotgun Managers, Tacticians, and Bystanders. *Organizational Dynamics* 12 (Winter): 58–67.
Pfeffer, *Power in Organizations*, Chap. 5.
Porter, L. W., R. W. Allen, and H. L. Angle. 1981. The Politics of Upward Influence in Organizations. In *Research in Organizational Behavior*, Vol. 3, ed. L. L. Cummings and B. M. Staw. Greenwich, CT: JAI Press, pp. 181–216.

38. Pfeffer, *Power in Organizations*, pp. 150–54.

39. Eder, R. W., and D. B. Fedor. 1989. Impression Management: Its Interpretative Role in the Supervisor-Employee Feedback Process. In *Impression Management in the Organization*, ed. R. A. Giacalone and P. Rosenfeld. Hillsdale: Lawrence Erlbaum Associates, Chap. 20. This edited collection discusses many other aspects of impression management in organizations.
Fandt, P. M., and G. R. Ferris. 1990. The Management of Information and Impressions: When Employees Behave Opportunistically. *Organizational Behavior and Human Decision Processes* 45: 140–58.
Gardner, W. L., and M. J. Martinko. 1988. Impression Management in Organizations. *Journal of Management* 15: 557–64.

40. Kipnis, D., and S. M. Schmidt. 1983. An Influence Perspective on Bargaining within Organizations. In *Negotiating in Organizations*, ed. M. H. Bazerman and R. J. Lewicki. Newbury Park: Sage Publishing, pp. 303–19.
Kipnis, D., S. M. Schmidt, and I. Wilkinson. 1980. Intraorganizational Influence Tactics: Explorations in Getting One's Way. *Journal of Applied Psychology* 65: 440–52.

41. Yukl, G., and C. M. Falbe. 1990. Influence Tactics and Objectives in Upward, Downward, and Lateral Influence Attempts. *Journal of Applied Psychology* 75: 132–40.

42. Ibid.

43. Ibid., p. 139.

44. Frost, Power, Politics, and Influence, pp. 523–25.

45. Ferris, G. R., P. L. Perrewé, W. P. Anthony, and D. C. Gilmore,. 2000. Political Skill at Work. *Organizational Dynamics* 28 (4): 25–37.
Ferris, G. R., W. P. Anthony, R. W. Kolodinsky, D. C. Gilmore, and M. G. Harvey. 2002. Development of Political Skill. In *Rethinking Management Education for the 21st Century*, ed. C. Wankel and R. DeFillippi. Greenwich, CT: Information Age Publishing, Chap. 1.
Ferris, G. R., D. C. Treadway, R. W. Kolodinsky, W. A. Hochwarter, C. J. Kacmar, C. Douglas, and D. D. Frink. 2005. Development and Validation of the Political Skill Inventory. *Journal of Management* 31: 126–52.

46. Developed from A. T. Cobb. 1986. Political Diagnosis: Applications in Organizational Development. *Academy of Management Review* 11: 482–96.
Griener and Schein, *Power and Organization Development*, Chap. 7.

47. Ferris, G. R., D. D. Frink, D. P. S. Bhawuk, J. Zhou, and D. C. Gilmore. 1996. Reactions of Diverse Groups to Politics in the Workplace. *Journal of Management* 22: 23–44.

48. Christie, R., and F. L. Geis. 1970. *Studies in Machiavellianism*. New York: Academic Press.
    Frost, Power, Politics, and Influence, p. 516.
    Guterman, S. S. 1970. *The Machiavellians: A Social Psychological Study of Moral Character and Organizational Milieu*. Lincoln: University of Nebraska Press.
    Wilson, D. S., D. Near, and R. R. Miller. 1996. Machiavellianism: A Synthesis of the Evolutionary and Psychological Literatures. *Psychological Bulletin* 119: 285–99.

49. Machiavelli, N. 1940. *The Prince and the Discourses*. New York: Modern Library, pp. 64–65.

50. Developed from Griener and Schein, *Power and Organization Development*, Chap. 5.

51. Ibid.

52. DePaulo, P. J., B. M. DePaulo, J. Tang, and G. W. Swaim. 1989. Lying and Detecting Lies in Organizations. In *Impression Management in the Organization*, ed. R. A. Giacalone and P. Rosenfeld. Hillsdale: Lawrence Erlbaum Associates, Chap. 23.
    Lewicki, R. J. 1983. Lying and Deception: A Behavioral Model. In *Negotiating in Organizations*, ed. M. H. Bazerman and R. J. Lewicki. Beverly Hills: Sage Publishing, pp. 68–90.

53. Developed from R. O'Day. 1974. Intimidation Rituals: Reactions to Reform. *The Journal of Applied Behavioral Science* 10: 373–86.

54. Developed from G. Hofstede. 1991. *Cultures and Organizations: Software of the Mind*. New York: McGraw-Hill.
    Hofstede, G. 1990. The Cultural Relativity of Organizational Practices and Theories. In *Managing Organizations: Text, Readings and Case*, ed. D. Wilson and R. Rosenfeld. London: McGraw-Hill, pp. 392–405.
    Hofstede, G. 2001. *Culture's Consequences: Comparing Values, Behaviors, Institutions, and Organizations Across Nations*, 2nd edn. Thousand Oaks: Sage Publishing.

55. Developed from G. F. Cavanagh, D. J. Moberg, and M. Velasquez. 1981. The Ethics of Organizational Politics. *Academy of Management Review* 6: 363–74.
    Velasquez, M., D. J. Moberg, and G. F. Cavanagh. 1983. Organizational Statesmanship and Dirty Politics: Ethical Guidelines for the Organizational Politician. *Organizational Dynamics* 12 (Autumn): 65–80.

56. Velasquez, Moberg, and Cavanagh, Organizational Statesmanship and Dirty Politics, p. 80.

Chapter 16

STRESS IN ORGANIZATIONS

After reading this chapter, you should be able to:

- Describe the body's natural responses to stressful events.
- Discuss some stress response models.
- Assess why stress is not always bad for people.
- Describe the sources of stress in modern living.
- Identify burnout as a special case of stress.
- Compare individual and organizational strategies of stress management.
- Assess why working in another country presents unique sources of stress.
- Debate the ethical issues raised by stress in organizations.

Stress is an unavoidable feature of modern living. Everyday events, such as crossing a street or an annoying draft, are sources of stress. An exciting event such as college graduation can also cause stress. Stress is not always bad for us, especially if we prepare our physical and psychological systems to cope with it.[1]

A person experiences **stress** when an event in her environment presents a constraint, an opportunity, or an excessive physical or psychological demand.[2] The first condition for stress occurs when a constraint blocks a person's efforts to reach a desired goal. The individual can experience stress while trying to overcome the constraint. The second condition for stress is more positive. An opportunity from the person's environment may present her with a chance to get something she values. The third condition for stress returns to the negative. Some event in the person's environment presents excessive physical or psychological demands. The individual experiences stress while trying to satisfy those demands.

The word stressor refers to an object or event in a person's physical and social environment that can cause a stress response. Potential stressors are present in the environments a person passes through during daily activities. These environments include the work environment, the nonwork environment, and life transitions.

A person's perceptual process decides whether the presence of a stressor leads to a stress response.[3] One person may perceive a stressor as a challenge to overcome; another person may perceive the same stressor as a threat.

The stress response has both physiological and psychological aspects. These psychophysiological responses lead to behavior focused on the stressor.[4] The physiological response to perceived stress is an integrated set of bodily functions that prepare the body to respond to the stressor. The bodily changes ready a person to either fight the stressor or run from it. Although the response involves a complex network of neurophysiological reactions (described later), the immediate reaction to perceived stress happens fast.

Some amount of stress can energize and motivate a person to behave in desired ways. As noted earlier, stress can be a response to an opportunity. It can help move a person toward valued results offered by the opportunity. Stress is also useful in times of threat or danger. When threatened, a person's adrenaline flows and her heart rate increases, preparing her to face the threat.

People have different stress responses to events in their environment. Some people quickly feel high amounts of stress. Others feel less stress or no stress

Chapter Overview

The General Adaptation Syndrome: "Fight or Flight"

The Psychological Demands and Decision Latitude Model

An Integrated Model of Stress
Stressors
Stress Response
Behavioral Response
Distress and Eustress Results
Moderators

Burnout

Stress Management: Individual and Organizational Strategies
Individual Strategies
Organizational Strategies

International Aspects of Stress in Organizations

Ethical Issues about Stress in Organizations

at all. Variations in stress responses are related to a person's skills, abilities, and experiences with those events.[5]

Understanding stress, especially stress in organizations, is important because it can have both positive and negative effects. For individuals, dysfunctional stress is associated with increased cardiac risk and the abuse of alcohol or other drugs. For organizations, dysfunctional stress is associated with high absenteeism rates, high turnover, reduced productivity, and poor decision making.[6]

The optimal stress level varies from person to person. All of us can benefit from understanding our stress responses and learning how to manage stress to reduce its negative effects. If you are a manager now, expect to be one in the future, or would like to better understand your manager, you need to know how people respond to stressors and how that response can vary.

Different models of stress give you different insights about your stress response and the responses of others. The next three sections describe some models that will help you understand stress in your life.

THE GENERAL ADAPTATION SYNDROME: "FIGHT OR FLIGHT"

The **general adaptation syndrome** is an early model of stress response. This model views the stress response as a natural human adaptation to a stressor in the individual's physical or psychological environment. A person adapts to the stressor by choosing behavior that lets her either change the stressor (a fight response) or leave the stressor (a flight response). This general model of stress is well documented in medical research.[7]

The stress response unfolds in three closely related stages. The first stage is **alarm**. The body prepares to fight or adjust to the stressor by increasing heart rate, respiration, muscle tension, and blood sugar.

The second stage is **resistance**. The body tries to return to a normal state by adapting to the stressor. The adaptation can be closing a window to prevent an irritating draft or quickly stepping back on the sidewalk to avoid an oncoming car.

When a person repeatedly experiences a stressor or constantly resists a stressor, the body moves to the third stage of stress, **exhaustion**. During the exhaustion stage, the body begins to wear down from exposure to the stressor. If a person experiences the stressor long enough and does not effectively manage the source of stress, then stress-related illnesses can appear (high blood pressure, headaches, ulcers, insomnia, and the like). The damaging effects of stress occur in this stage of the stress response both for the individual and for the organization. Later sections of this chapter describe ways of building your body's resilience to stress, so the exhaustion stage does not occur.

The stress response leads to either distress or eustress. **Distress** is the dysfunctional result of stress. A person suffers distress when she does not successfully adapt to the stressor or does not remove the stressor from her environment. **Eustress** is a positive result of stress that occurs when the person has successfully adapted to the stressor or when the degree of stress has not exceeded her ability to adapt to it. A later section focuses on managing stress to avoid distress and to get eustress.

We all have experienced the general adaptation syndrome. Recall some event in the past that alarmed you—turning into a dark alley, riding a horse that suddenly reared, hitting the brakes on a car to avoid an oncoming truck, or suddenly discovering a major error in a report due to your boss in one hour. In such circumstances, you should have experienced the reactions described by the syndrome: Your heart rate increased; the palms of your hands became sweaty; and you started to breathe faster. These were all natural responses invoked by your central nervous system's reactions to a threat. Stress is a natural human response to a condition that is overwhelming, either for a moment or for a long time.

THE PSYCHOLOGICAL DEMANDS AND DECISION LATITUDE MODEL

The psychological demands and decision latitude model (or the demand/control model) uses two constructs to explain the stress effects of people's jobs.[8] The first is **job demands**, which include the work pace, amount of work, and conflicting work requirements. The job demands in the model are psychological demands, not physical demands. Although a job may have high physical demands that lead to fatigue, the psychological demands can lead to a stress response. A person may tire because of the work pace, but also can feel anxiety about keeping up the pace and getting work done on time.

The second construct in the model is **job decision latitude**, a two-part construct consisting of a worker's decision authority and the different skills used on the job. Decision authority can vary from a low level to a high level of authority where a person is almost autonomous in doing her work. A job's skill requirements also vary from jobs requiring low skill to those requiring highly skilled people. Individuals with high job-related skills can often choose which skills to apply and at which moment. An example of the latter is a skilled automobile mechanic who diagnoses an automobile's problems and applies her skills to the problem solution.

Stress results when a job is high in demands and low in decision latitude. Here, the worker does not have the authority to behave in ways that let her successfully manage the job demands. An example is a customer service representative of a public utility who handles customer complaints but has almost no authority to fix the target of the complaint. The least stress comes from a job high in decision latitude and low in demand, such as the job of a forester. This job presents few psychological demands. A worker also can control work activities and the skills used in doing the job.

Some model predictions and explanations remain controversial in the stress research community. Empirical research among diverse populations of workers, and in different countries, largely supports the descriptions noted here.[9]

AN INTEGRATED MODEL OF STRESS

Figure 16.1 shows an integrated model of stress that describes sources of stress and the conditions under which those sources evoke a stress response. It combines many pieces from stress research to form a detailed model of stress responses.[10] Because the whole model has not been empirically tested, it is useful mainly as a tool for analyzing and managing stress in your life and as a management tool for managing stress in organizations.

Some parts of the model have solid footing, such as the role of perception in filtering stressors and the role of some moderators.[11] The evidence is strong for the moderating effects of Type A personalities, social support, diet, and exercise.[12] There is also research evidence of some gender differences in distress reactions. Men and women experience different types and degrees of stress, partly depending on the pattern of their multiple work and nonwork roles.[13]

Stressors

Stressors are the antecedents of stress. They occur in work experiences, nonwork experiences, and various life transitions.[14] As a person's perceptual processes filter the stressors, a stress response results. If the person perceives a stressor as excessively demanding or as a harmful constraint, distress results. If the person perceives a stressor as a challenge or an exciting opportunity, eustress results. Both distress and eustress have the different results shown in Figure 16.1.

Work stressors include deadlines, work overload, shift work, job security, political behavior, and the physical environment. Nonwork stressors include financial problems, relocation, and dual careers. Life transition stressors include the death of a loved one, divorce, or children leaving home.

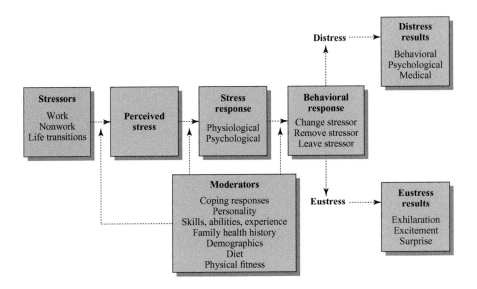

▪ **Figure 16.1:** Integrated Model of Stress

Stress Response

The sympathetic nervous system, the parasympathetic nervous system, and the endocrine system play integrated roles in the **physiological stress response**.[15] Seconds after perceiving a stressor, messages stream from the cortex to the hypothalamus and to the pituitary gland. The endocrine system increases the levels of several hormones in the bloodstream, including acetylcholine, cortisol, adrenaline, and noradrenaline. These hormones increase fatty acid and glucose levels in the bloodstream. Heart rate and blood pressure rise, as the heart pumps more blood to the brain and muscles. Breathing rate increases as the sympathetic nervous system and the endocrine system ready the body to face the stressor.

The general **psychological stress response** includes increased apprehension and alertness. An individual's specific psychological response can be either positive or negative. A positive response includes feelings of exhilaration, excitement, challenge, and opportunity. A negative response includes feelings of anxiety, fear, and threat. Although the physiological stress response is about the same for all of us, people vary in their psychological response to perceived stress. This is where you can begin to see how stress can have negative effects.

Behavioral Response

Now that the person is ready to act, she must choose the right **behavioral response** for the stressor. Her choices include removing the stressor, changing the stressor, or leaving the presence of the stressor.

Stressful situations often do not leave much time for decision. For example, a pilot faced with an in-flight emergency often has little time to decide what to do. The stress response readies the pilot to respond quickly; training and experience let the pilot make the right choices. Even in less dramatic situations, an individual must still act. We all face the dilemma of choosing the right behavior for a specific stressor. The wrong choice can lead to distress; the right choice can lead to eustress.

Distress and Eustress Results

Distress happens when a person does not choose the right behavior to manage the stress response, is predisposed to distress, becomes overwhelmed by the stressor, or has not built resilience to common stressors. The results of distress are the effects usually associated with the word stress.

The **behavioral results** include high levels of smoking, drug use, appetite disorders, proneness to accidents, violence, and decreased job peformance.[16] Behavioral distress effects can reach into a person's nonwork life, affecting family and other relationships, spouse and child abuse, sleep patterns, and sexual functioning. The **psychological results** of distress include severe anxiety, alienation, depression, and psychosomatic effects such as speech difficulties. You may have experienced the latter when starting a class presentation and discovering you had no voice. After a while, the anxiety passed and your voice returned. You temporarily experienced an unfortunate psychological result of distress.

Stress researchers have linked heart disease, stroke, backaches, ulcers, and headaches to distress. Some **medical results** are tied to the behavioral reactions described earlier. For example, increases in smoking and drug use can cause heart problems or a stroke. The natural stress response includes a rise in serum cholesterol and blood pressure. Each of these natural effects, if sustained over time, can lead to a stroke or a heart attack. Some research also suggests possible negative effects on the immune system.

Stressful life events probably do not lead directly to physical disorders such as stroke and heart disease. Stressors likely intertwine in complex and not yet well-understood ways with other parts of a person's lifestyle.[17] More varied research designs using multiple measurement methods will help clarify our understanding of stress in organizations and other parts of people's lives.[18]

Eustress is the exhilaration and excitement that comes with winning a competition, an unexpected high course grade, the birth of a child, a windfall of money, or an unexpected gift. The list of eustress events could go on and on. One person's source of eustress can be another person's source of distress. Consider the different reactions of people to a promotion at work. Some people grow and develop from a promotion (eustress). Others incur severe medical and psychological disorders such as hypertension and chronic depression (distress).[19]

Moderators

Several personal characteristics act as moderators of perceptions and behavioral responses to stressors. The moderators include coping responses; personality; skills, abilities, and experience; family health history; demographics such as age; family responsibilities; diet; and physical fitness.[20] Such moderators can change the relationships shown earlier in Figure 16.1. A physically fit person, for example, may have a less severe response to perceived stress than a person who is not physically fit. Senior executives with the high political skill described in Chapter 15, "Power and Political Behavior," might have a less negative response to their job's stressors than an executive with low political skill.[21]

People's coping responses to a stressor can affect their reaction to the stressor.[22] A **coping response** changes the stressor or how the person interprets the stressor. The two broad types of coping response are problem-focused coping and emotion-focused coping. **Problem-focused coping** changes the reason the stressor exists. For example, a person can change lighting in a work area to reduce glare. **Emotion-focused** coping changes a person's perception or interpretation of a stressor. For example, a person can attribute a coworker's negative comments to that person's experienced stress.

Stress researchers have identified eight coping responses. The following defines each response and gives a brief example:

■ **Confrontive coping:** The person makes aggressive efforts to change a situation, often with anger. Confrontive coping includes risky behavior such as taking an action that has uncertain results. Example: Fighting for what you want.

■ **Distancing:** The person psychologically detaches from or adds positive meaning to a situation. Example: Trying to forget the situation.

■ **Self-control:** The person takes steps to manage her actions and feelings. Example: Keeping feelings inside.

■ **Seeking social support:** The person goes to other people for emotional support or more information about the situation. Example: Talking to friends.

■ **Accepting responsibility:** The person highlights her role in creating the situation and tries to make it better. Example: Apologizing and then taking a positive action.

■ **Escape-avoidance:** The person tries to get away from the stressor, coupled with wishful thinking. Example: Staying away from people.

■ **Planful problem solving:** The person analyzes the situation and takes steps to improve it. Example: Develop a plan to fix the situation and then take action.

■ **Positive reappraisal:** The person focuses on personal improvements from addressing the situation. Example: Feelings of personal growth because of the situation.

People use most of the coping responses in stressful situations. If the person decides that she can fix the situation, there is a tendency to use a problem-focused approach such as planful problem solving. If the person decides that she cannot affect the situation, there is a tendency to use an emotion-focused approach such as positive reappraisal or escape-avoidance.

Stress researchers have associated two personality types with differences in perceptions of stressors and responses to them.[23] **Low hardiness personalities** assess stressors pessimistically. They view stressful life events as unchangeable disruptions to the normal course of their behavior. Their reaction follows from their alienation from events, a feeling of having little control over events, and a view of stressors as a threat. Low hardiness personalities try to escape from stressors, not change them.

High hardiness personalities assess stressors optimistically. They view stressful events as challenges to overcome. Their reaction comes from goal commitment, a feeling of control over events, and a view of stressors as a challenge. High hardiness personalities take decisive action to change the stressors, not escape from them. Research evidence points to commitment and control as consistently related to positive stress responses.[24]

For example, students typically face many stressors toward the end of a semester or quarter. Research papers are due as finals week approaches. Low hardiness personalities will likely see these events as threatening and try to avoid them for as long as possible. Such delays make the stressors worse because they meet their deadlines by working long, weary hours. High hardiness personalities will likely see the same events as a challenge and try to organize their schedules to meet deadlines in a timely way. The response of the high hardiness personality can help reduce the amount of distress she experiences.

The second personality type studied by stress researchers is the Type A described in Chapter 5, "Perception, Attitudes, and Personality." A **Type A personality** is aggressive, can quickly become hostile, focuses excessively on achievement, and has a keen sense of time urgency. Type A personalities like to move fast and often do more than one activity concurrently. Some aspects of the Type A personality predict coronary heart disease; other aspects predict high performance. Hostility is strongly associated with coronary heart disease.[25] Striving for achievement is strongly associated with performance.[26]

The opposite personality type is the **Type B personality**. Such people feel less time urgency, often stopping to ponder their achievements and reflect on where they are headed. They have high self-esteem, a characteristic that distinguishes them from Type A personalities. They are even-tempered and are not bothered by everyday events.

A Type A's hurried approach to life can lead to a perception of stressors as constraints and not opportunities. Type A personalities want accomplishments and can readily perceive blockages even when no constraints are present. A Type B's more even-tempered approach lets the person see more opportunities than constraints. Type A personalities can also increase the demands made on them.[27] In short, the Type A personality is more likely to feel distress than a Type B personality. Some research results also suggest that Type A personalities with low hardiness have the greatest risk of suffering the ill effects of distress.[28]

Other moderators include **skills, abilities, and experience**. A person experienced with similar stressors will have less distress than a person for whom a stressor is new.

A **family health history** often can suggest whether a person is predisposed to the negative health effects of distress. Medical histories of hypertension, high serum cholesterol levels, and ulcers point to a chance of experiencing the ill effects of stress.

Some **demographics** point to a greater likelihood of experiencing certain stressors or experiencing distress. Working people with family responsibilities often feel many work and nonwork stressors simultaneously. They often feel pressures to get ahead in a career while also raising children, maintaining social relationships, and managing a home. Work stress can spill over into the nonwork domain, and the reverse. This form of "stress contagion" can have harmful effects on everyone involved.[29]

Biological age also changes a person's perception of stress and the response to a stressor. With age comes experience, which can reduce the experience of distress as described earlier. The aging process also changes the body's physical response to a stressor. An older person, for example, is more likely to have increased blood pressure from a stressor than a younger person.

The saturated fat and sodium content of a person's **diet** can affect the long-term results of stress. Excessive sodium intake contributes to high blood pressure. Excessive saturated fat adds to serum cholesterol levels.

Physical fitness can increase a person's resilience to stressors. A physically fit person is less likely to feel the harmful effects of distress than a person who is less fit.[30]

BURNOUT

Burnout is a chronic state of emotional exhaustion that comes from an unrelenting series of on-the-job pressures with few positive experiences. Burnout is a special case of distress and is the term often used to refer to stress. People in jobs with high levels of interpersonal interaction or in jobs that require helping other people can experience work-related burnout.[31]

Occupations with high levels of burnout include nurses, customer service representatives, and social workers. Jobs with low burnout include research physicists, forest rangers, and laboratory technicians. Intermediate levels of burnout result from jobs such as librarian, receptionist, and sales representative.[32] People who experience burnout usually are emotionally invested in their work, derive a major part of their self-esteem from their work, and have few interests away from work. They also have high-performance standards for themselves, especially for what they can do to help others.

Burnout follows the process shown in Figure 16.2. Repeated exposure to work stressors results in emotional exhaustion. For example, nurses who tend the same terminally ill patients can become emotionally exhausted. Depersonalization of relationships follows emotional exhaustion as a distancing coping response. This response views the people served as objects instead of people, a way of building an impersonal barrier to the stressor. The final stage of the burnout process is reduced personal accomplishment. People at this stage lose interest in their work, are less efficient, and have little initiative.

The burnout process produces many individual and organizational results. Individual results include headaches, mood swings, cynicism, increased use of drugs and alcohol, self-questioning, and family conflicts. Organizational results include inflexibility in dealing with organizational clients, negative work attitudes, increased absenteeism, decreased work efficiency, and lower work performance.[33]

The research evidence about the effects of burnout is especially compelling. Chronic exposure to stressors in the workplace is associated with serious ill effects.[34] One researcher summarized burnout as follows: "Burnout seems more widespread, of longer duration, and has more somber consequences than many observers believe."[35]

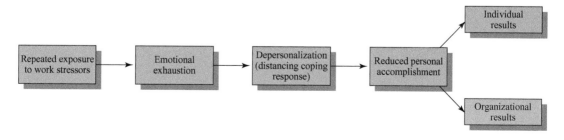

▪ **Figure 16.2:** The Burnout Process

STRESS MANAGEMENT: INDIVIDUAL AND ORGANIZATIONAL STRATEGIES

Stress management has a goal of maintaining stress at an optimal level for the individual and the organization. Not all stress should be reduced, because some stressors are unavoidable, and some amount of stress is not bad for many people.[36]

Individual and organizational stress management strategies fall into three groups. **Stress reduction strategies** aim to decrease the number of stressors affecting a person. **Stress resilience strategies** try to increase a person's ability to endure stressors and not feel dysfunctional results. **Stress recuperation strategies** aim to help the person bounce back from the stress response without physical harm. Some research suggests that combined individual and organizational strategies have the most positive effects on reducing stress effects on individuals.[37]

The stress management strategies described in this section have been widely discussed in the popular press and by medical practitioners and stress researchers. Some reviews of the stress research literature show mixed results for these strategies.[38] Other reviews of empirical stress research point to positive effects of many strategies described in this section.[39] The effectiveness of diet, aerobic exercise, and physical fitness are well understood. Existing empirical research points to their recuperative and resilience effects.[40]

Individual Strategies

Individual stress management strategies can help a person gain control over stress. This section presents the strategies but does not give a step-by-step description of each strategy. The associated citations provide those details.

Stress reduction strategies decrease the amount of stress a person experiences. Some strategies are obvious, old, and deceptively simple. The most obvious is to avoid events and circumstances that cause distress. If you do not enjoy crowds, then do your holiday shopping when crowds are few. If you do not enjoy driving in heavy traffic and congestion, then avoid such traffic.

Planning is a key element in stress avoidance. Knowing what to expect, and knowing potential stressors, helps a person prepare for them. If the stressors are unavoidable, planning helps the person prepare for them. You often cannot avoid traffic congestion, but you can plan and choose routes that give you the least amount of stress.

Entering a new organization and new job often is a stressful experience. Learning about the organization and job before accepting a position prepares a person for new stressors. A company's annual reports and business press accounts can give you some clues.

A less obvious source of stress that people can avoid is food. Some chemicals are in the environment and are hard to avoid. Others come from the foods we eat. Caffeine, nicotine, alcohol, and other drugs are stressors, especially in excess.[41] A person who omits such substances from her diet or uses them in moderation can significantly reduce those stressors.

This chapter earlier emphasized the role of perception in deciding whether stressors were present. A person can use perceptual processes to reduce stress. A person can isolate herself effectively (psychological withdrawal) from potential stressors to reduce their harmful effects. People in naturally stressful occupations, such as emergency room personnel, develop the ability to block perceptually the excess of stressors in their work. An alternative is to selectively ignore some stressors by looking for positive elements in the situation. For example, if you find traffic congestion stressful, you can think of it as an opportunity to watch humanity in action.[42] Lastly, some stressors simply are an inevitable part of certain experiences. Certified public accountants (CPAs) know the days before income tax deadlines are long, hard, and tiring. The experienced CPA recognizes the inevitable and does not try to resist those stressors.

Time-management skills help many people manage the multiple demands placed upon them in both work and nonwork settings.[43] Such skills include setting priorities between multiple tasks and developing a schedule for doing important tasks. Time-management skills include reducing interruptions while working, limiting the length of telephone calls, and reducing the number and length of meetings.

A situation's stressors may so overwhelm a person that the only way out is to leave the situation. Leaving can take various forms ranging from a job transfer to complete withdrawal from the organization.

Stress resilience strategies help a person develop physical and psychological stamina against potentially harmful stressors. The most widely recommended stress resilience strategies feature exercise, diet, and weight control.

Aerobic exercise (physical activity lasting 20 to 30 minutes) raises the heart rate, increases respiration, and raises the metabolic rate. Walking, swimming, cycling, jogging, mountain climbing, vigorous racket games, cross-country skiing, and aerobic dancing are all forms of aerobic exercise. Such exercising can be done both inside and outside. For example, a skiing machine or a stationary bicycle can be used indoors. Stress resilience comes from heart and lung conditioning, decreased blood pressure, and decreased serum cholesterol.[44]

Other exercise includes recreational sports, such as bowling, and nonstrenuous activities, such as gardening and light weight lifting. All such activities offer diversions from earlier stressful events. Weight lifting can also improve muscle tone and general conditioning. By helping improve a person's self-image, weight lifting can help her face potential stressors with confidence.

A proper diet, combined with a regular exercise program, helps a person's stress resilience by increasing her physical and psychological stamina and helps manage weight.[45] A balanced diet low in sodium and saturated fats helps keep blood pressure and serum cholesterol within acceptable bounds.

Stress recuperation strategies help people rejuvenate physically and psychologically, especially after severe distress. The methods all feature some type of activity ranging from vigorous exercise to positive thinking.

The preceding section described aerobic exercise as a way to build resilience to stress. It is also a good way to recuperate from distress. Some evidence shows that vigorous exercise causes hormonal secretions that lead to relaxed feelings.[46] The recuperative effects of exercise are a form of natural biochemical relaxation.

Relaxation training is a major element of recuperative strategies. As the name implies, relaxation training teaches people how to relax. The methods include ancient forms of meditation found in Eastern religions and modern secular methods of relaxation such as clinically standardized meditation. Some techniques emphasize physical relaxation; others emphasize mental relaxation. Likewise, some techniques can be self-taught; others require a trained instructor. All relaxation techniques stimulate the same physiological mechanism called the relaxation response.[47] The relaxation response is a natural physical process that includes decreased respiratory, heart, and metabolic rates.

Meditation is another way to reach a relaxed state,[48] but it is treated separately from relaxation training because of its mystical connotations. Most people have experienced meditation; it is simply focused awareness. That focus can be on anything, including objects, sounds, and images. Meditation techniques teach people how to focus their awareness in healthy ways. Such focused awareness leads to profound relaxation and recuperation from distress.

Other forms of stress recuperation feature rest, diversion, and a balanced work/nonwork lifestyle. Getting enough rest prepares a person for inevitable stressors. Three-day weekends and extended vacations give a person a chance to rest, recover, and immerse in other activities. A person with a balanced work and nonwork life can recover from work distress by being involved in interests outside of work. Many people also find eustress in nonwork activities, which can compensate for the distress of work activities. For example, the quiet of stamp collecting may compensate for the distress of an air traffic controller's demanding work. Competition in a marathon may compensate for the distress of an assembly-line worker's excessively routine work.[49]

Organizational Strategies

The goal of **organizational stress management** strategies is to reach an optimal level of stress required by the organization's goals. That level of stress varies according to individual differences and organizational needs.[50] Some organizational stress management strategies use stress and coping inventories to assess employee stress before and after they complete the strategy.[51]

Stress reduction strategies include training programs, personnel policies, job design, and organizational design. Training programs can focus on job-related training that improves a person's ability to do a job. Such training can improve the fit between a person's abilities and the demands of the job. It also is a way of reducing stress from role overload. Other training programs can teach people time and stress management. Time management includes a set of techniques and procedures that help people manage time effectively. Stress management training can include any individual stress reduction and stress recuperation techniques that lend themselves to formal training, including relaxation training and meditation.

Organizations can design their selection, placement, and career-development policies and procedures to help people with stress reduction. These procedures should be designed to improve person–job fit by identifying skill requirements and skill availability among employees. Selection, placement, and career-development policies also include removing people from dysfunctionally stressful situations. Such people can be placed in situations better suited to their skills, abilities, and interests. Organizations can enhance their policies and procedures by sponsoring self-assessment and career-development workshops, which can help people learn about their skills, abilities, and interests.

The job design discussion in Chapter 9, "Job Design and Intrinsic Rewards," presented a job redesign approach that can help managers create a better fit between people and their jobs. Improved fit reduces stressors that come from the work itself.[52] An earlier section of this chapter, "The Psychological Demands and Decision Latitude Model," also offered guidelines for job redesign. Increasing decision latitude and decreasing job demands can reduce distress.

Managers can use some organizational design options to reduce stress. Many people perceive centralized organizations as distressful because of the degree to which they are controlled and the lack of discretion they have while working. Decentralized organizations and self-managing work teams let people have more autonomy, reducing stressors from feelings of little self-control.[53]

Physical work conditions and the physical layout of the workplace can reduce stressors. Some obvious improvements are controlling noise, setting the proper ambient temperature, and removing noxious odors. The physical layout of the workplace can help or hinder social interaction. By changing the layout, managers can help build cohesive groups and social support networks.

Managers can also help reduce nonwork stressors for their employees. Flexible work schedules can make it easier for employees with school-age children to manage their responsibilities. Flexible work schedules also help reduce stressors from daily commuting in cities with high traffic congestion. Day-care benefits or day-care centers at work are helpful for employees with preschool children.

Organizations can use the individual **stress resilience** strategies of physical exercise, diet, and weight control to help their employees resist the effects of distress. An on-site exercise center lets employees exercise without traveling far from their workplace. Such exercise centers can also have trained instructors who design exercise programs for stress resilience.

Company cafeterias can offer diet options that let employees maintain a stress-resilient diet. Providing foods low in sodium and saturated fat lets employees choose something other than the usual high-sodium, high-fat dishes. Organizations can offer complete programs of diet and exercise, giving their employees guidance on the right balance of each.

The exercise centers that help develop stress resilience also promote **stress recuperation**. Strong aerobic exercise following a stressful day lets people recuperate from stress before going home. Working off the effects of stress before leaving the workplace helps prevent work stress from spilling over to an employee's nonwork life. Organizations can also support stress breaks during the work day to help their employees rebound from unavoidable distress.

Some training programs used for stress reduction also apply to stress recuperation. Organizations can offer on-site or off-site relaxation training and meditation workshops. In either case, offering such training during regular work hours enhances its availability and makes it a significant employee benefit.

Employee assistance programs can offer stress-oriented therapy or counseling programs that focus on behavioral changes, such as altering Type A behaviors, drug and alcohol abuse, and cigarette smoking. Counseling programs within organizations supplement stress management training. They usually are available to help people who cannot manage stress effectively by themselves.

INTERNATIONAL ASPECTS OF STRESS IN ORGANIZATIONS

An organization's international activities raise stress issues in three areas: (1) business trips to other countries, (2) relocation to another country for an extended time, and (3) returning home. Each area commonly adds to stress.[54]

Traveling to another country exposes a person to several potential stressors. Crossing time zones, adjusting sleep patterns, entering a different culture, and learning how to move about in that culture all add to stress levels. People's stress response will vary, of course. If they perceive travel as a source of stress, they are likely to have a distress reaction and feel apprehensive. Other people may have a eustress reaction and view the experience as a challenge. Both sets of people have a stress response, but with different results.

A stronger and more lasting source of stress is relocation to another country for an extended time.[55] The expatriate enters the new culture and experiences the culture shock common to traveling to any new country. Staying longer, moving an entire family, staying in living quarters other than a hotel, and possibly having servants who do household chores intensify culture shock. The ways and mores of a new culture cascade upon the expatriate and her family. Different rules of behavior, new relationships, and a different language all must be mastered quickly if the expatriate is to function effectively in the new environment. This crush of information acts as a form of role overload and exposes the expatriate to many stressors.

Because the expatriate's family often joins in the move, the family unit meets new nonwork stressors early. Family members severed ties with friends and relatives back home. Spouses or partners are left alone for extended periods as the expatriates immerse themselves in mastering new task environments. Children must adapt to new schools and new environments. School-age children are gone during the day, leaving a spouse or partner to master relationships with servants and to shop in unfamiliar stores. The entire family often sees big differences in its quality of life and in its social and physical environment. All these together are nonwork stressors surrounding the expatriate and her family.

The culture-shock stressors can be particularly grueling for expatriate spouses or partners, especially women.[56] Women foreigners often cannot work for pay in the host country. They may have many free daytime hours, during which they try to interact with members of the local population who may be unaccustomed to female foreigners, and face long periods of loneliness and boredom. If she left a job or career behind, she has lost something that gave meaning to her life. These factors are significant stressors for an expatriate's spouse or partner and can add stress to their relationship.

After expatriates adapt to behavioral differences in a new country, they may face a new challenge when they return to their home country to continue their career in a domestic operation of the same company. Returning home presents the repatriate with another set of stressors.[57]

Repatriates often assume that nothing will have changed while they were gone. Yet, during the repatriate's time overseas, the repatriate has changed, as have family members, relatives, friends, and coworkers in the home country. While living abroad, expatriates often recall only positive features of their home culture. Returning to their home country can cause as much culture shock as entering a foreign country. Many stressors are the same. The ways and mores of the home country are different from those of the country just left and may be different from what the employee remembers. Any negative features forgotten while gone will have a particularly shocking effect.

ETHICAL ISSUES ABOUT STRESS IN ORGANIZATIONS

Many states allow work-based stress claims under worker compensation laws, raising the specter of high social and economic costs of work-based stress.[58] The following are some ethical issues that could be raised about stress in work organizations:

■ Managers often decide to change a work environment. The change might involve technology, organizational design, or the physical aspects of the organization, including company relocation. Such changes can adversely affect the environmental fit for some, but not all, employees. Do managers have an ethical duty to reduce potential stress by preparing their employees for changes? Do managers have an ethical duty to avoid making changes that would cause high stress for employees although the changes are good for the company?

■ A person's physical work environment can present many stressors. The Occupational Safety and Health Administration (OSHA) has set standards for many stressors, including noxious fumes, radiation, and unsafe working conditions. Is it unethical for managers to knowingly expose workers to such hazards to reduce operating costs?

■ An organization's selection and placement policies can affect the quality of the person's environmental fit.[59] The likelihood of improved fit can occur if both the potential recruit and the organization have accurate information about each other. Is it unethical for an organization to knowingly distort information about the job, the organization, or the likely career path for the recruit? Is it unethical for a recruit to knowingly distort information about herself to improve her prospects of a job offer?

■ When harmful stress appears to result from a poor environmental fit, is the organization required to provide career counseling or to help the person find a better fitting job inside or outside the organization?[60]

■ Knowledge about work and nonwork stressors can help a manager understand the total stress effects on an employee. How much should an individual reveal about her nonwork world to an organization? Should managers concern themselves with nonwork stressors when judging the total stressor exposure of an employee? To what extent is it unethical to ask about an employee's nonwork life?

SUMMARY

Stress is an unavoidable aspect of modern living. People experience stress when an event in their environment presents a constraint, an opportunity, or an excessive physical or psychological demand. Not all stress is bad. Some stress can energize a person to behave in desired ways.

Different theories of stress can give you varying insights about the stress response. The general adaptation syndrome proposes a "fight or flight" response. Varying types of job qualities as stressors are the central feature of the psychological demands and decision latitude model. The integrated model of stress is the most comprehensive of the three models discussed in this chapter. It describes stressors as occurring in work experiences, in nonwork experiences, and during major life transitions. The model includes the role of perception in filtering stressors. A stressor can be exciting to one person and a source of harm to another. The model describes moderators of the stress response such as personality, skills, family health history, demographics, diet, and physical fitness. The integrated model also describes the results of both distress and eustress.

Burnout is a chronic state of emotional exhaustion stemming from an unrelenting series of on-the-job pressures with few moments of positive experience. Burnout is work-related distress usually experienced by people in jobs that require helping other people.

Stress management includes individual and organization strategies to manage stress. Different strategies aim to reduce stress, increase stress resilience, and help people recuperate from stress.

Stressors can arise from the international activities of organizations. Three areas in particular contribute to stress: (1) business trips to other countries, (2) relocation to another country for an extended time, and (3) returning home.

Many ethical issues surround stress in organizations. This section emphasized the roles of managers, nonmanagers, and organizational policies in dealing with sources of stress. The ethical issues often pivot on the amount of knowledge people have about stressors in their work environments.

REVIEW AND DISCUSSION QUESTIONS

REVIEW AND DISCUSSION QUESTIONS
16

1 Review the stressors described in the chapter. Which stressors play the biggest role in your life now? Which stressors do you expect to play big roles in the future?

2 Not all stress is bad for people. Eustress is possible and exhilarating for many. Discuss the conditions under which you believe you experience eustress. Compare those conditions to the conditions of eustress for some of your friends.

3 Discuss the role of perception in the stress response. You may find it useful to review the perception portion of Chapter 5 and discuss its implications for understanding the stress response.

4 What are the moderators of the stress response? What portions of the integrated model of stress do the moderators affect? How? Discuss each moderator and relate it to yourself.

5 Review the stress management section. Which methods are easiest for you to follow now? Which methods should you consider in the future? As a manager, which methods can you put into effect for others?

6 Travel and transfer to foreign locations are potential stressors for many people. Discuss your experiences with foreign travel or foreign assignments. Which parts of those experiences were the most recurring stressors?

7 Discuss the ethical issues about stress in organizations. Are these real issues to which modern managers should attend? Why or why not?

TAKE FIVE: OB ALIVE: *BROADCAST NEWS* (1987)

16 TAKE FIVE

Three sharply different personalities interact to produce the evening televised news. Jane Craig (Holly Hunter) is the compulsive news producer. Tom Grunick (William Hurt) is the smooth news anchor. Aaron Altman (Albert Brooks) is a veteran news reporter. A romantic triangle develops among them, adding to the film's comedic flavor.

These scenes start in DVD Chapter 5, "Insecurity and Desperation," 0:20:28 and continue into DVD Chapter 6, "Bill Smiled!" They begin in the television editing room with a sound of a tape rewinding. The scenes end after Aaron Altman says, "He did smile."

Consider the following questions and observations while viewing the scenes: Which characters experience distress? Which characters experience eustress? Do they have functional or dysfunctional responses to their stress experiences?

REFERENCES
AND NOTES

16

REFERENCES AND NOTES

1. Selye, H. 1956. *The Stress of Life*. New York: McGraw-Hill, p. vii.
2. Background sources for this chapter are:
   Beehr, T. A. 2013. *Psychological Stress in the Workplace*. New York: Routledge.
   Cooper, C. P., P. J. Dewe, and M. P. O'Driscoll. 2001. *Organizational Stress: A Review and Critique of Theory, Research, and Applications*. Thousand Oaks: Sage Publications.
   Ganster, D. C., and L. Murphy. 2000. Workplace Interventions to Prevent Stress-Related Illness: Lessons from Research and Practice. In *Industrial and Organizational Psychology: Linking Theory with Practice*, ed. C. L. Cooper and E. A. Locke. Oxford: Blackwell, Chap. 2.
   Ganster, D. C., and C. C. Rosen. 2013. Work Stress and Employee Health: A Multidisciplinary Review. *Journal of Management* 39: 1085–1122.
   Glaser, R., and J. Kiecolt-Glaser. 1994. *Handbook of Human Stress and Immunity*. San Diego: Academic Press.
   Griffin, M. A., and S. Clarke. 2011. Stress and Well-Being at Work. In *APA Handbook of Industrial and Organizational Psychology*, Vol. 3, ed. S. Zedeck. Washington, DC: American Psychological Association, Chap. 10.
   Kahn, R. L., and P. Byosiere. 1992. Stress in Organizations. In *Handbook of Industrial and Organizational Psychology*, ed. M. D. Dunnette and L. M. Hough. Palo Alto: Consulting Psychologists Press, pp. 571–650.
   Lazarus, R. S. 1993. From Psychological Stress to the Emotions: A History of Changing Outlooks. *Annual Review of Psychology* 44: 1–21.
   Quick, J. C., C. L. Cooper, D. L. Nelson, J. D. Quick, and J. H Gavin. 2003. Stress, Health, and Well-Being at Work. In *Organizational Behavior: The State of the Science*, 2nd edn, ed. J. Greenberg. Mahwah: Lawrence Erlbaum Associates, Chap. 2.
   Quick, J. C., and J. D. Quick. 1984. *Organizational Stress and Preventive Management*. New York: McGraw-Hill.
   Sonnentag, S., and M. Frese. 2003. Stress in Organizations. In *Handbook of Psychology: Industrial and Organizational Psychology*, ed. W. C. Borman, D. R. Ilgen, and R. J. Klimoski. Hoboken: John Wiley & Sons, Chap. 18.
3. Matteson, M. T., and J. M. Ivancevich. 1979. Organizational Stressors and Heart Disease: A Research Model. *Academy of Management Review* 4: 347–57.
4. Gregson, O., and T. Looker. 1996. The Biological Basis of Stress Management. In *Stress Management and Counseling: Theory, Practice, Research and Methodology*, ed. S. Palmer and W. Dryden. London: Cassell, Chap. 2.
   Schuler, R. S. 1980. Definition and Conceptualization of Stress in Organizations. *Organizational Behavior and Human Performance* 25: 184–215.
   Theorell, T. 1993. Medical and Physiological Aspects of Job Interventions. In *International Review of Industrial and Organizational Psychology*, Vol. 8, ed. C. L. Cooper and I. T. Robertson. Chichester: John Wiley & Sons, Chap. 5.

5. Lazarus, R. S. 1966. Stress As a Psychological Problem. In *Psychological Stress and the Coping Process*. New York: McGraw-Hill, Chap. 1.

6. Ganster and Murphy, Workplace Interventions.
Quick and Quick, *Organizational Stress*, Chap. 1.

7. Developed from Selye, *The Stress of Life*.
Selye, H. 1983. The Stress Concept: Past, Present, and Future. In *Stress Research*, ed. C. L. Cooper. New York: John Wiley & Sons, pp. 1–19. (Dr. Hans Selye did the basic psychophysiological research about human stress responses, to which he gave the name *general adaptation syndrome*. The phrase "fight or flight" came from the earlier stress research done by – Cannon.)
See W. B. Cannon. 1909. The Influence of Emotional States on the Functions of the Alimentary Canal. *The American Journal of Science* 137: 480–87.
Cannon, W. B. 1929. Organization for Physiological Homeostasis. *Physiological Review* 9: 339–430.

8. Developed from the following sources:
Karasek Jr., R. A. 1979. Job Demands, Job Decision Latitude, and Mental Strain: Implications for Job Redesign. *Administrative Science Quarterly* 24: 285–308.
Karasek, Jr., R. A. 1981. Job Socialization and Job Strain: The Implications of Two Related Psychosocial Mechanisms for Job Design. In *Working Life: A Social Science Contribution to Work Reform*, ed. R. Gardell and G. Johansson. New York: John Wiley & Sons, pp. 75–94.
Karasek Jr., R. A. 1989. Control in the Workplace and Its Health-Related Aspects. In *Job Control and Worker Health*, ed. S. L. Sauter, J. J. Harrell and C. L. Cooper. Chichester: John Wiley & Sons, pp. 129–59.
Karasek, Jr., R. A., and T. Theorell. 1990. *Healthy Work: Stress, Productivity, and the Reconstruction of Working Life*. New York: Basic Books.

9. Fox, M. L., D. J. Dwyer, and D. C. Ganster, 1993. Effects of Stressful Job Demands and Control on Physiological and Attitudinal Outcomes in a Hospital Setting. *Academy of Management Journal* 36: 289–318.
Ganster and Murphy, Workplace Interventions.
Schnall, P. L., D. Baker, and P. A. Landsbergis. 1994. Job Strain and Cardiovascular Disease. *Annual Review of Public Health* 15: 381–411.

10. Developed from Quick and Quick, Organizational Stress.
Matteson and Ivancevich, Organizational Stressors and Heart Disease.
Matteson, M. T., and J. M. Ivancevich. 1987. Job-Related Stress: A Managerial Framework. In *Controlling Work Stress: Effective Human Resource and Management Strategies*. San Francisco: Jossey-Bass, Chap. 2.
Schabracq, M. J., and C. L. Cooper. 1998. Toward a Phenomenological Framework for the Study of Work and Organizational Stress. *Human Relations* 51: 625–48.

11. Kasl, S. V., and C. L. Cooper. 1987. *Stress and Health: Issues in Research Methodology*. New York: John Wiley & Sons.

12. McMichael, A. J. 1978. Personality, Behavioural, and Situational Modifiers of Work Stressors. In *Stress at Work*, ed. C. L. Cooper and R. Payne. Chichester: John Wiley & Sons, Chap. 5.
Quick and Quick, *Organizational Stress*.

13. Benschop, R. J., R. Geenen, P. J. Mills, B. D. Naliboff, J. K. Kiecolt-Glaser, T. B. Herbert, G. van der Pompe, G. E. Miller, K. A. Matthews, G. L. R. Godaert, S. L. Gilmore, R. Glaser, C. J. Heijnen, J. M. Dopp, J. W. J. Bijlsma, G. F. Solomon, and J. T. Cacioppo. 1998. Cardiovascular and Immune Responses to Acute Psychological

Stress in Young and Old Women: A Meta-Analysis. *Psychosomatic Medicine* 60: 290–96.

Langan-Fox, J. 1998. Women's Careers and Occupational Stress. In *International Review of Industrial and Organizational Psychology*, Vol. 13, ed. C. L. Cooper and I. T. Robertson. Chichester: John Wiley & Sons, Chap. 8.

14. Developed from C. Chang, C. C Rosen, and P. E. Levy. 2009. The Relationship between Perceptions of Organizational Politics and Employee Attitudes, Strain, and Behavior: A Meta-Analytic Examination. *Academy of Management Journal* 52 (4): 779–801.

Cooper, C. L., and J. Marshall. 1978. Sources of Managerial and White Collar Stress. In *Stress at Work*, ed. C. L. Cooper and R. Payne. Chichester: John Wiley & Sons, Chap. 3.

Gotlib, I. H., and B. Wheaton, eds. 1997. *Stress and Adversity Over the Life Course: Trajectories and Turning Points*. Cambridge: Cambridge University Press.

Kets de Vries, M. F. R. 1999. Organizational Sleepwalkers: Emotional Distress at Midlife. *Human Relations* 52: 1377–401.

Miller, B. K., M. A. Rutherford, and R. W. Kolodinsky. 2008. Perceptions of Organizational Politics: A Meta-Analysis of Outcomes. *Journal of Business and Psychology* 22: 209–22.

Schabracq and Cooper, Toward a Phenomenological Framework.

Spurgeon, A., and C. L. Cooper. 2000. Working Time, Health, and Performance. In *International Review of Industrial and Organizational Psychology*, Vol. 15, ed. C. L. Cooper and I. T. Robertson. Chichester: John Wiley & Sons, pp. 189–222.

Westman, M., and A. D. Vinokur. 1998. Unraveling the Relationships of Distress Levels within Couples: Common Stressors, Empathic Reactions, or Crossover via Social Interaction? *Human Relations* 51: 137–56.

15. Gregson and Looker, The Biological Basis of Stress Management.

16. Developed from the following sources and other citations in this section:

Cohen, S., and T. Herbert. 1996. Health Psychology: Psychological Factors and Physical Disease from the Perspective of Human Psychoneuroimmunology. *Annual Review of – Psychology* 47: 113–42.

Cooper, C. L., and Marshall, J. 1976. Occupational Sources of Stress: A Review of the Literature Relating to Coronary Heart Disease and Mental Ill Health. *Journal of Occupational – Psychology* 49: 11–28.

Fletcher, B. 1993. *Occupational Stress, Disease and Life Expectancy*. Chichester: John Wiley & Sons.

Fried, Y., A. Shirom, S. Gilboa, and C. L. Cooper. 2008. The Mediating Effects of Job Satisfaction and Propensity to Leave on Role Stress–Job Performance Relationships: Combining Meta-Analysis and Structural Equation Modeling. *International Journal of Stress Management* 15: 305–28.

Gilboa, S., A. Shirom, Y. Fried, and C. Cooper. 2008. A Meta-Analysis of Work Demand Stressors and Job Performance: Examining Main and Moderating Effects. *Personnel Psychology* 61: 227–71.

Klainin, P., and Y. L. Lin. 2009. Stress and Health Outcomes: The Mediating Role of Negative Affectivity in Female Health Care Workers. *International Journal of Stress Management* 16: 45–64.

LePine, J. A., N. P. Podsakoff, and M. A. LePine. 2005. A Meta-Analytic Test of the Challenge Stressor–Hindrance Stressor Framework: An Explanation for Inconsistent Relationships among Stressors and Performance. *Academy of Management Journal* 48: 764–75.

Örtqvist, D. and J. Wincent. 2006. Prominent Consequences of Role Stress: A Meta-Analytic Review. *International Journal of Stress Management* 13: 399–422.

Podsakoff, N. P., J. A. LePine, and M. A. LePine. 2007. Differential Challenge Stressor–Hindrance Stressor Relationships With Job Attitudes, Turnover Intentions, Turnover, and Withdrawal Behavior: A Meta-Analysis. *Journal of Applied Psychology* 92: 438–54.

Schabracq and Cooper, Toward a Phenomenological Framework.

Vitkovic, L., and S. H. Koslow, eds. 1994. *Neuroimmunology and Mental Health.* Rockville: U.S. Department of Health and Human Services (DHHS publication no. [NIH] 94–3774).

17. Ganster, D. C., and J. Schaubroeck. 1991. Work Stress and Employee Health. *Journal of Management* 17: 235–71.

Kasl, S. V. 1983. Pursuing the Link Between Stressful Life Experiences and Disease: A Time for Reappraisal. In *Stress Research: Issues for the Eighties*, ed. C. L. Cooper. New York: John Wiley & Sons, pp. 79–102.

Kasl, S. V. 1986. Stress and Disease in the Workplace: A Methodological Commentary on the Accumulated Evidence. In *Health and Industry: A Behavioral Medicine Perspective*, ed. M. F. Cataldo and T. J. Coates. New York: John Wiley & Sons, pp. 52–85.

18. Sullivan, S. E., and R. S. Bhagat. 1992. Organizational Stress, Job Satisfaction and Job Performance: Where Do We Go From Here? *Journal of Management* 18: 352–74.

19. Podsakoff, LePine, and LePine. Differential Challenge Stressor–Hindrance Stressor Relationships with Job Attitudes. A "challenge stressor," as defined in this study, has close ties to the "eustress" concept. Their research found positive reactions to challenge stressors.

Quick, Cooper, Nelson, Quick, and Gavin. Stress, Health, and Well-Being at Work, pp. 79–80.

Quick and Quick, *Organizational Stress*, Chap. 3.

20. Developed from Cooper, Dewe, and O'Driscoll, *Organizational Stress*, Chap. 5.

Cooper and Marshall, Sources of Managerial and White Collar Stress, pp. 97–101.

Ganster and Schaubroeck, Work Stress and Employee Health.

McGrath, J. E. 1976. Stress and Behavior in Organizations. In *Handbook of Industrial and Organizational Psychology*, ed. M. D. Dunnette. Chicago: Rand McNally, pp. 1351–96.

Quick and Quick, *Organizational Stress*, pp. 63–73.

Schuler, Definition and Conceptualization of Stress, pp. 192–95.

21. Perrewé, P. L., G. R. Ferris, D. D. Frink, and W. P. Anthony. 2000. Political Skill: An Antidote for Workplace Stressors. *The Academy of Management Executive* 14: 115–23.

22. Developed from Cooper, Dewe, and O'Driscoll, *Organizational Stress*, Chap. 6.

Folkman, S., R. S. Lazarus, C. Dunkel-Schetter, A. Delongis and R. J. Gruen. 1986. Dynamics of a Stressful Encounter: Cognitive Appraisal, Coping, and Encounter Outcomes. *Journal of Personality and Social Psychology* 50: 992–1003.

Lazarus, *Psychological Stress and the Coping Process.*

Lazarus, From Psychological Stress to the Emotions.

Parker, J. D. A., and N. S. Endler. 1996. Coping and Defense: A Historical Review. In *Handbook of Coping: Theory, Research, Applications*, ed. M. Zeidner and N. S. Endler. New York: John Wiley & Sons, pp. 3–23.

Wethington, E., and R. C. Kessler. 1991. Situations and Processes of Coping. In *The Social Context of Coping*, ed. J. Eckenrode. New York: Plenum Press, pp. 13–29.

23. DeNeve, K. M., and H. Cooper. 1998. The Happy Personality: A Meta-Analysis of 137 – Personality Traits and Subjective Well-Being. *Psychological Bulletin* 124: 197–229.

Ganellen, R. J., and P. H. Blaney. 1984. Hardiness and Social Support as Moderators of the Effects of Life Stress. *Journal of Personality and Social Psychology* 47: 156–63.

Kobasa, S. C. 1982. The Hardy Personality: Toward a Social Psychology of Stress and Health. In *Social Psychology of Health and Illness*, ed. G. S. Sander and J. Suls. Hillsdale: Lawrence Erlbaum Associates, pp. 3–32.

Maddi, S. R., and S. C. Kobasa. 1984. *The Hardy Executive: Health Under Stress*. Homewood: Dow Jones-Irwin.

Orr, E., and M. Westman. 1990. Does Hardiness Moderate Stress, and How? A Review. In *Learned Resourcefulness: On Coping Skills, Self-Control, and Adaptive Behavior*, ed. M. Rosenbaum. New York: Springer, pp. 64–94.

24. Hull, J. G., R. R. Van Treuren, and S. Virnelli. 1987. Hardiness and Health: A Critique and Alternative Approach. *Journal of Personality and Social Psychology* 53: 518–30.

Orr and Westman, Does Hardiness Moderate Stress.

25. Booth-Kewley, S., and H. S. Friedman. 1987. Psychological Predictors of Heart Disease: A Quantitative Review. *Psychological Bulletin* 101: 343–62.

Ganster, D. C., J. Schaubroeck, W. E. Sime, and B. T. Mayes. 1991. The Nomological Validity of the Type A Personality Among Employed Adults. *Journal of Applied Psychology* 76: 143–68.

Lyness, S. A. 1993. Predictors of Differences Between Type A and B Individuals in Heart Rate and Blood Pressure Reactivity. *Psychological Bulletin* 114: 266–95.

Mathews, K. A. 1988. Coronary Heart Disease and Type A Behaviors: Update on and Alternative to the Booth-Kewley and Friedman (1987) Quantitative Review. *Psychological Bulletin* 104: 373–80.

26. Mathews, K. A. 1982. Psychological Perspectives on the Type A Behavior Pattern. *Psychological Bulletin* 91: 292–323.

Mathews, K. A., R. L. Helmreich, W. E. Beanne, and G. W. Lucker. 1980. Pattern A, Achievement-Striving, and Scientific Merit: Does Pattern A Help or Hinder? *Journal of Personality and Social Psychology* 39: 962–67.

27. Froggatt, K. L., and J. L. Cotton. 1987. The Impact of Type A Behavior Pattern on Role Overload Induced Stress and Performance Attributions. *Journal of Management* 13: 87–90.

28. Rhodewalt, F., and S. Agustsdottir. 1984. On the Relationship of Hardiness to the Type A Behavior Pattern: Perception of Life Events versus Coping with Life Events. *Journal of Research in Personality* 18: 212–23.

29. Langan-Fox, Women's Careers and Occupational Stress.

Westman and Vinokur, Unraveling the Relationships of Distress Levels within Couples.

30. Quick and Quick, *Organizational Stress*, pp. 249–52.

31. Cooper, Dewe, and O'Driscoll, *Organizational Stress*, Chap. 4.

Cordes, C. L., and T. W. Dougherty. 1993. A Review and Integration of Research on Job Burnout. *Academy of Management Review* 18: 621–56.

Freudenberger, H. J. 1974. Staff Burn-Out. *Journal of Social Issues* 30: 159–65. This source is the first mention in the social and behavioral science research literature of the word *burnout*. Freudenberger worked in 1970s free clinics, where he observed repeated burnout responses among staff and volunteers. It is an enjoyable article with excellent observations on burnout. He also describes many helpful preventive measures.

Griffin and Clarke, Stress and Well-Being, p. 364.

Jackson, S. E., R. L. Schwab, and R. S. Schuler. 1986. Toward an Understanding of the Burnout Phenomenon. *Journal of Applied Psychology* 71: 630–40.

Maslach, C. 1982. *Burnout: The Cost of Caring*. Englewood Cliffs: Prentice Hall.

Maslach, C., and M. P. Leiter. 1997. *The Truth About Burnout: How Organizations Cause Personal Stress and What to Do About It*. San Francisco: Jossey-Bass.

Maslach, C., and M. P. Leiter. 2005. Stress and Burnout: The Critical Research. In *Handbook of Stress Medicine and Health*, 2nd edn, ed. C. L. Cooper. London: CRC Press, pp. 153–70.

Maslach, C., W. B. Schaufeli, and M. P. Leiter. 2001. Job Burnout. *Annual Review of Psychology* 52: 397–422.

Shirom, A. 1989. Burnout in Work Organizations. In *International Review of Industrial and Organizational Psychology*, Vol. 4, ed. C. L. Cooper and I. T. Robertson. Chichester: John Wiley & Sons, pp. 25–48.

32. Cordes and Dougherty, A Review, pp. 643–44.

Maslach, Schaufeli, and Leiter, Job Burnout.

Moss, L. 1981. *Management Stress*. Reading, MA: Addison-Wesley.

33. Cordes and Dougherty, A Review.

Witt, L. A., M. C. Andrews, and D. S. Carlson. 2004. When Conscientiousness Isn't Enough: Emotional Exhaustion and Performance Among Call Center Customer Service Representatives. *Journal of Management* 30: 149–60.

34. Golembiewski, R. T. 1989. Burnout as a Problem at Work: Mapping Its Degree, Duration, and Consequences. *Journal of Managerial Issues* 1: 86–97.

Kahill, S. 1988. Symptoms of Professional Burnout: A Review of the Empirical Evidence. *Canadian Psychology/Psychologie Canadienne* 29: 284–97.

Lee, R. T., and B. E. Ashforth. 1996. A Meta-Analytic Examination of the Correlates of the Three Dimensions of Job Burnout. *Journal of Applied Psychology* 81: 123–33.

Maslach, *Burnout*.

Maslach and Leiter, *The Truth About Burnout*, Chap. 1.

35. Golembiewski, Burnout as a Problem at Work, p. 86.

36. Developed from the following sources:

Charlesworth, E. A., and R. G. Nathan. 1984. *Stress Management: A Comprehensive Guide to Wellness*. New York: Ballantine Books.

Cooper, C. L., and S. Cartwright. 1996. Stress Management Interventions in the Workplace: Stress Counselling and Stress Audits. In *Stress Management and Counselling: Theory, Practice, Research and Methodology*, ed. S. Palmer and W. Dryden. London: Cassell, Chap. 7.

Ellis, A. 1978. What People Can Do for Themselves to Cope with Stress. In *Stress at Work*, ed. C. L. Cooper and R. Payne. Chichester: John Wiley & Sons, Chap. 8.

Freudenberger, Staff Burn-Out. This easy-to-read source describes the special case of burnout and ways to manage it from an individual and organizational perspective.

Ganster and Murphy, Workplace Interventions.

Griffin and Clarke, Stress and Well-Being, pp. 379–84.

Leiter, M. P., and C. Maslach. 2005. *Banishing Burnout: Six Strategies for Improving Your Relationship with Work*. San Francisco: Jossey-Bass. This source gives a highly readable discussion of ways of reducing burnout in one's life.

McLean, A. A. 1979. *Work Stress*. Reading, MA: Addison-Wesley.

Ornish, D. 1984. *Stress, Diet, and Your Heart*. New York: Penguin Putnam Inc.

Quick and Quick, *Organizational Stress*.

Richardson, K. M., and H. R. Rothstein. 2008. Effects of Occupational Stress Management Intervention Programs: A Meta-Analysis. *Journal of Occupational Health Psychology* 13: 69–93.

Schabracq and Cooper, Toward a Phenomenological Framework.

Sonnentag and Frese, Stress in Organizations, pp. 474–79.

Note: The Academy of Management Executive, May 2000, Vol. 14, No. 2 is a special issue devoted to executive stress and stress management. It is an excellent supplement to this chapter's discussion of stress management.

37. Munz, D. C., J. M. Kohler, and C. I. Greenberg. 2001. Effectiveness of a Comprehensive Worksite Stress Management Program: Combining Organizational and Individual Interventions. *International Journal of Psychiatry in Medicine* 6: 133–46.

38. Druckman, D., and R. Bjork. 1991. *In the Mind's Eye: Enhancing Human Performance*. Washington, DC: National Academy Press.

Newman, J. E., and T. A. Beehr. 1979. Personal and Organizational Strategies for Handling Job Stress: A Review of Research and Opinion. *Personnel Psychology* 32: 1–41.

39. Ganster and Murphy, Workplace Interventions.

Munz, Kohler, and Greenberg, Effectiveness of a Comprehensive Worksite Stress Management Program.

Rahe, R. H., C. B. Taylor, R. L. Tolles, L. M. Newhall, T. L. Veach, and S. Bryson. 2002. A Novel Stress and Coping Workplace Program Reduces Illness and Health Care Utilization. *Psychosomatic Medicine* 40: 478–86.

Richardson and Rothstein, Effects of Occupational Stress Management Intervention Programs.

40. Druckman and Bjork, *In the Mind's Eye*.

*Note: The Academy of Management Ex*ecutive, May 2000, Vol. 14, No. 2 is a special issue devoted to executive stress and executive health. Several articles emphasized the important of exercise and diet. See especially C. P. Neck and K. H. Cooper. 2000. The Fit Executive: Exercise and Diet Guidelines for Enhancing Performance. *The Academy of Management Executive* 14: 72–83 and D. L. Nelson and R. J. Burke. 2000. Women Executives: Health, Stress, and Success. *The Academy of Management Executive* 14: 107–21.

Quick and Quick, *Organizational Stress*, Chaps. 3, 11.

41. Charlesworth and Nathan, *Stress Management*.

42. Pearlin, L. I., and C. Schooler. 1978. The Structure of Coping. *Journal of Health and Social Behavior* 19: 2–21.

43. Lakein, A. 1973. *How to Get Control of Your Time and Your Life*. New York: Peter H. Wyden.

44. Quick and Quick, *Organizational Stress*, pp. 249–52.

45. Ornish, *Stress, Diet, and Your Heart*.

Neck and Cooper, The Fit Executive.

Nelson and Burke, Women Executives.

46. Gambert, S. R., T. C. Hagen, T. L. Garthwaite, E. H. Duthie, Jr., and D. J. McCarty. 1981. Exercise and the Endogenous Opioids. *New England Journal of Medicine* 305: 1590–91.

47. Benson, H. 1975. *The Relaxation Response.* New York: William Morrow.

48. Davidson, R. J., J. Kabat-Zinn, J. Schumacher, M. Rosenkranz, D. Muller, S. Santorelli, F. Urbanowski, A. Harrington, K. Bonus, and J. F. Sheridan. 2003. Alterations in Brain and Immune Function Produced by Mindfulness Meditation. *Psychosomatic Medicine* 65: 564–70.
    Ornish, *Stress, Diet, and Your Heart*, Chap. 10.
    Quick and Quick, *Organizational Stress*, pp. 236–38, 241–43.

49. Champoux, J. E. 1981. A Sociological Perspective on Work Involvement. *International Review of Applied Psychology* 30: 65–86.

50. Developed from C. L. Cooper and S. Cartwright. 1997. An Intervention Strategy for Workplace Stress. *Journal of Psychosomatic Research* 43: 7–16.
    Cooper, Dewe, and O'Driscoll, *Organizational Stress*, Chap. 7.
    O'Donnell, M. R., and J. S. Harris, eds. 1994. *Health Promotion in the Workplace.* Albany: Delmar Publishers.
    Quick and Quick, *Organizational Stress*, Chaps. 8, 9.

51. Rahe, R. H., and R. L. Tolles. 2002. The Brief Stress and Coping Inventory: A Useful Stress Management Instrument. *International Journal of Stress Management* 9: 61–70. This source describes the brief version of the Stress and Coping Inventory (SCI) that is an efficient inventory for organizational stress management strategies. Rahe, R. H., T. L. Veach, R. L. Tolles, and K. Murakami. 2000. The Stress and Coping – Inventory: An Educational and Research Instrument. *Stress Medicine* 16: 199–208.
    There also is a Japanese version of the SCI. See I. Fukunishi, T. Nakagawa, H. Nakagawa, Y. Sone, N. Kaji, T. Hosaka, and R. H. Rahe. 1995. Validity and Reliability of the Japanese Version of the Stress and Coping Inventory. *Psychiatry and Clinical Neurosciences* 49: 195–99.

52. Edwards, J. R., and C. L. Cooper. 1990. The Person-Environment Fit Approach to Stress: Recurring Problems and Some Suggested Solutions. *Journal of Organizational Behavior* 11: 293–307.

53. See this chapter's earlier section, "The Psychological Demands and Decision Latitude Model," and its references, for support of this observation.

54. Developed from N. J. Adler, with A. Gundersen. 2008. *International Dimensions of Organizational Behavior*, 5th edn. Mason: Thomson South-Western, Part. 3.
    Black, J. S., M. E. Mendenhall, and H. B. Gregersen. 1992. *Global Assignments: Successfully Expatriating and Repatriating International Managers.* San Francisco: Jossey-Bass.

55. Developed from Adler, with Gundersen, *International Dimensions of Organizational Behavior*, Part. 3. See this source for more detail.
    Kraimer, M. L., and S. J. Wayne. 2004. An Examination of Perceived Organizational Support as a Multidimensional Construct in the Context of an Expatriate Assignment. *Journal of Management* 30: 209–37. This source has an excellent review of the expatriate adjustment research literature. The research clearly points to significant stressors in that adjustment process.

56. Adler, with Gundersen, *International Dimensions of Organizational Behavior*, Chap. 9.

57. Adler, N. J. 1981. Reentry: Managing Cross-Cultural Transitions. *Group and Organization Studies* 6: 341–56.

Adler, with Gundersen, *International Dimensions of Organizational Behavior*, Chap. 10.

Howard, C. 1974. The Returning Overseas Executive: Culture Shock in Reverse. *Human Resources Management* 13: 22–26.

58. Grover, R. 1991. Say, Does Workers' Comp Cover Wretched Excess? *Business Week* (July 22): 23.

59. Suggested by R. V. Harrison. 1978. Person-Environment Fit and Job Stress. In *Stress at Work*, ed. C. L. Cooper and R. Payne. Chichester: John Wiley & Sons, Chap. 8.

60. Ibid.

Part 4 Case

Abstract

Bob Marvin, president of Motor Parts Corporation (MPC), feels a great deal of conflict and frustration about how to deal with the behavior of one of his vice presidents, Al Shepherd. Al's wife, Ruth, has recently had a recurrence of a malignant brain tumor, and Al is spending more and more time away from work to be with her. Bob believes that Al's increasing absence from work and his preoccupation with his wife's problem is causing Al's performance to suffer. In addition, Bob thinks Al's behavior is beginning to affect the morale and performance of others who work with Al. Bob is even beginning to question Al's commitment to the organization.

Bob has chosen not to confront Al directly because he does not want to seem insensitive. Instead, he has asked Mike Jones, a management professor and planning consultant to MPC, as well as a good friend to both Al and Bob, to speak with Al. Al was quite open about his feelings with Bob. Al believed that he was performing his job duties adequately and expressed his loyalty to the company.

When Mike Jones reports the results of his conversation with Al, Bob becomes more puzzled about what to do. Later, when Bob finds out that Al is in Detroit at his mother's house (who is ill), he becomes really frustrated. (What Bob does not know is that Al is in Detroit closing the deal on a major account for MPC.) Mike asks Bob to talk to Al in a more straightforward way.

MOTOR PARTS CORPORATION*

Bob Marvin, president of Motor Parts Corp. (MPC), felt a great deal of conflict and frustration as he chaired the strategic planning meeting of his senior management team. Al Shepherd, his executive vice president, had just arose from the conference table and excused himself, saying:

> I'm sorry but we have had a change in our chemotherapy appointment and I have to meet Ruth.

Ruth, Al's wife, had just recently learned that she had a recurrence of a malignant brain tumor. The prior bout, over only two years ago, had been difficult. Al was completely involved with his wife's fight against her illness. He had become about as expert as a layman could become on the disease, the many methods of fighting it, and the best institutions and physicians. He had

---

* **Source:** Reprinted with the permission of Richard D. Freedman, Distinguished Service Professor of Management Emeritus, Leonard N. Stern School of Business, New York University. Copyright © 1995 by Richard D. Freedman.

accompanied her to virtually all medical appointments and procedures. When asked about her condition he would report to colleagues at great length and in technical detail. He was consumed by her situation. It had been a year since she had been given a clean bill of health when they were devastated to learn about her relapse. Now, the odds were against her. The doctors suggested a variety of alternative treatments, but at best her chances of surviving two years were less than one in three.

Bob, with great self-restraint, did not want to react at the meeting, and as hard as it was he tried to work around some of the issues that most directly affected Al.

Bob couldn't help but notice increasing, and less subtle references by others in the meeting to problems they had working around Al. After all, the organization had to go on. They all had their jobs to do, and while none had problems as severe as Al, many of them had their own serious problems. Jay Unger, VP Marketing, had a son who had recently been expelled from college and was in rehabilitation with a drug dependency problem. Pete Arnell was in the middle of a divorce. Bob himself had his own problems, real problems.

At the end of the meeting he asked Mike Jones, who had happened to be at the meeting, to return with him to his office. Mike is a management professor at the university and a consultant to MPC on planning issues.

> What am I going to do about Al? As you know, after me, he has the most important job in this company. In fact, on a day-to-day basis he probably has the most critical job since all functions except for Finance, Legal, and Public Relations report directly to him. For the past few months he has been out of the office as much as he has been in it. Even worse, numerous meetings have been set to coincide with his schedule only to be aborted at the last second because he had to leave to take his wife to a medical appointment.
>
> Now I just heard that our national sales meeting that has to be set up months in advance can't be scheduled because he is not certain about a procedure she has scheduled for about that time period.
>
> His job requires considerable travel to regional offices and he just has not been doing enough of it. We have a number of new regional managers who are not getting enough guidance. We have some regional managers who are not doing a good job. They require closer supervision, if not replacement. Instead of dealing with these issues directly he is delegating supervisory chores to the two senior staff people in his department. For example, I know Joe Roderick is a great planner and earlier in his career he was a regional manager at Major Parts, but he is not their boss. I don't want lines of authority confused. I told that to Al when we created those staff positions.
>
> You know that I try to keep in contact with our major customers. I have picked up hints that some of our regional people are just not performing adequately. He is not on top of things. Just look at how poor some of our regions are performing—Detroit and San Francisco are good examples. Our

business is as dependent on service as price and quality. We can't afford not to be on top of things.

Just think about today. Here we are under all of this pressure from our Board to develop a new five-year plan. Even though our performance has been, on a relative basis, the best in the industry, they keep warning me that a company of our size has to do even better if it is going to avoid a takeover.

And you know we haven't been cheap. Salaries have risen around here faster than any place in the industry. I think that is only fair given performance. No one has done better than Al in the eight years that he has been here. He started at a rather low pay level and now is the highest paid executive in a comparable position in the industry.

Even though I have always had problems with his attention to detail and some of the people he has hired, I have no complaint about overall results. But we have to continue to improve.

By the way, you know that this is only part of the problem with Al. He's got to be one of the softest guys I've ever met. He stays home when he's got a bad cold, when there's a few inches of snow in his driveway. He was out a week last year with an ear infection. He is out about as much as any senior manager I've ever known.

You really have to wonder sometimes about his commitment. Some Board members have picked this up. To be honest, if something happened to me I don't think he would be a serious candidate for my job, even though they think he is very talented.

Mike couldn't help but think while Bob was talking. "If someone didn't know Bob they would think him quite callous if they overheard what he just said, but Bob is really a good person in his own way." He had known Bob for over 20 years. Their careers ran in parallels. Mike had been a consultant for three organizations that employed Bob, each watched the other move up their respective professions.

Bob was a rather shy person who frequently had to work in public. So he masked his shyness in formality. Although he encouraged subordinates to demonstrate initiative, he tended to carefully scrutinize their work, even the work of those in whom he had developed considerable confidence. He wanted things done the "right" way. He was often characterized as a perfectionist. He was as meticulous in his dress as his work. Despite his success, he was quite insecure. He worried most of the time.

Bob held himself to the same standard as others. It was an unusual evening or weekend that he would not spend much of his time working on the thick pile of papers he would take home and dictating one of the dozen or so memos that he would send to subordinates every day. He tried to overcome his natural reticence in public by carefully developed presentations. There were times that he could spend half a day preparing a 10-minute presentation to his Board. One problem with the approach was that he came across to some as stiff and cold. People who did not know him well thought of him as a rather dry and formal person, even bureaucratic. Bob had few friends. Those few who managed to get close to him over the years know him as a caring and brilliant executive.

Bob said little to Al because he wanted to be supportive, and he certainly did not want to be perceived by Al as not caring or putting his job ahead of his family. After all, no one spent more time thinking about family issues than Bob. So what he did was constantly send Al reminders about unresolved issues, press him for dates, and urge him to make trips in the field.

"Well what have you said to him?" asked Mike.

> I have stressed to him how important some of the meetings are and I have tried to alert him to some of the critical issues he has to handle.
>
> He has indicated that he has been working on many of the problems at home and over the phone. He says he is in constant contact with his people over the telephone and that there are very few problems that he is not able to deal with. But that is simply not true.
>
> You've known him for a long time. Why don't you talk to him and give me your assessment?

The next week Mike asked Al out to lunch after they worked on the planning issues. Before lunch Mike couldn't help but review his impressions of Al. Al was like many people he had known who came up through sales. He was one of the most enjoyable people you could want to be around. He had an endless supply of the latest jokes—although he could be somewhat indiscreet as to who he told what joke. He was warm and friendly and showed great interest in the problems of the people he worked with—including his subordinates. He genuinely enjoyed helping his subordinates, although he was so busy that the lack of contact with him was a constant source of complaint. While this was a significant problem before the recurrence of Ruth's malignancy, now it was serious. Being liked was important to Al. His feelings would be hurt when he would hear about or sense the disapproval of a colleague. An ongoing source of conflict between Bob and Al was the fact that while Bob thought rules and regulations were meant to be followed, Al was inclined to overlook the rules, both for himself and others if the job was being done. Al was basically an optimistic person; he tended not to worry about the future, unless he had a specific problem he was forced to confront. He felt no need to control his subordinates if they were producing. After all, he had said to Mike many times what is the difference if he took time off if the job was being done?

After chatting for a while about issues that they were working on together Mike turned the conversation to Ruth's health. Al was quite hopeful about a new treatment available at the Morris Clinic. In fact, he had pulled strings with influential people and had a famous expert examine her. He advised an operation that would give her a one chance in three probability for surviving three years. Without the operation she had about a 15 percent probability. The operation would be in two months and she would have to remain at the hospital for a month. Of course, he would stay with her.

Mike asked about other relatives who could share the load. Their two children were away at college and he did not think it would be right to ask them. They were under enough stress at school and with their mother's illness. She had one sister who had two young teenagers so she could not help. Of course, he would not even consider leaving her alone.

Mike then asked: "Given all of the important issues you are working on and the people who look to you for supervision, how will you deal with your work responsibilities?"

Al said. "No problem, I've thought it through. First, I will set up in the regional office. I will try to be available for three hours a day, when I can leave Ruth. When there are significant problems with regional managers I'll fly them in to see me. After all, what's the difference if I fly out to see them or they come in to see me? As you know we hired Joe Roderick to handle major staff responsibilities like planning and executive development. He's had many years of supervisory experience, so he can handle any other issues that come up. So you can see that we ought to be able to handle the problems.

I guess I ought to tell you that this illness has been very troubling, very difficult for me to handle. I haven't been sleeping well for weeks. The same thing happened the last time. So I've been getting up at 3 or 4:00 a.m. every day. I have been using that time very productively. It is incredible how much work you can get done through the computer tie in to the office when everything is so quiet."

Mike had the feeling that there was a lot more to the story than he was getting from Al, so he responded that, "It is clear that you've given this a lot of thought. But don't tell me what your plans are, tell me how you feel about things. The fact that you are having trouble sleeping is understandable, but it's also suggestive of deeper issues."

Al replied that, "It is very difficult for me now. I know that I am not 100 percent into my job. But let me remind you about what happened about a year-and-a-half ago. The presidency of Delta Corp., our major competitor, opened when Arnie Wyman had the sudden heart attack. Their Board hired that executive search firm to find candidates, and the partner managing the account knew me and wanted me to go on their short list. You'll surely remember that I came to you as a friend and discussed the situation with you. Everyone said I would be the prime candidate for the job."

"After thinking it over I decided not to interview with them. There were a lot of factors involved, of course. But in the end the determining factor was how MPC, and Bob in particular, treated me when we were having all those health problems. I felt, and I feel, part of a family. Families take care of their own in times of trouble. Mike, money can't buy that."

Mike later spoke to Bob about his lunch with Al. He tried to be descriptive and nonevaluative, urging Bob to speak to Al directly. Yet, after the discussion Bob seemed fixated on one point. He wondered whether Al's reference to being recruited away was a cryptic warning or a genuine statement of emotion. Or was it some combination?

Two weeks later Mike was in the office working with managers on some rather complex planning issues when he was called out of a meeting to take a long distance call from Al. Al was calling from Detroit where MPC had one of its most important regional offices and which happened to be his home town.

While going over some of the planning issues Al interrupted the conversation, saying "Mike, I have to interrupt, I'm so excited, you'll never guess what happened last night. You know how long and hard we've been working on the Delta Corp. account. Tim Reynolds, our Detroit regional manager, finally set things up and we met with Delta's senior management team. We got the account! It will be at 5 least $15,000,000 this year—almost 2% of our sales goal! Don't tell Bob, I want to break the news to him. This account was a real high priority for him."

A few hours later, toward the end of the day, Mike was just completing a meeting with Bob, when Bob said to him:

"You'll never guess the latest with Al. He is in Detroit. I tried to get him in the office yesterday morning on a very important issue, but Tim Reynolds said that he hadn't been in. He said that Al was at his mother's house. You remember that his dad died last year and his mother is alone and is in the early stages of Alzheimer's. He didn't get back to me until the late afternoon. Then he told me that he had to cancel some important meetings back here because he had to spend Friday in Detroit. It's obvious that he is taking advantage again. On top of everything else. I'm really frustrated."

"Well," Mike said, "Why don't you think about discussing it with him in a more straightforward way?"

Bob replied, "What's the use? You heard what he said. He has us over a barrel. He is staying with us because we treat him like family."

"Bob, are you being sarcastic?"

Part 5

ORGANIZATIONAL DESIGN AND ORGANIZATIONAL CHANGE

Part 5 closes the book with two chapters that discuss organizational design and organizational change.

Chapter 17, "Organizational Design," describes the contingency view, which states that an organization's strategy, external environment, technical process, and size affect its design. The chapter discusses several generic forms of organizational design. Each form features different degrees of hierarchy and different management behaviors.

The chapter continues with descriptions of several specific forms of organizational design. They include the common and widely used functional, divisional, and hybrid designs; a complex form called matrix; and several evolving forms. Organizational design by function collects major activities of an organization into almost homogeneous groups. Organizational design by division divides the organization's activities according to customers served, operating locations, and the like. Some organizational designs feature a combination of the functional and divisional forms.

Organizational design by matrix is a complex form that aligns an organization along two dimensions. One dimension focuses on the organization's functional activities. The other dimension focuses on projects that serve the organization's customers.

Several evolving forms of organizational design are growing in use. Self-managing work teams let managers build an organization around decentralized teams. Process organizational design moves away from a hierarchical view and says organizations are a series of interconnected processes. Virtual organizations use networks to build connections between the host organization and many other organizations.

Chapter 18, "Organizational Change and Development," describes the forces for and against change and the difference between planned and unplanned change. Two models of planned organizational change exist. The evolutionary model sees change happening incrementally over time. The revolutionary model views change as unfolding over periods of stability followed by bursts of change activity. Chapter 18 then describes organizational development, a systematic, phased approach to planned change that uses much knowledge from the social and behavioral sciences.

Chapter 17

ORGANIZATIONAL DESIGN

After reading this chapter, you should be able to:

- Analyze how an organization's design coordinates its activities and gets information to decision makers.
- Describe the contingency factors of organizational design.
- Distinguish among the organizational design effects of strategy, external environment, technical process, and size.
- Discuss some generic forms of organizational design.
- Explain the design features of functional, divisional, hybrid, and matrix organizational forms.
- Compare the characteristics of several organizational forms that are likely to evolve in the future.
- Appreciate some international and ethical issues that surround the design of organizations.

Organizational design is the way managers structure their organization to reach the organization's goals.[1] The allocation of duties, tasks, and responsibilities among departments and individuals is an organizational design element. Other structural and design elements include reporting relationships and the number of levels in the organization's hierarchy.

Managers can choose from many types of organizational design. Some modern organizational designs rely on computer and communication technologies. Others draw on well-established designs that managers and organizations have used for many years. Whatever the organizational design chosen, they all have a simple enduring quality—they are hierarchies that depend on authority relationships.[2]

Organizational charts show an organization's formal design. They show the organization's current configuration or a future configuration that the organization's managers want. These charts typically use boxes to show positions in the organization and lines connecting the boxes to show reporting relationships.[3] Figure 17.1 shows an organizational chart for a hypothetical manufacturing company. The chart quickly shows how managers have divided the major organization tasks and the major reporting relationships. For example, manufacturing, engineering, and marketing report to one person, the Operations Vice President. Such grouping emphasizes the close ties needed in modern manufacturing among those who design, build, and market products.

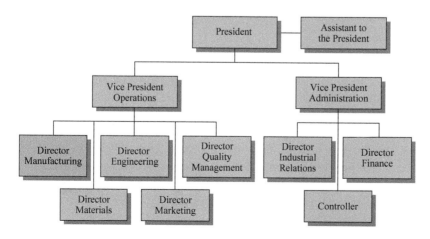

■ **Figure 17.1:**   Organization Chart of a Manufacturing Company

Organizational charts are incomplete pictures of an organization's division of labor. They do not show all communication links, integrating mechanisms, behavioral processes, and informal arrangements within the organization.[4] Nevertheless, organizational charts are useful for showing an organization's basic intended design.

The design of an organization is much more than the lines and boxes on an organizational chart. "[I]t is a pattern of interactions and coordination that links the technology, tasks, and human components of the organization to ensure that the organization accomplishes its purpose."[5] Organizational design includes the different ways organizations divide their work between people and work units.

Organizational design's goals are (1) get information to the right places for effective decision making and (2) help coordinate the organization's interdependent parts. When the organization's design is not right for what it is doing, managers might not get the information they need to predict problems and make effective decisions.[6] They also might not react quickly enough to problems because the existing organizational design blocks needed information. The existing structure might not do an effective job of monitoring changes in the external environment. It might fail to signal managers that a decision is needed now because of such environmental changes.

THE CONTINGENCY FACTORS OF ORGANIZATIONAL DESIGN

Managers often assess four contingency factors before deciding to design or redesign an organization. The factors are the external environment, the organization's strategy, its technical process, and its size. Each factor alone can affect design decisions, or they can act as a collection of forces that both press for design choices and constrain them. Managers can choose from the different designs, described later in this chapter, to reach the organizational performance levels they desire.[7]

Overview

The external environment includes the organization's competitors, customers, suppliers, distributors, government regulators, legislation affecting the company, countries of operation, labor unions, culture, and the like. An organization's strategy describes goals and the ways managers expect to reach those goals. Technical process is the organization's system for producing its products or services. The organization's size (number of employees) directly affects organizational design and changes the effects of other contingency factors.

Organizations are open systems with permeable boundaries. A system is a set of interdependent parts forming an organic whole. Open systems can act on their external environment and are affected by activities in that environment. Open systems have transactions and exchanges with various parts of their external environment. Closed systems have no such transactions. They are self-contained and operate independently of their external environment. This chapter assumes modern organizations are open systems that interact with their environments.

Figure 17.2 shows some relationships among the contingency factors. The external environment of an organization is dynamic and can change, forcing managers to form a new strategy for dealing with the change. Carrying out that strategy can require a change in some aspect of the organization's design, technical process, or both. The figure shows organizational size affecting several factors. A later section, "Organization Size," describes some effects of organization size. Managers who successfully align and balance these factors often get higher organizational performance than those who do not.[8]

Figure 17.2 shows organizational culture surrounding the relationships among the contingency factors. Organizational culture forms the context within which managers decide about organizational design and redesign. For example, an organization's culture can be a source of resistance to change (see Chapter 4, "Organizational Culture"). Managers must understand their organization's existing culture before beginning to redesign the organization.

Strategy

An organization's strategy is the organization's long-term goals and the way it plans to reach those goals. Strategy also specifies how managers should allocate resources to reach long-term goals. An organization's strategy might need to change as its external environment changes.[9]

The strategic planning process plays a mediating role among the external environment, the organizational design, and the organization's technical process.

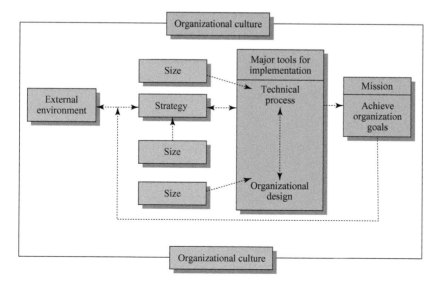

Figure 17.2: Relationships among the Contingency Factors of Organizational Design

For example, the strategic planning process can react to uncertainty in a product's market by increasing product innovation. The product innovation then leads to changes in the organization's design or technical process that help the organization carry out the innovation successfully.[10] Empirical research[11] strongly supports this "structure follows strategy" view.[12]

Another view, "strategy follows structure," sees strategy linked less directly to organizational design.[13] An organization's design is the environment within which managers form their strategy. The existing organizational design affects the managers' perceptions of opportunities and threats outside the organization. The existing design can help shape an effective strategy, or it can be a constraint. Empirical research offers limited support for the "strategy follows structure" view. Changes in structure must be large before changes in strategy follow. Because both views of strategy can affect the design of an organization, Figure 17.2 links strategy and organizational design with a two-headed arrow.

External Environment

Managers often assess the uncertainty in their organization's external environment when considering design decisions.[14] Managers can respond to uncertainty in two ways. They can design the organization to increase information about the environment or they can make the organization more flexible in its response to the environment. Information plays a key role because it can reduce risk in a manager's predictions about the future.

Two elements contribute to **environmental uncertainty**.[15] The first element is the complexity of the external environment. A simple environment has a few similar elements. A complex environment has many different elements that managers must monitor. Think of environmental complexity as a continuum that ranges from **simple to complex**.

The second element that adds uncertainty to an organization's environment falls on a continuum ranging from **static to dynamic**. A static external environment is unchanging or changes slowly; a dynamic external environment has many fast-moving events that could conflict with each other. The degree of change creates uncertainty in predicting future environmental states.

The external environment's four possible states have varying degrees of uncertainty. Each state is a point on an environmental continuum that ranges from certainty to uncertainty. A **simple-static** environment has the lowest uncertainty; a **complex-dynamic** environment has the highest uncertainty. Both **simple-dynamic** and **complex-static** environments are about midway between the other two. The unexpected explosive growth in Internet commerce, for example, has created a complex-dynamic environment for much of the retail industry.[16]

Technical Process

The technical process converts an organization's inputs (material, human, monetary) into outputs.[17] The process can be mechanical, as in manufacturing organizations, or it can be a service to clients, as in banks, hospitals, or insurance companies. The process also can be largely mental, as in organizations that solve problems or create new ideas, products, and services. Research and development (R&D) organizations, advertising agencies, and software development companies are examples of the latter.

Technical process design can predetermine much of the people's behavior who work in the process. Technical processes vary in work pace, worker control, complexity, routine, predictability, and interdependence within the process. The technical process decides both what is done and the pace at which it is done.

The research examining relationships between the technical process and organizational design has aroused much controversy.[18] Questions about how to measure and classify technical processes muddy conclusions we can draw from published reports. Studies strongly disagree about technology's importance as a contingency factor of organizational design.[19] Some studies support it as a factor; other studies do not.

With these cautions in mind, some conclusions emerge from systematically reviewing the research literature.[20] Routine technologies feature centralized decision making that uses formal written rules and procedures to guide decisions. Such centralization is more characteristic of small organizations than large organizations. Organizations that use routine technologies and have many professional employees use fewer formal procedures than organizations with fewer professionals. Organizations that use complex, nonroutine technologies have more departments, fewer levels of authority, and more participation in decision making than organizations that use more routine technologies. Modern manufacturing technologies, for example, let managers move decision authority to lower levels than was possible in the past.[21]

Organization Size

An organization's size can affect many aspects of the organization and its management. Organizations usually develop more formal written rules and procedures as they increase in size. Large organizations have more management levels and more structured work activities than small organizations, and they often use a decentralized form.[22]

Large organizations can have more diverse activities that need more coordination than small organizations.[23] Managers in large organizations make decisions guided by written rules and procedures. Small organizations can have an informal decision process and a simpler design.[24] Small organizations also have fewer diverse activities, fewer formal written procedures, and narrower spans of control (number of people reporting to a manager).

An organization's size moderates the technical process's effects on organizational design. Technical process is more strongly associated with organizational design in small organizations than in large organizations. People in the technical process have less control over work procedures in large organizations than in small ones.[25]

GENERIC FORMS OF ORGANIZATIONAL DESIGN

Researchers have proposed two sets of generic forms of organizational design that have empirical support in organizational design literature. The first set features two generic organization forms: mechanistic and organic. The second set features four generic forms: defender, prospector, analyzer, and reactor.

Mechanistic and Organic Organizations

Recall that organizations' external environments can fall on a continuum ranging from certainty to uncertainty. Two different types of organizational design are right for the two different environments.[26]

A mechanistic organization fits a highly certain external environment. Mechanistic organizations have the following characteristics:

▪ Clearly specified tasks.
▪ Precisely defined member rights and obligations.
▪ Hierarchical control, authority, and communication structure.
▪ Vertical interaction and communication.

Mechanistic organizations have predictable, formal internal relationships and rely on written rules and procedures. This organizational design suits recurring events to which organizational members can give standardized responses.

An organic organization fits an uncertain external environment. Organic organizations have the following characteristics:

▪ Loosely defined roles.
▪ Continually redefine tasks through interaction with other organization members.
▪ Rely on individual's commitment to organization goals to direct activities of organization members instead of relying on authority and control.
▪ Decentralize control and decision making.
▪ Fast decision-making processes.[27]
▪ Lateral and vertical communication.

Organic organizations process information better than mechanistic organizations.[28] Less-defined roles and continually redefining tasks give people flexibility to respond to changing events. Decentralized decision making helps people deal with the different situations presented by a changing external environment. A speedy decision process helps managers keep up with fast environmental shifts.

Defender, Prospector, Analyzer, and Reactor Organizations

The second configuration typology describes four organizational forms: defender, prospector, analyzer, and reactor.[29] The defender and prospector organizations anchor the end points of a continuum with the analyzer midway between them. The reactor is not on the continuum because this typology views it as a maladapted organization form.

Defender organizations succeed in stable environments with well-defined market segments for their products and services. They develop a committed customer base that lets them provide a predictable flow of products or services to the marketplace. Because their environment is stable, defenders have a competitive cost advantage that comes from specialization, repeated use of well-understood technical processes, and low costs of product manufacturing or service delivery. The defender's organizational design features well-defined functions, centralization, and formal procedures. They use a long-range planning process because their external environments change slowly. Many companies producing products with strong brand recognition, such as Jaguar automobiles, are defender organizations.

Prospector organizations succeed in dynamic environments that are unpredictable and fast-changing. They prosper by continually watching their external environment to find new markets. Prospectors focus on developing new products or services that fit fast-changing customer needs, desires, and expectations. Because they focus on developing new products and services, prospectors often change their external environment as well as respond to it. Prospector organizations have high decentralization, little task specialization, few management levels, and high interdependence between people and work units. Their technical processes emphasize flexibility so they can quickly introduce new products. Changes in the external environment have few negative effects on prospectors because they constantly monitor, adapt, and change the environment. Their constant quest for newness brings internal change that prevents them from enjoying the stable organizational design and stable technical processes advantages. Successful personal computer (PC) companies, such as Acer in Taiwan, are examples of prospector organizations.

Analyzer organizations have features of both prospector and defender organizations. To keep costs low, they strive for efficiency in their technical processes for producing stable products and services. They develop new products and services to maintain a competitive edge in changing markets. Analyzer organizations constantly scan their external environment for successful new products and services from prospectors. They then quickly introduce their own versions to capture market share. Because these organizations feature both stability and change, one part of their organizational design is routine, formal, and centralized. Another part features temporary task groups, decentralization, and few formal procedures. Major drug manufacturers such as Whitehall Laboratories invest in R&D for new products while successfully marketing established products such as Advil®.

Reactor organizations have an unbalanced configuration of external environment, organizational design, strategy, and technical process. Managers of reactor organizations have poorly adapted to environmental changes over time. Poor adaptation can occur for three reasons: (1) lack of a clear strategy that is widely known throughout the organization, (2) a technical process and organizational design that are not well linked to a strategy, or (3) management's insistence on keeping a strategy, technical process, or organizational design that is no longer right for a changed environment.

The first three organizational forms have a balanced configuration of external environment, strategy, technical process, and organizational design. Some research points to greater success for organizations with balanced configurations.[30] The last organizational form, the reactor, is less effective than the others.

SPECIFIC FORMS OF ORGANIZATIONAL DESIGN

The three major forms of organizational design are functional, divisional, and matrix. Managers also can combine functional and divisional designs into a hybrid design to get the best features of each. The divisional structure has several variations, creating an extensive list of design choices.

Several newer forms of organizational design are evolving and beginning to see widespread use. Those forms focus on teams or processes or link widely dispersed organizations and individuals to form an extended organization.

Managers do not use formulas to guide their design choices.[31] Each design has advantages and disadvantages, and managers try to choose the design that offers the most benefits and the fewest limitations.[32] Understanding the advantages and disadvantages of each design lets the manager use informed judgment when picking the basic configuration for an organization and variants within it.

Organizational Design by Function

Organizational design by **function** groups an organization's tasks according to the organization's activities. A functional configuration divides the organization into major units or departments such as accounting, finance, manufacturing, engineering, management information systems, and the like. Functional configurations can vary from one organization to another and usually depend on its goals and tasks.[33]

The strategy of a functional organization focuses on a few products or services in well-defined markets with few competitors. Functional organizational designs work well in stable, simple external environments with little uncertainty. The technical process is routine and depends little on the other parts of the organization. Standardized products or services let the organization apply the technical process repeatedly, according to well-defined procedures.

Look again at Figure 17.1, the organizational chart for the hypothetical manufacturing company described earlier. This company has a clear functional design with each function shown below the two vice presidents. The functions include manufacturing, engineering, marketing, finance, and industrial relations. Each box in the figure is a major element that the company feels is important for it to function effectively.

Although the chart is not detailed, it gives you some idea of the environmental sectors that the company considers important. Each major function helps align the company with each sector. For example, marketing focuses on the customer, a key element in the success of many firms. Marketing does not manufacture products. This department tries to sell the products using promotions in different media such as print advertising and television advertising.

The organizational chart also shows the combined use of line and staff within a functional design. Operations is the line organization shown in Figure 17.1. The functions within Operations are the major operating tasks of designing and manufacturing the product. The remaining staff functions serve in support and advisory roles to the line organization. Finance supports Operations by focusing on money sources for plant expansion. Industrial Relations supports the entire company by trying to maintain a committed workforce.

Functional organizations emphasize the technical skills of those within each function. The organization rewards behavior associated with the function's technical contribution. Individuals work in an environment populated with others who share common backgrounds and views. Such homogeneity can lead to narrow views of the function's contribution to the organization. Carried to its extreme, the emphasis on a functional contribution can produce dysfunctional behavior for the organization and limited career opportunities. For example, a person with a long career in the finance function could view all organizational operations as involving only finance and not consider any other function such as marketing.

A functional design has several strengths. It emphasizes specialization within the organization by grouping similar activities into single units or departments. The design brings specialists together in one place. Most accountants are in the accounting function, most financial analysts are in the financial function, and most engineers are in the engineering function. Such groups let collegial relationships develop among specialists. The groups encourage special skills development and information sharing. Career paths for the specialists are clear. A person who begins as a junior accountant can follow a career path within the accounting function to as high as he aspires.

The functional design's weaknesses partly derive from its strengths. Its weaknesses start to show when the organization's external environment shifts to a state that is ill-suited to a functional design. A functional design usually does not help managers respond quickly to external changes. The emphasis on specialization promotes a tunnel-vision view of each function's goal. Engineers do engineering; financial analysts do financial analysis; and so forth. The environment can shift, however, requiring a broader view and review of the organization's strategy. Getting a broader view can be difficult within a functional design, especially if it has existed for some time.

Organizational Design by Division

Organizational design by **division** uses decentralization as its basic approach. The basis of the decentralized divisions can be the organization's products, services, locations, customers, programs, or technical processes. A divisional design is especially useful for a strategy focused on different products or services.

It is useful when the strategy calls for high customer or client satisfaction with the organization's products or services. Some organizations are so complex in their relationship with their external environment that they simultaneously use several different bases for a divisional structure.

Organizations often evolve from a functional design to a divisional form. As the external environment changes, managers might need to diversify the organization's activities to stay competitive. As they add new activities, managers might find that the functional design does not let them manage as efficiently as they must. The solution often tried is moving or evolving the present functional form to a divisional design.[34]

An organization needs a divisional structure when it faces a complex, fast-changing external environment with moderate-to-high uncertainty. Technical processes in divisional organizations often are nonroutine and depend on other parts of the organization. Organizations with continuous process technologies, such as oil and chemical refineries, often use a divisional form. The divisional form focuses attention on costly and potentially dangerous processes. A divisional structure also is a common way to manage large organizations.

Colgate-Palmolive Co. uses a divisional structure based on its major operating areas around the world. The company's products face distinctly different markets in different world regions. Marketing of Colgate-Palmolive products in the United States likely is different from marketing products in Latin America or in the Asia-Pacific region.

Colgate-Palmolive's international divisions face sharply different legal and cultural environments in Europe, Latin America, and the Asia-Pacific countries. Grouping international operations into divisions separate from domestic operations lets the international divisions develop specialized skills and abilities for dealing with international questions that do not arise in domestic operations. The divisional organization helps Colgate-Palmolive respond and adapt to differences in product type, product marketing, and cultural differences of its various international locations.

Divisional organizational design emphasizes people's decision-making autonomy throughout the organization. Individuals at various levels can become more involved in the organization's basic activities. Decentralized organizations also put individuals in contact with people from many parts of the organization. Such organizations put more demands on individuals' interpersonal skills than functional organizations. They also often reward behavior that furthers the decentralization goals. Such behavior can focus on a product, customer, service, or location.

Several strengths characterize a divisional design. The organization easily adapts to differences in products, services, clients, locations, and the like. Products can differ not only in how they are manufactured, but also in how they are marketed. Products, services, and customers are highly visible in a divisional structure. The names of products or a broad class of products often appear in the company's organizational chart.

The divisional structure's weaknesses come partly from its decentralized qualities. Economies of scale are lost because many organization functions, such as accounting, human resources, and purchasing, are duplicated within each division. Technical specialization is not as focused as in a functional design. Specialists in one division cannot talk readily with similar specialists in another division. Applying human resource and purchasing policies uniformly is also difficult because decentralized functions are dispersed among the divisions.

Hybrid Organizational Design

Managers often combine functional and divisional designs to form a hybrid organization. They use this hybrid form to get the benefits and reduce the weaknesses of the two configurations used separately. Divisions are used in the same way described earlier. The divisions decentralize some functions, and the headquarters location centralizes others. The centralized functions often are the costly ones for the organization.[35]

Many design factors of a hybrid design are the same as those for a divisional organization. Many products or services are involved. Often the organization needs to use resources efficiently and to adapt to changes in the external environment. An organization's size is a design factor because a small organization often cannot bear the cost of maintaining a corporate headquarters and related staff.

Unilever de Argentina S.A. uses a hybrid design. The functional areas provide specialized support activities such as human resources and finance to each division and the entire company. Human resources includes safety, hygiene, and management development. The financial function includes company-wide finance, accounting, and auditing. The divisions focus activities according to specific market areas, such as personal care products and foods. Each division includes marketing and sales activities focused on the products assigned to the division.

Organizations that combine functional and divisional forms make behavioral demands similar to both types of organizations. Individuals in different parts of the organization fulfill different sets of demands. Those in the functional areas are rewarded for behavior associated with their technical expertise. The functional specialists supporting division operations are rewarded for achieving division goals. The two sources of pressure (that is, activities that lead to rewards) for different types of behavior are not always consistent. Such inconsistency can lead to conflict about the functional specialist's role.

A hybrid design has the divisional organization's strengths of focus on products and customers, and adapts well to complex environments. Economies of scale are possible in some functional areas. Expensive shared resources are not decentralized and duplicated at high cost to the organization.

The hybrid design's weaknesses follow directly from trying to get the best features of both the functional and the divisional forms. The hybrid organization shares the divisional organization's weaknesses of focusing on divisional goals and applying organizational policies in a nonuniform way. An added weakness is the potential for high administrative overheads if the staff at corporate headquarters expands without control. A high potential for conflict exists between decentralized divisions and centralized corporate headquarters units. Division managers want autonomy to do what they believe they do well. Centralized units might want to control divisions even when doing so is not effective.

Matrix Organizational Design

Organizations often use a **matrix** design when two sectors of the external environment demand management attention. For example, if the organization produces products using advanced technology and its customers have highly specialized needs, both changes in technology and changes in customer needs require management's attention.[36] Organizations also often move to a matrix form after other organizations in their region or industry have adopted it.[37]

The word *matrix* evolved during the 1950s within the U.S. aerospace industry to describe the grid-like organizational design used in project management. This design rejects the long-standing recommendation of unity of command with each employee getting direction from only one boss. Matrix organizational designs have multiple authority structures so that many people report to two managers.

Figure 17.3 shows a simple matrix organizational design. People from different functional areas of the company (the top row) are assigned to various projects (the left column). Each person assigned to a project reports to at least two supervisors or managers. One supervisor is in the functional area and the other is in a project.

The mixture of people from the functional areas varies according to project needs. Some projects, such as Project Office C, need people from all functional areas. Other projects, such as Project Office A and B, need people only from some functional areas. After a person finishes a project, he returns to the functional area.

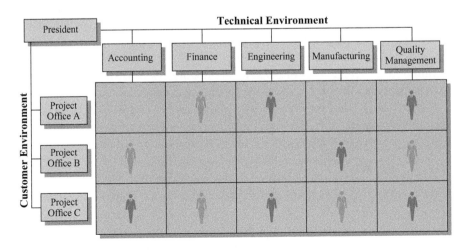

■ **Figure 17.3:** Simple Matrix Organizational Design

Multiple reporting relationships are a basic feature of matrix organizations, distinguishing them from the forms discussed earlier. Although reporting to two or more managers might appear odd, many people have experienced this relationship as children when both their mother and father have authority. Children often skillfully navigate these multiple authority relations.

The following are the conditions under which an organization might choose a matrix design:

■ Pressures from the external environment for a **dual focus**. The example from the aerospace industry described fast changes in technology and customer needs. Those pressures moved managers to adopt the matrix form's multiple focus.

■ **High uncertainty** within multiple external environment sectors. Multiple elements in the external environment are changing fast, creating high uncertainty about future environmental states. High uncertainty creates a strong need for more information.

■ **Constraints** on human and physical resources. Most organizations have constraints on expanding their human or physical resources. This is especially true when the resources are expensive specialists or costly technical equipment. The matrix organizational form encourages sharing those resources and allows the flexibility to meet competing requests.

Managers can design a matrix organization in different ways.[38] Some organizations use a matrix form within specific functional areas only. Such an arrangement is common in a marketing department. Managers responsible for a brand or group of brands bring all the marketing skills together to focus on the products. Other organizations use temporary matrix forms to complete specific projects, with the matrix organization disbanding after project completion. Still other organizations have the matrix form as a permanent feature of their organizational design.

Matrix organizations place high demands on managers' skills. Because of a matrix organization's high conflict potential, managers need well-developed conflict-management skills. When managers have poor conflict-management skills, matrix organizations become seriously dysfunctional. (See Chapter 11, "Conflict in Organizations," for a complete discussion of conflict and conflict management.)

Matrix organizations demand coordination, cooperation, and communication. The communication often is face-to-face and in groups or teams. Both managers and nonmanagers must have high levels of interpersonal skill to function successfully in matrix organizations. Individuals who do not like high levels of human contact will find matrix organizations uncomfortable.

The strengths of matrix organizations include responsiveness, flexibility, efficient use of costly resources, and potentially high levels of human motivation and involvement.[39] The dual focus of matrix organizations lets management respond quickly to changes in market or product demand. Matrix organizations share scarce and often expensive human and physical resources among different projects. Individuals in a matrix organization can get information about a total project, not only about their particular specialty.

A matrix organization's weaknesses include the ambiguity caused by dual or multiple authority relationships for many people. Ambiguity in authority relationships can encourage power struggles among managers who compete for dominance. People reporting to both a functional and a project manager can experience opposing demands from the two managers. Matrix organizations are also complex systems with high conflict potential. Such conflict can reach dysfunctionally high levels. These weaknesses can cause significant stress for people in such organizations.

Evolving Forms of Organizational Design

Managers are trying several new ways of designing their organizations. Some forms focus on teams and work processes. Others try to balance the formal and informal parts of an organization. The most unusual form, the virtual organization, links widely scattered organizations to form a network focused on a specific goal.

Self-Managing Teams

Many changes unfolding in the external environment of organizations emphasize the need to focus on customers and have the flexibility to respond to changing needs. Managers are moving decisions to lower levels in their organizations to meet both requirements. The need to meet diverse local requirements becomes even more important as organizations increasingly become more global in outlook.[40]

An organization that relies on **self-managing teams** (see Chapter 10, "Groups and Intergroup Processes") uses decentralization to move decisions to the teams. The teams have decision authority for product design, process design, and customer service. Such teams give the organization needed flexibility and tailor responses to specific customers. Many self-managing teams also feature people from different functions in the organization. In this way, the teams deliberately use functional differences in thinking to get more creative solutions to problems.

Decentralization and self-managing teams help managers flatten their organizations by removing one or more management levels. The result is often a nimble organization poised to meet the changing opportunities and constraints in the external environment.

Process Organizational Design

Process organizational design discards the idea of packaging duties and tasks offered by a functional or divisional approach. Instead, it asks managers to view their organization as a series of interconnected processes that weave across functions. Such process organizations are "flexible groupings of intertwined work and information flows that cut horizontally across [the organization], ending at points of contact with customers."[41] Organizations try to get a strategic advantage from the intense customer focus of a process organizational design.

A process organizational design focuses people on process results, not on their skills or functions. People are assigned responsibility for all or part of a process in which they use multiple skills. They also have the decision authority to act within their process.[42] People assigned to processes keep reporting in their functional area such as engineering and marketing. They also report to a process manager, giving them the dual-manager experience that exists in a matrix organization. Process managers must coordinate and cooperate with functional managers to maintain successful, efficient processes that satisfy customer desires.[43]

Insurance companies often process insurance applications with a stepwise process that goes from function to function. Individual clerks do repetitive tasks focused on a small part of the process. The steps include checking the application, rating it, and offering the customer a quotation. One insurance company changed its organizational design from functional to process.[44] Individual case managers were assigned to each application. They processed the entire application with the help of individual computers and expert systems that guided the manager through the process. The case manager went to someone for help only when an application raised major issues that required advice from a physician or an underwriter. The company reduced its processing time from an average of 5 to 25 days to 2 to 5 days. The company also increased its responsiveness to customers because a case manager had all the information he needed to answer a customer's questions.

The Virtual Organization

A **virtual organization** is a network of companies or individuals that focuses on reaching a specific target or responding to new opportunities. The networks can be temporary or permanent and are flexible so they can respond to fast environmental changes. Information technology, the Internet, and the World Wide Web link network members wherever they are in the world.[45]

The term *virtual organization* borrows its metaphor from computer technology. Virtual memory is a computer programming technique that gives a programmer more memory than is actually available on the computer. Software simulates memory by using space on a disk drive. When the program runs, it is unaware that the software gives it virtual memory instead of real memory.

The metaphor carries to the virtual organization. Any company that lacks a particular skill or resource enters an agreement with a company or person (consultant or contract employee) with that skill or resource. Information technology links the companies and individuals so they can operate as though they were a single organization. The skills, talents, and resources needed to reach the goal define the number of elements in a virtual organization network.

Unlike the designs discussed earlier, members of a virtual organization network have little direct control over the functions done by other network members. This approach to organizational design requires new behaviors from managers. High trust in network members is a central feature of a virtual organization. Conflict management and negotiation behaviors play a key role because of required cooperative relationships among parts of the network. Interdependencies among virtual organization members require them to work together to reach a mutually desired goal.[46]

Ford and Chrysler have formed formidable virtual links with their suppliers. These companies give nearly real-time production updates so suppliers can ship only what is needed when it is needed. Wal-Mart has formed electronic connections with suppliers to keep its inventories low. Perhaps the best-known virtual organization is Amazon.com, a virtual store with no inventory, electronic ordering, and electronic links to its customers.[47]

INTERNATIONAL ASPECTS OF ORGANIZATIONAL DESIGN

The international context of organizations increases the complexity of their external environments. The external environment elements described earlier multiply when an organization moves into the global arena. Countries vary in cultural orientation, labor laws, consumer preferences, buying and selling traditions, and economics. Multiple country operations can increase the environmental complexity of multinational organizations even further.[48]

Functional and divisional designs may be more congruent with the values of countries that want to avoid uncertainty and accept hierarchical differences in power, such as many Latin countries and Japan.[49] Countries that avoid ambiguity are not likely to accept a design with little predictability of human behavior. Matrix organizations typically have multiple authority relations and high ambiguity, making them unacceptable in countries such as Belgium, France, and Italy.

Cultures vary in how successfully they use self-managing teams. U.S. managers increasingly emphasize these teams as they shift to quality management. Managers in many Scandinavian countries also use self-managing teams with great success. Swedish and Norwegian organizations have restructured their work systems around self-managing teams,[50] an approach consistent with their more socially oriented values, need for quality interpersonal relationships, and little emphasis on competition.[51]

The virtual organization can use communications and computer technology to link organizations around the world. Members of such alliances can use an organizational design consistent with local culture values. As global relationships of this type increase, they will add to the complexity of managing in the international environment.

ETHICAL ISSUES AND ORGANIZATIONAL DESIGN

Managers face several ethical issues when considering the external environment of their organizations or when assessing strategic options. They can affect their external environments by lobbying activities. Such efforts are common in the United States, where they are considered both legal and ethical. Bribing government officials, however, is illegal under U.S. law.

Managers face constant choices about using new technologies in their organization's technical processes. Such changes can affect an organization's employment levels and create stress for those who need to learn new ways of working. The ethical issues center on the stress effects of such changes and the effects on displaced workers.

Strategic responses to environmental shifts also raise ethical questions. Many organizations have been pressed to become smaller, leaner, and more efficient to stay competitive. A utilitarian analysis focuses on the net benefits of management's actions. For example, many people gain from an organization slimming down, including shareholders, customers, and the remaining employees. The employees who lost their jobs are a clear cost. In the utilitarian view, management's actions were ethical if the total benefits exceeded the costs.

Matrix organizations often produce conflict and ambiguity. Moving to a process view of organizations usually requires large-scale organizational change. The virtual organization asks people to enter new and unusual relationships. Each move implies some ethical issues about the stress effects on people affected by these changes.

SUMMARY

Organizational design refers to the way managers structure organizations by assigning tasks and responsibilities to departments and individuals and by defining reporting relationships among them. The design of an organization helps get information to the right places for effective decision making and helps coordinate the interdependent parts of the organization.

The contingency factors of organizational design are strategy, external environment, technical process, and size. An organization's external environment can change, requiring managers to form a new strategy. That new strategy is then carried out by changing the technical process, organizational design, or both. Routine technologies centralize decision making and use written rules and procedures to guide decisions. Complex, nonroutine technologies can have more complex organizational forms with more departments or divisions than routine technologies.

Several generic organizational forms add to our understanding of organizational design. Mechanistic organizational forms work well in a static environment; organic forms work well in a dynamic environment. Other generic forms are defender, prospector, analyzer, and reactor organizations. The first three work well in different external environments. Reactor organizations have an unbalanced configuration of external environment, organizational design, strategy, and technical process.

Functional organizational design puts specialists together and separates them from other specialists. Such organizations emphasize developing and using technical skills, an emphasis that can distract members from the larger goals of the organization.

Organizations designed by divisions stress a particular set of products, markets, services, technologies, and the like. Such organizations are decentralized, with authority for decisions dispersed throughout the organization. Divisional organizations can be flexible and responsive to a changing environment. The emphasis on the division's work, however, can divert attention from the total organization's goals.

Matrix organizations are the most complex form of organization described in this chapter. Dual-authority relationships in many parts of the organization are their most distinctive feature. Matrix organizations are flexible and often constantly changing. Evidence suggests that the matrix form does not fit the values of all cultures, implying that multinational organizations should use it with caution.

Evolving organizational forms feature self-managing teams and organizations designed around processes. A third form, the virtual organization, uses technology to connect far-flung parts of the organization. Managers are using these new designs to build organizations that respond faster and more effectively to shifting constraints and opportunities.

An organization's international context can greatly increase the external environment's complexity. Operations in multiple countries further increase that complexity. Different organizational forms will best fit different country cultures.

Ethical issues center on management's shifts in strategic focus and the positive and negative effects on present employees. Moving to the evolving organizational forms also raises ethical questions about the people effects of such changes.

<table>
<tr><td>REVIEW
AND
DISCUSSION
QUESTIONS

17</td><td>

REVIEW AND DISCUSSION QUESTIONS

1 What are the major contingency factors of organizational design? How are they related to each other? Discuss modern examples of each contingency factor.

2 Why are mechanistic organizations right for a static environment? Why do organic organizations fit well with a dynamic environment? Which organization form likely will be dominant in the future?

3 Why do organizations often combine organization by function and organization by division? What advantages do organizations get from this more complex hybrid form?

4 What are the characteristics of defender, prospector, analyzer, and reactor organizations? What types of environments does each organizational form best fit? What are the unique qualities of a reactor organization?

5 Discuss the characteristics of matrix organizations. What environmental conditions contribute to choosing this complex organizational design? What skills do people need to successfully work in and manage a matrix organization?

</td></tr>
</table>

6 Review the section describing the evolving forms of organizational design. Which forms appear especially appealing, challenging, and motivating? Why?

7 Review the chapter's international and ethics sections. Discuss the ethical issues that surround organizational design questions in different countries. Should managers choose a design according to the local culture or according to their home culture?

TAKE FIVE: OB ALIVE: *CASINO* (1995)

17
TAKE FIVE

Martin Scorcese's *Casino* is his complex and beautifully photographed study of 1970s' Las Vegas gambling casinos. They have organized crime connections which combine with ambition, sex, greed, and drugs to destroy a gambling empire. The film includes strong performances by Sharon Stone, Robert De Niro, and Joe Pesci.

These scenes appear within DVD Chapter 2, "The Truth about Las Vegas," starting at 0:21:03 and playing to the chapter's end. It begins with a close-up shot of casino executive Sam "Ace" Rothstein (Robert De Niro). His voice-over says, "In Vegas, everybody's gotta watch everybody else." The scenes end after Rothstein describes the surveillance people as ex-cheats who know every trick in the house.

When viewing these scenes, watch for the organizational design concepts discussed in this chapter. Ask yourself: Which organizational design forms do these scenes show? Do this scenes show the organizational design processes of differentiation and integration?

REFERENCES AND NOTES

REFERENCES
AND NOTES
17

1. Burton, R. M., B. Obel, and G. DeSantis. 2011. *Organizational Design: A Step-by-Step Approach*, 2nd edn. New York: Cambridge University Press.
Butler, R. J. 1991. *Designing Organizations: A Decision-Making Perspective*. New York: Routledge.
Davis, M. R., and D. A. Weckler. 1996. *A Practical Guide to Organization Design*. Menlo Park: Crisp Publications.
Flamholtz, E. G., and Y. Randle. 1998. Designing Organizational Structure: Understanding the Fundamentals. In *Changing the Game: Organizational Transformations of the First, Second, and Third Kinds*, ed. E. G. Flamholtz and Y. Randle. New York: Oxford University Press, Chap. 8.
Huber, G. P. 2011. Organizations: Theory, Design, Future. In *APA Handbook of Industrial and Organizational Psychology*, ed. S. Zedeck. Washington, DC: American Psychological Association, Chap. 5.
Kramer, R. J. 1996. *Organizing for Global Competitiveness: A Research Summary*. New York: Conference Board.
Nadler, D. A., and M. L. Tushman. 1997. *Competing by Design: The Power of Organizational Architecture*. New York: Oxford University Press.

2. Leavitt, H. J. 2003. Why Hierarchies Thrive. *Harvard Business Review* (March): 96–102.

Leavitt, H. J. 2007. Big Organizations Are Unhealthy Environments for Human Beings. *Academy of Management Learning and Education* 62: 253–63.

3. White, K. K. 1963. *Understanding the Company Organization Chart*. New York: American Management Association.

4. Krackhardt, D., and J. R. Hanson. 1993. Informal Networks: The Company Behind the Chart. *Harvard Business Review* 71 (July–August): 104–11.

5. Duncan, R. 1999. What Is the Right Organization Structure? Decision Tree Analysis Provides the Answer. *Organizational Dynamics* 7 (Winter): 59–80. (Quotation taken from p. 59.)

6. Ibid., pp. 77–79.

7. Bluedorn, A. C. 1993. Pilgrim's Progress: Trends and Convergence in Research on Organizational Size and Environments. *Journal of Management* 19: 163–91.

Donaldson, L. 2001. *The Contingency Theory of Organizations*. Thousand Oaks: Sage Publishing.

Galunic, D. C., and K. M. Eisenhardt. 1994. Renewing the Strategy–Structure–Performance Paradigm. *Research in Organizational Behavior* 16: 215–55.

Gresov, C., and R. Drazin. 1997. Equifinality: Functional Equivalence in Organization Design. *Academy of Management Review* 22: 403–28.

Pennings, J. M. 1992. Structural Contingency Theory: A Reappraisal. *Research in Organizational Behavior* 14: 267–309.

Randolph, W. A., and G. G. Dess. 1984. The Congruence Perspective of Organizational Design: A Conceptual Model and Multivariate Research Approach. *Academy of Management Review* 9: 114–27.

8. Galunic and Eisenhardt, Renewing the Strategy–Structure–Performance Paradigm.

9. Chandler, A. D., Jr. 1962. *Strategy and Structure: Chapters in the History of the Industrial Enterprise*. Cambridge, MA: MIT Press, p. 13.

Galbraith, J. R., and R. K. Kazanjian. 1968. *Strategy Implementation: Structure, Systems, and Process*. St. Paul: West Publishing Company, p. 1.

Mintzberg, H. 1987. The Strategy Concept I: Five Ps for Strategy. *California Management Review* 30 (Fall): 11–24.

Mintzberg, H. 1987. The Strategy Concept II: Another Look at Why Organizations Need Strategies. *California Management Review* 30 (Fall): 25–32.

Porter, M. E. 1998. *On Competition*. Boston: Harvard Business Review Book Series.

10. Miller, D., C. Dröge, and J. Toulouse. 1988. Strategic Process and Content as Mediators between Organizational Context and Structure. *Academy of Management Journal* 31: 544–69.

11. Amburgey, T. L., and T. Dacin. 1994. As the Left Foot Follows the Right? The Dynamics of Strategic and Structural Change. *Academy of Management Journal* 37: 1427–52.

12. Chandler, *Strategy and Structure*, p. 14.

13. Keats, B. W., and M. A. Hitt. 1988. A Causal Model of Linkages Among Environmental Dimensions, Macro Organizational Characteristics, and Performance. *Academy of Management Journal* 31: 570–98.

Miller, Dröge, and Toulouse, Strategic Process and Content.

Russell, R. D., and C. J. Russell. 1992. An Examination of the Effects of Organizational Norms, Organizational Structure, and Environmental Uncertainty on Entrepreneurial Strategy. *Journal of Management* 18: 639–56.

14. Jaffee, D. 2001. The Environment and the Organization. In *Organization Theory: Tension and Change*. Boston: McGraw-Hill Higher Education, Chap. 9.

    Scott, W. R. 1992. The Organization of Environments: Network, Cultural, and Historical Elements. In *Organizational Environments: Ritual and Rationality*, ed. J. W. Meyer and W. R. Scott. Newbury Park: Sage Publishing, Chap. 7.

15. Duncan, What Is the Right Organization Structure?

16. Green, H. 1999. 'Twas the Season for E-Splurging. *Business Week* (January 18): 40, 42.

17. Developed from Jaffee, *Organization Theory*, Chap. 8.

    Scarbrough, H., and J. M. Corbett. 1992. *Technology and Organization: Power, Meaning, and Design*. New York: Routledge.

    Scott, W. R. 1990. Technology and Structure: An Organization-Level Perspective. In *Technology and Organizations*, ed. P. S. Goodman, L. S. Sproull, and Associates. San Francisco: Jossey-Bass, pp. 109–43.

18. Fry, L. W. 1982. Technology–Structure Research: Three Critical Issues. *Academy of Management Journal* 25: 532–52.

    Kolodny, H., M. Liu, B. Stymne, and H. Denis. 1996. New Technology and the Emerging Organizational Paradigm. *Human Relations* 49: 1457–87.

19. Aldrich, H. E. 1972. Technology and Organizational Structure: A Reexamination of the Findings of the Aston Group. *Administrative Science Quarterly* 17: 26–43.

    Hulin, C. L., and M. Roznowski. 1985. Organizational Technologies: Effects on Organizations' Characteristics and Individuals' Responses. In *Research in Organizational Behavior*, ed. L. L. Cummings and B. M. Staw. Greenwich, CT: JAI Press, pp. 39–85.

20. Fry, Technology–Structure Research.

    Miller, C. C., W. H. Glick, Y. Wang, and G. P. Huber. 1991. Understanding Technology–Structure Relationships: Theory Development and Meta-Analytic Theory Testing. *Academy of Management Journal* 34: 370–99.

21. Dean, J. W., Jr., S. J. Yoon, and G. I. Susman. 1992. Advanced Manufacturing Technology and Organization Structure: Empowerment or Sub-ordination? *Organization Science* 3: 203–29.

22. Bluedorn, Pilgrim's Progress.

    Grinyer, P. H., and M. Yasai-Ardekani. 1981. Strategy, Structure, Size, and Bureaucracy. *Academy of Management Journal* 24: 471–86.

    Khandwalla, P. N. 1974. Mass Output Orientation of Operations Technology and Organizational Structure. *Administrative Science Quarterly* 19: 74–97.

    Miller, Dröge, and Toulouse, Strategic Process and Content.

23. Blau, P. M., C. M. Falbe, W. McKinley, and P. K. Tracy. 1976. Technology and Organization in Manufacturing. *Administrative Science Quarterly* 21: 20–40.

24. Zwerman, W. L. 1970. *New Perspectives on Organization Theory*. Westport: Greenwood Publishing Corporation.

25. Aldrich, Technology and Organizational Structure.

    Hickson, D. J., D. S. Pugh, and D. C. Pheysey. 1969. Operations Technology and Organization Structure: An Empirical Reappraisal. *Administrative Science Quarterly* 14: 378–97.

    Inkson, J. H. K., D. S. Pugh, and D. J. Hickson. 1970. Organization Context and Structure: An Abbreviated Replication. *Administrative Science Quarterly* 15: 318–29.

    Pugh, D. S., D. J. Hickson, C. R. Hinnings, and C. Turner. 1968. Dimensions of Organization Structure. *Administrative Science Quarterly* 13: 65–105.

26. Burns, T., and G. M. Stalker. 1961. *The Management of Innovation*. London: Tavistock.
Galunic and Eisenhardt, Renewing the Strategy–Structure–Performance Paradigm.

27. Eisenhardt, K. M. 1989. Making Fast Strategic Decisions in High-Velocity Environments. *Academy of Management Journal* 32: 543–76.
Galunic and Eisenhardt, Renewing the Strategy–Structure–Performance Paradigm.
Judge, W. Q., and A. Miller. 1991. Antecedents and Outcomes of Decision Speed in Different Environmental Contexts. *Academy of Management Journal* 34: 449–63.

28. Pennings, Structural Contingency Theory.

29. Miles, R. E., and C. C. Snow. 1978. *Organizational Strategy, Structure, and Process*. New York: McGraw-Hill.

30. Doty, D. H., W. H. Glick, and G. P. Huber. 1993. Fit, Equifinality, and Organizational Effectiveness: A Test of Two Configurational Theories. *Academy of Management Journal* 36: 1196–250.

31. Galbraith, J. R. 1971. Matrix Organization Designs. *Business Horizons* 14 (February): 29–40.

32. Cichocki, P., and C. Irwin. 2011. *Organization Design: A Guide to Building Effective Organizations*. London: Kogan Page Limited.
Davis and Weckler, *A Practical Guide*, Chap. 2.
Flamholtz and Randle, Designing Organizational Structure.

33. Developed from Duncan, What Is the Right Organization Structure?
Jelinek, Organization Structure.

34. Developed from Duncan, What Is the Right Organization Structure?
Donaldson, *The Contingency Theory of Organizations*, pp. 771–81.
Fligstein, N. 1985. The Spread of the Multidivisional Form among Large Firms, 1919–1979. *American Sociological Review* 50: 377–91.
Hoskisson, R. E., C. W. L. Hill, and H. Kim. 1993. The Multidivisional Structure: Organizational Fossil or Source of Value? *Journal of Management* 19: 269–98.
Huber, Organizations, pp. 131–46.
Jelinek, Organization Structure.
Palmer, D. A., P. D. Jennings, and X. Zhou. 1993. Late Adoption of the Multidivisional Form by Large U.S. Corporations: Institutional, Political, and Economic Accounts. *Administrative Science Quarterly* 38: 100–31.

35. Developed from R. L. Daft. 2004. Designing Organizations for the International Environment. In *Organization Theory and Design*, 8th edn. Mason: South-Western, Chap. 6.

36. Developed from L. R. Burns. 1989. Matrix Management in Hospitals: Testing Theories of Matrix Structure and Development. *Administrative Science Quarterly* 34: 349–68.
Burns, L. R., and D. R. Wholey. 1993. Adoption and Abandonment of Matrix Management Programs: Effects of Organizational Characteristics and Interorganizational Networks. *Academy of Management Journal* 36: 106–38.
Davis, S. M., and P. R. Lawrence. 1977. *Matrix*. Reading, MA: Addison-Wesley.
Davis, S. M., and P. R. Lawrence. 1978. Problems of Matrix Organizations. *Harvard Business Review* 56 (May–June): 131–42.

Ford, R. C., and W. A. Randolph. 1992. Cross-Functional Structures: A Review and Integration of Matrix Organization and Project Management. *Journal of Management* 18: 267–94.

37. Burns and Wholey, Adoption and Abandonment of Matrix Management Programs.
38. Larson, E. W., and D. H. Gobeli. 1987. Matrix Management: Contradictions and Insights. *California Management Review* 29 (Summer): 126–38.
39. Developed from Davis and Lawrence, *Matrix*.
    Duncan, What Is the Right Organization Structure? pp. 59–80.
    Larson and Gobeli, Matrix Management.
40. Developed from M. H. Safizadeh. 1991. The Case of Workgroups in Manufacturing Operations. *California Management Review* 33 (Summer): 61–82.
    Mohrman, S., S. Cohen, and A. Mohrman. 1995. *Designing Team-Based Organizations*. San Francisco: Jossey-Bass.
    Scott Morton, M. S., ed. 1991. *The Corporation of the 1990s: Information Technology and Organizational Transformation*. New York: Oxford University Press.
41. Hammer, M., and S. Stanton. 1999. How Process Enterprises *Really* Work. *Harvard Business Review* (November–December): 108–18. (Quotation from p. 108.)
42. Ibid.
43. Hammer, M. 1990. Reengineering Work: Don't Automate, Obliterate. *Harvard Business Review* 68 (July–August): 104–11.
    Hammer, M., and J. Champy. 1993. *Reengineering the Corporation: A Manifesto for Business Revolution*. New York: HarperCollins.
44. Hammer, Reengineering Work, pp. 106–7.
45. Boudreau, M.-C., K. D. Loch, D. Robey, and D. Straud. 1998. Going Global: Using Information Technology to Advance the Competitiveness of the Virtual Transnational Organization. *Academy of Management Executive* 12: 120–28.
    Chesbrough, H. W., and D. J. Teece. 1996. When Is Virtual Virtuous? *Harvard Business Review* 74 (January–February): 65–73.
    Davidow, W. H., and M. S. Malone. 1992. *The Virtual Corporation*. New York: HarperCollins.
    Dutton, W. H. 1999. The Virtual Organization: Tele-Access in Business and Industry. In *Shaping Organization Form: Communication, Connection, and Community*, ed. G. DeSanctis and J. Fulk. Thousand Oaks: Sage Publishing, Chap. 16.
    Upton, D. M., and A. McAfee. 1996. The Real Virtual Factory. *Harvard Business Review* 74 (July–August): 123–33.
    Venkatraman, N., and J. Henderson. 1998. Real Strategies for Virtual Organizing. *Sloan Management Review* 40 (Fall): 33–48.
46. Duarte, D. L., and N. T. Snyder. 2001. *Mastering Virtual Teams*. San Francisco: Jossey-Bass.
    Handy, C. 1995. Trust and the Virtual Organization. *Harvard Business Review* 73 (May–June): 40–50.
47. Venkatraman and Henderson, Real Strategies for Virtual Organizing.
48. Sundaram, A. K., and J. S. Black. 1992. The Environment and Internal Organization of Multinational Enterprises. *Academy of Management Review* 17: 729–57.
49. Hofstede, G. 1991. *Cultures and Organizations: Software of the Mind*. New York: McGraw-Hill.
    Hofstede, G. 2001. *Culture's Consequences: Comparing Values, Behaviors, Institutions, and Organizations across Nations*, 2nd edn. Thousand Oaks: Sage Publishing.

Laurent, A. 1983. The Cultural Diversity of Western Conceptions of Management. *International Studies of Management and Organization* 13: 75–96.

50. Berggren, C. 1992. *Alternatives to Lean Production: Work Organization in the Swedish Auto Industry*. Ithaca, NY: Cornell University Press. (Cornell International Industrial and Labor Relations Report No. 22.)

51. Hofstede, G. 1980. Motivation, Leadership, and Organization: Do American Theories Apply Abroad? *Organizational Dynamics* 9: 42–63.
Hofstede, *Culture's Consequences*, Chap. 6.

Chapter 18

ORGANIZATIONAL CHANGE AND DEVELOPMENT

After reading this chapter, you should be able to:

- Analyze the pressures on managers to change their organizations.
- Compare unplanned and planned organizational change.
- Describe the forces for and against change as a force field around the organization's present state.
- Explain the phases and targets of planned change in organizations.
- Compare the evolutionary and revolutionary models of planned change.
- Describe reasons for resistance to organizational change.
- Discuss the role of leadership in planned organizational change.
- Explain the organizational development techniques managers can use to change their organizations.
- List the phases of organizational development.
- Identify some international aspects of organizational change and development.
- Discuss some ethical issues that surround organizational change and development.

Organizational change involves moving from the organization's present state to a future or target state.[1] The future state can include a new strategy, changes in the organization's culture, introduction of a new technology, and so on. These are just a few examples; many other possible future states exist.

Organizations vary in their readiness for change. Some can quickly go forward with change; others will hold back and proceed slowly with change.

Many sources of pressure push managers to change their organizations. Such pressures for change will undoubtedly continue in the future, making understanding how organizational change takes place and what it does to people in organizations necessary. You also will need to know the probable effects you will feel as a member of a changing system. You will be better prepared to adapt to such change, or cope with it, if you understand the change processes of organizations.

As a manager or nonmanager, you might also need to change all or part of an organization in the future. Successfully changing an organization requires knowing how to manage change and how to deliberately cause change. Because people and organizations often resist organizational change, managers need to know how to reduce such resistance.

FORCES FOR AND AGAINST CHANGE

Forces for change that press managers to change the organization can come from outside or inside the organization.[2] Competition for market share can force managers to change the organization's strategy and then its structure to carry out that strategy. Threats of acquisition can induce management to change the organization's structure and internal processes to inhibit the takeover effort. If managers are to respond to the increased interest in global markets and the need to compete across many borders, they need to consider major changes in their organizations.[3] Increasing workforce diversity and growing interest in managing for quality are also forces for change.

Internal forces for change appear as dissatisfaction, discontent, felt stress, loss of control over internal processes, and dysfunctionally high conflict. Decision processes may have become dysfunctionally slow; turnover and absenteeism may be high; and communication among different parts of the organization may have almost stopped. Such problems, or combinations of them, can press managers to try to change their organizations.

Forces for change often face **forces against change**. The opposing forces can lie inside or outside the organization. Resistance to change inside the organization comes from individuals and groups who do not want the change to happen. A later section of this chapter describes many reasons people resist change in organizations.

Outside the organization, special interest groups, such as consumer groups and unions, may oppose organizational change. Managers also might oppose major organizational changes because they believe their organization will move away from a widely accepted configuration for their industry. For example, accounting organizations typically use a partnership organizational form and likely would resist pressures to move to some other organizational form.[4]

Managers can respond to change pressures in two ways. They can deny the importance of the pressures for change and continue to manage as they have in the past. They also can accept the need for change and move forward with a deliberate, planned change effort.

Figure 18.1 shows the forces for and against change acting as a force field[5] around the present state of the organization. This chapter describes how managers and other change agents can affect that force field and move the organization to a desired new state.

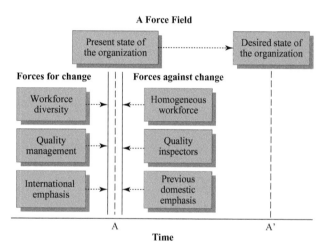

Figure 18.1: Forces For and Against Change

UNPLANNED AND PLANNED ORGANIZATIONAL CHANGE

Organizational change is either unplanned or planned. **Unplanned change** occurs when pressures for change overwhelm the efforts to resist change. Management may not have expected such change. Because management and the organization were not ready for change, the pressures can result in uncontrolled, if not chaotic, change effects on the organization.

Planned change is a systematic management effort to move an organization, or a subsystem, to a new state. It includes deliberately changing the organization's design, technology, tasks, people, information systems, and the like. Although managers try to follow a plan for change, it does not always move forward smoothly. The change effort is often blocked, causing managers to rethink their goals and plans.[6]

Planned change defines the organization's future, diagnoses the organization's present state, and manages the process that moves the organization from its present state to the desired future state.[7] A change agent guides the change process, helping managers bring about planned organizational change. The change agent is a consultant, who may be external to the organization or part of a staff function that specializes in helping managers carry out planned organizational change.

TARGETS OF PLANNED ORGANIZATIONAL CHANGE

The **targets** of a planned organizational change effort are as varied as organizations. The early phases of planned change establish the need for change and identify the target that needs changing to reach the desired future state. The target can be an organization's culture, decision processes, or communication processes. Managers might need to change a task's design or the organization's design. They might want to introduce technologies or adopt a new strategy for the organization. Managers should choose the target only after carefully assessing the current state of the organization and the need for change.[8]

MODELS OF PLANNED ORGANIZATIONAL CHANGE

The reasons for organizational change, the scope of change, and the intensity of change vary. Change can happen because managers react to environmental shifts or because they anticipate the future state of the organization's environment. Managers find planned change a difficult task. As noted by a prominent organizational change scholar, "Planned organization change is messy and never as clear as we have written in our books and articles."[9]

Sometimes change happens incrementally, letting the organization evolve from its present state to a future state. Such incremental change does not affect all organizational systems. For example, an organization might change its pay scale to stay market competitive. Change can also have more dramatic effects on an organization. A strategic shift, for example, can have almost revolutionary effects on an entire organization by affecting organizational design, job design, the informal organization, and support processes. Researchers have proposed two contrasting models of planned organizational change to explain these two types of change: the evolutionary model and the revolutionary model. The models describe different change processes for evolutionary and revolutionary change.[10]

Evolutionary Model of Organizational Change

Evolutionary change happens incrementally over time as managers adapt an organization's design and processes to changes in its external environment. This view of planned organizational change dominated academic and practitioner thinking until the early 1980s. The **evolutionary model** of organizational change sees change happening in small bits that add to a total amount of change.

The evolutionary model's phases of change[11] begin with a manager or other change agent who develops a **need for change** among those affected. The change agent then tries to **move** the organization (or a part of it) toward the changed state. During the last phase, the change agent tries to **stabilize the change** and make it a part of the organization. The phases do not have distinct boundaries. Each phase blends into the next phase in the sequence. Although the three phases often occur during a planned change effort, organizational change does not always happen in a linear fashion. Unexpected events can occur along the way, forcing a return to an earlier phase.

Microsoft's recognition that it was not ready for the sweeping effects of the Internet on how people communicate with PCs is an example of evolutionary change.[12] The company announced in 1994 that it would offer software to allow easy Internet access. For the industry giant, producing such software and adding new support systems for it were small changes in the company's massive array of products and systems.

Revolutionary Model of Organizational Change

The **revolutionary model** sees organizational change as unfolding over long periods of stability followed by bursts of major change activities.[13] It is massive change affecting many parts of an organization. After the big changes occur, the organization settles into another stable period.

Figure 18.2 shows the revolutionary change process and lists the main parts of this type of organizational change. Three concepts anchor the revolutionary

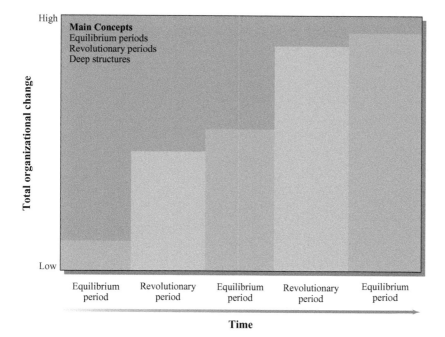

Figure 18.2: Revolutionary Model of Organizational Change

change model: equilibrium periods, revolutionary periods, and deep structures. During **equilibrium periods**, an organization moves steadily toward its mission and goals. **Revolutionary periods** feature feverish change activities aimed at changing an organization's strategic direction. **Deep structures** are enduring features of an organization's culture, design, processes, and relationships with its external environment that let the organization succeed.

Research focused on revolutionary organizational change suggests that two events can trigger a revolutionary period: (1) dissatisfaction with the organization's performance; and (2) strong feelings among organization members that it is time for change.[14]

The first event is a response to a felt misfit between the organization's deep structure and its current environment, technical process, product or service mix, and current organizational members. Dissatisfaction develops following clear organizational failure or when many believe failure is imminent.

The second event can happen when organizational members feel uneasy with the current equilibrium period and feel little forward movement of the organization. Although little research has focused on this event, some results suggest that it can happen in new venture organizations.[15] Managers seem to reach a milestone in the development of the new organization, sense a need for major change, and embrace it—starting a new turbulent period.

Revolutionary change characterizes organizations that must shift direction. Usually such changes happen under strong leadership at the top of the organization.[16] One fledgling entrepreneurial firm achieved such great success with its first information technology product that it launched a second one in a different area. The product met with limited market success and was draining organizational resources. The two founders quickly saw a need for change. They rallied the organization through its revolutionary period. The organization held to its deep structure—its core technological competence—with which everyone identified. As a result, the organization successfully passed through the revolutionary period to a new equilibrium period.[17]

Revolutionary change has several closely related cousins in the research literature. Some researchers refer to change of this magnitude as chaos, quantum change, frame-breaking change, radical change, eruptive change, transformational change, and discontinuous change. These views of change have the common characteristics of massive organizational change that is difficult to do and manage.[18]

RESISTANCE TO CHANGE

People in organizations often **resist** both planned and unplanned organizational change. Although the target of the change may be the design of the organization, people's jobs, or the underlying technology, the change also affects social systems in the organization. People develop long-standing and familiar social interaction patterns. When an organizational change affects these social networks, strong resistance can develop. The resistance can be a lack of cooperation with the change effort, deliberate sabotage of the change effort, or dysfunctionally high conflict levels. A particular change effort will lead to specific types of resistance.[19]

Reasons for Resistance to Change

Organizational change resistance occurs for several reasons. Some people might perceive the change as causing them to lose something valued. For example, a change could reduce an individual's or a group's social status. If the individual or group valued their status, they are likely to resist the change. The change could also create a feeling of future unfairness in rewards and sanctions distribution.

Misunderstandings about the intended change goal or lack of trust between the change target and the change agent can create resistance reactions. Misunderstandings can arise because the change agent did not fully explain the goal of the change. Lack of trust might develop because the change agent is an outsider or comes from a part of the organization that the target has long distrusted.

Resistance to change can also occur when all parties involved in the change do not share a common perception about the value of the change. The change agent and the change target often have different expectations about the effects of the change. Later, this section discusses how such differences make resistance to change a valuable tool for managing change.

The people who are the change target may have low tolerance for change and the uncertainty associated with it. People vary in their ability to change their behavior quickly. Those who resist change because of low tolerance may believe the change is good for them and the organization, but they simply cannot alter their behavior as fast as the change requires.

Managers' Orientation to Resistance to Change

Managers can react to resistance to change in two ways. They can treat the resistance as a problem to overcome or view it as a signal to get more information about the reasons for the resistance.[20] Managers who view resistance as a problem to overcome might try to forcefully reduce it. Such coercive approaches often increase the resistance.[21]

Alternatively, managers may see resistance as a signal that the change agent needs more information about the intended change.[22] The targets that will be affected by the change may have valuable insights about its effects. An alert change agent will involve the targets in diagnosing the reasons for the resistance. In this way, managers can use resistance to change as a tool to get needed information.

Should managers and change agents see the absence of resistance to change as a stroke of good fortune? Many reasons suggest that they should not. The absence of resistance is also a signal to managers and change agents to get more information.[23] A change that is automatically accepted can be less effective than one that has been resisted and actively debated. The resisters play an important role by focusing the change agent's attention on potentially dysfunctional aspects of the proposed change.[24]

Managing the Change Process to Reduce Resistance

Resistance reactions might focus on the change, the method of change, or the change agent. The method or methods used to reduce resistance partly depend on the target of the resistance to change.[25]

Resistance often develops when the change agent and the target of change differ strongly in such characteristics as education level, physical appearance, values, and language. Using change agents with characteristics congruent with those of the target reduces resistance reactions.[26] For example, if the target of the change effort was a group of people who dress informally at work, a change agent would be ill-advised to wear formal business clothes.

Using dramatic ceremonies and symbols to signal disengagement from the past can quickly move a system forward with little resistance.[27] The ceremony can include recognition of a job well done on some program that is ending. This approach to managing a change effort can be especially effective in industries such as aerospace, where shifts in technology make old programs obsolete. Ceremoniously burying the old program and launching the new one can go a long way to reducing resistance to change.

Communicating information about the change is another way to head off resistance.[28] The communications can be written or oral, presented to groups or to single individuals. Extensive conversations between managers and each person reporting to her will help the change process. The communication should explain the reasons for the change, how it will happen, and the effects it will have on various groups in the organization. Especially with highly technical change, an explanation in simple and understandable terms helps reduce resistance reactions.

Involving the key people who will be affected by the proposed change also helps reduce resistance. They should be involved early in the change effort, especially in diagnosing the system to assess whether change is needed. This suggestion does not mean inviting members of the target system to participate simply to give them a superficial sense of contributing to the change. Their involvement is necessary to get crucial information from those most intimately involved in the target system. Such information lets managers and change agents design an effective change effort.

Managers can support a major change effort by committing enough resources to make the change easier on those affected. Ample resources are particularly important if the change involves moving to a new and complex technology. Managers can expect resistance reactions when people must learn new, more complex ways of doing their work. Management can head off such resistance by committing enough resources to train people to use the new technology.

When a powerful person or group is a potential source of resistance, negotiation may be necessary. These people may not be powerful enough to prevent the change, but they can create a significant source of resistance. Negotiations are common in situations asking for change in work behavior from unionized employees. Changes in a union contract might be needed to get major changes in the way work is done.

A more indirect and politically based approach than the methods described involves manipulating (in various ways) those who are the target of change. Co-optation is a political tactic that aims to gain endorsement of the change from important individuals or groups by inviting such people to play a role in designing the change effort. Co-optation is different from involvement, described earlier. Here, the change agent is not seeking information to build an effective change program. The change agent or manager wants the important person or group to accept the change program. Of course, co-optation can backfire on the manager or change agent. The co-opted individual or group could affect the design of the change effort to benefit the individual or the group at the expense of the organization's goals.

Managers and change agents sometimes have no other choice than to force change onto the target system. Such a coercive reaction often happens when the change must come quickly or when the change is undesirable to the target system. Pressing or forcing a system to change also can increase resistance to change, making the manager or change agent's job even more difficult.

LEADERSHIP AND ORGANIZATIONAL CHANGE

Chapter 12, "Leadership and Management," describes the difference between leadership and management in organizations. Leaders can change organizations; managers operate with what they now have. As implied in Chapter 12, leaders play a major role in organizational change.[29]

A leader's vision of an organization's future can play a compelling role in successful organizational change.[30] A vision offers powerful imagery of the future. Recall the Chapter 12 discussion of leadership and vision: An effective vision is "future oriented, compelling, bold, aspiring, and inspiring, yet believable and achievable."[31]

Several types of leaders discussed in Chapter 12 can create strong changes in organizations. A leader with the leadership mystique has a sense of mission (vision), can build a power base for change, and has a will to survive and persevere during stormy periods. Transformational leaders use their charismatic qualities to inspire followers in pursuit of desired changes. Charismatic leaders combine an inspirational vision with the leader's charisma to move organizations out of a turbulent period to a new equilibrium period. All three types of leaders usually know what is in the organization's roots that they want to keep for the future. Without leaders at many levels in an organization, successful change is unlikely.

ORGANIZATIONAL DEVELOPMENT

Organizational development is a long-term, systematic, and prescriptive approach to planned organizational change. Although it uses a system-wide view, it can focus on single subsystems of an organization. Organizational development applies the social and behavioral science theories and concepts to organizational change. It also uses behavioral science knowledge as the source of techniques to cause change.[32]

The following statement by one of its key proponents describes the goals of organizational development:

(1) enhancing congruence among organizational structure, processes, strategy, people, and culture;
(2) developing new and creative organizational solutions; and
(3) developing the organization's self-renewing capacity.[33]

The self-renewing emphasis distinguishes organizational development from other approaches to planned organizational change.[34] Organizational development views organizations as complex social and technical systems. An organizational development effort can focus on human processes in the organization, or the organization's design, job design, technology, and many other aspects of the organization.

A careful examination of organizational development's goals reveals its prescriptive feature.[35] Organizational development tries to create an organization with the flexibility to change its design according to the nature of its tasks and external environment. It builds mechanisms within the organization that let members get feedback about the state of the organization. The feedback then encourages all members to focus on continuous improvement.

Organizational development views conflict as an inevitable part of organization life. It tries to build a culture that says conflict can be positively managed to reach the organization's goals. The culture also needs a norm that says people with knowledge, not only those in appointed decision-making roles, should have authority and influence in decision making. Organizational development asks organization members to take charge of their destiny and to be involved in the change process.

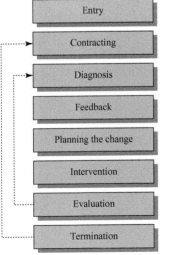

Figure 18.3: Organizational Development Phases

Organizational Development Phases

Organizational development unfolds in a series of phases as shown in Figure 18.3. Each phase flows into the next phase. These are **phases**—not steps—because no clear boundaries exist between them.[36]

The figure suggests that organizational development unfolds in a forward-moving fashion. Information developed during the effort, however, may suggest changes in the process. For example, during the evaluation phase, managers might discover that they need more data from the diagnosis phase. The arrows linking later to earlier phases in the figure show that phases can repeat.

The following description of the phases assumes that an internal or external consultant is involved in the organizational development effort. Such consultants typically have training and experience that let them serve as key resources to the managers trying to use organizational development. Not all organizational development efforts use consultants. Small organizations and those with limited resources, for example, tend not to use them.

Entry

The first phase, entry, is the point at which the consultant has direct client contact. The client usually begins the contact, especially if working with an external consultant. Internal consultants might also make the first contact because helping managers in their organization is often part of their job description.

This phase includes all the dynamics of building a client–consultant relationship. Key elements include evaluating each other and concluding that the client and consultant can develop a compatible working relationship.

Contracting

If both parties judge the entry phase as successful, they then move to the contracting phase. An organizational development contract can range from an oral agreement to a document that legally binds both parties. The contract describes each party's expectations and outlines what each party will do during the organizational development program.[37] Neither party should look upon the organizational development contract as a static agreement. As the organizational development program unfolds, both parties should reexamine or renegotiate the contract.

Diagnosis

During the diagnosis phase, the consultant gets information about the client system and diagnoses its current state. An alert consultant begins the diagnosis phase as early as the first contact with the client. Initially, the diagnosis might involve observing the client's behavior and reactions and the client system's physical characteristics. Later, the diagnosis can include collecting data systematically using interviews, surveys, and company records. The consultant summarizes the results of the analysis and diagnosis in preparation for providing feedback to the client system.

Feedback

The consultant then has a series of feedback meetings with client system members. The number of meetings depends on the scope of the organizational development program. If the program focuses only on one workgroup, the consultant would meet first with the manager or supervisor of the group and then with the other group members. If more groups are targeted, more meetings will be needed.

Feedback meetings typically include several steps. First, the consultant presents an analysis of data collected in the diagnosis phase. A discussion follows in which the consultant answers questions and clarifies the presentation as needed. The consultant then gives a preliminary diagnosis of the client system.

This step has the distinctive organizational development feature of client collaboration. The consultant and the client system members work together to arrive at a diagnosis of the client system's current state. The client's active involvement can lead to changes in the consultant's original diagnosis.

Planning the Change

The diagnosis and feedback phases, when done well, lead to **planning the change** required in the client system. The planning phase can occur during the feedback meeting if the change is simple or the client system is small. Often this phase happens at a later time.

The client and consultant collaborate during the planning phase. They identify alternative courses of action and the effects of each alternative. After picking the change alternatives, they lay out the steps needed to bring about that change. A distinctive feature of the planning phase in organizational development is that the client decides the nature of the change program—not the consultant.

Intervention

After the change program is underway, the consultant and client collaboratively intervene in the client system to move it to the desired future state. The **intervention** can include activities such as changes in job and organizational design, a conflict-reduction program, or management training. A later section, "Organizational Development Interventions," describes some available organizational development interventions.

During this phase, the consultant helps the intervention and predicts dysfunctional results. Client system members may resist the intervention. Involving these people in the diagnosis and feedback phases should reduce resistance at the intervention phase. The able consultant helps the client interpret the resistance and develop methods to reduce it, if they jointly decide they should.

Evaluation

Activities in the **evaluation** phase focus on whether the organizational development effort had the effect the client wanted. The evaluation can range from simply asking whether the client feels pleased to conducting a well-designed research effort to show empirically the intervention's effects. Any evaluation, whatever its depth, should be done independently of the consultant who helps develop the organizational development program. The evaluation should also give the client system information about the next steps to take.

Termination

The consultant's involvement with a specific intervention **terminates** at some point. If the intervention did not move the client system to the desired end state, the consultant's relationship may end completely. If the intervention was successful, and the client system changes and develops, an external consultant's direct involvement with the client ends, although some contact usually remains.

In contrast, internal consultants usually stay with their part of the organization and continue some involvement with the client system. Their involvement, however, is usually not as strong as in earlier phases of the organizational development effort.

Both external and internal organizational development consultants want the client system to become independent of the consultant. The goal of independence is consistent with the consultant's role of helping the client system become self-reliant in its change and development. Independence does not mean the consultant has no further contact with the client. Effective organizational development consultants often develop long-term relationships with clients, moving from one organizational development project to another within the same organization.

Organizational Development Interventions

Organizational development practitioners have many interventions from which to choose when trying to help a client system improve its functioning. Organizational development interventions are systematic techniques drawn from the behavioral sciences that can help bring about planned organizational change and development.[38]

Earlier chapters of this book have detailed descriptions of many of the interventions described. The citations associated with this section also have detailed descriptions of each intervention.

Human process interventions focus on interpersonal, intragroup, and intergroup processes, such as conflict, communication, and decision making. The goals of human process interventions include reducing dysfunctionally high conflict, making interpersonal processes more effective, and enhancing human value fulfillment in an organization. Practitioners using human process interventions assume that improving an organization's human processes will help the organization function more effectively.[39]

Structural and technological interventions focus on the organization's design, the jobs within it, and the addition of new technology to the organization. Each intervention has the goal of improving human productivity and organizational effectiveness. Chapter 17, "Organizational Design," and Chapter 9, "Job Design and Intrinsic Rewards," have extended discussions of this class of interventions.[40]

The technological portion of this intervention class includes any technology that can change the functioning and effectiveness of an organization's processes. Introducing extensive factory automation or a PC network can change the way people work and interact with each other. Although this intervention class aims to change structure or technology, it also directly affects the human processes of an organization.

Human resource management interventions draw on an organization's personnel practices. These include aspects of motivation and rewards, career planning and development, and stress management. For example, managers could associate bonuses and promotions with behavior that leads to continuous quality improvement.

Human resource management interventions target individuals. Goal setting and giving rewards, for example, aim to shape the person's behavior in the direction desired by the organization. Practitioners who use human resource management interventions expect changes in individual behavior and performance to lead to improved organization effectiveness.

Strategy interventions focus on an organization's responses to shifts in its external environment. These responses include strategic shifts to gain a competitive advantage, and changes in the organization's culture to create values and beliefs more congruent with the organization's new environment. For example, a big shift in the environment of American organizations is an emphasis on managing for the quality of their products or services. Such a shift includes viewing quality as a strategic advantage and changing the organization's culture to value quality as part of everyone's job.[41]

Organizational development efforts using multiple interventions often get the most change.[42] Combinations of team building, structural interventions, and worker involvement in goal setting can have positive effects. Survey feedback used alone can have little effect.[43] Research results show the effects as clearly positive for quantity and quality of work, but less positive for turnover and absenteeism. The strongest interventions were of the structural/technological and human resource management type. Effects were also stronger in small organizations than in large organizations.[44] Multiple interventions can also positively affect employee attitudes, although team building and goal setting used alone can do the same. Effects usually are stronger for supervisory than for nonsupervisory employees.[45]

INTERNATIONAL ASPECTS OF ORGANIZATIONAL CHANGE AND DEVELOPMENT

The intellectual roots of organizational development are mainly in the United States, with some branches coming from England, northern Europe, and Scandinavia.[46] Many organizational development assumptions and values reflect the values of those cultures. These assumptions and values are highly different from the assumptions and values found in other nations.

Latin American countries often have less egalitarian social values than the United States. Workers have strong loyalty to their superior and see a directive management style as both correct and appropriate. Social class distinctions are also strong in Latin American countries, as is the belief that superiors are more competent than subordinates.[47]

French, Italian, and Russian managers view organizations as hierarchically oriented systems of authority relations. Swedish and U.S. managers usually do not see organizations as strongly hierarchical. French and Italian managers often view organizations as political systems in which they try to gain power for themselves. The French also have a manipulative perspective about organizational change.[48]

Russian managers prefer having a clear plan to which everyone can commit. They do not share the Western view that a plan describes a starting point and can have different courses of action. Russian workers expect clear top-down direction. Any organizational change comes from centralized direction and workers do not expect their involvement in the change process.[49]

Countries vary in the degree of uncertainty they find tolerable and in their approaches to conflict. People in southern European and Latin American countries prefer to avoid uncertainty. Those in the Scandinavian countries can tolerate more uncertainty. People in Latin American countries also use nonconfrontational approaches to managing conflict.[50]

ETHICAL ISSUES ABOUT ORGANIZATIONAL CHANGE AND DEVELOPMENT

Organizational change and development activities present both the client system and the consultant with several possible ethical dilemmas. These dilemmas can lead to less effective and possibly harmful organizational development programs.[51]

One dilemma follows from misrepresentation of an organizational development consultant's capabilities, skills, or experience. The misrepresentation may occur to ensure that the consultant gets a fee from the potential client. Client system managers may misrepresent themselves and the nature of their problems because they are reluctant to expose their shortcomings to the consultant, other managers in the organization, or competitors.

Ethical issues surround using data in an organizational development effort. Usually, the data are collected under conditions of confidentiality and voluntarism. Any violation of either condition is a breach of ethics. Such data should not be used punitively against those who provided it.

Another type of ethical dilemma involves the manipulation or coercion of people in the client system. The issue here is whether individuals are asked to change their values and behavior without full awareness and consent. Several organizational development interventions described earlier are powerful techniques for changing people. Ethical considerations require that participants in an organizational development intervention be informed of the potential effects on them. Both forced participation and failure to inform participants about potential effects of an intervention are breaches of ethics.

SUMMARY

SUMMARY
18

Organizational change includes both unplanned and planned change. Unplanned change happens when forces for change overwhelm the organization. Planned organizational change is deliberate and unfolds in a series of phases that are not always distinct from each other. Planned change efforts can have different targets, including the organization's culture, decision processes, task design, and organizational design. It can proceed in incremental steps (evolutionary change) or at a fast pace (revolutionary change).

People resist change for many reasons. Managers may view resistance to change as a problem to overcome or as a new source of information about the organization. The chapter described some ways to manage the change process to reduce resistance.

Organizational development is a systematic approach to planned change using social and behavioral science theories and concepts. Organizational development occurs in a series of phases. It often uses data to assess the organization's current state and to diagnose the organization to identify needed changes.

Managers and consultants can choose from four classes of organizational development interventions: (1) human process interventions; (2) structural and technological interventions; (3) human resource management interventions; and (4) strategy interventions.

Organizational development has its intellectual roots mainly in the United States with some branches in England, northern Europe, and Scandinavia. The consultants' assumptions and values, and the nature of many interventions, reflect the values of those cultures. Those assumptions and values can differ from the assumptions and values found in many other nations.

Several ethics issues emerged from the discussion of organizational change and development. They center on misrepresentation by a client or consultant, data confidentiality, and full awareness and consent to behavioral changes by people who will experience the changes.

REVIEW AND DISCUSSION QUESTIONS

REVIEW
AND
DISCUSSION
QUESTIONS

18

1   Discuss the nature of planned and unplanned organizational change. What are the characteristics of each? What are some targets of planned change?

2   Planned organizational change can follow either the evolutionary model or the revolutionary model of change. Discuss the main features of each model. When would a manager follow one model instead of the other? Which of these have you experienced?

3   This chapter described the different orientations managers can have to resistance to change. Which orientation do you personally hold? Which orientations have you seen in your work experiences?

4   Discuss the role of leadership in organizational change. You might want to review part of Chapter 12 to refresh your views of leadership. Are there any current examples of leadership and organizational change in the business press? Discuss your experiences with leadership, or lack of leadership, and organizational change.

5   Review the phases of organizational development. What are the major issues faced by both the client system and the organizational

development consultant in each phase? Which ethical dilemmas most likely appear in each phase?

6 Discuss the major classes of organizational development interventions. What are the goals of each? Which interventions are likely to have the most lasting effects?

7 Review the section describing the international aspects of organizational change and development. Discuss the constraints different cultures put on an organizational development consultant. What opportunities also might exist because of culture differences?

TAKE FIVE: OB ALIVE: *ALONG CAME POLLY* (2004)

Meet Reuben Feffer (Ben Stiller), a highly focused Senior Risk Assessment Analyst. Also meet Polly Prince (Jennifer Anniston) who is not highly focused. Romantic interactions develop between them, as Reuben stretches himself into new behavioral areas.

You view parts of DVD Chapter 11, "Salsa!" and DVD Chapter 13, "Pillow Talk." The portion from Chapter 11 begins at 0:44:19. Reuben says, "Okay, it's just I'm just really, truthfully not the kind of guy ..." It ends as Polly nods her head.

The second film sequence is DVD Chapter 13. It begins with Reuben saying, "Ok, so throw pillows go in this cabinet here." This sequence ends after Reuben sticks the knife into the mattress (Stop: 0:50:18).

Keep the following questions in mind while viewing these film sequences: Who is the change target in these sequences? Are there any examples of resistance to change? Which model of organizational change discussed in this chapter best fits the dynamics shown in the film sequences?

REFERENCES AND NOTES

1. Beckhard, R., and R. T. Harris. 1987. *Organizational Transitions: Managing Complex Change*. Reading, MA: Addison-Wesley.
   Beckhard, R., and W. Pritchard. 1992. *Changing the Essence: The Art of Creating and Leading Fundamental Change in Organizations*. San Francisco: Jossey-Bass.
   Burke, W. W. 1995. Organization Change: What We Know, What We Need to Know. *Journal of Management Inquiry* 4: 158–71.
   Burke, W. W. 2014. *Organization Change: Theory and Practice*, 4th edn. Thousand Oaks: SAGE Publications.
   Burke, W. W. 2014. Organizational Change. In *The Oxford Handbook of Organizational Climate and Culture*, ed. B. Schneider and K. M. Barbera. New York: Oxford University Press, Chap. 24.
   Goodstein, L. D., and W. W. Burke. 1991. Creating Successful Organizational Change. *Organizational Dynamics* 19 (Spring): 5–17.

Stevens, G. W. 2013. Toward a Process-Based Approach of Conceptualizing Change Readiness. *The Journal of Applied Behavioral Science* 49: 333–60.

Stouten, J., D. M. Rousseau, and D. DeCremey. Successful Organizational Change: Integrating the Management Practice and Scholarly Literatures. *Academy of Management Annals* 12: 752–88. This article gives an excellent discussion and summary of the organizational change literature.

2. Beer, M., and A. E. Walton. 1987. Organizational Change and Development. In *Annual Review of Psychology*, Vol. 38, ed. M. R. Rosenzweig and L. W. Porter. Palo Alto: Annual Reviews, pp. 339–67.

   For good summaries of the research literature, see S.S. Gordon, W. H. Stewart, Jr., R. Sweo, and W. A. Luker. 2000. Convergence versus Strategic Reorientation: The Antecedents of Fast-paced Organizational Change. *Journal of Management* 26: 911–45 and L. J. Martins. 2011. Organizational Change and Development. In *APA Handbook of Industrial and Organizational Psychology*, Vol. 3, ed. S. Zedeck. Washington, DC: American Psychological Association, Chap. 20.

3. Beckhard and Harris, *Organizational Transitions*, Chap. 2.

4. Greenwood, R., and C. R. Hinnings. 1996. Understanding Radical Organizational Change: Bringing Together the Old and the New Institutionalism. *Academy of Management Review* 21: 1022–54.

5. Lewin, K. 1951. *Field Theory in Social Science*. New York: Harper & Row, pp. 172–74.

6. Beer and Walton, Organizational Change and Development.

7. Beckhard and Harris, *Organizational Transitions*, pp. 29–30.

8. French, W. L., C. H. Bell, Jr., and R. A. Zawacki, eds. 2000. *Organization Development, and Transformation*. Boston: McGraw-Hill Higher Education.

   Pearce, C. L., and C. P. Osmond. 1996. Metaphors for Change: The ALPs Model of Change Management. *Organizational Dynamics* 24 (Winter): 23–34.

9. Burke, Organization Change, p. 159.

   Burke, *Organization Change*.

10. Gersick, C. J. G. 1991. Revolutionary Change Theories: A Multilevel Exploration of the Punctuated Equilibrium Paradigm. *Academy of Management Review* 16: 10–36.

    Gordon, Stewart, Sweo, and Luker, Convergence versus Strategic Reorientation, pp. 911–13.

    Tushman, M. L., W. H. Newman, and E. Romanelli. 1986. Convergence and Upheaval: Managing the Unsteady Pace of Organizational Evolution. *California Management Review* 29: 29–44.

11. Developed from Beckhard and Harris, *Organizational Transitions*.

    Beer and Walton, Organizational Change and Development, pp. 359–60.

    Burke, W. W. 1987. *Organizational Development: A Normative View*. Reading, MA: Addison-Wesley.

    Burke, W. W. 2014. *Organization Change*.

    Lippitt, R., J. Watson, and B. Westley. 1958. *Dynamics of Planned Change*. New York: Harcourt, Brace.

    Miller, D., R. Greenwood, and B. Hinings. 1997. Creative Chaos Versus Munificent Momentum: The Schism between Normative and Academic Views of Organizational Change. *Journal of Management Inquiry* 6: 71–78.

12. Miller, M. J. 1994. Bill Gates Ponders the Internet. *PC Magazine* (October 11): 79–80.

13. Developed from W. W. Burke and G. H. Litwin. 1992. A Causal Model of Organizational Performance and Change. *Journal of Management* 18: 523–45.

Gersick, Revolutionary Change Theories.

Nutt, P. C., and R. W. Backoff. 1997. Organizational Transformation. *Journal of Management Inquiry* 6: 235–54.

Romanelli, E., and M. L. Tushman. 1994. Organizational Transformation as Punctuated Equilibrium: An Empirical Test. *Academy of Management Journal* 37: 1141–66.

Tushman, Newman, and Romanelli, Convergence and Upheaval.

14. Gersick, Revolutionary Change Theories.

15. Ibid., pp. 25–26.

Tushman, M. L., and E. Romanelli. 1985. Organizational Evolution: A Metamorphosis Model of Convergence and Reorientation. In *Research in Organizational Behavior*, ed. L. L. Cummings and B. M. Staw. Greenwich, CT: JAI Press, pp. 171–222.

16. Pascale, R., M. Millemann, and L. Gioja. 1997. Changing the Way We Change. *Harvard Business Review* 75 (November–December): 127–39.

17. Lichtenstein, B. B. 2000. Self-Organized Transitions: A Pattern amid the Chaos of Transformative Change. *Academy of Management Executive* 14: 128–41.

18. Amis, J., T. Slack, and C. R. Hinings. 2004. The Pace, Sequence, and Linearity of Radical Change. *Academy of Management Journal* 47: 15–39.

Finstad, N. 1998. The Rhetoric of Organizational Change. *Human Relations* 51: 717–40.

Flamholtz, E. G., and Y. Randle. 1998. *Changing the Game: Organizational Transformations of the First, Second, and Third Kinds*. New York: Oxford University Press.

Miller, Greenwood, and Hinings, Creative Chaos Versus Munificent Momentum.

Plowman, D. A., L. T. Baker, T. E. Beck, M. Kulkarni, S. T. Solansky, and D. V. Travis. 2007. Radical Change Accidentally: The Emergence and Amplification of Small Change. *Academy of Management Journal* 50: 515–43.

Roach, D. W., and D. A. Bednar. 1997. The Theory of Logical Types: A Tool for Understanding Levels and Types of Change in Organizations. *Human Relations* 50: 671–99.

Thiétart, R. A., and B. Forgues. 1995. Chaos Theory and Organization. *Organization Science* 6: 19–31.

19. Developed from these citations and others noted throughout the "Resistance to Change" section:

Drummond, H. 1998. Go and Say, "We're Shutting": Ju Jutsu as a Metaphor for Analyzing Resistance. *Human Relations* 51: 741–59.

Jellison, J. M. 1993. *Overcoming Resistance: A Practical Guide to Producing Change in the Workplace*. New York: Simon & Schuster.

Kotter, J. P., and L. A. Schlesinger. 1979. Choosing Strategies for Change. *Harvard Business Review* 57 (March–April): 106–14.

Lawrence, P. R. 1954. How to Deal with Resistance to Change. *Harvard Business Review* (May–June): 49–57.

Leana, C. B., and B. Barry. 2000. Stability and Change as Simultaneous Experiences in Organizational Life. *Academy of Management Review* 25: 753–59.

Piderit, S. K. 2000. Rethinking Resistance and Recognizing Ambivalence: A Multidimensional View of Attitudes Toward an Organizational Change. *Academy of Management Review* 25: 783–94.

Quinn, R. E. 1996. *Deep Change: Discovering the Leader Within*. San Francisco: Jossey-Bass. This source also examines why people have passive reactions to change and lose their passion for working in an organization that has experienced profound change.

Shapiro, D. L., and B. L. Kirkman. 1999. Employees' Reaction to the Change to Work Teams: The Influence of "Anticipatory" Injustice. *Journal of Organizational Change Management* 12: 51–66.

Townley, B. 2002. The Role of Competing Rationalities in Institutional Change. *Academy of Management Journal* 45: 163–79.

20. Lawrence, How to Deal with Resistance to Change.

21. Lewin, *Field Theory in Social Science*.

22. Ford, J. D., L. W. Ford, and A. D'Amelio. 2008. Resistance to Change: The Rest of the Story. *Academy of Management Review* 33: 362–77.

Lawrence, How to Deal with Resistance to Change.

23. Albanese, R. 1970. Overcoming Resistance to Stability. *Business Horizons* 13 (April): 35–42.

24. Klein, D. 1976. Some Notes on the Dynamics of Resistance to Change: The Defender Role. In *The Planning of Change*, 3rd edn., ed. W. G. Bennis, K. D. Benne, R. Chin, and K. E. Corey. New York: Holt, Rinehart and Winston, pp. 117–24.

Morrison, E. W., and F. J. Milliken. 2000. Organizational Silence: A Barrier to Change and Development in a Pluralistic World. *Academy of Management Review* 25: 706–25.

Piderit, Rethinking Resistance and Recognizing Ambivalence.

25. Developed from Drummond, Go and Say, "We're Shutting."

Jellison, *Overcoming Resistance*.

Jick, T. D. 1995. Accelerating Change for Competitive Advantage. *Organizational Dynamics* 24 (Summer): 77–82.

Kotter and Schlesinger, Choosing Strategies for Change.

Lawrence, How to Deal with Resistance to Change.

Miller, Greenwood, and Hinings, Creative Chaos Versus Munificent Momentum.

26. Rogers, E. M., with F. F. Shoemaker. 1971. *Communication of Innovations*. New York: Free Press.

27. Burke, *Organizational Development*, pp. 118–19.

28. Fernandez, S., and H. G. Rainey 2006. Managing Successful Organizational Change in the Public Sector. *Public Administration Review* 66: 168–76.

Ford, J. D., and L. W. Ford. 1995. The Role of Conversations in Producing Intentional Change in Organizations. *Academy of Management Review* 20: 541–70.

Gagné, M., Koestner, R., and Zuckerman, M. 2000. Facilitating Acceptance of Organizational Change: The Importance of Self-Determination. *Journal of Applied Social Psychology* 30: 1843–52.

Morrison and Milliken, Organizational Silence.

Young, G. J. 2000. Managing Organizational Transformations: Lessons from the Veterans Health Administration. *California Management Review* 43 (Fall): 66–82.

29. Kotter, J. P. 1996. *Leading Change*. Boston: Harvard Business School Press.

Lawler, E. E. III, and C. G. Worley. 2006. *Built to Change: How to Achieve Sustained Organizational Effectiveness*. San Francisco: Jossey-Bass.

30. Baum, J. R., E. A. Locke, and S. A. Kirkpatrick. 1998. A Longitudinal Study of the Relation of Vision and Vision Communication to Venture Growth in Entrepreneurial Firms. *Journal of Applied Psychology* 83: 43–54.

31. Levin, I. M. 2000. Vision Revisited: Telling the Story of the Future. *The Journal of Applied Behavioral Science* 36: 91–107. (Quotation taken from p. 92.)

32. Austin, J., and J. Bartunek. 2003. Theories and Practices of Organization Development. In *Handbook of Psychology*, Vol. 12: *Industrial and Organizational Psychology*, ed. D. Borman, D. Ilgen, and R. Klimoski. New York: John Wiley & Sons, Chap. 13.

Beckhard, R. 1969. *Organizational Development: Strategies and Models*. Reading, MA: Addison-Wesley.

Burnes, B., and B. Cooke. 2012. Review Article: The Past, Present and Future of Organization Development: Taking the Long View. *Human Relations* 65: 1395–429.

Cummings, T. G., and C. G. Worley. 2014. *Organization Development and Change*, 10th edn. Stamford: Cengage Learning.

French, Bell, and Zawacki, *Organization Development*.

Weick, K. E., and R. E. Quinn. 1999. Organizational Change and Development. *Annual Review of Psychology* 50: 361–86.

33. Beer, M. 1980. *Organizational Change and Development: A Systems View*. Santa Monica: Goodyear Publishing, p. 27.

34. French, Bell, and Zawacki, *Organization Development*.

35. Beckhard, *Organizational Development*.

36. Developed from Burke, *Organizational Development*, pp. 68–79.

Kolb, D. A., and A. L. Frohman. 1970. An Organizational Development Approach to Consulting. *Sloan Management Review* 12 (Fall): 51–65.

37. Weisbord, M. R. 1973. The Organizational Development Contract. *OD Practitioner* 5: 1–4.

38. Developed from Cummings and Worley, *Organization Development and Change*.

French, W. L., and C. H. Bell. 1999. *Organization Development: Behavioral Science Interventions for Organization Improvement*, 6th edn. Upper Saddle River: Prentice Hall.

Pannarayan, S., T. V. Rao, and K. Sing, eds. 1998. *Organizational Development: Interventions and Strategies*. Thousand Oaks: Sage Publishing.

39. Friedlander, F., and L. D. Brown. 1974. Organizational Development. In *Annual Review of Psychology*, Vol. 25, ed. M. R. Rosenzweig and L. W. Porter. Palo Alto: Annual Reviews, pp. 313–41.

Schein, E. H. 1987. *Process Consultation, Vol. 2: Lessons for Managers and Consultants*. Reading, MA: Addison-Wesley.

40. Nicholas, J. M., and M. Katz. 1985. Research Methods and Reporting Practices in Organizational Development: A Review and Some Guidelines. *Academy of Management Review* 10: 737–49.

Porras, J. I., and R. C. Silvers. 1991. Organizational Development and Transformation. In *Annual Review of Psychology*, Vol. 42, ed. M. R. Rosenzweig and L. W. Porter. Palo Alto: Annual Reviews, pp. 51–78.

41. Garvin, D. A. 1988. *Managing Quality: The Strategic and Competitive Edge*. New York: Free Press.

42. Robertson, P. J., D. R. Roberts, and J. I. Porras. 1993. Dynamics of Planned Organizational Change: Assessing Empirical Support for a Theoretical Model. *Academy of Management Journal* 36: 619–34.

43. Nicholas, J. M. 1982. The Comparative Impact of Organizational Development Interventions on Hard Criteria Measures. *Academy of Management Review* 7: 531–42.

Porras, J. I. 1975. The Comparative Impact of Different OD Techniques and Intervention Intensities. *Journal of Applied Behavioral Science* 15: 156–78.

Porras, J. I., and P. O. Berg. 1978. The Impact of Organizational Development. *Academy of Management Review* 2: 249–66.

44. Bettenhausen, K. L. 1991. Five Years of Group Research: What Have We Learned and What Needs to Be Addressed. *Journal of Management* 17: 345–81.
    Guzzo, R. A., R. D. Jette, and R. A. Katzell. 1985. The Effects of Psychologically Based Intervention Programs on Worker Productivity: A Meta Analysis. *Personnel Psychology* 38: 275–91.

45. Neuman, G. A., J. E. Edwards, and N. S. Raju. 1989. Organizational Development Interventions: A Meta-Analysis of Their Effects on Satisfaction and Other Attitudes. *Personnel Psychology* 42: 461–83.

46. Faucheux, C., G. Amado, and A. Laurent. 1982. Organizational Development and Change. In *Annual Review of Psychology*, Vol. 33, ed. M. R. Rosenzweig and L. W. Porter. Palo Alto: Annual Reviews, pp. 343–70.
    French and Bell, *Organization Development*.

47. Bourgeois, L. J., III, and M. Boltvinik. 1981. OD in Cross Cultural Settings: Latin America. *California Management Review* 23 (Spring): 75–81.

48. Faucheux, Amado, and Laurent, Organizational Development and Change.
    Michailova, S. 2000. Contrasts in Culture: Russian and Western Perspectives on Organizational Change. *Academy of Management Executive* 14: 99–112.

49. Michailova, Contrasts in Culture.

50. Hofstede, G. 1991. *Cultures and Organizations: Software of the Mind*. New York: McGraw-Hill.
    Hofstede, G. 2001. *Culture's Consequences: Comparing Values, Behaviors, Institutions, and Organizations across Nations*, 2nd edn. Thousand Oaks: Sage Publishing.

51. Connor, P. E., and L. K. Lake. 1994. *Managing Organizational Change*. New York: Praeger.
    Walter, G. A. 1984. Organizational Development and Individual Rights. *Journal of Applied Behavioral Science* 20: 423–39.
    White, L. P., and K. C. Wooten. 1983. Ethical Dilemmas in Various Stages of Organizational Development. *Academy of Management Review* 13: 690–97.

Part 5 Case

Abstract

The general manager of the production division of a Latin American export company is considering what to do about cross-functional teams and the quality council, both central to the implementation of total quality management (TQM). The company is the Tropical Export Company that produces LITEP—an acronym that refers to the labor intensive tropical export product grown in Playa Negra and exported by the company. The company is a U.S.-based multinational corporation with extensive production operations in Latin America that produces LITEP for industrialized markets, mainly North America and Europe. Several production divisions are located in the Central American country of Morazan. Each employs approximately 5,500 to 6,500 employees of whom around 500 to 550 are salaried; the rest are union members. The divisions are focused on exported volume of high-quality LITEP. Quality is vital to the customer and volume is the key to lowering costs and increasing productivity.

USING LEADERSHIP TO PROMOTE TQM*

Case Setting

The Tropical Export Company is a U.S.-based multinational corporation with extensive production operations in Latin America that produce LITEP—an acronym for the labor intensive tropical export product grown and exported by the company—for industrialized markets, mainly North America and Europe. The company is one of the 3–4 major players in the industry. Several production divisions are located in the Central American country of Morazan. Each employs approximately 5,500 to 6,500 employees of whom around 500 to 550 are salaried; the rest are union members. The divisions are focused on exported volume of high-quality LITEP. Quality is vital to the customer and export volume is the key to lowering costs and increasing productivity.

The village-like, relatively closed, company towns created social situations where the distinction between one's work and social roles was blurred. The company was very figural in the gestalt of workers' lives in Playa Negra, the production division where the case occurred.

Adoption of TQM

Playa Negra was one of the first sites within the company where TQM was implemented, beginning with a training program. The objectives of the training program were to understand how to work within a TQM culture and learn the

---

* **Source:** Copyright © Asbjorn Osland. Reprinted with the permission of Asbjorn Osland.

basic steps in beginning a TQM program to shift attention from inspecting the final product to analyzing the processes used to produce and ship LITEP. The transition from traditional quality inspection of the final product to TQM's continuous improvement of work processes involved the following changes:

1. include the internal customers in the analysis and revision of work processes;
2. focus on the prevention of quality problems rather than inspection;
3. manage the process rather than the results; managers were to work with subordinates in problem solving;
4. develop participative employees rather than passive subordinates;
5. provide basic analytical tools (e.g., Pareto charts, "fishbone" or cause-effect diagrams, control charts, histograms, and flow charts) to teams of subordinates who would analyze problems and make presentations to managers committed to listening rather than deciding based on intuition; and
6. assure continuous improvement of work processes that should ultimately be reflected in higher quality scores and customer satisfaction in the market rather than relying on a commodity—low cost producer approach.

There was no connection established between the TQM program and compensation; it was viewed as part of the participants' duties. However, executives did have bonuses tied to the achievement of TQM objectives.

The TQM process was housed in a structure parallel to the hierarchy and consisted of the following:

1. a quality council, made up of department heads and supervisors;
2. a full-time TQM coordinator who had fairly extensive experience within operations; he had worked for the company in purchasing, the controller's office, and operational roles for six years; and
3. the quality action—also called continuous improvement—teams, made up of a variety of people with particular expertise or involvement in a specific process that was designated for improvement by the quality council.

Such a parallel structure was necessary because the TQM process was not perceived as a replacement for the regular machine bureaucracy that had relentlessly met production targets for decades.

In Playa Negra, in addition to the introductory seminars given by the TQM coordinator, dozens of employees attended workshops conducted by external consultants. Topics covered included facilitation skills, leadership in participative workplaces, and statistical process control.

The General Manager's Questions

Armando, the general manager of Playa Negra, sat wondering how to proceed. He understood that TQM doctrine emphasized the importance of a relatively autonomous quality council and the need for cross-functional teams. Yet he was puzzled how to proceed in a culturally appropriate fashion. The dilemma was to strike a balance that would allow TQM to flourish while preserving enough continuity to maintain an organizational foundation that members found satisfying and consistent with their culturally determined expectations of the organization.

The quality council was to provide leadership to the TQM process. However, the council had done next to nothing for 18 months. Armando, the general manager, had quietly sat through the meetings as an observer. The controller, a relatively young expatriate, had led the council meetings.

Everyone, including Armando, was frustrated with the lack of progress. As Armando saw it, he had three alternatives:

1. He could continue within the council as he had for the past 18 months, basically an observer, in the hopes that the council would eventually coalesce around some highpriority project.
2. He could aggressively push his TQM agenda within the council. A colleague in another production division, Karl, had done this and was pleased that the quality council was pursuing the projects that were high on his list of priorities. The general manager's control over the organization was extreme due to the power Latin society gives to heads of organizations and the role the company had carved out for the position in its century of neocolonialist domination of the Latino workforce. Karl, a European with long family links to the company and extensive production experience and competence, observed that even if he asked a question, the Latino council members would try to infer what his desires were and would try to please him. Karl's view was that it would take too long for the council to become truly autonomous and he had decided to use the culturally acceptable role of strong leadership to use the council as a vehicle to achieve his ends. He once confided to Armando that the council was a "manager's council." Both Armando and Karl, as general managers in a very competitive industry, were pressured by their superiors to complete numerous specific projects. Their annual bonuses, of up to 30% of their base pay, depended on achievement of these objectives. Thus, it was understandable why Karl would feel compelled to do what he was doing. Plus, the general manager's role is so powerful that using it to achieve the ends of TQM seemed better to Karl than "sitting around" through endless meetings.
3. A subsidiary, Packing, Inc., that provided plastic and cardboard packaging materials to Playa Negra, had a different approach. The assistant manager, who reported to the general manager and was second-in-command, assumed leadership of the quality council. The general manager was only allowed to attend when the council had completed analyzing an issue and wanted to present their recommendations to him. The assistant manager found that when the general manager observed, the other executives were preoccupied with what they thought he might want rather than analyzing a problem independent of the general manager. Armando wondered if he would get too distant from the process with this method. He was accustomed to assuming strong leadership.

Based on the advice of both the external and the corporate TQM consultants and his internal TQM coordinator, Armando had attempted to establish quality action teams with members from various functions who were to collaboratively problem solve and thereby improve interdepartmental communication. However, the department heads had resorted to "turf" conscious behaviors and were not allowing their subordinates, who were on the quality action teams, to cooperate with other departments without passing things up the hierarchy for review, thereby slowing the process down and involving the more turf conscious department heads. Armando saw three alternatives:

1. He knew he could order the department heads to do as he told them. In the past, when he led change efforts, he aggressively pursued what he wanted to accomplish by bringing his immediate subordinates along and disseminating the information associated with the change throughout the organization. He followed up with consistent monitoring and encouragement. However, if he aggressively pushed the concept of cross-functional teams, he was worried that if he was to be transferred, the department heads would abandon TQM as they would not have a sense of ownership of the process because they would not have internalized the TQM philosophy.
2. He could allow the department heads to revert back to functional teams and then later attempt to convince them of the utility of cross-functional teams and functional interdependence between departments.
3. He was also considering naming respected middle managers to head the teams who would then choose the members of the quality action teams from their own departments and other departments, based on the team leader's relationship with the prospective members and their perceived competence relating to the problem addressed.

The corporate TQM consultant, Bob, who had encouraged Armando to push the cross-functional teams and also to keep the quality council on track, was doing a training program that day. Armando invited him and the internal TQM coordinator, Francisco, to play a round of golf after work and discuss how they should proceed with the TQM process.

The Golf Game

Armando sat on the verandah of the club and watched Francisco and Bob walk toward him. Though they were not very good golfers, he enjoyed playing with them because it was a more relaxed way to discuss things with them. He had developed confidence in their ability to provide him with assistance but felt that they were mistaken by following TQM as though it were an ideology or an off-the-shelf recipe for the latest potion of managerial self-help. Armando had grown leery of such rigidity as he knew the extremely strong organizational culture of a 70-year-old LITEP production division and the uniqueness of Latino culture forced him to modify managerial interventions developed in the U.S.

Armando greeted them, "Well, are you ready to wager a few pesos on the game? I'll give you 2-to-1 odds and bet 300 pesos."

Francisco and Bob looked at one another and shrugged assent. They knew they would lose but were also familiar with the custom of wagering and losing to the general manager.

They played a few holes and exchanged small talk about families and politics. Armando began the discussion, "I read your report, Bob. I understand that I have the power and authority to kick the council in the rear and get it moving, or the TQM budget might be at risk given the austerity campaign our financial wizards have imposed on us due to the falling P/E ratio. I also agree that I could force the department heads to adopt the cross-functional approach we've discussed for the quality action teams. I know that you believe such teams are essential due to the need for interdependent groups and cross-functional communication. But, I worry about jamming things down their throats because I could be transferred at any time to another production division and my successor might simply throw out the whole process if it's not strongly entrenched and supported by the department heads and supervisors."

Bob responded, "Your position is such a powerful one that I think you can get away with it and I think there's enough support in corporate to lean on the incoming general manager to follow the playbook we've laid out."

Francisco and Armando exchanged furtive glances and smiles. They were continually amazed that the U.S. corporate offices believed they could simply order the Latin American production divisions to follow some policy. If they followed everything corporate said there would be no production. They would either be paralyzed by strikes or have on going conflict with the local government. Armando understood how the company's neocolonialist past had fostered the arrogance that confused decision making but also understood that sometimes he had to be cautious in aggressively pushing things that didn't seem to fit with the peculiar culture of the LITEP production divisions.

Armando mused about Bob's reference to the power given the role of the general manager. "From a cultural standpoint, I know my Central American compatriots would accept my autocratic authority. I understand that the 'in-group,' as you call my department heads and supervisors, will do as I say. However, this same bond also works within departments and creates a powerful 'in-group' feeling that works against cross-functional teams."

As Armando prepared to drive, Bob thought how struck he had been by the loyalty, commitment, and obedience that characterized the organizational culture. He had likened it to the military. People did as they were told. They hesitated to contradict their superiors. They expressed high levels of commitment to the company. Turnover was practically nonexistent; people spent their lives working for LITEP, Inc.

Bob was also aware that the general managers, including Armando, enjoyed great power and respect because they had passed all the tests laid before them in their careers and deserved their designation as general manager. They had mastered various jobs and tasks over the 15 years or more that it usually took to become a general manager. When they attained the level of general manager, they were generally recognized as competent production and operations specialists who also had soundly developed managerial and political skills.

Armando drove within 25 yards of the hole. While walking up the fairway they continued chatting. Armando said, "We can't spell out everything. You seem to want to follow a recipe or some doctrine you heard from Deming, Juran, or one of the other TQM gurus. It doesn't work that way. Aside from our culture being very different than where you saw TQM work in the U.S., things are in such an upheaval now that conditions are too unpredictable to spell every step out." Armando understood that this uncertainty allowed the general manager great power as there were no established rules and procedures to solve such nonroutine problems.

Francisco listened and thought about Armando. He believed that Armando had highly developed political skills and charismatic leadership qualities. As a large fit man, he struck an imposing image. During meetings, he frequently stood and walked around the room speaking with a thundering voice and waved his arms to emphasize a point. He combined an engaging manner with total authority; one could speak frankly with him and challenge him with solid arguments, yet one was always aware of his authority. Francisco asked Armando, "What is it about TQM that you like?"

Armando thought for a few moments and replied, "I enjoy getting a large organization to do what I want it to do. I see TQM as an opportunity to try something new. You learn from your bosses but you want to do more. TQM gave me that opportunity. I have nothing to fear from more employee participation or the involvement that comes with TQM. If you know the business, you can help people problem solve in a manner that enables them to develop. By giving people authority, they will come to you and seek your input. This gives me more power than I would have had if I simply had told a passive work force what to do. I want a proactive group seeking answers. But I never submit anything to a group for their input when I already know the answer. You don't have to tell people you're in charge—they know it."

Francisco thought of all the conversations he had had with company colleagues about the power of the general manager. In one club in another LITEP producing country Francisco had visited, he saw a photo of a former American general manager (who later became the regional vice president) wearing two six-shooters, prominently displayed as part of the club's memorabilia. He also recalled the Spanish businessman who had said that many years ago he bought the first car owned by a "civilian" (i.e., non-company), a geographically isolated division. When it was delivered on the company train, the general manager initially refused to allow it to be unloaded saying he hadn't given his authorization.

As though he sensed what Francisco was thinking about, Armando continued, "If you think I'm autocratic you should have seen the first American general manager I worked for. He had a boat called 'Solo Mio' ('only mine') that nobody touched, except to keep it ready for his personal and exclusive use. This was how company employees grew to feel a general manager should behave."

Armando continued, "You must recall that our employees are not professionally educated specialists with strong ties outside Playa Negra. Sure, there are professional engineers, accountants, and some college educated production specialists, but most of the supervisors do not have much education. Instead they learned their jobs within the company. This made them heavily socialized within Playa Negra—an army of enlisted men, if you will. And I'm their general."

Bob thought about how power was most evident within hierarchical interaction with subordinates. He recalled how the need to dominate subordinates was commonly expressed by superiors. Once a subordinate threatened to quit if he did not receive a raise in his salary to increase it to a level comparable to that of others. His manager swore Bob to secrecy and said, "Julian is very good." Bob believed that the correct inference was that subordinates should not be told by their superiors how valuable they were because such knowledge would give them power.

Bob thought also of how for one department head, hierarchy was more than simple power associated with a senior position. It had a raw element to it wherein his authority could not be questioned. He expressed the explicit desire that his subordinates fear him. His preference for primitive domination was extreme but such a desire for control over subordinates was not unusual in traditional LITEP culture. He actually asked Bob to do a survey feedback of his department to find out if his subordinates held a sufficient degree of fear for him.

They continued playing. Bob and Francisco were soundly beaten. They paid the obligatory "round fee" to Armando. As Armando walked to his car, Francisco said to Bob, "He'll do what he wants but I think he has a point about not pushing the council too hard. If he's replaced, the new general manager could throw everything out the window.

Also, I'm having a devil of a time getting the department heads to support the cross-functional teams."

Bob countered, "Yes, but we know Armando could make things happen if he wanted to and also I strongly believe that the corporate offices won't allow any new general manager, in the event Armando is transferred, to regress to the bad old days and drop his support of TQM."

INDEX

Note: Information in figures and tables is indicated by page numbers in *italics* and **bold**.